World Wide Web Enhanced
Brief Edition

Gary B. Shelly
Thomas J. Cashman
Gloria A. Waggoner
William C. Waggoner

Contributing Authors

Misty E. Vermaat
Tim J. Walker
John F. Repede

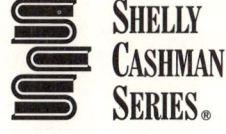

 COURSE TECHNOLOGY
ONE MAIN STREET
CAMBRIDGE MA 02142

an International Thomson Publishing company   I(T)P

CAMBRIDGE · ALBANY · BONN · CINCINNATI · LONDON · MADRID · MELBOURNE
MEXICO CITY · NEW YORK · PARIS · SAN FRANCISCO · TOKYO · TORONTO · WASHINGTON

© 1997 Course Technology
One Main Street
Cambridge, Massachusetts 02142

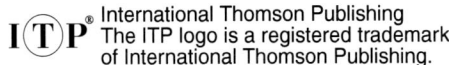
International Thomson Publishing
The ITP logo is a registered trademark
of International Thomson Publishing.

Printed in the United States of America

For more information, contact Course Technology:

Course Technology One Main Street Cambridge, Massachusetts 02142, USA	International Thomson Editores Campos Eliseos 385, Piso 7 Colonia Polanco 11560 Mexico D.F. Mexico
International Thomson Publishing Europe Berkshire House 168-173 High Holborn London, WC1V 7AA, United Kingdom	International Thomson Publishing GmbH Konigswinterer Strasse 418 53227 Bonn, Germany
Thomas Nelson Australia 102 Dodds Street South Melbourne Victoria 3205 Australia	International Thomson Publishing Asia Block 211, Henderson Road #08-03 Henderson Industrial Park Singapore 0315
Nelson Canada 1120 Birchmont Road Scarborough, Ontario Canada M1K 5G4	International Thomson Publishing Japan Hirakawa-cho Kyowa Building, 3F 2-2-1 Hirakawa-cho, Chiyoda-ku Tokyo 102, Japan

All rights reserved. No part of this work may be reproduced or used in any form or by any means—
graphic, electronic, or mechanical, including photocopying, recording, taping, or information and retrieval systems—
without prior written permission from the publisher.

ISBN 0-7895-1300-5

SHELLY CASHMAN SERIES® and **Custom Edition**® are trademarks of International Thomson Publishing, Inc. Names of all other products mentioned herein are used for identification purposes only and may be trademarks and/or registered trademarks of their respective owners. International Thomson Publishing, Inc. and Course Technology disclaim any affiliation, association, or connection with, or sponsorship or endorsement by, such owners.

2 3 4 5 6 7 8 9 10 BC 10 9 8 7

Contents in Brief

	Preface	**x**
CHAPTER 1	**An Overview of Using Computers**	**1.1**
	SPECIAL FEATURE	
	TIMELINE: Milestones in Computer History	**1.36**
CHAPTER 2	**Software Applications: User Tools**	**2.1**
CHAPTER 3	**The System Unit**	**3.1**
CHAPTER 4	**Input and Output**	**4.1**
CHAPTER 5	**Data Storage**	**5.1**
CHAPTER 6	**Communications and Networks**	**6.1**
CHAPTER 7	**The Internet and the World Wide Web**	**7.1**
	SPECIAL FEATURE	
	Guide to World Wide Web Sites	**7.41**
CHAPTER 8	**Operating Systems and System Software**	**8.1**
	SPECIAL FEATURE	
	How to Purchase, Install, and Maintain a Personal Computer	**8.34**
	Index	**I.1**
	Photo Credits	

Contents
DISCOVERING COMPUTERS
A Link to the Future, World Wide Web Enhanced Brief Edition

Preface	**x**

An Overview of Using Computers

Objectives	**1.1**
Computer and Information Literacy	**1.2**
What Is a Computer?	**1.4**
What Are the Components of a Computer?	**1.4**
Input Devices	1.4
System Unit	1.6
Output Devices	1.6
Storage Devices	1.7
Communications Devices	1.7
Peripheral Devices	1.7
What Does a Computer Do?	**1.7**
Why Is a Computer so Powerful?	**1.8**
Speed	1.8
Reliability	1.8
Accuracy	1.8
Storage	1.8
Communications	1.8
Connectivity	**1.9**
Categories of Computers	**1.10**
Personal Computers	1.10
Servers	1.13
Minicomputers	1.14
Mainframe Computers	1.14
Supercomputers	1.15
Computer Software	**1.16**
System Software	1.17
User Interface	1.17
Application Software	1.18
What Are the Elements of an Information System?	**1.19**
An Example of How One Company Uses Computers	**1.20**
Reception	1.20
Sales	1.21
Marketing	1.21
Shipping and Receiving	1.22
Manufacturing	1.22
Product Design	1.23
Accounting	1.23
Human Resources	1.24
Information Systems	1.24
Executive	1.25
Summary of How One Company Uses Computers	1.25
Summary of an Overview of Using Computers	**1.25**
Computers at Work: Shopping for an Auto Online	**1.26**
In the Future: From the Global Village to the Local Village	**1.27**
review	1.28
terms	1.30
yourTurn	1.31
hotTopics	1.32
outThere	1.33
winLabs	1.34
webWalk	1.35

SPECIAL FEATURE

TIMELINE
Milestones in Computer History — **1.36**

Software Applications: User Tools

Objectives	**2.1**
The Operating System and User Interface	**2.2**
Software Applications	**2.4**
Word Processing Software	2.4
Desktop Publishing Software	2.12
Spreadsheet Software	2.14
Database Software	2.21
Presentation Graphics Software	2.24
Communications Software and Web Browsers	2.26
Electronic Mail Software	2.27
Personal Information Management Software	2.28
Personal Finance Software	2.29
Project Management Software	2.29
Accounting Software	2.30
Groupware	2.30
Computer-Aided Design (CAD) Software	2.31
Multimedia Authoring Software	2.32
Integrated Software and Software Suites	2.32
Object Linking and Embedding (OLE)	**2.34**
Learning Aids and Support Tools for Application Users	**2.36**
Summary of Software Applications	**2.37**
Computers at Work: Shortcuts to Creating Documents	**2.38**
In the Future: Software by Subscription	**2.39**
review	2.40
terms	2.42
yourTurn	2.43
hotTopics	2.44
outThere	2.45
winLabs	2.46
webWalk	2.47

CONTENTS vii

The System Unit

Objectives	**3.1**
What Is the System Unit?	**3.2**
How Data Is Represented in a Computer	**3.3**
ASCII and EBCDIC	3.4
Unicode	3.4
Parity	3.5
The Components of the System Unit	**3.6**
Motherboard	**3.7**
Microprocessor and the CPU	**3.7**
The Control Unit	3.8
The Arithmetic/Logic Unit	3.8
Registers	3.8
The System Clock	3.8
Word Size	3.9
Microprocessor Comparison	3.10
Upgrade Sockets	**3.10**
Memory	**3.11**
RAM	3.11
ROM	3.13
CMOS	3.13
Memory Speed	3.13
Coprocessors	**3.14**
Buses	**3.14**
Expansion Slots	**3.15**
Ports and Connectors	**3.16**
Parallel Ports	3.16
Serial Ports	3.18
Bays	**3.18**
Power Supply	**3.18**
Sound Components	**3.18**
Summary of the Components of the System Unit	**3.19**
Machine Language Instructions	**3.19**
Types of Processing	**3.21**
Pipelining	3.21
Parallel Processing	3.21
Neural Network Computers	3.22
Number Systems	**3.22**
The Decimal Number System	3.22
The Binary Number System	3.23
The Hexadecimal Number System	3.24
Summary of Number Systems	3.24
How Computer Chips Are Made	**3.25**
Summary of the System Unit	**3.27**
Computers at Work: How Many Computers Do You See Each Day?	**3.28**
In the Future: 2,000 MIPS by the Year 2000	**3.29**
review	**3.30**
terms	**3.32**
yourTurn	**3.33**
hotTopics	**3.34**
outThere	**3.35**
winLabs	**3.36**
webWalk	**3.37**

Input and Output

Objectives	**4.1**
What Is Input?	**4.2**
The Keyboard	**4.2**
Pointing Devices	**4.5**
Mouse	4.5
Trackball	4.6
Touchpad	4.6
Pointing Stick	4.7
Joystick	4.7
Pen Input	4.8
Touch Screen	4.9
Light Pen	4.10
Digitizer	4.10
Graphics Tablet	4.11
Source Data Automation	**4.12**
Image Scanner	4.13
Optical Recognition	4.14
Magnetic Ink Character Recognition (MICR)	4.17
Data Collection Devices	4.17
Terminals	**4.18**
Other Input Devices	**4.19**
Sound Input	4.19
Voice Input	4.19
Biological Feedback Input	4.21
Digital Camera	4.21
Video Input	4.22
Electronic Whiteboards	4.22
What Is Output?	**4.23**
Types of Output	**4.23**
Reports	4.23
Graphics	4.25
Audio Output	4.25
Video Output	4.26
Display Devices	**4.27**
Monitors	4.27
Flat Panel Displays	4.29
Resolution	4.30
How Images Are Displayed on a Monitor	4.31
Printers	**4.32**
Impact Printers	4.32
Nonimpact Printers	4.34
Plotters	4.38
Special-Purpose Printers	4.39
Other Output Devices	**4.40**
Data Projectors	4.40
Computer Output Microfilm	4.41
Facsimile (Fax)	4.42
Multifunction Devices	4.42
Summary of Input and Output	**4.43**
Computers at Work: Helping People with Special Needs	**4.44**
In the Future: The Widespread Use of Voice Input	**4.45**

review	4.46
terms	4.49
yourTurn	4.50
hotTopics	4.51
outThere	4.52
winLabs	4.53
webWalk	4.54

CHAPTER 5

Data Storage

Objectives	**5.1**
What Is Storage?	**5.2**
Magnetic Disk Storage	**5.3**
Floppy Disks	5.3
Hard Disks	5.8
Disk Cartridges	5.11
Maintaining Data Stored on a Disk	5.12
CD-ROM and Optical Disks	**5.14**
Magnetic Tape	**5.16**
Cartridge Tape Devices	5.16
Reel-to-Reel Tape Devices	5.17
Storing Data on Magnetic Tape	5.18
Other Types of Storage Devices	**5.19**
PC Cards	5.19
RAID Storage Systems	5.19
Mass Storage Systems	5.21
Special-Purpose Storage Devices	5.21
Summary of Storage	**5.23**
Computers at Work: HSM: Hierarchical Storage Management	**5.24**
In the Future: Holographic Storage	**5.25**
review	5.26
terms	5.28
yourTurn	5.29
hotTopics	5.30
outThere	5.31
winLabs	5.32
webWalk	5.33

CHAPTER 6

Communications and Networks

Objectives	**6.1**
What Is Communications?	**6.2**
Examples of How Communications Is Used	**6.2**
Electronic Mail (E-mail)	**6.2**
Voice Mail	**6.2**
Facsimile	**6.2**
Telecommuting	6.2
Videoconferencing	6.3
Groupware	6.4
Electronic Data Interchange	6.4
Global Positioning Systems (GPSs)	6.5
Bulletin Board Systems (BBSs)	6.5
Online Services	6.6
The Internet	6.7
A Communications System Model	**6.8**
Transmission Media	**6.9**
Twisted-Pair Cable	6.9
Coaxial Cable	6.9
Fiber-Optic Cable	6.10
Microwave Transmission	6.11
Wireless Transmission: Radio and Light Waves	6.12
An Example of a Communications Channel	6.14
Line Configurations	**6.14**
Point-to-Point Lines	6.14
Multidrop Lines	6.15
Characteristics of Communications Channels	**6.16**
Types of Signals: Digital and Analog	6.16
Transmission Modes: Asynchronous and Synchronous	6.17
Direction of Transmission: Simplex, Half-Duplex, and Full-Duplex	6.18
Transmission Rate	6.18
Communications Software	**6.19**
Communications Equipment	**6.19**
Modems	6.19
Multiplexers	6.20
Front-End Processors	6.21
Network Interface Cards	6.21
Wiring Hubs	6.22
Gateways	6.22
Bridges	6.22
Routers	6.22
Communications Networks	**6.23**
Local Area Networks (LANs)	6.23
Wide Area Networks (WANs)	6.26
Network Configurations	**6.27**
Star Network	6.27
Bus Network	6.28
Ring Network	6.29
Communications Protocols	**6.29**
Ethernet	6.30
Token Ring	6.31
An Example of a Communications Network	**6.32**
Summary of Communications and Networks	**6.33**
Computers at Work: GPS: Tool of the Modern Traveler	**6.34**
In the Future: Anywhere, Anytime Voice and Data Communications	**6.35**
review	6.36
terms	6.39
yourTurn	6.40
hotTopics	6.41
outThere	6.42
winLabs	6.43
webWalk	6.44

CONTENTS ix

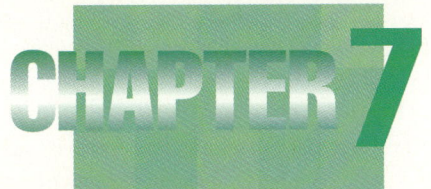

CHAPTER 7

The Internet and the World Wide Web

Objectives	**7.1**
What Is the Internet?	**7.2**
History of the Internet	**7.3**
How the Internet Works	**7.4**
Internet Addresses	**7.6**
The World Wide Web (WWW)	**7.7**
How a Web Page Works	7.7
Web Browser Software	7.9
Multimedia on the Web	7.11
Searching for Information on the Web	7.16
Intranets and Firewalls	**7.17**
Other Internet Services	**7.19**
E-mail	7.19
FTP	7.20
Gopher	7.21
Telnet	7.22
Usenet	7.23
Internet Relay Chat (IRC)	7.24
Network Computers	**7.25**
Network Computers for Business	7.25
Network Computers for the Home	7.26
Summary of Network Computers	7.27
How to Connect to the Internet and the World Wide Web	**7.28**
Computers at Work: Doing Business on the World Wide Web	**7.30**
In the Future: The Future of the Internet and the World Wide Web	**7.31**
review	**7.32**
terms	**7.35**
yourTurn	**7.36**
hotTopics	**7.37**
outThere	**7.38**
winLabs	**7.39**
webWalk	**7.40**

SPECIAL FEATURE

Guide to World Wide Web Sites   7.41

CHAPTER 8

Operating Systems and System Software

Objectives	**8.1**
What Is System Software?	**8.2**
What Is an Operating System?	**8.2**
Functions of an Operating System	**8.4**
Process Management	8.4
Memory Management	8.7
Input and Output Management	8.8
System Administration	8.10
Loading an Operating System	**8.12**
Popular Operating Systems	**8.14**
DOS	8.14
Windows 3.x	8.15
Windows 95 and Beyond	8.16
Windows CE	8.16
Windows NT	8.17
Macintosh	8.17
OS/2	8.18
UNIX	8.18
NetWare	8.19
Utilities	**8.19**
Language Translators	**8.23**
Summary of Operating Systems and System Software	**8.23**
Computers at Work: The Social Interface	**8.24**
In the Future: The Next User Interface	**8.25**
review	**8.26**
terms	**8.28**
yourTurn	**8.29**
hotTopics	**8.30**
outThere	**8.31**
winLabs	**8.32**
webWalk	**8.33**

SPECIAL FEATURE

How to Purchase, Install, and Maintain a Personal Computer   8.34

PREFACE

Discovering Computers: A Link to the Future, World Wide Web Enhanced Brief Edition is intended for use in a one-quarter or one-semester introductory computer course. No experience with computers is assumed. The material presented provides the most in-depth treatment of introductory computer subjects ever found in a textbook. Students will finish the course with a complete understanding of computers, how to use computers, and how to access information on the World Wide Web. The objectives of this book are as follows:

- Present the fundamentals of computers and computer nomenclature, particularly with respect to personal computer hardware and software and the World Wide Web
- Make use of the World Wide Web as a repository of the latest information in an ever-changing discipline
- Present the material in a visually appealing and exciting, easy-to-understand manner with a format that invites students to learn
- Give students an in-depth understanding of why computers are essential components in the business world and society in general
- Use a fully integrated, hands-on approach to foster an appreciation of the World Wide Web
- Focus on the computer as a valuable productivity tool
- Recognize the personal computer's position as the backbone of the computer industry and emphasize its use as a stand-alone and networked device
- Provide exercises and lab assignments that allow students to interact with a computer and actually learn by using the computer and the World Wide Web
- Present strategies for purchasing, installing, and maintaining a personal computer system

Distinguishing Features

The distinguishing features of this textbook include the following:

The Proven Shelly and Cashman Pedagogy

More than two million students have learned about computers using Shelly and Cashman computer fundamentals textbooks. This new and exciting book is our best work ever. With World Wide Web integration, extraordinary visuality, currency, and the Shelly and Cashman touch, students and teachers alike will find this to be the finest textbook they have ever used.

World Wide Web Enhanced

Each of the Shelly and Cashman computer fundamentals books has included significant educational innovations that have set them apart from all other textbooks in the field. *Discovering Computers* continues this tradition of innovation with its integration of the World Wide Web. The purpose of integrating the World Wide Web into the book is to: (1) offer students additional information on a topic of importance; (2) provide currency; and (3) underscore the relevance of the World Wide Web as a basic information tool that can be used in all facets of society. The World Wide Web is integrated into the book in two central ways:

- Throughout the text, marginal annotations titled *inCyber* provide suggestions on how to obtain additional information via the World Wide Web on an important topic covered on the page.
- Every end-of-chapter page in the book has been stored as a Web page on the World Wide Web. While working on an end-of-chapter page, students can display the corresponding Web page to obtain additional information on a term or exercise and to study for exams. See page xv for more information.

This textbook, however, does not depend on Web access in order to be used successfully. The Web access adds to the already complete treatment of topics within the book.

Visually Appealing

Using the latest technology, the pictures, drawings, and text have been artfully combined to produce a visually appealing and easy-to-understand book. Pictures and drawings reflect the latest trends in computer technology. The pictures, which were chosen for their pedagogical value, allow students to see the actual hardware, software, and other subjects being described in the book. The state-of-the-art drawings are geared toward simplifying the more complex computer concepts. Finally, the text on each page was set to make the book easy to read. This combination of pictures, drawings, and text sets a new standard for computer textbook design.

Latest Computer Trends

The terms and technologies your students see in this book are those they will encounter when they start using computers. Only the latest application software packages are shown throughout the book. New topics and terms include network computers, intranets, firewalls, HTML, Java, Windows CE, T1 lines, ISPs, TCP/IP, MAEs, IP address, and much more.

Chapter on The Internet and the World Wide Web

Chapter 7 covers the Internet and World Wide Web, which is the fastest growing area of computer technology. Topics include how the Internet works; browsers; URLs; search tools; firewalls; intranets; and Internet services.

Computers at Work and In the Future

Each chapter ends with two full pages devoted to features titled *Computers at Work* and *In the Future*. *Computers at Work* presents an example of how the concepts in the chapter are being used today. *In the Future* describes an application that will be available in the future using concepts presented in the chapter.

Shelly Cashman Series Interactive Labs

Fourteen unique, hands-on exercises, developed specifically for this book and free to adopters, allow students to use the computer to learn about computers. Each Lab exercise takes students about 15 minutes to step through. Assessment is available. The exercises are described in detail on page xvi. These same exercises are available with audio for purchase under the title, *Exploring Computers: A Record of Discovery 2nd Edition* (ISBN 0-7895-2839-8).

End-of-Chapter Exercises

Unlike other books on the subject of computer fundamentals, a major effort was undertaken in *Discovering Computers* to offer exciting, rich, and thorough end-of-chapter material to reinforce the chapter objectives and assist you in making your course the finest ever offered. As indicated earlier, each and every one of the end-of-chapter pages is stored as a Web page on the World Wide Web to provide your students in-depth information and alternative methods of preparing for examinations. Each chapter ends with the following:

- **review** This section summarizes the chapter material for the purpose of reviewing and preparing for examinations. Links on the Web page provide additional current information.
- **terms** This listing of the key terms found in the chapter together with the page on which the terms are defined will aid students in mastering the chapter material. A complete summary of all key terms in the book, together with their definitions, appears in the Index at the end of the book. On the Web page, students can click terms to view a definition of the term and a picture of the term.

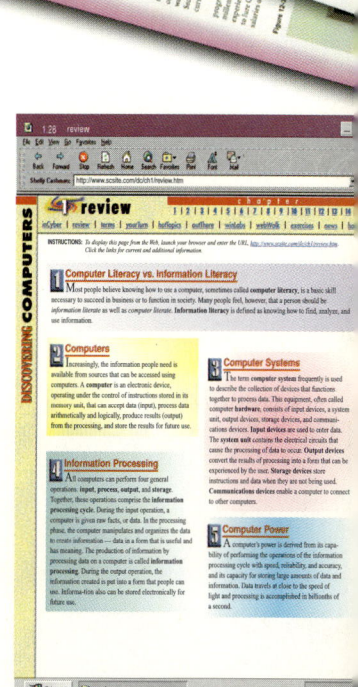

- **yourTurn** Fill-in and short-answer questions, together with a figure from the chapter that must be labeled, reinforce the material presented within the chapter. Students accessing the Web page can click a question to see a suggested answer.
- **hotTopics** The computer industry is not without its controversial issues. At the end of each chapter, several scenarios are presented that challenge students to critically examine their perspective of technology in society. The Web pages provide links to further challenge students.
- **outThere** Computers are found everywhere. This section provides many out-of-the-classroom projects that send students to the World Wide Web or out of the academic area where interesting discoveries about computers will take place.
- **winLabs** To complete their introduction to computers, students must interact with and use a computer. A series of Windows 95 Lab exercises are presented for student use. Many of these exercises also can be completed in a Windows 3.1 environment. Beginning with the simplest exercises within Windows, students are led through a series of activities that, by the end of the book, will enable them to be proficient in using Windows. Also included in this section are exercises that have students complete the Shelly Cashman Series Interactive Labs.
- **webWalk** In this section, students gain an appreciation for the World Wide Web by visiting interesting and exciting Web pages and completing suggested tasks. The last exercise sends students into a Chat room where they can discuss topics presented in the book with other students throughout the world.

Timeline: Milestones in Computer History

A colorful, highly informative eight-page timeline following Chapter 1 steps students through the major computer technology developments over the past 50 years, including the most recent advances and a glimpse of the future.

Guide to World Wide Web Sites

More than 100 popular Web sites are listed and described in a new guide to Web sites that follows Chapter 7.

Student Guide: How to Purchase, Install, and Maintain a Personal Computer

A nine-page student guide following Chapter 8 introduces students to purchasing, installing, and maintaining a desktop or laptop personal computer.

Instructor's Support Material

A comprehensive instructor's support package accompanies this textbook in the form of two CD-ROM packages. The two packages, which are titled Instructor's Resource Kit (IRK) and Course Presenter, respectively, are described in the following sections. Both packages are available free to adopters. Two additional products also are available for purchase — a *Study Guide* and *Exploring Computers: A Record of Discovery 2nd Edition*. These products are described on the following pages.

Instructor's Resource Kit (IRK)

The Instructor's Resource Kit (IRK) includes teaching and testing aids. The CD-ROM (ISBN 0-7895-1299-8) is available through your Course Technology representative or by calling 1-800-648-7450. The contents of the IRK are listed below.

- **ElecMan (Electronic Instructor's Manual)** ElecMan is made up of Microsoft Word files. The ElecMan files include the following for each chapter: chapter objectives; chapter overview; detailed lesson plans with page number references; teacher notes and activities; answers to the *winLabs* exercises; test bank (100 true/false, 50 multiple-choice, and 70 fill-in-the-blank questions per chapter); and transparency references. The transparencies are available in Figures on CD-ROM. The test bank questions are numbered the same as in Course Test Manager. You can print a copy of the chapter test bank and use the printout to select your questions in Course Test Manager. You also can use your word processor to generate quizzes and exams from the test bank.
- **Figures on CD-ROM** Illustrations for every picture, table, and screen in the textbook are available in electronic form. Use this ancillary to present a slide show in lecture or to print transparencies for use in lecture with an overhead projector. If you have a personal computer and LCD device, this ancillary can be a powerful tool for presenting your lectures.
- **Course Test Manager** This comprehensive LAN-based testing and assessment system helps instructors design and administer pretests, practice tests, and actual tests. This Windows-based program permits students to take tests online, where test results are available immediately after completion of the exam. Online test scheduling, automatic statistics collection and analysis, and printed tests are only a few of the features.
- **Offline Web Companion** The Offline Web Companion includes a fully functional copy of the Microsoft Internet Explorer 3 Web browser and all the *inCyber* Web pages referenced in the margins of the book. This system allows your students to access the *inCyber* Web pages without being connected to the Internet.
- **Interactive Labs** Eighteen hands-on Interactive Labs exercises that take students about fifteen minutes each to step through help solidify and reinforce computer concepts. Student assessment requires students to answer questions about the contents of the Interactive Labs.
- **winLabs Solutions** These files contain the solutions to the *winLabs* exercises including answers to the assessment questions for the Shelly Cashman Series Interactive Labs.

Course Presenter

Course Presenter (ISBN 0-7895-4262-5) is a multimedia lecture presentation system for *Discovering Computers* that provides PowerPoint slides for every subject in each chapter. Use this presentation system to present well-organized lectures that are both interesting and knowledge-based. Fourteen presentation files are provided for the book, one for each chapter. Each file contains PowerPoint slides for every subject in each chapter together with *optional choices* to show any figure in the chapter as you step though the material in class. More than 40, current, two- to three-minute video clips that reinforce chapter material also are available for *optional presentation*. Course Presenter provides consistent coverage for multiple lecturers.

Study Guide for Discovering Computers: A Link to the Future, World Wide Web Enhanced

This highly popular supplement includes a variety of activities that help students recall, review, and master introductory computer concepts. The *Study Guide* compliments the end-of-chapter material with short answer, fill-in, and matching questions and other challenging exercises (ISBN 0-7895-2849-5).

Exploring Computers: A Record of Discovery 2nd Edition

Exploring Computers: A Record of Discovery 2nd Edition is a supplement to *Discovering Computers*. It may be used in combination with the textbook to augment your students' learning process. With this journal and CD-ROM, students chronicle, analyze, and extend their experiences with an audio version of the Interactive Labs (ISBN 0-7895-2839-8).

Shelly Cashman Online

Shelly Cashman Online is a World Wide Web service available to instructors and students of computer education. Visit Shelly Cashman Online at http://www.scseries.com. Shelly Cashman Online is divided into four areas:

- **Series Information**   Information on the Shelly Cashman Series products.
- **The Community**   Opportunities to discuss your course and your ideas with instructors in your field and with the Shelly Cashman Series team.
- **Teaching Resources**   This area includes password-protected data, course outlines, teaching tips, and ancillaries such as ElecMan.
- **Student Center**   Dedicated to students learning about computers with Shelly Cashman Series textbooks and software. This area includes cool links and much more.

Acknowledgments

The Shelly Cashman Series would not be the most successful computer textbook series ever published without the contributions of outstanding publishing professionals. First, and foremost, among them is Becky Herrington, director of production and designer. She is the heart and soul of the Shelly Cashman Series, and it is only through her leadership, dedication, and untiring efforts that superior products are produced.

Under Becky's direction, the following individuals made significant contributions to this book: Ginny Harvey, series administrator and manuscript editor; Peter Schiller, production manager; Ken Russo, Mike Bodnar, Stephanie Nance, and Greg Herrington, graphic artists; Patti Koosed, editorial assistant; Nancy Lamm, proofreader; Sarah Evertson of Image Quest, photo researcher; and Cristina Haley, indexer.

Special thanks go to Jim Quasney, our dedicated series editor; Lisa Strite, senior product manager; Lora Wade, associate product manager; Scott MacDonald, editorial assistant; and Sarah McLean, marketing director.

Our sincere thanks go to Dennis Tani, who together with Becky Herrington, designed this book. In addition, Dennis performed all the layout and typography, executed the magnificent drawings contained in this book, and survived an impossible schedule with goodwill and amazing patience. We are in awe of Dennis's incredible work. We also salute Dennis Tani for a wonderful cover design, and both Dennis and Stephanie Nance for the graphics that appear on the cover.

Thanks go to Barbara Ellestad, Michael McQuead, Harry Rosenblatt, and Tim Sylvester, for reviewing the manuscript and to Mike Waggoner for his assistance with Chapter 7.

The efforts of our three contributing authors, John Repede, Misty Vermaat, and Tim Walker, on the chapter-ending material helped make this book extraordinary.

We hope you find using this book an exciting and rewarding experience.

Gary B. Shelly
Thomas J. Cashman
Gloria A. Waggoner
William C. Waggoner

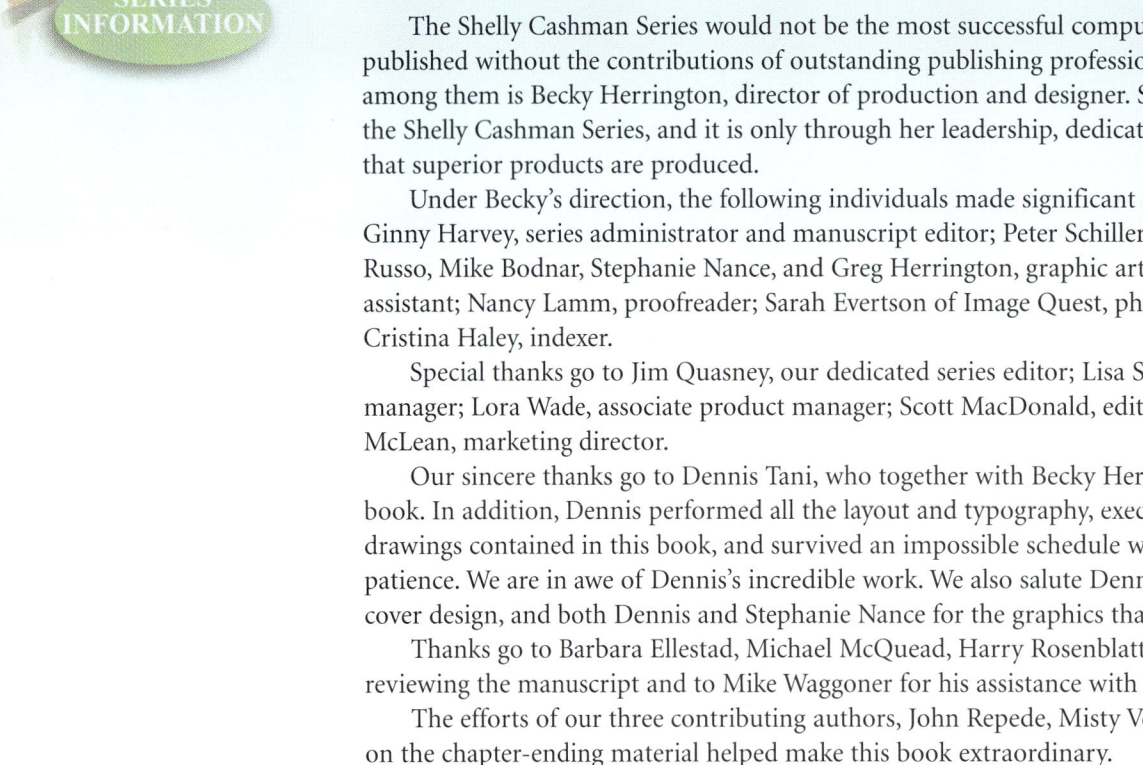

Notes to the Student

If you have access to the World Wide Web, you can obtain current and additional information on topics covered in this book in two ways:

1. Throughout the book, marginal annotations called *inCyber* specify subjects about which you can obtain additional current information. Enter the designated URL and then click the appropriate term on the Web page.

2. Each chapter ends with seven sections titled *review*, *terms* (Figure 1), *yourTurn*, *hotTopics*, *outThere*, *winLabs*, and *webWalk*. The pages in your book are stored as Web pages on the Web. You can visit them by starting your browser and entering the URL in the Shelly Cashman address box at the top of the page. When the Web page displays, you can click any of the links on the page to broaden your understanding of the topics discussed and to obtain the most current information about the topic.

You also can use the sections titled *terms* and *yourTurn* to prepare for examinations. In the *terms* section, display the Web page in your browser and then scroll through the terms. If you do not know the definition of a term, click the term on the Web page for its definition and a picture relating to it. If you click the rocket ship, a Web page will display additional current information about the term. In the *yourTurn* section, determine your answer to a question and then click the blank line to see the suggested answer.

Each time you reference a Web page from *Discovering Computers*, a navigation bar displays (Figure 1). To display a section within a chapter, click the chapter number and then click the section name. For instance, in Figure 1, to display the *outThere* page for Chapter 5, click chapter number 5 and then click outThere. If the chapter number you want already displays in the navigation bar (example: chapter number 1 in Figure 1), then simply click the section you want.

The exercises link displays a page containing links to all exercises in all chapters of the book. The news link displays pages that contain daily news about topics in each chapter of the book. The home link displays the home page for the *Discovering Computers* book. On the home page, if you click any of the section names, a page displays that contains links to the section for all chapters in the book. The index link contains an index/glossary for the entire book, together with definitions and appropriate pictures.

> *inCyber* annotations provide additional current information on a topic
>
> **inCyber**
>
> For information on aspects of the Internet, including search tools, chat rooms, and home page creation, visit the Discovering Computers Chapter 1 inCyber page (http://www.scsite.com/dc/ch1/incyber.htm) and click Internet.

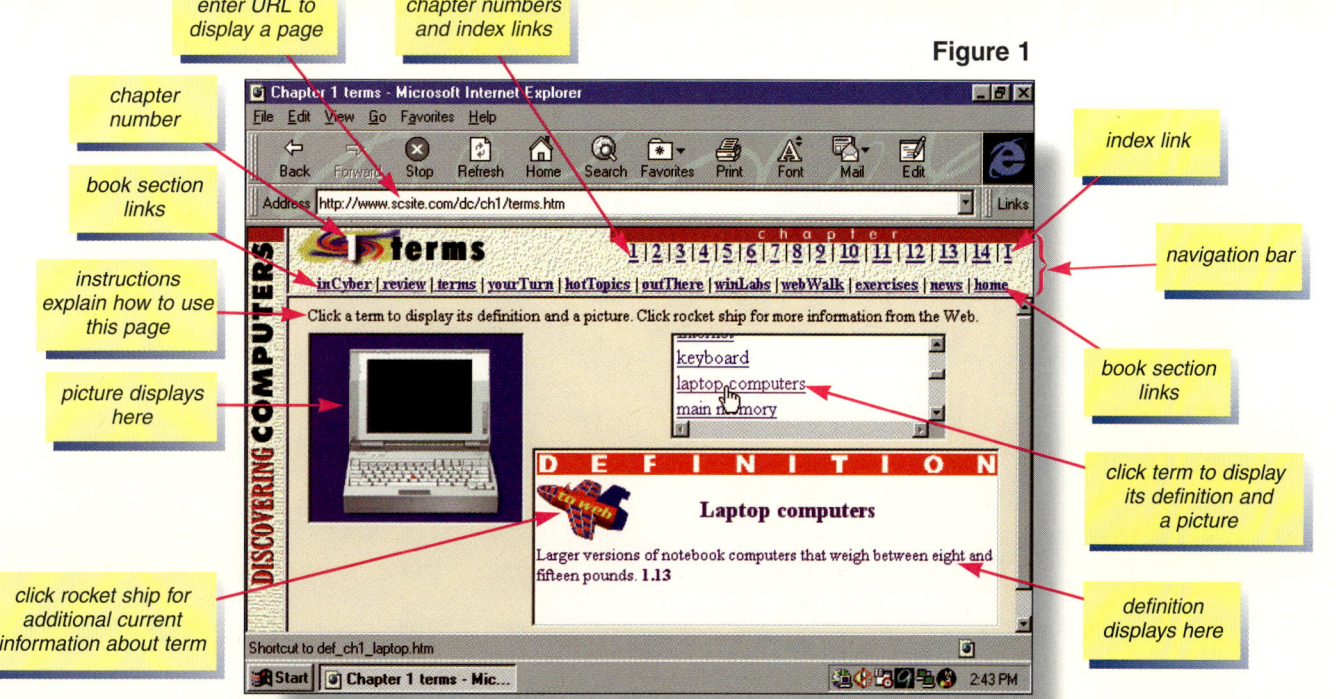

Figure 1

Shelly Cashman Series Interactive Labs

Each of the chapters in this book includes the *winLabs* hands-on exercises. The 14 Shelly Cashman Series Interactive Labs described below are included in the *winLabs* section. These Interactive Labs, which each take the students approximately 15 minutes to complete using a personal computer, help them gain a better understanding of a specific subject covered in the chapter.

Shelly Cashman Series Interactive Labs

Lab	Function	Page
Using the Mouse	Master how to use a mouse. The Lab includes exercises on pointing, clicking, double-clicking, and dragging.	1.34
Using the Keyboard	Learn how to use the keyboard. The Lab discusses different categories of keys, including the edit keys, function keys, ESC, CTRL, and ALT keys and how to press keys simultaneously.	1.34
Word Processing	Gain a basic understanding of word processing concepts, from creating a document to printing and saving the final result.	2.46
Working with Spreadsheets	Learn how to create and utilize spreadsheets.	2.46
Understanding the Motherboard	Step through the components of a motherboard and build one by adding components. The Lab shows how different motherboard configurations affect the overall speed of a computer.	3.36
Scanning Documents	Understand how document scanners work.	4.53
Setting Up to Print	See how information flows from the system unit to the printer and how drivers, fonts, and physical connections play a role in generating a printout.	4.53
Configuring Your Display	Recognize the different monitor configurations available, including screen size, display cards, and number of colors.	4.53
Maintaining Your Hard Drive	Understand how files are stored on disk, what causes fragmentation, and how to maintain an efficient hard drive.	5.32
Exploring the Computers of the Future	Learn about computers of the future and how they will work.	6.43
Connecting to the Internet	Learn how a computer is connected to the Internet. The Lab presents using the Internet to access information.	7.39
The World Wide Web	Understand the significance of the World Wide Web and how to use Web browser software and search tools.	7.39
Evaluating Operating Systems	Evaluate the advantages and disadvantages of different categories of operating systems.	8.32
Working at Your Computer	Learn the basic ergonomic principles that prevent back and neck pain, eye strain, and other computer-related physical ailments.	8.32

An Overview of Using Computers

OBJECTIVES

After completing this chapter, you will be able to:

- Explain the difference between computer literacy and information literacy
- Define the term computer
- Identify the major components of a computer
- Explain the four operations of the information processing cycle: input, process, output, and storage
- Explain how speed, reliability, accuracy, storage, and communications make computers powerful tools
- Identify the categories of computers
- Explain the difference between system software and application software
- Describe how the six elements of an information system work together

Computers play a key role in how individuals work and how they live. Even the smallest organizations have computers to help them operate more efficiently, and many individuals use computers at home for educational, entertainment, and business purposes. Computers also affect people's lives in many unseen ways. Buying groceries at the supermarket, using an automatic teller machine, or making a long-distance phone call all require using computers. The ability to use computers to communicate with other computers also is changing the way people work and live. Today, most computers have communications capabilities that enable them to access information and services around the world 24 hours a day, seven days a week.

As they have for a number of years, personal computers continue to make an increasing impact on our lives. At home, at work, and in the field, these small systems help us do our work faster, more accurately, and in some cases, in ways that previously would not have been possible.

Computer and Information Literacy

Today, most people believe that knowing how to use a computer, especially a personal computer, is a basic skill necessary to succeed in business or to function effectively in society. Given the increasing use and availability of computer systems, such knowledge will continue to be an essential skill. But is just knowing how to use a computer, sometimes called **computer literacy**, enough? Many people now believe that a person should be *information literate* as well as *computer literate*. **Information literacy** is defined as knowing how to find, analyze, and use information. It is the ability to gather information from multiple sources, select the relevant material, and organize it into a form that will allow you to make a decision or take a specific action.

For example, in shopping for a new car, you simply could visit several car dealers and talk to the salespersons about features of the model car in which you are interested. Even if you ask thorough questions and take written notes, your information will be limited to what you are told. As an information literate person, however, you will recognize the need to obtain relevant information about specific vehicles from a variety of sources before making any purchase decision. Such information might include vehicle list price, dealer cost, available options, repair history, and whether or not any recalls have been issued. This type of information is available in several consumer-oriented publications and automobile magazines. With these facts, you will be able to make a more *informed* decision on what car to buy (or not buy). So how do computers relate to information literacy? They relate because, increasingly, information on cars and other products, as well as information on finances, upcoming events, travel, and weather, is available from information sources that can be accessed using computers.

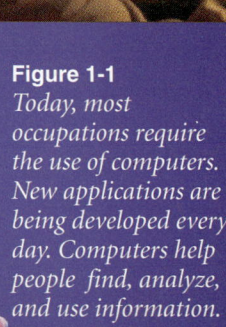

Figure 1-1
Today, most occupations require the use of computers. New applications are being developed every day. Computers help people find, analyze, and use information.

With communications equipment, computers can connect with online information service providers and the **Internet**, which is a global network of computers that houses information on thousands of subjects. Using a computer allows you to obtain up-to-the-minute information in a fast, efficient, and cost-effective manner. Computers have become the tools people use to access and manage information.

The purpose of this book is to give you the knowledge you need to understand how computers work and how computers and resources such as the Internet are used by people and organizations to gather, analyze and use information to make better decisions.

Chapter one will give you an overview of computer concepts. You will begin to learn what a computer is, how it processes data into information, and what elements are necessary for a successful information system. You also will begin to develop a basic vocabulary of computer terminology. While you are reading, remember that this chapter is an overview, and many of the terms and concepts that are introduced will be discussed in more detail in later chapters. Figure 1-1 shows a variety of computers, including personal computers, and their applications. As the photographs illustrate, many occupations now require the use of computers.

Computers affect your life every day and will continue to do so in the future. New uses for computers and improvements to existing technology are being developed continually. Learning about computers and their applications will help you to function effectively in society.

What Is a Computer?

The first question related to understanding computers and their impact on our lives is, "What is a computer?" A **computer** is an electronic device, operating under the control of instructions stored in its own memory unit, that can accept data (input), process data arithmetically and logically, produce results (output) from the processing, and store the results for future use. Most computers also include the capability to communicate by sending and receiving data to other computers and to connect to the Internet. While different definitions of a computer exist, this definition includes a wide range of devices with various capabilities. Often the term computer or **computer system** is used to describe a collection of devices that function together to process data. An example of a computer system is shown in Figure 1-2.

For details on new opportunities in the information age, visit the Discovering Computers Chapter 1 inCyber page (http://www.scsite.com/dc/ch1/incyber.htm) and click Opportunities.

What Are the Components of a Computer?

Data is input, processed, output and stored by specific equipment called computer **hardware**. This equipment consists of input devices, a system unit, output devices, storage devices, and communications devices.

Input Devices

Input devices are used to enter data into a computer. Two common input devices are the keyboard and the mouse. As the data is entered using the **keyboard**, it is temporarily stored in the computer's memory and displayed on the screen of the monitor. A **mouse** is a type of pointing device used to select processing options or information displayed on the screen. The mouse is used to move a small symbol that appears on the screen. This symbol, called a **mouse pointer** or **pointer**, can be many shapes but is usually in the shape of an arrow.

Figure 1-2
A typical personal computer system.

Monitor
Temporary visual display of information. Most work similarly to televisions by using electrical signals to illuminate dots on the screen that combine to form text and images. (output)

Speaker
Used to amplify audio output such as music. (output)

System Unit
Horizontal or vertical case that contains most of the computer system electronics including the main circuit board (motherboard), central processing unit (CPU), and memory.

Floppy Disk Drive
Used for removable storage media called floppy disks or diskettes. The most common floppy disk size is $3^1/_2$ inches, which can store up to 1.44 million characters. (storage)

CD-ROM Drive
Most CD-ROM drives use low-powered laser light to read information that has previously been stored on a high-capacity CD-ROM. Some CD-ROM units also can write information on a disk. CD-ROMs can store up to 680 million characters. (storage)

Modem
A communications device that converts signals to and from the computer so that they can travel over telephone lines to other computers. (communications)

Hard Disk Drive
A hard disk drive stores data on spinning non-removable platters. Hard disks come in different sizes that allow them to store more than a billion characters. A panel light indicates when the hard disk is storing or retrieving data. (storage)

Keyboard
The primary input device of most users. The keyboard consists of letter, number, function, and control keys. (input)

Mouse
A type of pointing device that controls the movement of a symbol on the screen called the mouse pointer. Moving the mouse pointer on the screen and pressing buttons on the mouse causes processing actions to take place. (input)

Printer
Produces a permanent copy of computer-generated text and images on paper or other materials. (output)

System Unit

The **system unit** is a box-like case that contains the electronic circuits that cause the processing of data to occur. The electronic circuits usually are part of or are connected to a main circuit board called the **motherboard** or **system board**. The system board includes the central processing unit, memory, and other electronic components. The **central processing unit (CPU)** contains a **control unit** that executes the instructions that guide the computer through a task and an **arithmetic/logic unit** (ALU) that performs math and logic operations. The CPU is sometimes referred to as the **processor**. Figure 1-3 shows an example of a CPU of a personal computer.

Memory, also called **RAM (Random Access Memory)** and **main memory,** temporarily stores data and program instructions when they are being processed.

Other electronics in the system unit include components that work with the input, output, and storage devices. Storage devices and communications devices often are mounted inside the system unit case.

inCyber

For an overview of PC hardware, including discussions of the CPU and memory, visit the Discovering Computers Chapter 1 inCyber page (http://www.scsite.com/dc/ch1/incyber.htm) and click Hardware.

Figure 1-3
This Intel Pentium Pro is used as the CPU for many personal computers. Its microscopic electronic circuits contain 5.5 million transistors that can process instructions in billionths of a second.

Output Devices

Output consists of the results of processing. **Output devices** convert the results into a form that can be understood by the user. Three commonly used **output devices** are a **printer**, a **monitor**, and **speakers**. The printer produces a permanent hard copy while a monitor produces a temporary onscreen display. Speakers are used for audio output.

Storage Devices

Storage devices, sometimes called **secondary storage** or **auxiliary storage devices**, store instructions and data when they are not being used by the system unit. Storage devices often function as an input source when previously stored data is read into memory. A common storage device on personal computers is a **floppy disk drive**, which stores data as magnetic areas on a small removable plastic disk called a **floppy disk**. Another secondary storage device is called a hard disk drive. A **hard disk drive** contains a high-capacity disk or disks that provide greater storage capacities than floppy disks. A **CD-ROM drive** uses a low-powered laser light to read data from removable CD-ROMs.

Communications Devices

Communications devices enable a computer to connect to other computers. A **modem** is a communications device used to connect computers over telephone lines. A **network interface card** is used with communications cable to connect computers that are relatively close together, such as those in the same building. A group of computers connected together is called a **network**.

Peripheral Devices

The devices just discussed are only some of the many types of input, output, storage, and communications devices that can be part of a computer system. Different types of devices will be discussed in more detail in later chapters. A general term for any device connected to the system unit is **peripheral device**.

> **inCyber**
>
> For details on hard disk drives, visit the Discovering Computers Chapter 1 inCyber page (http://www.scsite.com/dc/ch1/incyber.htm) and click Hard Disk.

What Does a Computer Do?

Whether small or large, computers can perform four general operations. These four operations are **input**, **process**, **output**, and **storage**. Together, they comprise the **information processing cycle**. Each of these four operations can be assisted by a computer's ability to communicate with other computers. Collectively, these operations describe the procedures that a computer performs to process data into information and store it for future use.

All computer processing requires data. **Data** refers to the raw facts, including numbers, words, images, and sounds, given to a computer during the input operation. In the processing phase, the computer manipulates and organizes the data to create information. **Information** refers to data that has been processed into a form that has meaning and is useful. The production of information by processing data on a computer is called **information processing**. During the output operation, the information that has been created is put into some form, such as a printed report, that people can use. The information also can be stored electronically for future use.

The people who either use the computer directly or use the information it provides are called **computer users**, **end users**, or simply **users**.

Why Is a Computer So Powerful?

The input, process, output, and storage operations that a computer performs may seem very basic and simple. The computer's power, however, is derived from its capability of performing these operations with speed, reliability, and accuracy, and storing large amounts of data and information. A computer's capacity to communicate with other computers increases its input, processing, output, and storage capabilities.

Speed

In a computer, operations occur through the use of electronic circuits contained on small chips. When data flows along these circuits, it travels at close to the speed of light. This allows processing to be accomplished in billionths of a second.

For more information on time and frequency issues, visit the Discovering Computers Chapter 1 inCyber page (http://www.scsite.com/dc/ch1/incyber.htm) and click Speed.

Reliability

The electronic components in modern computers are very reliable due to a low failure rate. The high reliability of the components enables the computer to produce accurate results on a consistent basis.

Accuracy

Computers can process even complex data precisely and accurately, and output error-free information. In fact, most instances of computer error usually can be traced back to other causes, often human mistakes.

Storage

Computers can store enormous amounts of data and keep that data readily available for processing. Using modern storage methods, the data can be quickly retrieved and processed and then re-stored for future use.

Communications

A computer that can communicate with other computers has many more options than a stand-alone computer. If a computer is able to communicate with a remote computer, it can share any of the four information processing cycle operations — input, process, output, and storage — with that remote computer. Communications capability is sometimes referred to as connectivity.

Figure 1-4
Use of the Internet has been made easier with browser programs such as Microsoft Explorer. Browsers allow you to access World Wide Web sites that have text, graphics, video, and sound and have hypertext links to other information and Web sites. This screen shows how Microsoft Explorer displays the first page of information (called a **welcome page**) located at the Web site of Microsoft Corporation, the developer of Microsoft Explorer.

Connectivity

Connectivity refers to the ability to connect a computer to other computers. The connection may be temporary, such as when a computer is connected to an **online** information service provider such as America Online, or permanent, such as when a computer is connected to a network of other computers. Connectivity has had a significant impact on the way people use computers. For many years, computers were used as stand-alone devices, limited to the hardware and software resources contained in that computer. Stand-alone computers, however, are becoming the exception.

Most business computers are connected to other computers as part of a network. Even home computers are increasingly used to access other computers to transfer data and to obtain information on practically any subject.

Today, millions of people use a global network of computers, called the **Internet**, to gather information, send messages, and obtain products and services (Figure 1-4). The **World Wide Web (WWW)** portion of the Internet consists of **Web sites**, which are computer sites that can be accessed electronically for information on thousands of topics. Web sites usually present their information in a **multimedia format** that combines text and graphics and can include video and sound. Internet **Web browser programs** enable users to display information and quickly connect to other Internet sites.

For more information on how various companies are benefiting from connectivity, visit the Discovering Computers Chapter 1 inCyber page (http://www.scsite.com/dc/ch1/incyber.htm) and click Connectivity.

For information on aspects of the Internet, including search tools, chat rooms, and home page creation, visit the Discovering Computers Chapter 1 inCyber page (http://www.scsite.com/dc/ch1/incyber.htm) and click Internet.

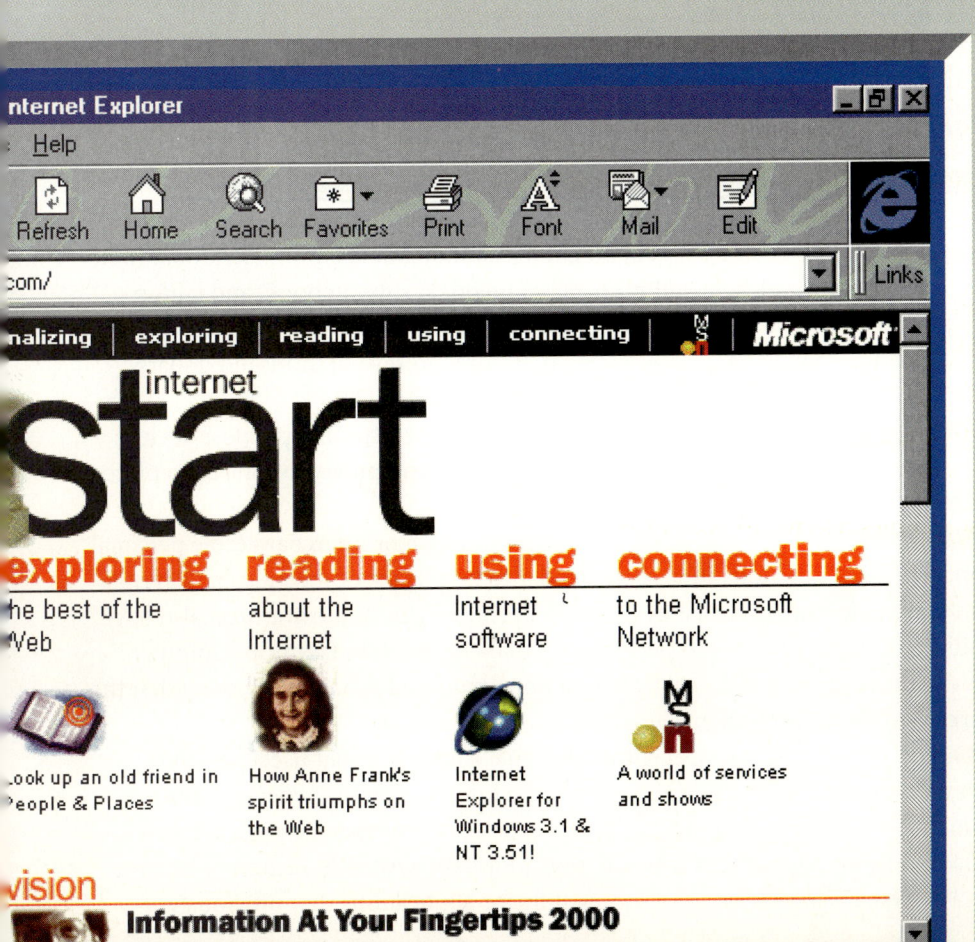

Categories of Computers

The five major categories of computers, which are personal computers, servers, minicomputers, mainframe computers, and supercomputers, are summarized in Figure 1-5.

Computers generally are classified according to their size, speed, processing capabilities, and price. Rapid changes in technology, however, make firm definitions of these categories difficult. This year's speed, performance, and price classification of one catagory may fit next year's classification of another category. Even though they are not firmly defined, the categories are frequently used and should be generally understood.

Category	Physical Size	Speed*	Number of Online Users	General Price Range
Personal Computer	hand-held to desktop or tower	1 to 200 MIPS	usually single user	hundreds to several thousand $
Server	tower or small cabinet	100 to 300 MIPS	2 to 1,000 users	$5,000 to $150,000
Minicomputer	small cabinet to several large cabinets	hundreds of MIPS	2 to 4,000 users	$15,000 to several hundred thousand $
Mainframe	partial to a full room of equipment	hundreds of MIPS	hundreds to thousands of users	$300,000 to several million $
Supercomputer	full room of equipment	thousands of MIPS	hundreds of users	several million $ and up

*speed rated in MIPS; each MIP equals one million instructions per second

Figure 1-5
This table summarizes some of the differences among the categories of computers. Because of rapid changes in technology, these should be considered general guidelines only.

Personal Computers

A **personal computer** (**PC**), also called **microcomputer** or **micro**, is a small system designed to be used by one person at a time. Classifications within this category, shown in Figure 1-6, include hand-held, palmtop, pen, notebook, subnotebook, laptop, desktop, tower, workstation, and network. Hand-held, palmtop, pen, notebook, subnotebook, and laptop computers are considered portable computers. Depending on their size and features, personal computer prices usually range from several hundred to several thousand dollars. The most expensive personal computers generally are less than $10,000.

Hand-held computers (Figure 1-6a) usually are designed for a specific purpose such as meter reading or inventory counting and are used by workers who move from place to place instead of sitting at a desk.

Palmtop computers (Figure 1-6b) often have several built-in or interchangeable personal information management functions such as a calendar to keep track of meetings and events, an address and phone file, and a task list of things to do. Some palmtop computers also have limited capabilities for typing notes and performing financial analysis. Palmtop computers do not have disk storage devices and usually have a non-standard keyboard, meaning that the keys are not arranged like a typewriter.

Pen computers (Figure 1-6c) are specialized portable computers that use a pen-like device to enter data. Sometimes the pen is used to write information on a special input screen and sometimes it is used as a pointing device to select a processing choice presented on the screen. Pen systems have special software that allows the system to recognize hand-written input. Pen systems have been used successfully for applications that previously

For information on hand-held computers, visit the Discovering Computers Chapter 1 inCyber page (http://www.scsite.com/dc/ch1/incyber.htm) and click Hand-held.

CATEGORIES OF COMPUTERS   1.11

required the user to fill out a paper form or checklist. One type of small pen input system is called a **personal digital assistant (PDA)** or **personal communicator** (Figure 1-6d). These hand-held devices are designed for workers on the go and often have built-in communications capabilities that allow the PDA to use voice, fax, or data communications.

Notebook computers (Figure 1-6e) are small enough to be carried in a briefcase but often are transported in their own carrying case. Notebooks are considered general-purpose computers because they can run most application software packages. They have standard keyboards and usually have at least one disk drive for storage. Notebooks usually weigh between four and eight pounds.

1-6a

1-6b

1-6c

1-6d
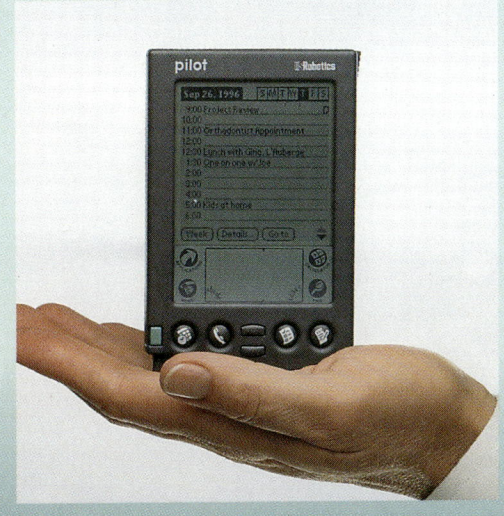

1-6e

Figure 1-6
These photographs show the many different types and sizes of personal computers. Shown are (a) hand-held, (b) palmtop, (c) pen, (d) personal digital assistant (PDA), (e) notebook,

(continued on next page)

1.12 CHAPTER 1 – AN OVERVIEW OF USING COMPUTERS

1-6f

1-6g
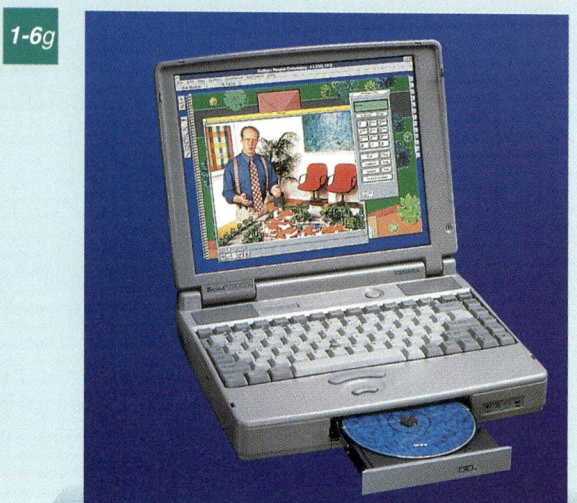

1-6h

1-6i

1-6j

1-6k

Figure 1-6 *(continued)*
(f) subnotebook, (g) laptop, (h) desktop, (i) tower, (j) workstation, (k) network.

Subnotebook computers (Figure 1-6f) are smaller versions of notebook computers and generally weigh less than four pounds. To save weight and space, some subnotebooks do not have disk drives and use special-purpose memory cards for storage.

Laptop computers (Figure 1-6g) are larger versions of notebook computers that weigh between eight and fifteen pounds. The extra weight comes primarily from hard disk storage devices and larger display screens.

Desktop computers (Figure 1-6h) are the most common type of personal computer and are designed to fit conveniently on the surface of a desk or workspace. Desktop computers have separate keyboards and display screens.

Tower computers (Figure 1-6i) are personal computers in an upright case. A full-sized tower case provides more room for expanding the system and adding optional equipment. The more powerful personal computers sometimes are only available in tower cases. A mini-tower case, approximately half the height of a full-sized tower case, usually has less expansion room than a desktop computer but takes up less room on the desk.

Workstations (Figure 6-j) are expensive, high-end personal computers that have powerful calculating and graphics capabilities. Workstations are frequently used by engineers to aid in product design and testing. The term **workstation** also is sometimes used to refer to a personal computer or terminal connected to a network.

Network computers (NC) (Figure 1-6k) are low-cost computers designed to work while connected to a network but not as stand-alone computers. Network computers have limited processing capability and little, if any, storage because these tasks are performed on the network server to which it is attached. Some network computers are designed to use a television monitor as their display device.

For more information on servers and network computers, visit the Discovering Computers Chapter 1 inCyber page (http://www.scsite.com/dc/ch1/incyber.htm) and click Server.

Servers

Server computers, shown in Figure 1-7, are designed to support a computer network that allows you to share files, application software, hardware, such as printers, and other network resources. The term **server** really describes how a computer is used. Technically, the term could be applied to any of the other categories of computers if they were used to support a network of other computers. In recent years, however, manufacturers have built computers specifically designed for network use and the term server is becoming widely used to describe this type of computer. Server computers usually have the following characteristics:

- designed to be connected to one or more networks
- the most powerful CPUs available
- multiple CPUs to share the processing tasks (one manufacturer's server can use up to 32 CPUs)
- large memory capacity
- large disk storage capacity
- high-speed internal and external communications capabilities

Small servers look like high-end personal computers and are priced in the $5,000 to $20,000 range. The more powerful servers look and function much like minicomputers and are priced as high as $150,000.

Figure 1-7
Server computers are designed to support a network of other computers. Servers allow the other computers to share data, application software, hardware resources such as printers, and other network resources. Small servers are powerful personal computers dedicated to a server function. The more powerful servers, however, are similar to minicomputers and are specifically designed for use on networks. The more powerful servers contain multiple CPUs, numerous hard disk drives, and large amounts of memory.

Minicomputers

Minicomputers, such as the one shown in Figure 1-8, are more powerful than personal computers and can support a number of users performing different tasks. Originally developed to perform specific tasks such as engineering calculations, their use grew rapidly as their performance and capabilities increased. Today, many businesses and other organizations use minicomputers to support their information processing requirements. These systems can cost from approximately $15,000 up to several hundred thousand dollars. The most powerful minicomputers are called superminicomputers.

Figure 1-8
Minicomputers are widely used in businesses to support multiple users.

Mainframe Computers

Mainframe computers, shown in Figure 1-9, are large systems that can handle hundreds of users connected at the same time, process transactions at a very high rate and, store large amounts of data. Mainframes usually require a specialized environment including separate air conditioning, cooling, and electrical power. Raised flooring is often built to accommodate the many cables connecting the system components underneath. The price range for mainframes is from several hundred thousand dollars to several million dollars.

Figure 1-9
Mainframe computers are large, powerful machines that can handle thousands of users concurrently and process immense volumes of data.

Supercomputers

Supercomputers, shown in Figure 1-10, are the most powerful category of computers and, accordingly, the most expensive. The capability of these systems to process hundreds of millions of instructions per second is used for such applications as weather forecasting, engineering design and testing, space exploration, and other jobs requiring long, complex calculations (Figure 1-11). These machines cost several million dollars.

For general information on supercomputer vendors, visit the Discovering Computers Chapter 1 inCyber page (http://www.scsite.com/dc/ch1/incyber.htm) and click Supercomputer.

Figure 1-10
Supercomputers are the most powerful and expensive computers. They often are used for applications that require complex calculations.

Figure 1-11
This simulated weather pattern was calculated on a supercomputer.

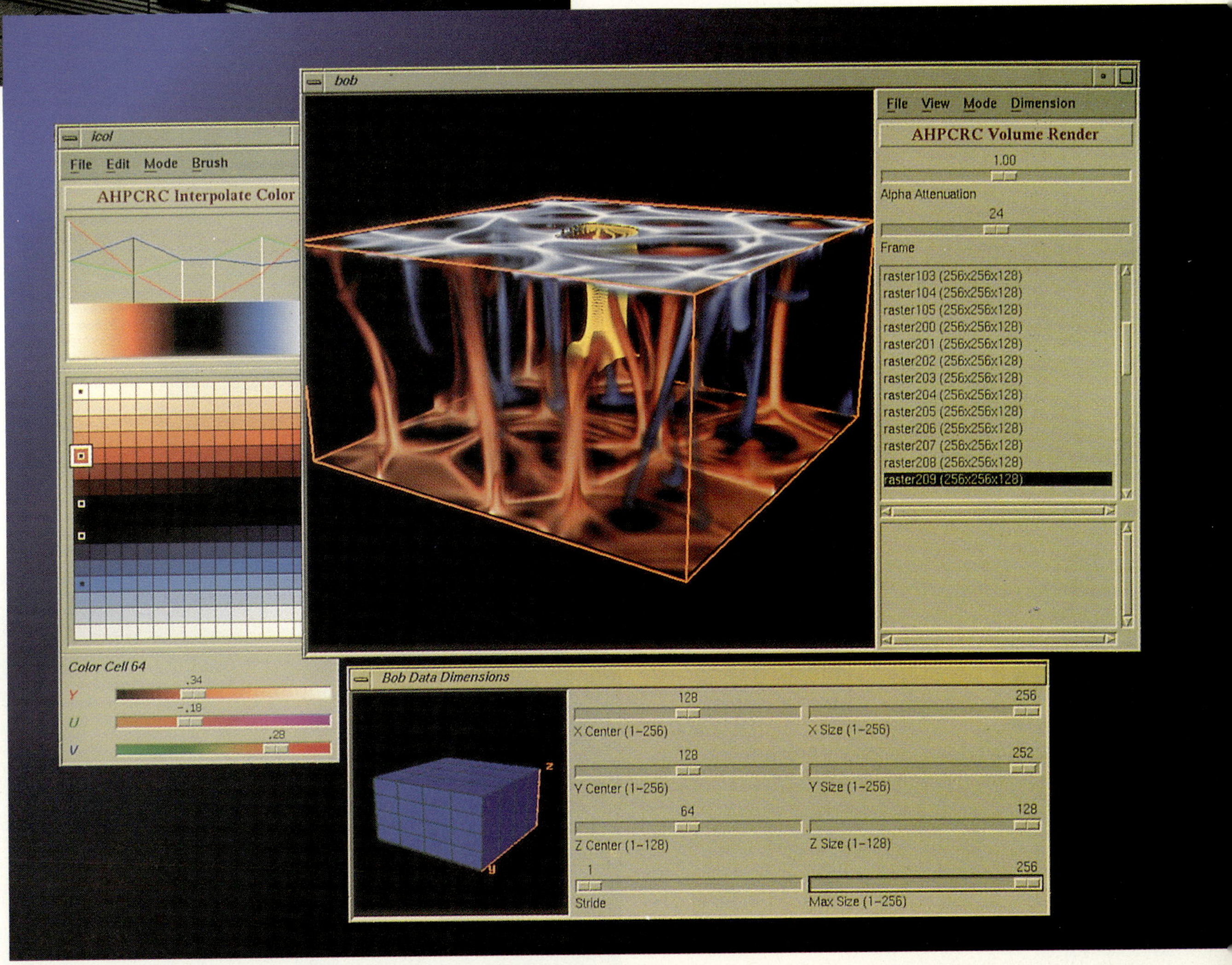

Computer Software

A computer is directed by a series of instructions called a **computer program** (lower screen in Figure 1-12b) that tells the computer what to do. Computer programs are commonly referred to as **software**. Before they can be performed, the program instructions must be loaded from disk into the memory of the computer. Many instructions are used to direct a computer to perform a specific task. For example, some instructions allow data to be entered from a keyboard and stored in memory; some instructions allow data in memory to be used in calculations such as adding a series of numbers to obtain a total; some instructions compare two values stored in memory and direct the computer to perform alternative operations based on the results of the comparison; and some instructions direct the computer to print a report, display information on the screen, draw a color graph on a screen, or store data on a disk.

Most computer programs are written by people with specialized training. These people, called **computer programmers**, write the instructions necessary to direct the computer to process data into information. The instructions must be placed in the correct sequence so the desired results will occur. Complex programs may require thousands of program instructions. Programmers often follow a plan developed by a **systems analyst** who works with both the user and the programmer to determine and design the desired output of the program.

Computer software is the key to productive use of computers. With the correct software, a computer can become a valuable tool. Software can be categorized into two types – system software and application software.

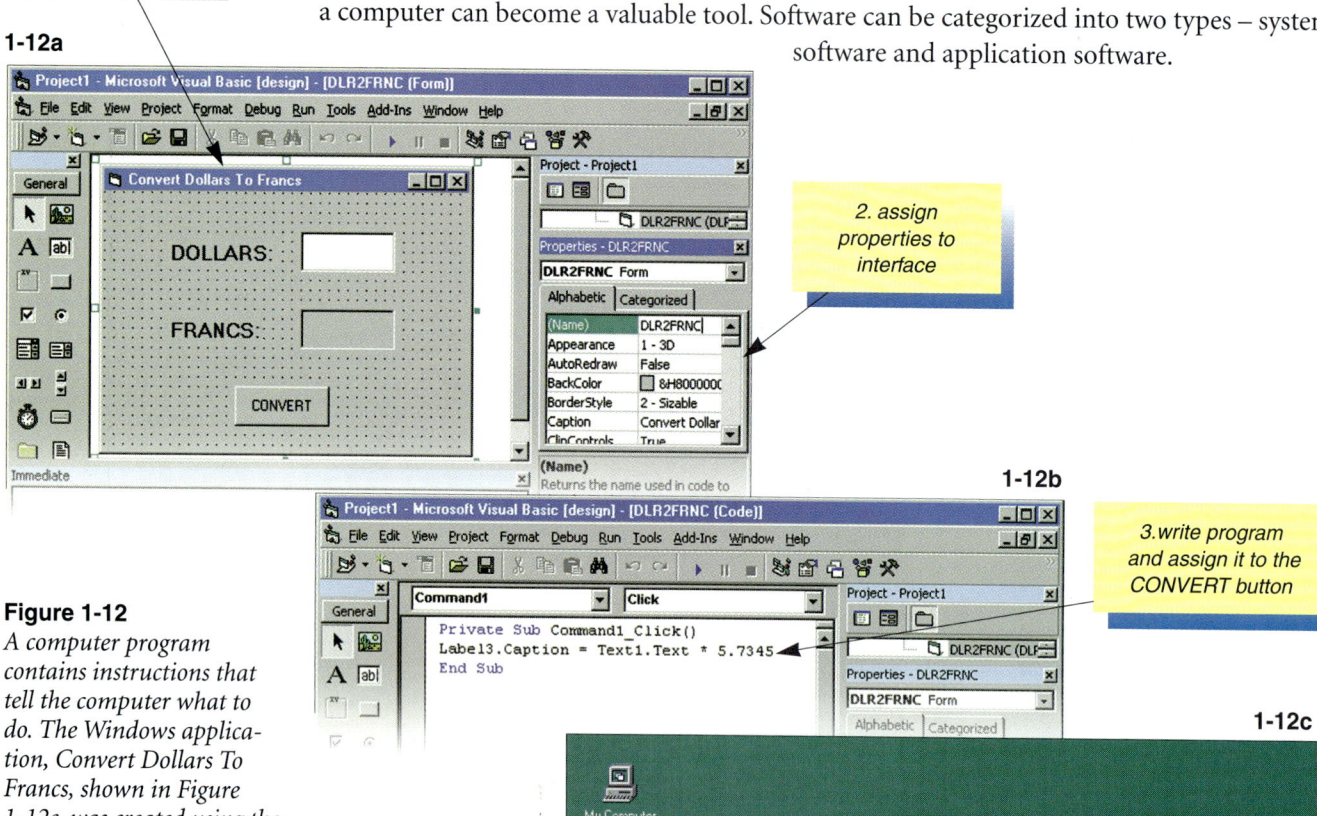

Figure 1-12
A computer program contains instructions that tell the computer what to do. The Windows application, Convert Dollars To Francs, shown in Figure 1-12c, was created using the programming language Microsoft Visual Basic. In Figure 1-12c, the user enters 520 (data) in the DOLLARS box, clicks the CONVERT button, and the computer displays the results 2981.94 (information) in the FRANCS box, following the instructions shown in Figure 1-12b. Creating a Windows application using Microsoft Visual Basic is a three-step process as shown in Figures 1-12a and 1-12b.

System Software

System software consists of programs that are related to controlling the actual operations of the computer equipment. An important part of the system software is a set of programs called the operating system. The instructions in the **operating system** tell the computer how to perform functions such as load, store, and execute a program and transfer data among the system devices and memory. For a computer to operate, an operating system must be stored in memory. Each time a computer is turned on, or restarted, the operating system is loaded from the hard disk and stored in memory. Many different operating systems are available for computers. An important part of the system software is the user interface.

User Interface

The **user interface** determines how you will interact with the computer. The user interface controls how information is presented on the screen and how you enter data and commands. Today, most computers use a graphical user interface. A **graphical user interface (GUI)** provides visual clues like small pictures, or icons, to help you. Each **icon** represents an application software program such as a word processor or a file or document where data is stored. Microsoft Windows 95 (Figure 1-13) is the latest version of Microsoft Windows, the most widely used graphical user interface for personal computers. Apple Macintosh computers also have a graphical user interface that is built into the Macintosh operating system.

For more information on the Windows 95 graphical user interface, visit the Discovering Computers Chapter 1 inCyber page (http://www.scsite.com/dc/ch1/incyber.htm) and click GUI.

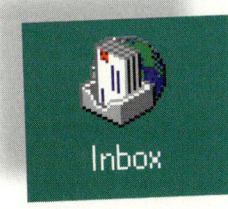

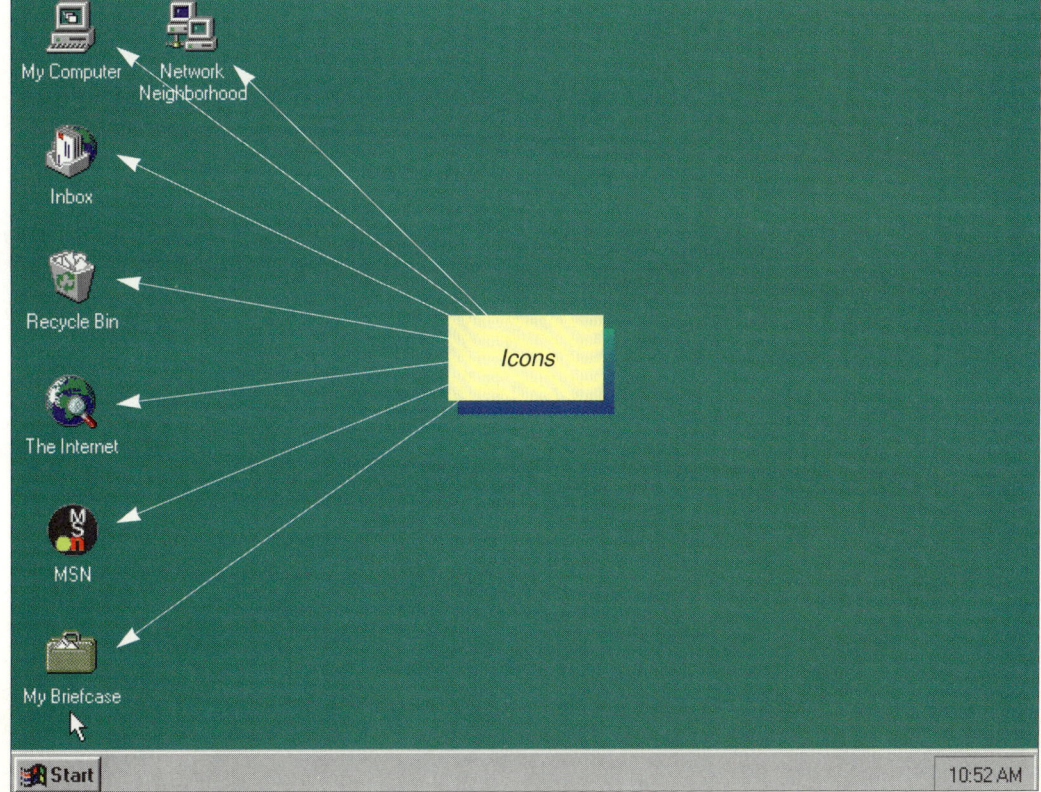

Figure 1-13
A graphical user interface, such as Microsoft Windows 95, makes the computer easier to use. The small pictures, or symbols, on the screen are called icons. The icons represent different processing options that you can choose. The icons (and the processing options) are selected by using a mouse or other pointing device.

Application Software

Application software consists of programs that tell a computer how to produce information. Application software resides permanently in storage, such as disk. You load a program into memory when you need to use it. When you think of the different ways that people use computers in their careers or in their personal lives, you are thinking of examples of application software. Business, scientific, and educational computer programs are all examples of application software.

Most computer users do not write their own programs. In some corporations, the information systems department develops custom software programs for unique company applications. Programs required for common business and personal applications can be purchased from software vendors or stores that sell computer products (Figure 1-14). Purchased programs often are referred to as **application software packages**, or simply **software packages**. Some of the more widely used personal computer software packages are word processing, desktop publishing, electronic spreadsheet, presentation graphics, database, communications, and electronic mail (e-mail) software.

For more information on application software packages, visit the Discovering Computers Chapter 1 inCyber page (http://www.scsite.com/dc/ch1/incyber.htm) and click Microsoft.

Figure 1-14
Many programs used for personal and business applications are purchased from computer stores.

1. Software

2. Hardware

3. Data

4. Users

5. Procedures

6. Information Systems Personnel

What Are the Elements of an Information System?

Obtaining useful and timely information from computer processing requires more than just the equipment and software described so far. Other elements required for successful information processing include accurate data, trained information systems personnel, knowledgeable users, and documented procedures. Together, these six elements – software, hardware, data, users, procedures, and information systems personnel – are referred to as an **information system** (Figure 1-15).

For an information system to provide accurate, timely, and useful information, each element in the system must be present and all of the elements must work together. The equipment must be reliable and capable of handling the expected workload. The software must have been carefully developed and tested, and the data entered for processing must be accurate. If the data is incorrect, the information produced from it will be incorrect.

Properly trained information systems personnel are required to run most medium and large computer systems. Even small networks of personal computers usually have a system administrator to manage the system. Users are taking increasing responsibility for the successful operation of information systems. This includes responsibility for the accuracy of both the input and output. In addition, users are taking a more active role in the development of computer applications. They work closely with information systems personnel in the development of computer applications that relate to their areas of work. Finally, all information processing applications should have documented procedures covering not only the computer operations but any other related procedures as well.

Figure 1-15
Six elements combine to make an information system: (1) software, (2) hardware, (3) data to be processed, (4) users who input the data and receive the output, (5) procedures to ensure data is processed accurately and consistently, and (6) information systems personnel to manage the computers.

An Example of How One Company Uses Computers

To show you how a typical mid-sized company might use computers, this section will take you on a visual and narrative tour of Dalton Corporation, a bicycle parts manufacturer. All of the computers at Dalton are joined together in a network that allows the computer users to communicate with one another and share information. In addition, Dalton operates an Internet Web site that provides product and selected company information (Figure 1-16). Customers, vendors, and other interested parties can access this information directly without having to speak to a Dalton employee.

Figure 1-16
Dalton's Internet Web site allows direct access to company and product information.

Reception

Before the installation of a computerized telephone system, a full-time operator was required to answer the telephone and direct the calls. Now, the computerized telephone system routes the calls to the appropriate person or department. If a caller does not want to leave a voice message or requests to talk to an operator, the call is routed to the receptionist (Figure 1-17). The receptionist can use the computer to determine the location of an employee. When employees leave their work areas for a meeting, lunch, or to travel away from the office, they record their destinations or reasons for being away using their computers. The employees can also record any special instructions to the receptionist, such as when they will return or to please hold their calls. If a caller wishes to leave a voice message, the computerized telephone system can play it back for the employee when he or she returns or calls in for messages.

Figure 1-17
The receptionist uses the computer system to locate employees away from their desks, to record messages, and to help with general administrative tasks.

Sales

The Dalton sales department consists of two groups: in-house sales representatives, who handle phone-in and mail-in sales orders and the field sales force, who make sales calls at customer locations. The in-house sales staff use headset telephones (Figure 1-18) so their hands are free to use their computer keyboards. Using the computer while they are on the telephone with a customer allows them to check product availability and the customer's credit status. A computer program also recommends products that complement the products ordered by the customer and displays information on special product promotions.

Outside sales representatives use notebook computers and special communications equipment and software to communicate with the Dalton main office. As with the in-house sales staff, they also can check product availability and customer credit status. If they receive a customer order, they can enter it into the Dalton computer system while they are still at the customer site. In addition, the field sales representatives can use the e-mail capability to check for or send messages.

Figure 1-18
Order entry personnel use the computer to check product availability for customers. The system automatically displays additional products the customer may need and information on special product promotions.

Marketing

The marketing department uses the computer system for a number of purposes. Desktop publishing, drawing, and graphics software are used to develop all marketing literature (Figure 1-19). Product brochures on bicycle parts, advertising materials, and product packaging are all produced in-house, saving considerable time and money. The customer service representatives all have computers that allow them to record a variety of customer inquiries. Recording the nature of each customer service inquiry provides for better follow-up (less chance of forgetting an unresolved inquiry) and enables the company to summarize and review why customers are calling. This helps the company identify and resolve potential problems at an early stage. The marketing department also uses a calendar program to schedule product promotions and attendance at trade shows (Figure 1-20).

Figure 1-19
The marketing departments of many companies use desktop publishing and drawing software to create product literature and advertising materials.

Figure 1-20
Calendar programs help users plan their schedules.

Shipping and Receiving

The shipping and receiving department uses the computer system to enter transactions that keep Dalton's inventory records accurate (Figure 1-21). Inventory receipts are first checked against computer records to make sure that Dalton receives only what was ordered. If the received goods match what was ordered, only a single entry has to be made to update the on-hand inventory and purchasing records.

Shipping transactions are also efficient. If all requested items are in stock, only a single entry is required to decrease the inventory and create the information that will be used to prepare the billing invoice. Shipping information, such as the method and time of shipment, can be added to the transaction record so the computer system can be used to provide an up-to-the-minute status of the customer's order.

Figure 1-21
Computers help companies maintain accurate inventory records.

Manufacturing

The manufacturing department uses the computer to schedule production and to record the costs of the items produced. Special manufacturing software matches the availability of production resources such as people, machines, and material against the desired product output. This information allows Dalton to schedule production efficiently and tells them when and how much to buy of the raw materials they need to produce their products. Actual labor, material, and machine usage is recorded on the manufacturing floor using special workstations designed to be used in industrial environments (Figure 1-22). This information is entered into the computer system automatically to update inventory, production, payroll, and cost accounting records.

Figure 1-22
Some computer workstations have been specially designed to withstand the heat, dust, and other conditions of a factory floor.

Product Design

The product design department uses computer-aided design (CAD) software to design new products (Figure 1-23). CAD software allows the designers to create and review three-dimensional models of new products on the computer before expensive molds are required. If a design is approved, the CAD software can automatically produce a list of the required parts.

Figure 1-23
Computer-aided design (CAD) software is used to design new products. As with word processing software, CAD programs make the design process easier by allowing you to make changes until you are satisfied.

Accounting

The accounting department is one of the largest computer system users. Many of the accounting records are the result of transactions entered in the user departments, such as shipping and receiving and manufacturing. These records are used to pay vendor invoices, bill customers for product sales, and process the Dalton employee payroll (Figure 1-24). The accounting transactions are summarized automatically to produce Dalton's financial statements, which are used internally to monitor financial performance and given to outside organizations such as banks.

Figure 1-24
Accounting departments were one of the first users of computer systems and still rely heavily on computers to summarize financial transactions.

Human Resources

The human resources department uses the computer system to keep track of information on existing, past, and potential employees (Figure 1-25). Besides the standard information required for payroll and employee benefits, the system keeps track of employees' job skills and training. This information enables the human resources department to review the records of existing employees first when a new job becomes available.

Figure 1-25
Human resources departments use computers to keep track of past, present, and potential employees.

Figure 1-26
Information systems personnel help maintain the computer system by using performance measurement software to monitor system use.

Information Systems

A primary responsibility of the information systems department is to keep the existing system running and determine when and if new equipment or software is required. To help answer these questions, the information systems personnel use diagnostic and performance measurement software that tells them how much the system is being used and if system problems are being encountered (Figure 1-26). A systems analyst works with users to design custom software for user applications for which application software packages do not exist. A computer programmer then uses this design to write the program instructions necessary to produce the desired processing results and output.

Executive

The senior management staff of Dalton Corporation (the president and three vice presidents) use the computer as an executive information system (EIS). The EIS summarizes information such as actual sales, order backlog, number of employees, cash on hand, and other performance measures into both a numeric and graphic display (Figure 1-27). The EIS is designed specifically for executives who may not work regularly with computers and want only to see summarized information.

Figure 1-27
Executive information system (EIS) software usually presents summarized data and often uses charts and graphs to convey information.

Summary of How One Company Uses Computers

The computer applications just discussed are only some of the many potential uses of the computers within Dalton Corporation. In addition, employees in each of the departments can use the computer for preparing correspondence, project and task management, budgeting, and sending messages via electronic mail. As shown in the Dalton Corporation example, computers are used throughout an organization. Employees use computers to perform a variety of tasks related to their job areas. Because of the widespread use of computers, most organizations prefer to hire employees with computer experience and knowledge.

Summary of an Overview of Using Computers

This chapter presented a broad introduction to concepts and terminology that are related to computers. You now have a basic understanding of what a computer is, how it processes data into information, and what elements are necessary for a successful information system. You also have seen some examples of different types of computers and how they are used. Reading and understanding the overview of using computers this chapter should help you to understand these topics as they are presented in more detail in following chapters.

CHAPTER 1 – AN OVERVIEW OF USING COMPUTERS

COMPUTERS AT WORK

Shopping for an Auto Online

Figure 1-28a

Shopping for a car or truck used to be a time-consuming process. Time was spent traveling to and from car dealers or locating the hard-to-find owner selling a used vehicle. Now, with a computer and a communications link, much of the work can be done online.

All of the major online services provide many resources for obtaining information on new and used vehicles. One of the best-looking references is CarPoint available on The Microsoft Network (MSN). CarPoint contains information and color photographs of more than 250 models from nearly 50 manufacturers. With CarPoint, you can browse through the models randomly or use built-in search capabilities to create a list that meets your specific desires. Once you have narrowed your choice to a specific model, you can request a report that gives detailed information on prices and other features. While the basic CarPoint information is free to MSN subscribers, the detailed reports cost $4.95 to download onto your computer.

Figure 1-28b

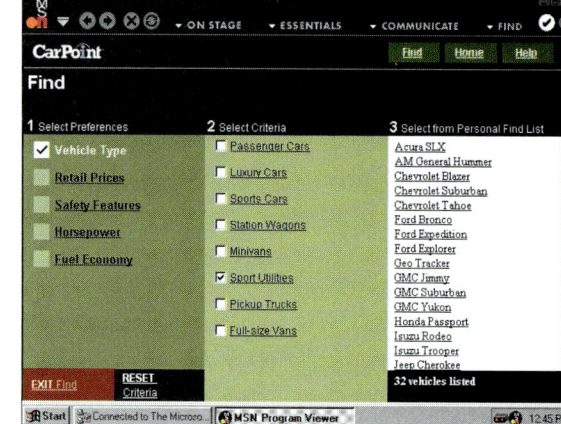

Not ready for a new car? Don't worry, even more information is available on used cars on various Internet Web sites. A good way to start gathering information is to do a keyword search on "cars" or "automotive." One Web site that may be familiar to vehicle shoppers is operated by the company that publishes the *Auto Trader* magazines (http://www.traderonline.com). Auto Trader® Online lets you search for a vehicle based on specific model and price range information. With Auto Trader® Online, you also can specify a beginning and ending year range. To localize the search, you can request to see only vehicles in a particular telephone area code, state, or region. The Auto Trader search returns a list of vehicles with two to four lines of description. Not shown are the seller's phone numbers. For $1.00, you can purchase the list with the phone numbers included. Auto Trader® Online also has information on new cars and has links to the Web sites of all the major car manufacturers. To verify that a used car price is reasonable, or to help determine the value of your car or truck, you can review the values published by *Edmund's Automobile Buyer's Guide* at its Internet site (http://www.edmunds.com/). Edmund's provides pricing and other information on the last ten years of most models.

Figure 1-28c

If you are ready to buy or lease a new vehicle, Auto-By-Tel operates an Internet buying and leasing service (http://www.autobytel.com). Enter the features and options of the vehicle you want, and Auto-By-Tel will find a local dealer willing to sell or lease it to you at a wholesale price.

You may not get as much exercise, but the ability to research, compare, locate, and finance a vehicle from the comfort of your computer chair does offer some advantages. About the only thing you cannot do online is kick the tires!

IN THE FUTURE

From the Global Village to the Local Village

Much of the information written about the Internet focuses on specific Web sites that provide specialized information or services. These Web sites are literally spread around the world and have contributed to the concept of an "electronic global village" where Internet citizens, sometimes called *netizens,* can access worldwide information resources. Another, however, more local trend is developing, that may offer more value to the average person.

Numerous cities are now establishing community networks whose primary goal is to provide information to local citizens. One of the leaders of this movement is Blacksburg, in southwestern Virginia. The Blacksburg Electronic Village (BEV) (http://www.bev.net) was started in 1994. The goal of the BEV is to link its citizens to each other and to local business, civic, and government organizations.

One of the widely used services is e-mail, which allows BEV users to keep in touch with each other and register their opinions on local issues with city and county representatives. The BEV Village Mall has almost 200 businesses, each with its own custom-designed presentation of products or services. Some businesses advertise and others allow users to place orders online. The Community Events and News section lists information about upcoming arts and entertainment. Other sections of the BEV offer information on health services, area museums, and local schools. To encourage people to use the network and to help struggling users, BEV offers an online Help Desk to anyone experiencing problems.

Although Blacksburg is recognized worldwide as the leading electronic community, others are not far behind. Other leading electronic communities include Palo Alto, California (http://www.city.paloalto.ca.us), Taos, New Mexico (http://laplaza.taos.nm.us), and Boulder, Colorado (http://bcn.boulder.co.us). The list of communities that offer at least some online information is growing rapidly. An Internet Web site exists that keeps track of community pages by state and provides information on how to create a community Web site.

What are the social implications of the electronic communities? Some people are concerned that the substitution of electronic meetings for face-to-face gatherings is not healthy. Others say that networks such as BEV make communicating with new people easier and often lead to face-to-face meetings. These same issues were raised in the past with other technological changes such as the telephone and television. You still may not be able to fight city hall, but at least in the future you can bombard them with e-mail.

Figure 1-29a

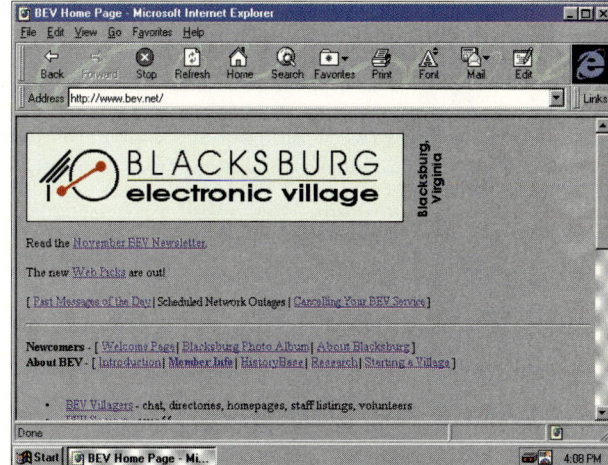

Figure 1-29b

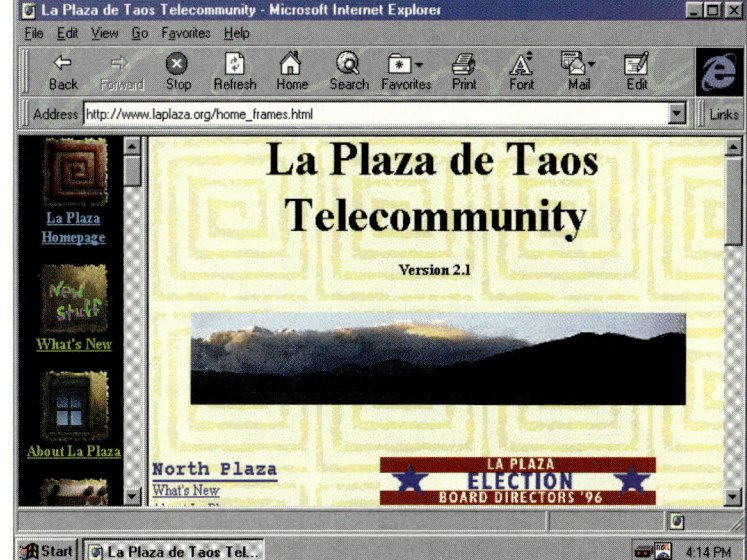

Figure 1-29c

review

chapter 1 | 2 | 3 | 4 | 5 | 6 | 7 | 8 | 9 | 10 | 11 | 12 | 13 | 14 | I

inCyber | review | terms | yourTurn | hotTopics | outThere | winLabs | webWalk | exercises | news | home

INSTRUCTIONS: *To display this page from the Web, launch your browser and enter the URL, http://www.scsite.com/dc/ch1/review.htm. Click the links for current and additional information.*

1 Computer Literacy vs. Information Literacy

Most people believe knowing how to use a computer, sometimes called **computer literacy**, is a basic skill necessary to succeed in business or to function in society. Many people feel, however, that a person should be *information literate* as well as *computer literate*. **Information literacy** is defined as knowing how to find, analyze, and use information.

2 Computers

Increasingly, the information people need is available from sources that can be accessed using computers. A **computer** is an electronic device, operating under the control of instructions stored in its memory unit, that can accept data (input), process data arithmetically and logically, produce results (output) from the processing, and store the results for future use.

3 Computer Systems

The term **computer system** frequently is used to describe the collection of devices that functions together to process data. This equipment, often called computer **hardware**, consists of input devices, a system unit, output devices, storage devices, and communications devices. **Input devices** are used to enter data. The **system unit** contains the electrical circuits that cause the processing of data to occur. **Output devices** convert the results of processing into a form that can be experienced by the user. **Storage devices** store instructions and data when they are not being used. **Communications devices** enable a computer to connect to other computers.

4 Information Processing

All computers can perform four general operations: **input**, **process**, **output**, and **storage**. Together, these operations comprise the **information processing cycle**. During the input operation, a computer is given raw facts, or data. In the processing phase, the computer manipulates and organizes the data to create information — data in a form that is useful and has meaning. The production of information by processing data on a computer is called **information processing**. During the output operation, the information created is put into a form that people can use. Information also can be stored electronically for future use.

5 Computer Power

A computer's power is derived from its capability of performing the operations of the information processing cycle with speed, reliability, and accuracy, and its capacity for storing large amounts of data and information. Data travels at close to the speed of light and processing is accomplished in billionths of a second.

review

chapter 1 | 2 | 3 | 4 | 5 | 6 | 7 | 8 | 9 | 10 | 11 | 12 | 13 | 14 | I

inCyber | review | terms | yourTurn | hotTopics | outThere | winLabs | webWalk | exercises | news | home

6 Connectivity

A computer's ability to communicate with other computers increases its input, processing, output, and storage capabilities. **Connectivity** refers to the ability to connect a computer to other computers, either temporarily or permanently. Today, millions of people use the **Internet**, a global network of computers, to gain information, send messages, and obtain products or services. The **World Wide Web (WWW)** portion of the Internet consists of computer sites, called **Web sites**, that can be accessed electronically for information on thousands of topics.

7 Personal Computers

Computers generally are classified according to their size, speed, processing capabilities, and price. Although rapid changes in technology make firm definitions difficult, computers can be grouped into five major categories: personal computers, server computers, minicomputers, mainframe computers, and supercomputers. **Personal computers** are small systems intended to be used by one person at a time. Classifications within this category include **hand-held, palmtop, pen, notebook, subnotebook, laptop, desktop, tower, workstation,** and **network.**

8 Other Computer Categories

Server computers are a category of computers designed to be part of a computer network. **Minicomputers** are more powerful than personal computers and can support a number of users performing different tasks. **Mainframe** computers can handle thousands of users at the same time, store large amounts of data, and process transactions at a very high rate. **Supercomputers**, the most powerful and expensive category of computers, are capable of processing hundreds of millions of instructions per second.

9 Computer Programs

A computer is directed by a series of instructions called a **computer program**, or **software**. Software can be categorized into two types: system software and application software. **System software** consists of programs related to controlling the actual operations of computer equipment. Important parts of system software are the **operating system**, which tells the computer how to perform basic functions, and the **user interface**, which determines how the user interacts with the computer. **Application software** consists of programs that tell a computer how to produce information. Purchased programs are called **application software packages**, or simply **software packages**.

10 Information Systems

Obtaining useful and timely information from computer processing requires equipment, software, accurate data, trained information systems personnel, knowledgeable users, and documented procedures. Together, these six elements are referred to as an **information system**. All of the elements must work together. Equipment has to be reliable and capable of handling the workload. Software must be carefully developed and tested. Data needs to be entered correctly. Trained information systems personnel are necessary to manage the system. Users are responsible for the accuracy of both input and output and are taking an active role in the development of computer applications. Finally, all information processing applications should have documented procedures covering computer and related operations.

terms

chapter 1 | 2 | 3 | 4 | 5 | 6 | 7 | 8 | 9 | 10 | 11 | 12 | 13 | 14 | I

inCyber | review | terms | yourTurn | hotTopics | outThere | winLabs | webWalk | exercises | news | home

INSTRUCTIONS: *To display this page from the Web, launch your browser and enter the URL, http://www.scsite.com/dc/ch1/terms.htm. Scroll through the list of terms. Click a term for its definition and a picture. Click the rocket ship for current and additional information about the term.*

laptop computers

DEFINITION

laptop computers
Larger versions of notebook computers that weigh between eight and fifteen pounds. **(1.13)**

application software (1.18)
application software packages (1.18)
arithmetic/logic unit (ALU) (1.6)
auxiliary storage devices (1.7)

CD-ROM drive (1.7)
central processing unit (CPU) (1.6)
communications devices (1.7)
computer (1.4)
computer literacy (1.2)
computer program (1.16)
computer programmers (1.16)
computer system (1.4)
computer users (1.7)
connectivity (1.9)
control unit (1.6)

data (1.7)
desktop computers (1.13)

end users (1.7)

floppy disk (1.7)
floppy disk drive (1.7)

graphical user interface (GUI) (1.17)

hand-held computers (1.10)
hard disk drive (1.7)
hardware (1.4)
home page (1.8)

icon (1.17)
information (1.7)
information literacy (1.2)

information processing (1.7)
information processing cycle (1.7)
information system (1.19)
input (1.7)
input devices (1.4)
Internet (1.3, 1.9)

keyboard (1.4)

laptop computers (1.13)

main memory (1.6)
mainframe computers (1.14)
memory (1.6)
micro (1.10)
microcomputer (1.10)
minicomputers (1.14)
modem (1.7)
monitor (1.6)
motherboard (1.6)
mouse (1.4)
mouse pointer (1.4)
multimedia format (1.9)

network (1.7)
network computers (NC) (1.13)
network interface card (1.7)
notebook computers (1.11)

operating system (1.17)
output (1.6, 1.7)
output devices (1.6)

palmtop computers (1.10)
pen computers (1.10)

peripheral device (1.7)
personal communicator (1.11)
personal computer (PC) (1.10)
personal digital assistant (PDA) (1.11)
pointer (1.4)
printer (1.6)
process (1.7)
processor (1.6)

RAM (Random Access Memory) (1.6)

secondary storage (1.7)
server (1.13)
server computers (1.13)
software (1.16)
software packages (1.18)
speakers (1.6)
storage (1.7)
storage devices (1.7)
subnotebook computers (1.13)
supercomputers (1.15)
system board (1.6)
system software (1.17)
system unit (1.6)
systems analyst (1.16)

tower computers (1.13)

user interface (1.17)
users (1.7)

Web browser programs (1.9)
Web sites (1.9)
workstations (1.13)
World Wide Web (WWW) (1.9)

chapter
1 | 2 | 3 | 4 | 5 | 6 | 7 | 8 | 9 | 10 | 11 | 12 | 13 | 14 | I

inCyber | review | terms | yourTurn | hotTopics | outThere | winLabs | webWalk | exercises | news | home

INSTRUCTIONS: *To display this page from the Web, launch your browser and enter the URL, http://www.scsite.com/dc/ch1/hot.htm Click the links for current and additional information to help you respond to the hotTopics questions.*

1 *Most people feel that knowing how to use a computer is an essential skill.* Nevertheless, when one thousand Americans were asked in a recent MIT poll which of eight inventions they could not live without, the personal computer tied for last, along with the blow-dryer. The automobile, lightbulb, telephone, television, aspirin, and microwave oven were all perceived as more indispensable than the personal computer. Is the belief in the importance of computer literacy inconsistent with the results of this poll? Why or why not? How might the characteristics of the people questioned have affected the results? How would you rank the importance of computers compared to the other inventions in the list? Why?

2 *Many technological innovations have been "double-edged swords," with both positive and negative* effects on society at large. The automobile, for example, has allowed people to travel freely and extended the availability of goods and services; at the same time, however, it has increased air pollution and contributed to thousands of serious accidents. Together with a classmate, present a debate on the effect computers have had on society. One of you should argue that their impact primarily has been positive, while the other should contend that their impact primarily has been negative. When the debate is over, see if you, together with all of your classmates, can reach a consensus regarding the overall impact of computers on society.

3 *Not only has computer literacy become an integral part of school curriculums, the* use of computers *also has affected other areas of study.* For example, an increasing number of elementary schools has abandoned the teaching of cursive writing, instead promoting keyboarding skills. Many students are learning how to type in first grade, even as they discover how to print. A noted educator points out that if something has to be eliminated — printing, cursive, or keyboard — then cursive is the logical choice. Many systems have rejected the traditional loops and flourishes of cursive in favor of a simpler style that can keep pace with computer keyboards. In what other ways might the use of computers change what schools teach? How will computers make your son's or daughter's elementary school education different from yours? In general, are these changes positive or negative? Why?

4 *In 1995, a problem-plagued computer system in Albany, New York, finally "crashed," losing* almost 26,000 photo driver's licenses. Affected motorists were given extensions and temporary licenses and asked to have their pictures retaken, at no additional cost and without having to wait in line again. Although the company leasing the system corrected the problem at no cost to the state, both motorists and state workers were inconvenienced by the system's failure. Despite the reliability of computers, everyone has heard of similar computer errors. Describe a situation with which you are familiar where a similar computer error occurred. Who, or what, was responsible for the error? What steps could be taken to ensure that the error does not happen again?

5 *Your school has been given a grant to purchase a supercomputer, a mainframe computer,* several minicomputers, and a number of personal computers. How do you think each category of computer would be best used in your school? Who should have access to each computer? If the money for personal computers had to be spent on three different types of personal computers, what kind do you think should be purchased and how should they be used?

1.33   outThere

outThere

chapter
1 | 2 | 3 | 4 | 5 | 6 | 7 | 8 | 9 | 10 | 11 | 12 | 13 | 14 | I

inCyber | review | terms | yourTurn | hotTopics | outThere | winLabs | webWalk | exercises | news | home

INSTRUCTIONS: *To display this page from the Web, launch your browser and enter the URL, http://www.scsite.com/dc/ch1/out.htm. Click the links for current and additional information.*

1 *For a few people, using a computer is still a novel experience. Increasingly,* however, computer use is becoming a fact of life. Does familiarity really breed contempt (as the old saying maintains)? Perhaps instead it engenders affection or only fosters indifference. Interview a person who uses a computer every day at work, and prepare a brief report on that person's feelings about computers. How does the person use the computer? Did he or she experience any initial anxiety when first confronting the computer? If so, did he or she overcome it? What type of training did the individual receive? With hindsight, what type of training would be recommended? How does a computer make the job easier or more difficult? Overall, how does the individual feel about computers?

2 *Computers have changed the way people access information. For example,* once avid newspaper readers now can turn instead to sites on the World Wide Web offered by their favorite tabloids. Some of the more recognizable names include *The New York Times*, the *Boston Globe*, *The Wall Street Journal*, the *San Francisco Chronicle*, and *USA TODAY*. How is the online rendering of a periodical different from the printed version? Purchase a newspaper that is represented on the World Wide Web and compare the printed paper to its Web site. How are they similar? How are they different? What are the advantages and disadvantages of each? In general, which do you prefer? Why?

3 *Are computers purchased by individuals from a broad spectrum, or does a certain type represent* most computer buyers? Visit a computer vendor and interview the manager or a salesperson about computer purchasers. Based on the interview, prepare a report on the demographics of computer buyers at that store. What gender are most buyers? In what age range do they fall? What is the average age group? What seems to be the typical educational level? What is the approximate average income of a typical buyer? Do buyers share any other characteristics? Why do most purchasers buy a computer?

4 *As the automobile led to the end of the horse and buggy, does* the growth of the Internet herald the demise of printed media? Probably not; in fact, many booksellers are turning to the Internet to promote their wares. Three of the largest bookstores online are Amazon, Chapter One, and Book Stacks Unlimited. Visit a bookstore Web site and compare searching for a book online to seeking a book in a traditional bookstore. Try looking for a particular title, a book by a certain author, and books on a specific subject. What are the advantages and disadvantages of shopping for a book online? How likely would you be to buy a book through a bookstore Web site? Why?

5 *Computers have had an important part in some major movies. How does Hollywood view* computers? Rent a videotape in which a computer plays a significant role — some examples are *2001: A Space Odyssey*, *War Games*, *Short Circuit*, *Virtuosity*, *Hackers*, and *The Net*. Watch the videotape, and then prepare a report on how the movie maker seems to view computers. What part do computers play in the movie? In general, are computers heroes, villains, or simply tools (for good or evil) of human characters? Why? What was the theme of the movie? What role, if any, did computers have in promoting the movie's theme?

Start outThere   1:05 AM

chapter

inCyber | review | terms | yourTurn | hotTopics | outThere | winLabs | webWalk | exercises | news | home

INSTRUCTIONS: *To display this page from the Web, launch your browser and enter the URL, http://www.scsite.com/dc/ch1/labs.htm. Click the links for current and additional information.*

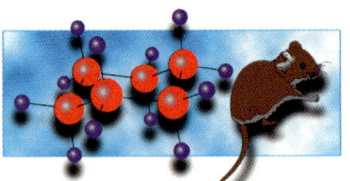

Shelly Cashman Series Mouse Lab

Click the Start button on the taskbar; point to Programs on the Start menu; point to Shelly Cashman Series Labs on the Programs submenu; and then click Interactive Labs on the Shelly Cashman Series Labs submenu. When the Shelly Cashman Series Labs screen displays (Figure 1-30), if Using the Mouse is not selected, press the UP ARROW or DOWN ARROW key to select it. Press ENTER. Carefully read the objectives. With your printer on, press the P key on the keyboard to print the questions. Fill out the top of the Questions sheet and then answer the questions.

Figure 1-30

Shelly Cashman Series Keyboard Lab

Follow the instructions in winLab 1 above to display the Shelly Cashman Series Labs screen. Click Using the Keyboard. Click the Start Lab button. When the initial screen displays, carefully read the objectives. With your printer on, click the Print Questions button. Fill out the top of the Questions sheet and then answer the questions.

Learning What's New in Microsoft Windows 95

Click the Start button on the taskbar, and then click Help on the Start menu. Click the Contents tab in the Help Topics: Windows Help dialog box. Double-click the Introducing Windows book; double-click the Welcome book; double-click the A List of What's New book (Figure 1-31); and then double-click the A new look and feel topic. Click each topic in the Windows Help window and then read the information. Answer the following questions as you step through the topics: (1) What are two uses of the Start button? (2) Where is the My Computer icon located? (3) How do you start Windows Explorer? (4) Are spaces legal characters in a file name? (5) How do you display a shortcut menu for an item? Click the Close button.

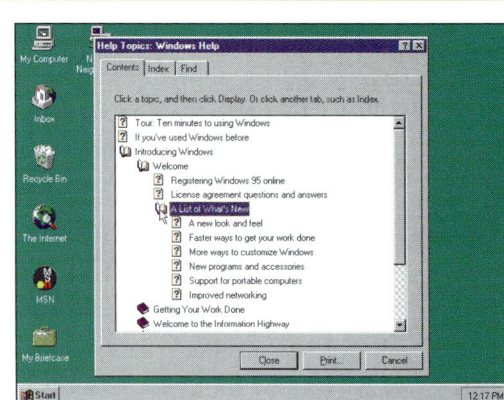

Figure 1-31

Improving Mouse Skills

Click the Start button on the taskbar; point to Programs; point to Accessories on the Programs submenu; point to Games on the Accessories submenu; and then click Solitaire on the Games submenu. When the Solitaire window displays, click its Maximize button. Click Help on Solitaire's menu bar, and then click Help Topics. Click the Contents tab, and then double-click the How to play Solitaire topic. Read and print the topic by clicking the Solitaire Help window's Options button, clicking Print Topic, and then clicking the OK button. Close the Solitaire Help window by clicking its Close button. Play the game of Solitaire. Quit Solitaire by clicking its Close button.

webWalk

chapter 1 | 2 | 3 | 4 | 5 | 6 | 7 | 8 | 9 | 10 | 11 | 12 | 13 | 14 | I

inCyber | review | terms | yourTurn | hotTopics | outThere | winLabs | webWalk | exercises | news | home

INSTRUCTIONS: *To display this page from the Web, launch your browser and enter the URL, http://www.scsite.com/dc/ch1/walk.htm. Click the exercise link to display the exercise.*

1. Information Literacy
Today, most people believe that knowing how to use a computer is a basic skill necessary to function successfully in society. Information literacy is knowing how to find, analyze and use information. You can increase your information literacy by completing this exercise.

3. Supercomputers
Supercomputers are the most powerful and expensive category of computers. These systems are capable of processing hundreds of millions of instructions per second. To view pictures of super-computers (Figure 1-32) and learn more about them, complete this exercise.

Figure 1-32

5. Information Mining
Complete this exercise to improve your Web research skills by using a Web search engine to find information related to this chapter.

6. Communications
A computer's ability to communicate with other computers increases its information retrieval capabilities. Complete this exercise to search a large database for information.

8. Connectivity
Connectivity has had a significant impact on the way people use computers. To see some future possibilities of coupling connectivity with the latest software technology, complete this exercise.

2. PDA Enhancements
One type of small pen input computer system is called a personal digital assistant (PDA). These hand-held devices often have built-in communications capabilities that allow the PDA to use voice, fax, or data communication. To learn about products designed to enhance PDAs, complete this exercise.

4. Computer Glossary
RAM, ROM, MIPS, FLOPS. If you are perplexed by all the computer buzzwords, you can complete this exercise to help you sort it all out (Figure 1-33).

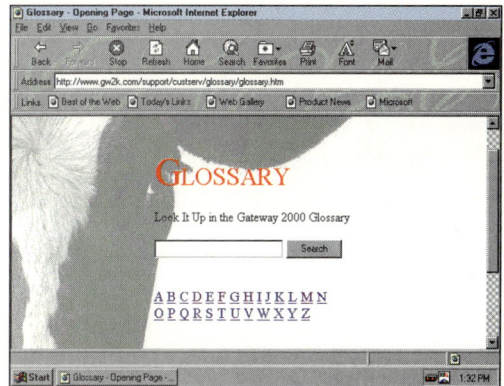

Figure 1-33

7. Web Commerce
Today, millions of people use the Internet to gain information, send messages, and purchase products and services. Complete this exercise to learn more about commerce on the Web.

9. Web Chat
Complete this exercise to enter a Web Chat discussion related to the issues presented in the hotTopics exercise.

TIMELINE
Milestones in Computer History

Dr. John V. Atanasoff and his assistant Clifford Berry designed and began to build the first electronic digital computer during the winter of 1937-38. Their machine, the Atanasoff-Berry-Computer, or ABC, provided the foundation for the next advances in electronic digital computers.

1937

1943

During the years 1943 to 1946, Dr. John W. Mauchly and J. Presper Eckert, Jr. completed the ENIAC (Electronic Numerical Integrator and Computer), the first large-scale electronic digital computer. The ENIAC weighed thirty tons, contained 18,000 vacuum tubes, and occupied a thirty-by-fifty-foot space.

1945

Dr. John von Neumann is credited with writing a brilliant report in 1945 describing several new hardware concepts and the use of stored programs. His breakthrough laid the foundation for the digital computers that since have been built.

1951

J. Presper Eckert, Jr., standing left, explains the operations of the UNIVAC I to newsman Walter Cronkite, right. This machine was the first commercially available electronic digital computer.

Public awareness of computers increased when, in 1951, the UNIVAC I, after analyzing only 5% of the tallied vote, correctly predicted that Dwight D. Eisenhower would win the presidential election.

IN 1951-52

after much discussion, IBM decided to add computers to its line of business equipment products. This led IBM to become a dominant force in the computer industry.

MILESTONES IN COMPUTER HISTORY   1.37

In 1952, Dr. Grace Hopper, a mathematician and commodore in the U.S. Navy, wrote a paper describing how to program a computer with symbolic notation instead of the detailed machine language that had been used.

Dr. Hopper was instrumental in developing high-level languages such as COBOL, a business application language introduced in 1960. COBOL uses English-like phrases and runs on most computers, making it one of the more widely used languages in the world.

1952

1953

The IBM model 650 was one of the first widely used computer systems. Originally, IBM planned to produce only 50 machines, but the system was so successful that eventually it manufactured more than 1,000.

Core memory, developed in the early 1950s, provided much larger storage capacities and greater reliability than vacuum tube memory.

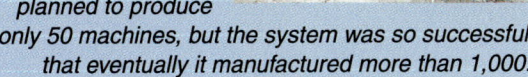

1957

FORTRAN (FORmula TRANslator) was introduced in 1957, proving that efficient, easy-to-use programming languages could be developed. FORTRAN is still in use.

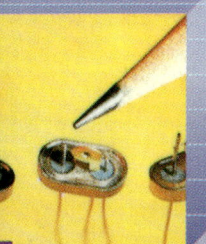

In 1958, computers built with transistors marked the beginning of the second generation of computer hardware. Previous computers built with vacuum tubes were first-generation machines.

1958

BY 1959 more than 200 programming languages had been created.

1.38 MILESTONES IN COMPUTER HISTORY

1960 From 1958 to 1964, the number of computers in the U.S. grew from 2,500 to 18,000.

1964 Third-generation computers, with their controlling circuitry stored on chips, were introduced in 1964. The IBM System/360 computers were the first third-generation machines.

In 1965, Dr. John Kemeny of Dartmouth led the development of the BASIC programming language. BASIC still is used widely on personal computers.

1965 Digital Equipment Corporation (DEC) introduced the first minicomputer in 1965.

1967

Pascal, a structured programming language, was developed by Swiss computer scientist Niklaus Wirth between 1967 and 1971.

1968 The software industry emerged in the 1960s. In 1968, Computer Science Corporation became the first software company to be listed on the New York Stock Exchange.

1969 ARPANET network established. Predecessor of the Internet.

MILESTONES IN COMPUTER HISTORY   1.39

1969 In 1969, under pressure from the industry, IBM announced that some of its software would be priced separately from the computer hardware. This "unbundling" allowed software firms to emerge in the industry.

1970

The fourth-generation computers built with chips that used LSI (large-scale integration) arrived in 1970. The chips used in 1965 contained as many as 1,000 circuits. By 1970, the LSI chip contained as many as 15,000.

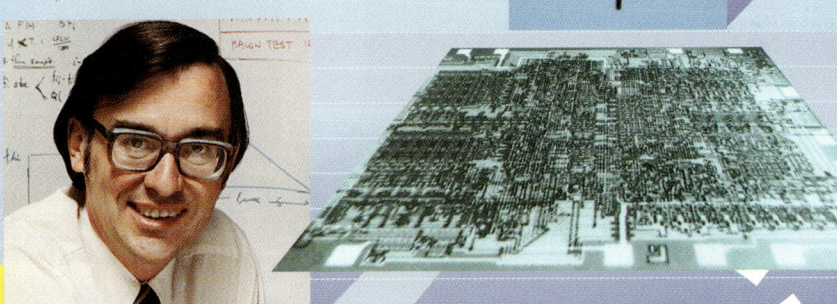

In 1971, Dr. Ted Hoff of Intel Corporation developed a microprocessor, or microprogrammmable computer chip, the Intel 4004.

1971

1975

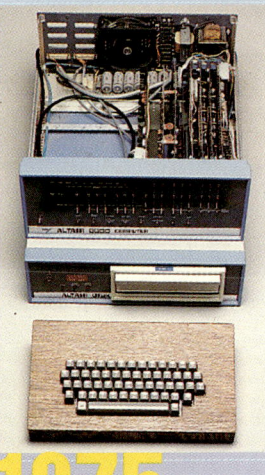

The MITS, Inc. Altair computer, sold in kits for less than $400, was the first commercially successful microcomputer.

Ethernet, developed at Xerox PARC (Palo Alto Research Center) by Robert Metcalfe, was the first local area network (LAN). Originally designed to link minicomputers, Ethernet was later extended to personal computers. The LAN allows computers to communicate and share software, data, and peripherals such as printers.

1975

In 1976, Steve Wozniak and Steve Jobs built the first Apple computer.

1976

1.40 MILESTONES IN COMPUTER HISTORY

1979
The first public online information services, CompuServe and the Source, were founded.

The VisiCalc spreadsheet program written by Bob Frankston and Dan Bricklin was introduced in 1979. This product originally was written to run on Apple II computers. Together, VisiCalc and Apple II computers rapidly became successful. Most people consider VisiCalc to be the singlemost important reason why personal computers gained acceptance in the business world.

1980
In 1980, IBM offered Microsoft Corporation's founder, Bill Gates, the opportunity to develop the operating system for the soon-to-be announced IBM personal computer. With the development of MS-DOS, Microsoft achieved tremendous growth and success.

1981
The IBM PC was introduced in 1981, signaling IBM's entrance into the personal computer marketplace. The IBM PC quickly garnered the largest share of the personal computer market and became the personal computer of choice in business.

1982
More than 300,000 personal computers were sold in 1981. In 1982, the number jumped to 3,275,000.

1983
Instead of choosing a person for its annual award, TIME magazine named the computer "Machine of the Year" for 1982. This event acknowledged the impact of the computer on society.

The Lotus 1-2-3 integrated software package, developed by Mitch Kapor, was introduced in 1983. It combined spreadsheet, graphics, and database programs in one package.

MILESTONES IN COMPUTER HISTORY   1.41

IBM introduced a personal computer, called the PC AT, that used the Intel 80286 microprocessor.

1984

Apple introduced the Macintosh computer, which incorporated a unique graphical interface, making it easy to learn.

1987

Several personal computers utilizing the powerful Intel 80386 microprocessor were introduced in 1987. These machines handled processing that previously only large systems could handle.

The Intel 486 became the world's first 1,000,000 transistor microprocessor. It crammed 1.2 million transistors on a sliver of silicon that measured .4" x .6" and executed instructions at 15 MIPS (million instructions per second) – four times as fast as its predecessor, the 80386 chip. The 80 designation used with previous Intel chips, such as the 80386 and 80286, was dropped with the 486.

1989

1990

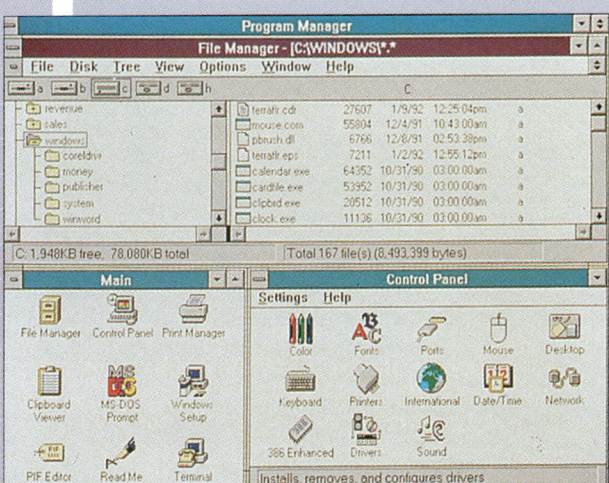

Microsoft released Windows 3.0, a substantially enhanced version of its Windows graphical user interface first introduced in 1985. The software allowed users to run multiple applications on a personal computer and more easily move data from one application to another. The package became an instant success, selling hundreds of thousands of copies.

MILESTONES IN COMPUTER HISTORY

BY 1990 more than 54 million computers were in use in the United States.

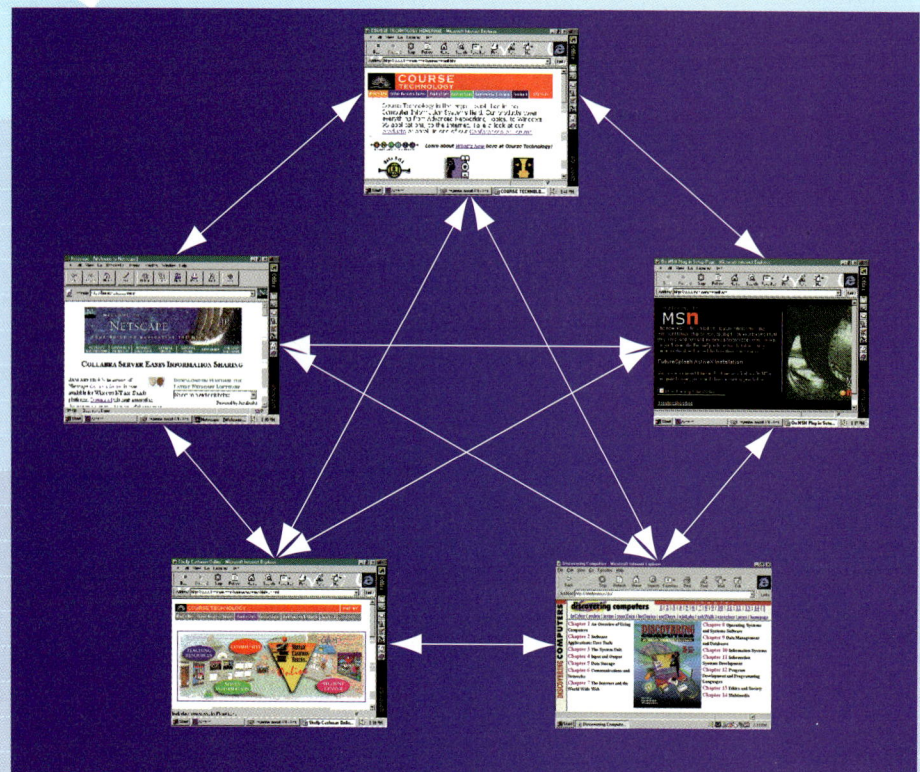

1991

World Wide Web standards released describing the framework for linking documents on different computers.

1992

Apple introduced a personal digital assistant (PDA) called the Newton MessagePad. This 7 1/4-by-4 1/2-inch personal computer incorporates a pen interface and wireless communications.

1993

Several companies introduced computer systems using the Pentium microprocessor from Intel. The Pentium chip is the successor to the Intel 486 microprocessor. It contains 3.1 million transistors and is capable of performing 112 million instructions per second (MIPS).

The Energy Star program, endorsed by the Environmental Protection Agency (EPA), encouraged manufacturers to build computer equipment that meets strict power consumption guidelines. Manufacturers meeting the guidelines then can display the Energy Star logo on their products.

MILESTONES IN COMPUTER HISTORY | 1.43

1993 Mosaic graphical Web browser was created by Marc Andreesen. This success ultimately led to the organization of Netscape Communications Corporation.

1995 Intel begins shipment of the Pentium Pro microprocessor, the successor to its widely used Pentium chip. The Pentium Pro microprocessor contains 5.5 million transistors and is capable of performing 250 million instructions per second (MIPS).

Microsoft releases Windows 95, a major upgrade to its Windows operating system, the leading graphical user interface for PCs. Windows 95 consists of more than 10 million lines of computer instruction developed by 300 person-years of effort. More than 50,000 individuals and companies tested the software before it was released.

IN 1996 2 out of 3 employees in the United States have access to a PC. 1 out of every 3 homes has a PC.

MORE THAN 50 million PCs were sold worldwide. More than 250 million are in use.

1997 50 million Internet and World Wide Web users; 15 million Internet host computers; Microsoft releases Office 97 with major Web enhancements integrated into Word, Excel, PowerPoint and Access.

"BY THE YEAR 2011, the microprocessor could have one billion transistors and might be capable of performing 100 billion instructions per second."

Dr. Andrew Grove, Chairman and CEO
Intel Corporation
"A Revolution in Progress"
COMDEX/Fall '96 Keynote Address

Software Applications: User Tools

OBJECTIVES

After completing this chapter, you will be able to:

- Define and describe a user interface and a graphical user interface

- Explain the key features of widely used software applications

- Explain the advantages of integrated software and software suites

- Explain object linking and embedding

- List and describe learning aids and support tools that help you to use personal computer software applications

CHAPTER 2

Today, understanding the applications commonly used on personal computers is considered a part of being computer literate. In fact, a working knowledge of at least some of these applications is now considered by many employers to be a required skill. Because of this, personal computer software applications are discussed early in this book. Learning about widely used applications will help you understand how people use personal computers in the modern world. Before discussing the applications, the operating system and the user interface are explained. The user interface controls how you work with the software and applies to all the applications. After learning about individual applications, you will learn about integrated software and software suites that combine several applications. The section on object linking and embedding will explain how data can be shared between applications. Finally, some of the aids and tools that are available to help you learn and use software applications are discussed.

The Operating System and User Interface

Before any application software is run, the operating system must be loaded from the hard disk into the memory of the computer and started. The **operating system** tells the computer how to perform functions such as processing program instructions and transferring data between input and output devices and memory. The operating system usually is loaded automatically from the hard disk when a computer is turned on and is always running until the computer is turned off. Once the operating system is loaded, application programs such as productivity software can be run.

All software, including the operating system, is designed to communicate with you in a certain way. The way the software communicates with you is called the user interface. A **user interface** is the way you tell the software what to do and the way the computer displays information and processing options to you. One of the more common user interfaces is the graphical user interface (GUI). The **graphical user interface**, or **GUI** (pronounced gooey), combines text and graphics to make the software easier to use. Graphical user interfaces include several common features such as icons, windows, menus, and buttons.

Icons are small pictures that are used to represent processing options, such as an application or a program, or documents, such as a letter (Figure 2-1).

A **window** is a rectangular area of the screen that is used to present information (Figure 2-1). Many people consider windows to be like multiple sheets of paper on top of a desk. In the same way that each piece of paper on the desk contains different information, each window on the screen contains different information. Just as papers can be moved from the bottom of a pile to the top of the desk when they are needed, windows can be displayed on a screen and moved around to show information when it is needed. The term Windows, with a capital W, refers to **Microsoft Windows**, the most popular graphical user interface for personal computers.

For information on Windows 95, visit the Discovering Computers Chapter 2 inCyber page (http://www.scsite.com/dc/ch2/incyber.htm) and click Windows 95.

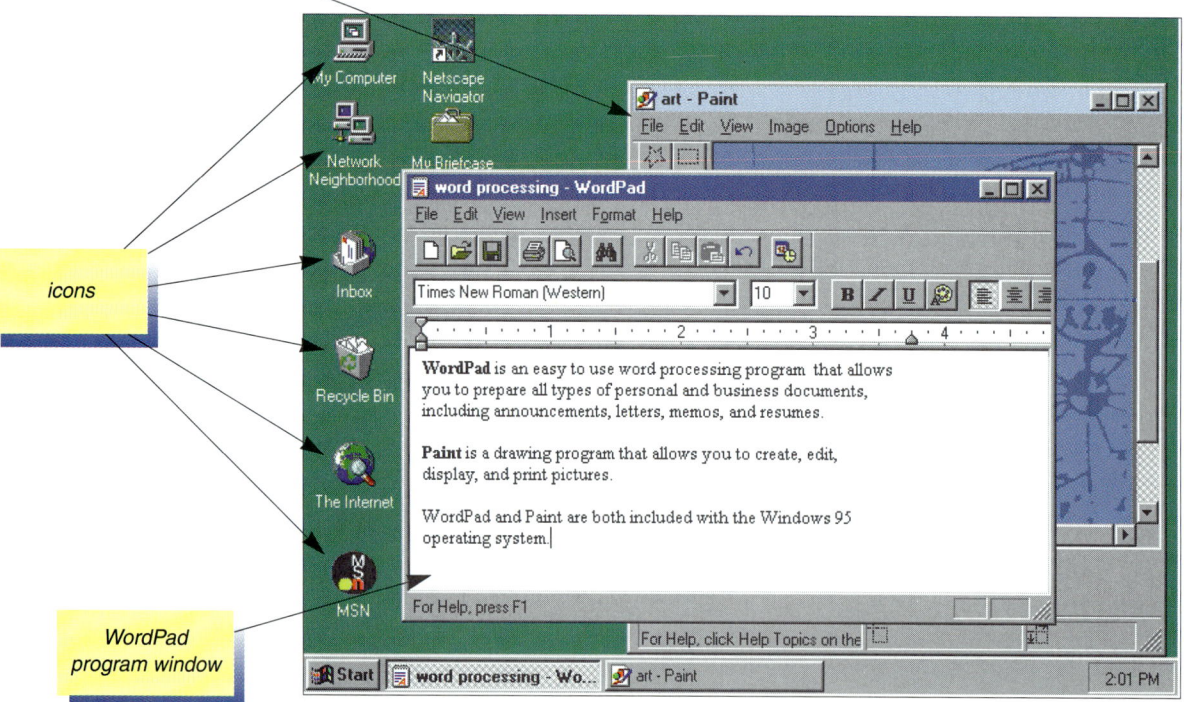

Figure 2-1
Two key features of a graphical user interface (GUI) are windows and icons. Windows are rectangular areas that present information. Icons are symbols that represent processing options or documents. In this screen, two windows are open: the WordPad program window in the foreground and the Paint program window in the background. Several windows can be open at the same time and moved from back to front so that all information on a window can be seen. The icons along the left side of the screen represent other applications that can be started.

A **menu** is a list of options from which you can choose. In a graphical user interface, menus often contain a list of related commands. **Commands** are instructions that cause the computer software to perform a specific action. For example, the menu shown in Figure 2-2 displays commands associated with the Windows 95 Start menu.

A **button** is an icon (usually a rectangular or circular shape) that when clicked, causes a specific action to take place. Buttons usually are clicked using a pointing device such as a mouse but some buttons such as OK and Cancel also can be activated by using the keyboard. Figure 2-3 shows several different types of buttons.

The features of a user interface make it easier for the user to communicate with the computer. You will see examples of these features and how they are used as you learn about the various personal computer applications.

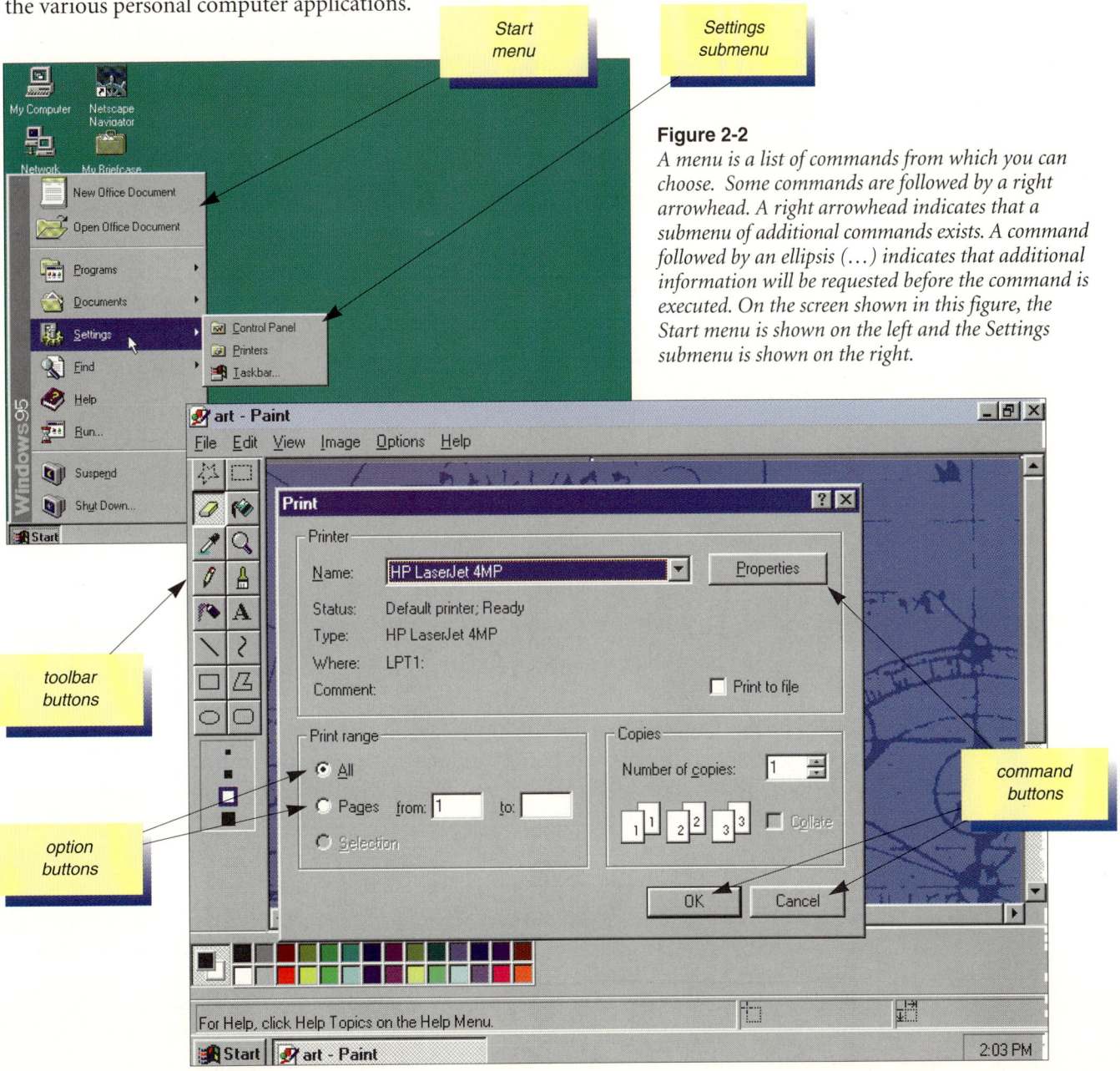

Figure 2-2
A menu is a list of commands from which you can choose. Some commands are followed by a right arrowhead. A right arrowhead indicates that a submenu of additional commands exists. A command followed by an ellipsis (...) indicates that additional information will be requested before the command is executed. On the screen shown in this figure, the Start menu is shown on the left and the Settings submenu is shown on the right.

Figure 2-3
A button is an icon that causes a specific action to take place. This screen shows several types of buttons. Many applications contain a row of buttons with icons called a toolbar. The icon indicates what happens when the button is clicked. For example, the selected button on the toolbar shown in this screen allows you to erase objects from a picture. The last two buttons allow you to add ellipses and rounded rectangles, respectively. Option buttons modify the action that will take place, such as printing all or a range of pages. Stand-alone buttons can contain text or icons and are referred to as command buttons.

Software Applications

The following sections of this chapter will introduce you to fifteen widely used personal computer software applications:

- Word processing
- Desktop publishing
- Spreadsheet
- Database
- Presentation graphics
- Web communications and browsers
- Electronic mail (e-mail)
- Personal information management
- Personal finance
- Project management
- Accounting
- Groupware
- Computer-aided design (CAD)
- Multimedia authoring
- Integrated software and software suites

With the exception of personal finance, which is primarily used by individuals, some organizations use all of the listed applications. Even though you personally may not use all of these applications, you should be at least familiar with their capabilities. These applications are discussed as they are used on personal computers, but most are available on computers of all sizes. The concepts you will learn about each application package on personal computers will also apply if you are working on a larger system. A software product within a category, for example, Microsoft Word, is called a *software package.*

Word Processing Software

The most widely used computer application is word processing. **Word processing** involves the use of a computer to produce or modify documents that consist primarily of text. Millions of people use word processing software every day to create letters, memos, reports, and other documents. A major advantage of using word processing to produce a document is the ability to easily change what has been done. Because the document is stored electronically, you can add, delete, or rearrange words, sentences, or entire sections. Newer word processors even have *intelligent* features that make changes to the document automatically.

Once completed, the document can be printed as many times as you like with each copy looking as good as the first. With older methods such as using a typewriter, making changes and reprinting a document takes much more time. Using word processing software also is a more efficient way of storing documents, because many documents can be stored on a disk. If computers are connected in a network, stored documents can be shared among users.

Today, most people perform word processing using personal computers or larger computer systems such as minicomputers or mainframes. These computers also can be used for other applications. **Dedicated word processing systems**, which can be used only for word processing, also exist, but are less frequently used.

Producing a document using word processing usually consists of four steps: creating, editing, formatting, and printing. A fifth step, saving the document, should be performed frequently throughout the process so that work will not be lost. In fact, most word processor programs have an optional **AutoSave** feature that automatically saves open documents at specified intervals. In the process of producing a document, the user may switch back and forth between these five steps.

Creating a Word Processing Document Creating a word processing document involves entering text, usually by using the keyboard. To aid in the process of creating a document, most word processing programs allow you to display the document on the screen exactly as it will look when it is printed. This capability is called WYSIWYG (pronounced whiz-e-wig). **WYSIWYG** is an acronym for What You See Is What You Get. Other common word processing features used during the creating step include word wrap, scrolling, and moving the insertion point.

- Word Wrap. **Word wrap** provides an automatic line return when the text reaches a certain position on a line in the document, such as the right-hand margin. Unlike a typewriter, you can continue typing and do not have to press a return or line feed key; the entered text automatically flows to the next line. Word wrap also operates when text is added to or deleted from lines.

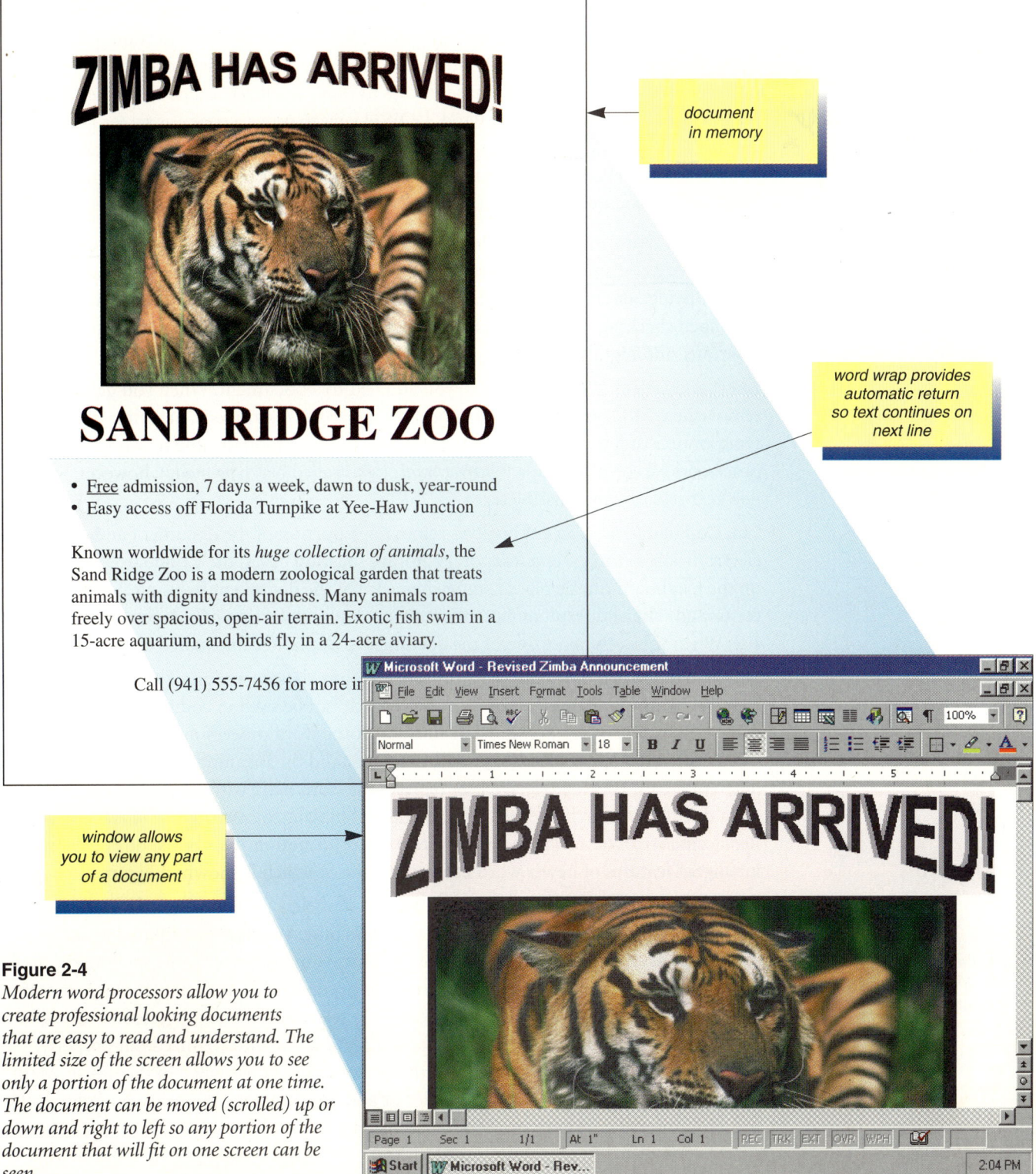

Figure 2-4
Modern word processors allow you to create professional looking documents that are easy to read and understand. The limited size of the screen allows you to see only a portion of the document at one time. The document can be moved (scrolled) up or down and right to left so any portion of the document that will fit on one screen can be seen.

- Scrolling. **Scrolling** is the process of moving the document so you can view any portion. Think of multipage documents as having been created on a continuous roll of paper. The screen can be thought of as a window that only allows a portion of the document to be seen. The document can be moved (scrolled) up or down behind the screen window. For wide documents, the screen can be scrolled left and right, as well. **Scroll tips**, small page labels beside the scroll box, show the current page as you scroll through a document, so you know how far you have scrolled through the document (Figure 2-4).

- Moving the insertion point. The **insertion point**, sometimes referred to as the **cursor**, is a symbol, such as a flashing vertical bar, that indicates where on the screen the next character will appear. The insertion point is moved by using a pointing device, such as a mouse, or the keyboard. The arrow keys on the keyboard move the insertion point one character or one line at a time. If you hold down an arrow key, the movement is repeated until you release the key. More efficient ways to move the insertion point farther and faster include using the PAGE UP and PAGE DOWN keys to move a page (or screen) at a time and the HOME and END keys to move to the beginning or end of a line. You can use other key combinations to move to the beginning of words or paragraphs, or to the start or end of the document.

    Editing a Word Processing Document Editing is the process of making changes in the content of a document. Word processing editing features include inserting and deleting; cutting, copying, and pasting; and searching and replacing. Additional editing features include spell checking; using a thesaurus; grammar checking; and adding revision marks, annotations, and highlighting.

- Insert and Delete. When you **insert**, you add text to a document. When you **delete**, you remove text. Most word processors normally are in the *insert mode*, meaning that as you type, any existing text is pushed down the page to make room for the new text. Word processors can be placed in a *typeover mode* (also called *overtype mode*), however, where new text replaces any existing text.

- Cut, Copy, and Paste. To **cut** involves removing a portion of the document and electronically storing it in a temporary storage location called the **Clipboard**. Whatever is on the Clipboard can be placed somewhere else in the document by using the **Paste** command. The end result of cut and paste is to move a portion of a document somewhere else. When you **copy**, a portion of the document is duplicated and stored on the Clipboard.

- Search and Replace. The **search** feature lets you find all occurrences of a particular character, word, or combination of words. Search can be used in combination with **replace** to substitute new letters or words for the old. Some word processing programs have advanced search and replace features that understand the meaning of words and their different forms. For example, if a user replaces the word *make* with the word *create* throughout a document, search and replace also changes *making* to *creating* and *made* to *created*. Replacement can be automatic or require user confirmation. This is just one of the many intelligent features of newer word processors, one of which is shown in Figure 2-5.

- Spelling Checker. A **spelling checker** allows you to review individual words, sections of a document, or the entire document for correct spelling. Words are compared to an electronic dictionary that is part of the word processing software. Some spelling checkers contain more than 120,000 words. If a match is not found, a list of similar words that may be the correct spelling is displayed. You can then select one of the suggested words; ignore the suggestions and leave the word unchanged; or add the unrecognized but properly spelled word to the dictionary so it will not be considered misspelled in the future. Many users customize their spelling dictionaries by adding company, street, city, and personal names so the software can check the correct spelling of those words.

---

inCyber

For details on spelling bees, visit the Discovering Computers Chapter 2 inCyber page (http://www.scsite.com/dc/ch2/incyber.htm) and click Spell.

While most spelling checkers operate as a separate process that can be started by the user, many word processors continually check the spelling of words as they are entered. Possible errors are shown on screen with red wavy underlines. To correct the misspelled words, you right-click the word (Figure 2-5). You can select a correct spelling from the shortcut menu that contains suggestions from the spelling checker dictionary.

- AutoCorrect. The **AutoCorrect** feature corrects common spelling errors automatically in words as they are entered. For example, if you enter the word, *teh*, the word processor automatically changes it to, *the*. AutoCorrect also corrects errors in capitalization. It will add capital letters to the names of days, remove capitals from words mistakenly capitalized in the middle of a sentence, and change two initial capital letters to just one. AutoCorrect is *smart* enough, however, not to change abbreviations such as CDs, PCs, and MHz. While spelling checkers and AutoCorrect can catch some misspelled words and repeated words such as *the the*, they cannot identify words that are used incorrectly. A thesaurus and grammar checker will help you to choose proper words and use them correctly.

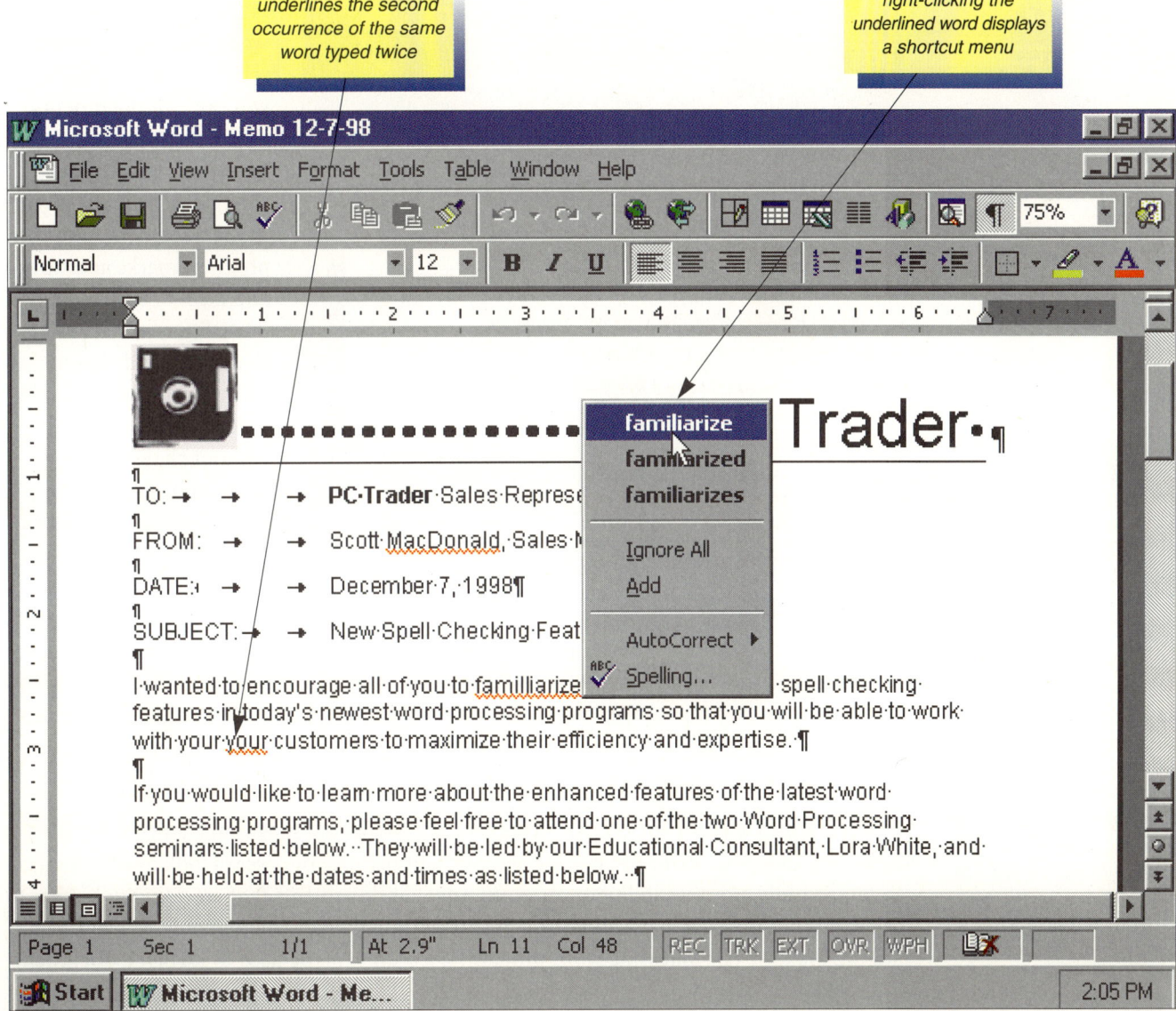

Figure 2-5
Some word processors check the spelling as you type. If you type a word that is not in the word processor's dictionary or you type the same word consecutively, the word processor marks the possible error with a red wavy underline or by some other means. If you right-click a marked word, the word processor displays a shortcut menu with a list of replacement words from which to select. The shortcut menu also includes a list of commands to help you correct the misspelled word in case the replacement words are not what you want.

To use writing tools, visit the Discovering Computers Chapter 2 inCyber page (http://www.scsite.com/dc/ch2/incyber.htm) and click Thesaurus.

- **Thesaurus.** A **thesaurus** allows you to look up synonyms (words with the same meaning) for words in a document while you are using your word processor. Using a thesaurus is similar to using a spelling checker. When you want to look up a synonym for a word, you click the word you want to check and then activate the thesaurus by using a keyboard command or a pointing device. The thesaurus software displays a list of possible synonyms. If you find a word you would rather use, you select the desired word from the list and the software automatically incorporates it in the document by replacing the previous word.

- **Grammar Checker.** A **grammar checker** is used to check for grammar, writing style, and sentence structure errors. This software can check documents for excessive use of a word or phrase, identify sentences that are too long, and find words that are used out of context such as *four* example.

- **Revision Marks, Annotations, and Highlighting Tools.** Most word processors provide several revision features so you can edit documents online (Figure 2-6). **Revision marks** allow changes to be made directly in the document. The program marks additions and deletions with underlines, strikethroughs, or different colors and fonts. **Annotations** can be used to make comments without changing the document. Annotation marks include your initials and a reference number within the document; the annotations are typed in an annotation pane. A **highlighting tool** lets you use color to call out key parts of a document for others. The tool provides different highlighter colors, so that several users can highlight different sections of a document. When the document is routed, others can easily scan for revision and annotation marks or highlighted text.

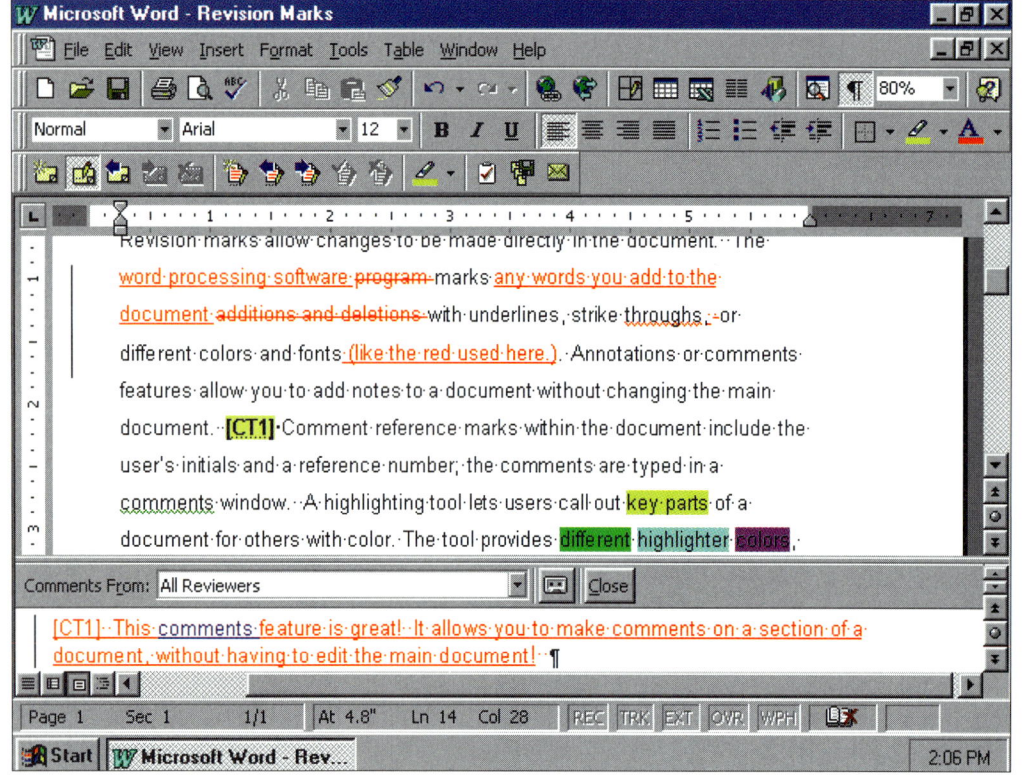

Figure 2-6
Most word processors provide revision features that allow you to mark additions and deletions with underlines, strikethroughs, or different colors and fonts. Annotations can be used to make comments without changing the document. Highlighting tools allow you to call out key parts of the document.

Formatting a Word Processing Document To **format** means to change the appearance of a document. Formatting is important because the overall look of a document can significantly affect its ability to communicate. For documents that are going to be sent to clients, it is not unusual to spend more time formatting the document than was spent entering the text. The following word processing features can be used to format a document (Figure 2-7).

- **Typeface, Font, and Style.** A **typeface** is a specific set of characters that are designed the same. Helvetica and Times New Roman are examples of typefaces. The size of a typeface is measured vertically in points. Each **point** is approximately 1/72 of an inch high. The text you are reading in this book is ten point type. A specific combination of typeface and

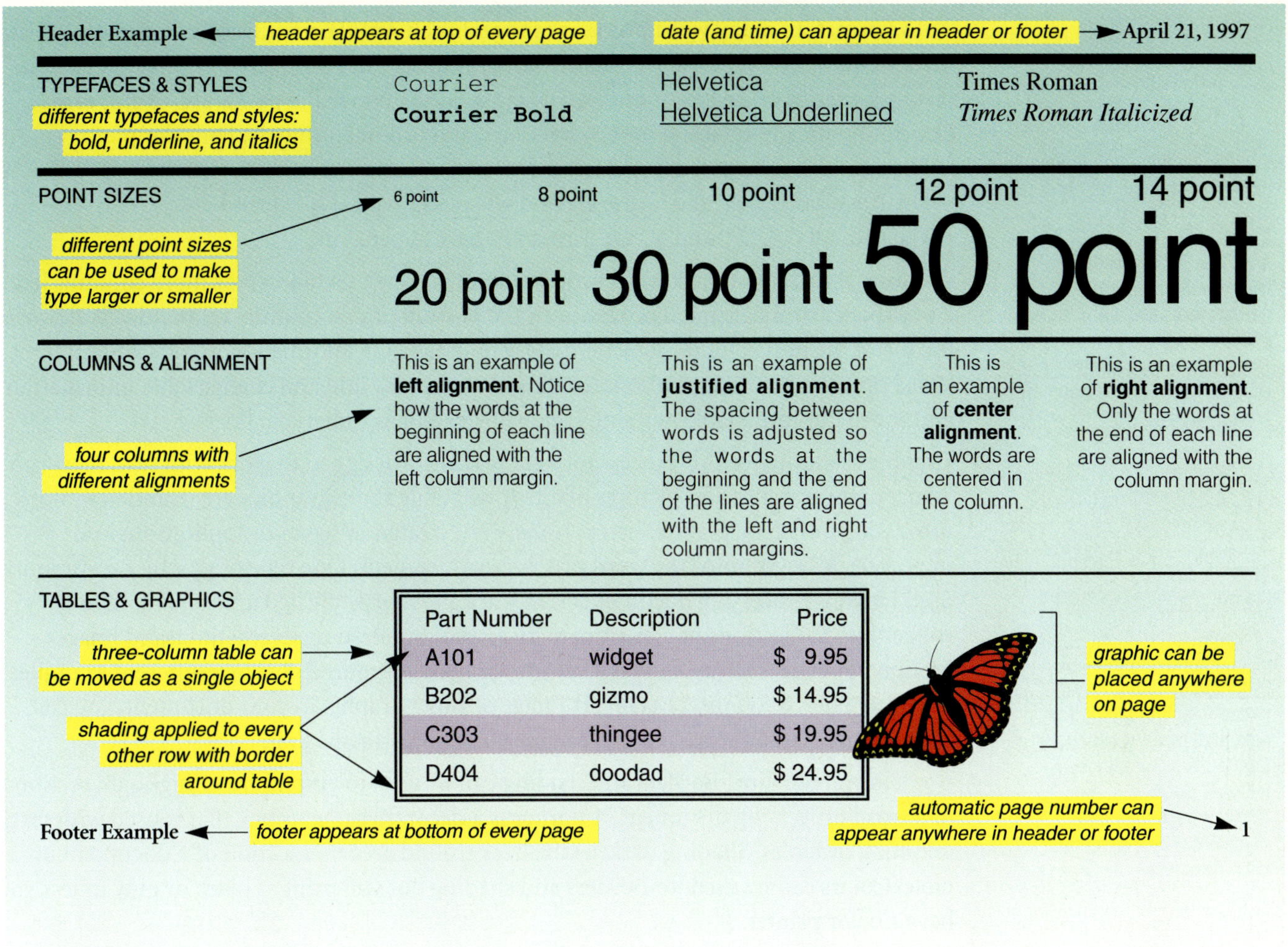

Figure 2-7
Examples of word processing formatting features.

point size is called a **font**, though it is common to hear and read of typefaces being called fonts. A particular **style**, such as **bold**, *italics*, or underlining, can be applied to a font to make it stand out.

- Margins and Alignment. **Margins** specify the space in the border of a page and include the left, right, bottom, and top margin. **Alignment**, also called **justification**, deals with how text is positioned in relation to a fixed reference point, usually a right or left margin. **Justified alignment** aligns text with both the left and right margins. **Left alignment** and **right alignment** align text with the left and right margins only. **Centered alignment** divides the text equally on either side of a reference point, usually the center of the page.

- Spacing. **Spacing** deals with how far apart individual letters (horizontal spacing) and lines of text (vertical spacing) are placed. With **monospacing**, each character takes up the same amount of horizontal space. With **proportional spacing**, wide characters, such as W or M, are given more horizontal space than narrow characters, such as I. When a document uses monospace letters, two spaces should be inserted after a period at the end of a sentence. By contrast, when a document has proportional spacing, only one space is placed after *all* punctuation. **Line spacing** specifies the vertical distance from the bottom of one line to the next line. Single and double line spacing are the most common, but in some word processing software, exact distances also can be specified.

inCyber

For a look at original fonts, visit the Discovering Computers Chapter 2 inCyber page (http://www.scsite.com/dc/ch2/incyber.htm) and click Font.

For samples of clip art available on the Internet, visit the Discovering Computers Chapter 2 inCyber page (http://www.scsite.com/dc/ch2/incyber.htm) and click Clip Art.

For information on using reference style templates, visit the Discovering Computers Chapter 2 inCyber page (http://www.scsite.com/dc/ch2/incyber.htm) and click Template.

- Auto Format. In many word processor programs an **AutoFormat** feature formats documents as you type. AutoFormat automatically creates numbered or bulleted lists and changes a series of dashes or underscores to a border above the paragraph. AutoFormat also automatically creates symbols, fractions, and ordinal numbers. For example,
  - The em dash symbol is created when you type, --, and the smiley when you type :).
  - The fractions $\frac{1}{2}$, $\frac{1}{4}$, and $\frac{3}{4}$ are created when you type 1/2, 1/4, and 3/4.
  - The ordinals 1st, 2nd, and 3rd are formatted with superscript.
- Columns and Tables. Most word processors can arrange text in two or more columns like a newspaper or magazine. The text from the bottom of one column automatically flows to the top of the next column. **Tables** are a way of organizing information in rows and columns. Word processors that support tables allow you to easily add and change table information and move the entire table as a single item, instead of as individual lines of text.
- Graphics. Although word processors were primarily designed to work with text, most can incorporate graphics and pictures of all types. While some **graphics** are included in word processing packages, graphics items usually are created in separate applications and imported (brought into) the word processing document. One type of graphics commonly used in word processing documents is **clip art**, previously created art that is sold in collections. Collections of clip art contain several hundred to several thousand images grouped by type, such as holidays, vehicle, or people. Figure 2-8 shows different examples of clip art. Once you insert a clip art image or other graphic in your document, you can move, resize, rotate, crop, and make some color adjustments to it.
- Borders and Shading. Borders and shading can be used to emphasize or highlight sections of a word processing document. A **border** is a decorative line or box that is used with text, graphics, or tables. **Shading** darkens the background area of a section of a document or table. Colors can by used for borders and shading but will print as black or gray unless you have a color printer.
- Page Numbers, Headers, and Footers. Most word processors can automatically apply page numbers to any location on the page. Page numbers can be started at a particular number and can appear in a font different than the main body of text. **Headers** and **footers** allow you to place the same information at the top or bottom of each page. A company name, report title, date, or page number, are examples of items that might appear in a header or footer.
- Built-in Styles. A **built-in style**, also called a **style sheet**, lets you save font and format information so it can be applied to new documents. Built-in styles usually are applied to a portion of a document, such as a heading, paragraph, or footnote. A **template** uses a

Figure 2-8
Clip art consists of previously created illustrations that can be added to documents. Clip art usually comes in collections of graphic images that are grouped by type. These clip art examples are from an animals and nature collection.

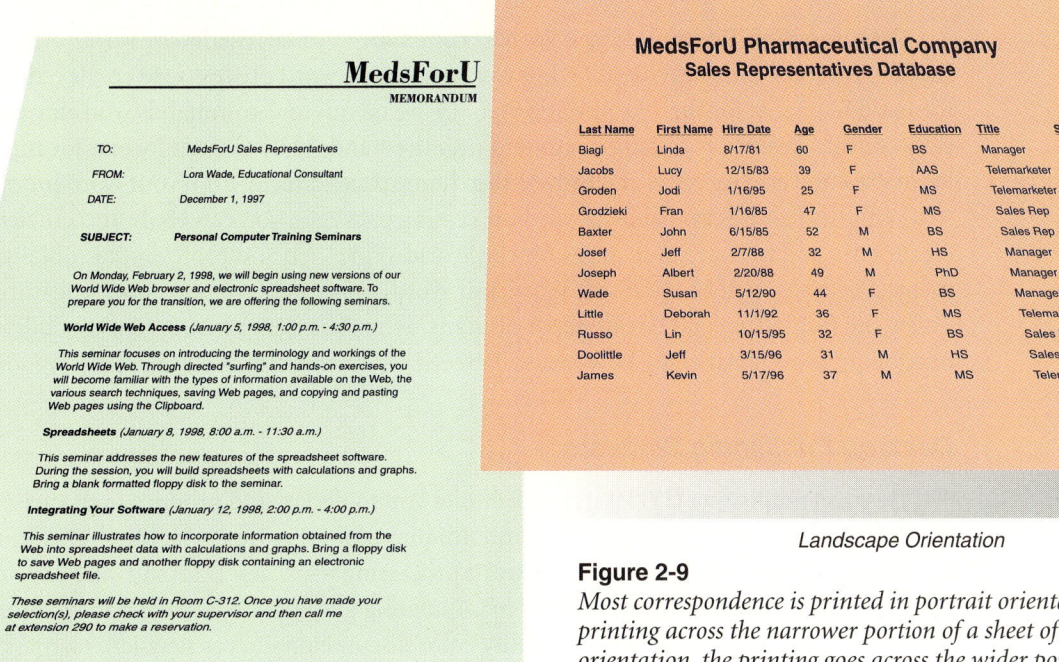

Landscape Orientation

Figure 2-9
Most correspondence is printed in portrait orientation, which is printing across the narrower portion of a sheet of paper. In landscape orientation, the printing goes across the wider portion of the paper.

Portrait Orientation

predefined style sheet, which contains font, style, spacing, and formatting information and usually includes text that is always used, such as title and headings. A memo, a fax cover sheet, and a newsletter are examples of documents that often originate using a template.

Printing a Word Processing Document Most word processors give you many options other than printing a single copy of the entire document.

- Number of Copies and Pages. The ability to print individual pages and a range of pages (for example, pages 2 through 7) usually is available. In addition, you can specify how many copies are to be printed.

- Portrait and Landscape. **Portrait** printing means that the paper is taller than it is wide. Most letters are printed in portrait orientation. **Landscape** printing means that the paper is wider than it is tall. Tables with a large number of columns often are printed in landscape orientation. See Figure 2-9 for examples.

- Print Preview. **Print preview** (Figure 2-10) allows you to see on the screen how the document will look when it is printed. In print preview, you can see one or more entire pages. Even though the text may be too small to read, you can review the overall appearance and decide if the page needs additional formatting.

Figure 2-10
Print preview allows you to see on the screen how the document will look when it is printed. This feature helps you decide if the overall appearance of the document is acceptable or if the document needs additional formatting.

Creating Web Pages Using a Word Processor Today, the major word processors support Internet connectivity, allowing you to use your word processor to create, edit, and format documents for the World Wide Web. Using menus and commands, you can automatically convert a word processing document into the standard document format for the World Wide Web. You also can view and browse Web home pages directly from your word processor.

With the features available in word processing packages, you can easily and efficiently create, edit, and format home pages for the World Wide Web and professional-looking documents. Packages such as Microsoft Word and WordPerfect may contain enough features to satisfy the formatting and layout needs of many users. The document design capabilities of desktop publishing packages, however, still exceed the capabilities of word processing software.

Desktop Publishing Software

Desktop publishing (DTP) software allows you to design and produce high-quality documents that contain text, graphics, and unique colors (Figure 2-11). Many DTP features have been incorporated into the better word processing packages. DTP software provides additional tools, however, especially for manipulating graphics, that make it the choice of people who regularly produce high-quality color documents such as newsletters, marketing literature, catalogs, and annual reports. Documents of this type were previously created by slower, more expensive traditional publishing methods such as typesetting.

DTP software is specifically designed for page composition and layout. **Page composition and layout**, sometimes called **page makeup**, is the process of arranging text and graphics on a document

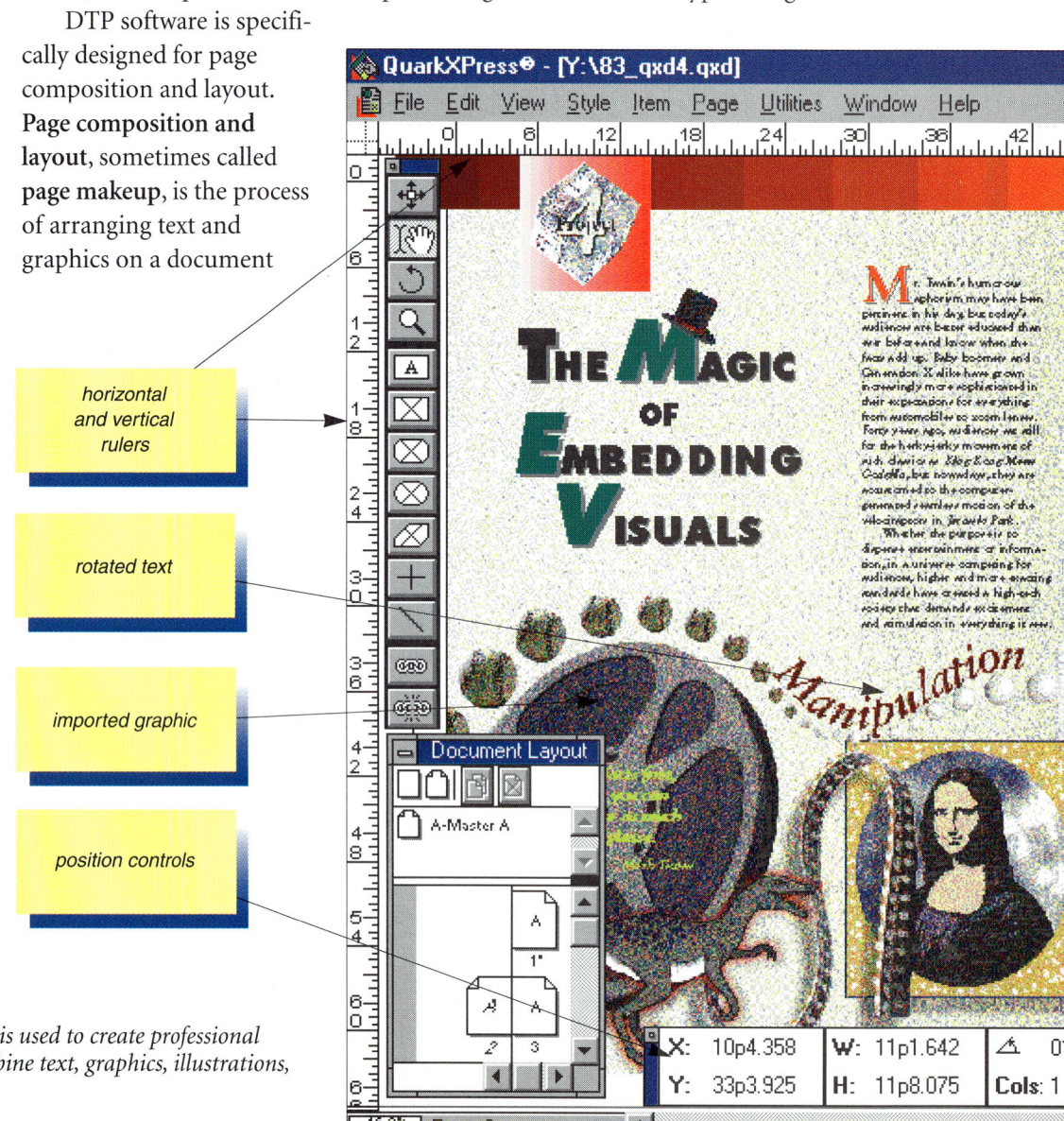

Figure 2-11
Desktop publishing software is used to create professional looking documents that combine text, graphics, illustrations, and photographs.

SOFTWARE APPLICATIONS   2.13

page. The text and graphics used by a DTP program are frequently imported from other software packages. For example, text is usually created with a word processor and then transferred into the desktop publishing package. Graphics objects, such as illustrations and photographs, also are imported from other software packages. **Illustration software** that is designed for use by artists, such as CorelDRAW! and Aldus Freehand, often is used to create graphics for DTP documents (Figure 2-12). Input devices, called scanners, can be used to convert photographs and art to import into DTP documents. Once a graphic is inserted in a document, a DTP program can crop, sharpen, and change the colors in the image.

DTP programs typically include **color libraries**, which are standard sets of colors used by designers and printers to ensure that colors will print exactly as specified. From these libraries, you can choose standard colors or specialty colors such as metallic or florescent colors. Tints or percentages of colors also can be added to any object or graphic.

Some of the other page composition and layout features that distinguish DTP software include the following (some of these features are illustrated in Figure 2-11):

- Ability to create master pages, which are non-printing pages that serve as templates
- Larger page sizes (up to 18" by 24")
- Page grids for aligning text and graphics
- Ability to stack and overlap multiple objects on a page
- Ability to *trap* objects to eliminate white space in a printed document

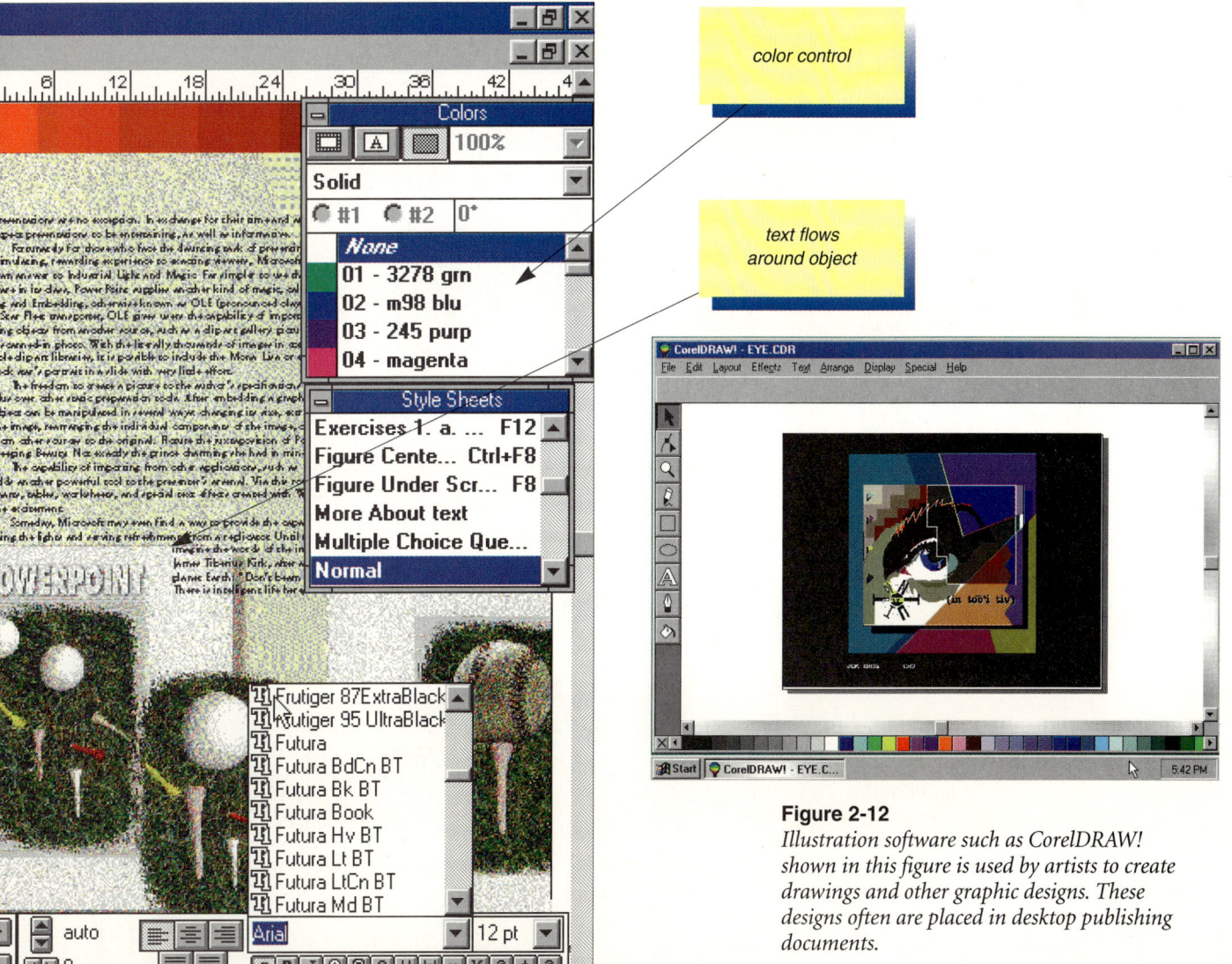

Figure 2-12
Illustration software such as CorelDRAW! shown in this figure is used by artists to create drawings and other graphic designs. These designs often are placed in desktop publishing documents.

The ability to print DTP documents relies on a page definition language. A **page definition language**, such as **PostScript**, describes the document to be printed in language the printer can understand. The printer, which includes a page definition language translator, interprets the instructions and prints the document. Using a page definition language enables a DTP document created on one computer system to be printed on another computer system with a different printer, so long as the second printer has a compatible page definition language.

With desktop publishing, you can create professional looking documents on your own computer and produce work that previously could be done only by graphic artists. By using desktop publishing, both the cost and time of producing quality documents are significantly decreased. Popular desktop publishing packages include PageMaker and QuarkXPress.

Spreadsheet Software

Spreadsheet software allows you to organize numeric data in a worksheet or in a tabular format called a **spreadsheet** or **worksheet**. Manual methods, those done by hand, have long been used to organize numeric data in this manner. You will see that the data in an electronic spreadsheet is organized in the same manner as it is in a manual spreadsheet (Figure 2-13).

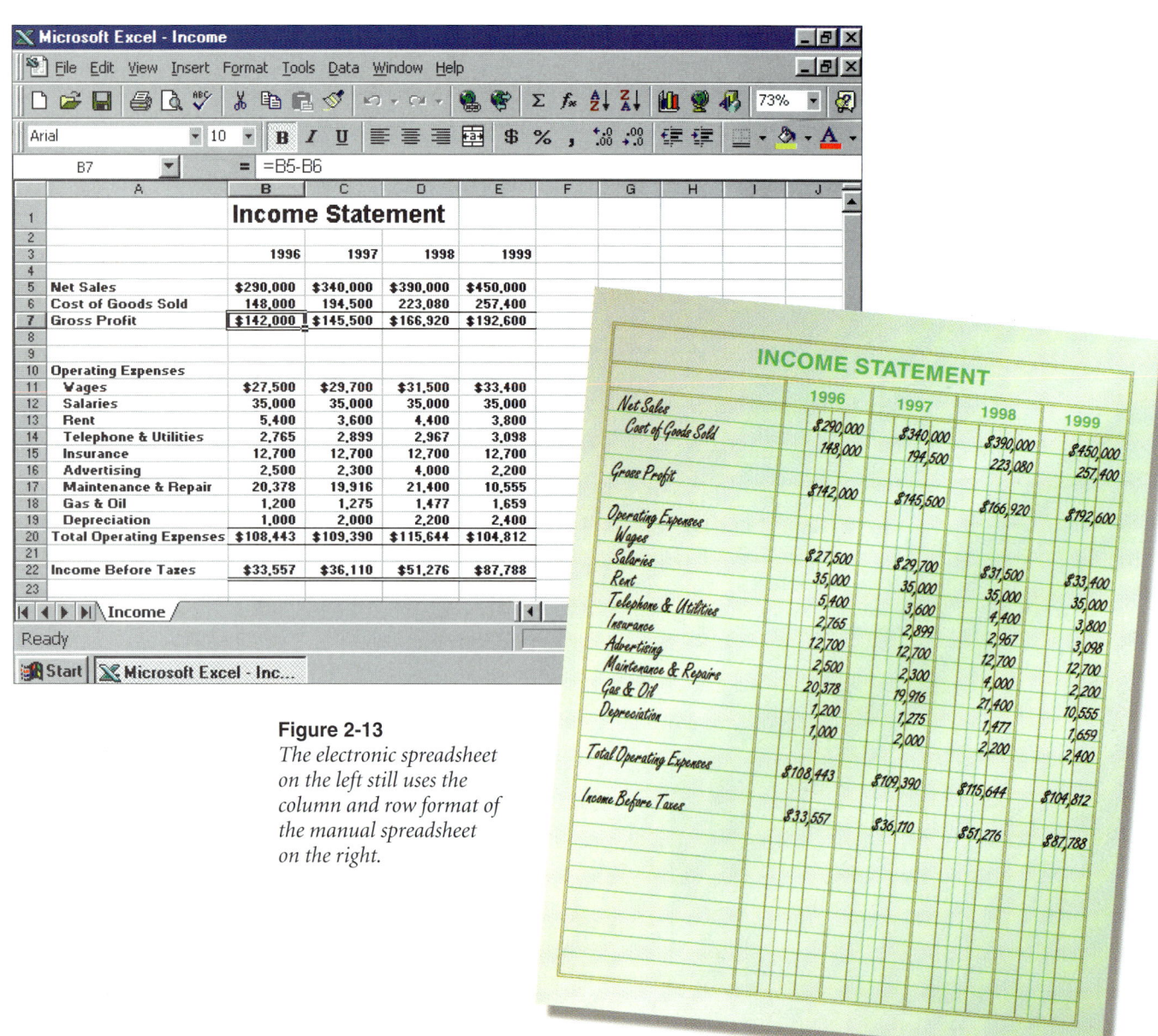

Figure 2-13
The electronic spreadsheet on the left still uses the column and row format of the manual spreadsheet on the right.

SOFTWARE APPLICATIONS 2.15

A spreadsheet file is like a notebook with up to 255 sheets (Figure 2-14). You access the different spreadsheets in a spreadsheet file by clicking the corresponding sheet tab. On each spreadsheet, data is organized vertically in **columns** and horizontally in **rows**. Columns are identified by a letter and rows by a number. Each spreadsheet has 256 columns and 16,384 rows. The column headings begin with A and end with IV. The row headings begin with 1 and end with 16,384. Only a small fraction of the active spreadsheet displays on the screen at one time. You can use the scroll bars, scroll arrows, and scroll boxes below and to the right of the window to view different parts of the active spreadsheet.

The intersection where a column and row meet is called a **cell** (Figure 2-14). Each of the spreadsheets in a spreadsheet file has more than 16,000,000 cells in which you can enter data. Cells are named by their location on the spreadsheet. As shown in Figure 2-14, the intersection of column E and row 7 is referred to as cell E7.

Cells may contain three types of data: labels (text), values (numbers), and formulas. The text, or **labels**, as they are called, identify the data and help organize the worksheet. Good spreadsheets contain descriptive titles. The rest of the cells in a spreadsheet may appear to contain numbers, or **values**. Some of the cells actually contain formulas, however. The **formulas** perform calculations on the data in the spreadsheet and display the resulting value

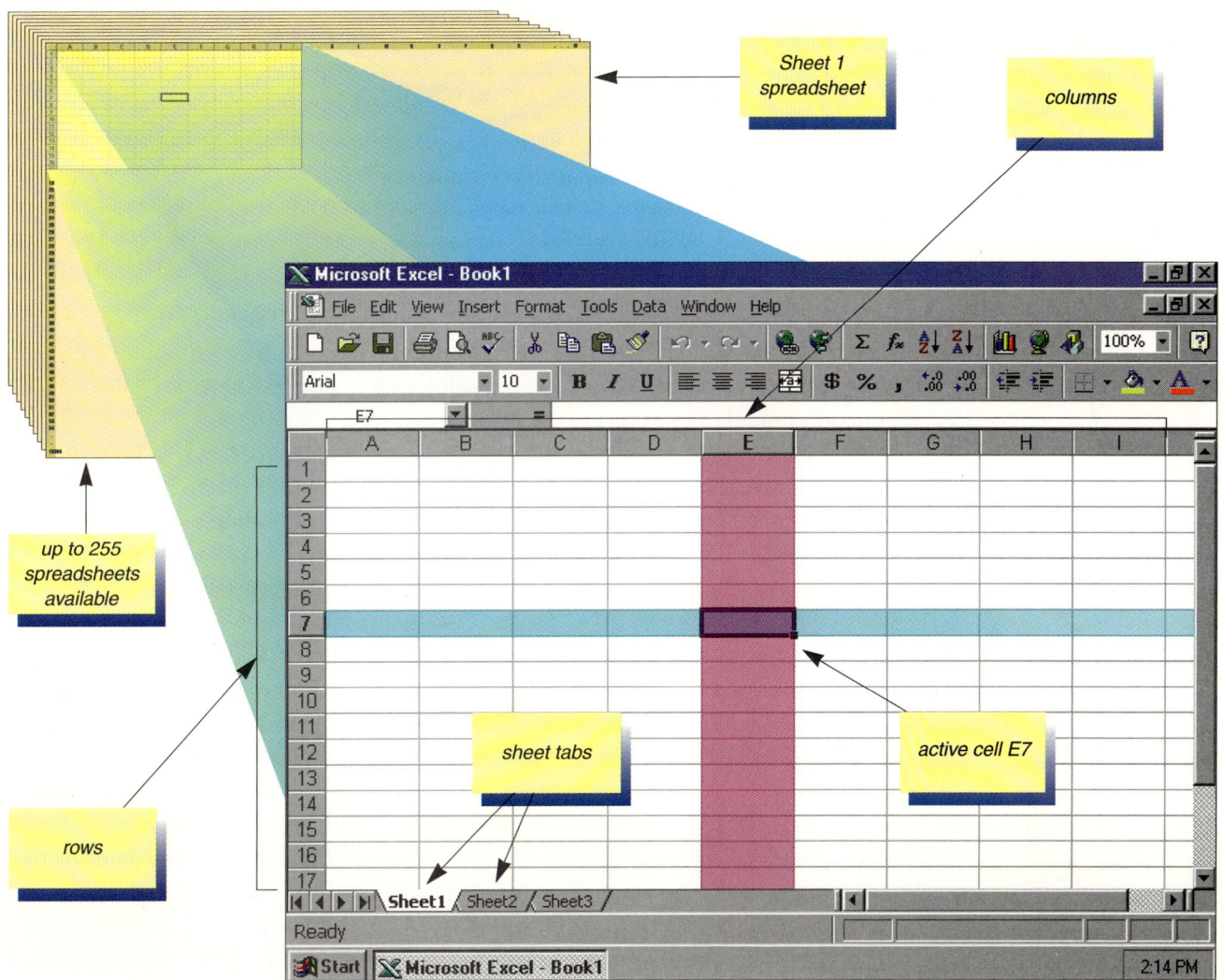

Figure 2-14
A spreadsheet file is like a notebook with up to 255 sheets. You view only a portion of a spreadsheet through a window which you can move to see other parts. On a spreadsheet, columns refer to the vertical lines of data and rows refer to the horizontal lines of data. Columns are identified by letters and rows are identified by numbers. The intersection of a column and row is called a cell.

SPREADSHEET FUNCTIONS

FINANCIAL
FV (rate, number of periods, payment)	Calculates the future value of an investment.
NPV (rate, range)	Calculates the net present value of an investment.
PMT (rate, number of periods, present value)	Calculates the periodic payment for an annuity.
PV (rate, number of periods, payment)	Calculates the present value of an investment.
RATE (number of periods, payment, present value)	Calculates the periodic interest rate of an annuity.

DAY & TIME
DATE	Returns the current date.
NOW	Returns the current date and time.
TIME	Returns the current time.

MATHEMATICAL
ABS (number)	Returns the absolute value of a number.
INT (number)	Rounds a number down to the nearest integer.
LN (number)	Calculates the natural logarithm of a number.
LOG (number, base)	Calculates the logarithm of a number to a specified base.
ROUND (number, number of digits)	Rounds a number to a specified number of digits.
SQRT (number)	Calculates the square root of a number.
SUM (range)	Calculates the total of a range of numbers.

STATISTICAL
AVERAGE (range)	Calculates the average value of a range of numbers.
COUNT (range)	Counts how many cells in the range have entries.
MAX (range)	Returns the maximum value in a range.
MIN (range)	Returns the minimum value in a range.
STDEV (range)	Calculates the standard deviation of a range of numbers.

LOGICAL
IF (logical test, value if true, value if false)	Performs a test and returns one value if the test is true and another value if the test is false.

Figure 2-15
Spreadsheet functions are predefined formulas that perform calculations or return information based on given data. This is just a partial list of some of the more common functions. Probably the most often used function is SUM, which is used to add a range of numbers.

in the cell containing the formula. You can create formulas or use functions that come with the spreadsheet software. **Functions** are stored formulas that perform common calculations, such as adding a range of cells or generating a value such as the time or date. Figure 2-15 is a list of functions found in most spreadsheet packages.

Another time-saving feature available in spreadsheets is a macro. A **macro** is a sequence of commands and keystrokes that are recorded and saved. When the macro is run, the sequence of commands and keystrokes is performed. Macros are used to reduce the number of keystrokes required for frequently performed tasks. Examples of tasks that might use macros are moving data from one spreadsheet to another or printing a portion of a spreadsheet.

This section illustrates how a spreadsheet works with steps to develop a simple spreadsheet to calculate the profit and profit percentage from four quarters of revenues and costs. As shown in Figure 2-16, the first step in creating the spreadsheet is to enter the labels, or titles. These should be short but descriptive, to help you organize the layout of the data in your spreadsheet.

The next step is to enter the values or numbers in the body of the spreadsheet. Figure 2-17 shows the value 125000 entered into cell B3. After entering the remaining data, the next step is to calculate the totals in cells F3 and F4. For some spreadsheets, formulas or functions are entered before the data.

In a manual spreadsheet, you would have to calculate each of the totals for the sales and cost in rows 3 and 4 by hand or with your calculator. To determine the sales totals in an electronic spreadsheet, you select the cells that you want to contain the totals (cells F3 and F4) and click the **AutoSum button** on the toolbar (Figure 2-18). The spreadsheet package is capable of determining that you want to sum by rows. The totals are calculated and displayed automatically (Figure 2-18).

SOFTWARE APPLICATIONS 2.17

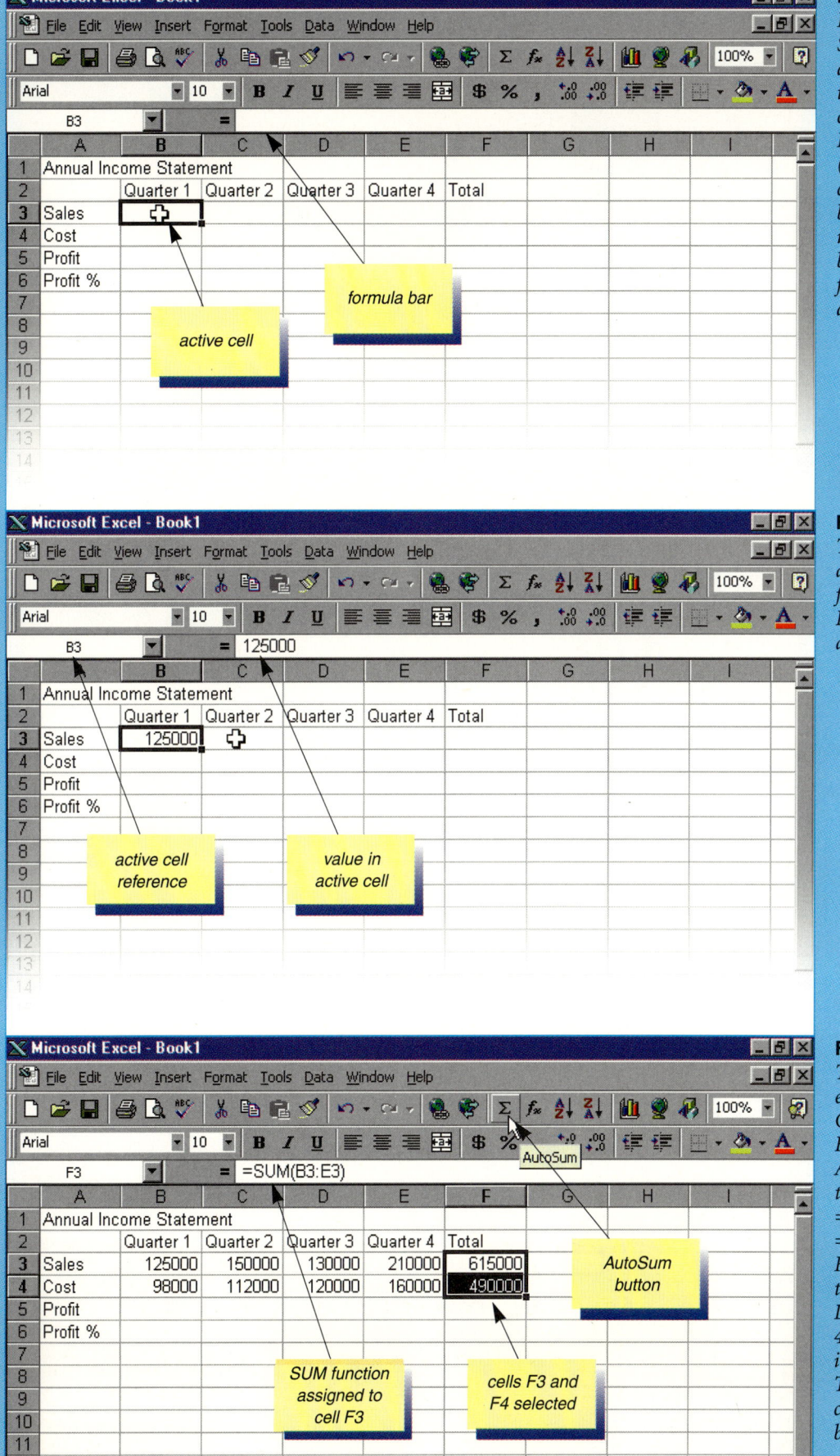

Figure 2-16
Labels such as Annual Income Statement, Quarter 1, Sales, and Cost are entered to identify the spreadsheet and the columns and rows of data. Here, the active cell is B3 (column B, row 3). The active cell is surrounded by a heavy border and its address displays in the formula bar. Nothing has been entered for this cell, so the formula bar shows only the cell address.

Figure 2-17
The value 125000 is entered and stored in cell B3. The formula bar shows the address, B3, and content, 125000, of the active cell.

Figure 2-18
The remaining values are entered in cells C3, D3, E3, B4, C4, D4, and E4. Cells F3 and F4 are selected. Clicking the AutoSum button on the toolbar assigns the formula =SUM(B3:E3) to cell F3 and =SUM(B4:E4) to cell F4. Cell F3 displays 615000, the sum of the values in the cells B3, C3, D3, and E3. Cell F4 displays 490000, the sum of the values in the cells B4, C4, D4, and E4. The SUM function assigned to cell F3 displays in the formula bar.

2.18 CHAPTER 2 – SOFTWARE APPLICATIONS: USER TOOLS

Figure 2-19
The formula to determine the Quarter 1 Profit in cell B5 is Quarter 1 Sales minus Quarter 1 Cost, or =B3 - B4. Thus, the formula =B3 - B4 is entered into cell B5 and the result 27000 displays. The formula to determine the Quarter 1 Profit % is Quarter 1 Profit divided by Quarter 1 Sales, or =B5 / B3 (the slash indicates division). Thus, the formula =B5 / B3 is entered into cell B6 and the result 21.60% displays. With cell B6 active, the formula =B5 / B3 displays in the formula bar.

Figure 2-20
This screen shows the completed spreadsheet. Once the formulas are assigned to cells B5 and B6, they are copied across rows 5 and 6 through column F. When you copy a formula, the spreadsheet program adjusts the cell addresses automatically. Hence, the formula in cell C5 is the same as the formula in cell B5, except that the cell addresses have been adjusted so the profit calculation in cell C5 pertains to the numbers immediately above cell C5.

Figure 2-21
The capability of a spreadsheet to recalculate totals automatically when data is changed is shown in this screen. This capability allows you to see quickly the total impact of changing one or more numbers in a spreadsheet. Using the spreadsheet shown in Figure 2-20, the value 150000 in cell C3 was changed to 110000. This one change results in five new values in cells containing formulas that use cell C3 directly or indirectly (cells C5, C6, F3, F5, and F6).

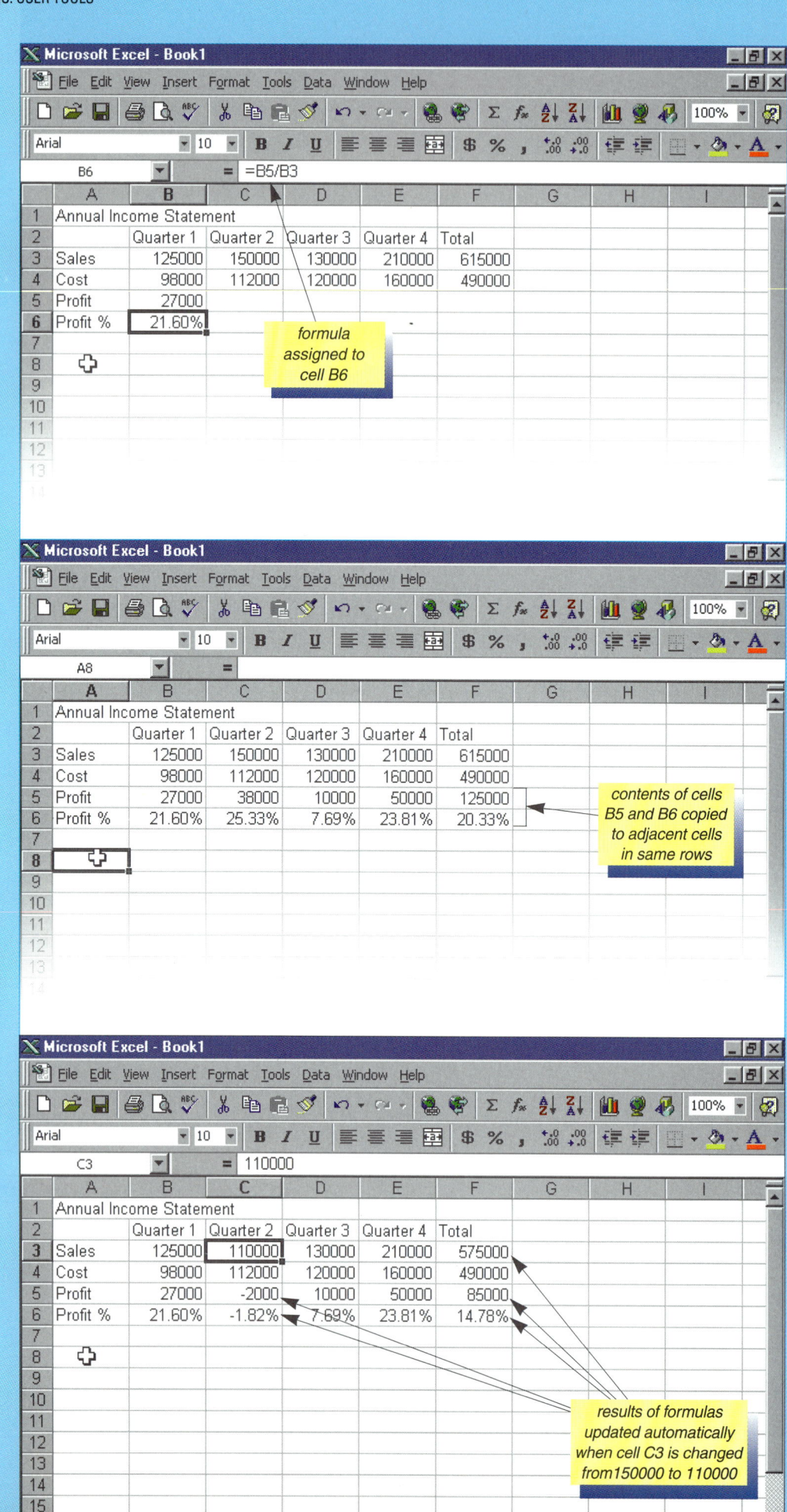

The next step is to determine the quarterly profits and total profits in row 5. The quarterly profit in cell B5 is equal to the first quarter sales in cell B3 minus the first quarter cost in cell B4. You can instruct the spreadsheet program to compute the first quarter profit by entering the formula =B3 - B4 in cell B5. The profit percent in cell B6 is equal to the first quarter profit in cell B5 divided by the first quarter sales or =B5 / B3. Figure 2-19 shows the results of entering these two formulas. With cell B6 selected, the formula =B5 / B3 displays in the formula bar.

Once a formula is entered into a cell, it can be copied to any other cell that requires a similar formula. Usually, when a formula is copied, the cell references are updated automatically to reflect the new location. For example, in Figure 2-20, when the formula in cell B5 is copied to cell C5, the formula changes from B3 - B4 to C3 - C4. This automatic updating of the formula is called **relative referencing**. If you are going to copy a formula but always want the formula to refer to the same cell location, you would use **absolute referencing**. For example, if you had a single tax rate that was going to be used to calculate taxes on the amounts in more than one cell, you would make an absolute reference to the cell containing the tax rate. To make a cell an absolute reference, you place a dollar sign in front of the column and row. In a formula, E5 would be an absolute reference to cell E5. As the formula is copied, the formula calculations are performed automatically. After copying the formula in cell B5 to C5, D5, E5, and F5 and copying the formula in cell B6 to C6, D6, E6, and F6, the spreadsheet is complete (Figure 2-20).

One of the more powerful features of spreadsheet software occurs when the data in a spreadsheet changes. To appreciate the capabilities of spreadsheet software, consider how a change is handled in a manual system. When a value in a manual spreadsheet changes, you must erase it and write a new value into the cell. You must also erase all cells that contain calculations referring to the value that changed and then you must recalculate these cells and enter the new result. For example, the row totals and column totals would be updated to reflect changes to any values within their areas. In a large manual spreadsheet, accurately posting changes and updating the values affected would be time consuming and new errors could be introduced. But posting changes on an electronic spreadsheet is easy. You change data in a cell simply by typing in the new value. All other values that are affected are updated automatically. Figure 2-21 shows that if you change the value in cell C3 from 150000 to 110000, five other cell values will change automatically. All other values and totals in the spreadsheet remain unchanged. On a computer, the updating happens almost instantly.

A spreadsheet's capability to recalculate when data is changed makes it a valuable tool for decision making. This capability is sometimes called **what-if analysis** because the results of different assumptions (*what-if we changed this ...*) can quickly be seen.

A standard feature of spreadsheet software is the ability to turn numeric data into a **chart** that graphically shows the relationship of numerical data. Visual representation of data in charts often makes it easier to analyze and interpret information. The types of charts provided by spreadsheet software are sometimes called **analytical graphics** or **business graphics** because they are used primarily for the analysis of numerical data by businesses. Figure 2-22 shows the chart types offered in one spreadsheet package. Most of these charts are variations on three basic chart types, line charts, bar charts, and pie charts.

Line charts are effective for showing a trend over a period of time, as indicated by a rising or falling line. If the area below or above a line is filled in with a color or pattern, it is called an area chart. **Bar charts** display bars of various lengths to show the relationship of data (Figure 2-23). The bars can be horizontal, vertical (sometimes called columns), or stacked on top of one another. **Pie charts**, so called because they look like pies cut into pieces, are effective for showing the relationship of parts to a whole. Pie charts often are used for budget presentations to show how much each part of the budget is a percentage of the total. To improve their appearance, most charts can be displayed or printed in a three-dimensional format.

Besides the ability to manipulate numbers, spreadsheet packages have many formatting features that can improve the overall appearance of the data. These features include the ability to change typefaces, sizes, and styles, add borders and lines, and use shading and colors to highlight data. Figure 2-24 shows the spreadsheet and chart with some of these features added.

Spreadsheets are one of the more popular software applications and have been adapted to a wide range of business and nonbusiness applications. Some of the popular packages used today are Microsoft Excel, Lotus 1-2-3, and Corel Quattro Pro.

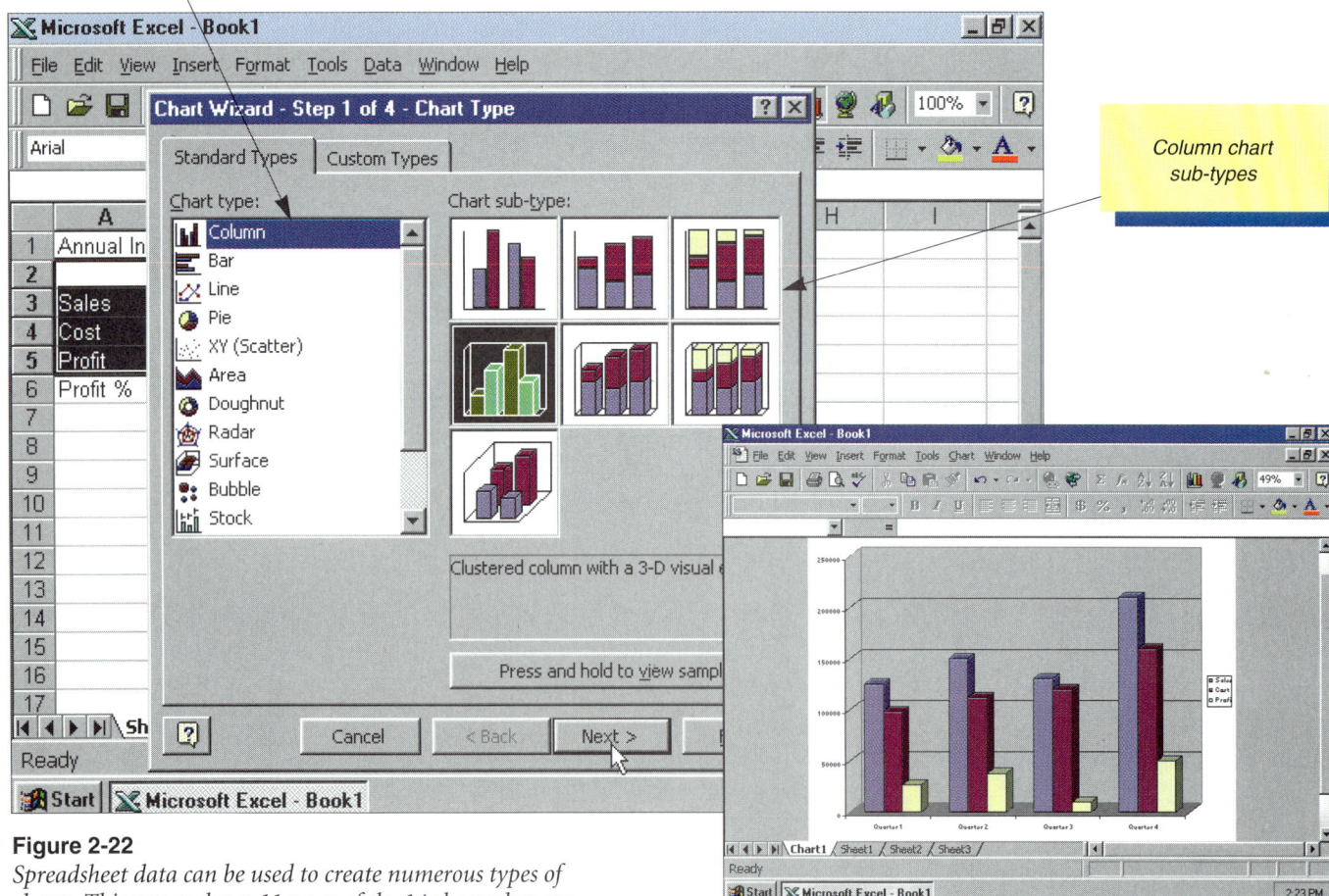

Figure 2-22
Spreadsheet data can be used to create numerous types of charts. This screen shows 11 types of the 14 charts that are available with the Microsoft Excel spreadsheet package.

Figure 2-23
A 3-D column chart can be created from spreadsheet data as shown on this Excel sheet.

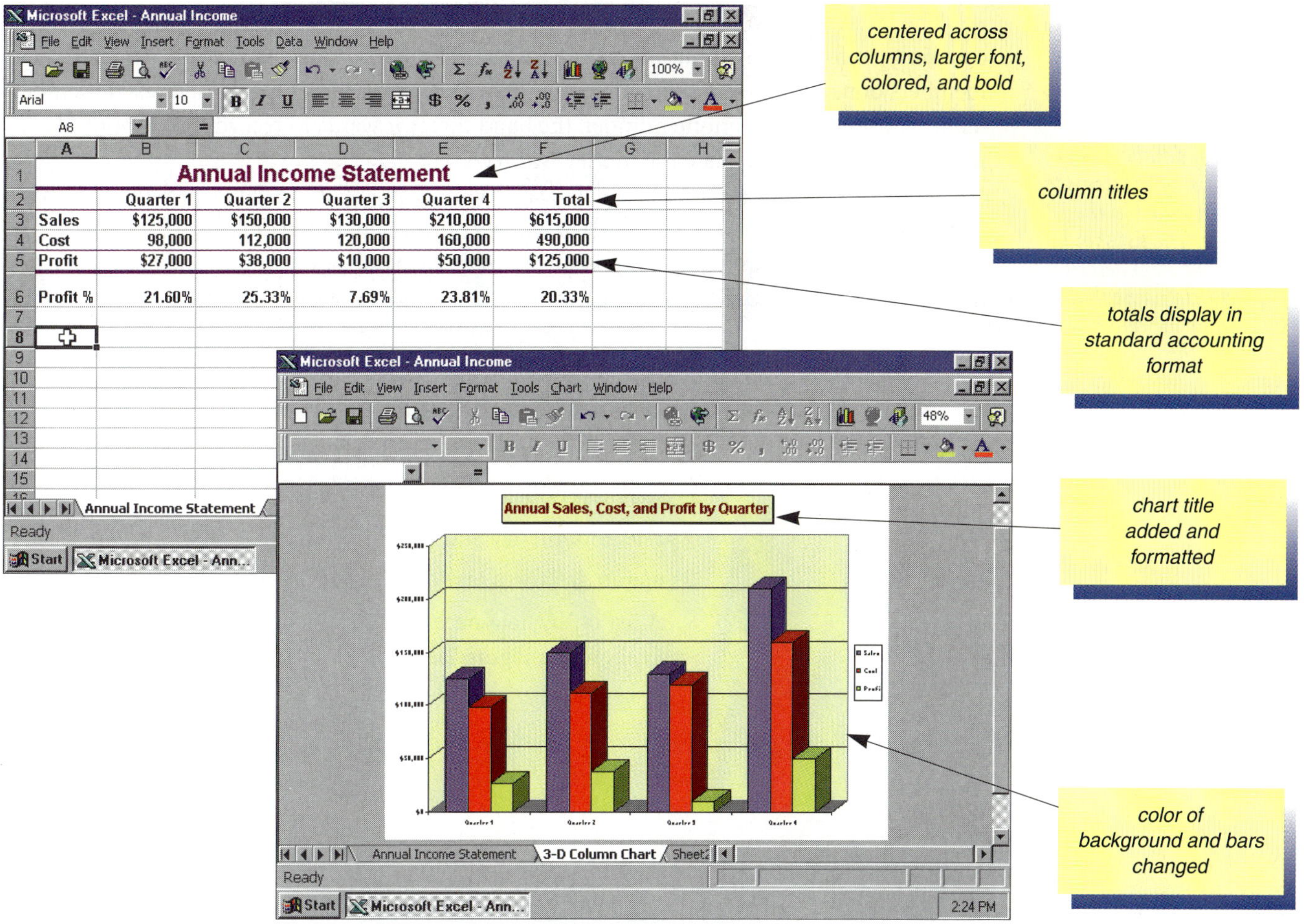

SOFTWARE APPLICATIONS 2.21

Figure 2-24
This spreadsheet and chart sheet show how the formatting features can improve the appearance of a spreadsheet and chart.

Database Software

A **database** refers to a collection of data that is stored in files. Although spreadsheet software can manage a small single-file database, most database applications require the use of database software. **Database software** allows you to create a database and to retrieve, manipulate, and update the data that you store in it. In a manual system (Figure 2-25), data might be recorded on paper and stored in a filing cabinet. In a database on the computer, the data will be stored in an electronic format on a storage device such as a disk.

When you use a database, you need to be familiar with the terms file, record, and field. Just as in a manual system, the word **file** is a collection of related data that is organized in records. Each **record** contains a collection of related facts called **fields**. For example, an address file might consist of records containing name and address information. All the data that relates to one name would be considered a record. Each fact, such as the street address or telephone number, is called a field.

Figure 2-25
A database is similar to a manual system, where related data items are stored in files.

2.22 CHAPTER 2 – SOFTWARE APPLICATIONS: USER TOOLS

The screens in Figures 2-26 through 2-29 present the development of a database containing information about the members of a college band booster club. The booster club members donate money to help fund band activities. Besides keeping track of each member's name, address, and telephone number, the band director wants to record the amount of money donated and the date the money was received.

A good way to begin creating a database is to make a list of the data you want to record. Each item that you want to keep track of will become a field in the database. Each field should be given a unique name that is short but descriptive. For example, the field name for a member's last name could be Last Name. The field name for a member's first name could be First Name. You also need to decide the length of each field and the type of data that each field will contain. The type of data could be any of the following:

- **alphanumeric**, letters, numbers, or special characters
- **numeric**, numbers only
- **currency**, dollar and cents amounts
- **date**, month, day and year information
- **memo**, freeform text of any type or length

A list of the data necessary for the band booster club is shown in Figure 2-26.

Figure 2-26
One of the first steps in creating a database is to make a list of the items that will be included in the database. The list should include the item description, a short field name that will be used by the database; the length of the item; and the data type. Most databases allow you to add, delete, or change fields after the database is created.

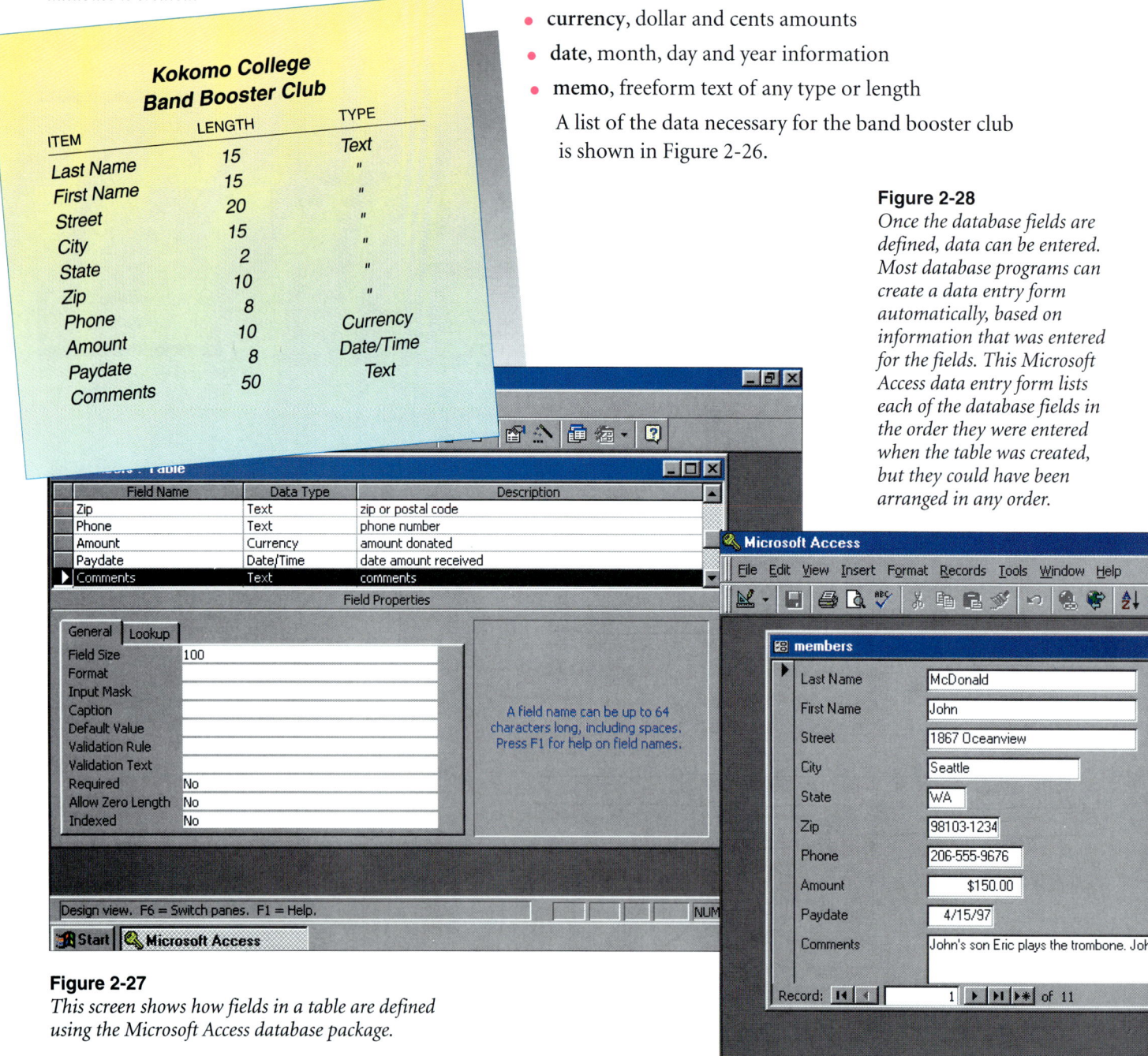

Figure 2-27
This screen shows how fields in a table are defined using the Microsoft Access database package.

Figure 2-28
Once the database fields are defined, data can be entered. Most database programs can create a data entry form automatically, based on information that was entered for the fields. This Microsoft Access data entry form lists each of the database fields in the order they were entered when the table was created, but they could have been arranged in any order.

SOFTWARE APPLICATIONS **2.23**

Each database program differs slightly in how it requires the user to enter, or define, fields. A field entry screen from Microsoft Access is shown in Figure 2-27.

After the database structure is created by defining the fields, individual database records can be entered. Usually, they are entered one at a time by using the keyboard. Most database programs, however, also have the ability to import data from other files. The field definitions specified for each field help you in entering the data. For example, designating the Paydate field as a date field prevents a user from entering anything other than a valid date. Comparing data entered against a predefined format or value is called **validation** and is an important feature of database programs. Figure 2-28 shows the entry screen for the band booster club data.

For an example of how athletes use databases for training purposes, visit the Discovering Computers Chapter 2 inCyber page (http://www.scsite.com/dc/ch2/incyber.htm) and click Athlete.

After the records are entered, the database can be used to produce information. All or some of the records can be selected and arranged in the order specified by the user. This is one of the more powerful features of a database; the ability to retrieve database information based on criteria specified by the user. For example, suppose the band director personally wanted to call and thank all the booster club members who donated more than $100. A report, called a **query** could be produced that listed the members names, phone numbers, and the amounts and dates donated. The report could be arranged so the largest donations were listed first. An example of such a report is shown in Figure 2-29.

As shown in the band booster club example, database software assists users in creating files and storing, manipulating, and retrieving data. Popular software packages that perform these functions include Microsoft Access, dBASE, FoxPro, and Paradox.

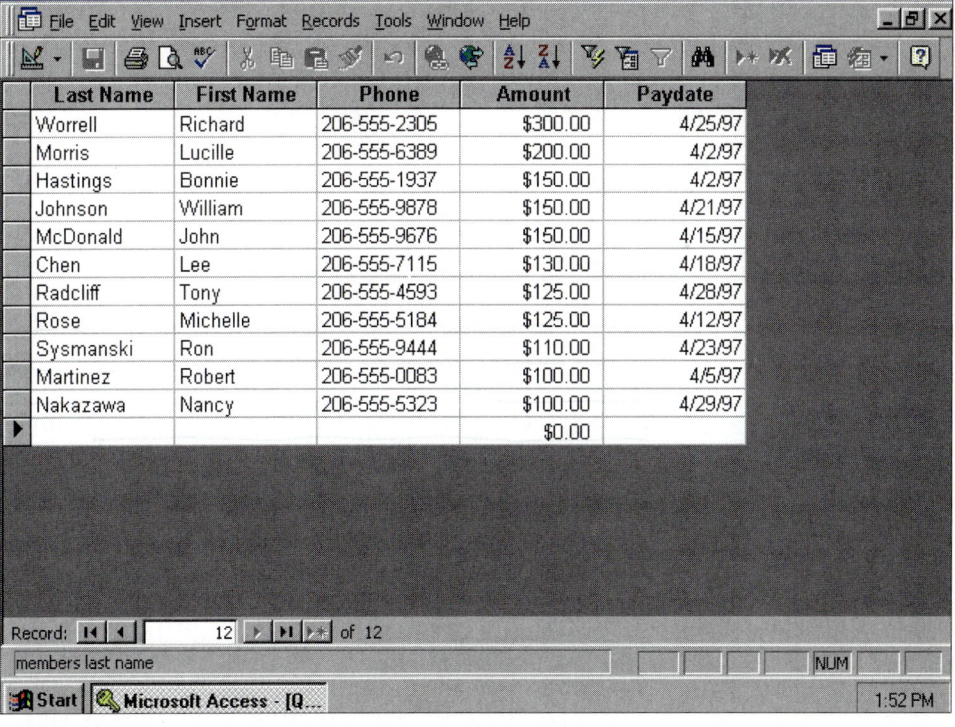

Figure 2-29
Database software can produce reports based on criteria specified by the user. For example, this screen shows the result of a request, called a query, that specified the name and phone number of each booster club member that contributed $100 or more. The records were sorted so the highest contributors are listed first. The results of the query can be displayed on the screen or printed.

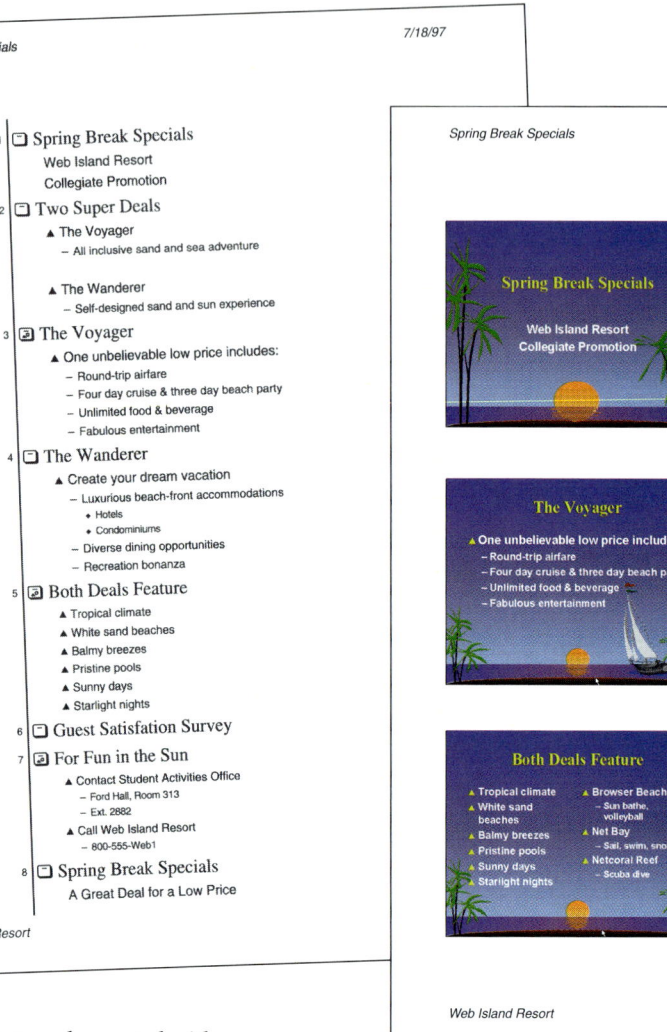

Figure 2-30
Presentation graphics software is used to prepare slides utilized in making presentations. The slides can be displayed on a computer, projected on a screen, or printed and handed out. The presentation graphics software includes many features to control graphics objects and color to make the slides more visually interesting.

Figure 2-31
Documents that can be created with presentation graphics software.

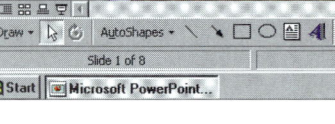

For tips on using graphics effectively in a presentation, visit the Discovering Computers Chapter 2 inCyber page (http://www.scsite.com/dc/ch2/incyber.htm) and click Presentation.

Presentation Graphics Software

Presentation graphics allow you to create documents called **slides** that are used in making presentations before a group. The slides can be displayed on a large monitor or projected on a screen (Figure 2-30). Presentation graphics go beyond analytical graphics by offering you a wider choice of presentation features. Some of the features included with presentation graphics packages are:

- Numerous chart types
- Three-dimensional effects for charts, text, and graphics
- Special effects such as shading, shadows, and textures
- Sound and animation
- Color control that includes preestablished groups of complementary colors for backgrounds, lines and text, shadows, fills, and accents
- Image libraries that include clip art graphics that can be incorporated into the slides. Usually the image libraries are business-oriented and include illustrations of factories, people, money, and other business-related art.

Besides the slides, presentation graphics packages create several other documents that can be used in a presentation (Figure 2-31). Outlines include just the text from each slide, usually the slide title and the key points. A notes page is used by the speaker making the presentation and includes a picture of the slide and any notes the speaker wants to see when he or she is discussing the slide. Audience handouts include images of two or more slides on a page that can be given to people who attended the presentation.

SOFTWARE APPLICATIONS 2.25

notes page

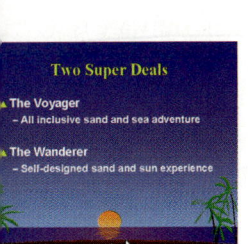
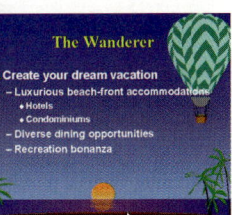
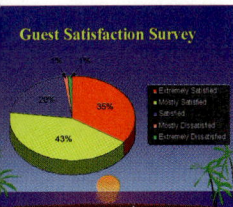
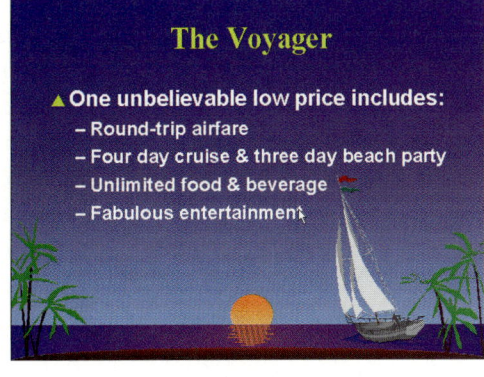

transparency

To help organize and present the slides, presentation graphics packages include slide sorters. A slide sorter presents a screen view similar to how 35mm slides would look on a photographer's light table (Figure 2-32). By using a mouse or other pointing device, you can arrange the slides in any order. When the slides are arranged in the proper order, they can be displayed one at a time by clicking the mouse or using the keyboard. The presenter also can set up the slides to be displayed automatically with a predetermined delay between each slide. Special effects also can be applied to the transition between each slide. For example, one slide might slowly dissolve as the other slide comes into view.

Using presentation graphics software allows you to efficiently create professional quality presentations that help communicate information more effectively. Studies have shown that people are more likely to remember information they have seen as well as heard and that they recall more information when it is presented in color. Popular presentation graphics packages include Microsoft PowerPoint, Aldus Persuasion, Lotus Freelance Graphics, and Compel.

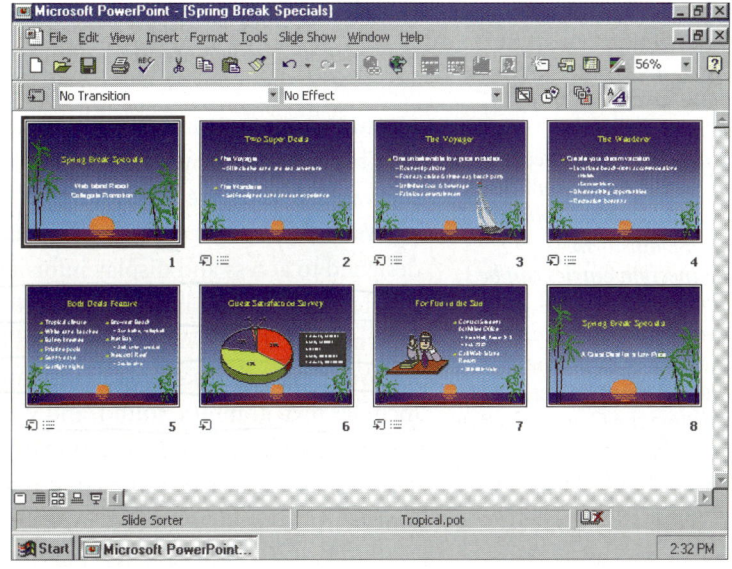

Figure 2-32
This slide sorter screen shows a miniature version of each slide. Using a pointing device or the keyboard, the slides can be rearranged to change their order of presentation.

Communications Software and Web Browsers

Perhaps more than any other application, communications software has tremendously changed the way people use computers in the last several years. **Communications software** is used to transmit data from one computer to another. For two computers to communicate, each must have data communications software, data communications equipment, and be connected by some type of link, such as a telephone line. Most communications packages have the ability to transmit and receive many different types of data, including text and graphics files, fax documents, and information obtained from online services or the Internet.

Besides transmitting and receiving the data, the communications software helps manage communications tasks by:

- Maintaining a directory of telephone numbers and settings for remote computers (Figure 2-33).
- Automatically dialing the number of the remote computer and establishing the communications connection.
- Automatically redialing if the line is busy. A time delay between communications attempts and a limit on the number of redial attempts also can be set.
- Automatically answering if another user calls your computer.

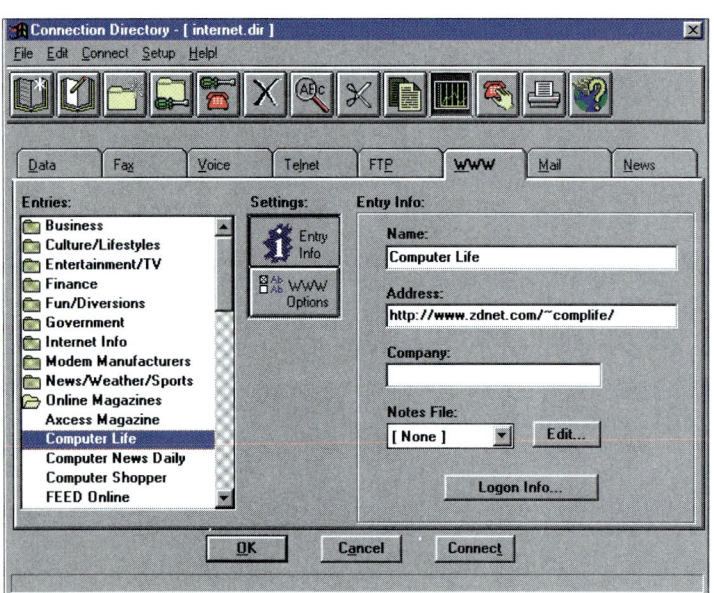

Figure 2-33
Communications software programs include directories that make it easier to connect with other computers. This screen shows the Procomm Plus communications software from Datastorm. Connection entries can be organized by type (e.g., data, fax, voice) and by category (e.g., business, finance, government). Clicking the Connect button at the bottom of the screen automatically makes the connection.

Communications software is frequently used by employees that are away from the office. Using communications software (and sometimes other packages such as electronic mail), remote employees can check their messages, send messages to other employees, check the quantity of inventory on hand, and enter orders that they have just received from customers.

Online Services Communications software also is used to access online services for news, weather, financial, and travel information. Online service companies such as The Microsoft Network and America Online provide a wide range of information and services for a small monthly fee. Other service companies provide detailed information in subject areas such as medicine, finance, or specific industries. Shopping is also available from several services. Online shoppers can read a description and, in many cases, see a picture of a product on their screen. Using a credit card, the product can be ordered. Most banks are now offering online banking. You can review recent financial transactions, transfer money from one account to another, and pay bills using your computer. All of these activities are made possible through the use of data communications software. Popular communications software packages are Procomm Plus and Crosstalk.

Web Browsers A **Web browser** is a special type of communications software that is designed to access and display information at Internet Web sites (Figure 2-34). Information at Internet Web sites is organized into what are called **Web pages**. The first page of information at each Web site is called the **home page**. The Web browser software interprets the Web page information and displays it on your computer screen in a format that usually includes text, graphics, sound, and video. Web browser software keeps track of Internet sites visited and can record the location of sites that you may want to revisit in the future. Netscape Navigator and Microsoft Internet Explorer are the most widely used browsers today.

SOFTWARE APPLICATIONS 2.27

Figure 2-34
Web browser software is used to access and display information at Internet Web sites. The site shown on this screen is used to search the Internet for information on a subject chosen by the user.

Electronic Mail Software

Electronic mail software, also called **e-mail**, allows you to send messages to and receive messages from other computer users (Figure 2-35). The other users may be on the same computer network or on a separate computer system reached through the use of communications equipment and software. Each e-mail user has an electronic mail box with an address to which the mail can be sent. To make the sending of messages more efficient, e-mail software allows you to send a single message to a distribution list consisting of two or more individuals. The e-mail software takes care of copying the message and routing it to each person on the distribution list. For example, a message sent to the Department Supervisors distribution list would be routed to each of the department supervisors. Most e-mail systems have a mail-waiting alert that notifies you by a message or sound that a message is waiting to be read even if you are working in another application.

Although e-mail was once used primarily within private organizations, today several communications

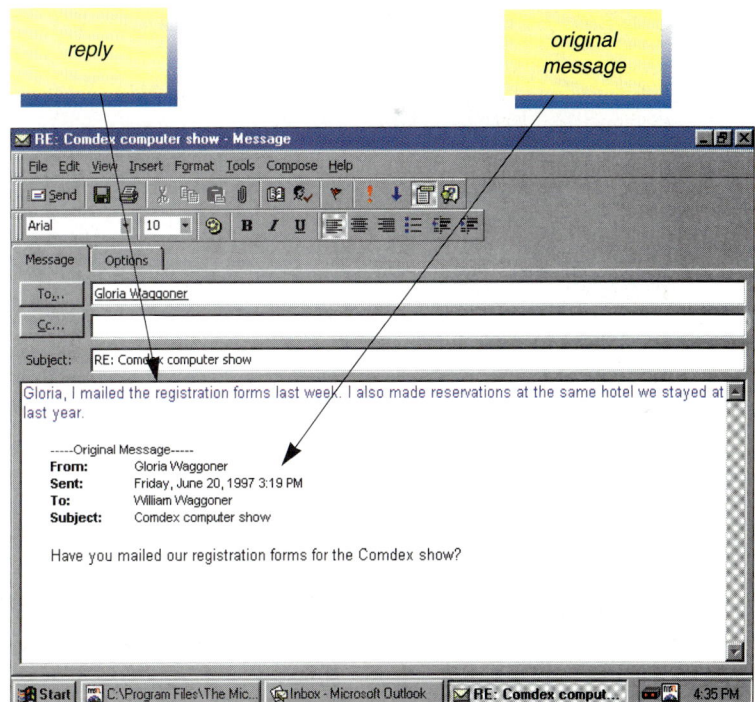

Figure 2-35
Electronic mail (e-mail) allows you to send and receive messages with other computer users. Each user has an electronic mail box to which messages are sent. This screen shows how a user can add a reply to a received message and then send the reply and a copy of the original message back to the person who sent the original message.

companies (such as MCI) and online services providers (such as America Online and CompuServe) provide public e-mail services for individuals. For a small monthly fee, you can receive mail from and send mail to others who have e-mail. Internet service providers such as the OnRamp Group and EarthNet offer e-mail as part of their standard service. Most Web browser software also includes e-mail capabilities. E-mail can be especially useful to people whose job keeps them away from the office. Remote workers can dial into their e-mail and send and receive messages at any time of the day. Because of its widespread use, informal rules, called e-mail etiquette, have been developed. These mostly common sense rules include:

- Keep messages short and to the point.
- Avoid using e-mail for trivia, gossip, or other non-essential communications.
- Keep the distribution list to a minimum.
- Avoid using all capitals letters – it is considered the same as yelling.
- It's okay (OK) for you (u) to (2) abbreviate as long as the abbreviation can be easily understood.
- Emoticons and acronyms also are used to show emotion (Table 2-1).
- Make the subject as meaningful as possible. Many e-mail systems list a summary of the mail and show only the subject, date, and sender.
- Read your mail regularly and clear messages that are no longer needed.

Popular e-mail packages are Microsoft Mail, Lotus cc:Mail, and Eudora.

EMOTICONS AND ACRONYMS

:)	Happy
:(	Sad
;)	Wink/Sarcasm
:O	Shouting/Shocked
:I	Indifferent
:P	Sticking out tongue
:D	Laughing
<g>	Grin
BTW	By the way
IMO	In my opinion
LOL	Laughing out loud

Table 2-1

Personal Information Management Software

Personal information management (PIM) software can help you keep track of the miscellaneous bits of personal information that each of us deals with every day. This information can take many forms: appointments, lists of things to do, telephone messages, notes about a current or future project, and so on. Individual programs that keep track of this type of information, such as electronic calendars, have been in use for some time. In recent years, however, such programs have been combined so that one package can keep track of all of a user's personal information.

Because of the many types of information that these programs can manage, it is difficult to precisely define personal information software. The category can be applied to programs that offer any of the following capabilities and features, however: appointment calendars, outliners, electronic notepads, data managers, and text retrieval. Some personal information software packages also include communications software capabilities such as phone dialers and e-mail. Appointment calendars allow you to schedule activities for a particular day and time (Figure 2-36). Most of them will warn you if two activities are scheduled for the same time. Outliners allow you to *rough out* an idea by constructing and reorganizing an outline of important points and subpoints. Electronic notepads allow you to record comments and assign them to one or more categories that can be used to retrieve the comments. Data managers are simple file management systems that allow the input, update, and retrieval of related records such as name and address lists or telephone numbers. Text retrieval provides the capability of searching files for specific words or phrases such as *Sales Meeting*. Three popular personal information management packages are Microsoft Schedule+, Ecco Pro, and Lotus Organizer.

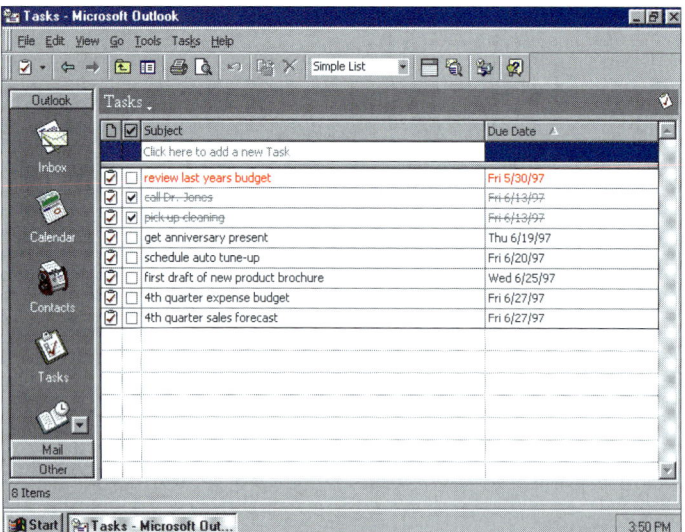

Figure 2-36
Personal information management (PIM) software helps organize and keep track of the many different types of information that people encounter each day. Microsoft Outlook, shown on this screen, allows you to keep track of appointments, events, task lists, and contacts.

Personal Finance Software

Personal finance software helps you track your income and expenses, pay bills, complete online transactions, and evaluate financial plans (Figure 2-37). Recording your financial transactions, especially expenses, helps you determine where, and for what purpose, your money is being spent. Reports can summarize transactions by category, by payee (such as the telephone company), or by time period (such as the last three months). Bill-paying features include the ability to print checks on your computer or have checks printed by an outside service. Several personal finance packages have agreements with credit card companies and banks that enable you to enter credit card transactions and bank account information automatically. You either receive a monthly transaction disk or download the data directly into your computer to obtain current credit card statements and account balances. Financial planning features include home and personal loan analysis, estimated income taxes, and how much money you should be saving for retirement. Other features included in many personal finance packages include home inventory, budgeting, tax related transactions, and investment tracking. Popular personal finance applications include Quicken and Microsoft Money.

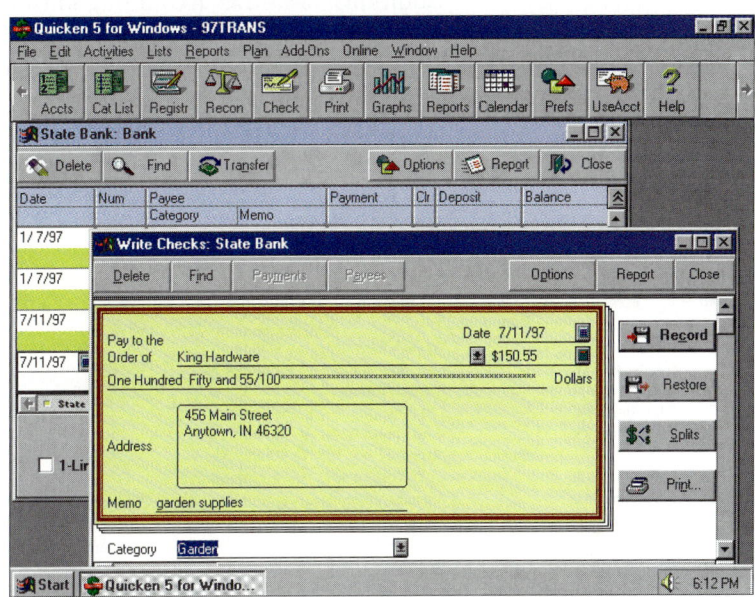

Figure 2-37
Personal finance software such as Quicken helps you track your income and expenses. This screen shows how checks are prepared.

Project Management Software

Project management software allows you to plan, schedule, track, and analyze the events, resources, and costs of a project (Figure 2-38). For example, a construction company might use this type of software to manage the building of an apartment complex or a campaign manager might use it to coordinate the many activities of a politician running for office. The value of project management software is that it provides a method for managers to control and manage the variables of a project to help ensure that the project will be completed on time and within budget. Popular project management packages include Timeline and Microsoft Project.

Figure 2-38
Project management software helps you plan and keep track of the tasks and resources necessary to complete a project. This screen shows part of a project plan for publishing a magazine. The more important tasks are listed in red. The bars in the upper right corner, called a Gantt chart, graphically indicate the duration of each task. The bottom portion of the screen identifies the resources required for the highlighted task; in this case, the hours needed from specific individuals.

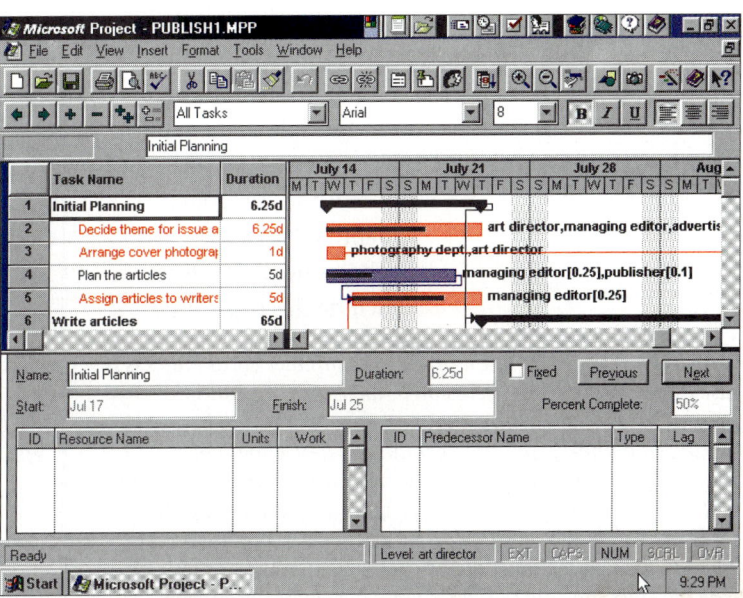

Accounting Software

Accounting software helps companies record and report their financial transactions (Figure 2-39). Some accounting tasks are similar to those handled by personal finance software: tracking income and expenses, writing checks, and recording transactions. Additional tasks that accounting software handles include the following:

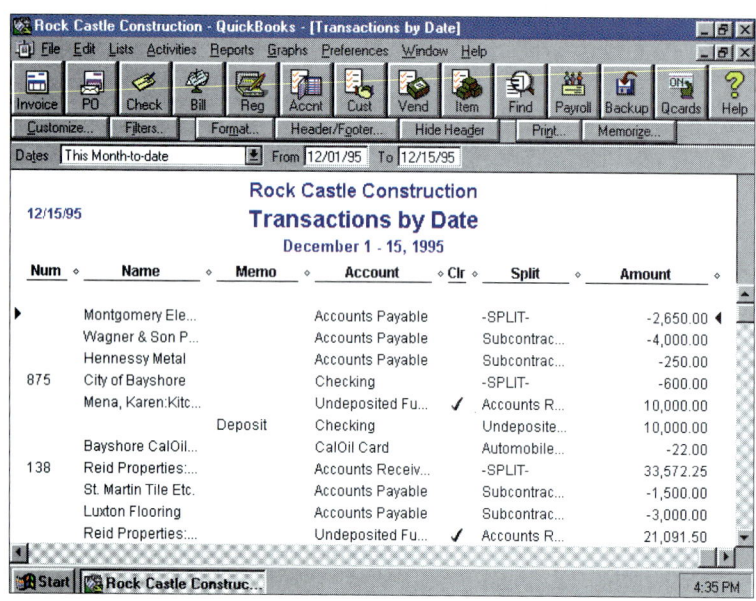

- Invoicing; preparing bills for products or services sold
- Accounts receivable; amounts owed by customers
- Accounts payable; amounts owed to suppliers
- Purchase orders; purchase commitments
- Payroll; amounts owed to employees
- Job costing; costs associated with a specific task, contract, or project
- Inventory; keeping track of unsold products
- General ledger; financial transaction summary

The listed features are provided by most accounting software packages. Some packages offer more sophisticated features such as multiple company reporting, foreign currency reporting, tracking the value of company assets, and forecasting the amount of raw materials needed for products. Accounting packages for small businesses range from less than one hundred to several thousand dollars. Accounting packages for large businesses can cost several hundred thousand dollars. Popular small business accounting packages include Intuit QuickBooks and Peachtree Accounting.

Figure 2-39
Accounting software helps businesses record and report financial transactions.

Groupware

Groupware is a loosely defined term applied to software that helps groups of people collaborate on projects and share information. Groupware is part of a broad concept called **workgroup technology** that includes equipment and software that help group members communicate, manage their activities, and make group decisions.

Some software applications discussed separately in this section, including e-mail and personal information management (PIM) software, also can be considered groupware. Other features and capabilities of groupware applications include:

- Group Editing; the ability for multiple users to revise a document with each set of revisions separately identified. Many word processing packages now include this capability.

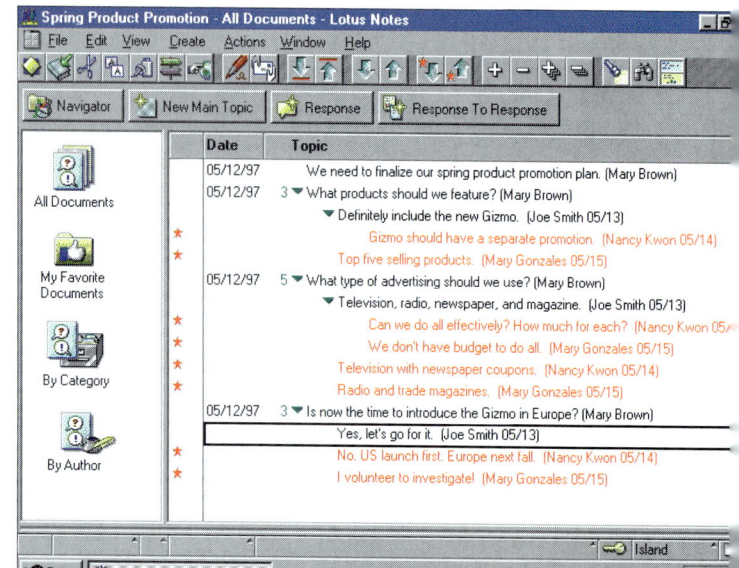

Figure 2-40
One of the capabilities of the groupware product Lotus Notes is a discussion database. A discussion database allows multiple persons to add their comments to a subject in the database in an organized manner, similar to conducting a meeting that participants need not attend at the same time or the same place. In the example shown on this screen, the original message has 5/12/97 in the date column and is left-aligned. Responses are shown indented and one line below the item to which they refer. The red stars indicate that a response has not yet been read.

- Group Scheduling; a group calendar that tracks the time commitments of multiple users and helps schedule meetings when necessary.
- Workflow Support; software that automates repetitive processes such as processing an insurance claim, in which multiple persons must review and approve a document.
- Discussion Database; an organized way to keep track of responses to a particular topic or subject.

One of the more widely used groupware packages is Lotus Notes (Figure 2-40). Notes uses a shared database approach to groupware. In addition, Notes includes e-mail and a programming language that can be used to develop customized groupware applications.

Computer-Aided Design (CAD) Software

Computer-aided design (CAD) software assists a user in creating a design for a product, such as a bicycle, or a structure, such as a building (Figure 2-41). CAD software eliminates the laborious drafting that used to be required. Changes to some or all of the design can be made and the results viewed instantly. Three-dimensional CAD programs can rotate the item being designed so you can view it from any angle. Variations of CAD programs have been developed for applications such as electronic circuit design, home remodeling, landscape design, and office furniture layout. AutoCAD and Parametric are two widely used CAD packages.

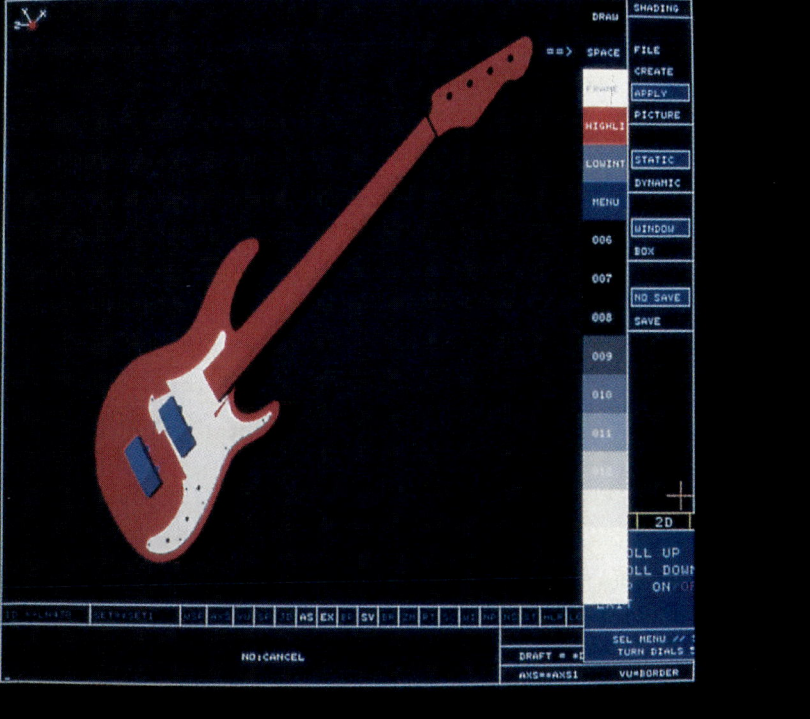

Figure 2-41
Computer-aided design (CAD) software helps users design products and structures.

Multimedia Authoring Software

Multimedia authoring software allows you to create a presentation that can include text, graphics, video, sound, and animation. A multimedia presentation is more than just a combination of these elements, however. A **multimedia presentation** is an interactive computer presentation in which you can choose what amount of material to cover and in what sequence it will be reviewed. For example, you may choose to click a video button to play a video or to skip the video and move to the next screen. Multimedia authoring software helps you create the presentation by controlling the placement of text and graphics and the duration of sounds, video, and animation. Multimedia ToolBook by Asymetrix Corporation is a widely-used multimedia authoring package (Figure 2-42).

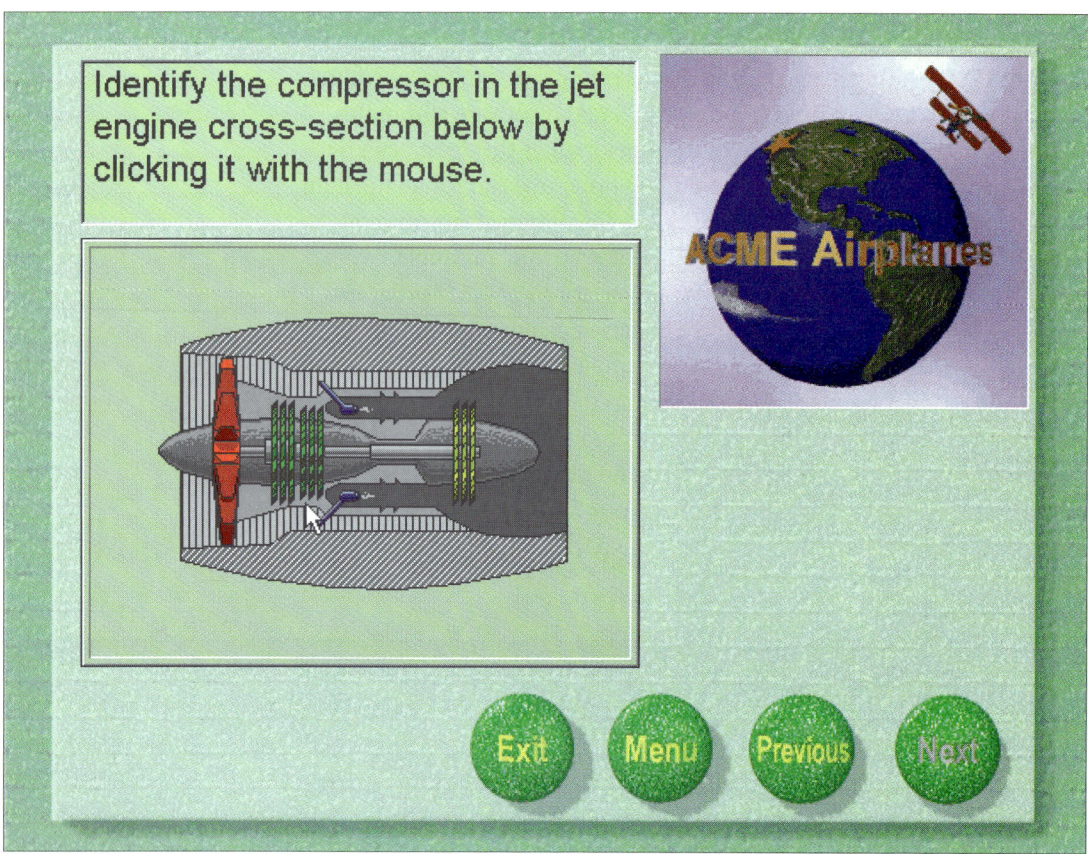

Figure 2-42
Multimedia authoring software enables a user to create a presentation using text, graphics, video, sound, and animation.

Integrated Software and Software Suites

Software packages such as databases and electronic spreadsheets are generally used independently of each other. But what if you wanted to place information from a database into a spreadsheet? You could reenter the database data in the spreadsheet. This would be time consuming, however, and errors could be introduced as you reentered the data. Integrated software and software suites are two approaches towards sharing information among applications.

Integrated software refers to software that combines applications such as word processing, spreadsheet, and database into a single, easy-to-use package. Many integrated packages also include communications capabilities. The applications that are included in integrated packages are designed to have a consistent command and menu structure. For example, the command to print a document looks and works the same in each of the integrated applications. Besides a consistent look and feel, a key feature of integrated packages is their capability of passing quickly and easily from one application to another. For example, revenue and cost information in a database on daily sales could be quickly loaded into a spreadsheet. The spreadsheet could be used to calculate gross profits.

Once the calculations are completed, all or a portion of the spreadsheet data can be passed to the word processing application to create a narrative report.

In their early days, integrated packages were criticized as being a collection of good but not great applications. To some extent this is still true. If you need the most powerful word processor or spreadsheet, you probably will not be satisfied with the capabilities of an integrated application. But for many users, the capabilities of today's integrated applications more than meet their needs. Besides the advantages of working well together, integrated applications are less expensive than buying comparable applications separately. Two popular integrated software packages are Microsoft Works (Figure 2-43) and ClarisWorks.

Similar to integrated software is a **software suite**, individual applications packaged in the same box and sold for a price that is significantly less than buying the applications individually. Although the use of suites was originally just a pricing strategy, suites are becoming more and more like integrated software. First the individual packages were just bundled together for a good price; now they are being modified to work better together and offer the same command and menu structures. For the developer, the advantages of products that look and work the same include shorter development and training time, and easier customer support. Another advantage is that customers who have learned one application package are more likely to buy a second package if they know it works in a similar manner. Popular software suites include Microsoft Office and Lotus SmartSuite.

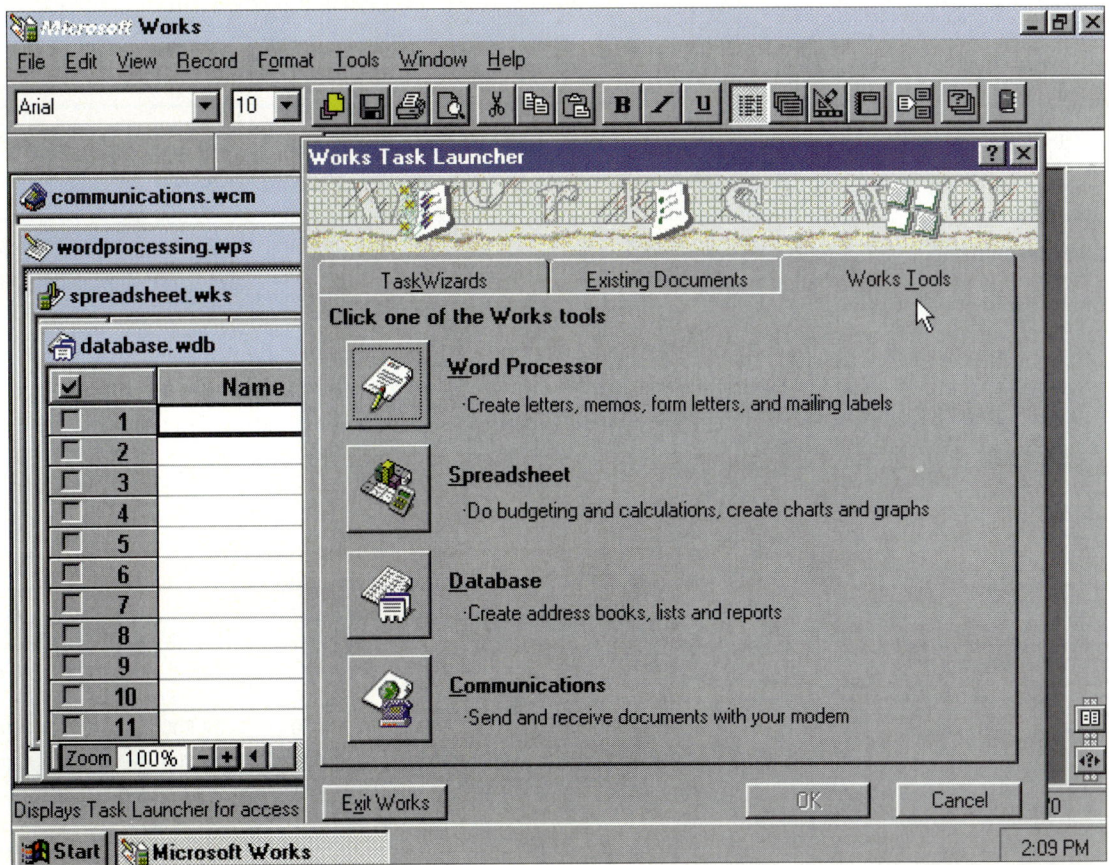

Figure 2-43
Microsoft Works provides word processing, spreadsheet, database, and communications capabilities in a single integrated software package.

Object Linking and Embedding (OLE)

Object linking and embedding, often referred to by the acronym **OLE** (pronounced oh-lay), are two ways to transfer and share information among software applications. To understand OLE, you first must understand something about objects. With regards to OLE, an **object** is any piece of information created with a Windows program. An object can be all or a portion of a document, a graphic, a sound file, or a video clip. Objects from one application, such as a spreadsheet document, can be placed in another application, such as a word processing document. When working with documents, the **source document** is the document from which the object originates, and the **destination document** is the document into which the object is placed. A document that contains objects from more than one application is called a **compound document**. The following numbers refer to Figure 2-44, which uses a spreadsheet and a word processing document to explain the difference between object embedding and object linking.

Figure 2-44
OLE (object linking and embedding).

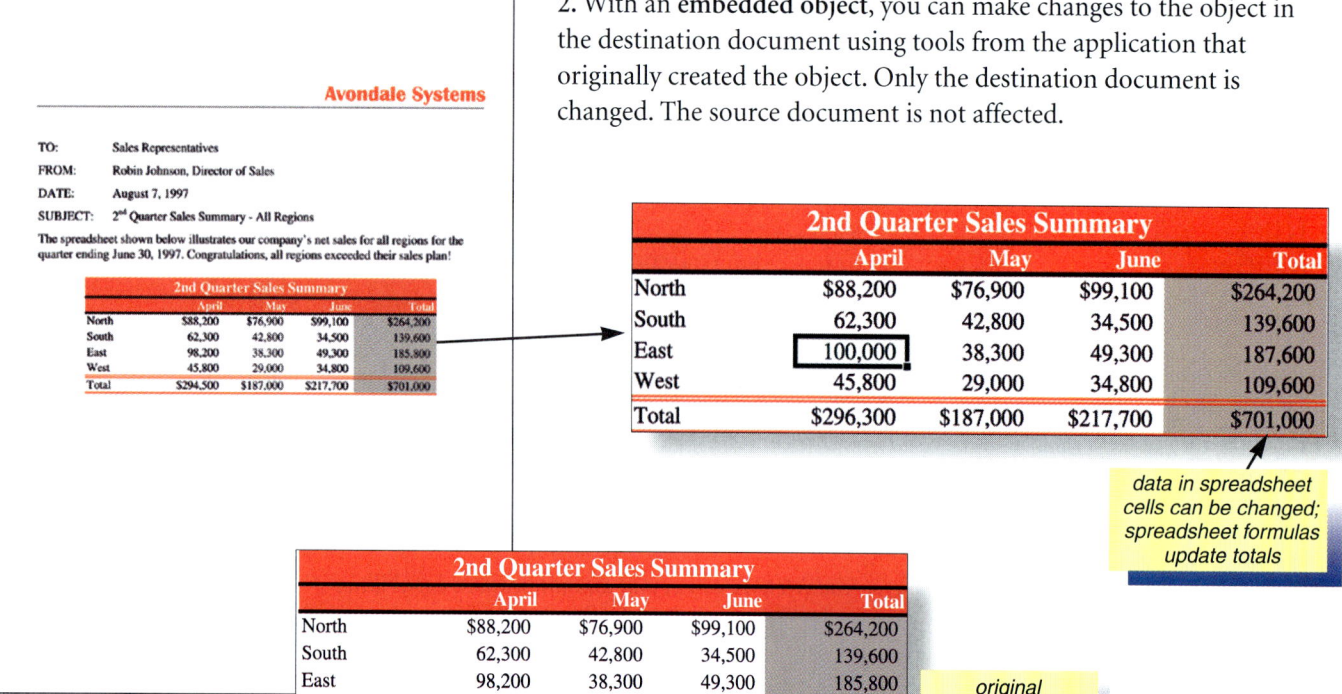

1. Both object linking and object embedding allow you to place all or a portion of a document into another document. This is similar to cut and paste using the Clipboard. With OLE, however, you have the added ability to make changes to the object while you are still working in the destination document. To select the object in the destination document, you double-click it using a pointing device.

2. With an **embedded object**, you can make changes to the object in the destination document using tools from the application that originally created the object. Only the destination document is changed. The source document is not affected.

OBJECT LINKING AND EMBEDDING (OLE) **2.35**

3. With a **linked object**, you make changes to the source document using the original software application. When the object is selected, the original software application is opened. After you make changes and save the source document, changes are reflected in both the source document and the linked destination document.

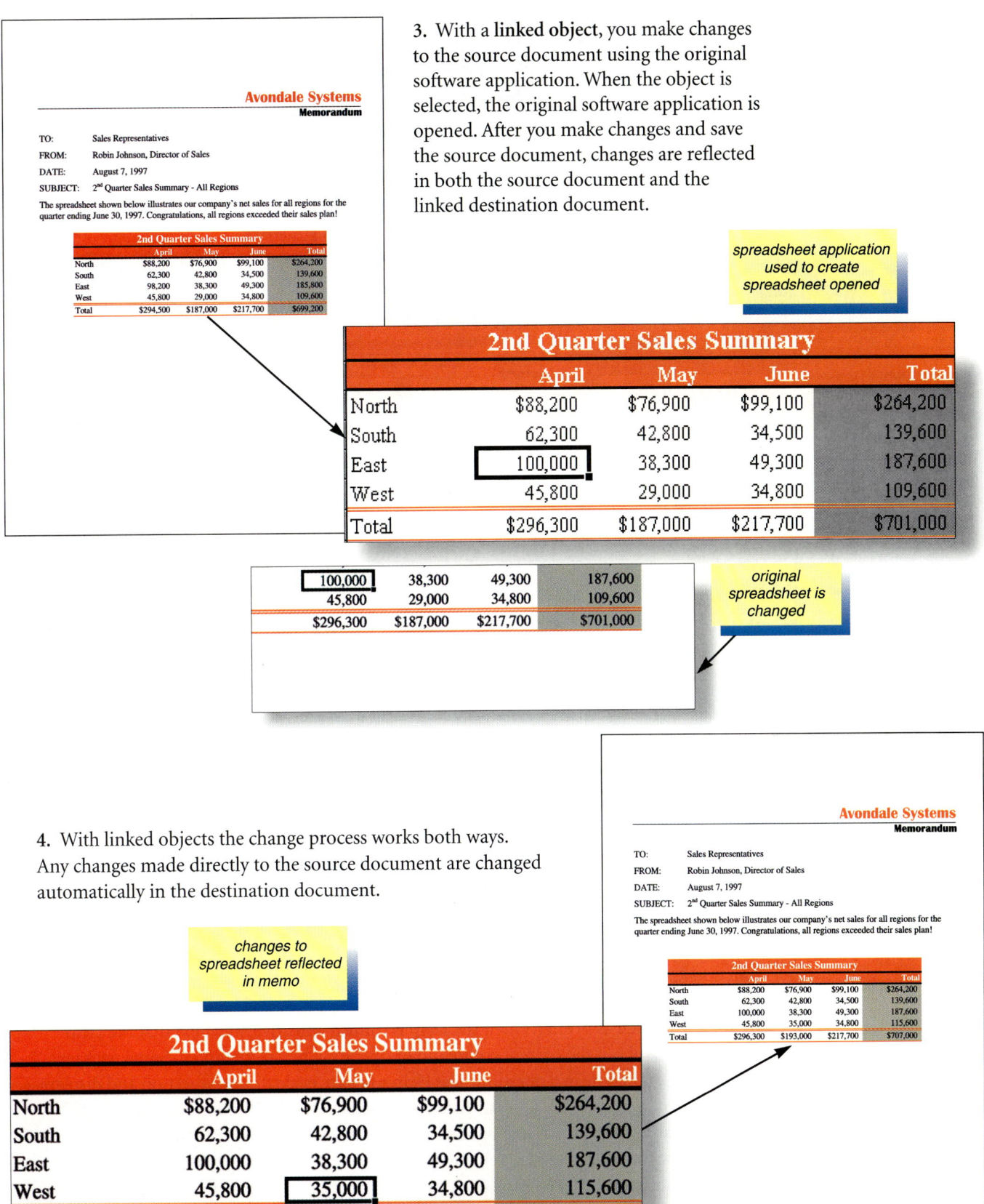

4. With linked objects the change process works both ways. Any changes made directly to the source document are changed automatically in the destination document.

OLE is particularly useful in situations where the overall form of a document stays the same, such as the memo in Figure 2-44, but the content of the document, such as the quarterly sales results, changes.

2.36   CHAPTER 2 – SOFTWARE APPLICATIONS: USER TOOLS

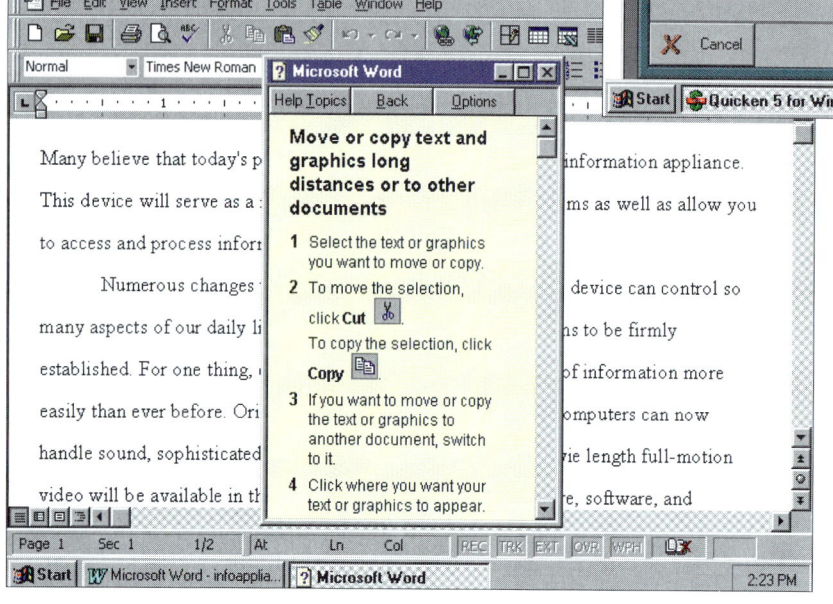

Figure 2-46
Software tutorials provide a step-by-step method of learning an application. This screen shows how the Quicken financial management tutorial explains how to set up a budget.

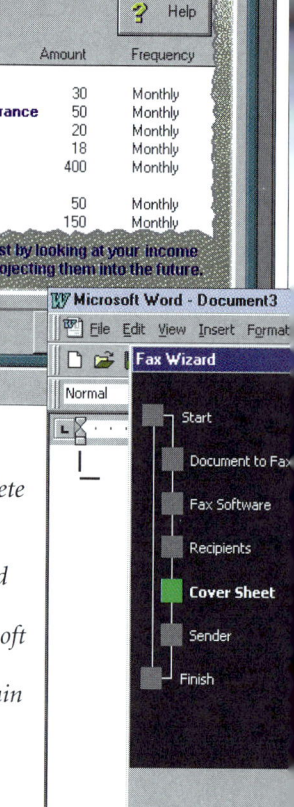

Figure 2-47
Wizards help you complete a task by asking you questions and then performing actions based on your answers. This screen shows the Microsoft Word Fax Wizard. The wizard prompts for certain information and then creates a fax cover page automatically. The resulting document can then be changed, if necessary.

Figure 2-45
Online Help provides assistance without having you leave your application.

Learning Aids and Support Tools for Application Users

Learning to use an application software package involves time and practice. In addition to taking a class to learn how to use a software application, several learning aids and support tools are available to help you, including online Help, tutorials, wizards, and trade books.

Online Help (Figure 2-45) refers to explanatory information that is available while you are using an application. In most packages, a function key or an on-screen button activates the Help feature. When you are using an application and have a question, using the help function key or button temporarily will overlay your work on the screen with information on how to use the package. Help topics can be accessed by topic, such as printing a document, or by keywords, such as printer. Often the Help is **context-sensitive**, meaning that the Help information is about the current command or operation being attempted. Some packages even allow you to type in a question. The Help software evaluates the question and displays a list of related topics. Many software developers believe that their online Help is so comprehensive that they have stopped shipping user's manuals along with the software. Many companies also have FAQs (Frequently Asked Questions) Web pages on the Internet to help you find answers to common questions.

Tutorials are step-by-step instructions using real examples that show you how to use an application (Figure 2-46). Some tutorials are written manuals, but more and more, tutorials are software-based, allowing you to use your computer to learn about a package.

A **wizard** is an automated assistant that helps you complete a task by asking you questions and then automatically performing actions based on your answers (Figure 2-47). Many software applications include wizards: word processing programs have wizards to help you create memorandums, meeting agendas, and letters; spreadsheet programs have chart and function wizards; and database programs have form and report wizards. These are just a few of the wizards available to help you learn and use these software programs effectively.

If printed documentation is included with a software package, often it is organized as reference material. This makes it helpful once you know how to use a package, but difficult to use when you are first learning it. For this reason, many **trade books** (Figure 2-48) are available to help you learn to use the features of personal computer application packages. These books can be found where software is sold and are usually carried in regular bookstores.

Summary of Software Applications

By reading this chapter, you have learned about user interfaces and several of the most widely used software applications. You have also read about some of the learning aids and support tools that are available for application software. Knowledge about these topics increases your computer literacy and helps you to understand how personal computers can help you in your career, school, and at home.

Figure 2-48
Trade books are available for all popular software applications.

CHAPTER 2 – SOFTWARE APPLICATIONS: USER TOOLS

COMPUTERS AT WORK

Shortcuts to Creating Documents

Before you invest the time to create a new document, you first should check to see if something similar already exists. Thousands of templates already have been created and are available from a variety of sources. Many of these templates are designed for general requirements common to many businesses, such as a fax cover sheet or a product invoice. Others templates are specific to particular professions such as legal or medical practices. The first place to look is in the template file included with your software application. Word processors usually have the most document templates, but spreadsheet, database, desktop publishing, and presentation graphics applications also include template files. If the standard templates do not represent your needs, ask your software supplier if add-on template packages are available. For example, Microsoft markets a Small Business Pack that consists of more than 40 easy-to-use templates, forms, and reports that assist businesses in everything from day-to-day operations to long range planning. Functional areas include financial, management, marketing, operations, planning, and sales.

Some documents, such as a contract or a lease agreement, need only a small amount of data changed each time they are prepared. Creation of these types of documents is made easier with document assembly programs that prompt you for the necessary data and insert it automatically in the document. Document assembly programs not only make preparation of routine documents faster, but they also reduce the possibility of leaving out key data.

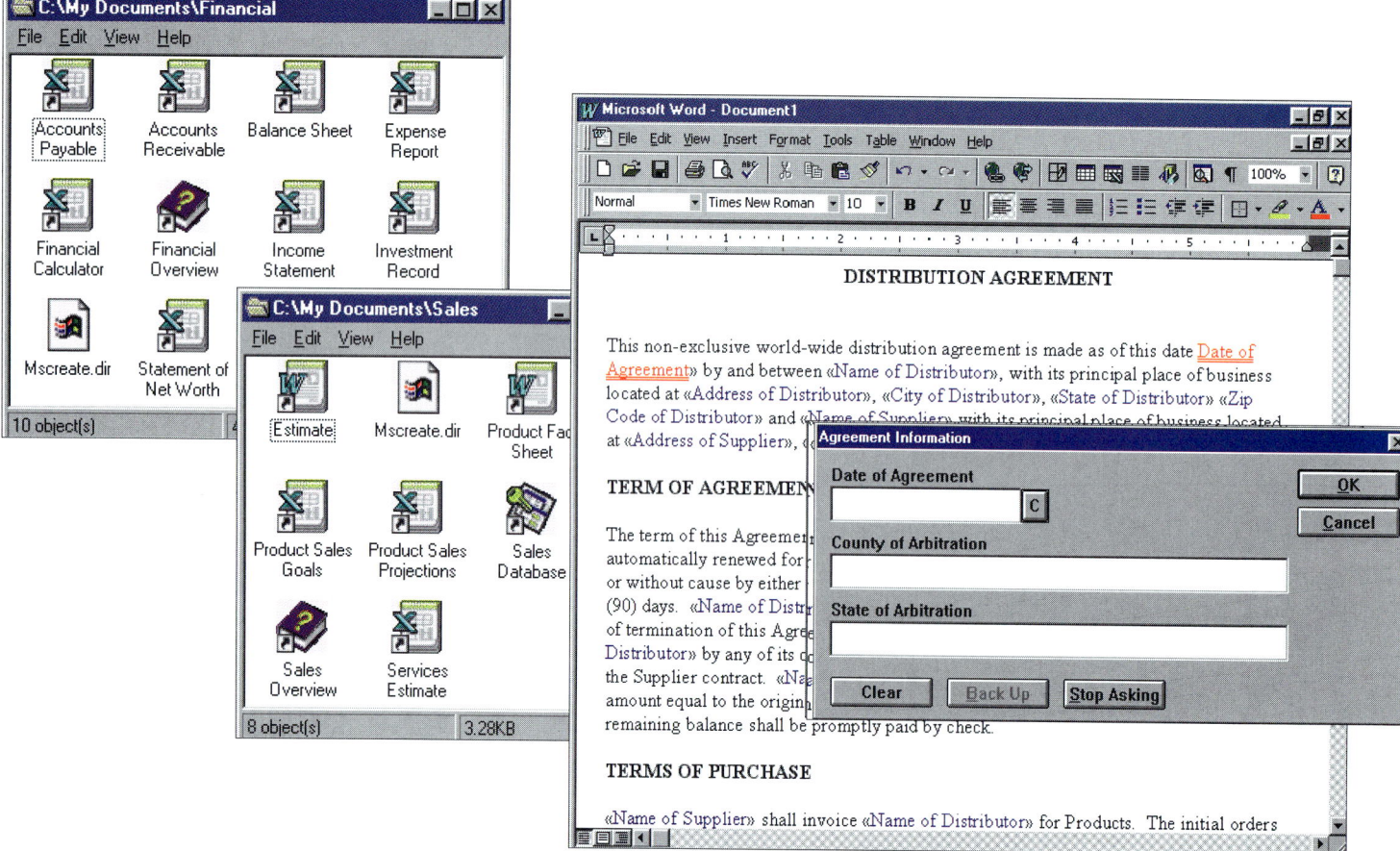

Figure 2-49

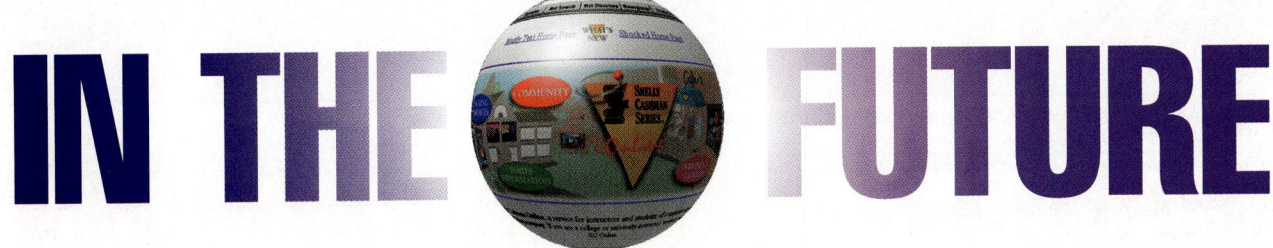

Subscription Software

In the future, will you pay an annual fee for application software packages, just as you pay for a magazine subscription? Some foresee this as the trend. Rather than paying a large one-time license fee for software, the vendor and the user may be better served by the user paying smaller amounts annually as long as he or she continues to use the software.

Software applications used to cost hundreds of dollars each. Some top-selling productivity applications had a list price of $500 or more. Intense competition lowered the prices of individual applications (and drove some developers out of business) and software suites have continued the downward per-package price trend. But today, software is even more expensive to produce and software developers have had to come up with other ways to generate revenue and lower support costs. One way to generate revenue is to charge maintenance or support fees. While some developers still provide toll-free support telephone numbers, most have gone to toll numbers. Even the toll-free numbers can be misleading. Often they connect to a person who will ask for a credit card number before you can talk to a technical support representative. Sometimes you are given the option of paying a flat fee; $25 is common, or paying $2 or $3 a minute for answers to your questions. You have to decide if it is a simple problem that is likely to be solved in a minute or two or if you would be better off with the flat fee. Some vendors use 900 area code numbers to charge your telephone number for pay-by-the-minute support. To lower costs, most vendors offer some type of online support. Some vendors offer online support from all of the following methods: dial-up bulletin boards, online service providers such as America Online, fax databases, and Internet Web sites. Many vendors now use these online methods to distribute software, especially corrections to known software problems.

Software Support Options

On the Internet • http://www.scseries.com
Answers to frequently asked questions (FAQs), technical bulletins, and other product support information are available 24 hours a day, 7 days a week at our Web site.

Fax Back • (208) 555-9876
Answers to many common installation and product questions are available 24 hours a day, 7 days a week from our fax-by-demand system.

Standard Support • (208) 555-1234
No charge support is available via a toll call Monday through Friday between 6:00 a.m. and 6:00 p.m. mountain time.

Priority Support
Priority support from support specialists is available 24 hours a day, 7 days a week. Two billing options are available:

(900) 555-4567 $2 per minute, $25 maximum. Charges appear on your telephone bill.

(800) 555-4321 $25 per incident. This service is billed to your credit card.

Figure 2-50

Upgrade fees are another way software companies generate revenues that help pay for ongoing development. Not too long ago, software upgrades came out every 18 to 36 months. Nowadays, some companies update their products several times a year. Many companies try for at least an annual upgrade. The upgrade fees usually are much less than the cost of buying the package new, but can still be substantial; sometimes more than $100. For a user with a lot of software, annual upgrade fees can be a significant ongoing expense. Some users are reluctant to upgrade each time the developer introduces a new version. Unless the new version has some feature the user needs, no practical incentive exists to upgrade. Most developers, however, stop supporting older versions of their product at some point in time. Usually, the last version is supported but versions two or more releases back often have limited or no support.

Overall, the tendency seems to be towards smaller but more frequent charges for software. Some developers have taken this approach to the point where they give away their software in hopes that you will install the product, become a dedicated user, and want to pay the subsequent upgrade and/or support charges. It's like the razor blade companies that give away their razors and make their profits selling replacement blades. To make it easier for the developer to receive the annual fees, some companies ask that you authorize the company to automatically charge a credit card. The annual fee has advantages to the user as well as the developer. If the developer has factored receiving annual fees into the software pricing, then you will obtain the product for a lower initial cost. Once the annual fee is paid, you do not have to worry about another $25 charge or speaking quickly to minimize a per-minute charge. All you have to worry about is whether the software vendor will answer the telephone!

review

chapter 2

1 | 2 | 3 | 4 | 5 | 6 | 7 | 8 | 9 | 10 | 11 | 12 | 13 | 14 | I

inCyber | review | terms | yourTurn | hotTopics | outThere | winLabs | webWalk | exercises | news | home

INSTRUCTIONS: *To display this page from the Web, launch your browser and enter the URL, http://www.scsite.com/dc/ch2/review.htm. Click the links for current and additional information.*

1 User Interface

An operating system tells the computer how to perform functions such as processing program instructions and transferring data. Once the operating system is loaded into the memory of a computer, application programs can be run. The **user interface** is the way all software, including the operating system, communicates with the user. A **graphical user interface (GUI)**, one of the more common user interfaces, combines text and graphics.

2 Software Applications

Application software consists of programs that tell a computer how to produce information. Individual software products are called **software packages**. Understanding software applications commonly used on personal computers is part of being computer literate.

3 Word Processing Software

Word processing requires the use of a computer to produce or modify documents that primarily consist of text. Producing a document using word processing generally consists of four steps: creating, editing, formatting, and printing. Creating involves entering text. **Editing** is the process of making changes in the content of a document. **Formatting** means changing the appearance of a document. Printing can be done utilizing many different options. Diverse features are used during each step to create professional-looking documents or home pages on the World Wide Web.

4 Desktop Publishing Software

Desktop publishing (DTP) software is used to design and produce high-quality documents that contain text, graphics, and unique colors. DTP software is designed specifically for **page composition and layout** (sometimes called **page makeup**), or the process of arranging text and graphics on the document page. A **page definition language** describes the document to be printed in language the printer can understand.

5 Spreadsheet Software

Spreadsheet software organizes numeric data in a table format called a **spreadsheet** or **worksheet**. Data is arranged vertically in **columns** and horizontally in **rows**. A **cell** is the intersection where a column and row meet. Cells may contain **labels** (text), **values** (numbers), and **formulas** that perform calculations. A spreadsheet's capabilities of recalculating when data is changed, called **what-if analysis**, and creating a **chart** that graphically shows the relationship of numerical data make it a valuable tool for decision making.

6 Database Software

A **database** is a collection of data stored in files. **Database software** is used to create a database and to retrieve, manipulate, and update the data kept in it. A **file** is a collection of related data stored in records. Each **record** contains a set of related facts called **fields**. The capability of retrieving information in a report, called a **query**, based on criteria specified by the user is one of the more powerful features of a database.

7 Presentation Graphics Software

Presentation graphics allows the user to create documents called **slides** that are utilized in making presentations before a group. Presentation graphics packages offer numerous chart types, three-dimensional effects, special effects, sound and animation, color control, and image libraries. A slide sorter helps to organize and present the slides. Presentation graphics packages also can be used to create outlines, notes pages, and audience handouts.

8 Communications Software, Web Browser, and Electronic Mail Software

Communications software is used to transmit data from one computer to another. Most communications packages transmit and receive different types of data, maintain a directory, automatically dial, automatically redial, and automatically answer. A **Web browser** is a type of communications software designed to access and display information that is organized into **Web pages** at Internet Web sites. **Electronic mail software**, also called **e-mail**, allows users to send messages to and receive messages from other computer users.

9 Personal Information Management and Personal Finance Software

Personal information management (PIM) software helps individuals keep track of miscellaneous bits of personal information. These packages may offer appointment calendars, outliners, electronic notepads, data managers, and text retrieval. **Personal finance software** helps you track your income and expenses, pay bills, and evaluate financial plans.

10 Project Management Software, Accounting Software, and Groupware

Project management software allows users to plan, schedule, track, and analyze the events, resources and costs of a project. **Accounting software** helps companies record and report their financial transactions. **Groupware** is a term applied to software that helps multiple users work together by sharing information.

11 Computer-Aided Design (CAD) and Multimedia Authoring Software

Computer-aided design (CAD) software assists a user in creating a design for a product or structure. Changes can be made to all or part of the design and the results viewed instantly. **Multimedia authoring software** allows you to create a presentation that can include text, graphics, video, sound, and animation.

12 Integrated Software and Software Suites

Integrated software refers to software that combines applications into a single, easy-to-use package. The applications are designed to have a consistent command and menu structure, and data can be passed quickly from one application to another. In a **software suite**, individual applications are packaged in the same box and sold for a price that is significantly less than buying the applications individually. The packages are modified to work better together and offer the same command and menu structures.

2 terms

chapter 1 | 2 | 3 | 4 | 5 | 6 | 7 | 8 | 9 | 10 | 11 | 12 | 13 | 14 | I

inCyber | review | terms | yourTurn | hotTopics | outThere | winLabs | webWalk | exercises | news | home

INSTRUCTIONS: *To display this page from the Web, launch your browser and enter the URL, http://www.scsite.com/dc/ch2/terms.htm. Scroll through the list of terms. Click a term for its definition and a picture. Click the rocket ship for current and additional information about the term.*

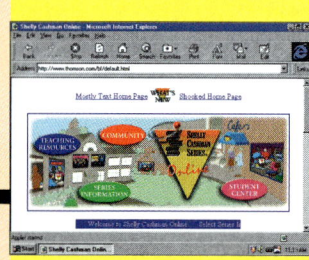

Web browser

DEFINITION

Web browser
Programs running on Internet-connected computers that enable users to access World Wide Web sites that have text, graphics, video, and sound and have hypertext links to other information and Web sites. (**2.26**)

absolute referencing (2.19)
accounting software (2.30)
alignment (2.9)
alphanumeric (2.22)
analytical graphics (2.20)
annotations (2.8)
AutoCorrect (2.7)
AutoFormat (2.10)
AutoSave (2.4)
AutoSum button (2.16)

bar charts (2.20)
border (2.10)
built-in style (2.10)
business graphics (2.20)
button (2.3)

cell (2.15)
centered alignment (2.9)
chart (2.20)
clip art (2.10)
Clipboard (2.6)
color libraries (2.13)
columns (2.13, 2.15)
commands (2.3)
communications software (2.26)
compound document (2.34)
computer-aided design (CAD) (2.31)
context-sensitive (2.36)
copy (2.6)
currency (2.22)
cursor (2.6)
cut (2.6)

database (2.21)
database software (2.21)
date (2.22)
dedicated word processing systems (2.4)
delete (2.6)
desktop publishing (DTP) (2.12)

destination document (2.34)

editing (2.6)
electronic mail software (2.27)
e-mail (2.27)
embedded object (2.34)

fields (2.21)
file (2.21)
font (2.9)
footers (2.10)
format (2.8)
formulas (2.15)
functions (2.16)

grammar checker (2.8)
graphical user interface (GUI) (2.2)
graphics (2.10)
groupware (2.30)

headers (2.10)
highlighting tool (2.8)
home page (2.26)

icons (2.2)
illustration software (2.13)
insert (2.6)
insertion point (2.6)
integrated software (2.32)

justification (2.9)
justified alignment (2.9)

labels (2.15)
landscape (2.11)
left alignment (2.9)
line charts (2.20)
line spacing (2.9)
linked object (2.35)

macro (2.16)
margins (2.9)
memo (2.22)
menu (2.3)
Microsoft Windows (2.2)
monospacing (2.9)
multimedia authoring software (2.32)
multimedia presentation (2.32)

numeric (2.22)

object (2.34)
object linking and embedding (2.34)
OLE (2.34)
online Help (2.36)
operating system (2.2)

page composition and layout (2.12)
page definition language (2.14)
page makeup (2.12)
paste (2.6)
personal finance software (2.29)
personal information management (PIM) software (2.28)
pie charts (2.20)
point (2.8)
portrait (2.11)
PostScript (2.14)
presentation graphics (2.24)
print preview (2.11)
project management software (2.29)
proportional spacing (2.9)

query (2.23)

record (2.21)
relative referencing (2.19)
replace (2.6)

revision marks (2.8)
right alignment (2.9)
rows (2.15)

scroll tips (2.6)
scrolling (2.6)
search (2.6)
shading (2.10)
slides (2.24)
software packages (2.4)
software suite (2.33)
source document (2.34)
spacing (2.9)
spelling checker (2.6)
spreadsheet (2.14)
style (2.9)
style sheet (2.10)

tables (2.10)
template (2.10)
thesaurus (2.8)
trade books (2.37)
tutorials (2.36)
typeface (2.8)

user interface (2.2)

validation (2.23)
values (2.15)

Web browser (2.26)
Web pages (2.26)
what-if analysis (2.19)
window (2.2)
wizard (2.36)
word processing (2.4)
word wrap (2.5)
workgroup technology (2.30)
worksheet (2.14)
WYSIWIG (2.5)

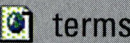

2 yourTurn

chapter 1 | 2 | 3 | 4 | 5 | 6 | 7 | 8 | 9 | 10 | 11 | 12 | 13 | 14 | I

inCyber | review | terms | yourTurn | hotTopics | outThere | winLabs | webWalk | exercises | news | home

INSTRUCTIONS: *To display this page from the Web, launch your browser and enter the URL, http://www.scsite.com/dc/ch2/turn.htm. Click a blank line for the answer. Click the links for current and additional information.*

Label the Figure

3. _____

4. _____

2. _____

1. _____

5. _____

6. _____

7. _____

Instructions: Identify each component of a graphical user interface.

Fill in the Blanks

Instructions: Complete each sentence with the correct term or terms.

1. A(n) _____ is the way the user tells the software what to do and the way the computer displays information and processing options to the user.
2. A(n) _____, which uses a predefined style sheet and usually includes standard text, can be used to produce certain types of word processing documents.
3. Spreadsheet cells may contain three types of data: _____ (text), _____ (numbers), and _____ that perform calculations and display the results.
4. With regard to OLE, a(n) _____ can be all or any portion of a document, a graphic, a sound file, or a video clip created with a Windows program.
5. Learning aids and support tools include _____, explanatory information available while using an application, _____, step-by-step instructions using real examples, _____, automated assistants that help complete a task, and _____, publications that help users learn features of personal computer application packages.

Short Answer

Instructions: Write a brief answer to each of the following questions.

1. What is a graphical user interface? Describe some common features of a graphical user interface. _____
2. How is desktop publishing software different from word processing software? _____
3. What spreadsheet capabilities make spreadsheet software a valuable tool for decision making? Why? _____
4. What are the advantages of integrated software and software suites? _____
5. What is object linking and embedding? How are linked objects different from embedded objects? _____

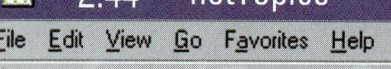 **hotTopics** chapter 2 | 1 | 2 | 3 | 4 | 5 | 6 | 7 | 8 | 9 | 10 | 11 | 12 | 13 | 14 | I

inCyber | review | terms | yourTurn | hotTopics | outThere | winLabs | webWalk | exercises | news | home

INSTRUCTIONS: *To display this page from the Web, launch your browser and enter the URL, http://www.scsite.com/dc/ch2/hot.htm. Click the links for current and additional information to help you respond to the hotTopics questions.*

1 *Increasingly sophisticated software applications not only have impacted* business, but recreation as well. For ten years, chess grand masters have used databases to analyze and replay past games. As the databases expand and database tools become more powerful, some chess aficionados fear that tournament games eventually will be reduced to replays of extensive computer analysis. How might another game, sport, or pastime be affected by a software application described in this chapter? What attributes may be lost through computer use? What could you do to maintain the diversion's positive qualities despite the use of computers?

2 *Many people believe that word processing software improves the quality* of written work by making it easier to create and edit documents. Some people argue, however, that word processing software has become a crutch, eliminating the need to learn the rudiments and nuances of language. These people insist that much of the work produced with word processors is indeed *processed*, lacking the beauty, artistry, and individuality of great literature. How do you think word processing software has influenced written communication? Does it result in better work or simply more correct, mediocre work? What word processing features most enhance the quality of written material?

3 *About 35 million people use e-mail while at work. Many of these people believe their* communications are private, but employees have been fired for using e-mail to gripe about their bosses. Although this may seem an invasion of privacy, courts have ruled that companies have a right to all the data in their computer networks. On the other hand, corporations have been sued for harassment because of the disparaging remarks executives have made over e-mail. Who should have access to electronic mail messages and records? Why? If, on an e-mail system, you *overheard* an employee's insulting assertions about the boss or an executive's distasteful comments about an employee, would you tell anyone? What if you heard someone planning to steal a product or reveal company secrets? Where do you draw the line?

4 *Over the past two decades, billions of dollars have been spent to computerize the classroom.* Despite this, many students still are computer illiterate when they graduate from high school. Various reasons are given for this failure — inadequately trained teachers, classrooms unable to handle new equipment, machines made obsolete by rapidly changing technology, and so on. Perhaps the most telling problem is that educators are not sure of the best use for computers. Drill and practice? Problem solving? Games? A growing number of instructors feel that students should be taught the software applications they will have to know to succeed in the workplace. From the applications presented in this chapter, make a list of five applications you think every student should learn, from most important to least important. Explain your ranking. At what level should each application be taught? Why?

5 *One of the catch phrases in education today is "learning styles," which is the belief that people* learn things best in different ways. How do you learn things most effectively? If you had to learn one of the software applications described in this chapter, which of the learning aids and support tools (online Help, tutorials, wizards, or trade books) would fit your learning style best? Why? Would the type of software application you were learning affect your choice of learning aid? Why or why not?

outThere

chapter 1 | 2 | 3 | 4 | 5 | 6 | 7 | 8 | 9 | 10 | 11 | 12 | 13 | 14 | I

inCyber | review | terms | yourTurn | hotTopics | outThere | winLabs | webWalk | exercises | news | home

INSTRUCTIONS: *To display this page from the Web, launch your browser and enter the URL, http://www.scsite.com/dc/ch2/out.htm. Click the links for current and additional information.*

1 *Each software application is characterized by certain key features, but every software package* in an application is not exactly the same. Different spreadsheet packages, for example, may use different methods to enter formulas, offer different functions, and have different ways to draw charts. People who use a software package at work often have strong feelings about the package's strengths and weaknesses. Interview someone who works with one of the software applications described in this chapter. Which software package does he or she use? Why was that package chosen? How did the person being interviewed learn to use the package? What does he or she like, or dislike, about the software? For what purpose does the individual use the package? If a friend of this person was choosing software to perform a similar task, would he or she recommend this software package? Why or why not?

2 *The most popular Web browser is Netscape Navigator, which is used by almost eighty percent of* people who surf the Web. Next in line is Microsoft's Internet Explorer, a distant second with a constituency of about ten percent. Internet Explorer is narrowing the gap, yet Netscape Navigator maintains that it is still a better browser. Information about both browsers can be found on the World Wide Web. Compare these two browsers, or another two browsers, and form your own opinion. What features are offered by both? What capabilities does one have that the other does not? What is the cost of each? Based on your evaluation, which Web browser do you think is better? Why?

3 *The relative merit of integrated software versus individual software packages sometimes is* perceived as quantity versus quality — integrated software provides more "bang for the buck" by combining several applications, but the capabilities of each component are eclipsed by individual software packages. Many feel, however, that integrated software is the best buy for average computer users. Visit a local computer software vendor and compare an integrated software package (such as Microsoft Works or ClarisWorks) to some individual software application packages. How much does the integrated software cost? How much would it cost to buy comparable application software packages individually? What are the differences, if any, between the capabilities of applications in the integrated software and those of individual software packages?

4 *Users of desktop publishing software frequently enhance their work with* scanned photographs or graphics. Now, the Internet is providing a new resource for desktop publishers. Companies such as Corbis, Picture Network International, Muse, and Liaison International offer archives of artwork and photographs. Information about all four companies can be found on the World Wide Web. What kind of illustrations are available? How are pictures on a specific subject located? How are the illustrations provided? What fees are involved? Would the cost be different for a high school student creating one paper than for a company? Which products do you prefer? Why?

5 *Although most software packages can be learned with online Help or tutorials, many people* prefer using trade books. Select a software application such as word processing, and visit a bookstore or software vendor to survey the trade books on that application. For what particular package (e.g., Word, WordStar, DisplayWrite, or WordPerfect) are the most titles available? How difficult would it be to learn each software package using the trade books at hand? Which trade book do you think is the best? Why? If you were going to purchase a software package solely on the basis of the related trade books, which package would you buy? Why?

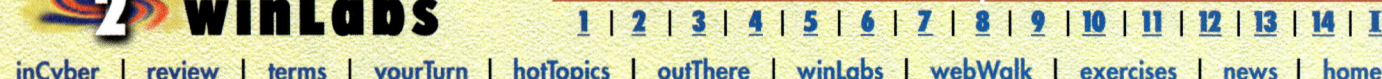

INSTRUCTIONS: *To display this page from the Web, launch your browser and enter the URL, http://www.scsite.com/dc/ch2/labs.htm. Click the links for current and additional information.*

1 Shelly Cashman Series Word Processing Lab

Follow the instructions in winLab 1 on page 1.34 to display the Shelly Cashman Series Labs screen. Click Word Processing. Click the Start Lab button. When the initial screen displays, carefully read the objectives. With your printer on, click the Print Questions button. Fill out the top of the Questions sheet and answer the questions.

2 Shelly Cashman Series Spreadsheet Lab

Follow the instructions in winLab 1 on page 1.34 to display the Shelly Cashman Series Labs screen. Click Working with Spreadsheets. Click the Start Lab button. When the screen displays, read the objectives. With your printer on, click the Print Questions button. Fill out the top of the Questions sheet and answer the questions.

3 Creating a Word Processing Document

Click the Start button on the taskbar; point to Programs on the Start menu; point to Accessories on the Programs submenu; and then click WordPad on the Accessories submenu. When the WordPad window displays, click its Maximize button. Type the first 2 paragraphs on page 2.4 under the heading Word Processing Software (see Figure 2-51). Press the TAB key to indent the first line of each paragraph. Press ENTER to begin a new paragraph. Do not bold or italicize any words. At the end of the second paragraph, press ENTER twice and then type your name.

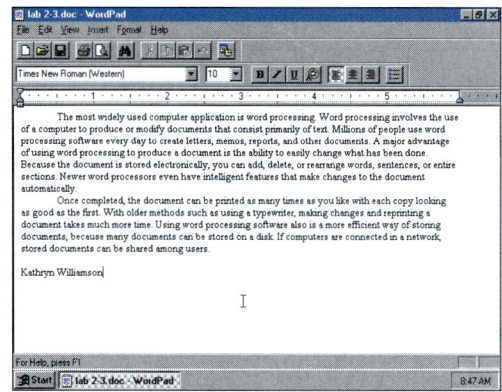

Figure 2-51

To correct errors in your document, move the I-beam mouse pointer to the location of the error and then click. Press the BACKSPACE key to erase to the left of the insertion point; press the DELETE key to erase to the right of the insertion point. To insert a character(s), click to the left of the point of insertion and then begin typing. If your screen does not display a toolbar, click View on the menu bar and then click Toolbar. When your document is correct, save it by inserting your student floppy disk into drive A and then clicking the Save button on the toolbar. In the Save As dialog box, type a:lab2-3 in the File name text box and then click the Save button. With your printer on, click the Print button on the toolbar to print the document. Close WordPad by clicking its Close button.

4 Using WordPad's Help

Open WordPad as described in winLab 3 above. Click Help on WordPad's menu bar and then click Help Topics. When the Help Topics: WordPad Help window displays, click the Contents tab, and then double-click the Working with Documents book. Click the Saving changes to a document topic; click the Print button; and then click the OK button. Click the WordPad Help window's Help Topics button to return to the Contents sheet. Click the Opening a document topic; click the Print button; and then click the OK button. Close any open Help windows and WordPad.

webWalk

chapter 2

| 1 | 2 | 3 | 4 | 5 | 6 | 7 | 8 | 9 | 10 | 11 | 12 | 13 | 14 | I |

inCyber | review | terms | yourTurn | hotTopics | outThere | winLabs | webWalk | exercises | news | home

INSTRUCTIONS: *To display this page from the Web, launch your browser and enter the URL, http://www.scsite.com/dc/ch2/walk.htm. Click the exercise link to display the exercise.*

1. Desktop Publishing
Desktop publishing software is designed specifically for page composition and layout. To increase your knowledge of desktop publishing software, complete this exercise.

2. Clip Art
Clip art consists of previously created illustrations that can be added to documents. A number of sources of clip art are available on the World Wide Web. To visit one of these sites, complete this exercise.

3. Online Help
Online Help refers to additional instructions that are available within application software. To learn more about your Web browser's online Help (Figure 2-52), complete this exercise.

4. Personal Information Management (PIM) Software
Personal information management (PIM) software helps you keep track of the miscellaneous bits of personal information that each of us deals with every day. You can learn about an innovative add-in to PIM software (Figure 2-53) by completing this exercise.

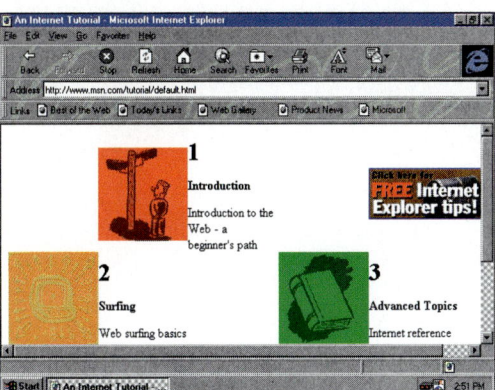

Figure 2-52

5. Information Mining
Complete this exercise to improve your Web research skills by using a Web search engine to find information related to this chapter.

6. Interactive Assistance Services
Interactive assistance can help you perform tasks online. Complete this exercise to experience the way the World Wide Web can provide assistance to you.

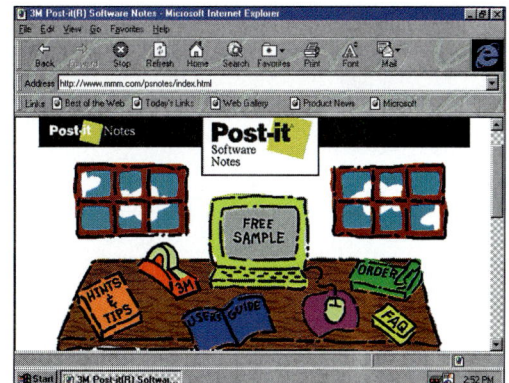

Figure 2-53

7. Financial Information Online
Online services for up-to-the-minute financial news is widely available on the Web. Complete this exercise to see one example of a financial information service.

8. Weather Forecast
Online weather information is available for travelers, pilots, picnickers, and anyone else whose plans are dependent on weather. To see one example of unique weather forecasts, complete this exercise.

9. Web Chat
Complete this exercise to enter a Web Chat discussion related to issues presented in the hotTopics exercises.

The System Unit

OBJECTIVES

After completing this chapter, you will be able to:

- Define a bit and describe how a series of bits in a byte is used to represent data
- Discuss how bit pattern codes are used to represent characters
- Identify the components of the system unit and describe their use
- Describe how the CPU uses the four steps of the machine cycle to process data
- Describe the primary use and characteristics of RAM and ROM memory
- Explain the difference between parallel and serial ports
- Describe a machine language instruction and the instruction set of a computer
- Describe various types of processing including pipelining, parallel processing, and neural networks
- Explain how computers use the binary number system
- Explain how a computer chip is made

CHAPTER 3

The information processing cycle consists of input, processing, output, and storage operations. When an input operation is completed and both a program and data are stored in memory, processing operations can begin. During these operations, the system unit executes, or performs, the program instructions and processes the data into information.

Chapter 3 examines the components of the system unit, describes how memory stores programs and data, and discusses the sequence of operations that occurs when instructions are executed on a computer. These topics are followed by a discussion of types of processing and number systems. How a computer chip is made is discussed at the end of the chapter.

What Is the System Unit?

The term computer usually means a combination of hardware and software that can process data and manage information. This term also is used more specifically to describe the system unit, because this is where the *computing* actually happens. It is in the system unit that the computer program instructions are executed and the data is manipulated. The system unit contains the central processing unit, or CPU, memory (also called random access memory, or RAM), and other electronics (Figure 3-1). To better understand how the system unit processes data, an explanation follows of how data is represented in a computer.

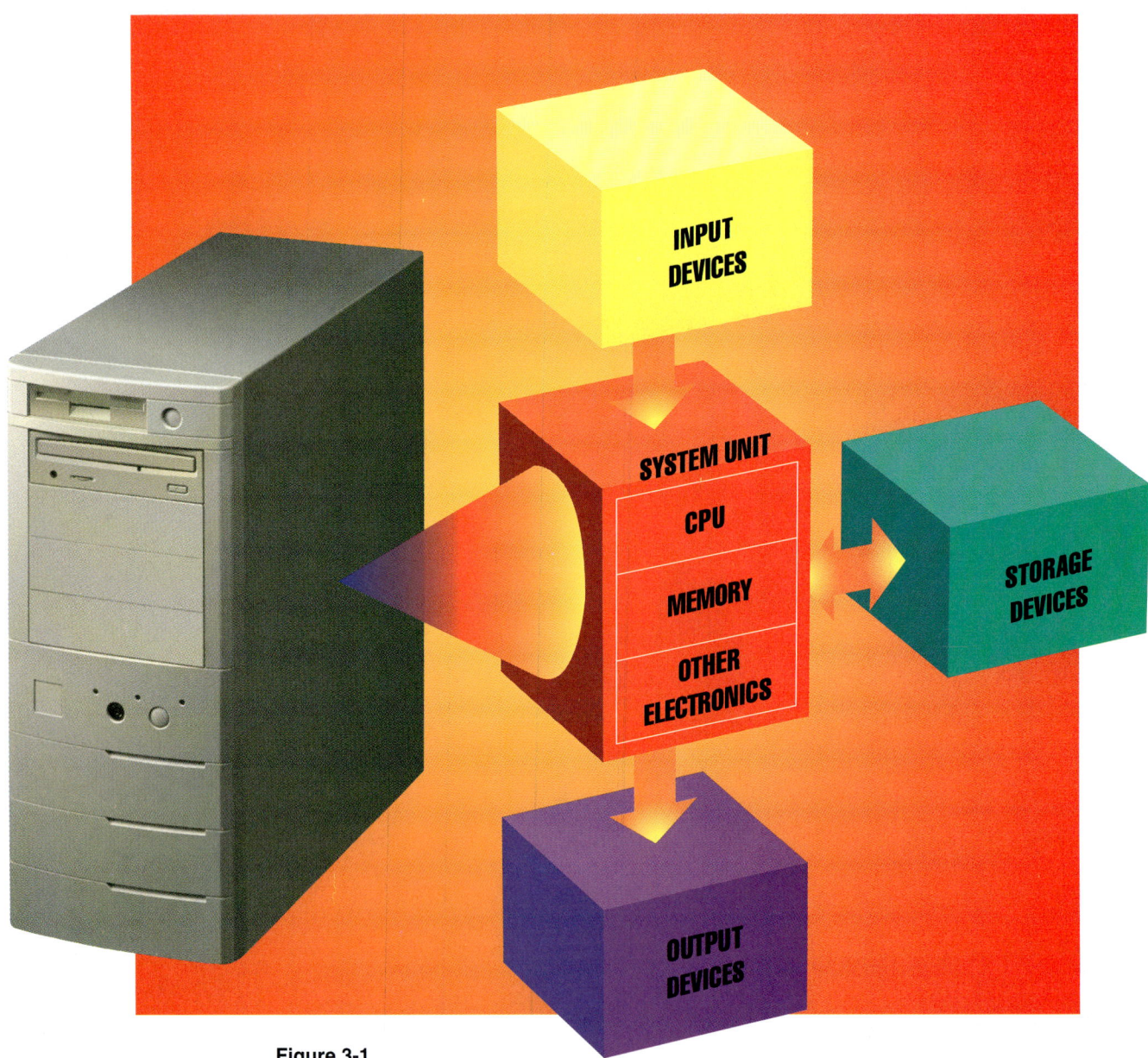

Figure 3-1
The system unit is the metal or plastic case that contains the central processing unit (CPU), memory, and other electronics. The system unit is connected to input devices such as a keyboard or mouse and output devices such as a monitor or printer. Storage devices such as a disk drive can be located either inside or outside the system unit case.

How Data Is Represented in a Computer

Most computers are **digital computers**, meaning that the data they process, whether it be text, sound, graphics, or video, is first converted into a digital (numeric) value. Converting data into a digital form is called **digitizing**. Other types of computers, called **analog computers**, are designed to process continuously variable data, such as electrical voltage.

You may be thinking that the digital values used by a computer are the digits 0 through 9. But in fact, only the digits 0 and 1 are used. Only two digits are used because they can be easily represented electronically by circuits in the computer being either off or on. A 0 is used to represent the electronic state of *off* and a 1 is used to represent the electronic state of *on*. Each off or on digital value is called a **bit**, the smallest unit of data handled by a computer. Bit is short for *binary digit* (Figure 3-2). By itself, a bit cannot represent much data. But in a group of eight bits, called a **byte**, 256 different possibilities can be represented by using all the combinations of 0s and 1s (Figure 3-3). This provides enough combinations so a unique code can be assigned to each of the characters that are commonly used such as, the digits 0 through 9, the uppercase and lowercase alphabet, foreign characters that require accent marks such as umlauts (¨) and tildes (~), and special characters such as punctuation marks. Several different coding schemes are used on computers.

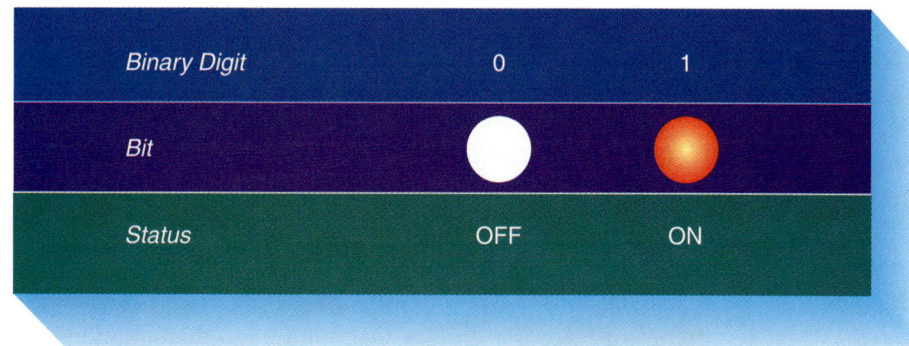

For details on digital computers, visit the Discovering Computers Chapter 3 inCyber page (http://www.scsite.com/dc/ch3/incyber.htm) and click Digital Computers.

Figure 3-2
A bit, the smallest unit of data handled by a computer, can represent either a 0 or 1 in the binary number system. A computer circuit represents the 0 or 1 electronically by being either off (representing the 0) or on (representing the 1).

Figure 3-3
A graphic representation of an eight-bit byte with four bits on and four bits off. The off bits (open circles) are represented by the binary digit 0 and the on bits (solid circles) are represented by the binary digit 1. This combination of bits represents the uppercase letter G.

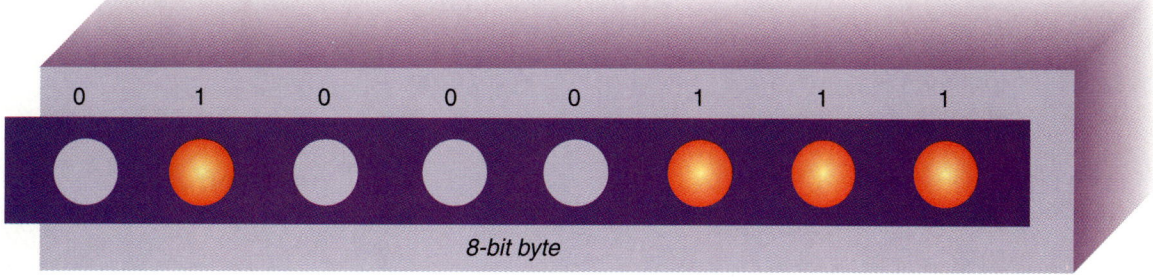

ASCII and EBCDIC

Two widely used codes that represent characters in a computer are the ASCII and EBCDIC codes. The **American Standard Code for Information Interchange**, called ASCII (pronounced ask-ee), is the most widely used coding system to represent data. ASCII is used on many personal computers and minicomputers. The **Extended Binary Coded Decimal Interchange Code**, or **EBCDIC** (pronounced eb-see-dick) is used primarily on mainframe computers. Figure 3-4 summarizes these codes. Notice how the combination of bits (0s and 1s) is unique for each character.

When the ASCII or EBCDIC code is used, each character that is represented is stored in one byte of memory. Other binary formats exist, however, that the computer sometimes uses to represent numeric data. For example, a computer may store, or *pack,* two numeric characters in one byte of memory. These binary formats are used by the computer to increase storage and processing efficiency.

Unicode

The 256 characters and symbols that are represented by ASCII and EBCDIC codes are sufficient for English and western European languages but are not large enough for Asian and other languages that use different alphabets. Further compounding the problem is that many of these languages used symbols, called **ideograms**, to represent multiple words and ideas. One solution to this situation is Unicode. **Unicode** is a 16-bit code that has the capacity to represent more than 65,000 characters and symbols. Unicode represents all the world's current languages using more than 34,000 characters and symbols (Figure 3-5). In Unicode,

SYMBOL	ASCII	EBCDIC
0	01100000	11110000
1	01100001	11110001
2	01100010	11110010
3	01100011	11110011
4	01100100	11110100
5	01100101	11110101
6	01100110	11110110
7	01100111	11110111
8	01101000	11111000
9	01101001	11111001
A	01000001	11000001
B	01000010	11000010
C	01000011	11000011
D	01000100	11000100
E	01000101	11000101
F	01000110	11000110
G	01000111	11000111
H	01001000	11001000
I	01001001	11001001
J	01001010	11010001
K	01001011	11010010
L	01001100	11010011
M	01001101	11010100
N	01001110	11010101
O	01001111	11010110
P	01010000	11010111
Q	01010001	11011000
R	01010010	11011001
S	01010011	11100010
T	01010100	11100011
U	01010101	11100100
V	01010110	11100101
W	01010111	11100110
X	01011000	11100111
Y	01011001	11101000
Z	01011010	11101001
!	00100001	01011010
"	00100010	01111111
#	00100011	01111011
$	00100100	01011011
%	00100101	01101100
&	00100110	01010000
(	00101000	01001101
)	00101001	01011101
*	00101010	01011100
+	00101011	01001110

Figure 3-4
This chart shows numeric, uppercase alphabetic, and several special characters as they are represented in ASCII and EBCDIC. Each character is represented in binary using a unique ordering of zeros and ones.

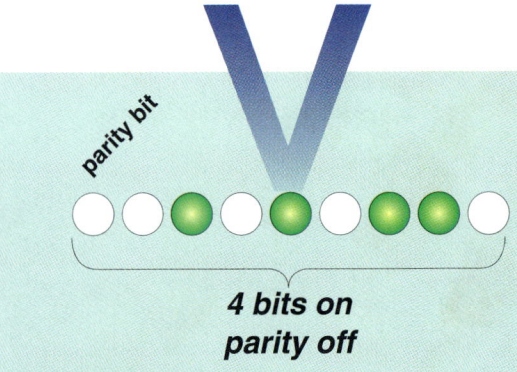

4 bits on parity off

30,000 codes are reserved for future use, such as ancient languages, and 6,000 codes are reserved for private use. Existing ASCII coded data is fully compatible with Unicode because the first 256 codes are the same. Unicode is currently implemented in several operating systems, including Windows NT and OS/2 and all major system developers have announced plans eventually to implement Unicode.

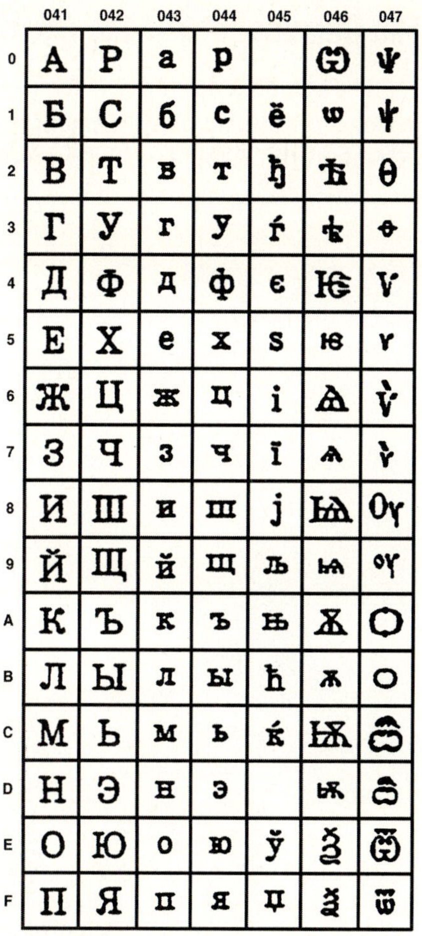

Parity

Regardless of whether ASCII, EBCDIC, or other binary methods are used to represent characters in memory, it is important that the characters be stored accurately. For each byte of memory, most computers have at least one extra bit, called a parity bit, that is used by the computer for error checking. A parity bit can detect if one of the bits in a byte has been inadvertently changed. While such errors are extremely rare (most computers never have a parity error during their lifetime), they can occur because of voltage fluctuations, static electricity, or a memory failure.

Computers are either odd- or even-parity machines. In computers with odd parity, the total number of *on* bits in the byte (including the parity bit) must be an odd number (Figure 3-6). In computers with even parity, the total number of on bits must be an even number. Parity is checked by the computer each time a memory location is used. When data is moved from one location to another in memory, the parity bits of both the sending and receiving locations are compared to see if they are the same. If the system detects a difference or if the wrong number of bits is on (e.g., an odd number in a system with even parity), an error message displays. Many computers use multiple parity bits that enable them to detect and correct a single-bit error and detect multiple-bit errors.

Figure 3-5
Unicode is a 16-bit character code developed to represent all the world's languages. This Cyrillic character set is part of the more than 34,000 characters that are currently represented in Unicode. The Unicode assigned code is along the top and left side of the chart.

inCyber

For an explanation of EBCDIC, visit the Discovering Computers Chapter 3 inCyber page (http://www.scsite.com/dc/ch3/incyber.htm) and click EBCDIC.

Figure 3-6
In a computer with even parity, the parity bit is turned on or off in order to make the total number of on bits (including the parity bit) an even number. Here, the letters V and A have an even number of bits so the parity bit is left off. The number of bits for the letter L is odd, so to achieve even parity, the parity bit is turned on.

The Components of the System Unit

The components of the system unit usually are contained in a metal or plastic case. For personal computers, all system unit components usually are in a single box. For larger and more powerful computers, the components may be housed in several cabinets. The components considered part of the system unit and discussed in the following sections include the motherboard, the microprocessor and CPU, upgrade sockets, memory, coprocessors, buses, expansion slots, ports and connectors, bays, the power supply, and sound components (Figure 3-7).

Figure 3-7
The components of the system unit are usually inside a plastic or metal case. This illustration shows how some of the components might be arranged in a typical PC.

MICROPROCESSOR AND THE CPU 3.7

Motherboard

The **motherboard**, sometimes called the **main board** or **system board**, is a circuit board that contains most of the electronic components of the system unit. Figure 3-8 shows a photograph of a personal computer motherboard and identifies some of the components. One of the main components on the motherboard is the microprocessor.

inCyber
For a detailed description of motherboards, visit the Discovering Computers Chapter 3 inCyber page (http://www.scsite.com/dc/ch3/incyber.htm) and click Motherboard.

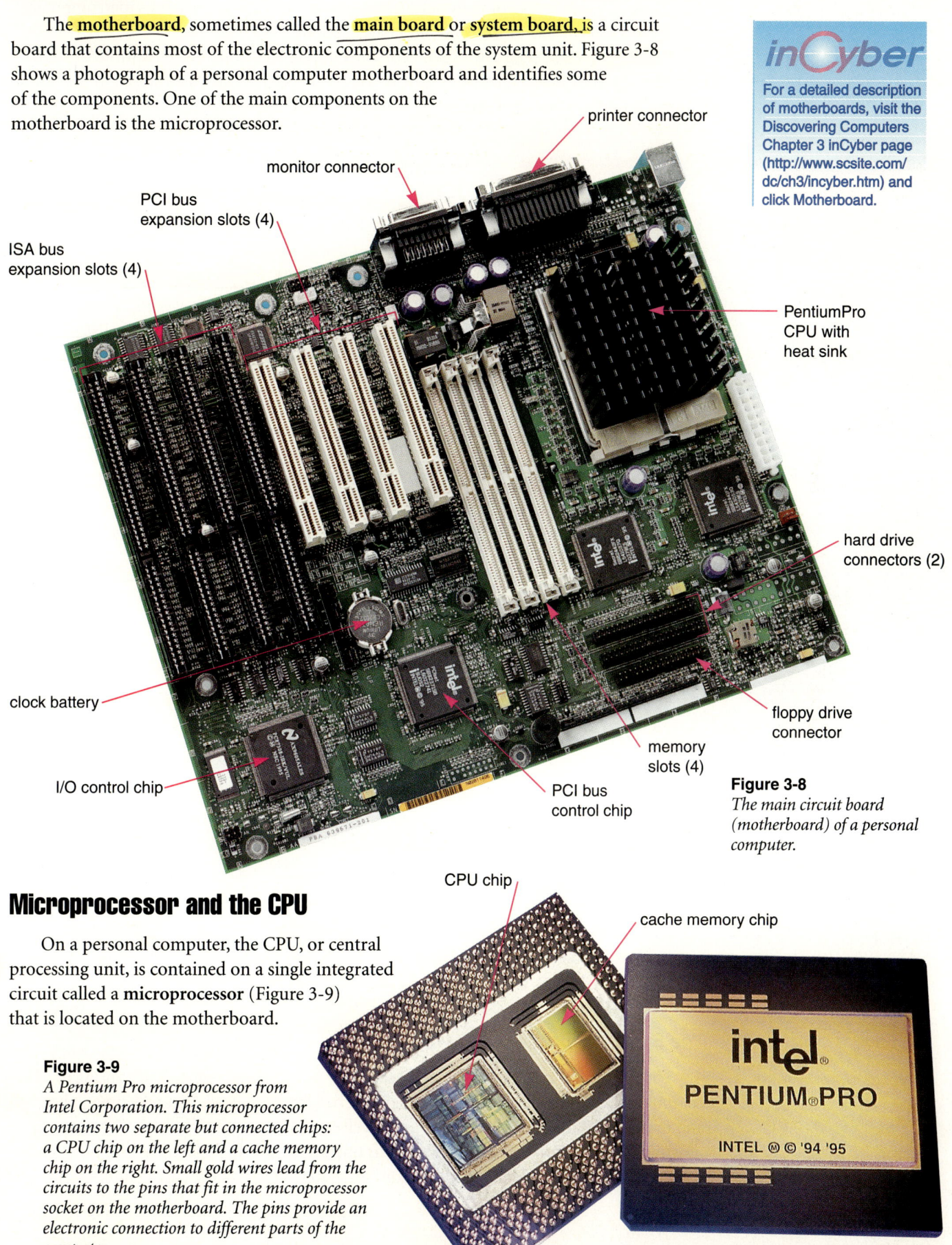

Figure 3-8
The main circuit board (motherboard) of a personal computer.

Microprocessor and the CPU

On a personal computer, the CPU, or central processing unit, is contained on a single integrated circuit called a **microprocessor** (Figure 3-9) that is located on the motherboard.

Figure 3-9
A Pentium Pro microprocessor from Intel Corporation. This microprocessor contains two separate but connected chips: a CPU chip on the left and a cache memory chip on the right. Small gold wires lead from the circuits to the pins that fit in the microprocessor socket on the motherboard. The pins provide an electronic connection to different parts of the computer.

An **integrated circuit,** also called a **chip or an IC,** is a complete electronic circuit that has been etched on a thin slice of material such as silicon. For mainframe and supercomputers, the CPU consists of one or more circuit boards (Figure 3-10).

The **central processing unit (CPU)** contains the control unit and the arithmetic/logic unit. These two components work together using the program and data stored in memory to perform the processing operations.

The Control Unit

The **control unit** can be thought of as the *brain* of the computer. Just as the human brain controls the body, the control unit *controls* the computer. The **control unit** operates by repeating the following four operations, called the **machine cycle** (Figure 3-11): fetching, decoding, executing, and storing. **Fetching** means obtaining the next program instruction from memory. **Decoding** is translating the program instruction into the commands that the computer can process. **Executing** refers to the actual processing of the computer commands, and **storing** takes place when the result of the instruction is written to memory. Fetching and decoding are called the **instruction cycle**. Executing and storing are called the **execution cycle**.

The Arithmetic/Logic Unit

The second part of the CPU is the **arithmetic/logic unit (ALU).** This unit contains the electronic circuitry necessary to perform arithmetic and logical operations on data. **Arithmetic operations** include addition, subtraction, multiplication, and division. **Logical operations** consist of comparing one data item to another to determine if the first data item is *greater than, equal to,* or *less than* the other. Based on the result of the comparison, different processing may occur. For example, two part numbers in different records can be compared. If they are equal, the part quantity in one record can be added to the quantity in the other record. If they are not equal, the quantities would not be added.

Figure 3-10
With PCs, the CPU is contained in a single microprocessor chip. With larger computers, the CPU operations are split among several chips and sometimes more than one circuit board.

For a discussion of the central processing unit components, visit the Discovering Computers Chapter 3 inCyber page (http://www.scsite.com/dc/ch3/incyber.htm) and click CPU.

Registers

Both the control unit and the ALU contain **registers,** temporary storage locations for specific types of data. Separate registers exist for the current program instruction, the address of the next instruction, and the values of data being processed.

The System Clock

The control unit utilizes the **system clock** to synchronize, or control the timing of, all computer operations. The system clock is not a conventional clock that tells time in hours and minutes, but rather a chip that generates electronic pulses at a fixed rate. The control unit and ALU are designed to complete their operations one step at a time with both starting each step at the same time. The pulses from the system clock set the pace. Think of the

MICROPROCESSOR AND THE CPU 3.9

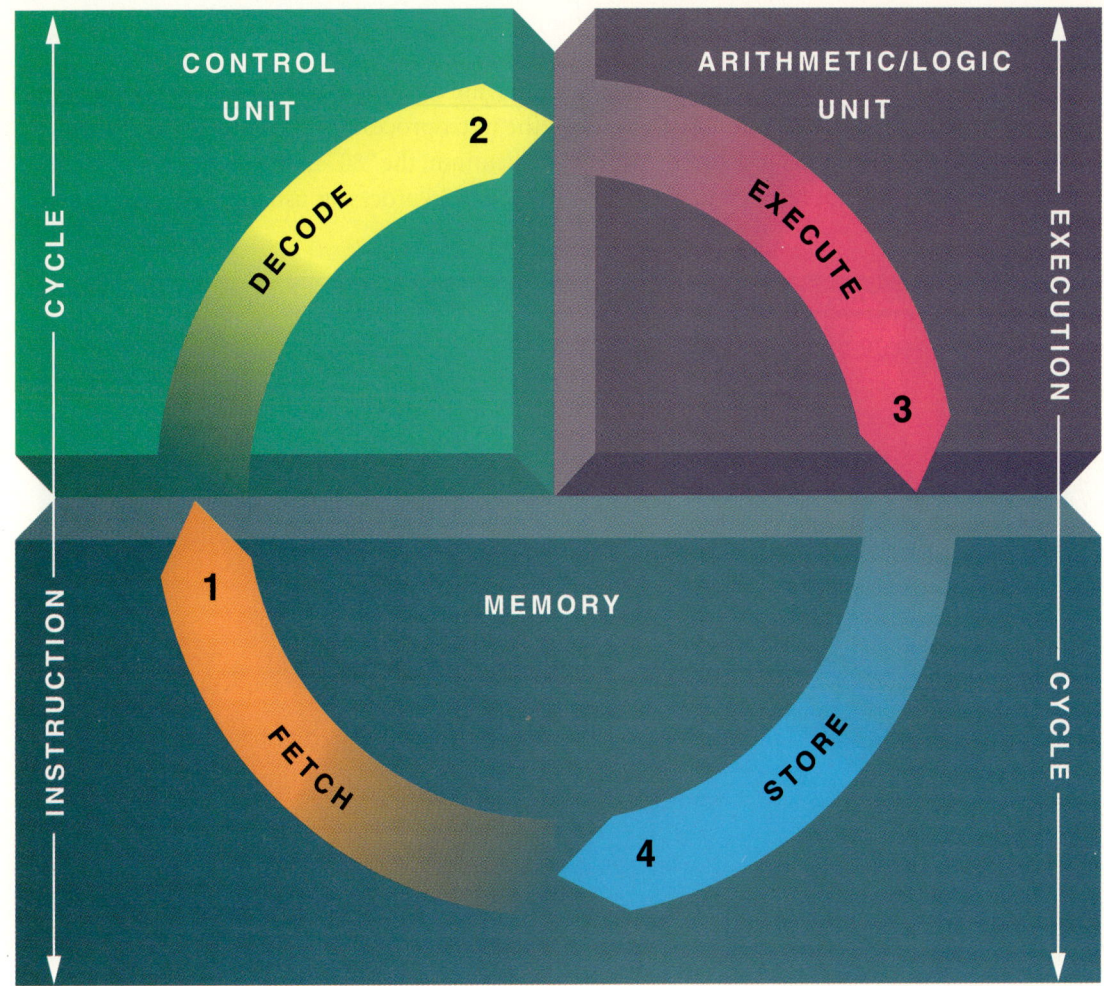

Figure 3-11
The machine cycle consists of four steps; fetching the next instruction, decoding the instruction, executing the instruction, and storing the result. Fetching and decoding are called the instruction cycle. Executing and storing are called the execution cycle.

control unit and ALU as members of a marching band that all take their steps to the beat of the system clock drummer. The pulse rate of the clock is measured in **megahertz** (abbreviated **MHz**). One megahertz equals one million pulses per second. The speed of the system clock varies among computers. Many personal computers can operate at speeds in excess of 100 megahertz.

Word Size

One aspect of the CPU that affects the speed of a computer is the word size. The **word size** is the number of bits that the CPU can process at one time. The word size of a machine is measured in bits. CPUs can have 8-bit, 16-bit, 32-bit, or 64-bit word sizes. A CPU with a 16-bit word size can manipulate 16 bits at a time. Sometimes, the word size of a computer is given in bytes instead of bits. For example, a word size of 16 bits may be expressed as a word size of two bytes because there are eight bits in a byte. Computers with a larger word size can process more data in the same amount of time than computers with a smaller word size.

Microprocessor Comparison

Personal computer microprocessors most often are identified by their model number or model name. Figure 3-12 summarizes some of the microprocessors currently in use. When discussing the three Intel processors prior to the Pentium, the "80" in the name/model number usually is not referred to. For example, the 80486 processor usually is referred to as a 486 processor.

Name	Date	Manufacturer	Word Size	Bus Width	Clock Speed (MHz)	MIPS*
Pentium Pro	1995	Intel	64	64	150-200	300
Pentium	1993	Intel	64	64	75-166	150
80486DX	1989	Intel	32	32	25-100	20-75
80386DX	1985	Intel	32	32	16-33	6-12
80286	1982	Intel	16	16	6-12	1-2
PowerPC	1994	Motorola	64	64	50-225	300
68040	1989	Motorola	32	32	25-40	15-35
68030	1987	Motorola	32	32	16-50	12
68020	1984	Motorola	32	32	16-33	5.5
Alpha	1993	Digital	64	64	150-333	275-1332

*MIPS: millions of instructions per second

Figure 3-12
A comparison of some of the more widely used microprocessors.

ZIF socket

Upgrade Sockets

Some motherboards contain a type of receptacle for microprocessors, called an upgrade socket (Figure 3-13), that can be used to install a more powerful CPU.

The CPU upgrade sockets enable a user to install a more powerful microprocessor and obtain increased performance without having to buy an entirely new system. With a CPU upgrade socket, the old microprocessor does not have to be removed. When the new microprocessor is installed, the old microprocessor is automatically disabled. Many, but not all, systems can install a more powerful microprocessor even if they do not have a separate CPU upgrade socket. For these systems, the old microprocessor is removed and replaced with the new microprocessor.

Figure 3-13
This motherboard includes an upgrade socket that can accept a more powerful Intel microprocessor. This particular type of socket is called a zero insertion force (ZIF) socket. The ZIF socket uses a lever to clamp down on the microprocessor pins and makes the installation of the chip easier. Other types of upgrade sockets require the microprocessor pins to be forced into the socket.

Memory

Memory refers to integrated circuits that temporarily store program instructions and data that can be retrieved. Memory chips are installed on the motherboard and also on similar circuit boards that control computer devices such as printers. Some memory is also designed directly into the CPU chip. Memory stores three items: the operating system and other system software that direct and coordinate the computer equipment; the application program instructions that direct the work to be done; and the data currently being processed by the application programs. Data and programs are transferred into and out of memory and data stored in memory is manipulated by computer program instructions.

The basic unit of memory is a byte, which, recall, consists of eight bits. Each byte in the memory of a computer has an address that indicates its location in memory (Figure 3-14). The number that indicates the location of a byte in memory is called a **memory address**. Whenever the computer references a byte, it does so by using the memory address, or location, of that byte.

The size of memory is measured in either kilobytes, megabytes, or gigabytes. A **kilobyte** (abbreviated as **K** or **KB**) is equal to 1,024 bytes, but for discussion purposes, is usually rounded to 1,000 bytes. A **megabyte** (abbreviated as **MB**) is approximately one million bytes or 1,000 kilobytes. A **gigabyte** (abbreviated as **GB**) is approximately one billion bytes or one million kilobytes. These terms are used when discussing the storage capacity of other devices such as disk drives, as well as discussing memory size. Three common types of memory chips are RAM, ROM, and CMOS.

For an explanation of various memory chips, visit the Discovering Computers Chapter 3 inCyber page (http://www.scsite.com/dc/ch3/incyber.htm) and click Memory.

Figure 3-14
Just like a mail box in a post office, each byte in memory is identified by a unique address.

RAM

RAM (random access memory) is the name given to the integrated circuits, or chips, that can be read and written by the microprocessor or other computer devices. RAM memory is said to be **volatile** because the programs and data stored in RAM are erased when the power to the computer is turned off. As long as the power remains on, the programs and data stored in RAM will remain intact until they are replaced by other programs and data. Programs and data that are needed for future use must be transferred from RAM to secondary storage before the power is turned off. A relatively new type of memory called **flash RAM** or **flash memory** can retain data even when the power is turned off. Flash memory is sometimes used instead of a disk drive in small portable computers.

CHAPTER 3 – THE SYSTEM UNIT

Today, most RAM memory is installed by using a **SIMM (single in-line memory module)** or a **DIMM (dual in-line memory module)**. A SIMM is a small circuit board that has multiple RAM chips on one side. Common SIMM sizes are 1, 2, 4, 8, and 16 megabytes of memory. A SIMM is installed directly on the motherboard. A DIMM is similar to a SIMM but has memory chips on both sides (Figure 3-15).

Many computers improve their processing efficiency by using high-speed RAM **cache** (pronounced cash) memory between the CPU and the main RAM memory to store the most frequently used instructions and data (Figure 3-16). When the processor needs the next program instruction or data, it first checks the cache memory. If the required instruction or data is in cache memory (called a *cache hit*), the processor will execute faster than if the instruction or data has to be retrieved from the slower RAM memory or from even slower storage. Most new microprocessors have some cache memory, called **level 1 (L1) or internal cache**, built into the microprocessor chip itself. Cache that is not part of the CPU chip is called **level 2 (L2) cache**. Level 2 cache is usually found on the motherboard. Intel's Pentium Pro microprocessor, however, includes a separate level 2 cache chip as part of its microprocessor package.

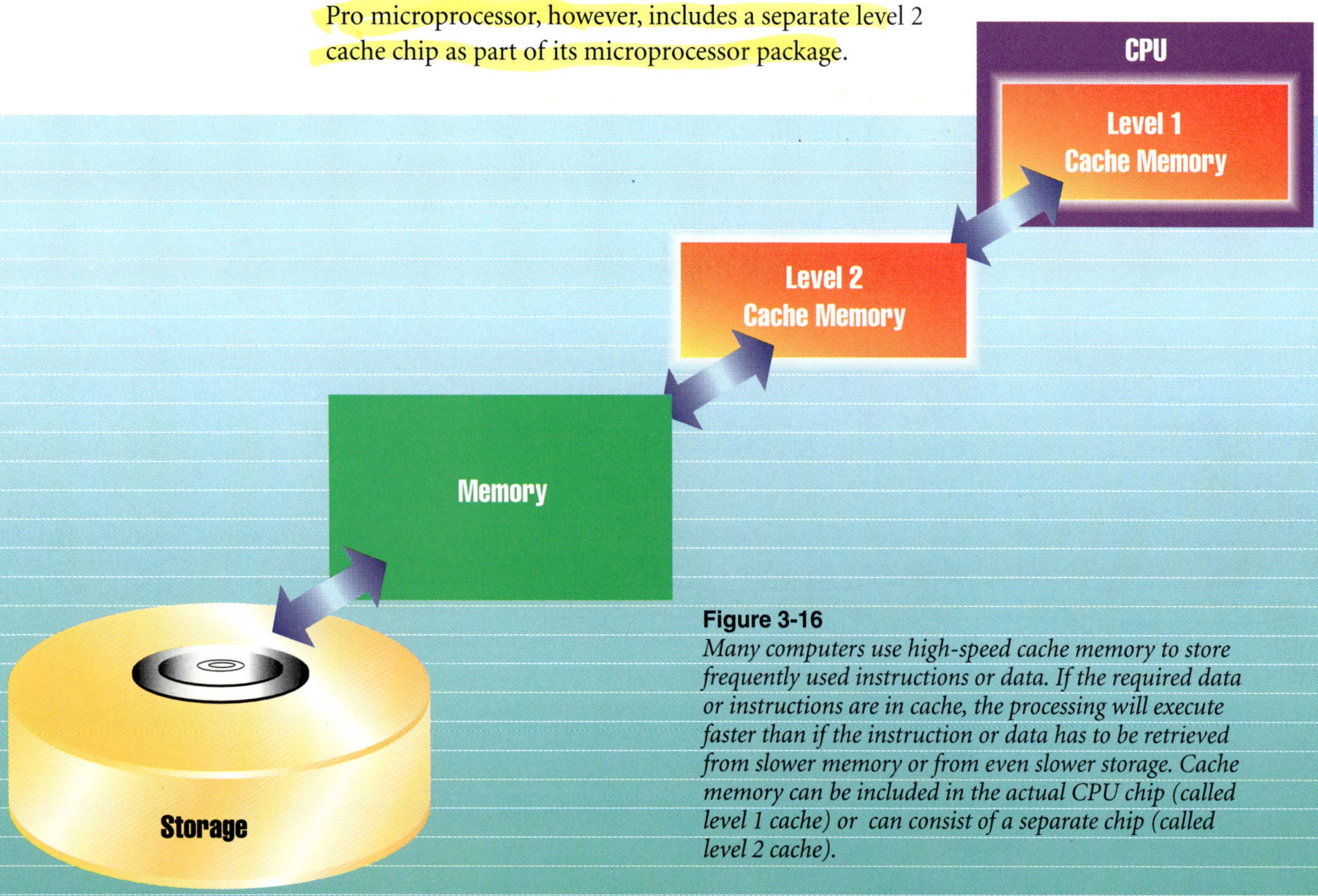

inCyber

For information on cache memory, visit the Discovering Computers Chapter 3 inCyber page (http://www.scsite.com/dc/ch3/incyber.htm) and click Cache.

Figure 3-15
This photo shows a DIMM (dual in-line memory module). DIMMs contain memory chips mounted on a small circuit board. Each chip represents one of the bit positions in a byte. Common DIMM sizes are 1, 2, 4, 8, and 16 megabytes.

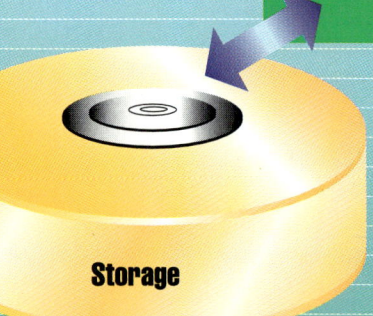

Figure 3-16
Many computers use high-speed cache memory to store frequently used instructions or data. If the required data or instructions are in cache, the processing will execute faster than if the instruction or data has to be retrieved from slower memory or from even slower storage. Cache memory can be included in the actual CPU chip (called level 1 cache) or can consist of a separate chip (called level 2 cache).

ROM

ROM (read only memory) is the name given to chips that store information or instructions that do not change. For example, ROM is used to store the startup instructions and data used when a computer is first turned on.

With ROM, instructions and data are recorded permanently in the memory when it is manufactured. ROM memory is described as **nonvolatile** because it retains its contents even when the power is turned off. The data or programs that are stored in ROM can be read and used, but cannot be altered, hence the name *read only*. Many of the special-purpose computers used in automobiles, appliances, and so on use small amounts of ROM to store instructions that will be executed repeatedly. Instructions that are stored in ROM memory are called **firmware** or **microcode**.

CMOS

CMOS (complementary metal-oxide semiconductor) memory (pronounced SEE-moss), is used to store information about the computer system, such as the amount of memory, the type of keyboard and monitor, and the type and capacity of disk drives. CMOS also operates the real-time clock on your computer that keeps track of the date and time. The system information in the CMOS memory is needed each time the computer is started. CMOS memory has very low electrical requirements and can be powered by a battery. Battery power enables CMOS memory to retain the stored information even when power to the computer is turned off (which is why your computer clock runs even when the computer is off). Unlike ROM memory, data in CMOS memory can be changed, such as when a new device is added to the computer system.

Memory Speed

Access speed is defined as the time it takes to find data and retrieve it. Because of different manufacturing techniques and materials, some types of memory are faster than others. The speed of memory is measured in **nanoseconds**, which is one billionth of a second (Figure 3-17). Most memory is comprised of **dynamic RAM (DRAM)** chips that have access speeds of 50 to 100 nanoseconds. RAM cache memory is faster and is comprised of **static RAM (SRAM)** chips with access times of 10 to 50 nanoseconds. Static RAM chips are not used for memory

Figure 3-17
Examples of a nanosecond (one billionth of a second).

How to Measure a Nanosecond
nanosecond = 1 billionth of a second

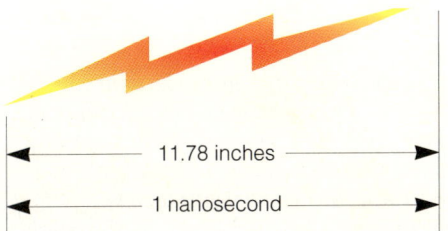

Because electricity travels at close to 186,000 miles per second, it can travel 11.78 inches in one nanosecond.

It takes about 1/10 of a second to blink your eye, the equivalent of 100 million nanoseconds. A computer can perform some operations in as little as 10 nanoseconds. Thus, in the time it takes to blink your eye, a computer can perform some operations 10 million times.

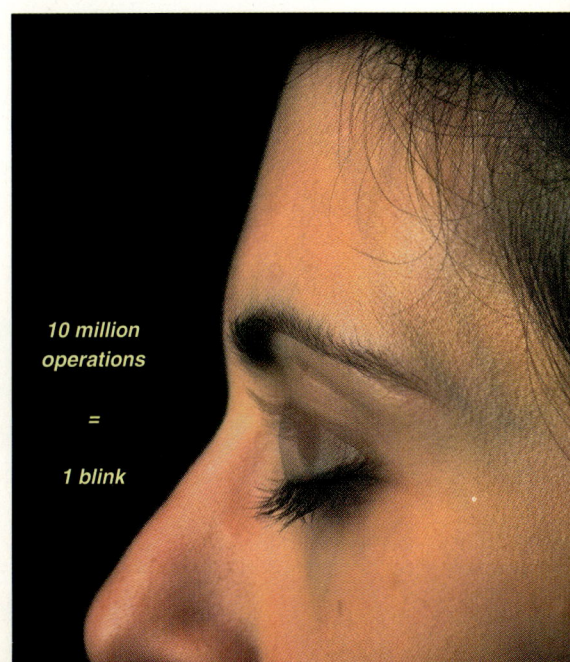

10 million operations = 1 blink

because they are larger than dynamic RAM chips and because they cost significantly more to manufacture. ROM memory has access times between 50 and 250 nanoseconds. Registers and level 1 cache designed into the CPU chip are the fastest type of memory with access times of 1 to 10 nanoseconds. For comparison purposes, accessing data on a fast hard disk takes between 10 and 20 milliseconds. One **millisecond** is a thousandth of a second. Thus, accessing information in memory with a 70 nanosecond access time is 2,500 times faster than accessing data on a hard disk with a 15 millisecond access time.

Coprocessors

One way computers can increase their efficiency is through the use of a **coprocessor**, which is a special microprocessor chip or circuit board designed to perform a specific task. For example, math coprocessors can be added to computers to greatly speed up the processing of numeric calculations. Other types of coprocessors are used to speed up the display of graphics and for communications. Some computers have coprocessors designed into the CPU.

For a description of coprocessors, visit the Discovering Computers Chapter 3 inCyber page (http://www.scsite.com/dc/ch3/incyber.htm) and click Coprocessor.

Buses

As previously explained, computers store and process data as a series of electronic bits. These bits are transferred internally within the circuitry of the computer along paths capable of transmitting electrical impulses. Sometimes these paths are actual wires and sometimes they are etched lines on the circuit board or within the CPU chip itself. Any path along which bits are transmitted is called a **bus**. Buses are used to transfer bits from input devices to memory, from memory to the CPU, from the CPU to memory, and from memory to output or storage devices. Separate buses are used for memory addresses, control signals, and data. One type of bus is called an expansion bus.

An **expansion bus** carries the data to and from the expansion slots where new system devices are added (Figure 3-18). Most expansion buses connect directly to memory. To obtain faster performance, some expansion buses bypass RAM and connect directly to the CPU. An expansion bus that connects directly to the CPU is called a **local bus**. Personal computers can have different types of expansion buses. Some computers have more than one type present. Figure 3-19 lists the more common expansion bus types on personal computers. It is important to know the type of expansion buses on your computer because some devices are designed to work with only one bus type.

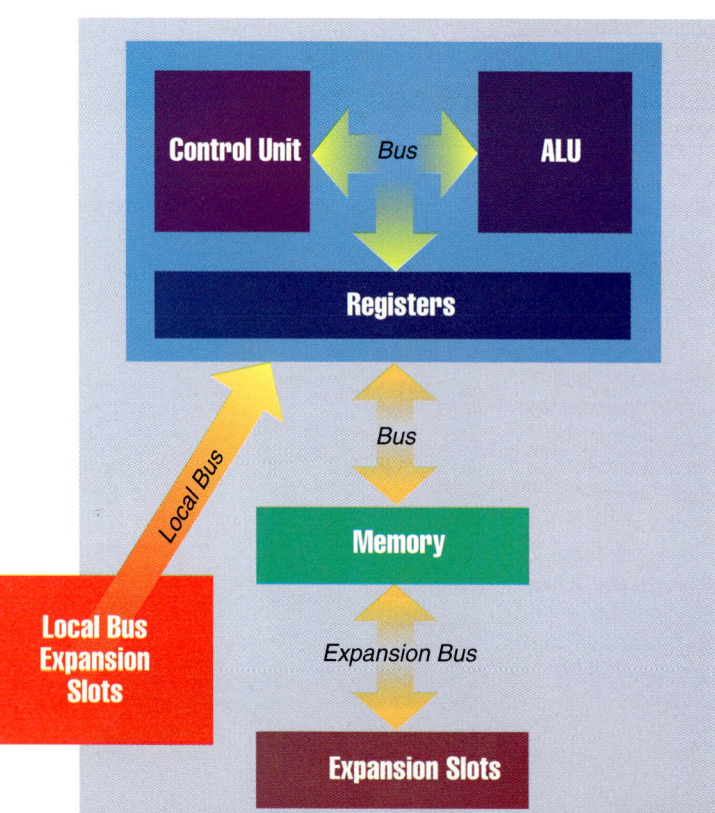

Figure 3-18
Buses are electrical pathways that carry bits from one part of the computer to another. Different buses exist for data, addresses, and control signals. The expansion bus carries data to and from the expansion boards that control peripheral devices and other components used by the computer. Many computers have a special type of expansion bus called a local bus. The local bus communicates directly with the CPU at a much faster rate than the standard expansion bus. The local bus is used for devices that require large amounts of data quickly such as monitors and disk drives.

Bus Name	Type	Bits	Description
PCI	local	32 or 64	Peripheral Component Interconnect local bus standard developed by Intel; also used on newer Macintosh computers
VESA or VL	local	32	local bus standard developed by Video Electronics Standards Association
EISA	standard	32	Extended Industry Standard Architecture developed by IBM clone manufacturers; backward compatible with ISA bus (ISA cards can run in EISA bus)
MCA	standard	16 or 32	Micro Channel Architecture developed by IBM for high-end PS/2 systems
ISA	standard	16	Industry Standard Architecture, sometimes called AT bus
XT	standard	8	developed for original IBM PC
NuBus	standard	32	high-performance expansion bus used in older Apple Macintosh computers

Figure 3-19
Types of expansion buses found on personal computers.

Buses can transfer multiples of eight bits at a time. A 16-bit bus has 16 lines and can transmit 16 bits at a time. On a 32-bit bus, bits can be moved from place to place 32 bits at a time, and on a 64-bit bus, bits are moved 64 bits at a time. The larger the number of bits that are handled by a bus, the faster the computer can transfer data. Think of a bus as a highway in which one 8-bit byte occupies one lane, and suppose a number in memory occupies four 8-bit bytes (32 bits). A 16-bit bus is like a two-lane highway; it can transfer data from memory to the CPU in two steps, transferring 16 bits at one time, 8 bits per lane. A 32-bit bus is like a four-lane highway; it can transfer the data from memory to the CPU in one step, transferring all 32 bits at one time, 8 bits in each of the four lanes. The fewer the number of transfer steps required, the faster the transfer of data occurs.

Expansion Slots

An **expansion slot** is a socket designed to hold the circuit board for a device such as a sound card that adds capability to the computer system. The circuit board for the add-on device is called an **expansion card** or **expansion board**. Expansion cards also are sometimes called **controller cards, adapter cards,** or **interface cards**. The expansion card usually is connected to the device it controls by a cable. The socket that holds the card is connected to the expansion bus that transmits data to memory or the CPU. Figure 3-20 shows an expansion card being placed in an expansion slot on a personal computer motherboard.

Figure 3-20
An expansion card being inserted into an expansion slot on the motherboard of a personal computer.

A special type of expansion slot is the PC Card slot. A **PC Card** is a thin credit card-sized device that can be inserted into a personal computer (Figure 3-21). PC Cards come in different thicknesses and often are used on portable computers for additional memory, storage, and communications capabilities. PC Cards conform to a specification developed by the Personal Computer Memory Card International Association, most often referred to by its initials, **PCMCIA**.

Ports and Connectors

A **port** is a socket used to connect the system unit to a peripheral device such as a printer or a modem. Most of the time, ports are on the back of the system unit (Figure 3-22), but they also can be on the front. Ports have different types of **connectors** that are used to attach cables to the peripheral devices. A matching connector is on the end of the cable that attaches to the port. Most connectors are available in two types, referred to as being male or female. Male connectors have one or more exposed pins, like the end of an electrical cord you plug into the wall. Female connectors have matching receptacles to accept the pins, like an electrical wall outlet. Figure 3-23 shows the different type of connectors you may find on a system unit. Ports can either be parallel or serial.

Parallel Ports

Parallel ports most often are used to connect devices that send or receive large amounts of data such as printers or disk and tape drives. **Parallel ports** transfer 8 bits (one byte) at a time using a cable that has eight data lines (Figure 3-24). The electrical signals in a parallel cable tend to interfere with one another over a long distance and therefore, parallel cables usually are limited to 50 feet. Personal computer parallel cables usually are 6- to 10-feet long. A special type of parallel port is the SCSI (pronounced scuzzy) port. **SCSI** stands for small computer system interface. A SCSI port can be used to attach seven to fifteen different devices to a single port. The devices are connected to the SCSI port and each other by a cable to form a continuous single line known as a *daisy chain*.

Figure 3-21
PC Cards are not much bigger than a credit card and fit in a small slot, usually on the side of a computer. PC Cards are used for additional memory, storage, and communications. Because of their small size, PC Cards often are used on portable computers. The card shown in this photo is a fax/data modem that can be connected to a telephone line.

inCyber
For an explanation of various PC Cards, visit the Discovering Computers Chapter 3 inCyber page (http://www.scsite.com/dc/ch3/incyber.htm) and click PC Card.

Figure 3-22
Ports are sockets used for cables that connect the system unit with devices such as a the mouse, the keyboard, and a printer. Usually, ports are on the back of the system unit and often are labeled.

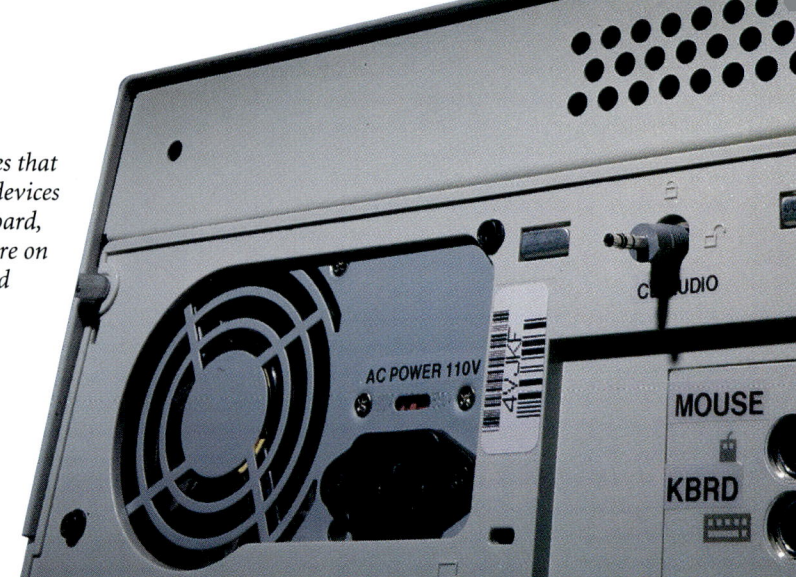

PORTS AND CONNECTORS **3.17**

Connector	Use
DB-9, 9-pin male	serial port, external modem
DB-9, 9-pin female	EGA & CGA video
DB-15, 15-pin female	VGA & EGA video
DB-25, 25-pin male	serial port, external modem
DB-25, 25-pin female	parallel port, printer, tape backup
36-pin female, mini ribbon	printer
5-pin 180° female DIN	keyboard, MIDI
RJ-11, 6-pin female, modular telephone	telephone, modem, LAN
BNC, male coaxial	LAN
6-pin male, mini DIN	mouse, keyboard

Figure 3-23
Examples of different types of connectors that are used to connect devices to the system unit. Adapters are available to join one type of connector with another.

Figure 3-24
Parallel ports transfer eight bits at a time using a cable that has eight data lines.

Serial Ports

A **serial port** transmits data one bit at a time (Figure 3-25). Serial ports are used to connect the mouse, the keyboard, and communication devices such as a modem. A special type of serial port called a **musical instrument digital interface**, or **MIDI** (pronounced *midd-dee*) port is a serial port designed to be connected to a musical device such as an electronic music keyboard. Because they transmit data one bit at a time, older serial ports, sometimes called RS-232 serial ports, transfer data at a much slower rate than parallel ports. One advantage of these serial ports, however, is that because of reduced electrical interference, their connecting cables can be up to 1,000 feet long. Newer technology, such as the **Universal Serial Bus (USB)**, has significantly increased data transfer rates and allows up to 128 devices to be connected to a serial port. With USB, one device, such as a keyboard or monitor, plugs directly into the serial port. Other devices then connect into additional expansion sockets built into the keyboard or monitor.

> **inCyber**
> For samples of MIDI files, visit the Discovering Computers Chapter 3 inCyber page (http://www.scsite.com/dc/ch3/incyber.htm) and click MIDI.

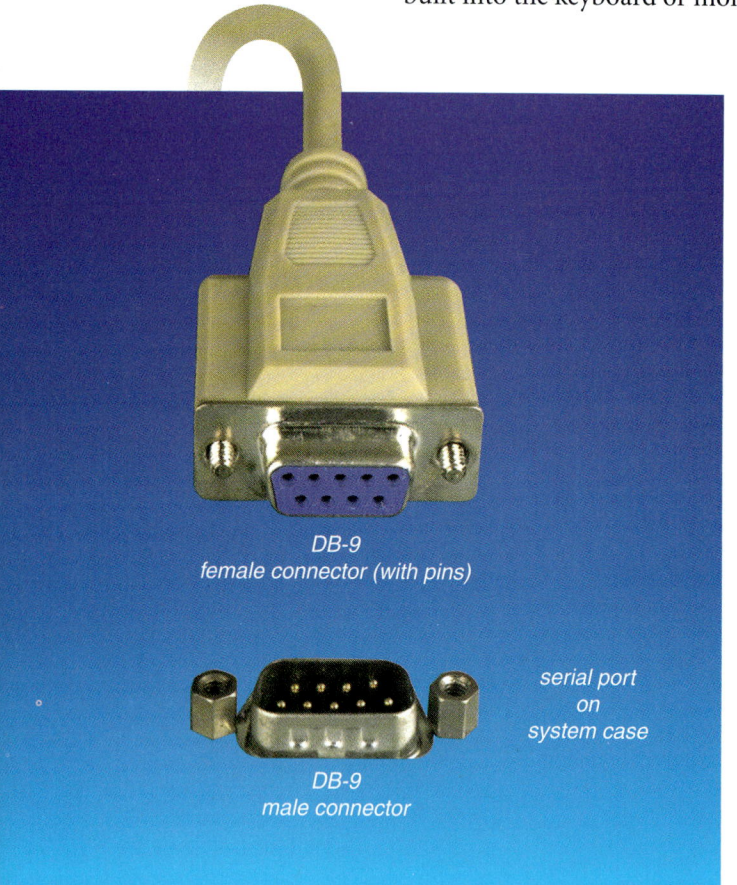

Figure 3-25
Serial ports transfer only one bit at a time and generally are slower than parallel ports. Separate data lines are used to transmit and receive data. Pin 2 is used to receive data and pin 3 is used to send data.

Bays

A **bay** is an open area inside the system unit used to install additional equipment. Because they often are used for disk drives, these spaces also are called **drive bays**. Mounting brackets called **rails** are sometimes required to install a device in a bay. Two or more bays side by side or on top of one another are called a **cage**. Figure 3-26 shows a personal computer with a three-bay cage. *External bays* have one end adjacent to an opening in the case. External bays can be used for devices that require loading and unloading of storage media such as floppy disks, tapes, and CD-ROMs. *Internal bays* are not accessible from outside the case and are used for hard disk drives.

Power Supply

The **power supply** converts the wall outlet electricity (115-120 volts AC) to the lower voltages (5 to 12 volts DC) used by the computer. The power supply also has a fan that provides airflow inside the system unit to help cool the components. The humming noise you hear when you turn on a computer usually is the power supply fan. Personal computer power supplies are rated by wattage and range from 100 to 250 watts. Higher wattage power supplies can support more electronic equipment.

Sound Components

Most personal computers have the capability of generating sounds through a small speaker housed within the system unit. Software allows you to generate a variety of sounds including music and voice. Some computers also have built-in microphones that allow you to record voice messages and other sounds. As you will see in the chapter on output devices, many users enhance the sound-generating capabilities of their systems by installing expansion boards, called **sound boards**, and by attaching higher quality speakers to their systems.

Summary of the Components of the System Unit

The previous sections have presented information about the various components of the system unit. You should now be able to identify these components and have a more complete understanding about how they operate. The next section will explain how the system unit processes data by executing machine language instructions.

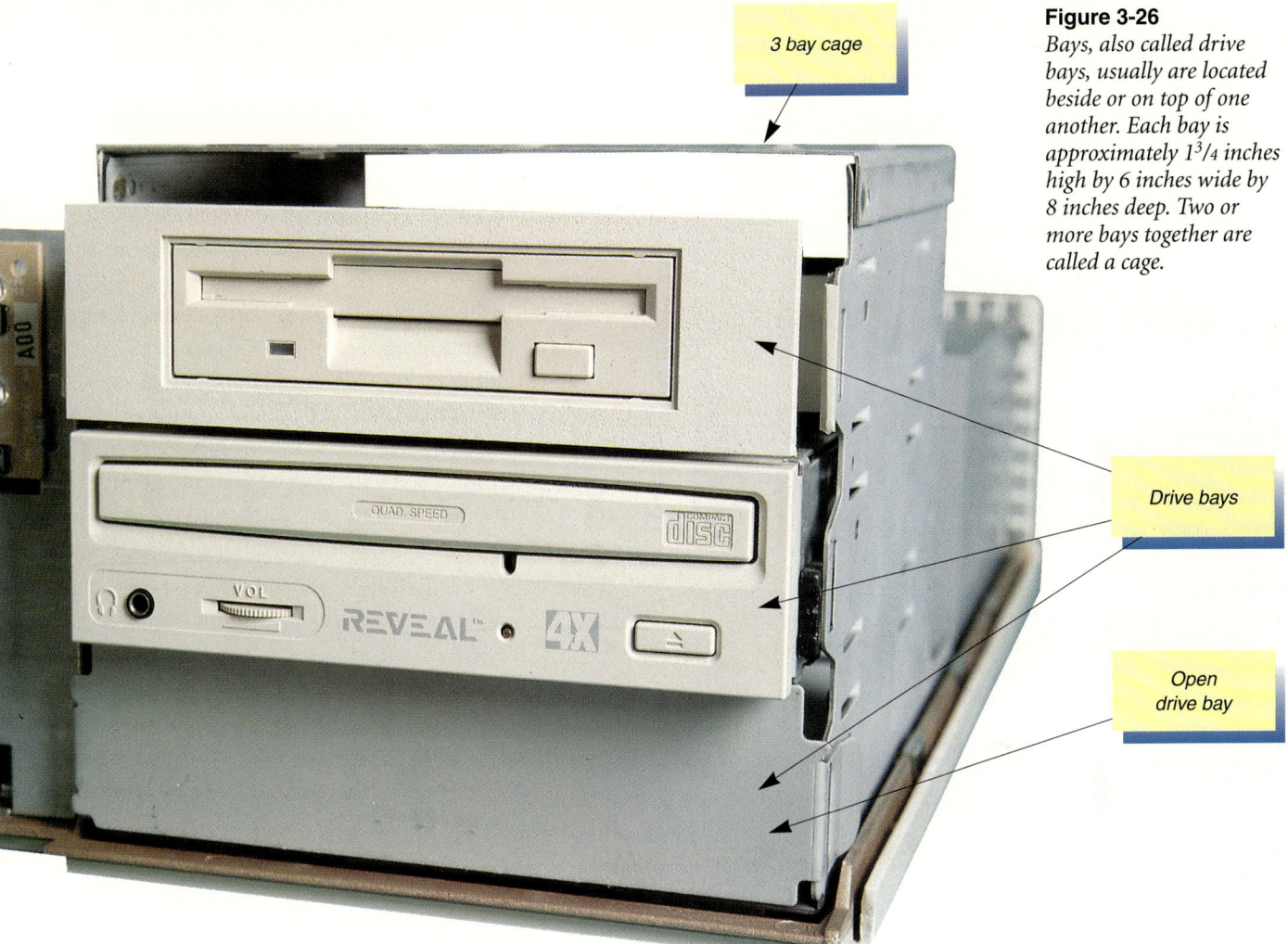

Figure 3-26
Bays, also called drive bays, usually are located beside or on top of one another. Each bay is approximately $1^3/4$ inches high by 6 inches wide by 8 inches deep. Two or more bays together are called a cage.

Machine Language Instructions

The system unit gets its directions from programs permanently stored in ROM or temporarily stored in RAM. To be executed, program instructions must be in a form that the CPU can understand, called a machine language instruction. A **machine language instruction** is binary data that the electronic circuits in the CPU can interpret and convert into one or more of the commands in the computer's instruction set. The instruction set contains commands, such as ADD or MOVE, that the computer's circuits can directly perform. Most computers have hundreds of commands in their instruction sets and are referred to as **CISC** computers for complex instruction set computing (or computers). Studies have shown, however, that as much as 80% of the processing is performed by a small number of frequently used instructions. Based on these findings, some manufacturers have designed CPUs based on RISC technology. **RISC**, which stands for reduced instruction set computing (or computers), involves reducing the instructions to only those that are most frequently used. Because a RISC computer is designed to execute the frequently used instructions more quickly, overall processing capability, or throughput, is increased.

A machine language instruction is composed of two parts. The first part is called an operation code or opcode for short. An **operation code** tells the computer what to do and matches one of the commands in the instruction set. The second part of the machine language instruction is an operand. An **operand** specifies the data or the location of the data that will be used by the instruction. A machine language instruction may have zero to three operands. Figure 3-27 shows an example of a machine language instruction that adds the number 20 to a register in the CPU.

In the early days, computers actually had to be programmed in machine language instructions using mechanical switches to represent each binary bit. Today, program instructions are written in a readable form using a variety of programming languages. The program instructions then are converted by the computer into machine language instructions. Programming languages and conversion methods are discussed in the chapter on programming languages.

The number of machine language instructions that a computer can process in one second is one way of rating the speed of computers. One **MIPS** equals one million instructions per second. Powerful personal computers today are rated at more than 100 MIPS. Another way of rating computer speed is the number of floating-point operations. Floating-point operations are a type of mathematical calculation. The term **megaflops (MFLOPS)** is used for millions of floating-point operations per second. **Gigaflops (GFLOPS)** is used for billions of floating-point operations per second.

MACHINE LANGUAGE INSTRUCTION

opcode	operand 1	operand 2
00000101	00100000	00000000
addition command	the value 32	data register in CPU

Figure 3-27
A machine language instruction consists of an operation code (opcode) and up to three operands. This machine language instruction adds the value 32 to a register.

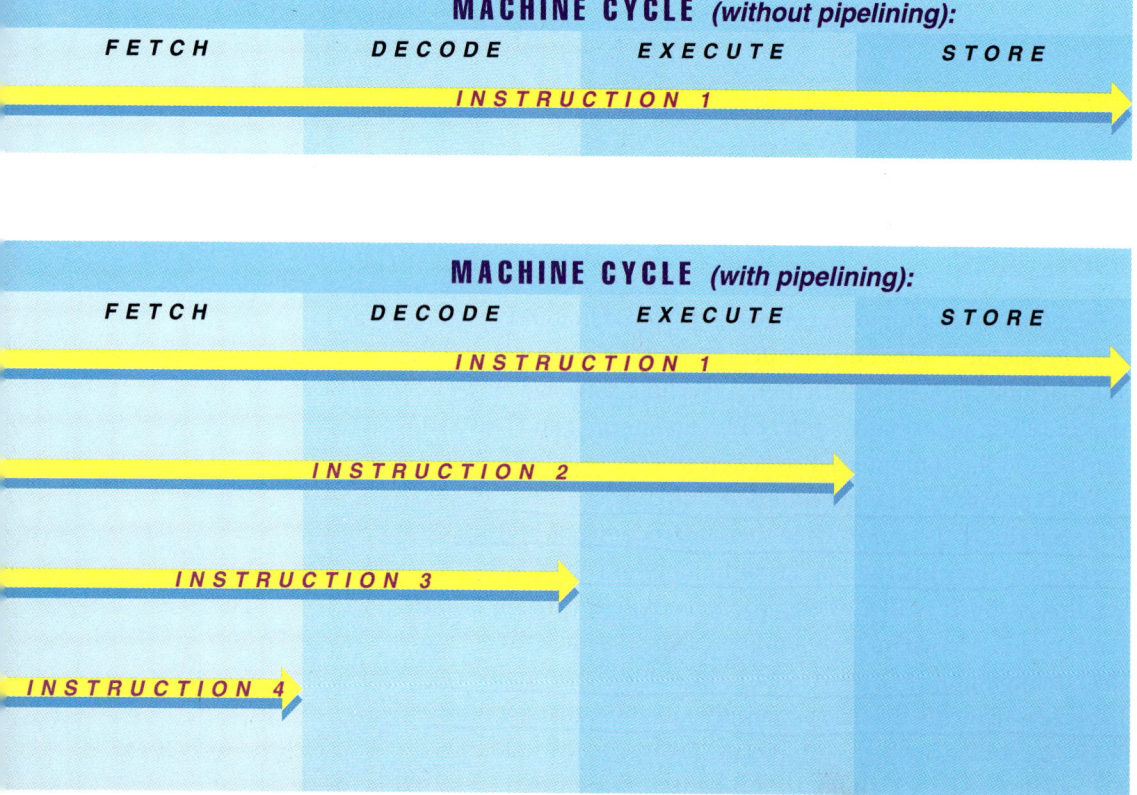

Figure 3-28
With conventional CPUs, an instruction moves through the complete machine cycle before the next instruction is started. With pipelining, the CPU starts working on another instruction each time the preceding instruction moves to the next stage of the machine cycle. In this pipelining example, three other instructions are partially completed by the time instruction 1 is finished. Some CPUs have more than one pipeline.

Types of Processing

In the discussion thus far, the emphasis has focused on computers with single CPUs processing one instruction at a time. The following section presents variations from this approach.

Pipelining

The central processing unit (CPU) in most computers processes only a single instruction at a time. The CPU waits until an instruction completes all four stages of the machine cycle (fetch, decode, execute, and store) before beginning work on the next instruction. With pipelining, a new instruction is fetched as soon as the preceding instruction moves on to the next stage. The result is faster throughput because by the time the first instruction is in the fourth and final stage of the machine cycle, three other instructions have been fetched and are at various stages of the machine cycle (Figure 3-28). Some CPUs, called **superscalar CPUs**, have two or more pipelines that can process instructions simultaneously.

For an explanation of pipelining, visit the Discovering Computers Chapter 3 inCyber page (http://www.scsite.com/dc/ch3/incyber.htm) and click Pipelining.

Parallel Processing

Another way to speed processing is to use more than one CPU in a computer. This method is known as parallel processing. **Parallel processing** involves the use of multiple CPUs, each with its own memory. Parallel processors divide up a problem so that multiple CPUs can work on their assigned portion of the problem simultaneously (Figure 3-29). As you might expect, parallel processors require special software that can recognize how to divide up problems and bring the results back together again. Parallel processors often are used in supercomputers. **Massively parallel processors (MPPs)** use hundreds or thousands of microprocessor CPUs to perform calculations.

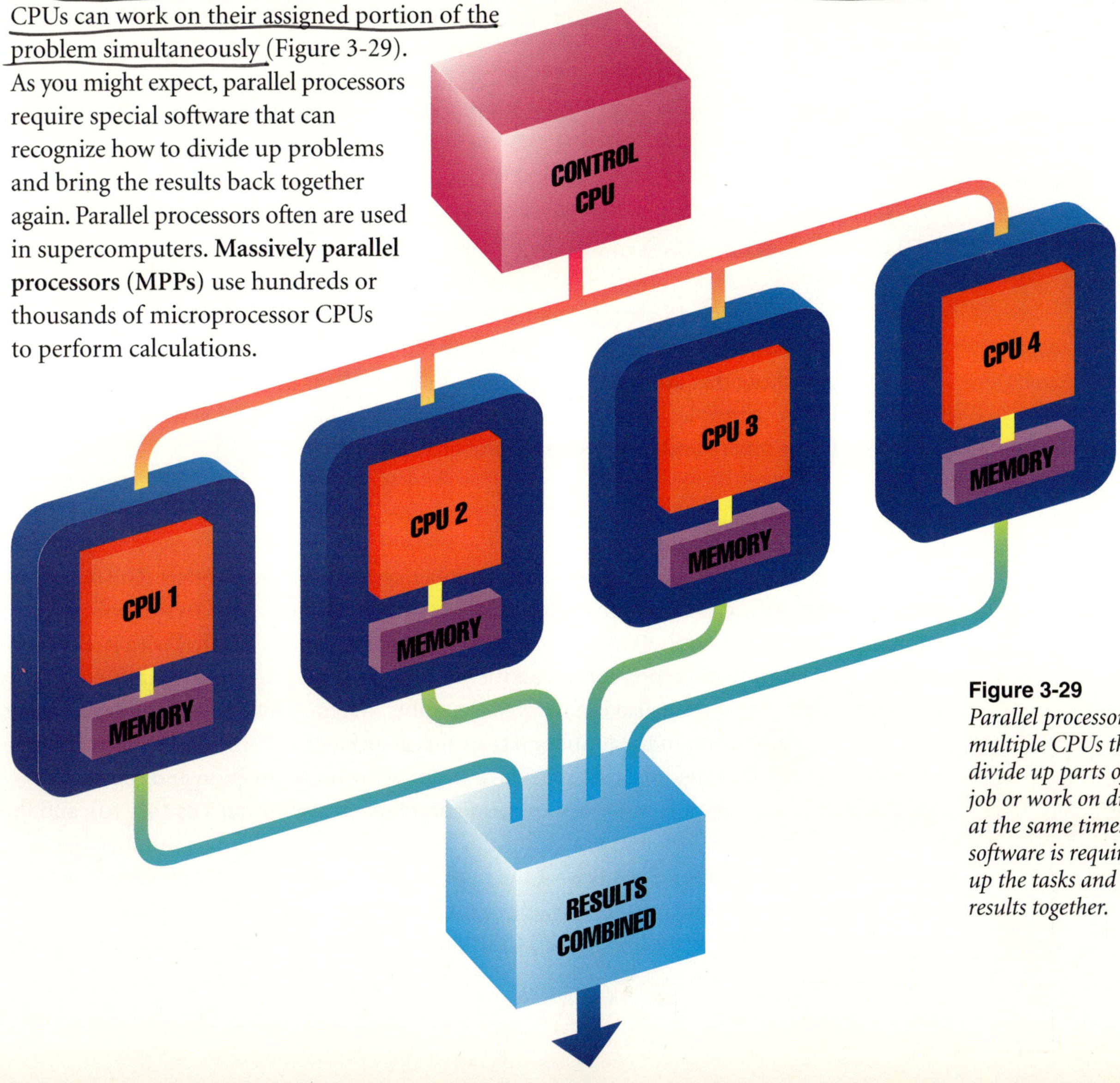

Figure 3-29
Parallel processors have multiple CPUs that can divide up parts of the same job or work on different jobs at the same time. Special software is required to divide up the tasks and bring the results together.

Neural Network Computers

Neural network computers use specially designed circuits to simulate the way the human brain processes information, learns, and remembers. Neural network chips form an interconnected system of processors that learn to associate the relative strength or weakness of inputs with specific results (output). Neural network computers are used in applications such as pattern recognition to correctly guess the identity of an object when only hazy or partial information is available. Other applications that use neural network computers are speech recognition and speech synthesis.

DECIMAL	BINARY	HEXADECIMAL
0	0000	0
1	0001	1
2	0010	2
3	0011	3
4	0100	4
5	0101	5
6	0110	6
7	0111	7
8	1000	8
9	1001	9
10	1010	A
11	1011	B
12	1100	C
13	1101	D
14	1110	E
15	1111	F

Figure 3-30
The chart shows the binary and hexadecimal representation of decimal numbers 0 through 15. In hexadecimal, notice how letters A through F represent the numbers 10 through 15.

Number Systems

This section describes the number systems that are used with computers. Whereas thorough knowledge of this subject is required for technical computer personnel, a general understanding of number systems and how they relate to computers is all most users need. As you have seen, the binary (base 2) number system is used to represent the electronic status of the bits in memory. It is also used for other purposes such as addressing the memory locations. Another number system that is commonly used with computers is **hexadecimal** (base 16). The hexadecimal system is used by the computer to communicate with a programmer when a problem with a program exists, because it would be difficult for the programmer to understand the 0s and 1s of binary code. Figure 3-30 shows how the decimal values 0 through 15 are represented in binary and hexadecimal.

The mathematical principles that apply to the binary and hexadecimal number systems are the same as those that apply to the decimal number system. To help you better understand these principles, this section starts with the familiar decimal system, then progresses to the binary and hexadecimal number systems.

The Decimal Number System

The decimal number system is a base 10 number system (*deci* means ten). The *base* of a number system indicates how many symbols are used in it. Decimal uses 10 symbols, 0 through 9. Each of the symbols in the number system has a value associated with it. For example, you know that 3 represents a quantity of three and 5 represents a quantity of five. The decimal number system also is a *positional* number system. This means that in a number such as 143, each position in the number has a value associated with it. When you look at the decimal number 143, you know that the 3 is in the ones, or units, position and represents three ones or (3 x 1); the 4 is in the tens position and represents four tens or (4 x 10); and the 1 is in the hundreds position and represents one hundred or (1 x 100). The number 143 is the sum of the values in each position of the number (100 + 40 + 3 = 143). The chart in Figure 3-31 shows how the positional values (hundreds, tens, and units) for a number system can be calculated. Starting on the right and working to the left, the base of the number system,

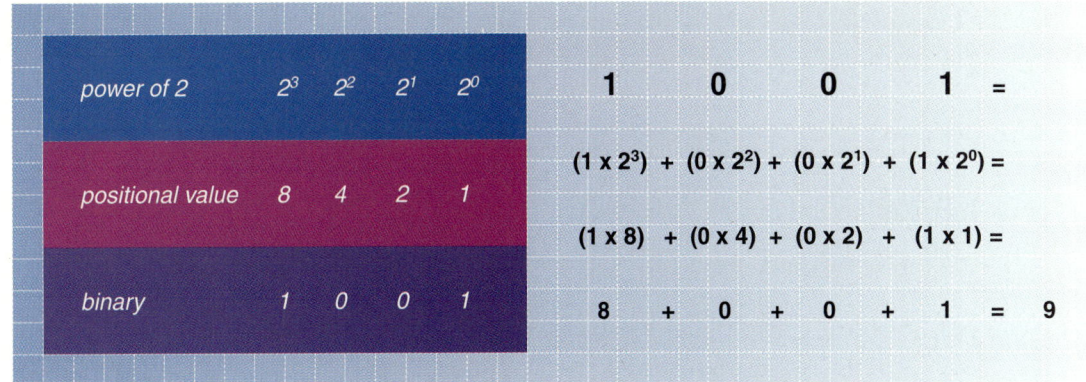

Figure 3-31
The positional values in the decimal number 143 are shown in this chart.

Figure 3-32
Each positional value in a binary number represents a consecutive power of two. Using the positional values, the binary number 1001 can be converted to the decimal number 9.

in this case 10, is raised to consecutive powers (10^2, 10^1, 10^0). These calculations are a mathematical way of determining the place values in a number system.

When you use number systems other than decimal, the same principles apply. The base of the number system indicates the number of symbols that are used, and each position in a number system has a value associated with it. The positional value can be calculated by raising the base of the number system to consecutive powers beginning with zero.

The Binary Number System

As previously discussed, binary is a base 2 number system (*bi* means two), and the symbols that are used are 0 and 1. Just as each position in a decimal number has a place value associated with it, so does each position in a binary number. In binary, the place values are successive powers of two (2^3, 2^2, 2^1, 2^0) or (8, 4, 2, 1). To construct a binary number, you place ones in the positions where the corresponding values add up to the quantity you want to represent; you place zeros in the other positions. For example, the binary place values are 8, 4, 2, and 1, and the binary number 1001 has ones in the positions for the values 8 and 1 and zeros in the positions for 4 and 2. Therefore, the quantity represented by binary 1001 is 9 (8 + 0 + 0 + 1) (Figure 3-32).

power of 16	16^1	16^0
positional value	16	1
hexadecimal	A	5

A 5 =
$(10 \times 16^1) + (5 \times 16^0)$ =
$(10 \times 16) + (5 \times 1)$ =
160 + 5 = 165

Figure 3-33
Conversion of the hexadecimal number A5 to the decimal number 165. Notice that the value 10 is substituted for the A during calculations.

positional value	8421	8421
binary	0100	1101
decimal	4	13
hexadecimal	4	D

Figure 3-34
Conversion of the ASCII code 01001101 for the letter M to the hexadecimal value 4D. Each group of four binary digits is converted to a hexadecimal symbol.

The Hexadecimal Number System

The hexadecimal number system uses 16 symbols to represent values (*hex* means six, *deci* means ten). These include the symbols 0 through 9 and A through F (Figure 3-30). The mathematical principles previously discussed also apply to hexadecimal (Figure 3-33).

The primary reason why the hexadecimal number system is used with computers is because it can represent binary values in a more compact and readable form and because the conversion between the binary and the hexadecimal number systems is very efficient. An eight-digit binary number (a byte) can be represented by a two-digit hexadecimal number. For example, in the ASCII code, the character M is represented as 01001101. This value can be represented in hexadecimal as 4D. One way to convert this binary number to a hexadecimal number is to divide the binary number (from right to left) into groups of four digits; calculate the value of each group; and then change any two-digit values (10 through 15) into the symbols A through F that are used in hexadecimal (Figure 3-34).

Summary of Number Systems

As mentioned at the beginning of the section on number systems, binary and hexadecimal are used primarily by technical computer personnel. A general user does not need a complete understanding of numbering systems. The concepts that you should remember about number systems are that binary is used to represent the electronic status of the bits in memory and storage. Hexadecimal is used to represent binary in a more compact form.

For an explanation of the hexadecimal number system, visit the Discovering Computers Chapter 3 inCyber page (http://www.scsite.com/dc/ch3/incyber.htm) and click Hexadecimal Number.

How Computer Chips Are Made

A computer chip is made by building layers of electronic pathways and connections by using conducting and nonconducting materials on a surface of silicon. The combination of these materials into specific patterns forms microscopic electronic components such as transistors, diodes, resistors, and capacitors; the basic building blocks of electronic circuits. Connected together on a chip, these components are referred to as an **integrated circuit**. The application of the conducting and nonconducting materials to the silicon base is done through a series of technically sophisticated chemical and photographic processes. Some of the manufacturing steps are shown in the following photographs.

A computer chip begins with a design developed by engineers using a computer-aided circuit design program (Figure 3-35). To better review the design, greatly enlarged printouts are prepared. Some chips take only a month or two to design while others may require a year or more. A separate design is needed for each layer of the chip. Most chips have at least four to six layers, but some have up to fifteen.

Although other materials can be used, the most common raw material used to make chips is silicon crystals (Figure 3-36) that have been refined from quartz rocks. The silicon crystals are melted and formed into a cylinder five to ten inches in diameter and several feet long (Figure 3-37). After being smoothed, the silicon ingot is sliced into **wafers** four to eight inches in diameter and 4/1000 of an inch thick.

Much of the chip manufacturing process is performed in special laboratories called **clean rooms**. Because even the smallest particle of dust can ruin a chip, the clean rooms are kept 1,000 times cleaner than a hospital operating

> **inCyber**
>
> For details on the Pentium chip, visit the Discovering Computers Chapter 3 inCyber page (http://www.scsite.com/dc/ch3/incyber.htm) and click Integrated Circuit.

Figure 3-35
Computer-aided design programs are used to create the chip design. Notice the enlarged design printouts in the background.

Figure 3-36
Silicon crystals are the most common raw material used to make the wafers that eventually will become computer chips.

Figure 3-37
Silicon crystals are melted and formed into a cylinder five to ten inches in diameter and several feet long. The ingot is sliced into wafers four to eight inches in diameter and 4/1000 of an inch thick.

Figure 3-38
To avoid contamination of the chip surface, manufacturing is performed in clean rooms 1,000 times cleaner than hospital operating rooms. Workers wear protective clothing called bunny suits.

Figure 3-39
A high-temperature diffusion oven bakes chemicals into the wafer.

Figure 3-40
In the photolithography process, a mask with a layer of chip design is used as a negative. A different mask is used for each layer of the chip. The mask protects specific areas of the wafer from exposure to ultraviolet light. The areas not exposed to ultraviolet light will be removed in the next manufacturing step. The mask may contain up to 100 images of the individual chip.

room. People who work in these facilities must wear special protective clothing called **bunny suits** (Figure 3-38).

After the wafer has been polished and sterilized, it is cleaned in a chemical bath. After cleaning, the wafers are placed in a **diffusion oven** where the first layer of material is added to the wafer surface (Figure 3-39). Other materials, called dopants, are added to the surface of the wafer in a process called **ion implantation**. The **dopants** create areas that will conduct electricity. Channels in these layers of materials are removed in a process called **etching**. Before etching, a soft gelatin-like emulsion called **photoresist** is added to the wafer.

During **photolithography**, an image of the chip design, called a mask, is used as a negative (Figure 3-40). The photoresist is exposed to the mask using ultraviolet light. Ultraviolet light is used because its short wavelength can reproduce very small details on the wafer. Up to 100 images of the chip design are exposed on a single wafer. The photoresist exposed to the ultraviolet light becomes hard and the photoresist covered by the chip design on the mask remains soft. The soft photoresist and some of the surface materials are etched away with hot gases leaving what will become the circuit pathways (Figure 3-41). The process of adding material and photoresist to the wafer, exposing it to ultraviolet light, and etching away the unexposed surface, is repeated using a different mask for each layer of the circuit.

SUMMARY OF THE SYSTEM UNIT   **3.27**

Figure 3-41
This microscopic view shows the electrical pathways that are created during the chip manufacturing process.

Figure 3-42
After the wafer manufacturing process is completed, the wafer is sliced into individual chips called die.

After all circuit layers have been added, individual chips on the wafer are tested by a machine that uses probes to apply electrical current to the chip circuits. In a process called **dicing**, the wafers are cut into individual chips called **die** (Figure 3-42). Die that have passed all tests are placed in a ceramic or plastic case called a **package** (Figure 3-43). Circuits on the chip are connected to pins on the package using gold wires (Figure 3-44). Gold is used because it conducts electricity well and does not corrode. The pins connect the chip to a socket on a circuit board.

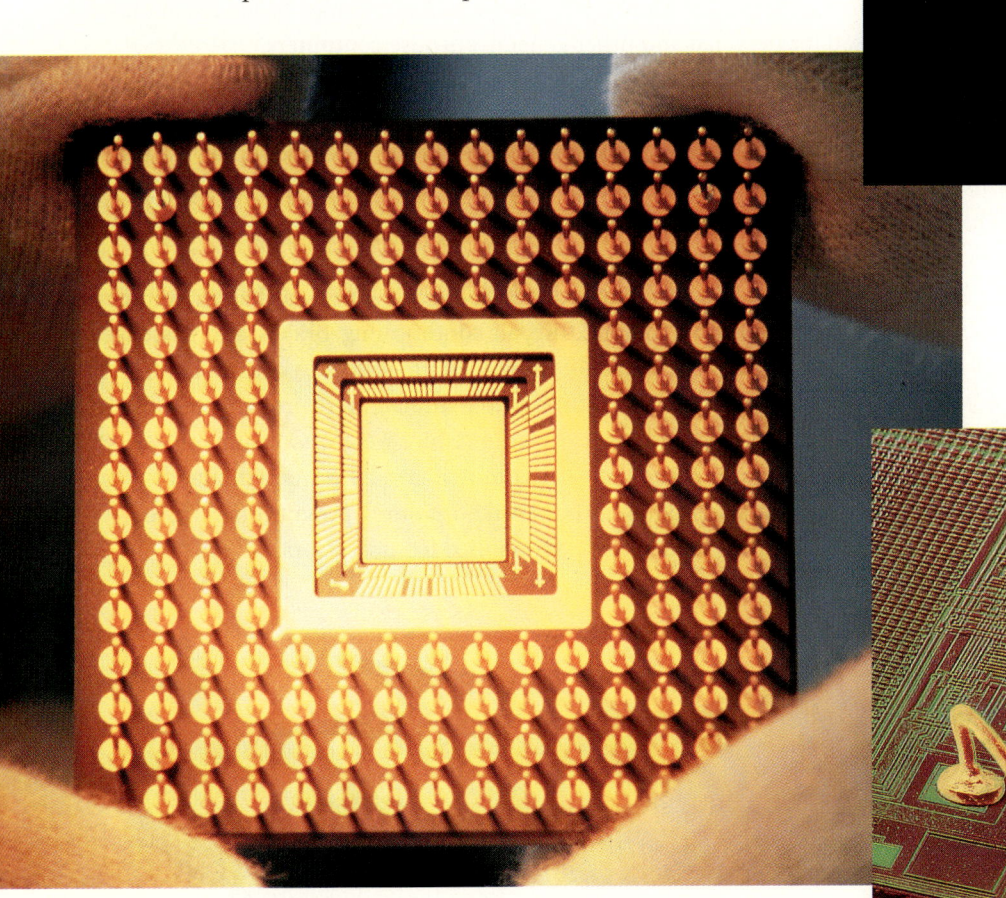

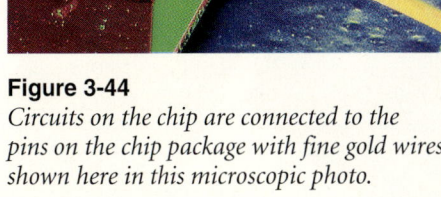

Figure 3-43
Completed die are placed in a ceramic or plastic case called a package. The gold-plated pins shown on the bottom of this package will connect to a socket on the computer motherboard.

Figure 3-44
Circuits on the chip are connected to the pins on the chip package with fine gold wires shown here in this microscopic photo.

Summary of the System Unit

This chapter examined various aspects of the system unit including its components, how programs and data are stored, and how the processor executes program instructions to process data into information. You also have studied various methods of processing, learned about the various number systems that are used with computers, and seen how computer chips are made. Knowing this material will increase your overall understanding of how processing occurs on a computer.

CHAPTER 3 – THE SYSTEM UNIT

COMPUTERS AT WORK

How Many Computers Do You See Each Day?

If you ask someone how many computers he or she uses each day, the answer usually is one or two; a computer at work or school and possibly another computer at home. In reality, most people use dozens of computers each day. These other computers, called **embedded processors**, are built into equipment such as radios, cellular telephones, microwave ovens, copiers, automatic teller machines, and automobiles. We do not think of these processors as computers because we cannot see them and because they play a supporting role in the overall function of the device of which they are a part. In terms of volume, 90% of the processor chips produced are used for embedded applications; only 10% are used for personal and other general-purpose computers.

The capabilities and prices of embedded processors vary greatly. Kitchen appliances, such as a coffee maker, use simple 4- or 8-bit processors that cost less than a dollar. A programmable industrial robot may require a 16-bit processor that costs $20. More sophisticated devices such as communications switching equipment may use the same 32-bit processor as those installed in the more powerful personal computers and servers. These processor chips cost more than $1,000 each. Custom designed processor chips such as those used for aircraft flight control systems can cost even more.

Automobile manufacturers currently are the largest users of embedded processors. A new car has an average of six embedded processors to monitor and control ignition, fuel mixture, air conditioning, brakes, and passenger restraint systems such as air bags. Some luxury cars have more than 40 embedded processors to control lights, suspension, traction, and navigation systems automatically. In the future, auto manufacturers probably will use fewer but more powerful processors that will be connected with fiber optics to reduce weight. Consumer electronic devices also are heavy users. Think about how many appliances and entertainment devices contain digital displays and the capability of programming them to meet your desired use. Alarm wake-up times, programmed radio stations, and yes, the blinking 12:00 on your VCR, all are made possible by embedded processors.

Figure 3-45

IN THE 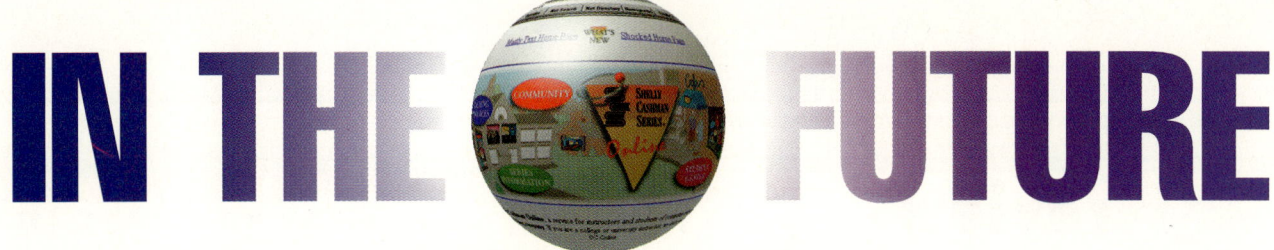 FUTURE

2,000 MIPS by the Year 2000

By the year 2000, Intel, the world's largest manufacturer of microprocessors, predicts it will have a CPU chip that can perform 2,000 MIPS; which is 2 billion instructions per second. This is almost seven times faster than most microprocessor CPUs currently available. To reach this performance level, Intel will have to continue to pack more transistors onto the slice of silicon that becomes the heart of the microprocessor. Intel's Pentium Pro processor has 5.5 million transistors. Its next generation processor, dubbed the P7, is estimated to have between 10 and 15 million transistors. The 2,000 MIPS processor will have between 50 and 100 million transistors spread among four or more integrated CPUs. To reach this level of transistor density, the size of the transistors will have to shrink below one-tenth of a micron. A micron is one-millionth of a meter. Current microprocessors have transistor sizes approximately .35 to .60 microns. For comparison purposes, an average human hair is 75 microns or approximately 150 times the size of current microprocessor transistors. The clock speed of the microprocessor also will have to improve, probably to more than 300 megahertz (each megahertz is one million cycles per second). Current microprocessors run at about 100 to 200 megahertz.

To reach these levels of transistor density and clock speed, microprocessor chip advances will have to continue to meet the prediction of Intel founder Gordon Moore. In 1965, Moore predicted that transistor density, and thus relative computing power, would double every 18 to 24 months. Called Moore's Law, this prediction has so far been amazingly accurate (Figure 3-46). To reach Intel's goal of the 2,000 MIPS chip by the year 2000, the law will have to hold true for a few more years.

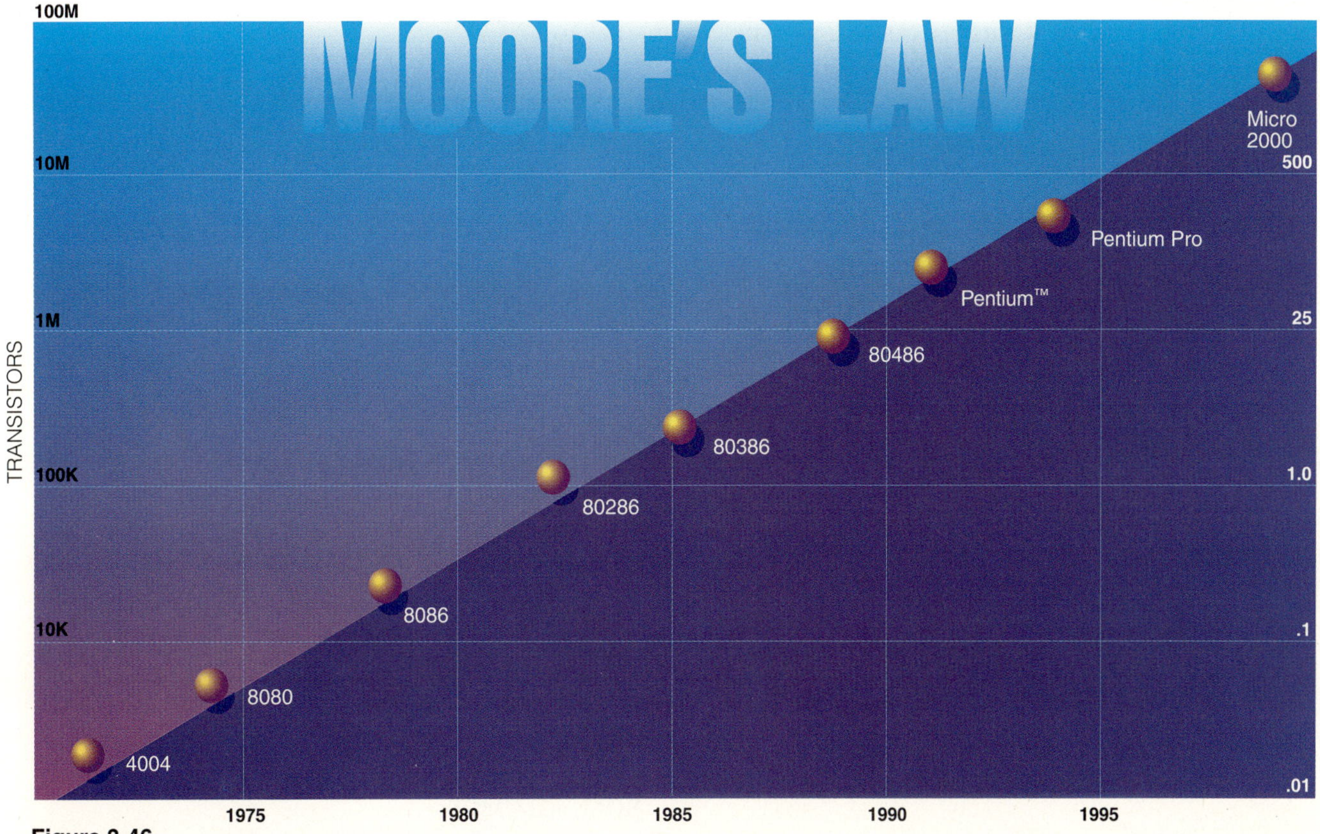

Figure 3-46

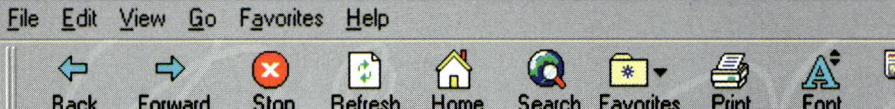

1 Bits and Bytes

Most computers are **digital computers,** meaning all the data they process is converted first into a digital (numeric) value. Only two digits are used because they can be represented by circuits being either off (0) or on (1). Each off or on digital value is called a bit, which is short for *bi*nary dig*it*. Using combinations of 0s and 1s in a group of eight bits, called a byte, a unique code can be assigned to 256 different data possibilities.

2 Bit Pattern Codes

Several different coding schemes are used on computers. The **American Standard Code for Information Interchange (ASCII)** is used on many personal computers and minicomputers. The **Extended Binary Coded Decimal Interchange Code (EBCDIC)** is used primarily on mainframe computers. With these codes, each character is stored in one byte (eight bits) of memory. **Unicode,** a 16-bit code that can represent more than 65,000 characters and symbols, can be used with all of the world's current languages. Every major system developer has announced plans to implement Unicode eventually.

3 Components of the System Unit

In the **system unit,** the computer program instructions are executed and the coded data is manipulated. Components considered part of the system unit include the motherboard, the microprocessor and CPU, upgrade sockets, memory, coprocessors, buses, expansion slots, ports and connectors, bays, the power supply, and sound components.

4 The Motherboard, Microprocessor, and CPU

The **motherboard** is a circuit board that contains most of the electronic components of the system unit. On a personal computer's motherboard is a single integrated circuit (chip), called a **microprocessor,** that holds the central processing unit. The **central processing unit (CPU)** contains the control unit and the arithmetic/logic unit, which work together to perform processing.

5 The Control Unit and the Arithmetic/Logic Unit

The **control unit** *controls* the computer by repeating four operations, called the **machine cycle.** The four operations are **fetching** program instructions from memory, **decoding** the instructions into commands the computer can process, **executing** the commands, and storing the results in memory. The **arithmetic/logic unit (ALU)** contains the electronic circuits to perform **arithmetic operations** (computations) and **logical operations** (comparisons) on data. Some motherboards contain a type of receptacle, called an **upgrade socket,** that can be used to install a more powerful CPU.

6 Memory

Memory refers to integrated circuits that temporarily store program instructions and data used by the CPU. Memory stores three items: the systems software, the application program instructions, and the data being processed. Memory size is measured in **kilobytes** (**K** or **KB**), **megabytes** (**MB**), or **gigabytes** (**GB**). Three common types of memory chips are RAM, ROM, and CMOS.

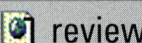

3:00 AM

3 review

chapter 1 | 2 | 3 | 4 | 5 | 6 | 7 | 8 | 9 | 10 | 11 | 12 | 13 | 14 | I

inCyber | review | terms | yourTurn | hotTopics | outThere | winLabs | webWalk | exercises | news | home

7 RAM vs. ROM

RAM (random access memory) is the name given to the integrated circuits containing data that can be read and written by the microprocessor or other computer devices. RAM is **volatile** because the programs and data stored in RAM are erased when the power is turned off. **ROM (read only memory)** is the name given to chips that store information or instructions that can be read and used, but cannot be changed. ROM is **nonvolatile** because it retains its contents even when the power is turned off. **CMOS (complementary metal-oxide semiconductor)** memory is used to store information about the computer system that is needed each time the computer is started.

8 Coprocessors, Buses, and Expansion Slots

Computers can increase their efficiency with a **coprocessor**, which is a special microprocessor chip or circuit board designed to perform a specific task. Within the circuitry of a computer, any path along which bits are transmitted is called a **bus**. An **expansion bus** carries data to and from **expansion slots**, which are sockets designed to hold the circuit board for a device that adds capability to the computer system.

9 Parallel Ports and Serial Ports

A **port** is a socket used to connect the system unit to a peripheral device. **Parallel ports**, which transfer eight bits (one byte) at a time, are used most often to connect devices that send or receive large amounts of data, such as printers or disk and tape drives. **Serial ports**, which transmit data one bit at a time, are used to connect the mouse, the keyboard, and communication devices.

10 Bays, the Power Supply, and Sound Components

A **bay** is an open area inside the system unit used to install additional equipment. The **power supply** converts the wall outlet electricity (115 to 120 volts AC) to the lower voltages (5 to 12 volts DC) used by the computer. Most personal computers have the capability of generating sounds through a small speaker, and some have a microphone to record messages.

11 Machine Language Instructions

Program instructions must be in **machine language**, which is binary data that the electronic circuits in the CPU can interpret and convert into one or more of the commands in the computer's instruction set. The **instruction set** contains commands that the computer's circuits can perform directly. The first part of a machine language instruction, called the **operation code**, tells the computer what to do and matches a command in the instruction set. The second part of the instruction, called an **operand**, specifies the data or the location of the data that will be used by the instruction.

12 Types of Processing

The CPU in most computers processes a single instruction at a time. The CPU waits until the instruction completes all four stages of the machine cycle before beginning to work on the next instruction. **Pipelining** speeds throughput by fetching a new instruction as soon as the preceding instruction moves on to the next stage. **Parallel processing** uses multiple CPUs, which each work simultaneously on a portion of the problem. **Neural network computers** apply specially designed circuits to simulate the way the human brain processes information, learns, and remembers.

3 terms — chapter

1 | 2 | 3 | 4 | 5 | 6 | 7 | 8 | 9 | 10 | 11 | 12 | 13 | 14 | I

inCyber | review | terms | yourTurn | hotTopics | outThere | winLabs | webWalk | exercises | news | home

INSTRUCTIONS: *To display this page from the Web, launch your browser and enter the URL, http://www.scsite.com/dc/ch3/terms.htm. Scroll through the list of terms. Click a term for its definition and a picture. Click the rocket ship for current and additional information about the term.*

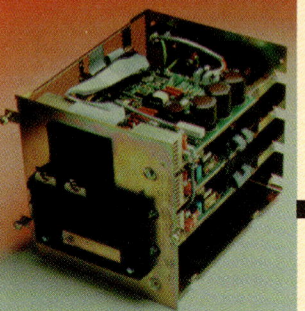

integrated circuit (IC) ▼

DEFINITION

integrated circuit (IC)
Also called a chip, or IC, is a complete electronic circuit that has been etched on a thin slice of material such as silicon. For mainframe and supercomputers, the CPU consists of one or more circuit boards. (3.8, 3.25)

access speed (3.13)
adapter cards (3.15)
American Standard Code for Information Interchange (ASCII) (3.4)
analog computers (3.3)
arithmetic operations (3.8)
arithmetic/logic unit (ALU) (3.8)

bay (3.18)
bit (3.3)
bunny suits (3.25)
bus (3.14)
byte (3.3)

cache (3.12)
cage (3.18)
central processing unit (CPU) (3.8)
chip (3.8)
CISC (3.19)
clean rooms (3.25)
CMOS (complementary metal-oxide semiconductor) (3.13)
connectors (3.16)
control unit (3.8)
controller cards (3.15)
coprocessor (3.14)

decoding (3.8)
dicing (3.27)
die (3.27)
diffusion oven (3.26)
digital computers (3.3)
digitizing (3.3)
DIMM (dual in-line memory module) (3.12)

dopants (3.26)
drive bay (3.18)
dynamic RAM (DRAM) (3.13)

etching (3.26)
even parity (3.5)
executing (3.8)
execution cycle (3.8)
expansion board (3.15)
expansion bus (3.14)
expansion card (3.15)
expansion slot (3.15)
Extended Binary Coded Decimal Interchange Code (EBCDIC) (3.4)

fetching (3.8)
firmware (3.13)
flash memory (3.11)
flash RAM (3.11)

gigabyte (GB) (3.11)
gigaflops (GFLOPS) (3.20)

hexadecimal (3.22)

ideograms (3.4)
instruction cycle (3.8)
instruction set (3.19)
integrated circuit (IC) (3.8, 3.25)
interface cards (3.15)
internal cache (3.12)
ion implantation (3.26)

kilobyte (K or KB) (3.11)

level 1 (L1) cache (3.12)
level 2 (L2) cache (3.12)
local bus (3.14)
logical operations (3.8)

machine cycle (3.8)
machine language instruction (3.19)
main board (3.7)
massively parallel processor (MPP) (3.21)
megabyte (MB) (3.11)
megaflops (MFLOPS) (3.20)
megahertz (MHz) (3.9)
memory (3.11)
memory address (3.11)
microcode (3.13)
microprocessor (3.7)
millisecond (3.14)
MIPS (3.20)
motherboard (3.7)
musical instrument digital interface (MIDI) (3.18)

nanoseconds (3.13)
neural network computers (3.22)
nonvolatile (3.13)

odd parity (3.5)
operand (3.20)
operation code (3.20)

package (3.27)
parallel ports (3.16)
parallel processing (3.21)
parity bit (3.5)
PC Card (3.16)

PCMCIA (3.16)
photolithography (3.26)
photoresist (3.26)
pipelining (3.21)
port (3.16)
power supply (3.18)

rails (3.18)
RAM (random access memory) (3.11)
registers (3.8)
RISC (3.19)
ROM (read only memory) (3.13)

SCSI (3.16)
serial port (3.18)
SIMM (single in-line memory module) (3.12)
sound board (3.18)
static RAM (SRAM) (3.13)
storing (3.8)
superscalar CPUs (3.21)
system board (3.7)
system clock (3.8)
system unit (3.2)

Unicode (3.4)
Universal Serial Bus (USB) (3.18)
upgrade socket (3.10)

volatile (3.11)

wafers (3.25)
word size (3.9)

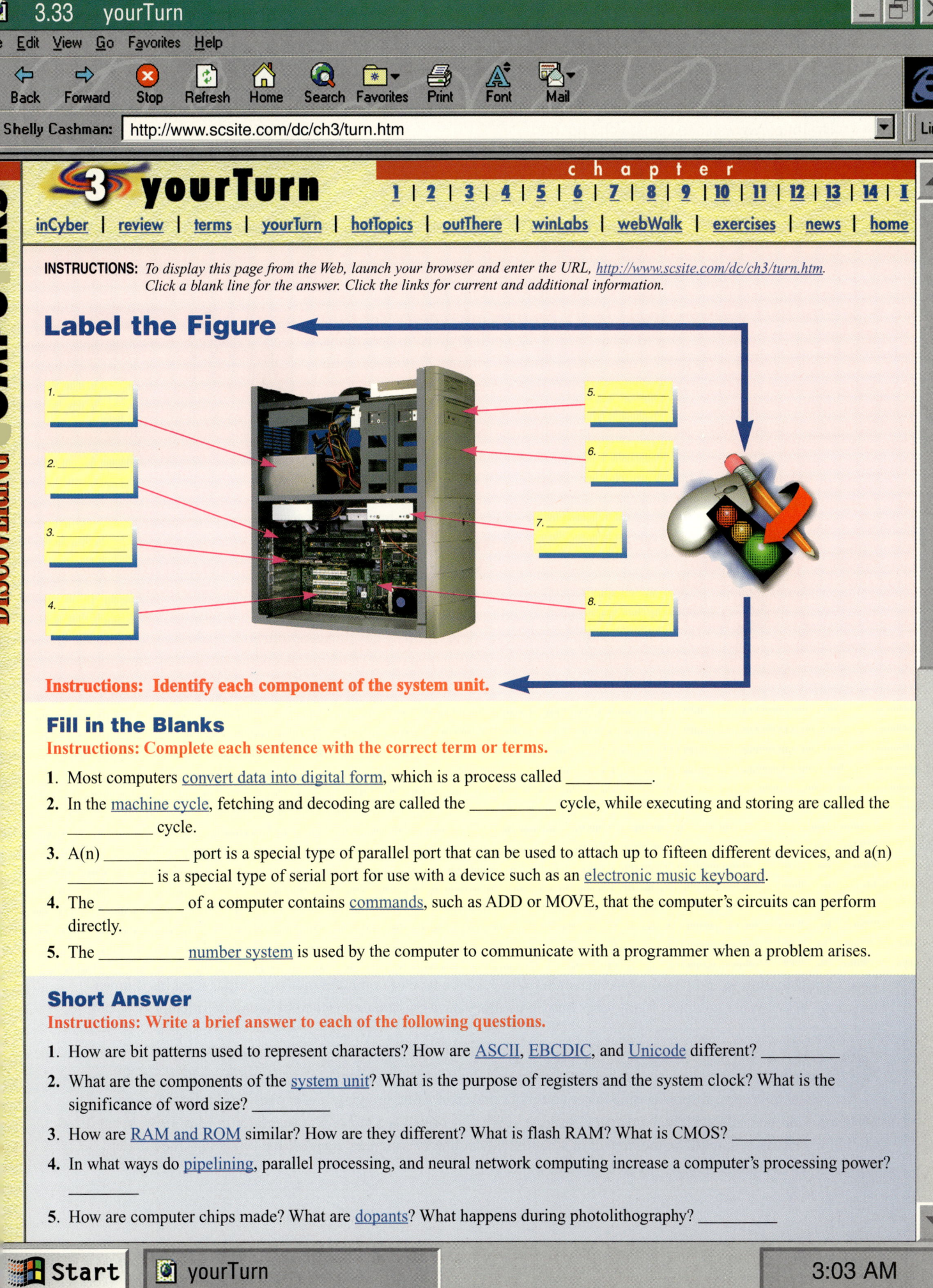

DISCOVERING COMPUTERS

3 hotTopics

chapter 1 | 2 | 3 | 4 | 5 | 6 | 7 | 8 | 9 | 10 | 11 | 12 | 13 | 14 | I

inCyber | review | terms | yourTurn | hotTopics | outThere | winLabs | webWalk | exercises | news | home

INSTRUCTIONS: *To display this page from the Web, launch your browser and enter the URL, http://www.scsite.com/dc/ch3/hot.htm. Click the links for current and additional information to help you respond to the hotTopics questions.*

1 *In 1994, a design flaw in Intel's Pentium microprocessor chip* caused a rounding error to occur once in nine billion division operations. For an average user, this would cause a mistake once in 27,000 years, but users demanded replacement chips. Intel eventually decided to supply replacements for anyone who wanted one. This decision cost Intel almost $500 million. Did people overreact? Does the demand for perfection divert funds that could be spent better elsewhere? (Intel's costs were equivalent to half a year's research and development budget.) How much perfection should be expected, and what should be its price?

2 *People sometimes take an anthropomorphic approach to animals and* objects, assigning them human-like qualities and attributes. The control unit, for example, has been described as the *brain* of a computer because the functions it performs are considered similar to those discharged by the human brain. Can the analogy be reversed? Pick a simple task that people do every day. In accomplishing this task, what actions resemble operations in the machine cycle (fetching, decoding, executing, and storing)? How? What actions are different from any machine cycle operations? Can any operations be omitted without affecting completion of the task? Why or why not?

3 *In February 1996, the forerunner of the modern computers had its 50th anniversary. That* progenitor, the ENIAC (Electronic Numerical Integrator and Computer), weighed thirty tons, filled a thirty-by-fifty-foot room, and contained more than 18,000 vacuum tubes. Although the ENIAC performed several important tasks, its capabilities are dwarfed by today's notebooks. What will computers be like 50 years from now? Which components are most likely to change? How? Which components are least likely to change? Why?

4 *Computers have several different types of memory chips, each of which stores different kinds* of information. Do people also have distinct types of memory, with characteristics similar to computer memory chips? Consider, for instance, how RAM, ROM, cache RAM, and CMOS are different. If your own memory was divided into four areas, each with traits comparable to one of the disparate computer memory chips, what kind of information would be stored in each area? Why? Which type of computer memory chip is least like human memory? Why? What qualities, if any, does human memory have that are unmatched by computer memory?

5 *As a general marketing rule, higher quality results in higher prices, and the cost of new* products rises as the product becomes more popular. Computers appear to challenge these dictums, however, as new microprocessors become faster and more powerful while growing less expensive. An Intel Pentium 133 MHz microprocessor chip, which cost $935 in June 1995, was priced at $257 only a year later in May 1996. What drives the fall in prices? What will be the impact of a continued decline in computer costs? What effect will the greater affordability of computers have on areas such as education?

chapter 3 outThere

1 | 2 | 3 | 4 | 5 | 6 | 7 | 8 | 9 | 10 | 11 | 12 | 13 | 14 | I

inCyber | review | terms | yourTurn | hotTopics | outThere | winLabs | webWalk | exercises | news | home

INSTRUCTIONS: *To display this page from the Web, launch your browser and enter the URL, http://www.scsite.com/dc/ch3/out.htm. Click the links for current and additional information.*

1 ***Many system unit manufacturers provide a toll-free telephone number*** that customers can call with <u>technical problems or questions</u>. If the service technician determines a difficulty is a hardware problem that the customer can fix, the technician might ask the customer to open the system unit and make some adjustments. For this reason, every computer user can benefit by being familiar with the inside of the system unit. If you own a personal computer or have access to a personal computer, unplug the power supply and take the cover off the system unit. Make a sketch of the system unit and try to identify each part. Compare your sketch and list with a classmate who has done this exercise with a different computer. How are the computers similar? How are they different?

2 ***In 1951, Remington Rand introduced the UNIVAC (UNIVersal Automatic Computer)*** for commercial use by a few businesses and scientists. The invention of the microchip, by Jack Kilby and Robert Noyce (founder of Intel) in 1959 led to computers becoming an indispensable part of offices and laboratories. The World Wide Web offers several accounts of the story of microprocessors. Prepare a brief report on the history of microprocessors. What developments have been most significant? Why? What microprocessor chips are on the cutting edge of today's technology? Considering the microprocessor's past, what developments do you anticipate in the future?

3 ***Perhaps the fastest growing portion of the personal computer market are*** <u>notebook computers</u>. About 8% of personal computer sales in 1984, <u>notebook computers</u> are expected to make up more than 35% of sales in the year 2000. How do notebook computers compare with desktop models? Use a computer catalog, call a mail-order computer vendor, or visit a computer retailer and find a notebook computer and a desktop computer with comparable system units. What is the price of each computer? Describe the system units. How are they similar? How are they different? Which computer is the better buy? Why?

4 ***Most authorities agree that <u>RISC</u> (reduced instruction set computing) processors are more*** efficient than the traditional CISC (complex instruction set computing) processors. Perhaps because of the large number of CISC computers, however, debate continues on the World Wide Web over the merits of RISC. A few wonder if RISC has gone too far, but others argue that RISC has not gone far enough. CISC computers typically have more than one hundred instructions in their instruction sets, while RISC computers have about fifty. Compare CISC and RISC. What are the advantages of each? What are the disadvantages? Which type of computer eventually will prevail?

5 ***Some people say that <u>Software drives hardware</u>. When purchasing a computer, this usually means*** your system unit and peripheral devices (hardware) must be capable of running your application programs (software). Visit a store that sells computer software and make a list of application programs you would like now and those you may want in the future. Examine the software packages and note the capabilities required of the system unit (type of microprocessor, amount of memory, and so on). What are the minimum system requirements you would demand in a personal computer? What system requirements would be sufficient to provide a *cushion* so you could be sure the system also could run other, or new, application packages?

winLabs

chapter | 1 | 2 | 3 | 4 | 5 | 6 | 7 | 8 | 9 | 10 | 11 | 12 | 13 | 14 | I

inCyber | review | terms | yourTurn | hotTopics | outThere | winLabs | webWalk | exercises | news | home

INSTRUCTIONS: *To display this page from the Web, launch your browser and enter the URL, http://www.scsite.com/dc/ch3/labs.htm. Click the links for current and additional information.*

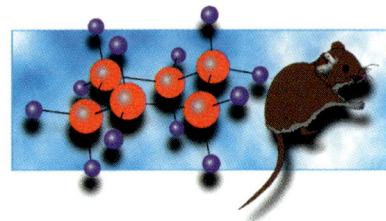

1 Shelly Cashman Series Motherboard Lab

Follow the instructions in winLab 1 on page 1.34 to display the Shelly Cashman Series Labs screen. Click Understanding the Motherboard. Click the Start Lab button. When the initial screen displays, carefully read the objectives. With your printer on, click the Print Questions button. Fill out the top of the Questions sheet and answer the questions. Close the Shelly Cashman Series Labs.

Setting the System Clock

Double-click the time on the taskbar. In the Date/Time Properties dialog box (Figure 3-47), click the question mark button on its title bar and then click the picture of the calendar. Read the information in the pop-up window and then click the pop-up window to close it. Repeat this process for the other areas of the dialog box and then answer the following questions: (1) What is the purpose of the calendar? (2) How do you change the time zone? (3) What is the difference between the OK and the Apply buttons? Close the Date/Time Properties dialog box.

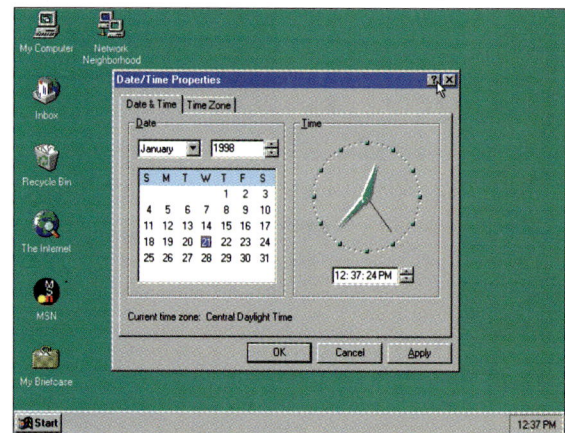

Figure 3-47

Using Calculator to Perform Number System Conversion

Click the Start button on the taskbar; point to Programs on the Start menu; point to Accessories on the Programs submenu; and then click Calculator on the Accessories submenu. Click View on the menu bar and then click Scientific to display the scientific calculator. Perform the following tasks: (1) Click Dec to select base 10. Enter **27843** by clicking the numeric buttons or using the numeric keypad. Click Hex. Write down the number that displays. Click Bin. Write down the result. Click C (the Clear button). (2) Convert the following decimal (base 10) numbers to hexadecimal (Hex) and binary (Bin) and write down each result: 5, 16, 33, 64, 2048, and 4000. (3) Convert the following hexadecimal (base 16) numbers to decimal (Dec) and binary (Bin) and write down each result: 42, 5AC, DDD, 97AE2, and 1D9A48. Close Calculator.

Using Help in a Dialog Box

Click the Start button on the taskbar; point to Settings on the Start menu; and then click Taskbar on the Settings submenu. In the Taskbar Properties dialog box, click the Taskbar Options tab; click the question mark icon on the title bar; and then click Show Clock. Right-click the pop-up window; click Print Topic on the shortcut menu; and then click the OK button to print the pop-up window contents. Click the pop-up window to close it and then close the Taskbar Properties dialog box. Answer the following questions: (1) How do you display and/or remove the clock from the taskbar? (2) When the clock displays on your taskbar, exactly what displays when you point to it?

webWalk

chapter 3 | 1 | 2 | 3 | 4 | 5 | 6 | 7 | 8 | 9 | 10 | 11 | 12 | 13 | 14 | I

inCyber | review | terms | yourTurn | hotTopics | outThere | winLabs | webWalk | exercises | news | home

INSTRUCTIONS: *To display this page from the Web, launch your browser and enter the URL, http://www.scsite.com/dc/ch3/walk.htm. Click the exercise link to display the exercise.*

1 Parallel Processing
In massively parallel processing (MPP), large numbers of processors divide the components of a problem into tiny fragments, with each processor working on a different fragment at the same time. Learn about applications of this technology by completing this exercise.

3 Memory Upgrades
Today's 32-bit operating systems, such as Windows 95 and Windows NT 4, require 16 MB of RAM just to run properly. Graphics and multimedia software can take as much as 32 MB or more to operate. Complete this exercise to learn about upgrading the memory of your PC.

4 PC Cards
The first credit-card sized PC cards were memory cards, but now, many PC cards are available, ranging from hard drives to network adapters. To learn about some of these cards, complete this exercise.

5 Information Mining
Complete this exercise to improve your Web research skills by using a Web search engine to find information related to this chapter.

7 RISC
As much as 80 percent of a PC's processing involves a small number of frequently used machine language instructions. Some manufacturers have taken advantage of this statistic by designing CPUs based on Reduced Instruction Set Computing (RISC). To learn more about RISC, complete this exercise.

9 Web Chat
Complete this exercise to enter a Web Chat discussion related to the issues presented in the hotTopics exercise.

2 Neural Networks
Artificial neural networks have become an accepted information analysis technology in a variety of disciplines. This has resulted in an assortment of commercial applications (Figure 3-48). To learn more about neural network applications, complete this exercise.

Figure 3-48

6 Microprocessors
Personal computer microprocessors most often are identified by their model number or model name. Complete this exercise to learn more about some of the widely used microprocessors.

8 Computer Chips
A computer chip is made by building layers of electronic pathways and connections using conducting and nonconducting materials on a surface of silicon. To learn how computer chips are made, complete this exercise.

Input and Output

OBJECTIVES

After completing this chapter, you will be able to:

- Define the four types of input and how the computer uses each type

- Describe the standard features of keyboards and explain how to use the arrow and function keys

- Explain how a mouse and other pointing devices work and how they are used

- Describe several different methods of source data automation

- Define the term output

- Describe different types of printed output

- Identify different types of display devices

- Explain the difference between impact and nonimpact printers

- Explain how images are displayed on a screen

- List and describe other types of output devices used with computers

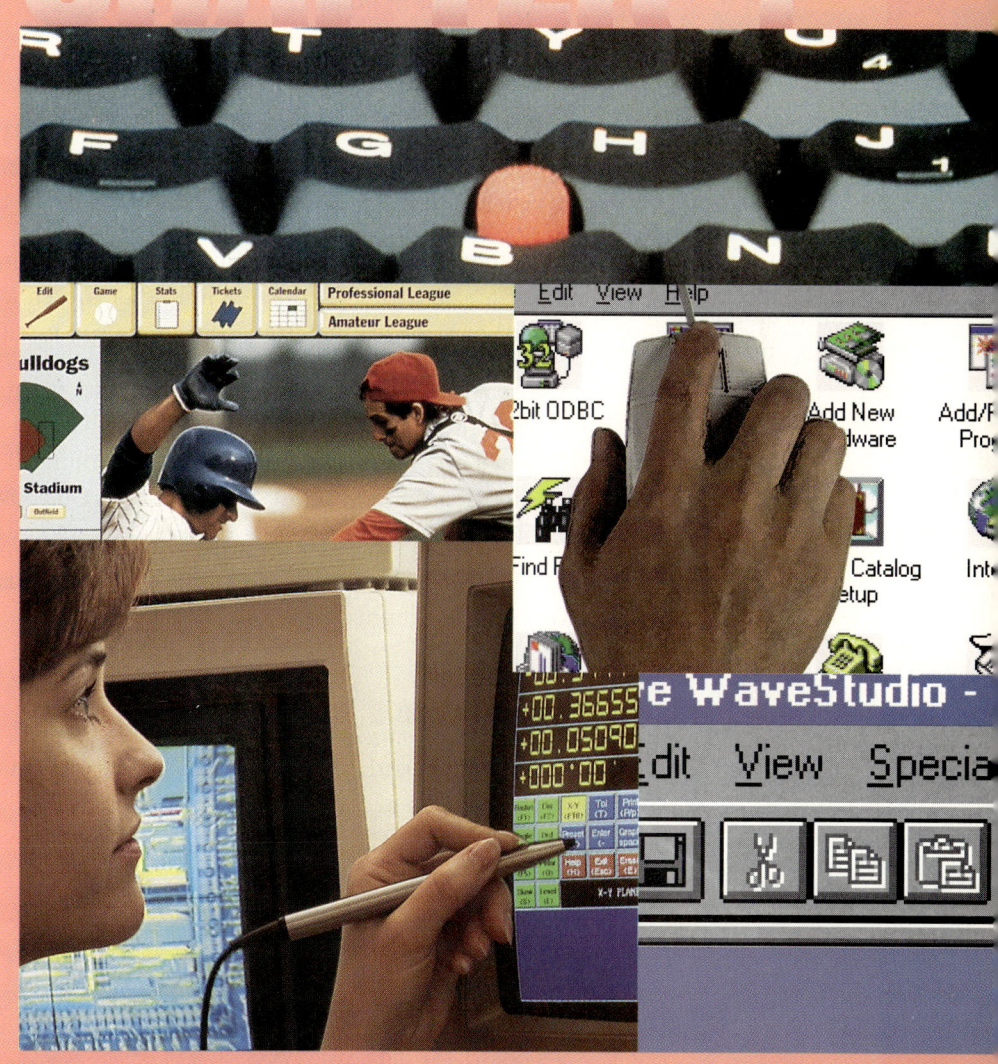

CHAPTER 4

Input and output devices are essential to most computer tasks. Input devices convert data into a form that the computer can understand and process. Output devices take processed or stored data and convert it into a form that you can understand. This chapter describes many of the more commonly used input and output devices. Devices that can be used for both input and storage, such as disk and tape drives, will be covered in the storage chapter.

What Is Input?

Input refers to the process of entering data, programs, commands, and user responses into memory. These four types of input are used by a computer in the following ways:

- **Data** refers to the raw facts, including numbers, letters, words, images, and sounds, that a computer receives during the input operation and processes to produce information. Although technically speaking, a single item of data should be called a *datum*, it is common and accepted usage to use the word data to represent both singular and plural. Data must be entered and stored in memory for processing to occur. Data is the most common type of input.

- **Programs** are instructions that direct the computer to perform the operations necessary to process data into information. The program that is loaded from storage into memory determines the processing that the computer will perform. When a program is first created, usually it is input by using a keyboard and a pointing device. Once the program has been entered and stored on a storage device, it can be transferred to memory by a command.

- **Commands** are keywords and phrases that you input to direct the computer to perform certain activities. Commands are either chosen with a pointing device, entered from the keyboard, or selected using another type of input device.

- **User responses** refer to the data that a user inputs to respond to a question or message from the software. Programs sometimes ask you to answer "Yes" or "No" to a question. Based on the answer, the computer program will perform specific actions. For example, choosing Yes in response to the message, Do you want to save this file?, will result in the file being saved to a storage device.

Input also can refer to the media (e.g. floppy disks, tape cartridges, documents) that contain these input types.

The Keyboard

The **keyboard** is the most commonly used input device. You input data to a computer by pressing the keys on the keyboard. Keyboards are connected to other devices that have screens, such as a personal computer or a terminal. As you enter data through the keyboard, the data displays on the screen.

function keys

THE KEYBOARD **4.3**

Most keyboards are similar to the one shown in Figure 4-1. The alphabetic keys are arranged like those on a typewriter. A **numeric keypad** is located on the right-hand side of most keyboards. The numeric keys are arranged in an adding machine or calculator format to allow you to enter numeric data rapidly.

Keyboards also contain keys that can be used to position the insertion point, or cursor, on the screen. An **insertion point**, or **cursor**, is a symbol, such as an underline character, rectangle, or vertical bar, that indicates where on the screen the next character entered will appear. The keys that move the insertion point are called **arrow keys** or **arrow control keys**. The arrow keys are the UP ARROW (↑), DOWN ARROW (↓), LEFT ARROW (←), and RIGHT ARROW (→). When you press any of these keys, the insertion point moves one space in the same direction as the arrow. In addition, many keyboards contain other control keys such as the HOME key, which you can press to move the insertion point to a beginning position such as the upper left position of the screen or document. The numeric keypad also can be used to move the insertion point. With most keys, if you hold them down, they will start to repeat automatically.

Most computer keyboards also contain keys that can alter or edit the text displayed on the screen. For example, the INSERT, DELETE, and BACKSPACE keys allow characters to be inserted into or deleted from data that displays on the screen. Pressing the CAPS LOCK key capitalizes all the letters you type.

The CAPS LOCK key is an example of a **toggle key**, which switches, or *toggles*, the keyboard between two different modes. The NUM LOCK key also is a toggle key. Pressing the NUM LOCK key turns the numeric keypad on or off. When the numeric keypad is on, you can use the keys to type numbers. When it is off, the same keys work like arrow keys and move the insertion point.

inCyber

For details on keyboards, visit the Discovering Computers Chapter 4 inCyber page (http://www.scsite.com/dc/ch4/incyber.htm) and click Keyboard.

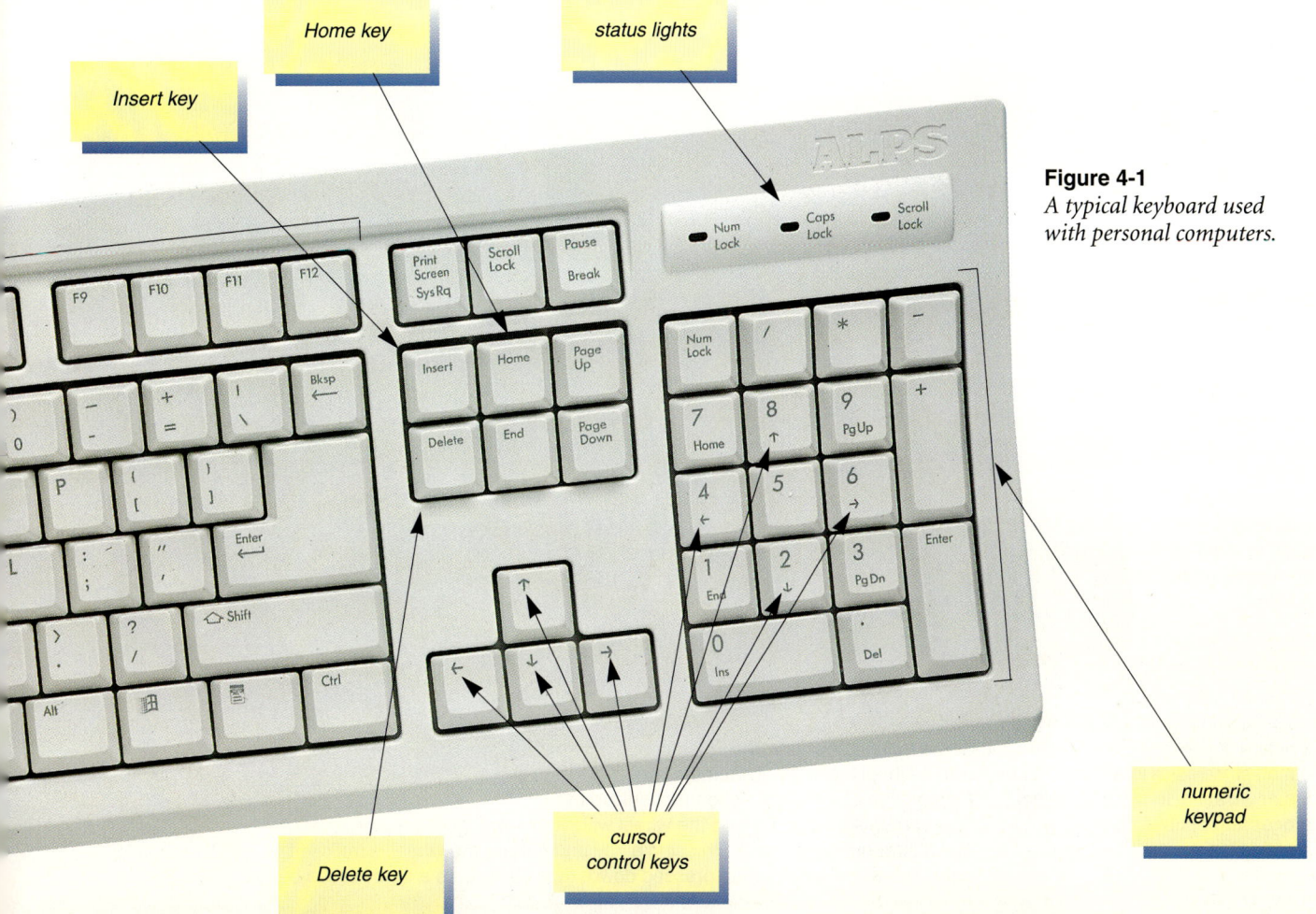

Figure 4-1
A typical keyboard used with personal computers.

Function keys are the keys located at the top of the keyboard that are programmed to initiate commands and accomplish certain tasks. Function keys are labeled with the letter F followed by a digit (Figure 4-1 on pages 4.2 and 4.3). When you are instructed to press F1, you should press function key F1, not the letter F followed by the number 1. For example, when you press the function key F1—which often is programmed as a Help key in word processor programs—the online Help window opens to provide assistance. Function keys also can save you time. For example, if you are typing on the keyboard, it may be faster to press the function key F7 than to move the mouse to click a button or menu command. Most application software packages are written so you can use a shortcut menu, a button, a menu, or a function key and obtain the same result.

Status lights in the upper right corner of the keyboard indicate if the numeric keypad, capital letters, and scroll lock are turned on.

The ESCAPE (ESC) key often is used by computer software to cancel an instruction or exit from a situation. The functions performed by the ESC key varies between software packages.

The disadvantage of using a keyboard as an input device is that training is required to use it efficiently. If you lack typing ability, you are likely to be at a disadvantage because of the time required to look for the appropriate keys. While other input devices are appropriate in some situations, you are encouraged to develop your keyboarding skills.

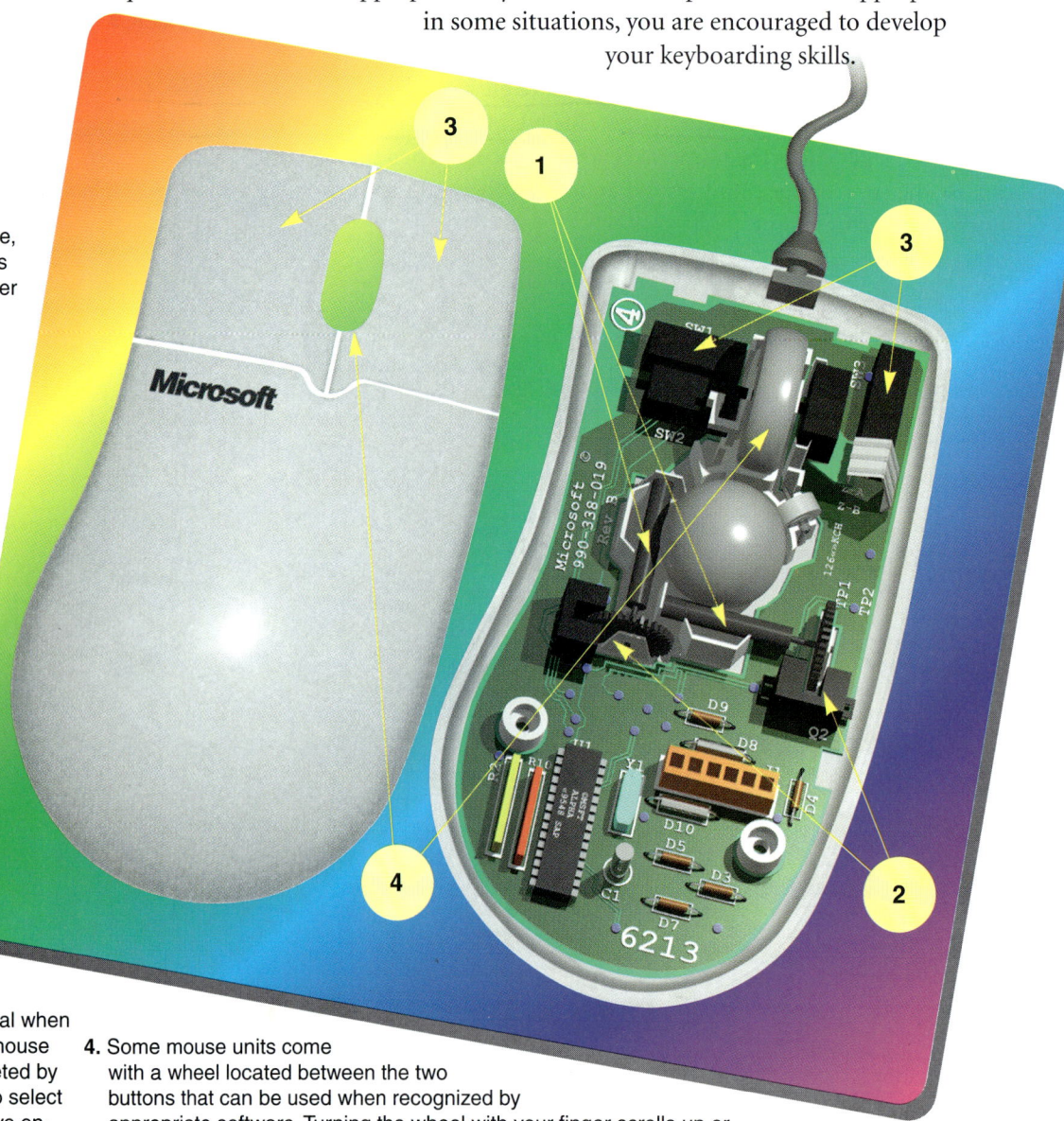

Figure 4-2
How a mouse works.

1. When you move the mouse, the ball rubs against rollers inside the mouse. One roller measures side-to-side motion and the other measures up-and-down motion.

2. The rollers are attached to encoder wheels that have metal contact points. Each time the encoder wheel contact points pass by the contact bar they send an electrical signal to the mouse software in the computer. The signals are translated into the direction and speed of the mouse and are used to move the on-screen mouse pointer.

3. Switches under each mouse button send a signal when a button is pressed. The mouse button signals are interpreted by the application software to select processing options or move on-screen objects.

4. Some mouse units come with a wheel located between the two buttons that can be used when recognized by appropriate software. Turning the wheel with your finger scrolls up or down through a document. Pressing a key and turning the wheel, scrolls left or right. The wheel also can be pressed down, thus serving as a third mouse button.

Pointing Devices

Pointing devices allow you to control an on-screen symbol, called the **mouse pointer** or **pointer**, that usually is represented by an arrowhead shaped marker (↖). You use the pointing device to move the insertion point to a particular location on the screen or to select available software options.

Mouse

A **mouse** is a small, palm-sized input device that you move across a flat surface, such as a desktop, to control the movement of the pointer on a screen. The mouse often rests on a **mouse pad**, which is a rectangular piece of cushioned material that provides better traction for the mouse than a desktop. On the bottom of the mouse is a mechanism, usually a small ball, that senses the movement of the mouse (Figure 4-2).

Electronic circuits in the mouse translate the movement of the mouse into signals that are sent to the computer. The computer uses the mouse signals to move the pointer on the screen in the same direction as the mouse (Figure 4-3). When you move the mouse left on the surface of the desktop or mouse pad, the pointer moves left on the screen. When you move the mouse right, the pointer moves right, and so on. The mouse usually is attached to the computer by a cable, but wireless mouse units also exist.

The top of the mouse contains one or more buttons. By using the mouse to move the pointer on the screen and then pressing, or **clicking**, the buttons on the mouse, you can perform actions such as pressing buttons, making menu selections, editing a document, and moving, or **dragging**, data from one location in a document to another. To press and release a mouse button twice without moving the mouse is called **double-clicking**. Double-clicking can be used to perform actions such as starting a program or opening a document. The function of the buttons can be changed to accommodate right- and left-handed people.

The primary advantage of a mouse is that it is easy to use. With a little practice, you can use a mouse to point to locations on the screen just as easily as using a finger.

Three disadvantages of the mouse exist. The first is that it requires empty desk space where it can be moved about. The second disadvantage is that you must remove a hand from the keyboard and place it on the mouse whenever the pointer is to be moved or a command is to be given. A third disadvantage is that mouse units must be cleaned to remove dust and dirt from the ball mechanism.

For details of the mouse pointing device, visit the Discovering Computers Chapter 4 inCyber page (http://www.scsite.com/dc/ch4/incyber.htm) and click Mouse.

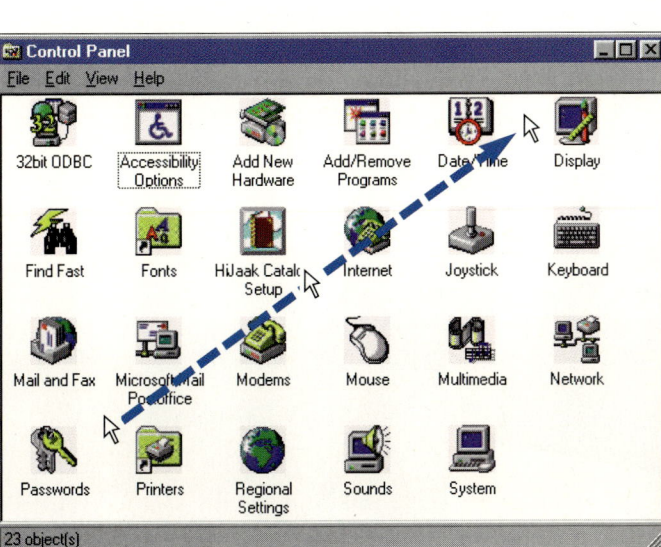
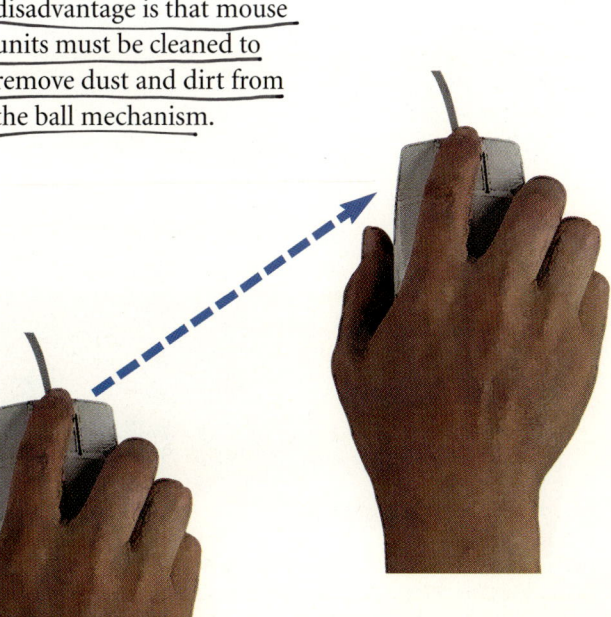

Figure 4-3
As the mouse is moved diagonally across a flat surface, the mouse pointer on the screen moves in a similar direction.

Trackball

A **trackball** is a pointing device like a mouse only with the ball on the top of the device instead of the bottom (Figure 4-4).

To move the pointer with a trackball, you rotate the ball in the desired direction. With a mouse, you have to move the entire device. To accommodate movement with both the fingers and palms of a hand, the ball on top of a trackball usually is larger than the ball on the bottom of a mouse. As with the mouse, the trackball occasionally needs to be cleaned. The main advantage of a trackball over a mouse is that it does not require clear desk space. Smaller trackball units have been designed for use on portable computers (Figure 4-5).

> For a detailed description of trackballs, visit the Discovering Computers Chapter 4 inCyber page (http://www.scsite.com/dc/ch4/incyber.htm) and click Trackball.

Figure 4-4
The trackball is like a mouse turned upside down. You rotate the ball to move the insertion point and then press one of the buttons on the side of the device.

Figure 4-5
Smaller trackball units often are used on portable computers.

Touchpad

A **touchpad**, sometimes called a **trackpad**, is a flat rectangular surface that senses the movement of a finger on its surface to control the movement of the insertion point (Figure 4-6). Most touchpads use an electronic grid underneath the surface of the pad to sense the location and movement of the finger. Some touchpads have buttons you can click like a mouse, while others have you indicate a click by tapping the finger on the touchpad surface. Touchpads often are built into portable computers, but stand-alone touch-pads that attach to any PC also are available.

Figure 4-6
Portable computers often use touch-pads to control the movement of the pointer. Electronics underneath the surface of the pad sense the movement of a finger and move the pointer in a corresponding direction.

Pointing Stick

A **pointing stick**, sometimes called a **trackpoint** or **an isometric pointing device**, is a small device shaped like a pencil eraser that moves the insertion point as pressure is applied to the device (Figure 4-7). Pointing stick devices are used on portable computers because they require little space. Another advantage is they require no cleaning as mouse units and trackballs do.

Figure 4-7
Pointing stick devices move the on-screen pointer by sensing the direction and amount of pressure applied to a small eraser-shaped device located within the keyboard.

pointing stick

Joystick

A **joystick** uses the movement of a vertical stem to direct the pointer. Joysticks often are used with computer games and have buttons you can press to activate certain events, depending on the software (Figure 4-8).

Figure 4-8
Joysticks often are used with computer games to control the actions of a vehicle or player.

Pen Input

Pen input devices have become increasingly popular in recent years and eventually may be part of most if not all computers. Almost all of the personal digital assistant (PDA) class of personal computers use a pen. One advantage is that people who have never used a computer adapt naturally to using a pen as an input device (Figure 4-9).

Pen input devices can be used in three ways: to input data using hand-written characters and shapes that the computer can recognize, as a pointing device like a mouse to select items on the screen, and to gesture, which is a way of issuing commands.

Pen computers use special hardware and software to interpret the movement of the pen. When the pen touches the screen, it causes two layers of electrically conductive material to make contact. The computer determines the coordinates for the contact point and darkens that location on the screen. The darkened area on the screen is referred to as **ink**. Hand-written characters are converted into computer text by software that matches the shape of the hand-written character to a database of known characters or shapes. If the software is unable to recognize a particular character, it asks you to identify it. Most **handwriting recognition software** can be taught to recognize an individual's unique style of writing. In addition to working with character input, graphic recognition software used on pen input devices can improve drawings by cleaning up uneven lines. Wavy lines can be straightened and circles can be made perfectly round. Perhaps the most natural use of the pen is as a pointing device. When used this way, the pen functions like a mouse. Pressing the pen against the screen once or twice is the same as clicking the buttons on a mouse.

Gestures are special symbols made with the pen that issue a command, such as delete text. As shown in Figure 4-10, many gestures are identical to those used for manual text editing. Gestures can be more efficient than using a mouse or keyboard because they not only identify where you want to make a change but also the type of change to be made.

Pen input devices already have been adapted to many applications that were previously not computerized. Any application where a form has to be filled out is a candidate for a pen input device. One of the larger markets for pen input devices is mobile workers, who spend most of their time away from their desks or offices.

inCyber

For a discussion of pen input devices, visit the Discovering Computers Chapter 4 inCyber page (http://www.scsite.com/dc/ch4/incyber.htm) and click Pen Input.

Figure 4-9
Pen input systems allow you to use a pen to enter data or select processing options without using a keyboard. This method is easy to learn by individuals who have worked with a pencil and paper.

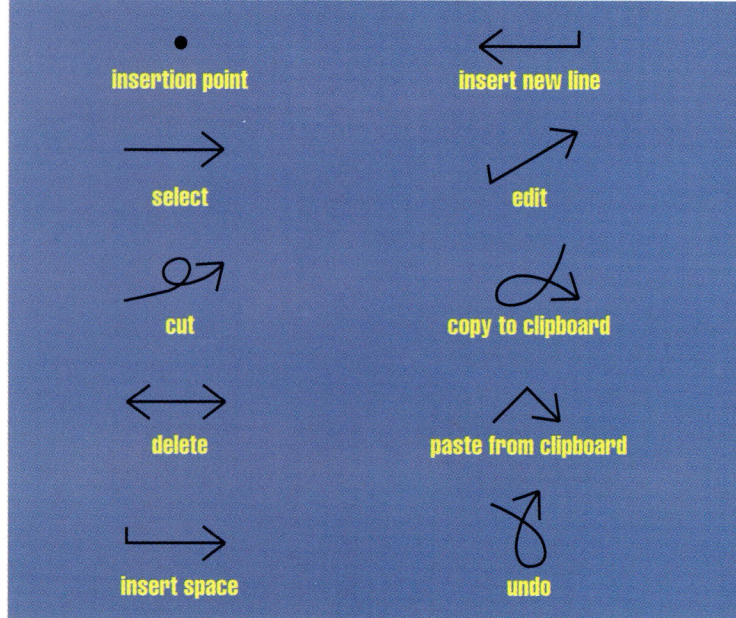

Figure 4-10
Gestures are a way of issuing commands with a pen. Gestures not only tell what you want done but also where you want to make a change. The arrows indicate the direction of the pen movement.

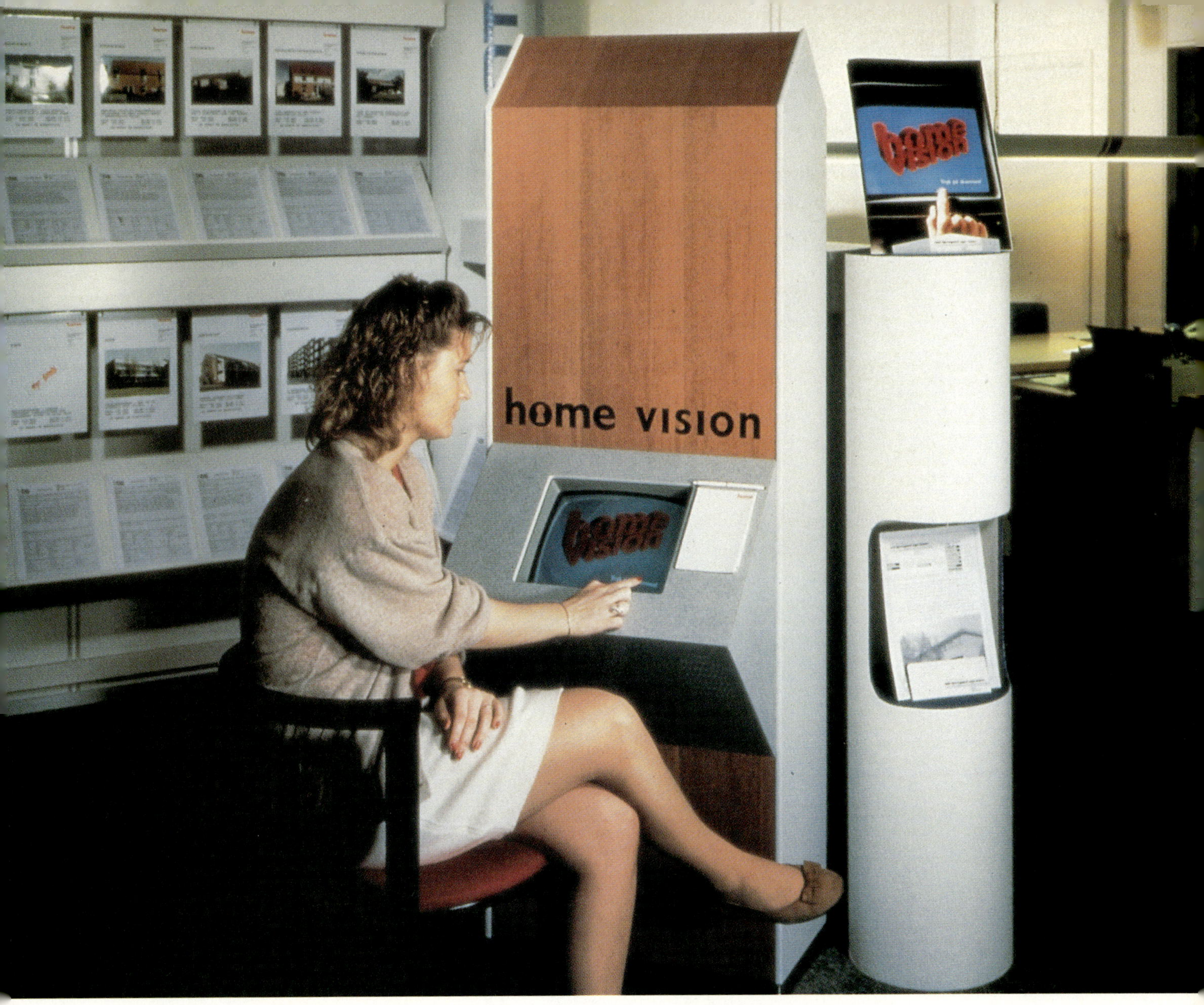

Touch Screen

A **touch screen** allows you to touch areas of the screen to enter data. They let you interact with a computer by the touch of a finger rather than typing on a keyboard or moving a mouse. You enter data by touching words or numbers or locations identified on the screen.

Several electronic techniques change a touch on the screen into electronic impulses that can be interpreted by the computer software. One technique uses beams of infrared light that are projected across the surface of the screen. A finger or other object touching the screen interrupts the beams, generating an electronic signal. This signal identifies the location on the screen where the touch occurred. The software interprets the signal and performs the required function.

Touch screens are not used to enter large amounts of data. They are used, however, for applications where you must issue a command to the software to perform a particular task or must choose from a list of options. Touch screens have been installed successfully in kiosks used to provide information in hotels, airports, and other public locations (Figure 4-11).

Figure 4-11
Touch screens frequently are used for information kiosks. Users touch the screen and receive information about the chosen topic.

For an explanation of touch screens, visit the Discovering Computers Chapter 4 inCyber page (http://www.scsite.com/dc/ch4/incyber.htm) and click Touch Screen.

Light Pen

A **light pen** is used by touching it on the display screen to create or modify graphics (Figure 4-12). A light cell in the tip of the pen senses light from the screen to determine the pen's location. You can use the light pen to select processing options or draw on the screen.

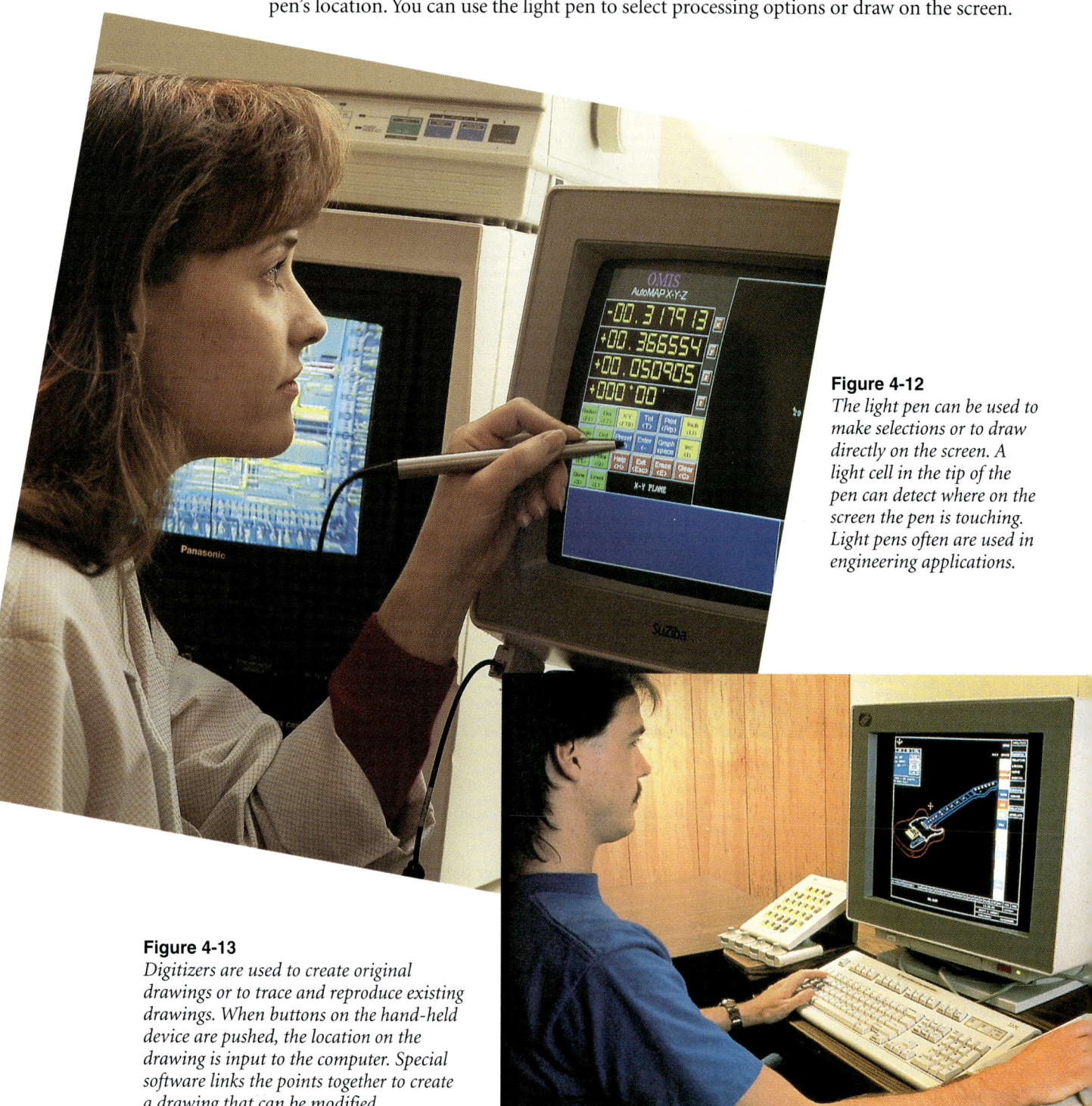

Figure 4-12
The light pen can be used to make selections or to draw directly on the screen. A light cell in the tip of the pen can detect where on the screen the pen is touching. Light pens often are used in engineering applications.

Figure 4-13
Digitizers are used to create original drawings or to trace and reproduce existing drawings. When buttons on the hand-held device are pushed, the location on the drawing is input to the computer. Special software links the points together to create a drawing that can be modified.

Digitizer

A **digitizer** converts points, lines, and curves from a sketch, drawing, or photograph to digital impulses and transmits them to a computer (Figure 4-13). You indicate the data to be input by using a pen-like stylus or pressing one or more buttons on the hand-held digitizer device. Mapmakers and architects use digitizers for their precision tracing capabilities.

POINTING DEVICES **4.11**

inCyber

For information on graphic tablets, visit the Discovering Computers Chapter 4 inCyber page (http://www.scsite.com/dc/ch4/incyber.htm) and click Graphics Tablet.

Figure 4-14
The color template on the graphics tablet allows you to select processing options by placing a hand-held device over the appropriate location on the tablet and pressing a button.

Graphics Tablet

A **graphics tablet** works in a manner similar to a digitizer, but it also contains unique characters and commands that can be generated automatically by the person using the tablet (Figure 4-14).

The graphics tablet and the digitizer both use absolute referencing. That is, each location on the tablet and digitizer corresponds to a specific location on the screen. The previously discussed touchpad, which looks like a small graphics tablet, uses relative referencing. On the touchpad, it does not matter where you first place your finger; the touchpad measures only the direction of the finger movement. Graphics tablets commonly are used in computer-aided design applications by architects and designers.

Source Data Automation

Source data automation, or **source data collection**, refers to procedures and equipment designed to make the input process more efficient by eliminating the manual entry of data. Instead of a person entering data using a keyboard, source data automation equipment captures data directly from its original form, such as an invoice or an inventory tag. The original form is called a **source document**. In addition to making the input process more efficient,

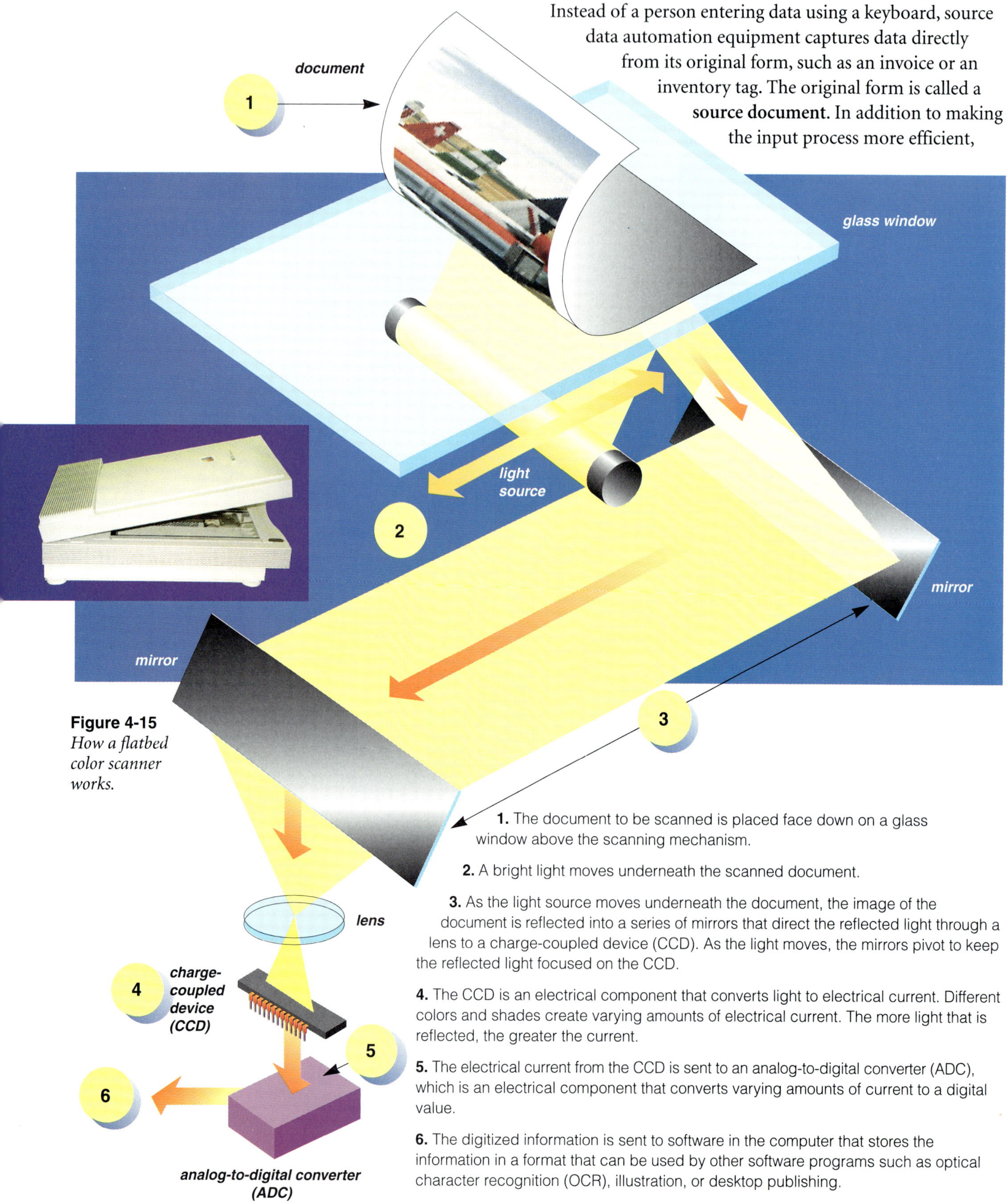

Figure 4-15
How a flatbed color scanner works.

1. The document to be scanned is placed face down on a glass window above the scanning mechanism.

2. A bright light moves underneath the scanned document.

3. As the light source moves underneath the document, the image of the document is reflected into a series of mirrors that direct the reflected light through a lens to a charge-coupled device (CCD). As the light moves, the mirrors pivot to keep the reflected light focused on the CCD.

4. The CCD is an electrical component that converts light to electrical current. Different colors and shades create varying amounts of electrical current. The more light that is reflected, the greater the current.

5. The electrical current from the CCD is sent to an analog-to-digital converter (ADC), which is an electrical component that converts varying amounts of current to a digital value.

6. The digitized information is sent to software in the computer that stores the information in a format that can be used by other software programs such as optical character recognition (OCR), illustration, or desktop publishing.

source data automation usually results in a higher input accuracy rate. The following section describes some of the equipment used for source data automation.

Image Scanner

An **image scanner**, sometimes called a **page scanner**, is an input device that can electronically capture an entire page of text or images such as photographs or art work (Figure 4-15).

Both monochrome and color units are available. The scanner converts the text or image on the original document into digital data that can be stored on a disk and processed by the computer. The digitized data can be printed, displayed separately, or merged into another document for editing. Hand-held devices that can scan a portion of a page also are available (Figure 4-16). **Image processing systems** use scanners to capture and electronically file documents such as legal documents or documents with signatures or drawings. These systems are like electronic filing cabinets that allow you to rapidly access and review exact reproductions of the original documents (Figure 4-17). Besides the actual image, these systems record information about the document such as the type of document, the date it was processed, and who submitted the document. This information can be used to retrieve the document image.

Figure 4-16
A hand-held scanner enters text or graphics less than a page wide. Software allows you to join separately scanned items to make up a complete page.

For a description of image scanners, visit the Discovering Computers Chapter 4 inCyber page (http://www.scsite.com/dc/ch4/incyber.htm) and click Image Scanner.

Figure 4-17
Image processing systems record and store an exact copy of a document. These systems often are used by insurance companies that may need to refer to any of hundreds of thousands of documents.

Optical Recognition

Optical recognition devices use a light source to read codes, marks, and characters and convert them into digital data that can be processed by a computer.

Optical Codes Optical codes use a pattern or symbols to represent data. The most common optical code is the bar code. A bar code consists of a set of vertical lines and spaces of different widths. The bar code usually is either printed on the product package or attached to the product with a label or tag. The bar code reader uses the light pattern from the bar code lines to identify the item. Several different types of bar codes exist, but the most familiar is the **universal product code** (UPC). The UPC bar code, used for grocery and retail items, can be translated into a ten-digit number that identifies the product manufacturer and product number (Figure 4-18).

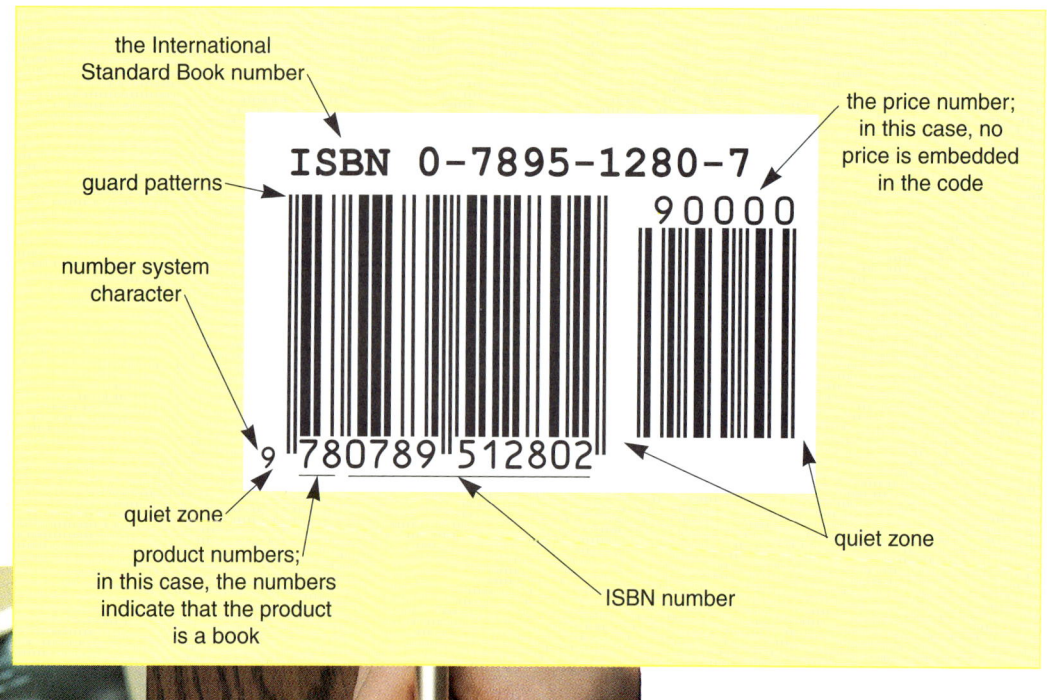

Figure 4-18
Bar codes are a type of optical code found on most grocery and retail items. The universal product code (UPC) bar code is the most common. The numbers printed at the bottom identify the manufacturer and the product and can be used to input the item if the bar code reader fails.

Figure 4-19
Three different types of bar code readers are shown here: a hand-held gun, a hand-held wand, and a stationary reader set in the counter of a grocery store.

Optical code scanning equipment includes light guns that can be aimed at the code and wands that are passed over the code. Grocery stores often use stationary units set in a counter. Figure 4-19 shows several different types of bar code readers.

Optical Mark Recognition (OMR) Optical mark recognition (OMR) devices often are used to process questionnaires or test answer sheets (Figure 4-20). Carefully placed marks on the form indicate responses to questions and can be read and interpreted by a computer program and matched against a previously entered answer key sheet.

Optical Character Recognition (OCR) Optical character recognition (OCR) devices are scanners that read typewritten, computer-printed, and in some cases hand-printed characters from ordinary documents. OCR devices range from large machines that can automatically read thousands of documents per minute to hand-held wands.

An OCR device scans the shape of a character, compares it with a predefined shape stored in memory, and converts the character into the corresponding computer code. The standard OCR typeface, called OCR-A, is illustrated in Figure 4-21. The characters can be read easily by both people and machines. OCR-B is a set of standard characters widely used in Europe and Japan.

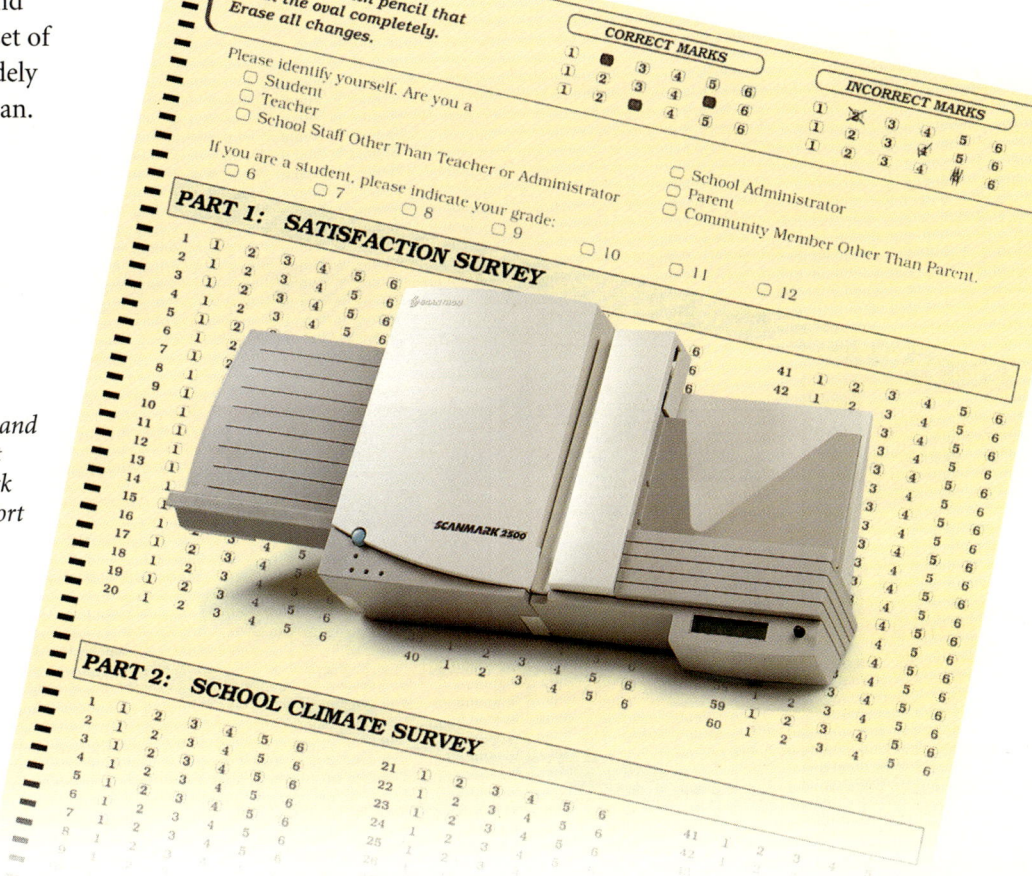

inCyber

For an explanation of optical character recognition devices, visit the Discovering Computers Chapter 4 inCyber page (http://www.scsite.com/dc/ch4/incyber.htm) and click OCR.

Figure 4-20
Optical mark recognition devices often are used for processing questionnaires and test answer sheets. For test scores, the reader can mark the incorrect answers, report the number of correct answers, and report the average score of all tests.

ABCDEFGHIJKLMNOPQRSTUVWXYZ
1234567890-=▮;',./

Figure 4-21
A portion of the OCR-A character set. Notice how the characters B and 8, S and 5, and the number 0 and the letter O, are designed differently so the reading device easily can distinguish between them.

OCR is frequently used for **turn-around documents**, which are documents designed to be returned (*turned around*) to the organization that created them. Examples of such documents are billing statements from credit card companies and department stores. The portion of the statement that you send back with your payment has your account number, total balance, and payment information printed in optical characters.

OCR Software OCR **software** is used with image scanners to convert text images into data that can be processed by word processing software. OCR software works as follows: First, the entire page of text is scanned. At this point, the page is considered a single graphic image, just like a picture, and individual words are not identified. Next, the software tries to identify individual letters and words. The methods used for word recognition are quite sophisticated and can include determining the most likely word based on previously identified words. Figure 4-22 shows how one OCR software package displays the status during the identification process. Modern OCR software has a very high success rate and usually can identify more than 99% of the scanned material. Finally, the OCR software displays the text that it could not identify. When you make the final corrections, the document can be saved in the application software format of your choice. Besides word processing files, OCR software can create spreadsheet and database files, as well.

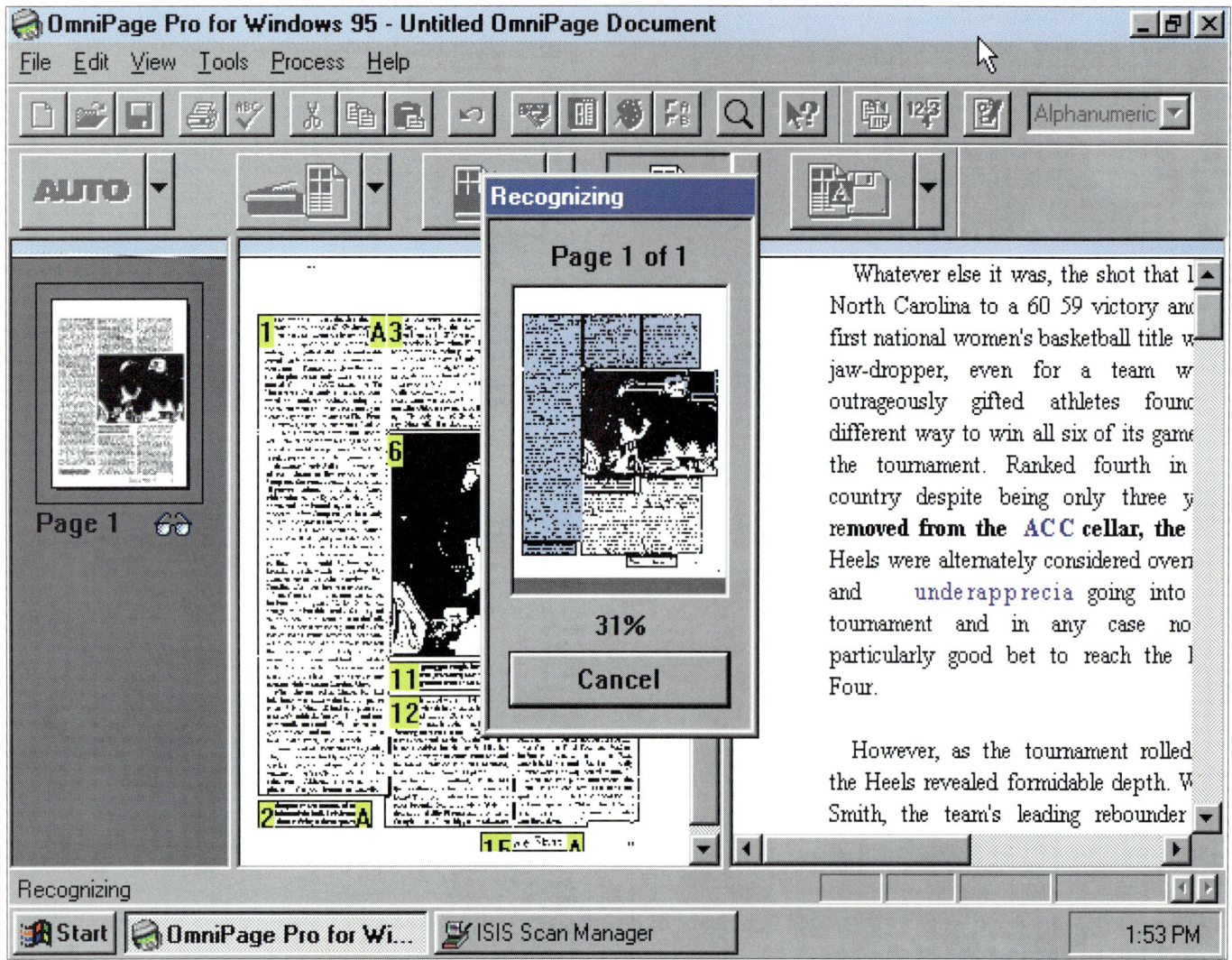

Figure 4-22
This screen shows OCR software in the process of converting a page of scanned text into data that can be input to word processing software. The entire page of text, including a photograph, was converted in less than ten seconds; much faster than the text could be entered using the keyboard.

Magnetic Ink Character Recognition (MICR)

Magnetic ink character recognition (MICR) characters use a special ink that can be magnetized during processing. MICR is used almost exclusively by the banking industry for processing checks. Blank (unused) checks already have the bank code, account number, and check number printed in MICR characters across the bottom. When the check is processed by the bank, the amount of the check is also printed in the lower right corner (Figure 4-23). Together, this information is read by MICR reader/sorter machines as part of the check-clearing process.

> **inCyber**
> For details on magnetic ink character recognition, visit the Discovering Computers Chapter 4 inCyber page (http://www.scsite.com/dc/ch4/incyber.htm) and click MICR.

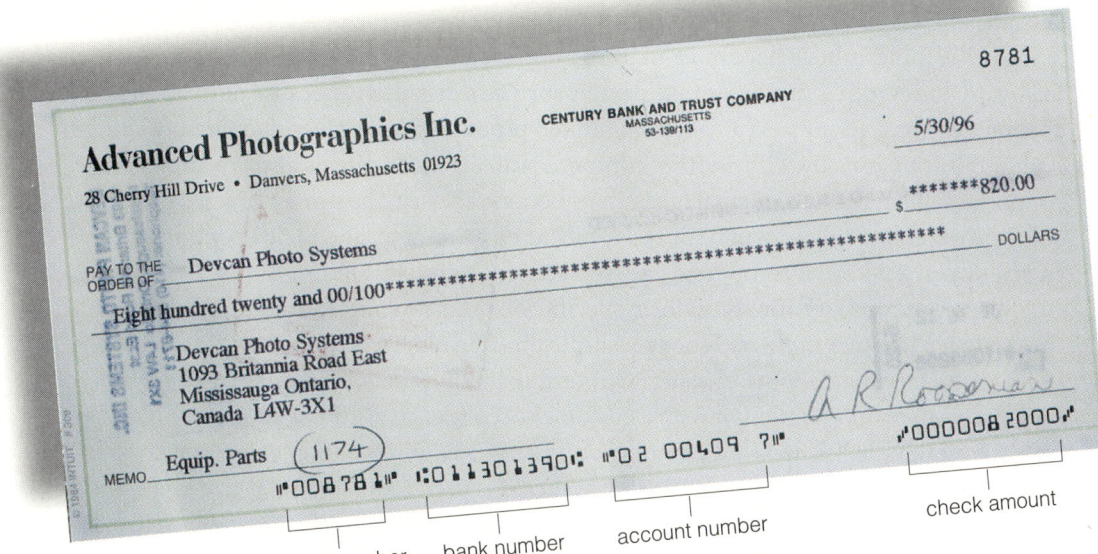

Figure 4-23
The MICR characters printed along the bottom edge indicate the bank, account number, and amount of the check. The amount in the lower right corner is added after the check is cashed. The other MICR numbers are pre-printed on the check.

Data Collection Devices

Data collection devices are designed and used for obtaining data at the site where the transaction or event being reported takes place. Often, data collection equipment is used in factories, warehouses, or other locations where heat, humidity, and cleanliness is difficult to control (Figure 4-24). Data collection equipment must be rugged and easy to use because often it is operated by persons whose primary task is not entering data.

Figure 4-24
Data collection devices often are used in factories and warehouses where heat, humidity, and cleanliness is difficult to control.

Terminals

Terminals, sometimes called **display terminals** or **video display terminals** (VDTs), consist of a keyboard and a screen. They fall into three basic categories: dumb terminals, intelligent terminals, and special-purpose terminals. The following sections explain each type.

A **dumb terminal** consists of a keyboard and a display screen you can use to enter and transmit data to or receive and display data from a computer to which it is connected. A dumb terminal has no independent processing capability or secondary storage and cannot function as an independent device (Figure 4-25). Dumb terminals often are connected to minicomputers, mainframe, or supercomputers that perform the processing and then send the output back to the dumb terminal.

Intelligent terminals have built-in processing capabilities and often contain not only the keyboard and screen, but also storage devices such as a disk drive. Because of their built-in capabilities, these terminals can perform limited processing tasks when they are not communicating directly with another computer. Intelligent terminals also are known as **programmable terminals** or **smart terminals** because they can be programmed by the software developer to perform basic tasks, including arithmetic and logic operations. In recent years, personal computers have replaced many intelligent terminals.

Special-purpose terminals perform specific jobs and contain features uniquely designed for use in a particular industry. The special-purpose terminal shown in Figure 4-26 is called a point-of-sale terminal. **Point-of-sale (POS) terminals** allow data to be entered at the time and place where the transaction with a customer occurs, such as in fast-food restaurants or hotels, for example. Point-of-sale terminals and serve as input to either computers located at the place of business or elsewhere. The data entered is used to maintain sales records, update inventory, make automatic calculations such as sales tax, verify credit, and perform other activities associated with the sales transactions and critical to running the business. Automatic teller machines (ATMs) are another kind of special-purpose terminal that allow you to complete financial transactions and other banking-related activities. You input data into the ATM using a bank card with a magnetic strip and a specialized keyboard. Both point-of-sale terminals and ATMs are designed to be easy to operate, requiring little technical knowledge.

Figure 4-25
A dumb terminal has no independent processing capability and cannot function as a stand-alone device. Dumb terminals usually are connected to larger computer systems.

Figure 4-26
Point-of-sale terminals usually are designed for a specific type of business, such as a restaurant, hotel, or retail store. Keys are labeled to assist the user in recording transactions.

Other Input Devices

Although characters (text and numbers) are still the primary form of input data, the use of sound and image data is increasing. To capture sound and image data, special input devices are required to convert the input into a digital form that can be processed by the computer. For personal computers, these input devices consist primarily of electronics contained on a separate card, such as a **sound card** or **video card**, that is installed in the computer. These cards convert the sound or video input into digital data that can be stored and processed by the computer.

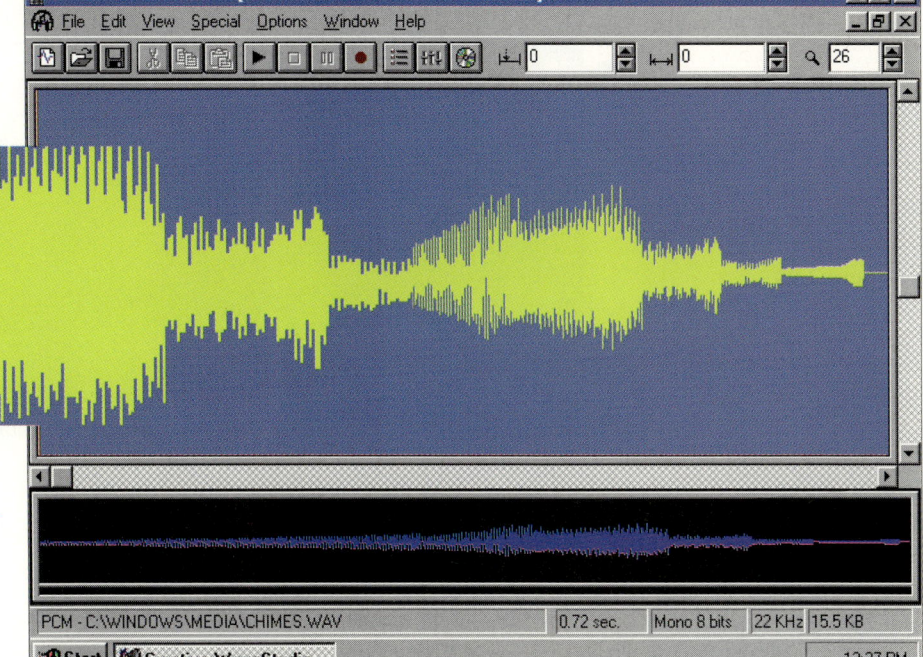

Sound Input

Sounds usually are recorded with a microphone connected to the sound card or by directly connecting a sound device, such as an electronic music keyboard, to the sound card. Sound editing software (Figure 4-27) allows you to change the sound after it is recorded.

Figure 4-27
Sound editing software allows you to change sounds that have been digitally recorded. Sounds can be copied, speeded up, slowed down, or have special effects added, such as echo or fade. This screen represents the sound of chimes reversed with echo added.

Voice Input

Voice input, sometimes referred to as speech or voice recognition, allows you to enter data and issue commands to the computer with spoken words (Figure 4-28). Some experts think that eventually voice input may be the most common way to operate a computer. Their belief is based on the fact that people can speak much faster than they can type (approximately 200 words per minute speaking and only 40 words per minute for the average typist). In addition, speaking is a more natural means of communicating than using a keyboard, which takes some time to learn. Many telephone directory assistance services now use voice input. You are asked to give the city and name of the person or business you are calling, and your voice command starts a database search to locate the appropriate telephone number.

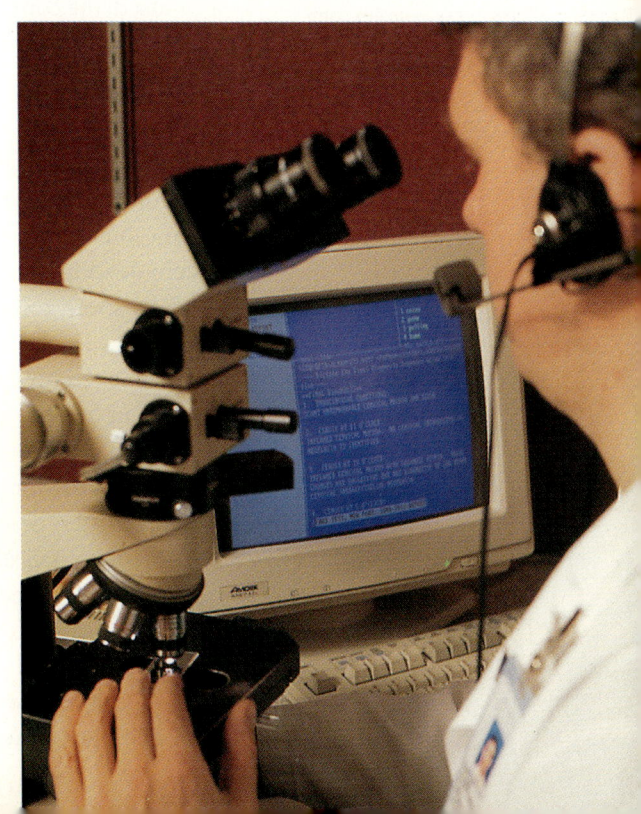

Figure 4-28
Many health professionals now use voice input to enter into the computer the numerous records that must be maintained on patients.

4.20 CHAPTER 4 – INPUT AND OUTPUT

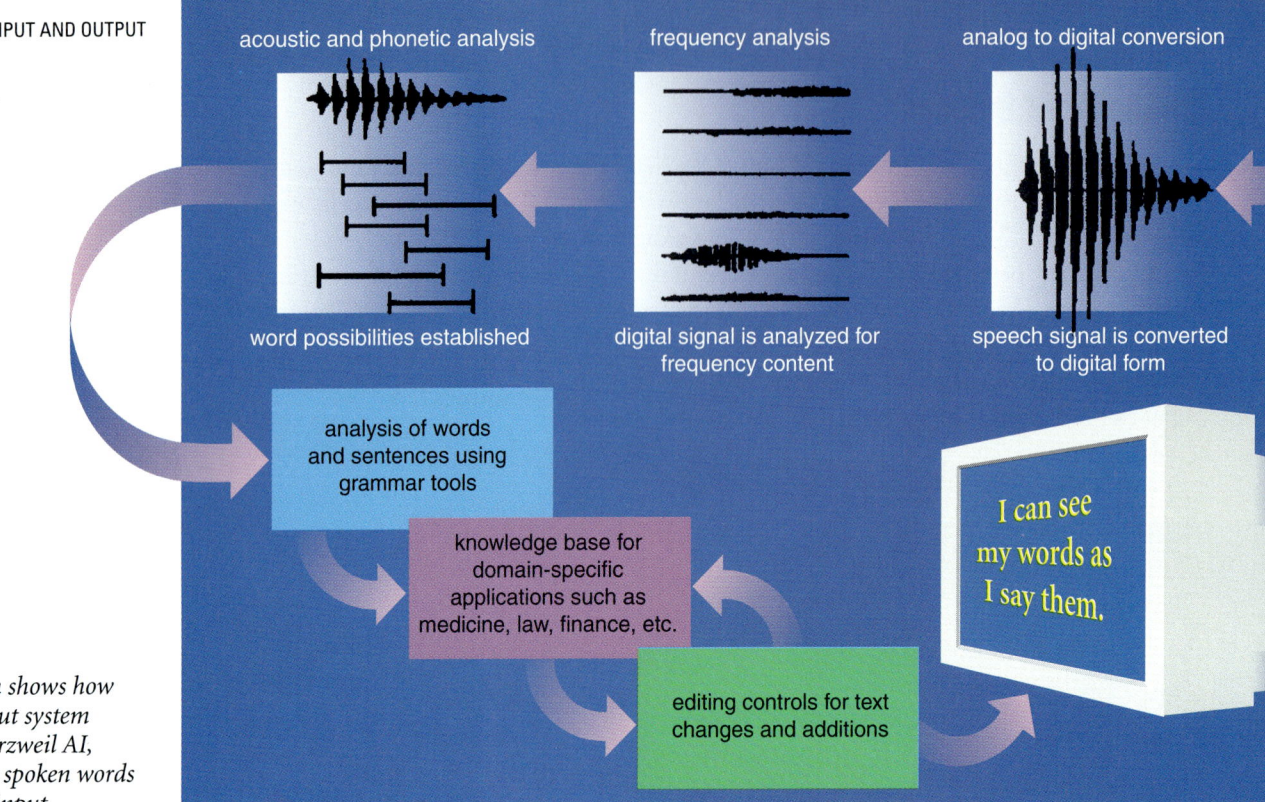

Figure 4-29
This diagram shows how one voice input system company, Kurzweil AI, Inc., converts spoken words to computer input.

For an explanation of voice input systems, visit the Discovering Computers Chapter 4 inCyber page (http://www.scsite.com/dc/ch4/incyber.htm) and click Voice Input.

Most voice input systems use a combination of hardware and software to convert spoken words into data that the computer can process. The conversion process used by one voice input system developer, shown in Figure 4-29, is as follows:

1. Your voice, consisting of sound waves, is converted into digital form by **digital signal processing** (**DSP**) circuits that are usually on a separate board that has been added to the computer.

2. The digitized voice input is compared against patterns stored in the voice systems database.

3. Grammar rules are used to resolve possible word conflicts. Based on how a word was used, the computer usually can identify the correct word in cases of words that sound alike such as *to*, *too*, and *two*.

4. Unrecognized words are presented to you to identify.

With many voice input systems, especially the lower cost systems with limited vocabularies, you have to train the system to recognize your voice. For each of the words in the vocabulary, you speak the word. After each word has been spoken several times, the system develops a digital pattern for the word that can be stored on a storage device. When you later speak a word to the system to request a particular action, the system compares the word to the words that were previously entered. When it finds a match, the software performs the activity associated with the word. Such systems are referred to as **speaker dependent** because each person who wants to use the system has to train it to his or her voice. Larger vocabulary systems can contain up to 50,000 words and training on individual words is not practical. Instead, developers include multiple patterns, called **voice templates**, for each word. These templates include male and female voices as well as regional accents. These systems are called **speaker independent** because most users will not have to train the system to their speech patterns.

Most speech-to-text systems in use today use **discrete-speech recognition** that requires you to pause slightly between each word. **Continuous-speech recognition** systems that allow you to speak in a flowing conversational tone are not yet widely used because they require more complex software and hardware to separate and make sense of the words. Low-cost

Figure 4-30
This digital camera is used to record digital photographs of documents, products, or people. The camera is connected to a video board installed in the computer.

continuous-speech recognition systems are expected to be available for personal computers by the year 2000.

Beyond continuous-voice recognition is what is called natural language voice interface. A **natural language voice interface** allows you to ask a question and have the computer not only convert the question to understandable words but to interpret the question and give an appropriate response. For example, think how powerful and easy it would be to use a system if you simply could ask, How soon can we ship 200 red aluminum frame mountain bikes to Boston? Think about how many different pieces of data the computer might have to pull together to generate a correct response. Such natural language voice recognition systems are not commercially available now but are being developed using powerful computers and sophisticated software.

Biological Feedback Input

Biological feedback input devices work in combination with special software to translate movements, temperature, or even skin-based electrical signals into input. Devices such as gloves, body suits, and eyeglasses are used for biological feedback input. Still another device uses a sensor placed around a user's finger. As the user changes his or her thoughts, the electrical signals coming from the user's skin change and are deciphered into movements on the computer screen. Biological feedback input devices allow for even more natural input than voice recognition systems.

Digital Camera

Digital cameras record photographs in the form of digital data that can be stored on a computer. No chemical-based film is used. Some digital cameras, called field cameras, are portable and look similar to traditional film cameras. Other digital cameras, called studio cameras, are stationary and are connected directly to a computer (Figure 4-30). Many companies use digital cameras to record images of their products for online catalogs on the World Wide Web or to record photos of their employees for personnel records.

Video Input

Video material is input to the computer using a video camera or a video recorder using previously recorded material. Video data requires tremendous amounts of storage space, which is why video segments, or *clips*, in personal computer applications often are limited to only a few seconds. Improvements in video electronics and software, and larger capacity storage devices will enable movie length video data to eventually become available. Video applications currently under development include video repair manuals. Rather than just looking at a photo or diagram, you can view narrated video clips on how to disassemble and repair a piece of equipment.

Electronic Whiteboards

An **electronic whiteboard** is a modified conference room whiteboard that uses built-in scanners to record text and drawings in a file on an attached computer (Figure 4-31). The drawing is recorded and displayed as it is created and can be printed or stored for future use. Unique reflective collars near the tips of the dry-erase marking pens allow the sensors to identify and record different colors. The eraser also has an identifying collar that enables the computer to delete previously entered data in areas that the eraser covers. Communications software enables the drawing to be transmitted to a remote location.

The input devices discussed in this chapter are summarized in Figure 4-32.

Figure 4-31
An electronic whiteboard captures whatever is written on the whiteboard surface and saves it as a file on an attached computer. The file can be printed, modified, incorporated into other documents, or transmitted to other locations.

Figure 4-32
This table summarizes some of the more common input devices.

INPUT DEVICE	DESCRIPTION
Keyboard	Most commonly used input device; special keys may include numeric keypad, arrow keys, and function keys
Mouse, Trackball, Touchpad, Pointing Stick	Used to move pointer and select options
Joystick	Stem device often used as input device for games
Pen Input	Uses pen to input and edit data and select processing options
Touch Screen	User interacts with computer by touching screen with finger
Light Pen	Can be used to select options or draw on screen
Digitizer	Used to enter or edit drawings
Graphics Tablet	Digitizer with special processing options built into tablet
Image Scanner	Converts text, graphics, or photos into digital input
Optical Recognition	Uses light source to read codes, marks, and characters
MICR	Used in banking to read magnetic ink characters on checks
Data Collection	Used in factories and warehouses to input data at source
Sound Input	Converts sound into digital data
Voice Input	Converts speech into digital data
Digital Camera	Captures digital image of subject or object
Video Input	Converts video into digital data
Electronic Whiteboard	Captures anything drawn on special whiteboard

What Is Output?

Output is data that has been processed into a useful form called information that can be used by a person or a machine.

Types of Output

The type of output generated from the computer depends on the needs of the user and the hardware and software that are used. Two common types of output are reports and graphics. These types of output can be printed on a printer or displayed on a screen. Printed output is called **hard copy** and output that is displayed on a screen is called **soft copy**. Other types of output include audio (sound) and video (visual images). Each of these types of output are discussed in the following sections.

Reports

A **report** is information presented in an organized form. Most people think of reports as items printed on paper or displayed on a screen. For example, word processing documents can be considered reports. Information printed on forms such as invoices or payroll checks also can be considered types of reports. One way to classify reports is by who uses them. An **internal report** is used by individuals in the performance of their jobs. For example, a daily sales report that is distributed to sales personnel is an internal report because it is used only by personnel within the organization. An **external report** is used outside the organization. Sales invoices that are printed and mailed to customers are external reports.

Reports also can be classified by the way they present information. The four types of common reports are: narrative reports, detail reports, summary reports, and exception reports.

Narrative reports may contain some graphic or numeric information, but are primarily text-based reports. These reports, usually prepared with word processing software, include the various types of correspondence commonly used in business such as memos, letters, and sales proposals. Detail, summary, and exception reports are used primarily to organize and present numeric-based information.

In a **detail report**, each line on the report usually corresponds to one record that has been processed. For example, companies that sell products keep a sales log that shows specific information about each sale. Detail reports contain a great deal of information and can be quite lengthy. They are usually required by individuals who need access to the day-to-day information that reflects the operating status of the organization. For example, people in the warehouse of a distributor should have access to the location and number of units on hand for

DETAIL INVENTORY REPORT
by Part Number

Part#	Description	Location	Quantity On Hand
87143	ink-jet printer	Portland	1,400
87143	ink-jet printer	San Francisco	80
87143	ink-jet printer	Seattle	550
89620	laser printer	Portland	750
89620	laser printer	Seattle	250
93042	17-inch monitor	Portland	635
93042	17-inch monitor	San Francisco	240
93042	17-inch monitor	Seattle	50

one line printed for each part at each location

Figure 4-33
This detail report shows quantities for each part number and each location.

each product. The Detail Inventory Report in Figure 4-33 on the previous page contains a line for each warehouse location for each part number. Separate inventory records exist for each line on the report. Many software programs generate audit trails when they output detail reports. Audit trails provide a way to track changes made to data so you can backtrack to find the origin of specific information that appears on a report. For example, an audit trail could show that David Williams changed the inventory record for laser printers in the Seattle warehouse at 1:14 p.m. on November 27.

As the name implies, a **summary report** summarizes data. It contains totals for certain values found in the input records. The report shown in Figure 4-34 contains a summary of the total quantity on hand for each part. The information on the summary report consists of totals for each part from the information contained in the detail report in Figure 4-33. Detail reports frequently contain more information than most managers have time to review. With a summary report, however, a manager can review information quickly in summarized form.

An **exception report** contains information that is outside of *normal* user-specified values or conditions, called the *exception criteria*. Records meeting this criteria are an *exception* to the majority of the data. For example, if an organization wants to know when to reorder inventory items to avoid running out of stock, it would design an exception report. The report would tell which inventory items fell below the reorder points and therefore need to be ordered. An example of such a report is shown in Figure 4-35.

Exception reports help you focus on situations that may require immediate decisions or specific actions. The advantage of exception reports is that they save time and money. In a large department store, for example, more than 100,000 inventory items may exist. A detail report containing all inventory items could be longer than 2,000 pages. To search through the report to determine the items whose on-hand quantity was less than the reorder point would be a difficult and time-consuming task. The exception report, however, could select these items, which might number 100 to 200, and place them on a two- to four-page report that could be reviewed in just a few minutes.

Reports are also sometimes classified by how often they are produced. **Periodic reports**, also called **scheduled reports**, are produced on a regular basis such as daily, weekly, monthly, or yearly. **Ad hoc** or **on-demand reports** are created whenever they are needed for information that is not required on a scheduled basis.

Figure 4-34
The summary report contains the total on-hand quantity for each part. The report can be prepared using the same records that were used to prepare the report in Figure 4-33.

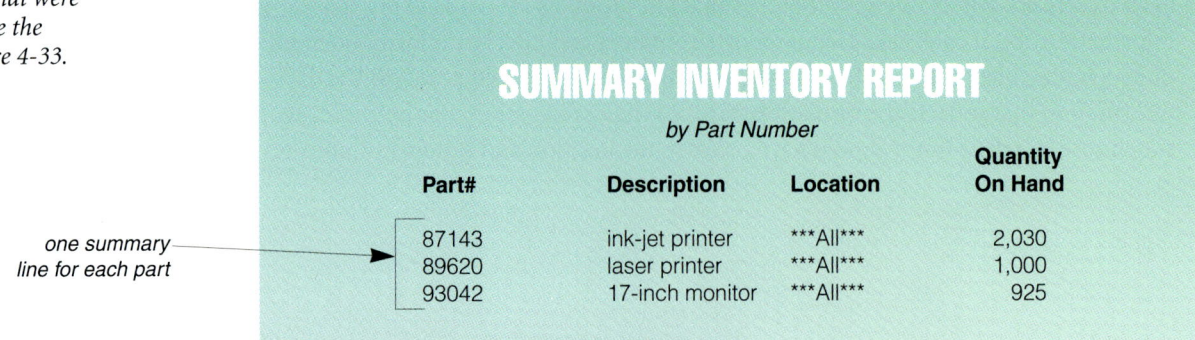

Figure 4-35
The exception report lists inventory items with an on-hand quantity below their reorder points. These parts could have been selected from thousands of inventory items. Only these parts met the exception criteria.

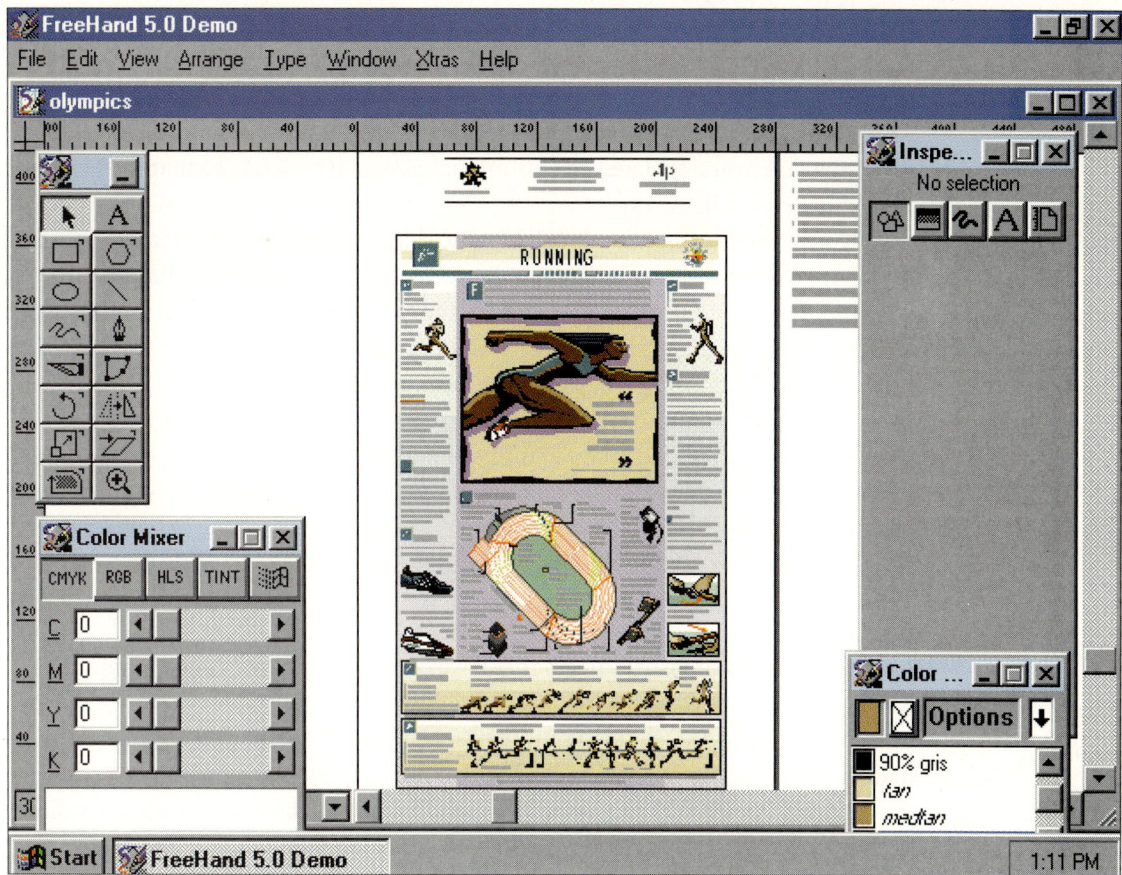

Figure 4-36
Computer drawing and paint programs often are used by professional artists to create advertising and marketing materials.

Graphics

Computer graphics are any non-text pictorial information. One of the early uses of computer graphics was for charts to help present and analyze numeric information. In recent years, computer graphics have gone far beyond charting capabilities. **Computer drawing programs** and **computer paint programs** allow an artistic user to create stunning works of art. These programs are frequently used for developing advertising and other marketing materials (Figure 4-36). Clip art and photographs also are considered types of computer graphics.

Audio Output

Audio output, consists of sounds, including words and music, produced by the computer. An audio output device on a computer is a speaker. Most personal computers come with a small (approximately two inch) speaker that usually is located behind an opening on the front or side of the system unit case. Increasingly, personal computer users are adding higher quality stereo speakers to their systems. The stereo speakers connect to a port on a sound card that works with sound, voice, and music software. Some PCs come with speakers built into the sides of the display unit.

Voice output is a type of audio output that consists of spoken words that are conveyed to you from the computer. Thus, instead of reading words on a printed report or monitor, you hear the words over earphones, the telephone, or other devices from which sound can be generated.

The data that produces voice output usually is created in one of two ways. First, a person can talk into a device that will encode the words in a digital pattern. For example, the words, *The number is*, are spoken into a microphone, and the computer software assigns a digital pattern to the words. The digital data is then stored on a disk. At a later time, the data can be retrieved from the disk and translated back from digital data into voice, so that the person listening will actually hear the words.

A second type of voice generation is called voice synthesis. **Voice synthesis** can transform words stored in memory into speech. The words are analyzed by a program that examines the letters stored in memory and generates sounds for the letter combinations. The software can apply rules of intonation and stress to make it sound as though a person were speaking. The speech is then played through speakers attached to the computer.

You may have heard voice output used by the telephone company directory assistance. Automobile and vending machine manufacturers are also incorporating voice output into their products. The potential for this type of output is great and it undoubtedly will be used in many products and services in the future.

Video Output

Video output consists of visual images that have been captured with a video input device, such as a VCR or camera, digitized, and directed to an output device such as a computer monitor (Figure 4-37). Video output also can be directed to a television monitor. Because standard televisions are not designed to handle a computer's digital signals, the video output has to be converted to an analog signal that can be displayed by the television. **High-definition television (HDTV)** sets are designed for digital signals and eventually may replace computer monitors.

Figure 4-37
This use of video output is like a video telephone system; it allows company employees to see the co-workers with whom they are talking.

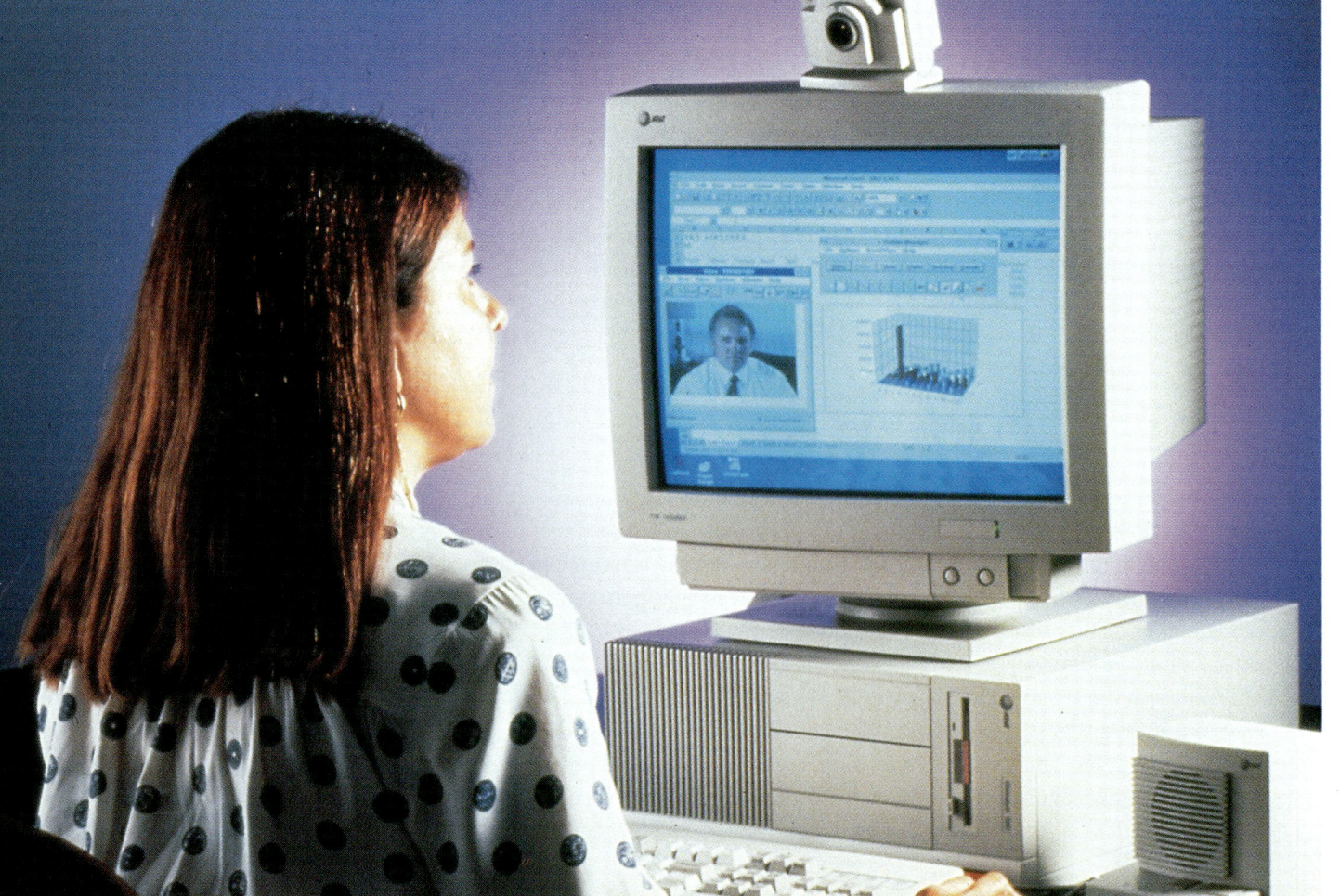

DISPLAY DEVICES **4.27**

Display Devices

A **display device** is the visual output device of a computer. The two most common types of display devices are monitors and flat panel displays.

For information on monitors, visit the Discovering Computers Chapter 4 inCyber page (http://www.scsite.com/dc/ch4/incyber.htm) and click Monitor.

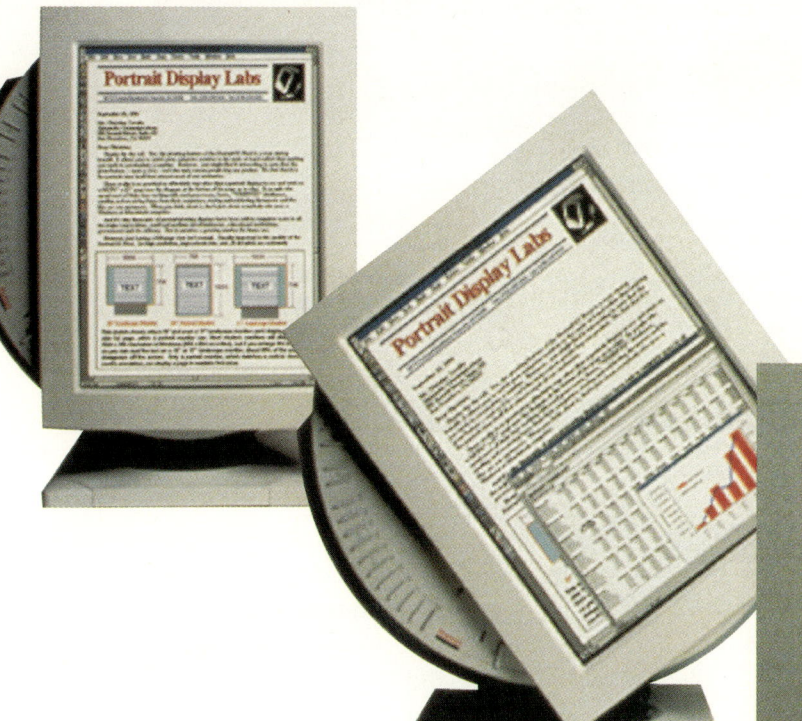

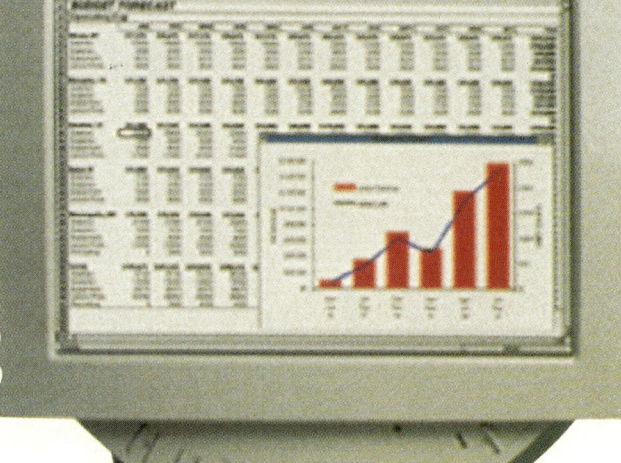

Monitors

A **monitor** looks like a television and consists of a display surface, called a screen, and a plastic or metal case to house the electrical components. A monitor differs from a terminal, discussed earlier in the section on input devices, in that a terminal also has a keyboard. A monitor often has a swivel base that allows the angle of the screen surface to be adjusted. The term **screen** is used to refer to both the surface of any display device and to any type of display device. An older term sometimes used to refer to a monitor or terminal is CRT. A **CRT**, which stands for **cathode ray tube**, is actually the large tube inside a monitor or terminal. The front part of the tube is the display surface or screen.

The more widely used monitors are equivalent in size to a 14- to 17-inch television screen. Monitors designed for use with desktop publishing, graphics, or engineering applications come in even larger sizes that can display full-sized images of one or sometimes two $8 1/2$-by-11-inch pages of data. One company even makes a monitor that can be tilted 90 degrees to display either long or wide pages or two pages side by side (Figure 4-38).

Figure 4-38
Portrait Display Labs manufactures a monitor that can be tilted 90 degrees to display long or wide pages or two pages side by side.

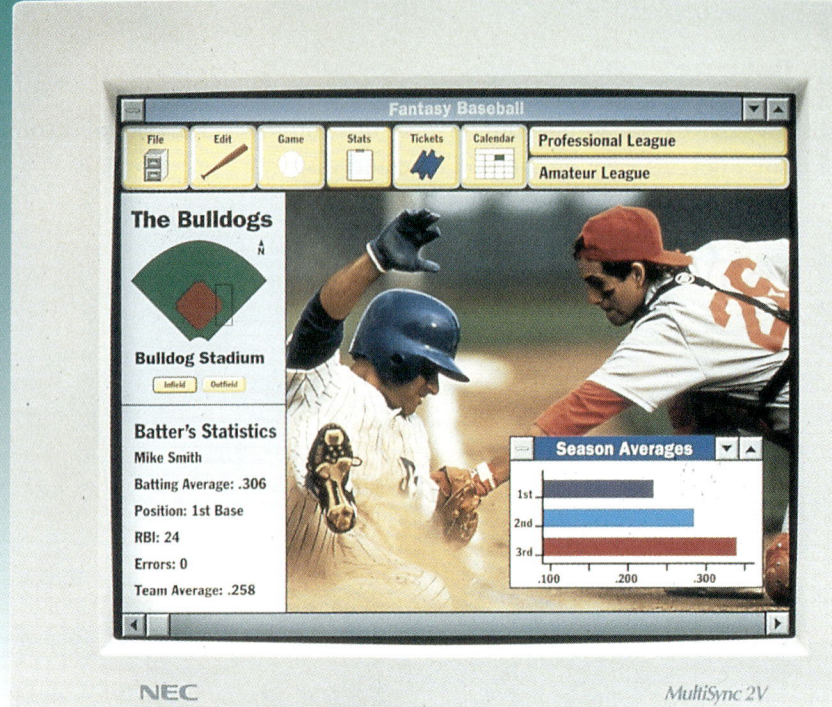

Figure 4-39
Color monitors are widely used because most of today's software is written to display information in color.

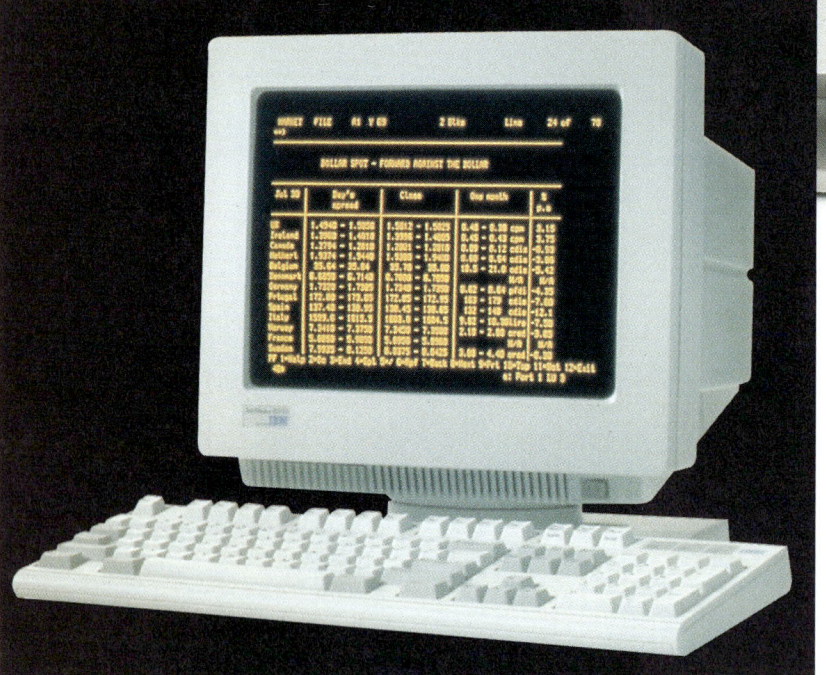

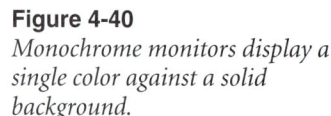

Figure 4-40
Monochrome monitors display a single color against a solid background.

A **color monitor** can display text or graphics in color (Figure 4-39). Color monitors are widely used with all types of computers because most of today's software is written to display information in color. The amount of colors a monitor can display at one time depends on the amount of memory installed on the video adapter board. The maximum number of colors that can be displayed is more than 16 million.

Monochrome monitors display a single color such as white, green, or amber characters on a black background (Figure 4-40) or black characters on a white background. Monochrome monitors are still used by business for order entry and other applications where color is not required and cost is a concern. Smaller, pen computers such as PDAs also often have monochrome monitors. Using a technique known as gray scaling, some monochrome monitors can display good quality graphic images. **Gray scaling** involves converting an image into different shades of gray like a black and white photograph.

Flat Panel Displays

A **flat panel display** is a thin display screen that does not use cathode ray tube (CRT) technology. Flat panel displays are most often used in portable computers, but larger units that can mount on a wall or other structure are also available. Two common types of technology used for flat panel displays are liquid crystal display (LCD) and gas plasma.

In a **liquid crystal display** (**LCD**), a liquid crystal is deposited between two sheets of polarizing material. When an electrical current passes between crossing wires, the liquid crystals are aligned so light cannot shine through, producing an image on the screen. LCD technology also commonly is used in digital watches, clocks, and calculators. **Active matrix** LCD screens use individual transistors to control each crystal cell. **Passive matrix** LCD screens use fewer transistors; one for each row and column. **Dual scan** is a type of passive matrix LCD screen frequently used on lower cost portable computers. Active matrix displays cost more but display a sharper, brighter picture (Figure 4-41).

Gas plasma screens substitute a neon gas for the liquid crystal material. Any locations on a grid of horizontal and vertical electrodes can be turned on to cause the neon gas to glow and produce the pixels that form an image. Gas plasma screens offer better display quality than LCD screens but are more expensive.

Figure 4-41
Active matrix LCD screens produce the best color display by using individual transistors to control each crystal cell.

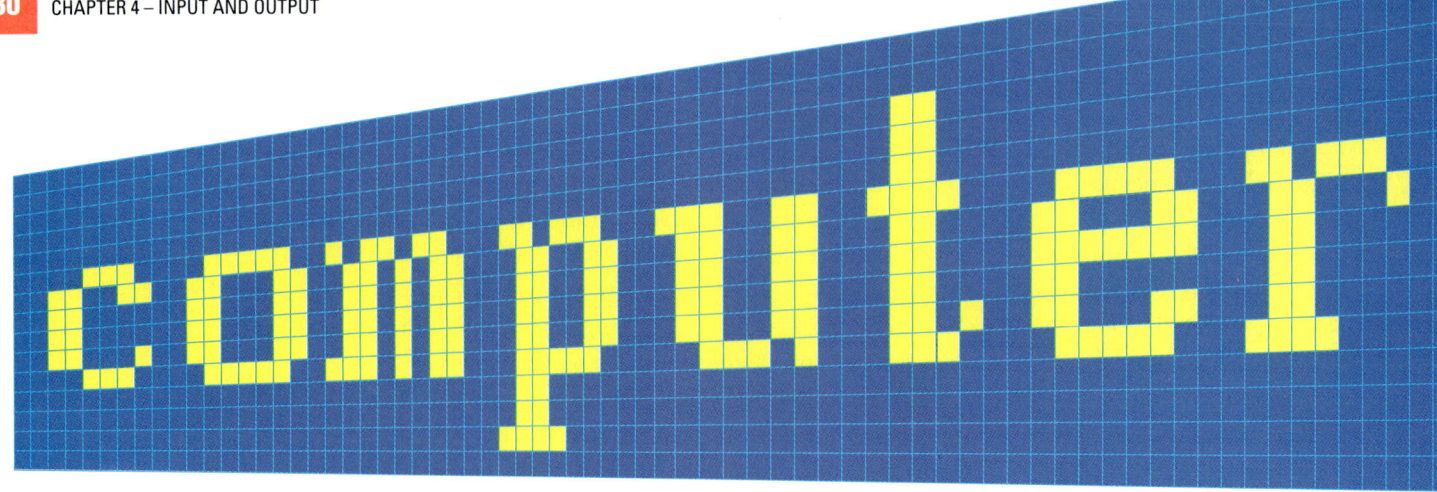

Figure 4-42
The word, computer, shown here is made up of individual picture elements (pixels). Each pixel can be turned on or off to form an image on the screen.

Resolution

Images are displayed on a monitor using patterns of lighted dots. Each dot that can be lighted is called a **picture element,** or **pixel** (Figure 4-42). The **resolution,** or clarity, of the image on a monitor is directly related to the number of pixels the monitor can display and the distance between each pixel. The distance between each pixel is called the **dot pitch.** In general, the greater the number of pixels and the smaller the dot pitch, the better the monitor resolution, because it means more pixels can be displayed. Pixels are the standard unit of measure for screen resolution. The number of pixels the monitor can display is expressed as the number of pixels horizontally and lines vertically on the screen, such as 640 (horizontal pixels) x 480 (vertical lines). The number of pixels actually displayed is determined by three things: the software program, the capability of the video adapter card, and the monitor itself.

Monitors and video adapter cards often are identified by the highest graphics display standard they support. Today, most monitors and video adapter cards support VGA and SVGA standards. **VGA (video graphics array)** devices can display a resolution of 640 x 480 pixels. **SVGA (super video graphics array)** devices can display resolutions even higher than 640 x 480 pixels. Common Super VGA resolutions are 800 x 600 and 1,024 x 768. Having a high-resolution monitor is important, especially when the monitor will be used to display graphics or other non-text information. High-resolution display can produce an image that is almost equivalent to the quality of a photograph (Figure 4-43).

Each of the video graphics standards have a specific frequency or rate at which the video signals are sent to the monitor. Some monitors are designed to only work with at a particular frequency and video standard. Other monitors, called **multiscanning** or **multisync monitors,** are designed to work within a range of frequencies and thus can work with different standards and video adapters.

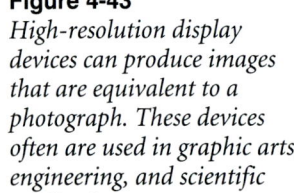

Figure 4-43
High-resolution display devices can produce images that are equivalent to a photograph. These devices often are used in graphic arts, engineering, and scientific applications.

DISPLAY DEVICES | **4.31**

How Images Are Displayed on a Monitor

Most monitors used with personal computers and terminals use cathode ray tube (CRT) technology. To show color on a monitor, each pixel must have three colored phosphor dots. These dots are the additive primary colors red, green, and blue. A separate electron gun is used for each color. By varying the intensity of the electron beam striking the phosphors, and making some colored dots glow more than others, many colors can be generated. When a color monitor produces an image, the following steps occur (Figure 4-44):

1. The image to be displayed on the monitor is sent electronically from the CPU to the video circuits (located on a video graphics card) to the cathode ray tube.

2. Electron guns at the rear of the tube generate electron beams towards the screen. The beams pass through holes in a metal screen called the *shadow mask*. The shadow mask helps align the beams so they hit the correct dots on the screen. The screen is coated with colored phosphor dots. Phosphor is a substance that glows when it is struck by the electron beam.

3. The yoke, which generates an electromagnetic field, moves the electron beams across and down the screen. Older **interlaced monitors** illuminate every other line (e.g., lines 1, 3, 5, and so on) and then return to the top to illuminate the lines they skipped (e.g., lines 2, 4, 6, and so on). It is an inexpensive way to illuminate the entire screen, but causes flicker. In newer **noninterlaced monitors**, each line is illuminated sequentially (e.g., lines 1, 2, 3, 4, and so on) so the entire screen is lighted more quickly and in a single pass. The speed at which the entire screen is redrawn is called the **refresh rate**.

4. The illuminated phosphor dots create an image on the screen.

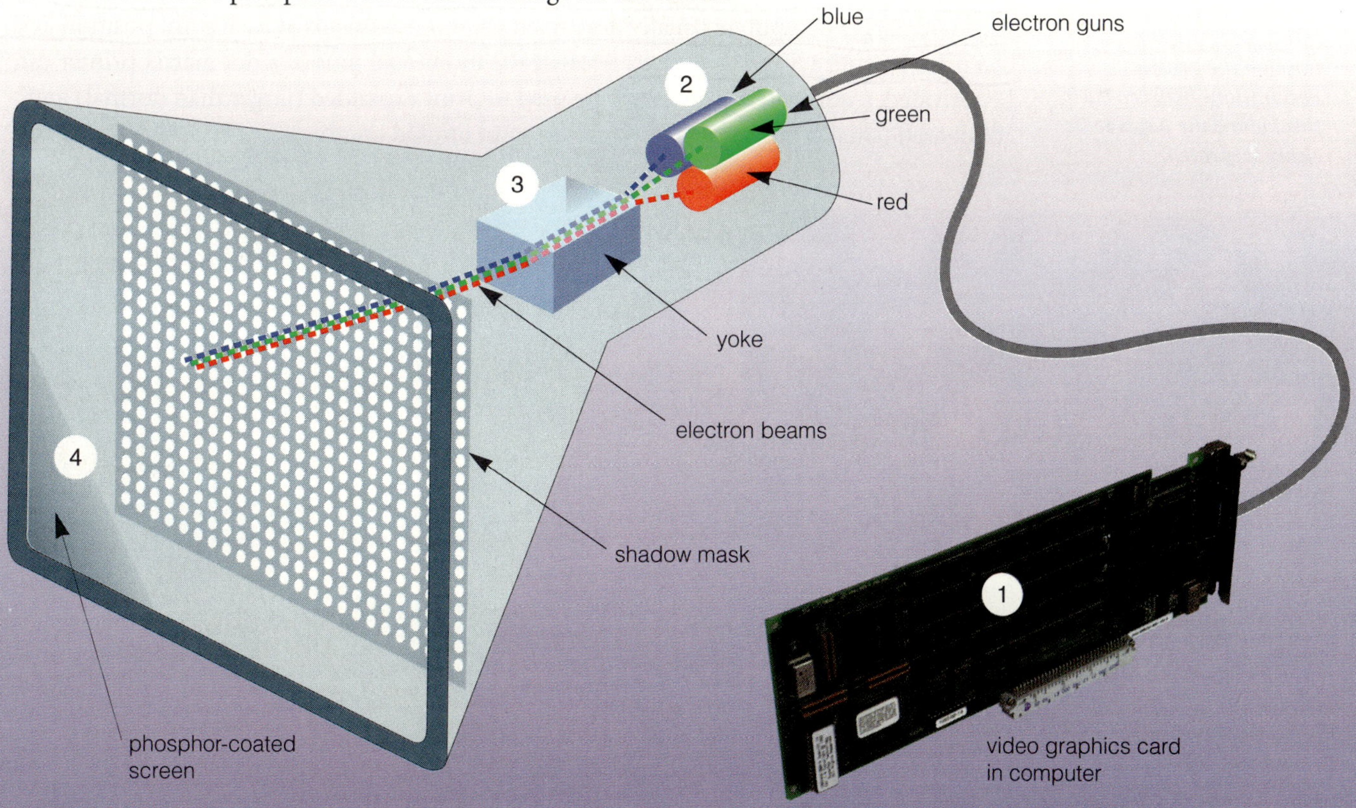

Figure 4-44
How an image is displayed. Each pixel on a color monitor screen is made up of three colored (red, green, and blue), phosphor dots. These dots can be turned on individually or in combinations to display a wide range of colors.

Printers

Printing requirements vary greatly among computer users. For example, home computer users might print only a hundred pages or fewer a week. Small business computer users might print several hundred pages a day. Users of mainframe computers, such as large utility companies that send printed bills to hundreds of thousands of customers each month, need printers that are capable of printing thousands of pages per hour. These different needs have resulted in the development of printers with varying speeds, capabilities, and printing methods. Generally, printers can be classified into two groups, impact or nonimpact, based on how they transfer characters to the paper.

Impact Printers

Impact printers transfer the image onto paper by some type of printing mechanism striking the paper, ribbon, and character together. Most impact printers use continuous-form paper. The pages of **continuous-form paper** are connected together for a continuous flow through the printer (Figure 4-45). The advantage of continuous-form paper is that it does not need to be changed frequently; thousands of pages come connected together. Some impact printers also use single-sheet paper. The advantage of using single-sheet paper is that different types of paper, such as letterhead, can be changed quickly.

Dot Matrix Printers A **dot matrix printer** produces printed images by striking wire pins against an inked ribbon. Its print head consists of a series of small tubes containing wire pins that, when pressed against a ribbon and paper, print small dots. The combination of small dots printed closely together forms the character. Most dot matrix printers used with personal computers have a single print head that moves across the page. Dot matrix printers used with larger computers usually have fixed print mechanisms at each print position and can print an entire line at one time. Because the individual pins of a dot matrix printer can be activated, a dot matrix printer can be used to print expanded (larger than normal) and condensed (smaller than normal) characters and limited graphics.

Figure 4-45
Sheets of continuous-form paper are connected together. Small holes on the sides of the paper allow sprockets to pull the paper through the printer. Perforations between each sheet allow the pages to be easily separated.

Dot matrix printers can contain a varying number of pins, depending on the manufacturer and the printer model. Print heads consisting of 9 and 24 pins (two vertical rows of 12) are most common. Figure 4-46 illustrates the formation of the letter G using a nine-pin dot matrix printer. The two rows of pins on a 24-pin print head are slightly offset (Figure 4-47) and can print overlapping dots that produce better quality output than a 9-pin printer.

The speed of impact printers with movable print heads is rated in **characters per second** (**cps**). Depending on the printer model, this speed varies between 50 and 700 cps. The speed of impact printers that print one line at a time is rated in **lines per minute (lpm)**. High-speed dot matrix printers can print up to 1,400 lpm.

Dot matrix are the least expensive printers but are less frequently used because they do not offer a high-quality output. Dot matrix printers often are used when multiple copies of a document, such as an invoice or an airline ticket, must be printed. Dot matrix printers range in cost from under $200 for small desktop units to more than $10,000 for heavy-use business models.

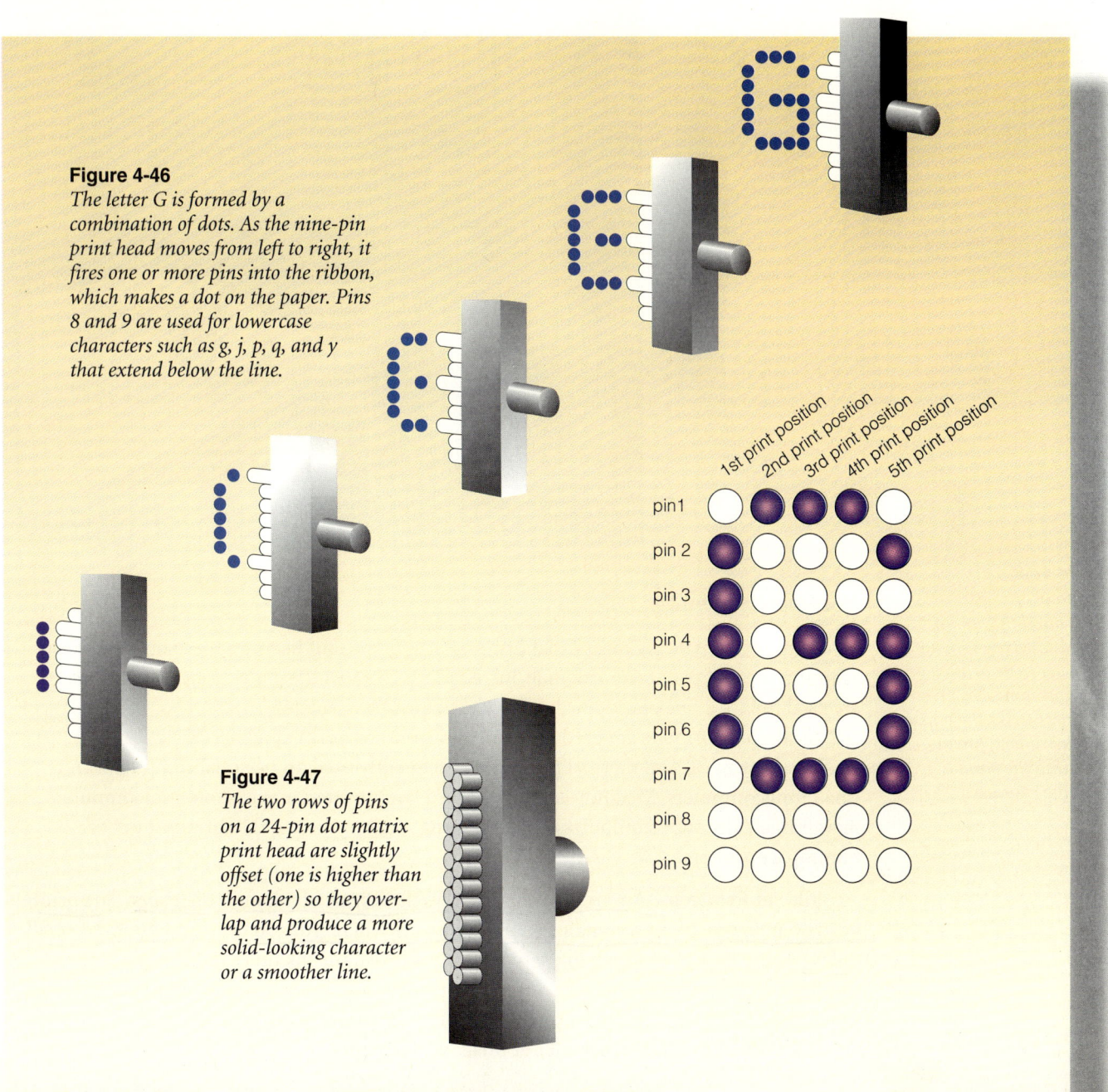

Figure 4-46
The letter G is formed by a combination of dots. As the nine-pin print head moves from left to right, it fires one or more pins into the ribbon, which makes a dot on the paper. Pins 8 and 9 are used for lowercase characters such as g, j, p, q, and y that extend below the line.

Figure 4-47
The two rows of pins on a 24-pin dot matrix print head are slightly offset (one is higher than the other) so they overlap and produce a more solid-looking character or a smoother line.

Band Printers Band printers are used for high-volume output on large computers systems. **Band printers** use a horizontal, rotating band containing numbers, letters of the alphabet, and selected special characters. The characters are struck by hammers located at each print position behind the paper and ribbon to create a line of print on the paper (Figure 4-48).

Interchangeable type bands with different fonts can be used on band printers. A band printer can produce up to six carbon copies, has good print quality, high reliability, and depending on the manufacturer and model of the printer, can print in the range of 600 to 2,000 lines per minute.

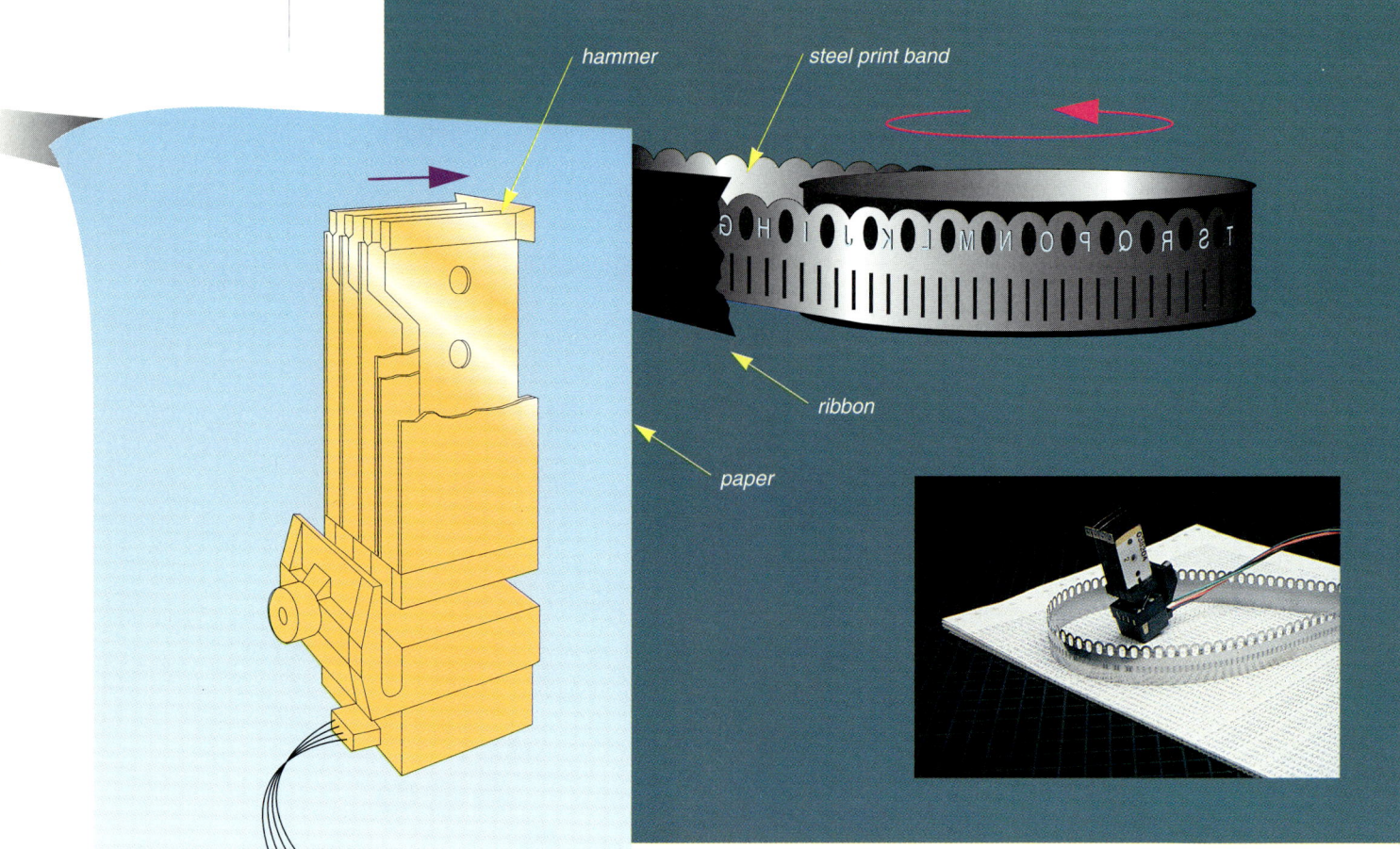

Figure 4-48
A band printer uses a metal band that contains solid characters. When the character to be printed on the band comes by, print hammers strike the paper and the ribbon, forcing them into the band to print the character.

Nonimpact Printers

Nonimpact printing means that printing occurs without having a mechanism striking against a sheet of paper. For example, ink is sprayed against the paper or heat and pressure are used to fuse a fine black powder into the shape of a character.

Nonimpact printers are used on small and large computer systems. Ink-jet printers, small laser printers, and thermal printers are frequently used on personal computers and small minicomputers. Medium- and high-speed laser printers are used on minicomputers, mainframes, and supercomputers. The following sections discuss the various types of nonimpact printers.

Ink-Jet Printers An ink-jet printer sprays tiny drops of ink onto the paper. The print head of an ink-jet printer contains a nozzle with anywhere from 50 to several hundred small holes (Figure 4-49). Although many more of them exist, the ink holes in the nozzle are similar to the individual pins on a dot matrix printer. Just as any combination of dot matrix pins can be activated, ink can be propelled by heat or pressure through any combination of the nozzle holes to form a character or image on the paper.

Ink-jet printers produce high-quality print and graphics and are quiet because the paper is not struck as it is by dot matrix printers. Standard weight copying machine paper is used for most ink-jet documents but heavier weight premium paper is recommended for better looking color documents. Lower quality paper can be too soft and cause the ink to bleed.

Figure 4-49
How a color ink-jet printer works.

1. The print head contains one black and at least one color ink cartridge. Some printers contain three separate color cartridges for the cyan (blue), yellow, and magenta (red) colors used for color printing.

2. An ink cartridge has anywhere from 50 to several hundred small ink nozzles, each less than half the width of a human hair. Each nozzle sprays only one color. Electrical contacts on the cartridge connect to the electronic circuits of the printer.

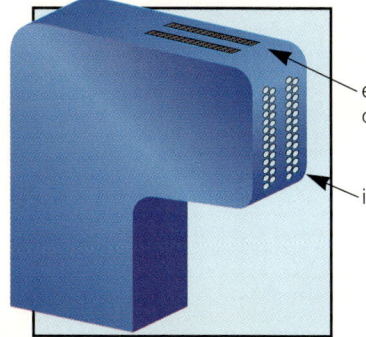

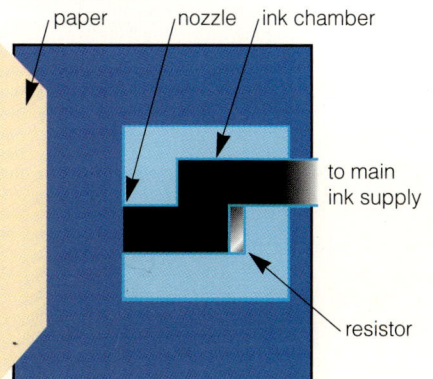

3. Each nozzle is connected to an ink chamber. The ink chambers are connected to the ink supply for each color.

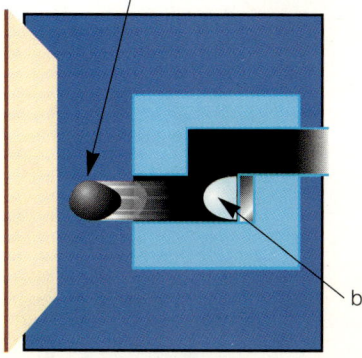

4. Several methods are used to force the ink through the nozzle and onto the paper. Using the thermal method illustrated here, a small resistor in the ink chamber is heated for several millionths of a second. The heat causes a bubble of ink to form and forces a drop out of the nozzle and onto the paper. Instead of the thermal method, some ink-jet printers use a vibrating crystal that forces the ink out the nozzle.

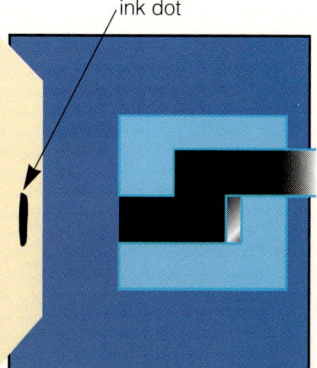

5. As the bubble collapses, fresh ink is drawn into the chamber from the main ink supply in the cartridge. Surface tension keeps the ink from dripping out of the nozzle.

4.36 CHAPTER 4 – INPUT AND OUTPUT

Overhead projector transparency sheets also can be printed. Ink-jet printers print text at rates from two to eight pages per minute. Graphics and color print at a slower rate. In recent years, color ink-jet printers have become the most popular type of color printer (Figure 4-50). Good-quality color ink-jet printers are available for less than $500.

Laser Printers The laser printer is a nonimpact printer that operates similarly to a copying machine. A laser printer converts data from the computer into a laser beam that is directed to a positively charged revolving drum by a spinning mirror (Figure 4-51). Each position on the drum touched by the beam becomes negatively charged and attracts the toner (powdered ink). The toner is transferred onto the paper and then fused to the paper by heat and pressure to create the text or image.

Some laser-type printers use light emitting diode (LED) arrays or liquid crystal shutters (LCS). With these methods, the light can expose thousands of individual points on the drum. Although the light exposure methods of LED and LCS printers are different from laser printers, they often are referred to as and classified with laser printers. All laser printers produce high-quality text and graphics suitable for business correspondence (Figure 4-52). Color laser printers are available but are expensive and not yet widely used.

inCyber
For details on laser printers, visit the Discovering Computers Chapter 4 inCyber page (http://www.scsite.com/dc/ch4/incyber.htm) and click Laser Printer.

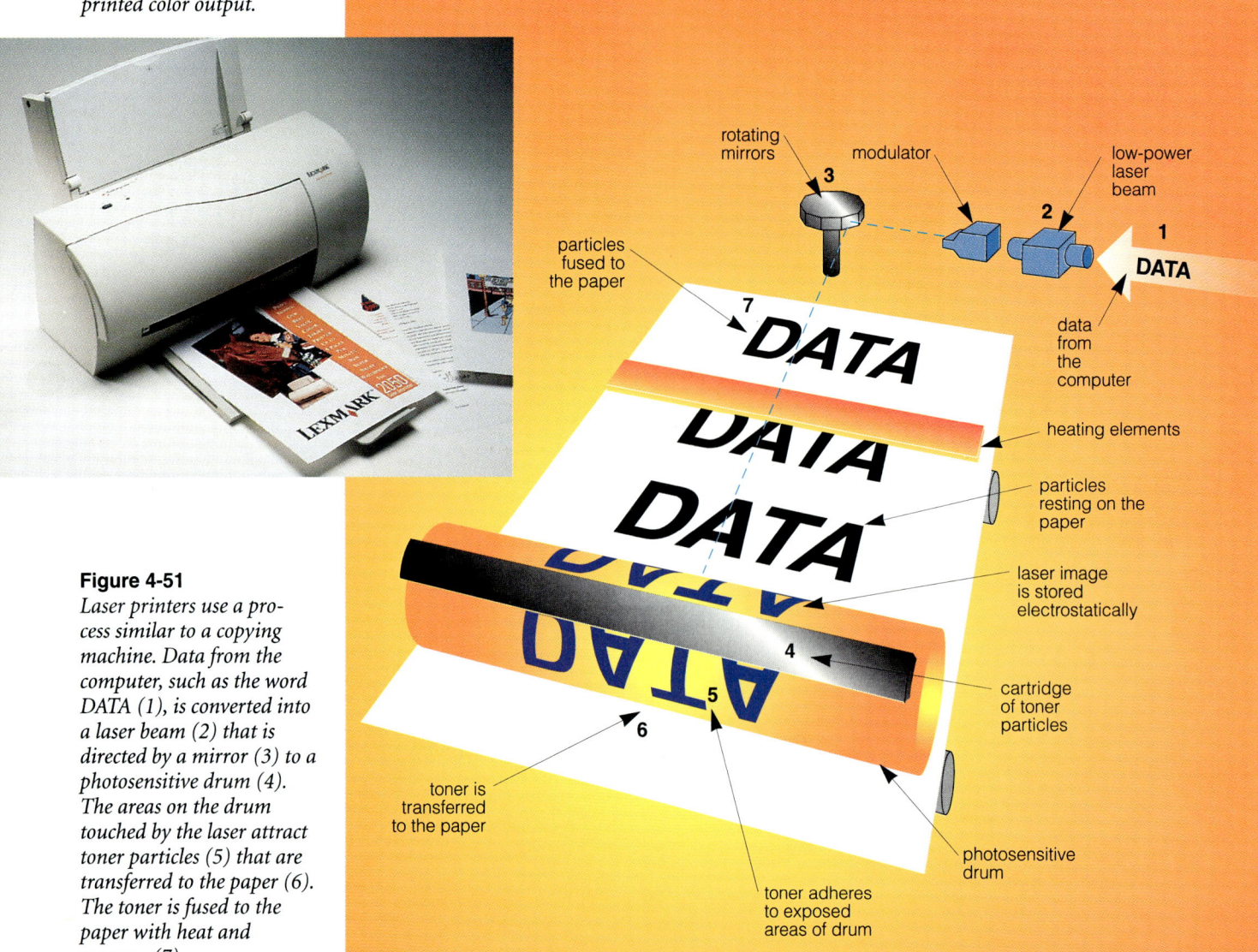

Figure 4-50
Color ink-jet printers have become an affordable way to produce good-quality printed color output.

Figure 4-51
Laser printers use a process similar to a copying machine. Data from the computer, such as the word DATA (1), is converted into a laser beam (2) that is directed by a mirror (3) to a photosensitive drum (4). The areas on the drum touched by the laser attract toner particles (5) that are transferred to the paper (6). The toner is fused to the paper with heat and pressure (7).

Laser printers are rated by their speed and resolution. Speed is measured in **pages per minute (ppm)**. Laser printers used with individual personal computers range from four to twelve pages per minute and start at less than $500. Laser printers supporting multiple users on a network or larger computer range from 16 to 50 pages per minute and cost from $10,000 to $100,000. High-speed laser printers costing as much as several hundred thousand dollars can produce output at the rate of several hundred pages per minute (Figure 4-53). Laser printer resolution is measured by the number of **dots per inch (dpi)** that can be printed. The more dots, the sharper the image. The resolution of laser printers ranges from 240 to 1,200 dpi with most printers currently offering 300 to 600 dpi. Laser printers usually use individual sheets of paper stored in a removable tray that slides into the printer case. Some laser printers have trays that can accommodate different sizes of paper while others require separate trays for letter and legal paper. Most laser printers have a manual feed slot where individual sheets and envelopes can be inserted. Transparencies also can be printed on laser printers.

Figure 4-52
Laser printers can produce high-quality text or graphics output.

Figure 4-53
High-speed laser printers can operate at speeds higher than 200 pages per minute. These printing systems can cost more than $200,000.

Thermal Printers Thermal printers, sometimes called **thermal transfer printers**, use heat to transfer colored inks from ink sheets onto the printing surface (Figure 4-54). Thermal printers can work with plain paper but produce the best results when higher quality smooth paper or plastic transparencies are used. A special type of thermal printer, using a method called **dye diffusion**, uses chemically treated paper to obtain color print quality equal to glossy magazine pages. Dye diffusion actually varies the color intensity of each dot placed on the page. Most color printers merely alter the pattern of cyan (blue/green), magenta (red/purple), yellow, and black dots to create the illusion of different colors. Thermal printers produce output at the rate of one to two pages per minute.

Figure 4-54
Thermal transfer printers are used to produce high-quality color output.

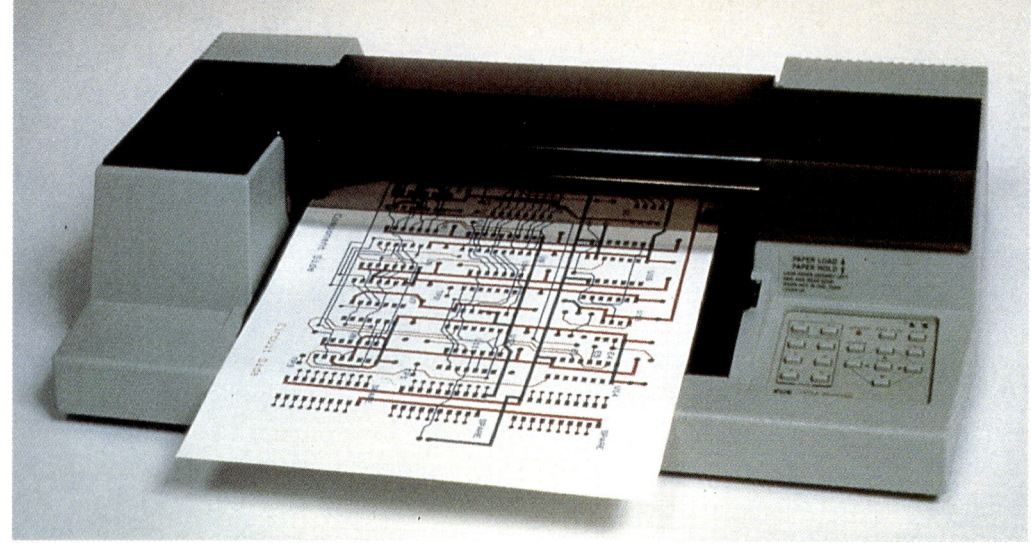

Figure 4-55
Color flatbed plotter.

Plotters

A **plotter** is an output device used to produce high-quality line drawings such as building plans, charts, or circuit diagrams. These drawings can be quite large; some plotters are designed to handle paper up to 40 inches by 48 inches, much larger than would fit in a standard printer. Plotters can be classified by the way they create the drawing. The two types are pen plotters and electrostatic plotters.

As the name implies, **pen plotters** create images on a sheet of paper by moving one or more pens over the surface of the paper or by moving the paper under the tip of the pens.

Two different kinds of pen plotters are flatbed plotters and drum plotters. When a **flatbed plotter** is used to plot, or draw, the pen or pens are instructed by the software to move to the down position so the pen contacts the flat surface of the paper. Further instructions then direct the movement of the pens to create the image. Most flatbed plotters have one or more pens of varying colors or widths. The plotter shown in Figure 4-55 is a flatbed plotter that can create color drawings.

A **drum plotter** uses a rotating drum, or cylinder, over which drawing pens are mounted. The pens can move to the left and right as the drum rotates, creating an image (Figure 4-56). An advantage of the drum plotter is that the length of the plot is virtually unlimited, because roll paper can be used. The width of the plot is limited by the width of the drum.

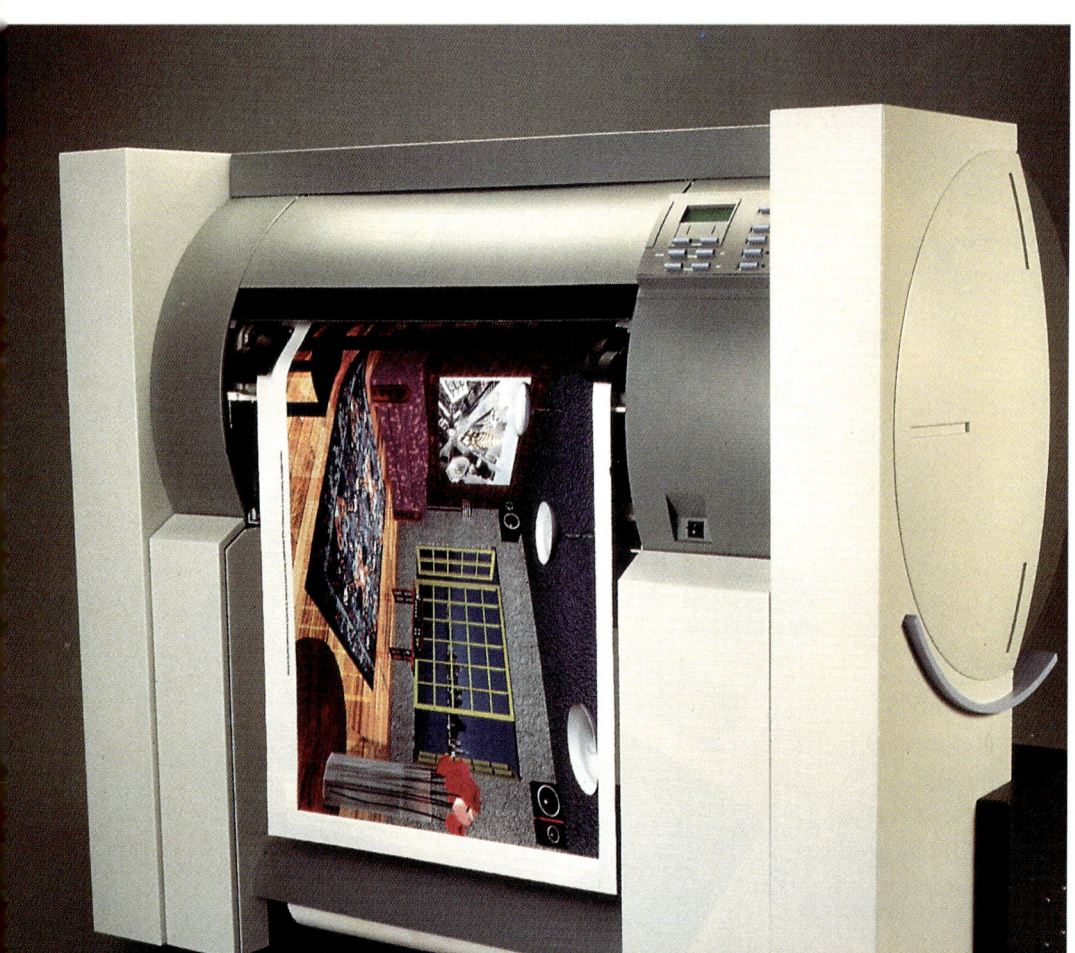

Figure 4-56
A drum plotter can handle larger paper sizes than a flatbed plotter.

With an **electrostatic plotter**, the paper moves under a row of wires (called styli) that can be turned on to create an electrostatic charge on the paper. The paper then passes through a developer and the drawing emerges where the charged wires touched the paper. The electrostatic printer image is composed of a series of very small dots, resulting in relatively high-quality output. In addition, the speed of electrostatic plotting is faster than with pen plotters.

Special-Purpose Printers

In addition to the printers just discussed, a number of other printers have been developed for special purposes. These include single label printers, bar code label printers, and portable printers. Figure 4-57 shows examples of these printers.

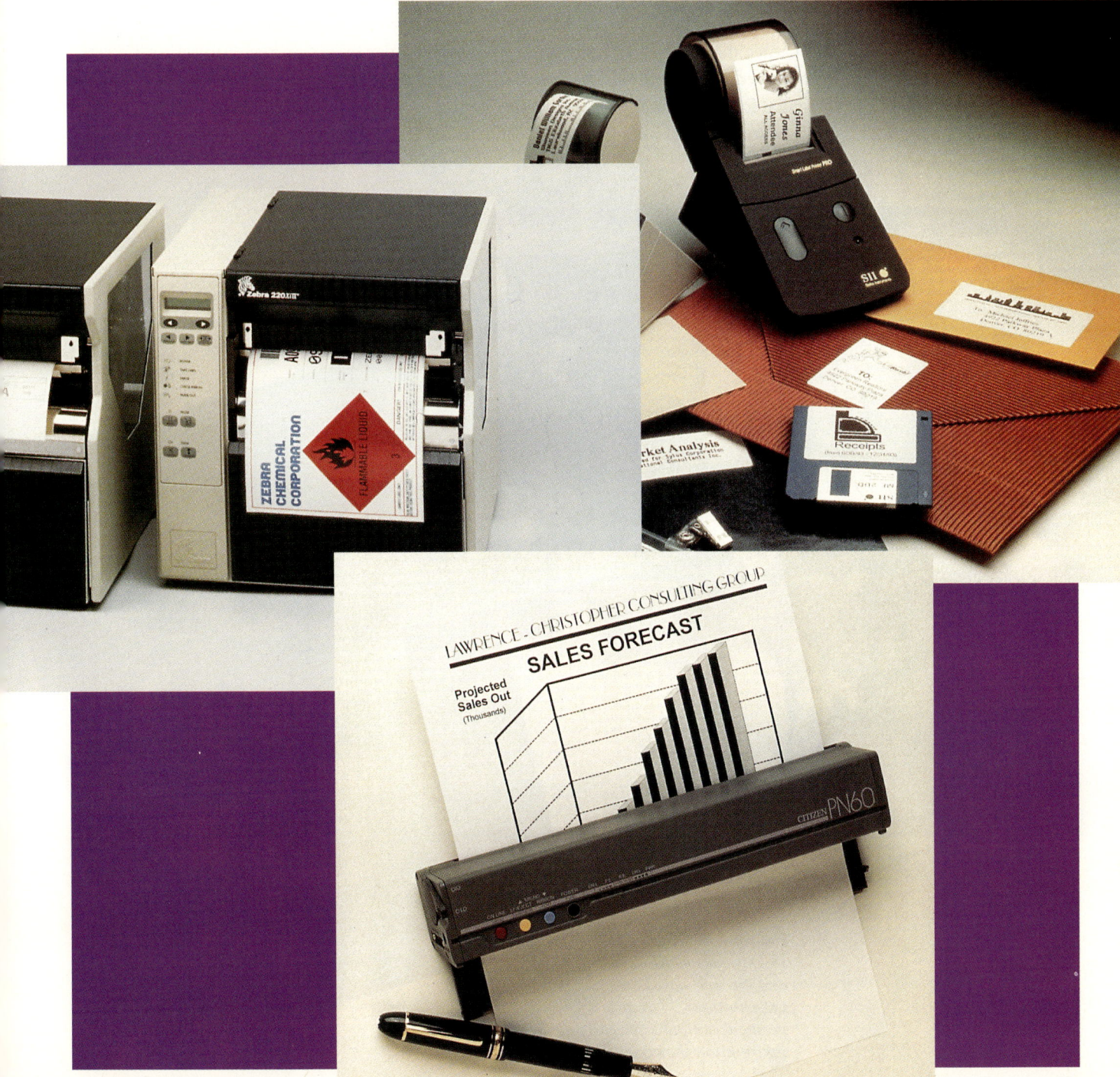

Figure 4-57
Other types of printers, from left to right, include a bar code label printer, a single label printer, and a printer designed for use with portable computers.

CHAPTER 4 – INPUT AND OUTPUT

Other Output Devices

Although display devices and printers provide the majority of computer output, other devices are available for particular uses and applications. These include data projectors and computer output microfilm devices.

Data Projectors

A variety of devices are available to take the image that displays on a computer screen and project it so it can be clearly seen by a room full of people. Smaller, lower cost units, called **LCD projection panels**, use liquid crystal display (LCD) technology and are designed to be placed on top of an overhead projector (Figure 4-58).

Self-contained **LCD projectors** have their own light source and do not require a separate overhead projector (Figure 4-59). The LCD projection panels and projectors are easily portable and can be located at different distances from the projection screen.

Larger, more expensive units use technology similar to large-screen projection TV sets; separate red, green, and blue beams of light are focused onto the screen. These units are designed for larger areas such as meeting rooms or auditoriums. The three-beam projectors must be focused and aligned for a specific distance and thus once installed, usually are not moved.

Figure 4-58
Projection panels are used together with overhead projectors to display computer screen images to a group of people.

Figure 4-59
LCD projectors are portable and are well suited for small room presentations. They attach directly to a personal computer and display the same information shown on the computer screen.

Figure 4-60
Microfiche often is used for reports that must be kept on file but do not have to be referred to frequently.

Computer Output Microfilm

Computer output microfilm (COM) is an output technique that records output from a computer as microscopic images on roll or sheet film. The images stored on COM are the same as the images that would be printed on paper. The COM recording process reduces characters 24, 42, or 48 times smaller than would be produced on a printer. The information then is recorded on **microfiche** sheet film or on 16mm, 35mm, or 105mm roll film (Figure 4-60).

Microfilm has several advantages over printed reports or other storage media for certain applications. Some of these advantages are:

1. Data can be recorded on the film faster than printers; up to 30,000 lines per minute.

2. Costs for recording the data are lower. Studies have shown that microfilm can be as little as one-tenth the cost of printing a report.

3. Less space is required to store microfilm than printed materials. Microfilm that weighs one ounce can store the equivalent of ten pounds of paper.

4. The cost to store a megabyte of information is less on microfilm than it is on disk.

To access data stored on microfilm, a variety of readers are available. They utilize indexing techniques to provide a quick reference to the data. Some microfilm readers can perform automatic data lookup, called **computer-assisted retrieval (CAR)**, under the control of an attached computer. With the indexing software and hardware available for microfilm, you usually can locate any piece of data in a database in less than ten seconds, at a far lower cost per inquiry than using an online inquiry system consisting of a computer system that stores the data on a hard disk.

Facsimile (Fax)

Facsimile, or **fax**, equipment is used to transmit and receive an image of a document over telephone lines. The document can contain text and graphics, can be hand-written, or be a photograph. Fax equipment is available as an external stand-alone machine (Figure 4-61) or as part of an internal data communications package, such as a modem and fax software, that can send and receive data and fax transmissions. Stand-alone fax machines optically scan a document and convert the image into digitized data that is transmitted. A fax machine at the receiving end converts the digitized data and prints a copy of the original image. Internal fax equipment can transmit computer prepared documents, such as a word processing letter, or documents that have been digitized with a scanner. Documents received by internal fax equipment can be displayed on a monitor or sent to the printer.

Multifunction Devices

A **multifunction device** (**MFD**) is a single piece of equipment that can print, scan, copy, and fax (Figure 4-62). The MFD offers two primary advantages: it requires less space and costs less money than separate units. In fact, the cost of an MFD often is less than the total of any two devices it is designed to replace. Personal units are available for around $1,000. Higher volume business models are available for between $2,000 and $3,000.

Figure 4-61
A facsimile (fax) machine can send and receive copies of documents to and from any location with phone service and another fax machine. Fax capabilities often are built into personal computer communications equipment.

Figure 4-62
A multifunction device is a single machine that has the capabilities of a printer, scanner, copier, and fax machine.

Many MFDs are based on a printer because it is the device that is used the most. Both laser and ink-jet technology are available. Print speeds are comparable to stand-alone printers. Perhaps the second most important feature is the copier capability. Older units sometimes offered what was described as *convenience copying*; 200 dot per inch (dpi) resolution that was barely adequate for text and inadequate for most graphics. Newer models offer 300 to 600 dpi resolution, comparable to good-quality, stand-alone copiers.

Scanner capability usually will mirror the capabilities of the copier. Both features use the same components to capture the document image. Scanner use has significantly increased in recent years because of desktop publishing applications and the improvement of OCR software for automatically entering scanned text. Some scanner manufacturers offer limited MFD capability by providing software that turns a scanner into a copier. A separate printer must be available to output the copied document. Fax features usually include the capability of faxing to or from a PC or directly to another fax machine. Speed dialing and the capability of sending a fax to a distribution list also are common features.

The one obvious risk of an MFD is that if the machine breaks down you lose all four functions. But given the space and cost advantages of MFDs, more and more users are willing to take the risk.

The output devices discussed in this chapter are summarized in Figure 4-63.

Summary of Input and Output

The input and output steps of the information processing cycle use a variety of devices to allow you to enter data and provide you with information. After reading this chapter, you should have a better overall understanding of computer input and output.

OUTPUT DEVICE	DESCRIPTION
Display Devices	
Monitor	Visual display like TV set
Flat panel display	Flat visual display used with portable computers
Printers - Impact	
Dot matrix	Prints text and graphics using small dots
Band	High-speed rotating band text-only printer
Printers - Nonimpact	
Ink jet	Sprays tiny drops of ink onto page to form text and graphics; prints quietly; inexpensive color printer
Laser	Works like a copying machine; produces very high quality text and graphics
Thermal	Uses heat to produce high-quality color output
Plotter	Designed for line drawing; often used for computer-aided design; some units can handle large paper sizes.
Data Projectors	Projects display screen image to a group
COM	Stores reduced-size image on sheet or roll film
Facsimile (fax)	Transmits and receives text and image documents over telephone lines
Multifunction Devices	Combines printer, fax, scanner, and copier

Figure 4-63
Summary of the more common output devices.

CHAPTER 4 – INPUT AND OUTPUT

COMPUTERS AT WORK

Helping People with Special Needs

For physically challenged and disabled individuals, working with standard computers either may be difficult or impossible. Fortunately, special software and hardware, called adaptive or assistive technology, enables many of these individuals to use computers productively and independently.

Adaptive technology covers a wide range of hardware and software products that help the user make the computer meet their special needs. For people with motor disabilities who cannot use a standard keyboard, a number of alternative input devices are available. Most of these devices involve the use of a switch that is controlled by any reliable muscle. One type of switch even can be activated by breathing into a tube. The switches are used with special software to select commands or input characters. For those who are unable to use their muscles to activate switches, a system exists that is controlled by eye movement. Called Eyegaze, the system uses a camera mounted on the computer and directed at one of the user's eyes. Using the movement of the user's eye, software determines where on the screen the user is looking to within $1/4$-inch accuracy. To activate a choice on the screen, the user has to stare at it for approximately $1/4$ of a second.

For blind individuals, voice recognition programs allow for verbal input. Software also is available that can convert text to Braille and send it to Braille printers. Both blind and non-verbal individuals use speech synthesis equipment to convert text documents into spoken words. For people with limited vision, several programs are available that magnify information on the screen.

The use of adaptive technology received further encouragement when the Americans with Disabilities Act (ADA) was enacted. Since 1994, the ADA requires that all companies with 15 or more employees make reasonable attempts to accommodate the needs of workers with physical challenges. Many employers are complying with the legislation by incorporating the use of personal computers and adaptive technology software and equipment.

Figure 4-64

IN THE FUTURE

The Widespread Use of Voice Input

Although speech recognition programs have improved significantly in recent years, voice input still is used in only a limited number of applications, such as helping people with disabilities. These existing systems use discrete word recognition that requires the user to pause between each word. Discrete speech works well for commands that use one or two words, such as *print or shut down*, but it is unnatural and tiring to use for dictation. Most experts agree that for voice input to be used widely, continuous speech recognition systems that accept natural (conversational) speech will have to be developed. To provide continuous speech recognition, however, computers with more power are required. In addition, voice recognition software will have to be significantly improved.

To understand human speech, a computer has to go through four steps; sound analysis, word recognition, sentence or thought construction, and statement context. Sound analysis is the easiest part. Sound waves are converted into the smallest units of speech called phonemes. During word recognition, the phonemes are joined together to form words. This can be a difficult task because conversational speech often runs one word into another. The problem becomes more difficult during sentence and thought construction. During this process, the identified words are joined together to make a logical statement. As your high school English teacher may have told you, people do not always speak or write in a logical manner using correct grammar. Statement context involves using past statements to provide information about a current statement. For example, say the computer reservation agent just had told you that no flights were available on the day you wanted to leave, June 20. If you said, How about the next day?, the computer should know that you now want to check the flights on June 21.

Some experts think that significant breakthroughs in natural speech recognition are just a few years away and that affordable systems will be available by the year 2000. The optimists, however, already are talking about the next human interface challenge: how to read lips!

Figure 4-65

chapter 4 review

1 | 2 | 3 | 4 | 5 | 6 | 7 | 8 | 9 | 10 | 11 | 12 | 13 | 14 | I

inCyber | review | terms | yourTurn | hotTopics | outThere | winLabs | webWalk | exercises | news | home

INSTRUCTIONS: *To display this page from the Web, launch your browser and enter the URL, http://www.scsite.com/dc/ch4/review.htm. Click the links for current and additional information.*

1 Types of Input

Input refers to the process of entering data, programs, commands, and user responses into memory. **Data** refers to the raw facts that a computer receives and processes to produce information. **Programs** are instructions that direct the computer to perform the necessary operations to process the data. **Commands** are key words and phrases that direct the computer to perform certain activities. **User response** refers to the data a user enters to respond to a question or message.

2 Keyboards

The **keyboard** is the most commonly used input device. Users enter data by pressing keys. Alphabetic keys are arranged like those on a typewriter. Most keyboards also have a **numeric keypad**. Other keys include **arrow keys** or **cursor control keys**, which are used to move the cursor, and **function keys**, which can be programmed to accomplish certain tasks.

3 The Mouse

Pointing devices control the movement of an on-screen symbol called the **mouse pointer**, or **pointer**. A **mouse** is a palm-sized pointing device. A mechanism, usually a ball, on the bottom of the mouse senses its movement. Electronic circuits translate the mouse's movement into signals that are sent to the computer and used to direct the pointer. Various actions can be performed by moving the pointer and then pressing one of the buttons on top of the mouse.

4 Trackballs, Touchpads, Pointing Sticks, and Joysticks

A **trackball** is a pointing device like a mouse only with the ball on top. A **touchpad** is a flat surface that controls the movement of the pointer by sensing the motion of a finger on its exterior. A **pointing stick** is a device shaped like a pencil eraser that moves the pointer as pressure is applied. A **joystick** uses the movement of a vertical stem to direct the pointer.

5 Other Pointing Devices

Pen input devices can input data with hand written characters, select items by pressing the pen against the screen, and use gestures, which are special symbols, to issue commands. A **touch screen** allows users to touch areas of the screen to enter data. A **light pen** can be used to select processing options or to draw on the screen. A **digitizer** converts shapes from a drawing or photograph to digital impulses and transmits them to a computer. A **graphics tablet** is similar to a digitizer, but it also contains unique characters and commands.

4 review

chapter 1 | 2 | 3 | 4 | 5 | 6 | 7 | 8 | 9 | 10 | 11 | 12 | 13 | 14 | I

inCyber | review | terms | yourTurn | hotTopics | outThere | winLabs | webWalk | exercises | news | home

6 Source Data Automation

Source data automation refers to procedures and equipment designed to make the input process more efficient by eliminating the manual entry of data, instead taking data directly from its original form. An **image scanner** electronically captures an entire page and converts the document into digital data that can be processed by a computer. **Optical recognition** devices use a light source to read optical codes, marks on forms, and characters from ordinary documents and convert them into digital data. **Magnetic ink character recognition (MICR)** uses a special ink that can be magnetized during processing. **Data collection devices** are designed and used for obtaining data at the site where the transaction or event being reported takes place.

7 Terminals

Terminals consist of a keyboard and a screen. **Dumb terminals** can be used to transmit data to or receive data from a connected computer, but have no independent processing capability. **Intelligent terminals** have built-in processing capabilities. **Special-purpose terminals** perform specific jobs and contain features uniquely designed for use in a particular industry.

9 Types of Output

Output is data that has been processed into a useful form called information. A **report** presents information in an organized form. Reports can be classified by who uses them (**internal reports** or **external reports**), by the way they present information (**narrative reports, detail reports, summary reports,** or **exception reports**), or by how often they are produced (**periodic reports** or **ad hoc reports**). **Computer graphics** are any non-text pictorial information. **Audio output** consists of sounds, including words and music, produced by the computer. **Video output** consists of visual images that have been captured with an input device, digitized, and directed to an output device.

8 Other Input Devices

Special input devices are required to convert sound and image data into digital form. For personal computers, these devices consist primarily of electronics contained on a **sound card** or a **video card**. Sounds usually are recorded with a microphone or by directly connecting a sound device. **Voice input** allows data and commands to be entered with spoken words. Digital cameras record photographs in the form of digital data. Video material is input using a video camera or a video recorder. An **electronic whiteboard** is a modified whiteboard that captures text and drawings in a file on an attached computer.

10 Display Devices

A **display device** is the visual output device of a computer. A **monitor** is a display device that looks like a television and consists of a display surface, called a **screen**, a plastic or metal case to house a **cathode ray tube (CRT)**, and the electrical components. A **flat panel display** is a thin display screen, most often used in portable computers, that does not employ CRT technology.

11 How Images are Displayed

When a color monitor produces an image, the image is sent electronically from the CPU to the video circuits and then to the cathode ray tube. Electron guns generate electron beams towards the colored phosphor dots that coat the screen. The beams pass through a shadow mask that helps align them so they hit the right dot. When struck by the electron beam, the phosphor dots glow. The yoke, an electromagnetic field, moves the beams across and down the screen, and the illuminated phosphors create the image.

12 Printers

Generally, printers can be classified in two groups. **Impact printers** transfer an image by some type of printing mechanism striking the paper, ribbon, and character together. Dot matrix printers and band printers are two types of impact printers. Nonimpact printers print without having a mechanism striking against a sheet of paper. Ink jet printers, page printers, and thermal printers are types of nonimpact printers.

13 Other Types of Output Devices

Plotters are used to produce high-quality line drawings. **LCD projection panels** and **LCD projectors** take the image that appears on a computer screen and project it. **Computer output microfilm (COM)** records output as microscopic images on roll or sheet film. **Facsimile (FAX)** equipment transmits and receives an image of a document over telephone lines. A **multifunctional device (MFD)** is a single piece of equipment that can print, scan, copy, and fax.

chapter 4 terms

    1 | 2 | 3 | 4 | 5 | 6 | 7 | 8 | 9 | 10 | 11 | 12 | 13 | 14 | I

inCyber | review | terms | yourTurn | hotTopics | outThere | winLabs | webWalk | exercises | news | home

INSTRUCTIONS: To display this page from the Web, launch your browser and enter the URL, http://www.scsite.com/dc/ch4/terms.htm. Scroll through the list of terms. Click a term for its definition and a picture. Click the rocket ship for current and additional information about the term.

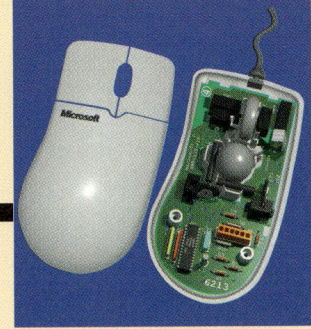

mouse ▼

DEFINITION

mouse
A small, palm-sized input device that you move across a flat surface, such as a desktop, to control the movement of the pointer on the screen (4.5)

active matrix (4.29)
arrow control keys (4.3)
arrow keys (4.3)
audio output (4.25)

band printer (4.34)
bar code (4.14)
biological feedback input (4.21)

cathode ray tube (CRT) (4.27)
characters per second (cps) (4.33)
clicking (4.5)
color monitor (4.28)
commands (4.2)
computer-assisted retrieval (CAR) (4.41)
computer drawing programs (4.25)
computer graphics (4.25)
computer output microfilm (COM) (4.41)
computer paint programs (4.25)
continuous-form paper (4.32)
continuous-speech recognition (4.20)
CRT (cathode ray tube) (4.27)
cursor (4.3)

data (4.2)
data collection devices (4.17)
detail report (4.23)
digital cameras (4.21)
digitizer (4.10)
discrete-speech recognition (4.20)
display terminals (4.18)
dot matrix printer (4.32)
dots per inch (dpi) (4.37)
double-clicking (4.5)
dragging (4.5)
drum plotter (4.38)
dual scan (4.29)
dumb terminal (4.18)
dye diffusion (4.37)

electronic whiteboard (4.22)
electrostatic plotter (4.39)
exception report (4.24)
external report (4.23)

facsimile (4.42)
fax (4.42)
flat panel display (4.29)
flatbed plotter (4.38)
function keys (4.4)

gas plasma (4.29)
gestures (4.8)
graphics tablet (4.11)

hard copy (4.23)
high-definition television (HDTV) (4.26)

image processing systems (4.13)
image scanner (4.13)
impact printers (4.32)
ink (4.8)
ink-jet printer (4.34)
input (4.2)
insertion point (4.3)
intelligent terminal (4.18)
interlaced monitors (4.31)
internal report (4.23)

joystick (4.7)

keyboard (4.2)

laser printer (4.36)
LCD projection panels (4.40)
LCD projectors (4.40)
light pen (4.10)
lines per minute (lpm) (4.33)
liquid crystal display (LCD) (4.29)

magnetic ink character recognition (MICR) (4.17)
microfiche (4.41)
monitor (4.27)
monochrome monitor (4.28)
mouse (4.5)
mouse pad (4.5)
mouse pointer (4.5)
multifunction device (MFD) (4.42)
multiscanning monitors (4.30)
multisync monitors (4.30)

narrative report (4.23)
nonimpact printing (4.34)
noninterlaced monitors (4.31)
numeric keypad (4.3)

OCR software (4.16)
on-demand report (4.24)
optical character recognition (OCR) (4.15)
optical codes (4.14)
optical mark recognition (OMR) (4.15)
optical recognition (4.14)
output (4.23)

page scanner (4.13)
pages per minute (ppm) (4.37)
passive matrix (4.29)
pen input (4.8)
pen plotter (4.38)
periodic report (4.24)
picture element (4.30)
pixel (4.30)
plotter (4.38)
pointer (4.5)
pointing stick (4.7)
point-of-sale (POS) terminal (4.18)
programmable terminal (4.18)
programs (4.2)

refresh rate (4.31)
report (4.23)
resolution (4.30)

scheduled report (4.24)
screen (4.27)
smart terminal (4.18)
soft copy (4.23)
sound card (4.19)
source data automation (4.12)
source data collection (4.12)
source document (4.12)
special-purpose terminal (4.18)
summary report (4.24)
SVGA (4.30)

terminals (4.18)
thermal printer (4.37)
thermal transfer printer (4.37)
toggle key (4.3)
touch screen (4.9)
touchpad (4.6)
trackball (4.6)
trackpad (4.6)
trackpoint (4.7)
turn-around documents (4.16)

universal product code (UPC) (4.14)
user responses (4.2)

VGA (video graphics array) (4.30)
video card (4.19)
video display terminals (VDTs) (4.18)
video input (4.22)
video output (4.26)
voice input (4.19)
voice output (4.26)
voice synthesis (4.26)
voice templates (4.20)

yourTurn

chapter 4
1 | 2 | 3 | **4** | 5 | 6 | 7 | 8 | 9 | 10 | 11 | 12 | 13 | 14 | I

inCyber | review | terms | yourTurn | hotTopics | outThere | winLabs | webWalk | exercises | news | home

INSTRUCTIONS: *To display this page from the Web, launch your browser and enter the URL,* http://www.scsite.com/dc/ch4/turn.htm. *Click a blank line for the answer. Click the links for current and additional information.*

Label the Figure

1. _____
2. _____
3. _____
4. _____
5. _____
6. _____
7. _____
8. _____

Instructions: Identify the components that produce an image.

Fill in the Blanks
Instructions: Complete each sentence with the correct term or terms.

1. Input refers to the process of entering _____, _____, _____, and _____ into memory.
2. The mouse, trackball, and touchpad are used to control an on-screen symbol called the _____ that usually is represented by a block arrow marker.
3. _____ is data that has been processed into useful information that can be used by a person or a machine.
4. _____ LCD screens, which use individual transistors to control each crystal cell, display sharper pictures than _____ LCD screens, which use one transistor for each row and column.
5. A(n) _____ is an output device that produces high-quality drawings such as maps, charts, or circuit diagrams.

Short Answer
Instructions: Write a brief answer to each of the following questions.

1. How is a computer keyboard like a typewriter? What keys can be found on most keyboards but not on traditional typewriters? What is the purpose of these keys? _____
2. What is source data automation? What is some of the equipment used for source data automation? For what purpose are optical codes, OMR devices, OCR devices, and OCR software used? _____
3. What is a report? What are three ways that reports can be classified? How are the types of reports within each classification different? _____
4. How are impact printers different from nonimpact printers? What are examples of each type of printer? How is the speed of each type of printer rated? _____
5. What are pixels? When purchasing a monitor, why are the number of pixels and the dot pitch important? _____

4 hotTopics

chapter 1 | 2 | 3 | 4 | 5 | 6 | 7 | 8 | 9 | 10 | 11 | 12 | 13 | 14 | I

inCyber | review | terms | yourTurn | hotTopics | outThere | winLabs | webWalk | exercises | news | home

INSTRUCTIONS: *To display this page from the Web, launch your browser and enter the URL, http://www.scsite.com/dc/ch4/hot.htm. Click the links for current and additional information to help you respond to the hotTopics questions.*

1. *After her first week of work at a fast-food restaurant, an Arizona* teenager was surprised to receive a check for $16,834. Her dreams of a new car quickly were dashed when it was discovered that her hourly pay rate had been entered incorrectly in the restaurant's computer. Reliable output requires accurate input. The acronym GIGO (Garbage In, Garbage Out) always applies. Data entered with some input devices is more likely to be accurate than data entered with others. What three input devices are most likely to produce accurate data? Why? What three input devices are most likely to produce inaccurate data? Why? What factors have the most effect on input accuracy?

2. *When Christopher Sholes invented the first practical commercial* typewriter in 1867, he purposely designed the keyboard to slow typists down and thus prevent keys from jamming. Having keys jam is no longer a problem, but more than a hundred years later, Sholes's sequence of letters, often called the QWERTY layout, continues to be used on most keyboards. Other arrangements have proved to be more effective. Trained typists using the Dvorak layout, which places the more used letters in the home row, can type up to three hundred percent faster than those using the QWERTY sequence. Why have these keyboards been slow to catch on? Will an arrangement other than the QWERTY layout ever become popular? Why?

3. *Almost everyone knows people who feel intimidated when forced to enter data into a computer.* Some input devices make it easy for even a novice to enter data, while others require instruction to be used efficiently. Which input device would be the easiest to use for someone who is uncomfortable with computers? Why? Which device requires the most training? Which input device would be the most important to learn how to use? Why? Which input device will be most commonplace fifty years from now? Will any device become an historical oddity, seen only in museums? Why?

4. *About 80 percent of today's movies are edited with a computer. Using video input devices,* directors can store more than a hundred miles of film on a hard drive. The click of a mouse then can access any scene, compare multiple versions, and seamlessly join the best shots. When the output is released, a scene might have a different background, or a group of a hundred may have been expanded into a crowd of thousands. Some directors, however, insist that the ease with which episodes can be cut and spliced has resulted in frenzied films that race too quickly from scene to scene. Perhaps worse, film editing, once a collaborative process, is now more of an individual effort. In general, do you think computers will have a positive or negative effect on movie making? Why? How else might the use of computers impact film making? What can be done to address the concerns of directors?

5. *When computers first were used in business, people predicted the "paperless office," where* nearly all documents would exist only electronically. Yet, much to the dismay of environmentalists, studies show that many of today's offices use more paper than in the past. Why, when it comes to paper, do you think computerized offices are often guilty of over-consumption? What impact might the World Wide Web have on paper use? What can be done to decrease the amount of paper used?

Start | hotTopics   4:05 AM

outThere

chapter 4

1 | 2 | 3 | 4 | 5 | 6 | 7 | 8 | 9 | 10 | 11 | 12 | 13 | 14 | I

inCyber | review | terms | yourTurn | hotTopics | outThere | winLabs | webWalk | exercises | news | home

INSTRUCTIONS: *To display this page from the Web, launch your browser and enter the URL, http://www.scsite.com/dc/ch4/out.htm. Click the links for current and additional information.*

1 *Manufacturers of notebook computers work hard to reduce the size of their* machines. One problem they face is that, because of the size of the human hand, keyboard keys cannot be made much smaller or placed much closer together and still be practical. Therefore, many manufacturers reduce the number of keys. Most desktop computer keyboards have 101 or more keys, but notebook computers often use fewer keys by making some perform multiple functions. Visit a computer vendor and compare the keyboards of desktop computers to the keyboards of notebook computers. How many keys are on each keyboard? What keys are on the desktop computer keyboard that are not on the other keyboards? How do the notebook computer keyboards handle the functions of these keys? Try each keyboard. Is one keyboard easier to use, or more comfortable, than the other? Why?

2 *The computer mouse comes in a wide range of shapes with a variety of capabilities. Among* the types of mouse units are the cordless mouse, ergonomic mouse, whimsically designed mouse, ring mouse (worn on the finger like a ring), and even a tough mouse that can be dropped from a five-story building, plunged under water, or run over by a truck without damage. Visit several Web sites to find out more about the different types of mouse units. Which mouse do you think is the most unusual? Why? Which mouse has the most capabilities? Which mouse is least expensive? Which is most expensive? How is the difference in price justified? Which mouse would you like most to own? Why?

3  *Optical codes are used by retail stores, supermarkets, and libraries. Some people* mistakenly believe that the optical code contains the name of a product or its price, but optical codes are only a link to a database in which this information is stored. Visit an organization that utilizes optical codes to find out how the codes are used. How are the codes read? How can the optical code data be input if the reader fails? What information is obtained when the optical code is scanned? How is the information used? In what way does the information benefit the organization or its clientele? What are the advantages of using optical codes? The disadvantages?

4 *Recently, a monitor was developed with an extremely dense display screen—seven million pixels.* Of course, this achievement is important only if you understand pixels and how their density is related to picture quality. To purchase the best monitor for your needs, it is important to be familiar with a number of terms and to recognize the significance of each. Visit several Web sites to learn more about things to consider when buying a monitor. What is the best screen size? How are screen size and resolution related? What are focus and convergence? What issues are involved in monitor safety? When you have finished reviewing monitor characteristics, make a list of the five most important factors when purchasing a monitor.

5 *While printers produce an image on a page from top to bottom, plotters can draw on any part of* a page at random, and then move to any other part. This capability makes plotters particularly valuable to people who produce maps or blueprints. Arrange to interview someone in an organization that uses plotters. What kind of plotter does the organization use? Why? For what purpose is the plotter used? What is the advantage (or disadvantage) of using a plotter compared to creating a drawing by hand? If possible, ask to see a demonstration of the plotter or an example of its work. What size paper is used? How long does it take to produce an image? How clear is the final drawing?

4 winLabs

chapter 1 | 2 | 3 | 4 | 5 | 6 | 7 | 8 | 9 | 10 | 11 | 12 | 13 | 14 | I

inCyber | review | terms | yourTurn | hotTopics | outThere | winLabs | webWalk | exercises | news | home

INSTRUCTIONS: *To display this page from the Web, launch your browser and enter the URL, http://www.scsite.com/dc/ch4/labs.htm. Click the links for current and additional information.*

1. Shelly Cashman Series Input Lab
Follow the instructions in winLabs 1 on page 1.34 to display the Shelly Cashman Series Labs screen. Click **Scanning** Documents. Click the Start Lab button. When the screen displays, read the objectives. With your printer turned on, click the Print Questions button. Fill out the top of the Questions sheet and then answer the questions.

2. Shelly Cashman Series Printer Lab
Follow the instructions in winLabs 1 on page 1.34 to display the Shelly Cashman Series Labs screen. Click Setting Up to **Print**. Click the Start Lab button. When the screen displays, read the objectives. With your printer turned on, click the Print Questions button. Fill out the top of the Questions sheet and then answer the questions.

3. Shelly Cashman Series Monitor Lab
Follow the instructions in winLabs 1 on page 1.34 to display the Shelly Cashman Series Labs screen. Click Configuring Your **Display**. Click the Start Lab button. When the screen displays, read the objectives. With your printer turned on, click the Print Questions button. Fill out the top of the Questions sheet and answer the questions.

4. Using the Mouse and Keyboard to Interact with an Online Program
Insert your Student Floppy Disk or see your instructor for the location of the **Loan Payment Calculator** program. Click the Start button on the taskbar, and then click Run on the Start menu to display the Run dialog box. In the Open text box, type the path and filename of the program. For example, type a:loancalc.exe and then press the ENTER key to display the Loan Payment Calculator window. Type 12500 in the LOAN AMOUNT text box. Click the YEARS right scroll arrow or drag the scroll box until YEARS equals 15. Click the APR right scroll arrow or drag the scroll box until APR equals 8.5. Click the Calculate button. Write down the monthly payment and sum of payments (Figure 4-66). Click the Clear button. What are the monthly payment and sum of payments for each of these loan amounts, years, and APRs? (1) 28000, 5, 7.25; (2) 98750, 30, 9; (3) 6000, 3, 8.75; and (4) 62500, 15, 9.25. Close Loan Payment Calculator.

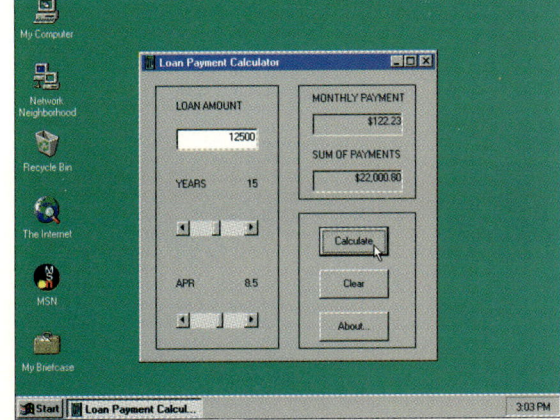

Figure 4-66

5. About Your Computer
Right-click the **My Computer** icon on the desktop. Click Properties on the shortcut menu. When the System Properties dialog box displays, click the Device Manager tab. Click View devices by type. Click the Print button. Click System summary in the Print dialog box and then click the OK button. Click the Cancel button in the System Properties dialog box.

4 webWalk

chapter 1 | 2 | 3 | 4 | 5 | 6 | 7 | 8 | 9 | 10 | 11 | 12 | 13 | 14 | I

inCyber | review | terms | yourTurn | hotTopics | outThere | winLabs | webWalk | exercises | news | home

INSTRUCTIONS: *To display this page from the Web, launch your browser and enter the URL, http://www.scsite.com/dc/ch4/walk.htm. Click the exercise link to display the exercise.*

1 User Responses
User responses refer to the data that a user enters to respond to a question or message from software. Learn about user responses to an automobile purchasing service (Figure 4-67) by completing this exercise.

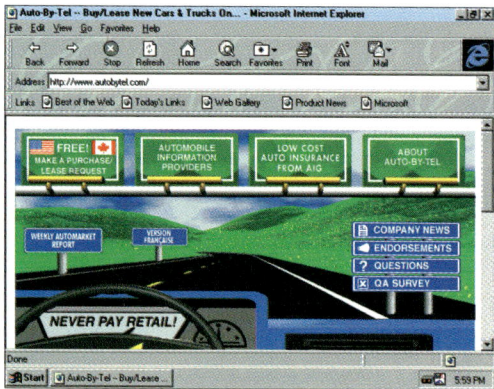

Figure 4-67

2 Input Devices
Input devices consist of hardware used to enter data, programs, commands, and user responses into computer memory. To learn about some unique input devices, complete this exercise.

3 Types of Output
The type of output generated from the computer depends on the needs of the user and the hardware and software that are used. To learn about the output of an interactive mapping service (Figure 4-68), complete this exercise.

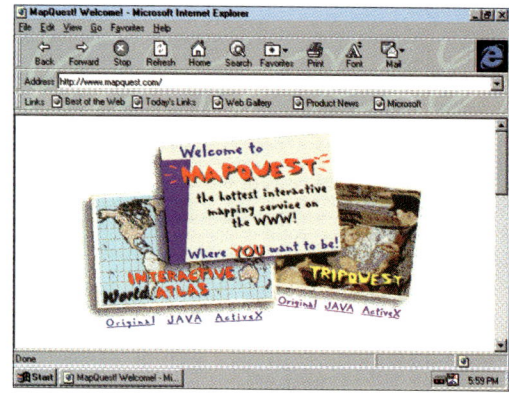

Figure 4-68

4 Output Devices
Output devices consist of hardware through which information can be communicated from the computer to the user. Complete this exercise to learn more about output devices.

5 Information Mining
Complete this exercise to improve your Web research skills by using a Web search engine to find information related to this chapter.

6 Displaying an Image
Each pixel on a color monitor screen is made up of three colored (red, green, blue) phosphor dots. These dots can be turned on in combinations to display a wide range of colors. Complete this exercise to learn more about RGB color values.

7 Digital Cameras
Digital cameras record photographs in the form of digital data. Complete this exercise to learn more about digital cameras and to see a "live" digital camera in action.

8 Computer Related Injuries
Keyboards are responsible for the vast majority of computer related injuries. Learn more about Carpal Tunnel Syndrome and other computer related injuries by completing this exercise.

9 Web Chat
Complete this exercise to enter a Web Chat discussion related to the issues presented in the hotTopics exercise.

Data Storage

CHAPTER 5

OBJECTIVES

After completing this chapter, you will be able to:

- Define storage
- Identify the major storage devices
- Explain how data is stored on floppy disks and hard disks
- Explain how data compression works
- Explain how data is stored on optical disks such as CD-ROMs
- Explain how magnetic tape storage is used with computers
- Describe other forms of storage: PC Cards, RAID, and mass storage devices
- Describe how special-purpose storage devices such as smart cards are used

Storage is the fourth and final operation in the information processing cycle. This chapter explains storage operations and the various types of storage devices that are used with computers. Combining what you learn about storage with your knowledge of input, processing, and output will allow you to complete your understanding of the information processing cycle.

What Is Storage?

It is important to understand the difference between how a computer uses memory and how it uses storage. As you have seen, memory, sometimes called RAM, temporarily stores data and programs that are being processed. **Storage**, also called **secondary storage** or **auxiliary storage**, stores data and programs when they are *not* being processed. Think of storage as a filing cabinet used to store files, and memory as your desk surface. When you need to work on a file, you take the file out of the filing cabinet (storage) and move it to your desk (memory). Although the term storage sometimes is used to refer to the temporary storage of data in memory, it commonly is used to refer to more permanent storage devices such as disk drives. Storage devices provide a more permanent form of storage than memory because they are **nonvolatile**, that is, data and programs held in storage are retained even when power is turned off. Most memory is **volatile**, which means that, when power is turned off, the data and programs stored in memory are erased.

The process of storing data is called **writing** or **recording data**, because the storage device records the data on the storage medium to save it for later use. The process of retrieving data is called **reading data**, because the storage device reads the data and transfers it to memory for processing.

Storage devices also can be used as both input and output devices. When a storage device transfers some of its stored data to the computer for processing, it is functioning as an input device. When a storage device receives information that has been processed by the computer, it is functioning as an output device.

Storage needs can vary greatly. Personal computer users might have a relatively small amount of data to be stored. For example, a database of names, addresses, and telephone numbers of two hundred customers of a small business might require only 100,000 bytes of storage (200 records x 500 characters per record). Users of large computers, such as banks or insurance companies, however, might need storage devices that can store trillions of bytes. In addition to data, software programs must be stored. Programs sometimes require tens to hundreds of megabytes of storage space. To meet the different needs of users, a variety of storage devices are available. Figure 5-1 shows how different types of storage devices and memory compare in terms of relative cost and speed. The storage devices named in the pyramid will be discussed in this chapter.

Figure 5-1
The pyramid chart compares the different types of computer storage and memory. Memory is faster than storage but is expensive and not practical to use for all storage requirements. Storage is less expensive per megabyte stored but is slower than memory. Many computer systems have two or more types of storage devices.

MAGNETIC DISK STORAGE 5.3

Magnetic Disk Storage

Magnetic disk is the most widely used storage medium for all types of computers. A **magnetic disk** consists of a round piece of plastic or metal, the surface of which is covered with a magnetic material. Data can be written to (recorded on) or read from the magnetic surface. Magnetic disk offers high storage capacity, reliability, and fast access to stored data. Types of magnetic disks include floppy disks, hard disks, and removable disk cartridges.

Floppy Disks

A **floppy disk**, also called a **diskette**, consists of a circular piece of thin mylar plastic (the actual disk), which is coated with an oxide material such as that used on audio and video recording tape. In the early 1970s, IBM introduced the floppy disk as a new type of storage. These early, eight-inch wide disks were called *floppies* because they were thin and flexible. The next generation of floppies looked much the same, but were only $5^{1}/_{4}$ inches wide. Today, the most widely used floppy disk is $3^{1}/_{2}$ inches wide (Figure 5-2). The flexible cover of the earlier disks has been replaced with a hard plastic outer covering. Although the $3^{1}/_{2}$-inch disk is not very flexible, the term floppy disk still is used.

In a $3^{1}/_{2}$-inch floppy disk, the circular piece of plastic used for recording is enclosed in a rigid plastic shell. Paper liners help keep the recording surfaces clean (Figure 5-3).

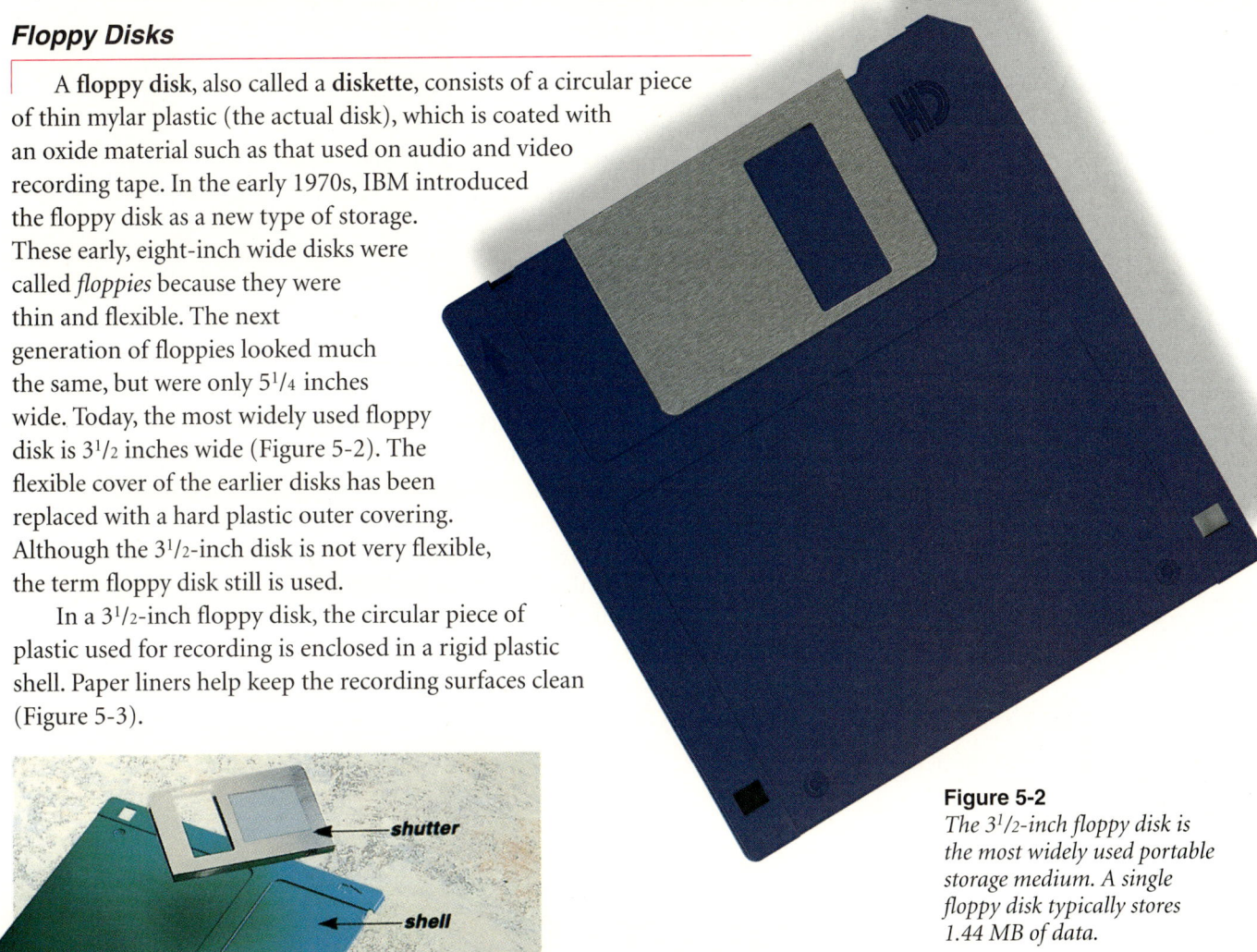

Figure 5-2
The $3^{1}/_{2}$-inch floppy disk is the most widely used portable storage medium. A single floppy disk typically stores 1.44 MB of data.

Figure 5-3
In a $3^{1}/_{2}$-inch floppy disk, the flexible plastic disk is enclosed between two liners that clean any microscopic debris from the disk surface and help to disperse static electricity. The outside cover is made of a rigid plastic material, and the recording window is covered by a metal shutter that slides to the side when the disk is inserted into the floppy disk drive.

inCyber
For details on floppy disks, visit the Discovering Computers Chapter 5 inCyber page (http://www.scsite.com/dc/ch5/incyber.htm) and click Floppy Disk.

A piece of metal called the shutter covers an opening in the rigid plastic shell. When the 3½-inch floppy disk is inserted into a floppy disk drive (Figure 5-4), the drive slides the shutter to the side to expose a portion of both sides of the recording surface.

Floppy disks are widely used with personal computers because they are convenient, portable, and inexpensive. Desktop PCs usually have permanently installed floppy disk drives. Portable computers often have removable floppy disk drives that can be replaced with other devices.

Figure 5-4
A user inserts a floppy disk into the floppy disk drive of a personal computer.

Formatting: Preparing a Floppy Disk for Use Before a floppy disk can be used for storage, it must be formatted. **Formatting** prepares the floppy disk for storage by defining the tracks, cylinders, and sectors on the recording surfaces of a floppy disk (Figure 5-5). A **track** is a narrow recording band forming a full circle around the floppy disk. A **cylinder** is the set of tracks that occupy the same position on the top and the bottom of the disk and have the same number. Cylinder 3, for example, contains track 3 on side 1 of the floppy disk and track 3 on side 2 of the floppy disk. A **sector** is a pie-shaped section of the floppy disk. A **track sector** is a section of track within a sector. Each track sector holds 512 bytes. For reading and writing purposes, track sectors are grouped into clusters. A **cluster** consists of two to eight track sectors (the number varies depending on the operating system).

Figure 5-5
Each track on a floppy disk is a narrow, circular band separated from other tracks by a small gap. Floppy disks typically have eighty tracks with the track closest to the outside edge numbered 0. The tracks are divided into 18 sectors. Each sector of track holds 512 bytes of data. Two or more sectors form a cluster, the smallest amount of space used to record data.

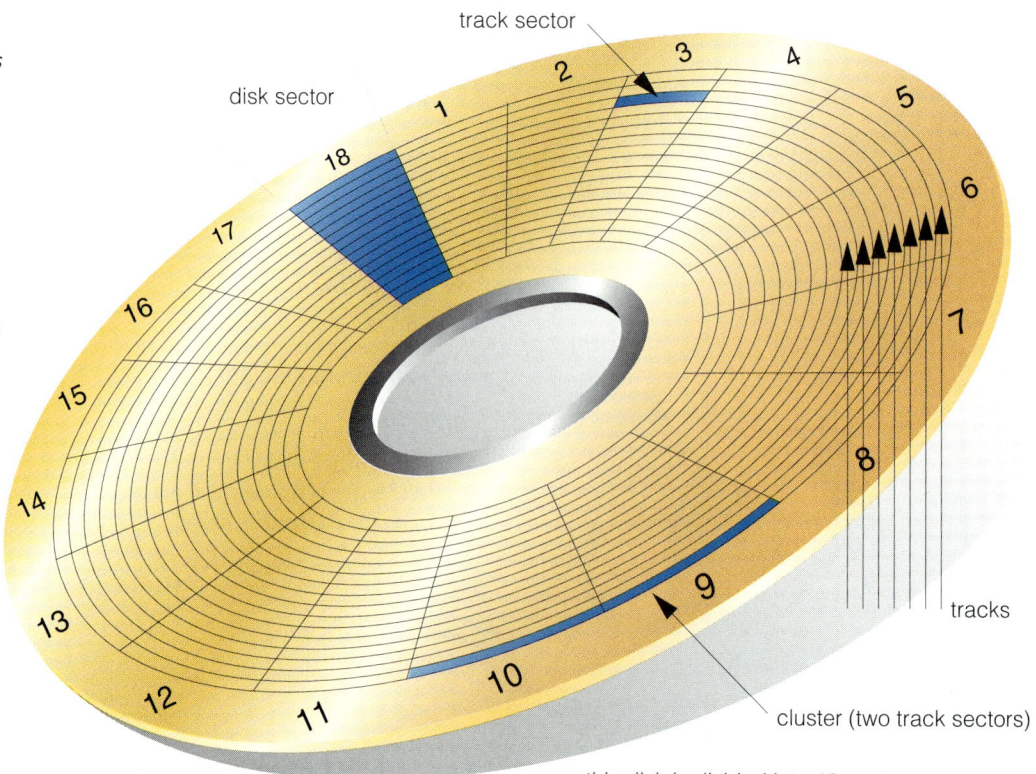

A cluster is the smallest unit of floppy disk space used to store data. Even if a file consisted of only a few bytes, one cluster would be used for storage. Although each cluster holds data from only one file, one file can be stored in many clusters.

The number of tracks and sectors created when a floppy disk is formatted varies according to the storage capacity of the floppy disk, the capabilities of the floppy disk drive used for formatting, and the specifications in the operating system software that does the formatting. An IBM-compatible system—one that is based on the design of the original IBM PC—usually formats 80 tracks and 18 sectors on each side of a 3$\frac{1}{2}$-inch floppy disk. Other computer systems, such as the Apple Macintosh, format disks differently than IBM-compatible systems.

The formatting process not only defines tracks on the recording surface, but also erases any data that is on the floppy disk, analyzes the recording surface for any defective spots, and establishes a directory that will be used to record information about files stored on the floppy disk. On most personal computers, this directory is called the file allocation table (FAT). For each file, the **file allocation table (FAT)** stores the file name, the file size, the time and date the file was last changed, and the cluster number where the file begins. On Windows 95 systems, the file allocation table is called the **virtual file allocation table (VFAT)**. When you ask a computer to list the files on a floppy disk, the information comes from the FAT file. FAT also keeps track of unused clusters and defective areas, if any, and is used when the computer writes new files to the floppy disk.

Figure 5-6
Data cannot be written on the 3$\frac{1}{2}$-inch floppy disk on the left, because the write-protect window in the corner of the floppy disk is open. A small piece of plastic covers the write-protect window of the 3$\frac{1}{2}$-inch floppy disk on the right, so data can be written on this floppy disk. The open hole at the opposite corner identifies this as a high-density disk.

open **closed**

To protect data from being erased accidentally during formatting or other writing operations, floppy disks have a write-protect window. A **write-protect window** is a small hole in the corner of the floppy disk (Figure 5-6). A piece of plastic in the window can be moved to open or close the window. If the write-protect window is closed, the drive can write on the floppy disk. If the window is open, the drive cannot write on the floppy disk. The write-protect window works much like the recording tab on a video tape: if the recording tab is removed, a video cassette recorder (VCR) cannot record on the video tape. Another hole on the opposite side of the disk does not have the sliding plastic piece. This open hole identifies the disk as a high-density floppy disk.

Floppy Disk Storage Capacity The amount of data you can store on a floppy disk depends on two factors: (1) the recording density and (2) the number of tracks on the floppy disk.

The **recording density** is the number of bits that can be recorded on one inch of track on the floppy disk. This measurement is referred to as **bits per inch (bpi)**. The higher the recording density, the higher the storage capacity of the floppy disk. Most floppy disk drives store the same amount of data in the longer outside tracks and the shorter inside tracks, despite the difference in size. Recording density, or bpi, is thus highest in the innermost track, and bpi is measured there. Some newer drives use a different recording method called multiple zone recording. **Multiple zone recording** (MZR) records data at the same density on all tracks. Because longer outside tracks must hold more data to achieve the same density as shorter inside tracks, the outside tracks sometimes contain extra sectors.

The second factor that influences the amount of data a floppy disk can store is the number of tracks on the recording surface. This measurement is referred to as **tracks per inch (tpi)**. As previously explained, the number of tracks on the disk depends on the size of the floppy disk, the drive used for formatting, and how the floppy disk was formatted.

The capacity of floppy disks varies and increases every two or three years as manufacturers develop new ways of recording data more densely. A **high-density (HD) floppy disk**, the most widely used $3^1/_2$-inch floppy disk, can store 1.44 MB of data—the equivalent of approximately 700 pages of 2,000 characters each. Higher and lower capacity $3^1/_2$-inch floppy disks also exist but are not as widely used.

Storing Data on a Floppy Disk Regardless of the type of floppy disk or the way it is formatted, the process of storing data on a floppy disk is essentially the same. When you insert a floppy disk into a floppy disk drive, a shaft connected to the drive motor engages the notches in the metal hub (Figure 5-7). As the drive writes to or reads from the floppy disk, the drive motor spins the circular plastic recording surface at approximately 300 revolutions

Figure 5-7
When you insert a floppy disk into a floppy disk drive, the notches in the metal hub are engaged by a drive motor shaft. A lever moves the shutter to one side so a portion of the floppy disk surface is exposed. As the computer reads from or writes to a floppy disk, the drive motor shaft spins the floppy disk at approximately 300 rpm. Read/write heads above and below the recording surface move in and out to read or write data.

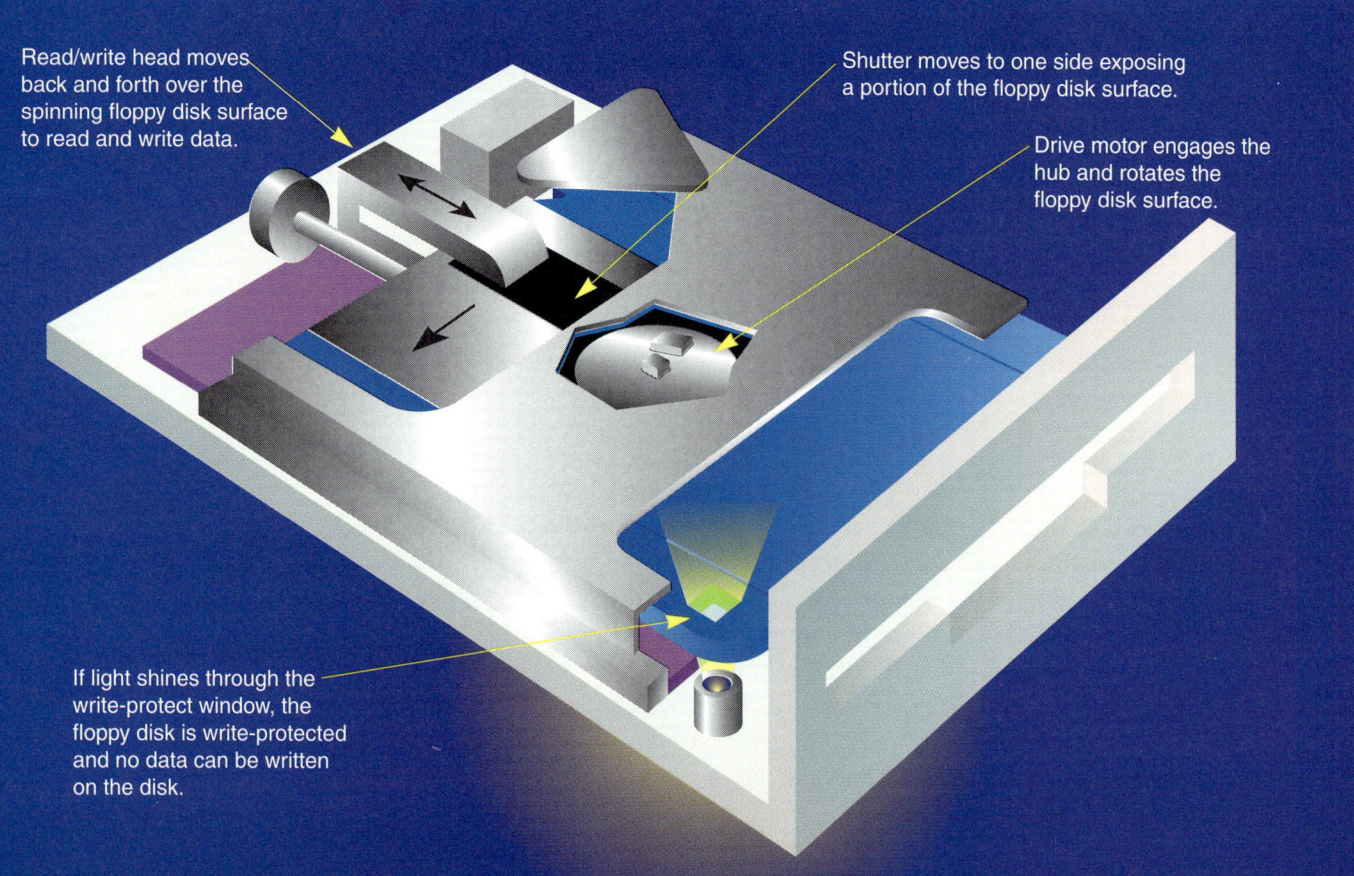

Read/write head moves back and forth over the spinning floppy disk surface to read and write data.

Shutter moves to one side exposing a portion of the floppy disk surface.

Drive motor engages the hub and rotates the floppy disk surface.

If light shines through the write-protect window, the floppy disk is write-protected and no data can be written on the disk.

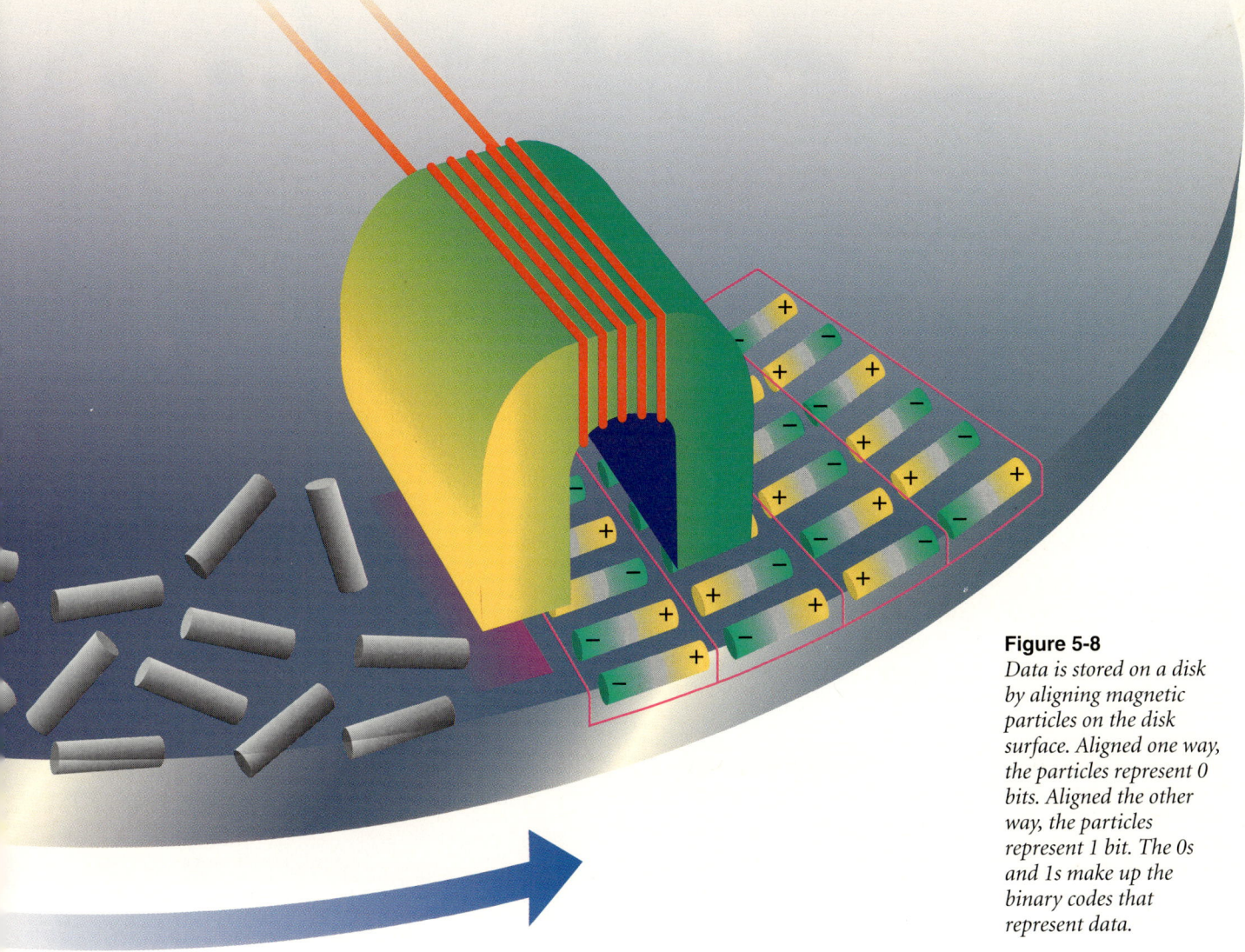

Figure 5-8
Data is stored on a disk by aligning magnetic particles on the disk surface. Aligned one way, the particles represent 0 bits. Aligned the other way, the particles represent 1 bit. The 0s and 1s make up the binary codes that represent data.

per minute (rpm). (If data is not being written or read, the disk does not spin.) A lever opens the shutter to expose a portion of the plastic recording surface.

Data is stored on tracks of the disk using the same binary code that is used to store data in memory, such as ASCII. To do this, a recording mechanism in the drive called the **read/write head** rests on the top and bottom surface of the rotating floppy disk, generating electronic impulses. These electronic impulses change the magnetic polarity, or alignment, of magnetic areas along a track on the disk (Figure 5-8). The plus or minus polarity represents the 1 or 0 bits being recorded. When reading data from the floppy disk, the read/write head senses the magnetic areas that have been recorded along the various tracks and transfers the data to memory. To access different tracks on the floppy disk, the drive moves the read/write head from track to track.

Data stored on a floppy disk must be retrieved and placed in memory to be processed. The time required to locate the data and transfer it to memory is called **access time**. Three factors determine the access time for a floppy disk drive.

1. **Seek time**, the time it takes to position the read/write head over the proper track.
2. **Rotational delay** (also called **latency**), the time it takes for the sector containing the data to rotate under the read/write head.
3. **Data transfer rate**, the time required to transfer the data from the disk to memory.

The access time for floppy disks is approximately 150 milliseconds—that is, data stored in a single sector on a floppy disk can be retrieved in about 1/6 of one second.

Figure 5-9
Guidelines for the proper care of floppy disks.

The Care of Floppy Disks With reasonable care, floppy disks provide an inexpensive and reliable form of storage. When handling floppy disks, you should avoid exposing them to heat, cold, magnetic fields, and contaminants such as dust, smoke, or salt air. One advantage of the 3 1/2-inch floppy disk is that its rigid plastic cover provides protection for the data stored on the plastic disk inside. Figure 5-9 illustrates the guidelines for the proper care of floppy disks.

Hard Disks

Hard disks provide faster access times and larger storage capacities than floppy disks. **Hard disks** consist of one or more rigid **platters** coated with a material that allows data to be recorded magnetically on the surface of the platters (Figure 5-10). The platters most often are made of aluminum, but some newer hard disks use glass or ceramic materials. The platters, the read/write heads, and the mechanism for moving the heads across the surface of the disk are enclosed in an airtight, sealed case. This helps to ensure a clean environment for the disk. Unlike floppy disks, most hard disks are permanently mounted inside the computer and are not removable.

Figure 5-10
This high-capacity disk drive from Western Digital can store 4.3 GB of data. The data is stored on both sides of four platters. The top and bottom of each platter surface is read from or written to by a read/write head at the end of an access arm (such as the one shown over the top platter).

Minicomputers and mainframes use hard disks called **fixed disks** or **direct-access storage devices (DASD)**. These hard disks are often larger versions of the hard disks used with personal computers and can be mounted in the same cabinet as the computer or enclosed in their own stand-alone cabinet (Figure 5-11).

While most personal computers are limited to two to four disk drives, minicomputers can support eight to sixteen disk drives, and mainframe computers can support more than one hundred high-speed disk drives.

Hard Disk Storage Capacity Data is stored on both sides of a hard disk platter. If a drive has one platter, two surfaces are available for data storage; if a drive has two platters, four surfaces are available for data storage; and so on. Naturally, the more platters a drive has, the more data it can store. Just as with a floppy disk, a hard disk must be formatted before it can store data. Before a hard disk is formatted, it can be divided into separate areas called **partitions**. Each partition can function as if it were a separate disk. Separate partitions sometimes are used to store data belonging to different branches of a large company or even to separate the programs and data of a single user. Separate partitions also sometimes are used for different operating systems. On personal computers, hard disk partitions usually are identified by different letters, starting with the letter C. The letters A and B are reserved for floppy disk drives.

The storage capacity of hard drives is measured in megabytes, gigabytes, or terabytes. Figure 5-12 summarizes these terms and their abbreviations. Common storage capacities for personal computer hard disk drives range from 500 MB to several gigabytes. Five hundred megabytes of storage is the equivalent of 250,000 printed pages with about 2,000 characters per page—a stack of paper almost 85 feet high.

Figure 5-11
A high-speed, high-capacity fixed disk drive in a stand-alone cabinet.

> **inCyber**
> For information about hard disks, visit the Discovering Computers Chapter 5 inCyber page (http://www.scsite.com/dc/ch5/incyber.htm) and click Hard Disk.

Storage Terminology

term	abbreviation	number	number of bytes
kilobyte	KB	1,000	thousand
megabyte	MB	1,000,000	million
gigabyte	GB	1,000,000,000	billion
terabyte	TB	1,000,000,000,000	trillion

Figure 5-12
Common storage terms. Some larger storage devices can store terabytes of data.

Storing Data on a Hard Disk Storing data on hard disks is much like storing data on floppy disks, except that hard disks usually have multiple platters. Hard disks rotate at a high rate of speed, usually 3,600 to 7,200 revolutions per minute. Hard disk read/write heads are attached to **access arms** that swing out over the correct track on the disk surface. The read/write heads float on a cushion of air and do not actually touch the surface of the disk. The distance between the head and the surface is approximately ten millionths of an inch. As shown in Figure 5-13, this close clearance leaves no room for any type of contamination. If some form of contamination is introduced, or if the alignment of the read/write heads is altered by something jarring the computer, a head crash can occur. A **head crash** is when a read/write head collides with the disk surface. A head crash usually results in a loss of data.

Figure 5-13
The clearance between a disk read/write head and the disk surface is about 10 millionths of an inch. Because of this small difference, contaminants, such as a smoke particle, a fingerprint, a dust particle, or a human hair, could render the drive unusable. Hard disk drives are sealed to prevent contamination.

Access time for a hard disk is between ten and twenty milliseconds. This is significantly faster than a floppy disk for two reasons. First, a hard disk spins ten to twenty times faster than a floppy disk drive. Second, a hard disk spins constantly, while a floppy disk starts spinning only when it receives a read or write command.

Some computers improve the apparent speed at which data is written to and read from a disk by using disk cache. Similar in concept to RAM cache, **disk cache** is an area of memory set aside for data most often read from the disk. Every time the CPU requests data from the disk, disk cache software looks for the data in the disk cache memory area first. If the requested data is in disk cache, it is transferred immediately to the CPU, and the slower disk read operation is avoided. In addition to tracking the data requested from the disk, disk cache software also reads adjacent clusters on the assumption that they might be needed next. Disk cache memory is updated every time a disk read takes place. Disk cache software also makes disk write operations more efficient by temporarily holding data to be written until the CPU is not busy.

The flow of data to and from the hard disk is managed by a collection of electronic circuits called the **hard disk controller**. The controller can be built into the disk drive or it can be a separate board in an expansion slot. For personal computers, two types of controllers are common, IDE and SCSI. **Integrated drive electronics (IDE)** controllers can operate one or two hard disk drives. Most motherboards have built-in IDE connectors that use a cable to attach directly to the disk drive. IDE controllers can transfer data to the disk at a rate of up to 10 MB per second. **Small computer system interface**, or **SCSI** (pronounced *scuzzy*), controllers can support multiple disk drives or a mix of other SCSI-compatible devices. SCSI devices connect to each other in a chain, with a cable between each device. SCSI controllers usually consist of a circuit board mounted in an expansion slot. They are faster than IDE controllers and can provide up to 100 MB per second transfer rates.

Disk Cartridges

Some hard disk drives, called disk cartridges, are removable. **Disk cartridges** (Figure 5-14) provide both the storage capacity and fast access times of hard disks and the portability of floppy disks. High-capacity disk cartridges can store more than one gigabyte of data and can be used to transport large files or to make copies of important files. Disk cartridges also can be used when data security is an issue. At the end of a work session, you can remove the disk cartridge and lock it up, leaving no data on the computer.

One unique type of disk cartridge is called a Bernoulli disk. The **Bernoulli disk cartridge** works with a special drive unit that uses a cushion of air to keep the flexible disk surface from touching the read/write head. The flexible disk surface reduces the chance of a head crash but causes the cartridges to eventually wear out.

> **inCyber**
>
> For an explanation of disk cartridges, visit the Discovering Computers Chapter 5 inCyber page (http://www.scsite.com/dc/ch5/incyber.htm) and click Disk Cartridge.

Figure 5-14
This removable disk cartridge can hold more than 1 GB of data. It can be used to back up a hard disk or transport large files.

5.12 CHAPTER 5 – DATA STORAGE

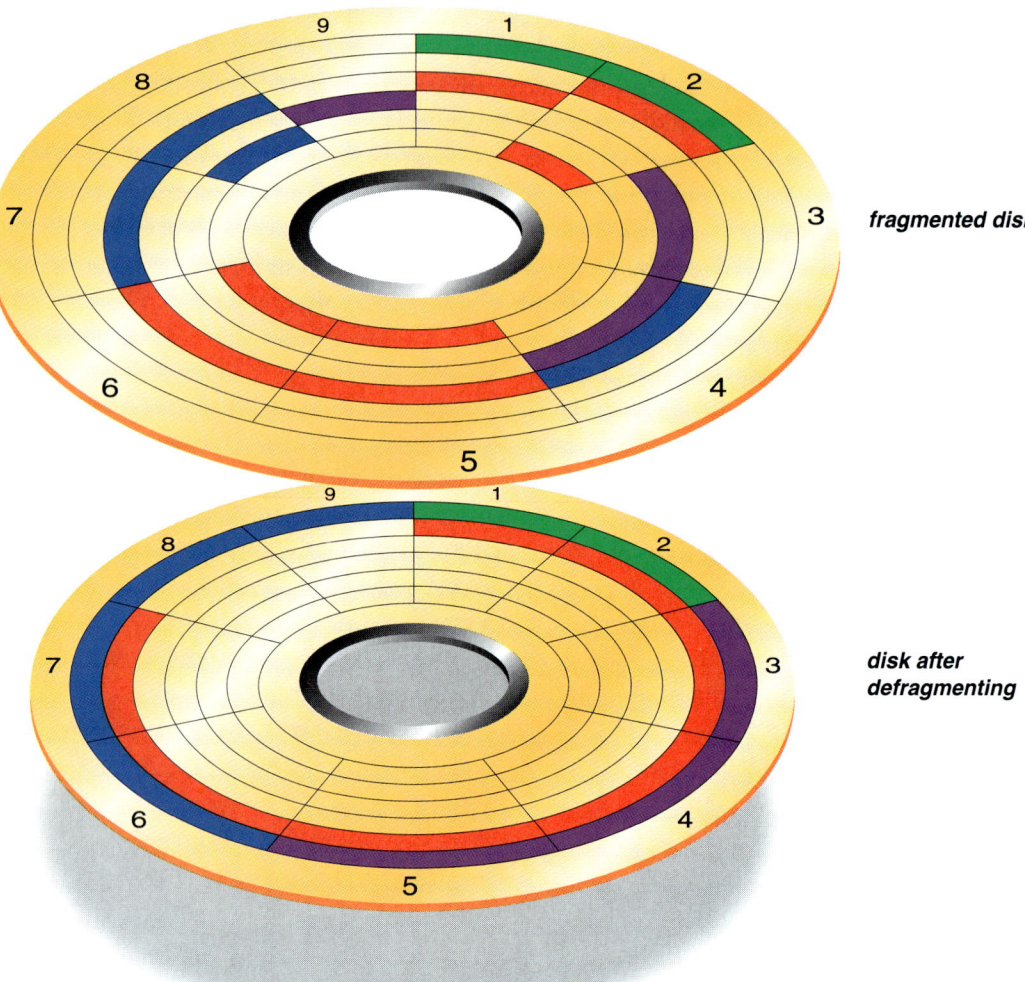

Figure 5-15
A fragmented disk has many files stored in non-contiguous clusters. This condition slows the retrieval of data from the disk. Defragmenting the disk reorganizes the files so they are located in contiguous clusters and speeds access time.

fragmented disk

disk after defragmenting

Maintaining Data Stored on a Disk

To prevent the loss of data stored on a disk, the two procedures that should be performed regularly are backup and defragmentation.

Backup   Backup is the process of creating a copy of important programs and data. Backup should be performed regularly for all data and as needed for important files. To back up a floppy disk, simply copy the data on one floppy disk to another floppy disk. To back up a large number of files or an entire hard disk, tape cartridges or disk cartridges commonly are used.

Defragmentation   When a computer stores data on a disk, it places the data in the first available cluster. While the computer tries to place data in clusters that are *contiguous* (all in a row), contiguous clusters are not always available. When a file is stored in clusters that are not next to each other, the file is said to be **fragmented**. The term fragmented also is used to describe the condition of a disk drive that has many files stored in noncontiguous clusters (Figure 5-15). Fragmentation causes the computer to run slowly, because reading data from several locations on the disk takes longer than if the data were all in one location. Defragmenting the disk solves this problem. **Defragmentation** reorganizes the data stored on the disk so that files are located in contiguous clusters. Defragmentation programs are available as part of system utility packages or as separate programs. Some operating systems also contain defragmentation programs.

For a discussion of backup procedures, visit the Discovering Computers Chapter 5 inCyber page (http://www.scsite.com/dc/ch5/incyber.htm) and click Backup.

MAGNETIC DISK STORAGE

Data Compression One way to store more data on a disk is to use data compression. **Data compression** reduces data storage requirements by substituting codes for repeating patterns of data. For example, consider the familiar Ben Franklin saying, "Early to bed, early to rise, makes a man healthy, wealthy, and wise." Including punctuation, this phrase includes 56 characters. As shown in Figure 5-16, by substituting special characters for repeating patterns, the original phrase can be compressed to only 30 characters, which is a reduction of 46%. Compression generally is stated as a ratio of the size of the original decompressed data divided by the size of the compressed data. The example shown, for instance, has a compression ratio of 1.9 to 1 (56 divided by 30). The codes substituted for the repeating patterns are filed in a table when the data is compressed. This substitution table is used to restore the compressed data to its original form, when necessary.

The type of compression described above is called *lossless compression* because no data is lost in the process. Lossless compression works best for text and numeric data that cannot lose data without losing some meaning. Compression ratios for lossless compression average 2 to 1 (the size of the data is reduced 50%). Other compression methods, called *lossy compression*, have higher compression ratios (up to 200 to 1), but do result in some data loss. Lossy compression methods typically are used to compress video images and sound. Video and sound both can lose data without a noticeable reduction in the overall quality of the output.

Lossy compression usually is performed with special hardware such as a video or sound expansion board. Disk compression programs such as Stacker can be installed to keep all files on a hard disk compressed automatically until they are needed for processing. Some file compression programs such as PKZIP compress and decompress data as directed by the user.

Compressed files often are used when files must be transferred over a communications line, such as a file that is downloaded from the Internet. Because it is smaller, a compressed file takes less time to transfer than a decompressed file.

For an explanation of data compression, visit the Discovering Computers Chapter 5 inCyber page (http://www.scsite.com/dc/ch5/incyber.htm) and click Data Compression.

DATA COMPRESSION

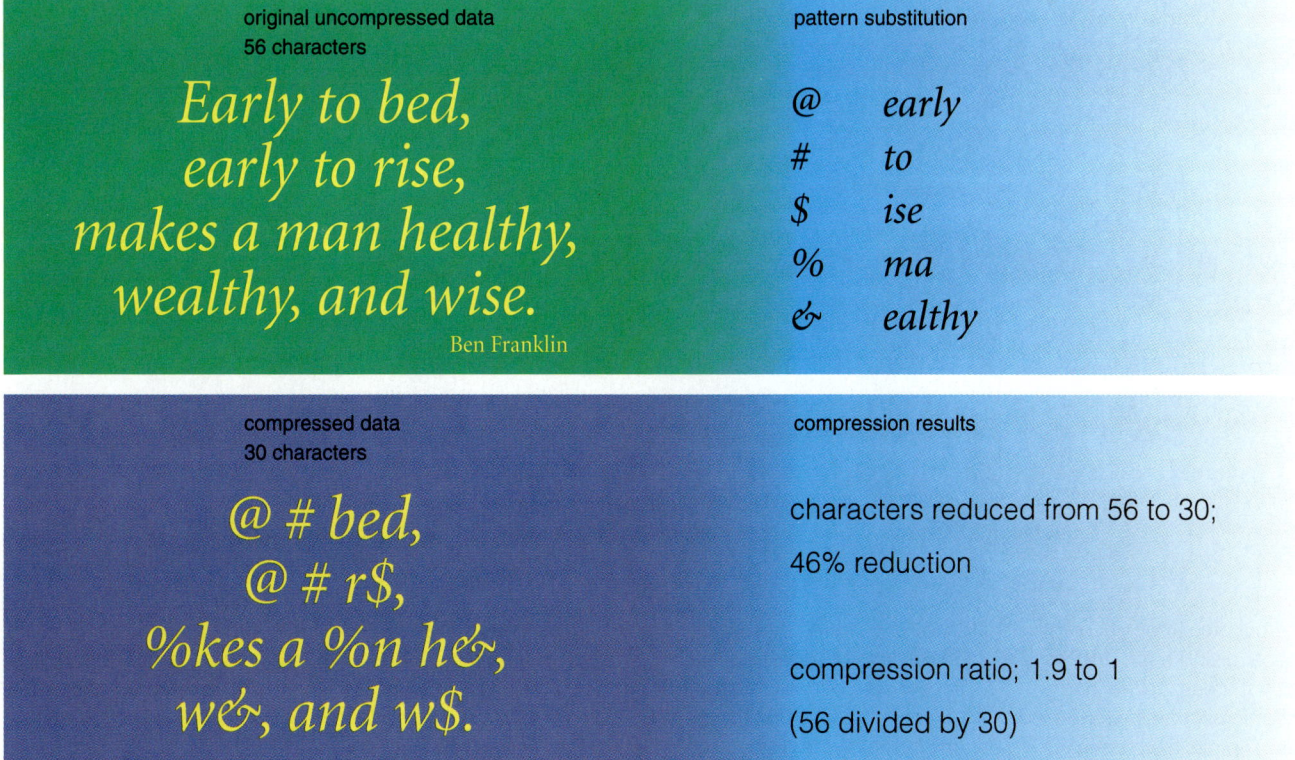

Figure 5-16
An example of data compression.

CD-ROM and Optical Disks

Large quantities of data can be stored on **optical disks**, which use laser technology to read from and write data to a plastic disk or platter. Data is written on an optical disk by a high-powered laser that burns microscopic holes on the surface of the disk. A lower powered laser reads the data from the disk by reflecting light off the disk surface. The reflected light is converted into a series of bits that the computer can process (Figure 5-17).

A full-size, 14-inch optical disk can store 6.8 billion bytes of information. Up to 150 of these disks can be installed in automated disk library systems called jukeboxes that provide more than one trillion bytes of storage. A smaller optical disk, just under five inches in diameter, is called a **CD-ROM**, an acronym for **compact disk read-only memory** (Figure 5-18). CD-ROMs use the same laser technology as the audio compact disks that are used for recorded music. In fact, if a computer is equipped with a CD-ROM drive, a sound card, and speakers, audio compact disks can be played in the CD-ROM drive.

A CD-ROM can store almost 650 MB of information, or about 450 times the data that can be stored on a high-density $3^1/_2$-inch floppy disk. This is enough space to store approximately 325,000 pages of typed data. A revised format for CD-ROM disks, called **DVD** (**digital video disk**), eventually will increase the capacity of CD-ROM size disks to 4.7 gigabytes.

For information about CD-ROMs, visit the Discovering Computers Chapter 5 inCyber page (http://www.scsite.com/dc/ch5/incyber.htm) and click CD-ROM.

Figure 5-17
How data is read from a CD-ROM.

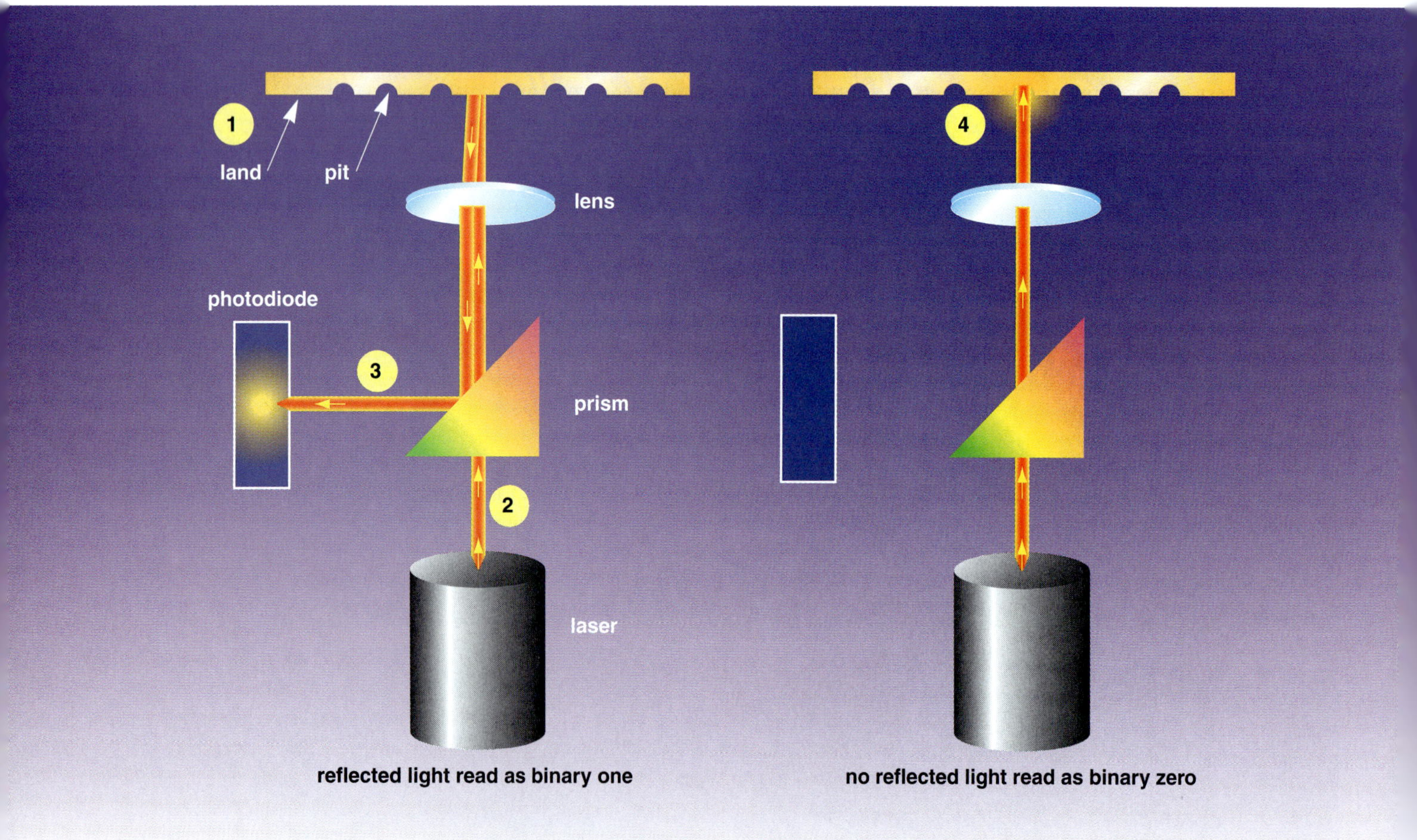

1. The bottom surface of an optical disk like a CD-ROM has flat areas, called lands, and microscopic holes, called pits. The pits have been burned into the surface with a high-powered laser.

2. A lower powered laser is used to read the optical disk. The laser beam passes through a prism and a lens that focuses the beam on the disk surface.

3. Lands reflect the laser beam back to the prism, which then directs the light to a photodiode, which is a component that converts light to an electrical signal. Reflected light is read as the binary bit 1.

4. Pits scatter the laser beam and no light is reflected to the photodiode. No reflected light is read as the binary bit 0.

The original CD-ROM drives were single-speed drives, but today, ten-speed, twelve-speed and sixteen-speed (abbreviated 10X, 12X, and 16X) are common. A CD-ROM drive's speed rating refers to how fast the drive can transfer data in relation to a standard established for CD-ROM drives used for multimedia applications. The original standard established a minimum transfer rate of 150 kilobytes per second (kbps). A 10X drive can transfer data at 1,500 kbps. A 12X drive can transfer data at 1,800 kbps and an 16X drive transfers data at 2,400 kbps, or 2.4 megabytes per second (mbps). The faster CD-ROM drives are especially useful for playing audio and video files.

Recordable CD-ROM drives, called **CD-R (compact disk-recordable)** drives, are growing in use. Multimedia developers who need the large storage capacities of CD-ROM and organizations that must store large volumes of data, for example, often use CD-R drives. A new type of erasable CD-ROM drive, called a **CD-E (compact disk-erasable)** drive, is not yet widely used because the technology is still relatively new.

Another type of erasable optical disk uses magnetic and optical technology to write and read data. **Magneto-optical (MO)** drives record data by using a magnetic field to change the polarity of a spot on a disk that has been heated by a laser. Another type of storage that combines optical and magnetic technologies is a special type of floppy disk, called a **floptical disk**. Flopticals use optical and magnetic technology to achieve higher storage rates (currently up to 120 MB) on a disk very similar to a standard 3^1/$_2$-inch magnetic floppy disk. A floptical disk drive uses a low-powered laser to read the data that is stored in closely spaced tracks. The closely spaced tracks allow for higher bpi and tpi densities. Another advantage of a floptical drive is its capability of reading standard 3^1/$_2$-inch floppy disks.

Figure 5-18
A CD-ROM can store hundreds of times as much information as a floppy disk of similar size. Many reference materials such as encyclopedias, catalogs, and telephone books now are published on CD-ROM instead of on paper.

For an examination of recordable CD-ROM drives, visit the Discovering Computers Chapter 5 inCyber page (http://www.scsite.com/dc/ch5/incyber.htm) and click CD-ROM Drive.

Magnetic Tape

During the 1950s and early 1960s, magnetic tape was the primary method of storing large amounts of data. Today, even though tape is no longer used as a primary method of storage, it is still a cost-effective way to store data that does not have to be accessed immediately. In addition, tape storage serves as the primary means of backup for most systems and often is used to transfer data from one system to another.

Magnetic tape consists of a thin ribbon of plastic. One side of the tape is coated with a material that can be magnetized to record the bit patterns that represent data. Tape is considered a **sequential storage** media because the computer must write and read tape records one after another (sequentially). For example, to read the 1,000th record on a tape, the tape drive must first pass over the previous 999 records. The more common types of magnetic tape devices use cartridges that contain one-quarter- to one-half-inch wide tape (Figure 5-19). Some older computer systems use reel-to-reel tape devices.

inCyber

For a description of magnetic tape, visit the Discovering Computers Chapter 5 inCyber page (http://www.scsite.com/dc/ch5/incyber.htm) and click Magnetic Tape.

Figure 5-19
Magnetic tape cartridges contain tape one-quarter- to one-half-inch wide.

Cartridge Tape Devices

A **cartridge tape** contains magnetic recording tape in a small, rectangular plastic housing. Tape cartridges containing one-quarter-inch wide tape are only slightly larger than audio cassette tapes and frequently are used for personal computer backup. Faster, higher-capacity, one-half-inch cartridge tapes are used for larger system backup. For personal computers, cartridge tape units are designed to be mounted internally in a bay or externally in a separate cabinet (Figure 5-20).

Figure 5-20
One-quarter-inch cartridge tapes often are used to backup the hard disks of personal computers. Tape drives can be internal units mounted in a drive bay or external units.

MAGNETIC TAPE **5.17**

For larger systems, cartridge tapes usually are mounted in their own cabinet. Cartridge tapes for larger systems are designed so multiple tapes can be loaded and unloaded automatically so that tape storage operations can take place unattended (Figure 5-21).

Figure 5-21
Cartridge tape units used for larger systems have automatic loaders that allow multiple tapes to be loaded and recorded without the need of an operator.

For an explanation of cartridge tape devices, visit the Discovering Computers Chapter 5 inCyber page (http://www.scsite.com/dc/ch5/incyber.htm) and click Cartridge.

Reel-to-Reel Tape Devices

Reel-to-reel tape devices have been replaced almost completely by cartridge tape devices but still may be found on large computer systems. **Reel-to-reel tape** devices use two reels, a supply reel to hold the tape that will be read from or written to (Figure 5-22), and a take-up reel to temporarily hold portions of the supply reel tape as it is being processed. As the tape moves from one reel to another, it passes over a read/write head, which is the electromagnetic device that reads and writes data on the tape. When processing is complete, tape on the take-up reel is wound back onto the supply reel.

Figure 5-22
Older style tape units use reels of tape. A full-sized reel is 10 1/2 inches wide and contains more than 2,000 feet of one-half-inch tape. A reel this size can hold about 200 MB of data.

Storing Data on Magnetic Tape

Binary codes such as ASCII and EBCDIC are used to represent data stored on magnetic tape. As with disk drives, tape drives have an electromagnetic read/write head that can read or write magnetic patterns on the tape representing bits. Several different methods are used to record bits on the tape (Figure 5-23).

Quarter-inch-cartridge (**QIC**) tape devices, often used with PCs, record data in narrow tracks along the length of the tape. When the end is reached, the tape reverses direction, and data is recorded in another track in the opposite direction. This method of recording up and down the length of the tape is called **longitudinal**, or **serpentine**, **recording**. QIC cartridges have between nine and 144 tracks and can store from several hundred megabytes to more than 10 GB of data on a single tape. **Digital audio tape** (**DAT**) drives use **helical scan technology** to record data across the width of the tape at a six-degree angle. Instead of using a stationary read/write head, DAT tape drives use a rotating head similar to a video cassette recorder. Older one-half-inch reel-to-reel tape drives record data across the width of the tape in nine channels; eight channels for eight data bits (one byte) and one parity bit.

Tape density is the number of bits that can be stored on one inch of tape. As with disk drives, tape density is expressed in bits per inch, or bpi. Cartridge tape densities range from 6,000 bpi to more than 60,000 bpi. The higher the density, the more data that can be stored on a tape. Some cartridges used on large systems can hold in excess of 40 GB of decompressed data.

For details on quarter-inch-cartridge (QIC) tape devices, visit the Discovering Computers Chapter 5 inCyber page (http://www.scsite.com/dc/ch5/incyber.htm) and click QIC.

Figure 5-23
Different methods of recording data on magnetic tape.

On most quarter-inch-cartridge (QIC) tapes, data is recorded in a single track along the length of the tape. When the end is reached, the tape reverses direction and data is recorded in another track in the opposite direction.

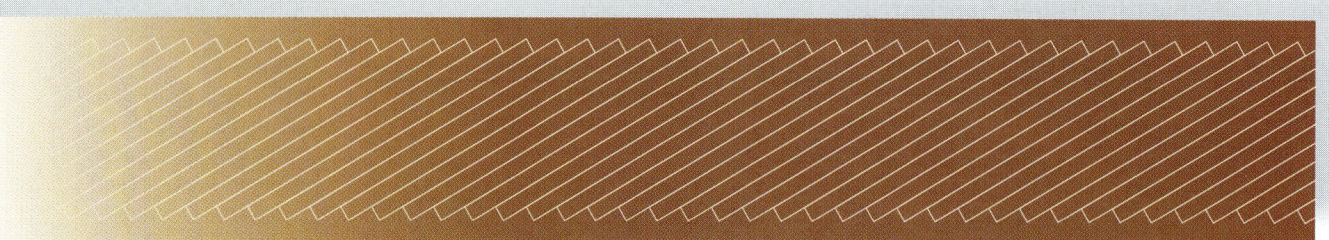

Digital audio tape (DAT) uses helical scan technology to record data in tracks at a six-degree angle to the tape.

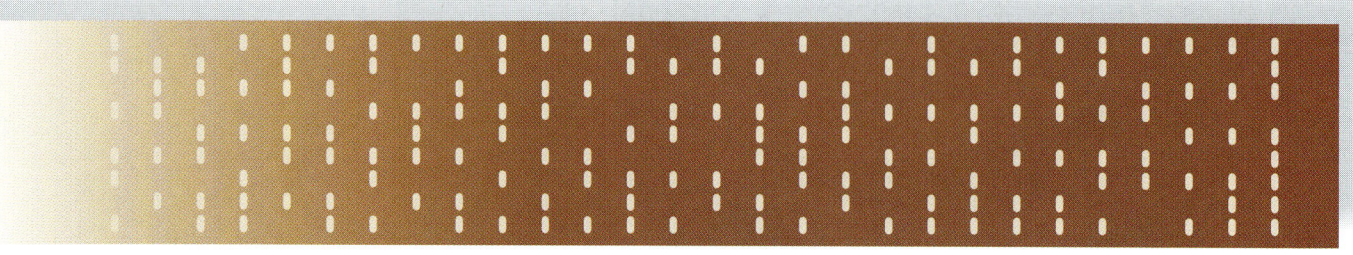

Older, one-half-inch reel-to-reel tape drives record data in nine channels: eight channels for data bits and one channel for a parity bit.

Other Types of Storage Devices

The conventional disk and tape devices just described comprise the majority of storage devices and media, but other means for storing data sometimes are used. These include PC Cards, RAID storage systems, and mass storage devices.

PC Cards

PC Cards are small, credit card-sized cards that fit into PC Card expansion slots. Different types and sizes of the cards are used for storage, communications, and additional memory. Most often, PC Cards are used with portable computers, but they also can be used with desktop systems. PC Cards used for storage are only 10.5mm (about .4 inches) thick, but they contain small rotating disk drives, each 1.3 inches in diameter, that can store more than 300 MB of data (Figure 5-24).

PC Cards are useful for storage if you work with more than one computer or share a computer with others. Your data can be stored on a PC Card and moved quickly to a different computer.

RAID Storage Systems

As computers became faster, writing data to and reading data from increasingly larger disks became a hindrance. Computers spent a large percentage of time waiting for data to go to or from the disk drive. Rather than trying to build even larger and faster disk drives, some disk manufacturers began to connect several smaller disks into an integrated unit that acted like a single large disk drive. A group of integrated small disks is called a **RAID** storage system, which stands for **redundant array of inexpensive disks**. RAID technology can be implemented in several ways, called *RAID levels*.

Figure 5-24
Type III PC Cards are used as small removable disk drives that can hold more than 300 MB of data.

For information about various PC Cards, visit the Discovering Computers Chapter 5 inCyber page (http://www.scsite.com/dc/ch5/incyber.htm) and click PC Card.

The simplest RAID method, called RAID level 1, uses one backup disk for each data disk (Figure 5-25). Each backup disk contains the same information as its corresponding data disk. If the data disk fails, the backup disk can be used as the data disk.

Because the disks contain duplicate information, RAID level 1 is sometimes called **disk mirroring**. RAID levels beyond level 1 divide data across more than one drive. Dividing a logical piece of data such as a record or word into smaller parts and writing those parts on multiple drives is called **striping** (Figure 5-26).

Parity information is an important part of RAID technology. It allows the system to rebuild, sometimes automatically, any information that is damaged on one of the data disks. Some RAID levels require a separate disk, called a parity or check disk, to track parity information. Other RAID levels store parity information directly on the data disk.

RAID storage systems offer a number of advantages over single large disk systems, called **SLEDs**, which stands for **single large expensive disks**. For one, data can be read from or written to RAID disks faster, because multiple read or write operations can take place at the same time. The biggest advantage, however, is the reduced risk of data loss. The ability to recreate damaged data is important to organizations that cannot afford to lose valuable stored information.

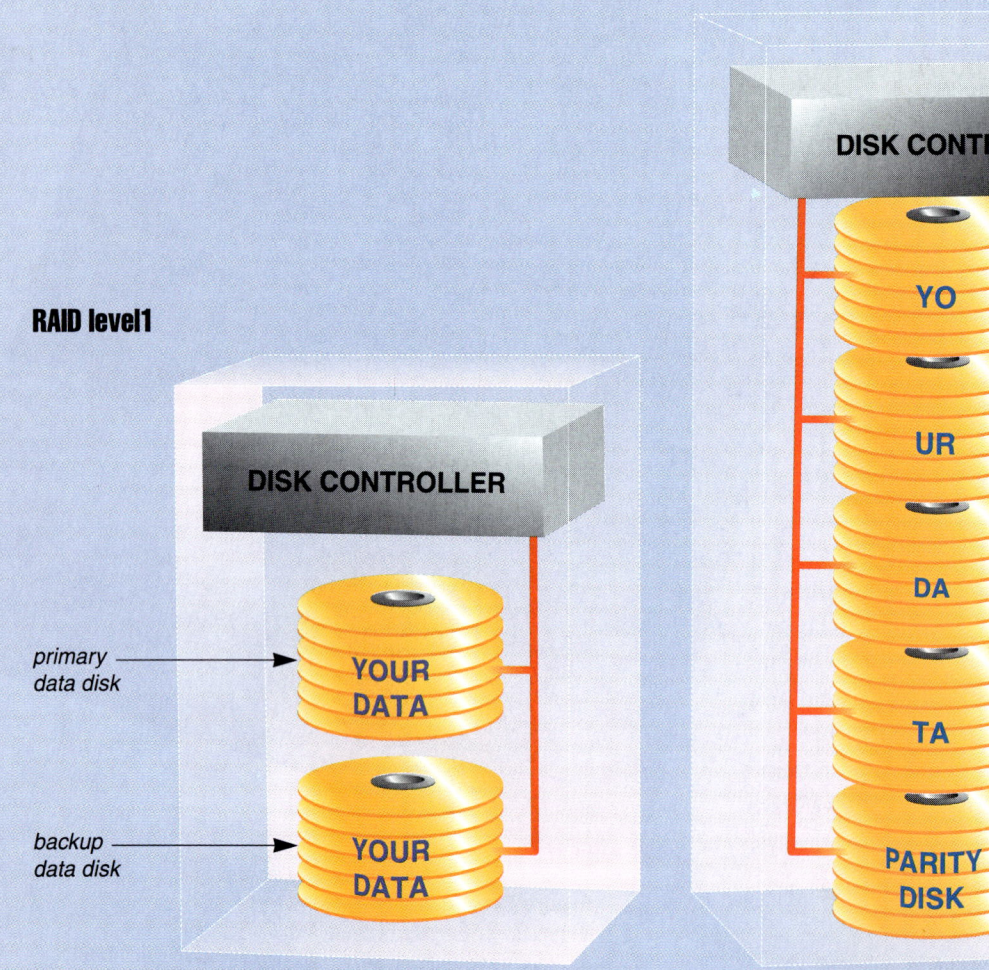
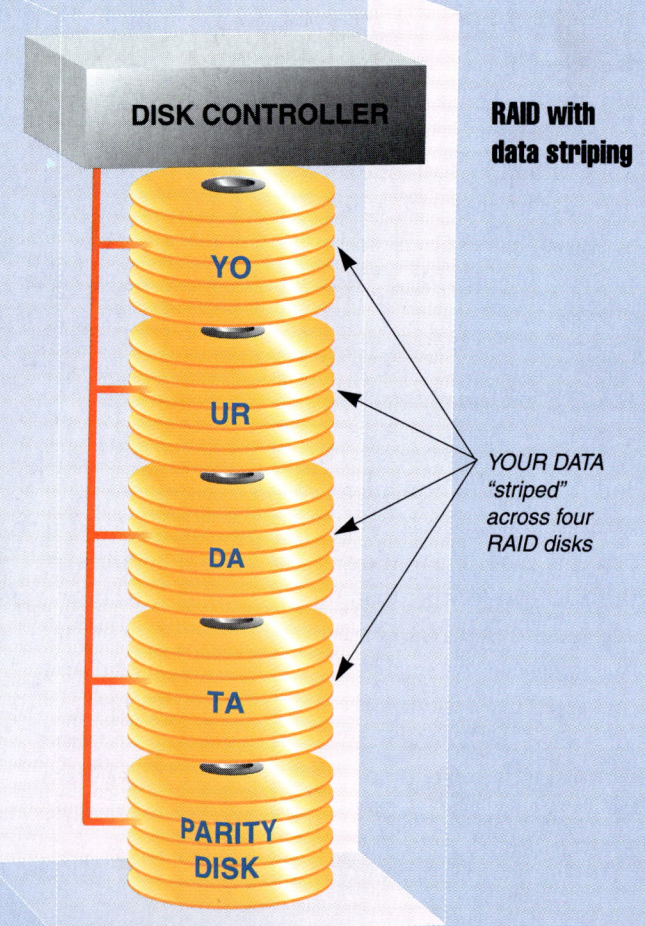

Figure 5-25
In RAID level 1, called disk mirroring, a backup disk exists for each data disk.

Figure 5-26
In RAID levels beyond level 1, data to be stored is divided into parts and written across several disks. This process is called striping. Some RAID levels call for additional parity disks that track information needed to recreate data if one of the data disks malfunctions.

Mass Storage Systems

Mass storage systems provide automated retrieval of data from a library of storage media, such as tape cartridges. Mass storage is ideal for extremely large databases that must allow fast access to all data, even though any one portion of the database may be used only infrequently. Mass storage systems can retrieve and begin accessing records within seconds and take up less room than conventional tape storage systems. Figure 5-27 shows a mass storage system that uses tape cartridges.

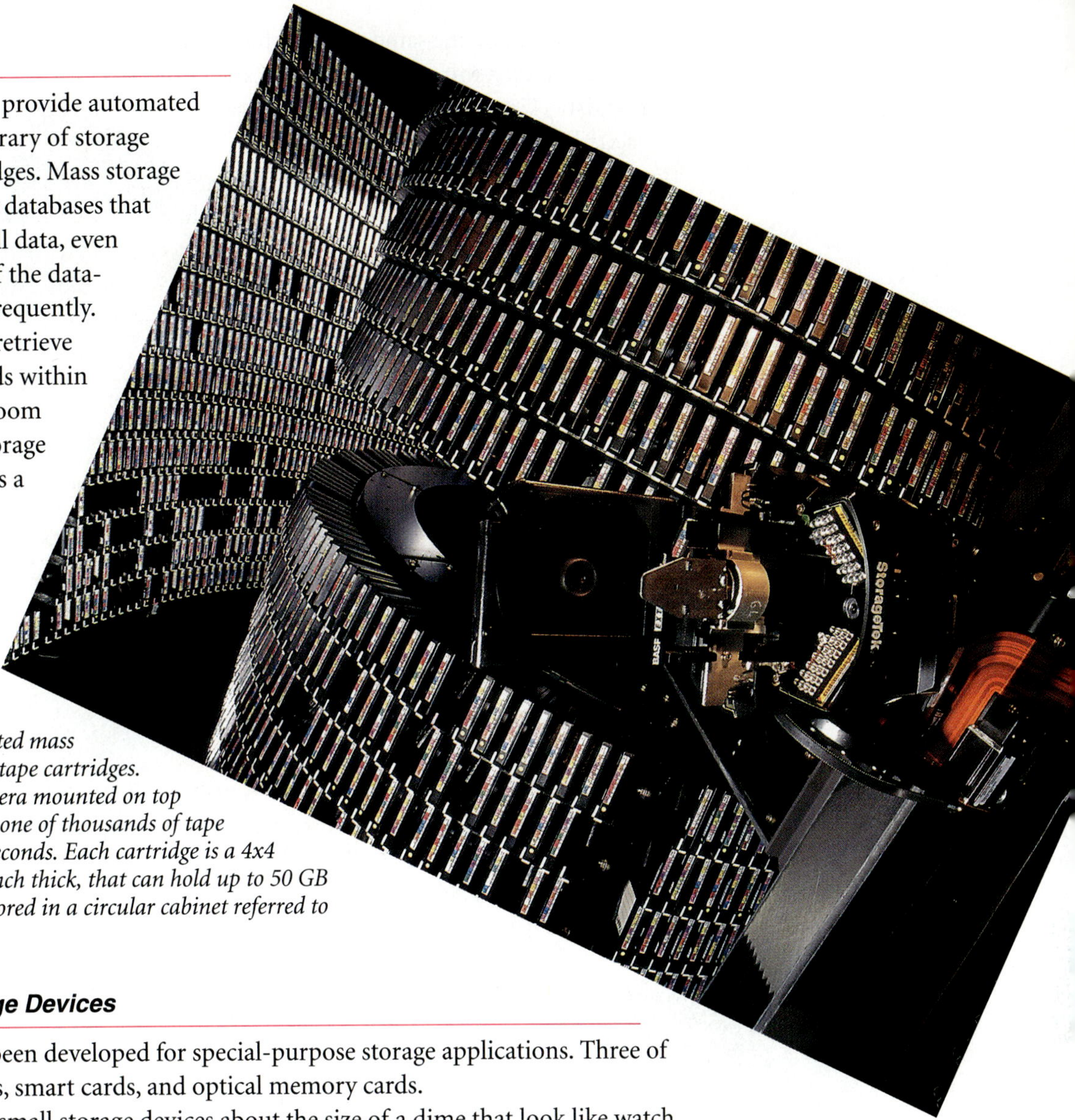

Figure 5-27
The inside of an automated mass storage system that uses tape cartridges. A robot arm with a camera mounted on top can access and load any one of thousands of tape cartridges in about 11 seconds. Each cartridge is a 4x4 inch square about one inch thick, that can hold up to 50 GB of data. The tapes are stored in a circular cabinet referred to as a silo.

Special-Purpose Storage Devices

Several devices have been developed for special-purpose storage applications. Three of these are memory buttons, smart cards, and optical memory cards.

Memory buttons are small storage devices about the size of a dime that look like watch batteries (Figure 5-28). Memory buttons currently can hold up to 8,000 characters of data, but storage capacities are increasing rapidly. To read or update data in the button, you touch the button with a small pen-like probe, which is attached to a hand-held terminal. A sound is generated to indicate that the read or write operation is complete. Memory buttons are used in applications where information about an item must travel with it. Examples are laboratory samples, shipping containers, and rental equipment.

Figure 5-28
Memory buttons can hold up to 8,000 bytes of information. The buttons are ideal in situations where it would be difficult to have related information travel with an item in paper form. The buttons can be read or updated using a pen-like probe attached to a hand-held terminal.

For details on smart cards, visit the Discovering Computers Chapter 5 inCyber page (http://www.scsite.com/dc/ch5/incyber.htm) and click Smart Card.

Smart cards are the same size and thickness of a credit card and contain a thin microprocessor capable of storing data (Figure 5-29). When a smart card is inserted into a specialized card reader, the information on the smart card can be read and, if necessary, updated. Smart cards often are used as prepaid telephone calling cards. Individuals buy smart cards with a specific amount of money stored in the card's microprocessor. Each time the card is used at a special pay telephone, the amount is reduced. An LCD display built into the phone indicates how much money remains in the card. Using smart cards provides convenience to the caller and eliminates the telephone company's need to collect coins regularly from the telephones. Smart cards also are used for employee time and attendance tracking (instead of time cards) and for security applications where detailed information about the card holder is stored in the card. It is estimated that 80% of conventional magnetic-stripe credit cards will be replaced by smart cards by the year 2001.

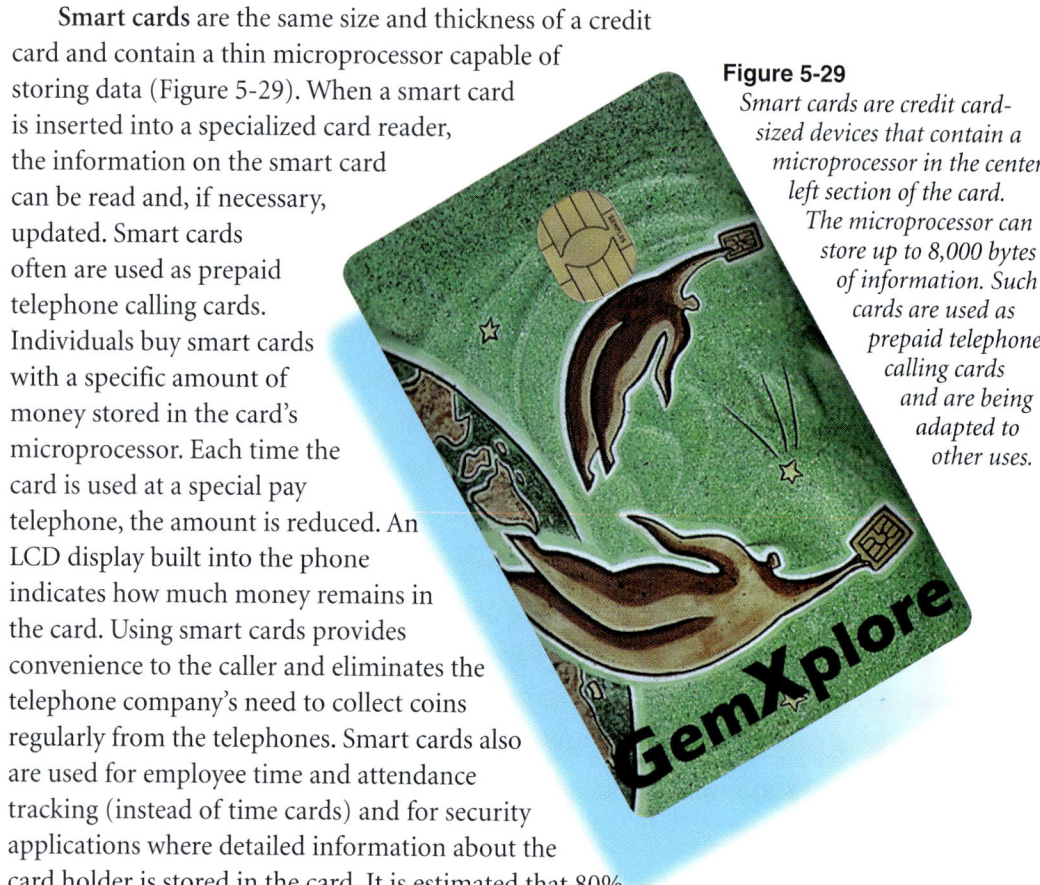

Figure 5-29
Smart cards are credit card-sized devices that contain a microprocessor in the center left section of the card. The microprocessor can store up to 8,000 bytes of information. Such cards are used as prepaid telephone calling cards and are being adapted to other uses.

Optical memory cards are plastic cards the size of a credit card that can store up to 4.1 MB of digitized text or images using a laser beam (Figure 5-30). Optical memory cards are useful as a storage medium that permits data to be added but not to be erased or rewritten. Applications of optical memory cards include storage of automobile records, security identification data, and personal medical information for diagnostic use.

Figure 5-30
This optical memory card can store up to 4.1 MB of data and images. It is the size and thickness of a credit card.

Summary of Storage

Storage is used to store data and programs that currently are not being processed by the computer. This chapter discussed the various types of storage used with computers. The chart in Figure 5-31 provides a summary of the storage devices covered. Adding what you have learned about these storage devices and storage operations in general to what you learned about the input, processing, and output operations will complete your understanding of the information processing cycle.

TYPE	SPACE WITH CAPACITY	DESCRIPTION
Magnetic Disk		
Floppy disk	1.44 MB	Thin, portable plastic storage media that is reliable and low cost.
Hard disk	500 MB to 5 GB	Fixed-platter storage media that provides large storage capacity and fast access.
Disk cartridge	100 MB to 1 GB	Removable hard disk unit that provides large storage capacity and is portable.
CD-ROM and Optical Disk	650 MB to 7 GB	High-capacity disks use lasers to read and record data.
Magnetic Tape		
Cartridge tape	120 MB to 4 GB	Tape enclosed in rectangular plastic housing.
Reel tape	200 MB	$1/2$-inch tape on 300- to 3,600-foot reel.
Other Storage Devices		
PC Card	40 MB to 300 MB	Credit card-sized disk used on portable computers.
RAID	5 GB to 40 GB	Multiple hard disks integrated into a single unit.
Mass storage	10 TB to 100 TB	Automated retrieval of storage media such as tape cartridges.
Special-Purpose Devices		
Memory button	8 KB	Stores data on chip in small metal canister.
Smart card	1 KB to 8 KB	Thin microprocessor embedded in plastic card.
Optical memory card	4 GB	Text and images stored in credit card-sized holder.

Figure 5-31
Summary of storage devices.

HSM: Hierarchical Storage Management

Even though per-megabyte storage costs continue to decrease, the amount of data companies need to store is increasing more quickly than ever. While companies want and need to keep such vast amounts of data readily accessible, the costs of keeping all of this data stored on a hard disk are high.

This problem continues to occur, despite the fact that hard disk storage costs have dropped significantly over the past few years. In 1990, hard disk storage cost $2 per megabyte; by 1996, the cost was down to $ .20 per megabyte. Experts estimate that the cost will be $ .02 per megabyte by the year 2000. The main reason for the lower cost is the capacity increase of hard disks. In 1997, the average PC hard disk stored 1.2 GB. By the year 2000, 5 GB to 10 GB disk drives will be standard.

Lower per-megabyte costs and higher capacities have encouraged users to store more data. In addition, users are storing more complex data that requires more storage space, such as images, compound documents with embedded graphics, and sound and video files. The bottom line is that, even with dramatically lower storage costs, more data than ever exists to store, and companies cannot afford to store all this data on hard disks.

To help with this problem, many companies are turning to **hierarchical storage management** (HSM), which is a way of automating the transfer of data to lower cost, but slower, forms of storage. HSM addresses the storage issue by automating the transfer of data to different categories and speeds of storage devices. The top category is online storage. **Online storage** means the computer has fast, direct access to the data. Online storage mainly consists of hard disks, but some companies use RAM disks for even faster access. Accessing data stored on online devices is almost instantaneous. The next category is called near-line storage. **Near-line storage** usually consists of high-capacity optical disks. Accessing near-line storage may take 10 to 20 seconds while the system finds the appropriate optical disk and loads the requested data. The third category is off-line storage. **Off-line storage** usually consists of automated tape libraries. Tape libraries used for HSM may take up to several minutes to access requested data. The lowest category is shelf storage. **Shelf storage** means that the data has been stored on a tape or other removable media and stored in a cabinet or rack. Accessing this data requires the tape (or other media) to be retrieved manually and loaded on a storage device.

With HSM, files moved from online devices still have a reference, called a *placeholder*, stored online. The placeholder tells the system where to find the data, be it online or on the shelf. The user determines the criteria for transferring data from online storage and can change them at any time. A specific criterion, for example, might be to move any file not requested for ninety days to off-line storage.

Fine-tuning the criteria for moving data from one category to another takes time and experience. Users get very frustrated if data they need is not available because it has been moved to shelf storage too quickly. The goal of HSM is to store data on the lowest cost device but still provide an appropriate level of data availability.

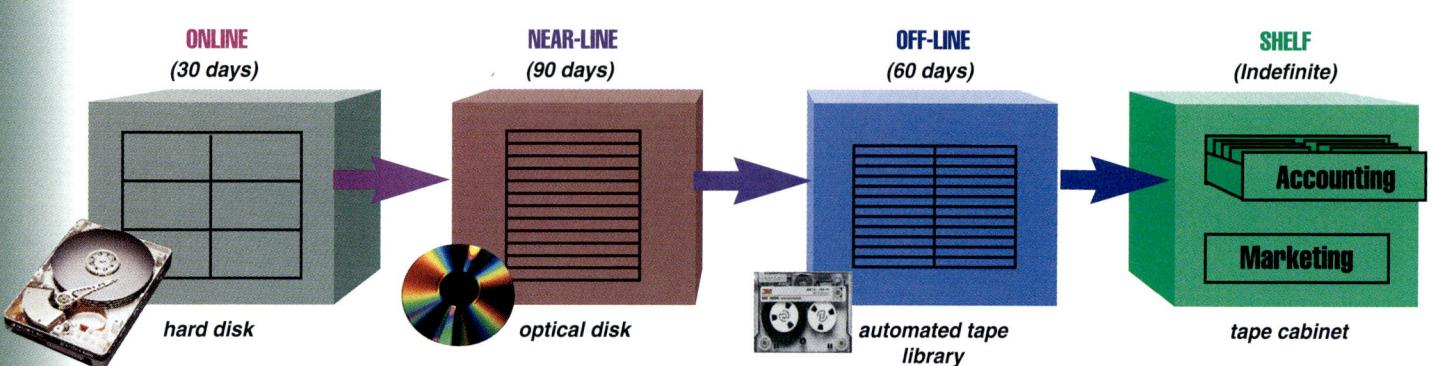

Figure 5-32
Hierarchical storage management (HSM) transfers data to different types and speeds of storage such as online, near-line, off-line, and shelf.

IN THE FUTURE

Holographic Storage

Early in the twenty-first century, around the year 2005, many experts believe that holographic storage devices will hold terabytes of data; the equivalent of a small library. These devices will store data as a hologram, which is a three-dimensional image in photosensitive material.

To record data, a single laser beam is split in two and directed toward the photosensitive material at right angles. Where the laser beams meet, the molecules are altered and the color changes from clear to blue. Blue molecules are considered 1 bits and the clear, unaltered molecules are considered 0 bits. To read information, a different colored laser beam is used. The reading laser beam interacts only with the blue molecules, making them briefly emit a red light. Sensors read the red light and transmit a 1 bit to the computer.

Several obstacles need to be overcome before holographic storage becomes commercially feasible. The first challenge is the size of the equipment required to record and read the material. The smallest size so far is approximately one-foot square. This may not seem that big but still it is much too large for personal computers. The second challenge is to find a suitable recording media. Early studies used chemically treated plastic cubes. The cubes have high storage capacities, more than six terabytes in the space of a sugar cube, but they require very low temperatures to retain their stored information. If the material is left at room temperature, it loses its information in a few hours. Even when it is cooled with liquid nitrogen, it retains its data only for a few months. Other materials lose data—it actually fades—when additional data is recorded. Recent research has focused on plastic discs similar to compact discs. These challenges are worth pursuing, however, because of the tremendous potential. In addition to storing large amounts of data in a small space, the estimated data transfer rates are more than 1,000 times faster than current magnetic disk drives.

Figure 5-33

review chapter

1 | 2 | 3 | 4 | 5 | 6 | 7 | 8 | 9 | 10 | 11 | 12 | 13 | 14 | I

inCyber | review | terms | yourTurn | hotTopics | outThere | winLabs | webWalk | exercises | news | home

INSTRUCTIONS: *To display this page from the Web, launch your browser and enter the URL,* **http://www.scsite.com/dc/ch5/review.htm** *Click the links for current and additional information.*

1 Storage

Storage, also called **secondary storage** or **auxiliary storage**, stores data and programs when they are not being processed. The process of storing data is called **writing** or **recording data**, and the process of retrieving data is called **reading data**. Storage devices also can be used as both input and output devices. Because storage needs vary, a variety of storage devices is available.

2 Magnetic Disk Storage

Magnetic disks, the most widely used storage medium, consist of a round piece of plastic or metal, the surface of which is covered with a magnetic material. Types of magnetic disks include floppy disks, hard disks, and removable disk cartridges.

3 Floppy Disks

A **floppy disk** is a circular piece of thin mylar plastic that is coated with an oxide material. In a 3½-inch floppy disk, the circular piece of plastic is enclosed in a rigid plastic shell. **Formatting** prepares a floppy disk for storage by defining the **tracks**, **cylinders**, and **sectors** on the disk surface. When storing data, a **read/write head** resting on the surface of the rotating floppy disk generates electronic impulses. These impulses change the alignment of magnetic areas along a track to represent the binary code used to store data in memory. To read data, the read/write head senses the magnetic areas that have been recorded and transfers the data to memory. The time required to locate data and transfer it to memory is called **access time**.

4 Hard Disks

Hard disks consist of one or more rigid platters coated with a material that allows data to be recorded magnetically on the surface of the platters. The platters, read/write heads, and **access arms** that move the heads across the disk surface are all enclosed in an airtight, sealed case. Storing data on hard disks is much like storing data on floppy disks except that hard disks usually have multiple platters; and the read/write heads float on a cushion of air and do not touch the disk surface. Access time for a hard disk is significantly less than access time for a floppy disk because a hard disk spins faster and, unlike a floppy disk, a hard disk is spinning constantly.

5 Removable Disks

Disk **cartridges** are removable hard disk drives that provide both the storage capacity and fast access times of hard disks and the portability of floppy disks. The **Bernoulli disk cartridge** works with a special drive unit that uses a cushion of air to keep the flexible disk surface from touching the read/write head.

6 Maintaining Data Stored on a Disk

To prevent the loss of data stored on a disk, two procedures should be performed regularly: backup and defragmentation. **Backup** is the process of creating a copy of important programs and data. **Defragmentation** reorganizes the data stored on a disk so that files are located in contiguous (adjacent) clusters.

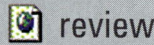

5 review

chapter
1 | 2 | 3 | 4 | 5 | 6 | 7 | 8 | 9 | 10 | 11 | 12 | 13 | 14 | I

inCyber | review | terms | yourTurn | hotTopics | outThere | winLabs | webWalk | exercises | news | home

7 Data Compression

Data compression reduces data storage space requirements by substituting codes for repeating patterns of data. Compression most often is stated as a ratio of the size of the original data divided by the size of the compressed data. In *lossless compression*, which is used for text and numeric data, no data is lost in the compression process. In *lossy compression*, which is used for video images and sound, compression ratios are higher, but some data is lost.

8 CD-ROM and Optical Disks

Optical disks, which use laser technology, can store large quantities of data. A high-powered laser writes data on an optical disk by burning microscopic holes on the disk surface. A lower powered laser reads the data by reflecting light off the disk surface. The reflected light is converted into a series of bits. A **CD-ROM** (an acronym for compact disk read-only memory) is a smaller optical disk that can store about 450 times the data that can be stored on a 3fi-inch floppy disk.

9 Magnetic Tape

Magnetic tape consists of a thin ribbon of plastic, one side of which is coated with a material that can be magnetized to record the binary codes that represent data. Tape is a **sequential storage** media because the computer must write and read records one after another. The most common types of magnetic tape devices use **cartridge tape**, but some older systems use **reel-to-reel tape**. **Quarter-Inch-Cartridge (QIC)** tape devices, often used on PCs, record data in narrow tracks along the length of the tape. Tape storage serves as a primary means of backup, a method of transferring data between systems, and a cost-effective way to store data that does not have to be accessed immediately.

10 Other Types of Storage

PC Cards are small, credit card-sized cards that fit into PC Card expansion slots. Most often, PC Cards are used with portable computers, but they also can be used with desktop systems. A **RAID** storage system uses a group of integrated small disks that act like a single large disk drive. RAID storage systems read and write data faster than single large disk systems and reduce the risk of data loss. **Mass storage** systems provide automated retrieval of data from a library of storage media. Mass storage is ideal for large databases that must allow fast access to all data.

11 Special-Purpose Storage Devices

Memory buttons are small storage devices about the size of a dime that look like watch batteries. Memory buttons are used in applications where information about an item must travel with it. **Smart cards** are the same size and thickness of a credit card and contain a thin microprocessor capable of storing data. Smart cards often are used as prepaid telephone calling cards, as employee time and attendance tracking cards, and as identification cards for security applications. **Optical memory cards** are plastic cards the size of a credit card that can store up to 4.1 MB of digitized text or images using a laser beam. Optical memory cards are useful as a storage medium that permits data to be added but not to be erased or rewritten.

chapter 5 terms

1 | 2 | 3 | 4 | 5 | 6 | 7 | 8 | 9 | 10 | 11 | 12 | 13 | 14 | I

inCyber | review | terms | yourTurn | hotTopics | outThere | winLabs | webWalk | exercises | news | home

INSTRUCTIONS: *To display this page from the Web, launch your browser and enter the URL, http://www.scsite.com/dc/ch5/terms.htm. Scroll through the list of terms. Click a term for its definition and a picture. Click the rocket ship for current and additional information about the term.*

hard disks

DEFINITION

hard disks
Consist of one or more rigid platters coated with a material that allows data to be recorded magnetically on the surface of the platters. (**5.8**)

access arms (5.10)
access time (5.7)
auxiliary storage (5.2)

backup (5.12)
Bernoulli disk cartridge (5.11)
bits per inch (bpi) (5.6)

cartridge tape (5.16)
CD-E (compact disk-erasable) (5.15)
CD-R (compact disk-recordable) (5.15)
CD-ROM (5.14)
cluster (5.4)
compact disk read-only memory (5.14)
cylinder (5.4)

data compression (5.13)
data transfer rate (5.7)
defragmentation (5.12)
digital audio tape (DAT) (5.18)
direct-access storage devices (DASD) (5.9)
disk cache (5.10)
disk cartridges (5.11)
disk mirroring (5.20)
diskette (5.3)
DVD (digital video disk) (5.14)

file allocation table (FAT) (5.5)
fixed disks (5.9)
floppy disk (5.3)
floptical (5.15)
formatting (5.4)
fragmented (5.12)

hard disks (5.8)
hard disk controller (5.10)
head crash (5.10)
helical scan technology (5.18)
hierarchical storage management (HSM) (5.24)
high-density (HD) floppy disk (5.6)

integrated drive electronics (IDE) (5.11)

latency (5.7)
longitudinal recording (5.18)
magnetic disk (5.3)
magnetic tape (5.16)
magneto-optical (MO) (5.15)
mass storage (5.21)
memory buttons (5.21)
multiple zone recording (MZR) (5.6)

near-line storage (5.24)
nonvolatile (5.2)

offline storage (5.24)
online storage (5.24)
optical disks (5.14)
optical memory cards (5.22)

partitions (5.9)
PC Cards (5.19)
platters (5.8)

Quarter-Inch-Cartridge (QIC) (5.18)

RAID (5.19)
read/write head (5.7)
reading data (5.2)
recording data (5.2)
recording density (5.6)
redundant array of inexpensive disks (5.19)
reel-to-reel tape (5.17)
rotational delay (5.7)

secondary storage (5.2)
sector (5.4)
seek time (5.7)
sequential storage (5.16)
serpentine recording (5.18)
SLEDs (5.20)
small computer system interface (SCSI) (5.11)
smart cards (5.22)
storage (5.2)
striping (5.20)

tape density (5.18)
track (5.4)
track sector (5.4)
tracks per inch (tpi) (5.6)

virtual file allocation table (VFAT) (5.5)
volatile (5.2)

write-protect window (5.5)
writing data (5.2)

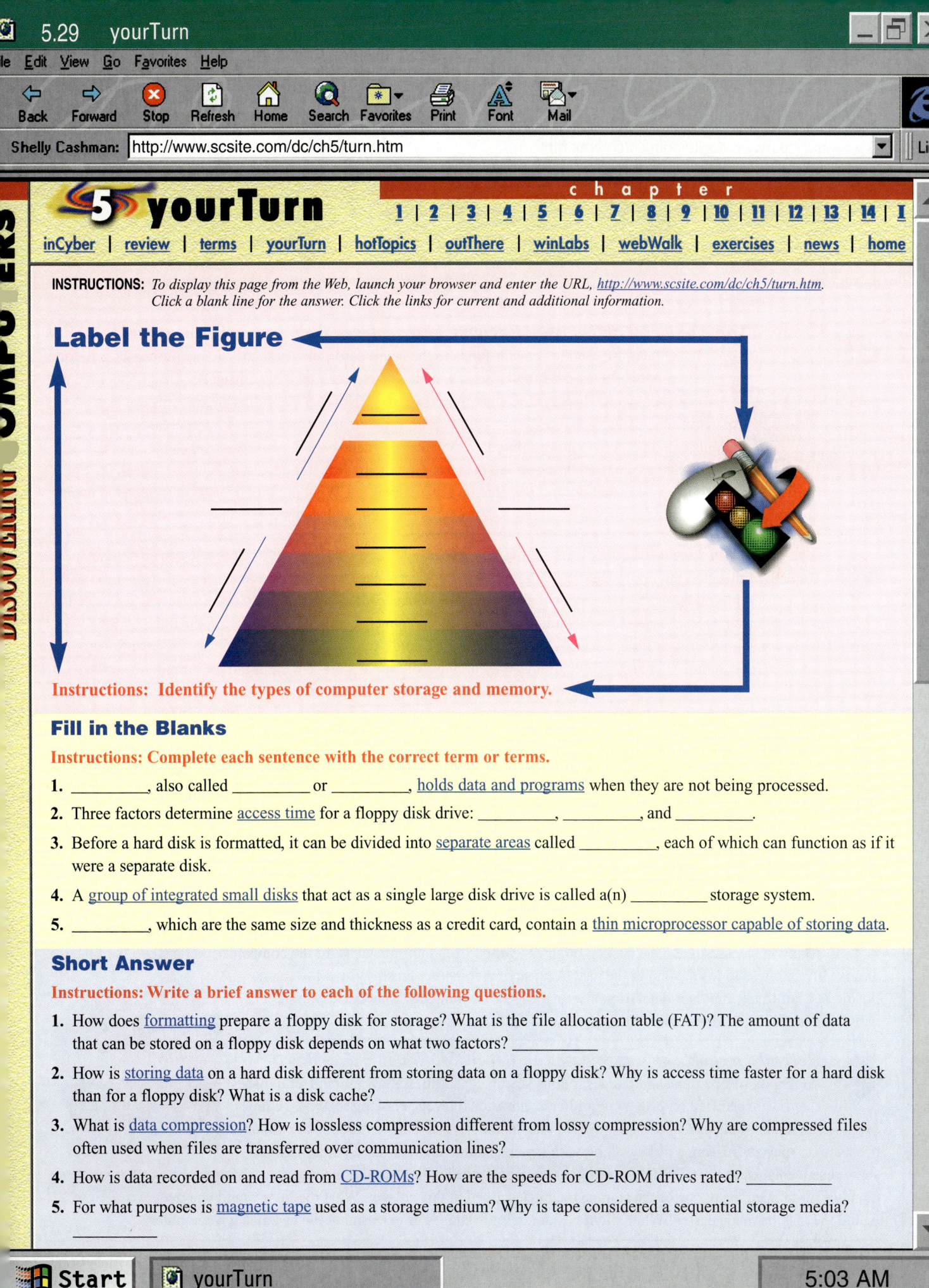

hotTopics

chapter 5 | 1 | 2 | 3 | 4 | 5 | 6 | 7 | 8 | 9 | 10 | 11 | 12 | 13 | 14 | I

inCyber | review | terms | yourTurn | hotTopics | outThere | winLabs | webWalk | exercises | news | home

INSTRUCTIONS: *To display this page from the Web, launch your browser and enter the URL, http://www.scsite.com/dc/ch5/hot.htm. Click the links for current and additional information to help you respond to the hotTopics questions.*

1. *Some residents of Swindon, England, have replaced their cash with smart cards.* Special machines are used to transfer funds to the smart card's microprocessor, and purchases are made simply by running the card through a store's reader. Money can be moved from one card to another, and a small balance reader displays the amount remaining. Advocates claim that smart cards are less expensive than using cash, checks, or credit cards; provide greater security; offer increased control (parents can restrict the types of purchases that can be made on a dependent's card); and serve as a safe form of payment for purchases on the Internet. Opponents fear fraud by savvy counterfeiters, lack of anonymity in transactions, and possible invasion of privacy. What are the greatest advantages of using smart cards? What are the disadvantages? Do you think smart cards ever will replace money? Why or why not?

2. *The history of personal computer storage is a tale of increasing speed, capacity, and durability.* Until IBM invented the floppy disk in 1970, magnetic tape cartridges were the primary means of storage. Tape soon was replaced by the 5¼-inch floppy disk, a magnetic disk sheathed in a flexible cloth-like cover, that stored more data and allowed it to be accessed more quickly. Gradually, the 5¼-inch floppy disk has been supplanted by the sturdier, more capacious 3½-inch floppy disk. What does the future hold? Ten years from now, will the 3½-inch floppy disk, or a version it, still be an important storage medium? Why or why not? What storage medium, if any, might be used instead? Why?

3. *The National Gallery in Washington, D.C., is a remarkable collection that contains works by* Italian, French, and American masters. The Gallery has recorded its entire collection on an optical disk. The disk images offer startling clarity — even brush strokes are visible. Users can display any work in the collection almost instantaneously, locate works based on a range of criteria, and magnify portions of a work on the screen. Is this the beginning of a trend? Will all galleries, archives, and museums eventually take advantage of optical disk technology to catalog their holdings? Why or why not? Who is most likely to use the optical disks? Despite their advantages, how might optical disks pale when compared with a visit to the institution itself?

4. *A recent study has shown that data loss costs American businesses approximately $4 billion* every year. Despite this, another study discovered that less than 33% of all companies regularly backup their files. Many businesses that have backup policies learned from their mistakes; of the companies that backup their data, almost 30% confess to losing data in the past because of a computer crash. Why do so many businesses fail to backup their data? If you were a CEO of a company, what backup policy would you establish? How would you ensure that the policy was carried out?

5. *Recently, a cookbook was released on CD-ROM. Not only does this* cookbook offer a thousand recipes, but its search capabilities allow users to find dishes that meet specified criteria — ingredients, nutritional levels, cooking methods, ethnic origins, and so on — in seconds. The CD-ROM also includes video demonstrations of culinary procedures, such as trussing a turkey, along with a meal planner and glossary. What might be some disadvantages of the CD-ROM cookbook when compared with its traditional counterpart? Imagine another task that could be simplified using one of the storage media described in this chapter. What medium would you use? Why? How would the task be made easier? What might be some disadvantages of performing the task using a computer?

5 outThere

chapter
1 | 2 | 3 | 4 | 5 | 6 | 7 | 8 | 9 | 10 | 11 | 12 | 13 | 14 | I

inCyber | review | terms | yourTurn | hotTopics | outThere | winLabs | webWalk | exercises | news | home

INSTRUCTIONS: *To display this page from the Web, launch your browser and enter the URL, http://www.scsite.com/dc/ch5/out.htm Click the links for current and additional information.*

1. ***The cost of floppy disks varies depending on such factors as recording*** density, manufacturer, and whether or not the disk already is formatted for an Apple or IBM-compatible personal computer. What type of floppy disk is the best buy? Visit a computer vendor and compare three floppy disks: the least expensive, the most expensive, and one priced in the middle of the range. Who manufactures each disk? How are the floppy disks similar? How are they different? Which disk is recommended by the store's salesperson? Why? If you were purchasing a floppy disk for your own use, would you buy one of these floppy disks or a different one? Why?

2. ***Digital video disks (DVDs) can store seven times as much information as*** CD-ROMs — more than two million pages of text, seven hours of music, or multiple complete versions of a popular movie. The disks can be copied a thousand times, and each duplicate is as clear as the original. DVD technology has existed for awhile, but various commercial considerations delayed its introduction. Manufacturers had to agree on a unified format to avoid a conflict like that between VHS and Beta that once afflicted the videocassette industry. An understanding between movie makers, who feared counterfeiting if the disks could be copied, and software writers, who opposed restrictions on copying, had to be reached. Visit sites on the World Wide Web to find out about DVD. Who is most likely to purchase DVD technology? Why? What features of DVD are most important? How will DVD be used? What is a DVD-RAM drive? When will software be published on DVD-ROM disks?

3. ***Some organizations, such as insurance companies, banks, libraries, and college registrars, are*** information intensive, meaning they must keep track of and manipulate large amounts of data. For these institutions, choosing a suitable storage medium is a crucial decision. Care must be taken so the medium selected is adequate, reliable, cost-effective, and appropriate. Visit an information-intensive organization and interview someone responsible for maintaining the organization's data. What are the organization's storage requirements? What type of storage medium is used? In what way does that medium meet the organization's needs? Have any problems with storage ever existed? If so, how where the problems remedied? What kinds of backup procedures are employed?

4. ***Many computer users support the saying "You never can have too much storage." Although*** some turn to hardware solutions to address the problem of adequate storage, other users look to software answers, such as hard disk partitions or data compression. Information about both partition software and data compression software is available on the World Wide Web. Visit some Web sites to find out more about hard disk partitions and data compression. How do partitions increase the capacity of hard disks? What kind of data compression (lossy or lossless) is most suitable for communications devices? What are the most well known data compression algorithms? How can compression ratios of different algorithms be compared?

5. ***As a result of expanding storage requirements for software and graphic files, new technologies*** are being developed that offer even greater storage capacity. These technologies include DVD, flash memory cards, glass disks, glass-ceramic disks, and wet hard drives. Using current computer magazines and sites on the Web, prepare a brief report on one or more of these new technologies. What does the technology entail? What benefits does it offer? Why? When is the technology likely to be available for general use?

5.32   winLabs

inCyber | review | terms | yourTurn | hotTopics | outThere | winLabs | webWalk | exercises | news | home

chapter 1 | 2 | 3 | 4 | 5 | 6 | 7 | 8 | 9 | 10 | 11 | 12 | 13 | 14 | I

INSTRUCTIONS: *To display this page from the Web, launch your browser and enter the URL,* http://www.scsite.com/dc/ch5/labs.htm. *Click the links for current and additional information.*

Shelly Cashman Series Secondary Storage Lab

 Follow the instructions in winLabs 1 on page 1.34 to display the Shelly Cashman Series Labs screen. Click Maintaining Your Hard Drive. Click the Start Lab button. When the initial screen displays, read the objectives. With your printer turned on, click the Print Questions button. Fill out the top of the Questions sheet and then answer the questions.

Examining My Computer

Right-click the My Computer icon in the upper-left corner on the desktop. Click Open on the shortcut menu. What is the drive letter for the floppy disk on your computer? What letter(s) are used for the hard drives on your computer? If you have a CD-ROM drive, what letter is used for it? Double-click the drive C icon in the My Computer window. What are the names of the folders (yellow folder icons) on your drive C? Close all open windows.

Working with Files

Insert your student floppy disk into drive A. Double-click the My Computer icon on the desktop. When the My Computer window displays, right-click the 3fi Floppy [A:] icon. Click Open on the shortcut menu. Click View on the menu bar and then click Large Icons. Right-click the lab2-3 icon. If lab2-3 is not on your floppy disk, ask your instructor for a copy. Click Copy on the shortcut menu. Click Edit on the menu bar and then click Paste. A new icon titled Copy of lab2-3 displays in the 3fi Floppy [A:] window (Figure 5-34). Right-click the Copy of lab2-3 icon and then click Rename on the shortcut menu. Type lab5-3 and then press ENTER. Right-click the lab5-3 icon and then click Print on the shortcut menu. Close the 3fi Floppy [A:] window.

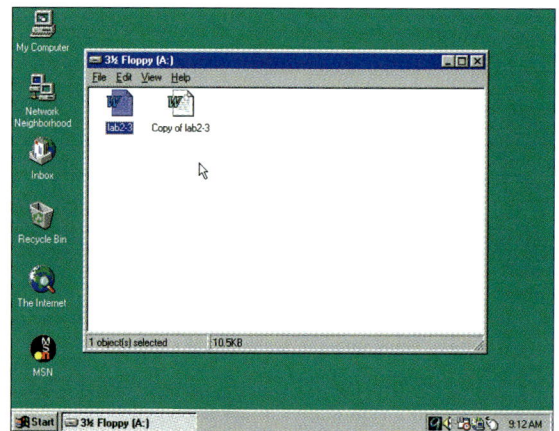

Figure 5-34

Using Help

 Click the Start button on the taskbar, and then click Help on the Start menu to display the Help Topics: Windows Help dialog box. Click the Contents tab, double-click How To..., and then double-click Work with Files and Folders. Click Finding a file or folder. Click the Options button and then click Print Topic. Click the OK button. Click the Help Topics button. One at a time, print each of the remaining Work with Files and Folders topics. Close any open Help window(s). Read the printouts.

webWalk

chapter 5 | 1 | 2 | 3 | 4 | 5 | 6 | 7 | 8 | 9 | 10 | 11 | 12 | 13 | 14 | I

inCyber | review | terms | yourTurn | hotTopics | outThere | winLabs | webWalk | exercises | news | home

INSTRUCTIONS: *To display this page from the Web, launch your browser and enter the URL, http://www.scsite.com/dc/ch5/walk.htm. Click the exercise link to display the exercise.*

1. Data Compression
One way to store more data on a disk is to use data compression. You can learn more about data compression by completing this exercise.

2. Audio File Storage
One common audio file format on the Web is the WAV format. Complete this exercise to learn about storage requirements for .wav sound files (Figure 5-35).

3. Video File Storage
One common video file format on the Web is the AVI format. To view some movie clips and learn about the storage requirements for .avi video files, complete this exercise.

4. Graphics File Storage
While GIF is still the dominant graphics format on the Web, JPEG is gaining ground fast. To view some dramatic pictures in .jpg format (Figure 5-36) and learn more about storage requirements for .jpg graphic files, complete this exercise.

Figure 5-35

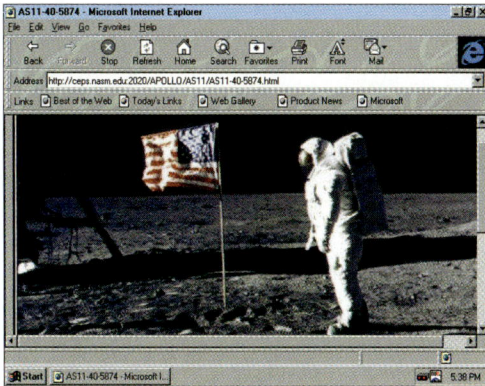

Figure 5-36

5. Information Mining
Complete this exercise to improve your Web research skills by using a Web search engine to find information related to this chapter.

6. Web file formats
Multimedia files on the Internet come in many different formats. Some Web browsers need "helper" applications, also called "viewers," to be able to display certain file formats. Complete this exercise to learn more about different file formats and viewers for Web browsers.

7. Flash Memory
Digital cameras, PDAs, handheld PCs, navigation systems, digital voice recorders and even cell phones are targets for new storage technologies. Flash memory is electronically erasable, programmable, read-only memory, so it is non-volatile. Complete this exercise to learn more about Flash memory.

8. Digital Video Disk (DVD)
Twenty times more data can fit on a DVD than a CD. This translates into richer sound and images than ever heard or seen before. By some estimates, DVD optical drives will be a $4 billion market by the year 2000. Complete this exercise to learn more about DVDs.

9. Web Chat
Complete this exercise to enter a Web Chat discussion related to the issues presented in the hotTopics exercise.

Communications and Networks

O B J E C T I V E S

After completing this chapter, you will be able to:

- Define the term communications
- Describe several uses of communications technology
- Describe the basic components of a communications system
- Describe the various transmission media used for communications channels
- Describe the different types of line configurations
- Describe how data is transmitted
- Describe the functions performed by communications software
- Describe commonly used communications equipment
- Explain the difference between local and wide area networks
- Explain the use of communications protocols

When computers were first developed, they were designed as stand-alone systems. As computers became more widely used, equipment and software were designed to transfer data from one computer to another. Initially, this capability was available only on large systems. Today, even the smallest hand-held computers can communicate with other computers. This change has taken place because of several reasons. For one, communications equipment and software, once expensive options, now are standard components in most computer systems. In addition, opportunities to use communications to access information increase almost daily. Online services and the Internet, for example, allow you to send messages to friends, read magazines on the World Wide Web, and obtain research data, news, and product information, twenty-four hours a day.

This chapter provides an overview of communications with an emphasis on the communication of data and information. The chapter explains some of the terminology, equipment, procedures, and applications that relate to computers and their use as communications devices. It also discusses how computers can be joined together into a network, which is a group of connected computers that multiplies the power of individual computers by allowing them to communicate and share hardware, software, data, and information.

What Is Communications?

Communications, sometimes called **data communications** or **telecommunications**, refers to the transmission of data and information between two or more computers, using a communications channel such as a standard telephone line.

Examples of How Communications Is Used

The ability to instantly and accurately communicate information is changing the way people do business and interact with each other. The following applications rely on communications technology:

- Electronic mail (e-mail)
- Voice mail
- Facsimile (fax)
- Telecommuting
- Videoconferencing
- Groupware
- Electronic data interchange (EDI)
- Global positioning systems (GPSs)
- Bulletin board systems (BBSs)
- Online services
- The Internet

Electronic Mail (E-mail)

Electronic mail (**e-mail**), described in Chapter 2, allows you to use a computer to transmit messages to and receive messages from other computer users. The other users may be connected to the same computer network or to a separate network reached through the use of communications equipment.

Voice Mail

For a glossary of communications terms, visit the Discovering Computers Chapter 6 inCyber page (http://www.scsite.com/dc/ch6/incyber.htm) and click Communications.

Voice mail allows callers to leave a voice message in a voice mailbox, much like leaving a message on an answering machine. The difference between voice mail and an answering machine is that a voice mail system digitizes the caller's message so it can be stored on a disk like other computer data. The party who was called then can listen to the stored message (by converting it from digital to audio form), reply to the message, or add comments and forward the message to another mailbox on the system.

Facsimile (Fax)

Facsimile, or **fax**, equipment, described in Chapter 4, is used to transmit a digitized image of a document over telephone lines. The document can contain hand-written or typed text, graphics, or even photographs. A fax machine scans the document and converts the image into digitized data, which is transmitted over a telephone line. The fax machine at the receiving end converts the digitized data back into its original image. Many PCs use fax equipment and a modem to send documents directly to a fax machine or to another PC. A person who receives the fax on his or her PC can print the document to create a hard copy.

Telecommuting

Telecommuting involves working at home and communicating with an office by using a personal computer and communications equipment and software (Figure 6-1). Using this equipment and software, a telecommuter can connect to the office's main computer or network to read and answer electronic mail, access databases, and transmit completed

Figure 6-1
Telecommuting allows you to work from your home or some other location away from the office.

For details on telecommuting, visit the Discovering Computers Chapter 6 inCyber page (http://www.scsite.com/dc/ch6/incyber.htm) and click Telecommuting.

projects. Telecommuting provides flexibility, allowing companies to increase employee productivity and, at the same time, meet the needs of individual employees. Telecommuting can reduce the time used to commute to the office each week; eliminate the need to travel during poor weather conditions; provide a convenient and comfortable work environment for disabled employees or workers recovering from injuries or illnesses; and allow employees to combine work with personal responsibilities such as child-care. Some predict that by the year 2000, ten percent of the work force will be telecommuters.

Videoconferencing

Videoconferencing is the use of computers, television cameras, and communications software and equipment to conduct *electronic meetings* with participants at different locations (Figure 6-2). Special software and equipment are used to digitize and compress

Figure 6-2
Videoconferencing is used to transmit and receive video and audio signals over standard communications channels. This meeting is being transmitted to a video conference center at another location. The people at the other location also are being recorded and transmitted and can be seen on the TV monitor.

the video image so it can be transmitted along with the audio over standard communications channels. The video images of moving objects do not transmit as clearly as they do over television channels, but they are clear enough to contribute to the discussion. Images of nonmoving objects such as charts and graphs transmit more clearly.

Videoconferencing originally was developed for large groups holding meetings in a room specially outfitted with videoconferencing equipment. More recently, desktop videoconferencing equipment has been developed to allow individual users to conduct videoconferences using a personal computer (Figure 6-3).

For information about videoconferencing, visit the Discovering Computers Chapter 6 inCyber page (http://www.scsite.com/dc/ch6/incyber.htm) and click Videoconferencing.

Groupware

Groupware, described in Chapter 2, is software that helps multiple users to collaborate on projects and share information. Groupware is part of a broad concept called **workgroup technology**, which includes equipment and software used by group members to communicate, manage their activities, and make group decisions. Other features and capabilities of groupware include group editing, group scheduling, group decision support, workflow software, and discussion databases. Some software applications discussed separately in this section, including e-mail and videoconferencing, also can be considered groupware.

Electronic Data Interchange (EDI)

Electronic data interchange (EDI) is the direct electronic exchange of documents from one business's computer system to another. EDI frequently is used by large companies to transmit routine business documents such as purchase orders and invoices. In some industries, such as the automotive industry, EDI is the standard way of doing repeat business with suppliers. EDI offers a number of advantages over paper documents, including the following:

- Reduced paper flow
- Lower transaction costs
- Faster transmission of documents
- Reduced data entry errors, because data does not need to be reentered at the receiving end

Some companies have developed sophisticated EDI applications in which orders are created automatically based on sales or inventory levels, transmitted electronically to a vendor, and shipped to the customer. The entire process requires almost no human intervention.

For information about electronic data interchange (EDI), visit the Discovering Computers Chapter 6 inCyber page (http://www.scsite.com/dc/ch6/incyber.htm) and click EDI.

Figure 6-3
Desktop videoconferencing equipment allows individual users to communicate with other employees on their computer network. Some systems also can connect to remote locations.

Global Positioning Systems (GPSs)

A **global positioning system** (**GPS**) uses receivers that pick up and analyze transmissions from several satellites to determine the geographic location of the earth-based GPS receiver. Depending on the equipment used, a GPS system can be accurate to within 50 feet. GPS systems often are used for tracking and navigation by all types of vehicles, such as cars, trucks, boats, and planes. Small GPS systems even have been designed for use with portable personal computers. Some GPS systems work with map software, which can measure the distance between two points and display the user's exact location and direction of travel on a map (Figure 6-4).

Figure 6-4
Global positioning system (GPS) equipment communicates with satellites to provide an exact fix on the user's location.

Bulletin Board Systems (BBSs)

An electronic **bulletin board system** (**BBS**) is a computer system that maintains a centralized collection of information in the form of electronic messages. Once you access a bulletin board system using a personal computer and communications equipment, you can add or delete messages, read existing messages, or upload and download software. BBSs are run by a person called the **system operator,** or **sys op,** who maintains and updates the bulletin board.

More than 60,000 BBSs exist in the United States. Some of these bulletin boards provide specific services; for example, many hardware and software vendors have set up BBSs to provide online support for their products. Other bulletin boards function as electronic meeting rooms for special-interest groups that use the BBS to share information about hobbies such as stamp collecting, games, music, genealogy, and astronomy. Still other BBSs are strictly social; for example, users meet new friends and conduct conversations by posting messages on the bulletin board. While most BBSs are local and serve a relatively small number of users, some regional and national BBSs attract a larger user base.

inCyber

For an explanation of global positioning systems (GPSs), visit the Discovering Computers Chapter 6 inCyber page (http://www.scsite.com/dc/ch6/incyber.htm) and click GPS.

Online Services

Online services, sometimes called **information services**, make information and services available to paying subscribers. Once you subscribe to an online service, you can access it by using communications equipment and software to connect to the service provider's computer system. Services that are available include electronic banking, shopping, news, weather, hotel and airline reservations, and investment information. Some specialized online services provide very specific information, such as legal reports. Other online services (Figure 6-5) provide a wide variety of information. Figure 6-6 is a list of the major online service providers.

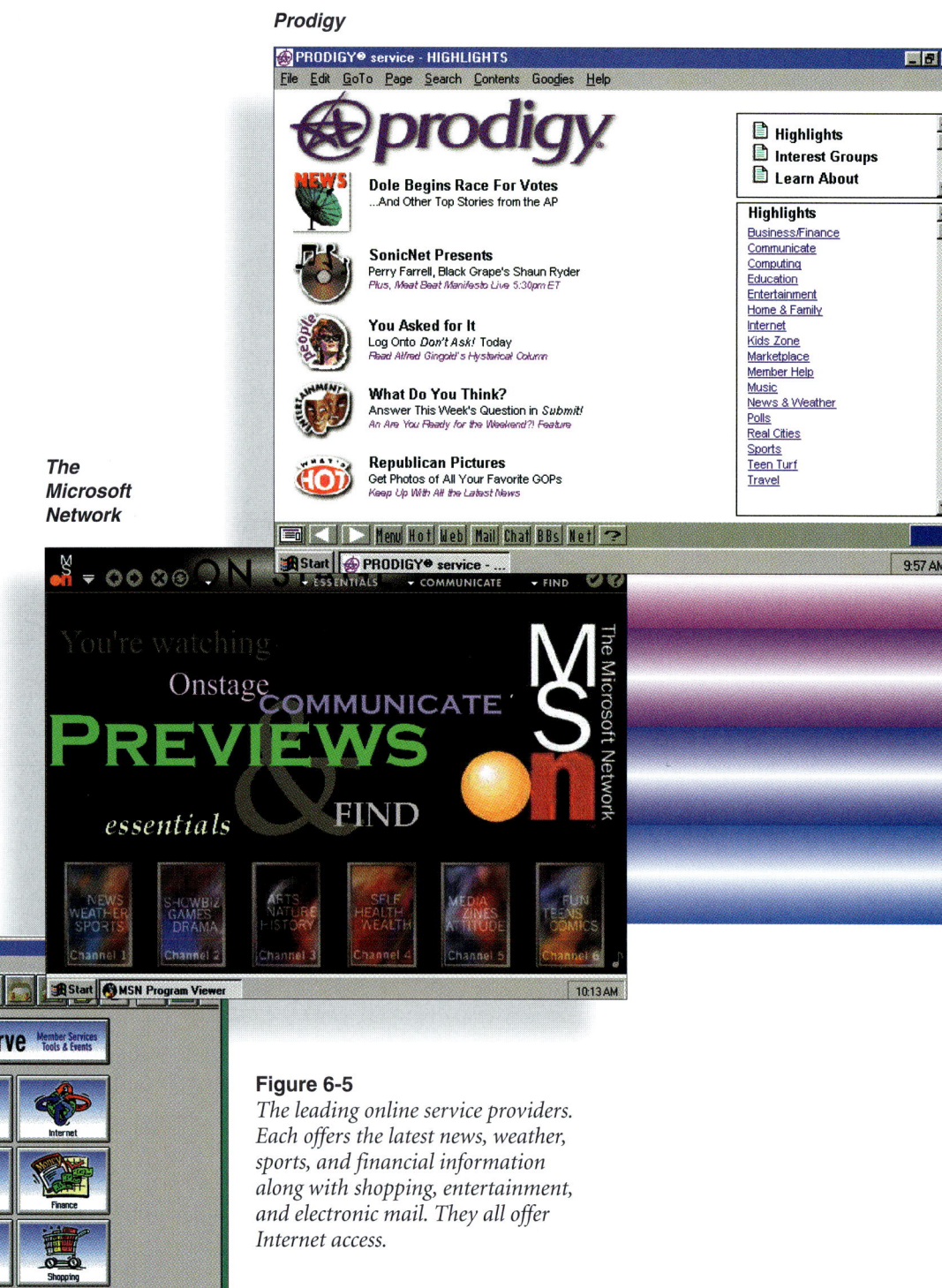

Figure 6-5
The leading online service providers. Each offers the latest news, weather, sports, and financial information along with shopping, entertainment, and electronic mail. They all offer Internet access.

America Online

NAME	DESCRIPTION	TELEPHONE NUMBER
America Online	Largest service provider. News, weather, shopping, finance, travel, and more.	800-827-6364
Prodigy	News, weather, shopping, finance, travel, and more.	800-776-3449
CompuServe	Most comprehensive of all services. Business oriented.	800-848-8199
The Microsoft Network	Newest service. News, weather, shopping, finance, travel, and more.	800-386-5550

Figure 6-6
The names and information telephone numbers of the major online information service providers.

The Internet

One of the more exciting uses of communications today is the Internet. The **Internet** is a global network of computer networks used daily by individuals and businesses to obtain information, send messages, order products and services, and more. Much like the telephone, the Internet is changing the way people communicate and share information. The history and uses of this growing communications application will be covered in more detail in Chapter 7.

A Communications System Model

Figure 6-7 shows the basic model for a communications system. This model consists of the following equipment:

- A computer or a terminal
- Communications equipment that sends (and usually can receive) data
- The communications channel over which data is sent
- Communications equipment that receives (and usually can send) data
- Another computer

The basic model also includes **communications software**, consisting of programs that manage the transmission of data between computers. For two computers to communicate with each other, each system must have compatible communications software. A **communications channel**, also called a **communications line**, **communications link**, or **data link**, is the path that the data follows as it is transmitted from the sending equipment to the receiving equipment in a communications system. Communications channels are made up of one or more transmission media.

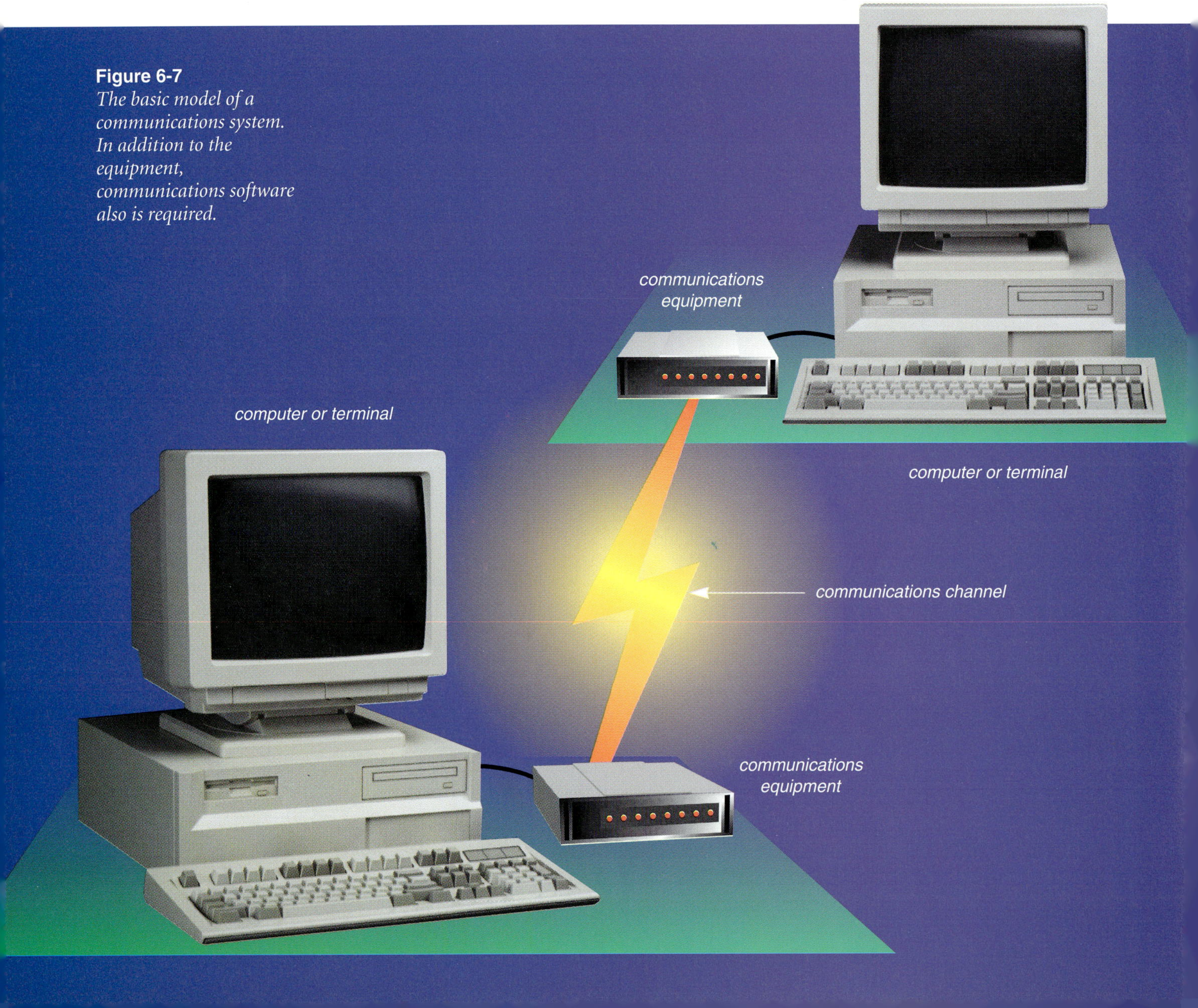

For an example of how companies use communications systems, visit the Discovering Computers Chapter 6 inCyber page (http://www.scsite.com/dc/ch6/incyber.htm) and click Communications System.

Figure 6-7
The basic model of a communications system. In addition to the equipment, communications software also is required.

TRANSMISSION MEDIA   6.9

Transmission Media

Transmission media are the physical materials or other means used to establish a communications channel. The two types of transmission media are physical cabling media, such as twisted-pair cable, coaxial cable, and fiber-optic cable and wireless media, such as microwaves and other radio waves and infrared light.

Twisted-Pair Cable

Twisted-pair cable (Figure 6-8) consists of pairs of plastic-coated copper wires that are twisted together. A thin layer of colored plastic insulates and identifies each wire; the wires then are twisted to reduce electrical interference. **Shielded twisted-pair (STP) cable** has a foil wrapper around each wire that further reduces electrical interference. **Unshielded twisted-pair (UTP) cable**, also called **10baseT cable**, does not have the foil wrapper. Because twisted-pair cable is an inexpensive transmission medium that can be installed easily, it commonly is used for telephone lines and data communications between computers.

1. wires are twisted to reduce electrical interference
2. color coding identifies individual and pairs of wires
3. plastic sheath protects wires
4. modular connector; RJ11 (4-wire) connector used for voice and low-speed (up to 1 Mbps) data transmission; RJ45 connector (8-wire) used for high-speed (10 to 100 Mbps) data transmission

Figure 6-8
Twisted-pair cable often is used to connect personal computers with one another. It is inexpensive and can be installed easily.

Coaxial Cable

A **coaxial cable**, often referred to as **coax** (pronounced *co-axe*), is a high-quality communications line that consists of a copper wire conductor surrounded by three layers: a nonconducting insulator surrounded by a woven metal outer conductor and a plastic outer coating (Figure 6-9). Because coaxial cable is more heavily insulated than twisted-pair, it is not susceptible to electrical interference and transmits data faster over longer distances.

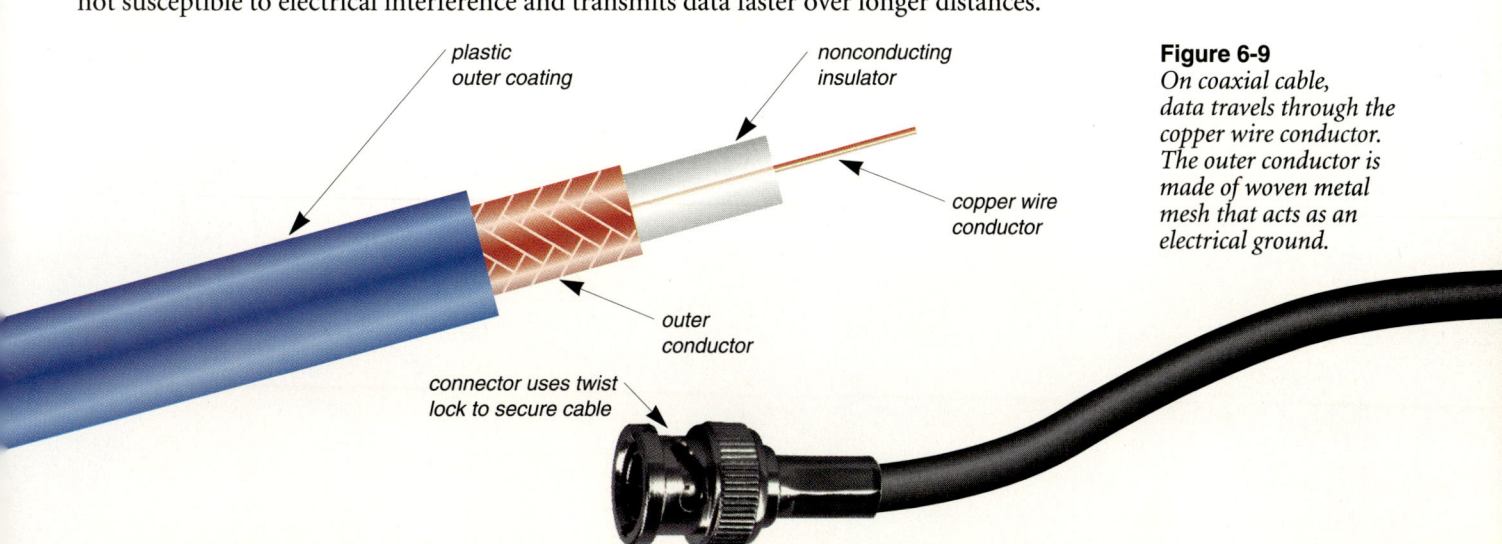

Figure 6-9
On coaxial cable, data travels through the copper wire conductor. The outer conductor is made of woven metal mesh that acts as an electrical ground.

Different grades and sizes of coaxial cable exist. One type of coaxial cable, for example, is used for cable television. Another type called **thinnet**, or **10base2 cable**, is a small diameter coaxial cable that often is used with computer networks.

Fiber-Optic Cable

Fiber-optic cable uses smooth, hair-thin strands of glass or plastic to transmit data as pulses of light (Figure 6-10). The major advantages of fiber-optic cables over wire cables include substantial weight and size savings and reduced electrical and magnetic interference. Another advantage is increased speed of transmission. A single fiber-optic cable can carry several hundred thousand voice communications simultaneously. Fiber-optic cable does, however, cost more than twisted-pair or coaxial cable and can be difficult to install and modify. Despite these limitations, many telephone companies use fiber-optic cable for new telephone lines because of its high-carrying capacity.

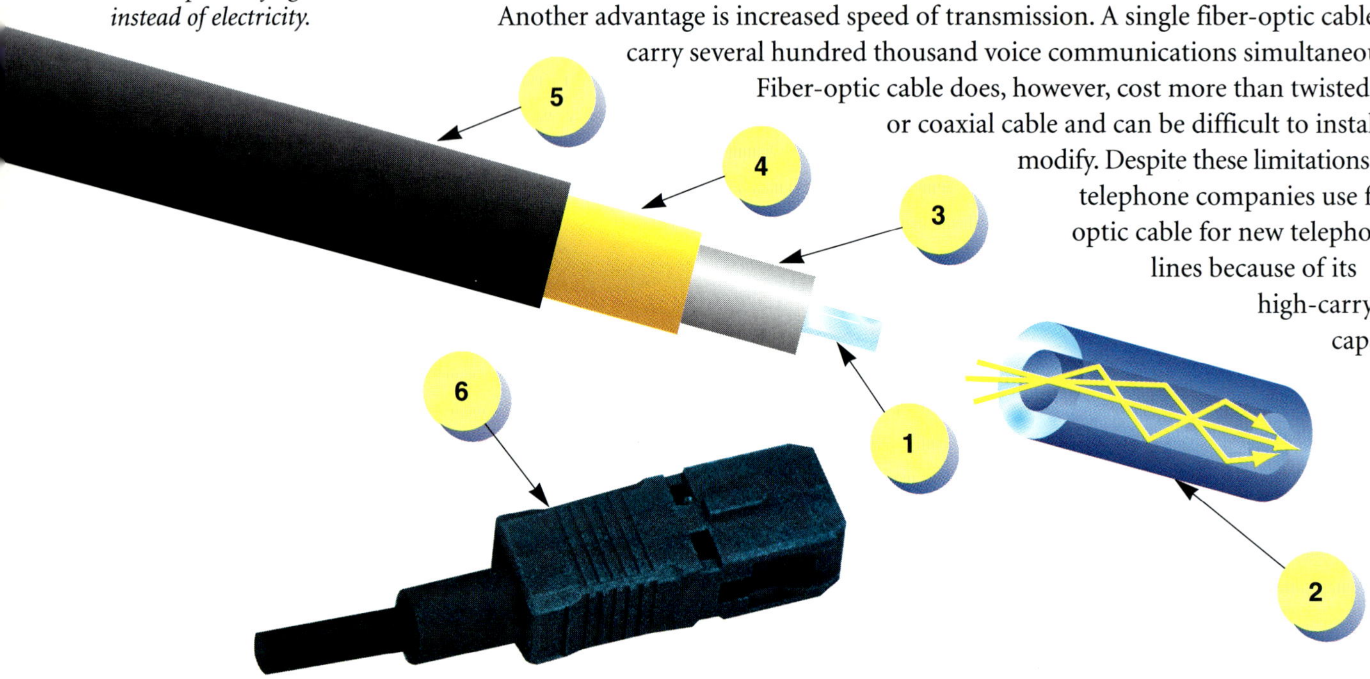

Figure 6-10
Fiber-optic cable is made up of hair-thin strands of glass or plastic that carry data as pulses of light instead of electricity.

1. optical fiber is made up of an inner and outer core of glass or plastic; the inner core is 100 to 200 millionths of an inch in diameter
2. inner core layer carries light signals; the surrounding outer layer of glass acts as a boundary and keeps the light signal within the inner core
3. plastic buffer layer protects optical fiber against ultraviolet light and gives cable rigidity
4. several layers of high-strength fabric provide reinforcement and protection against cuts
5. plastic jacket surrounds inner materials and provides outer protection
6. fiber-optic connector has latching mechanism to prevent disconnection

inCyber
For information about fiber-optic cable, visit the Discovering Computers Chapter 6 inCyber page (http://www.scsite.com/dc/ch6/incyber.htm) and click Fiber-Optic.

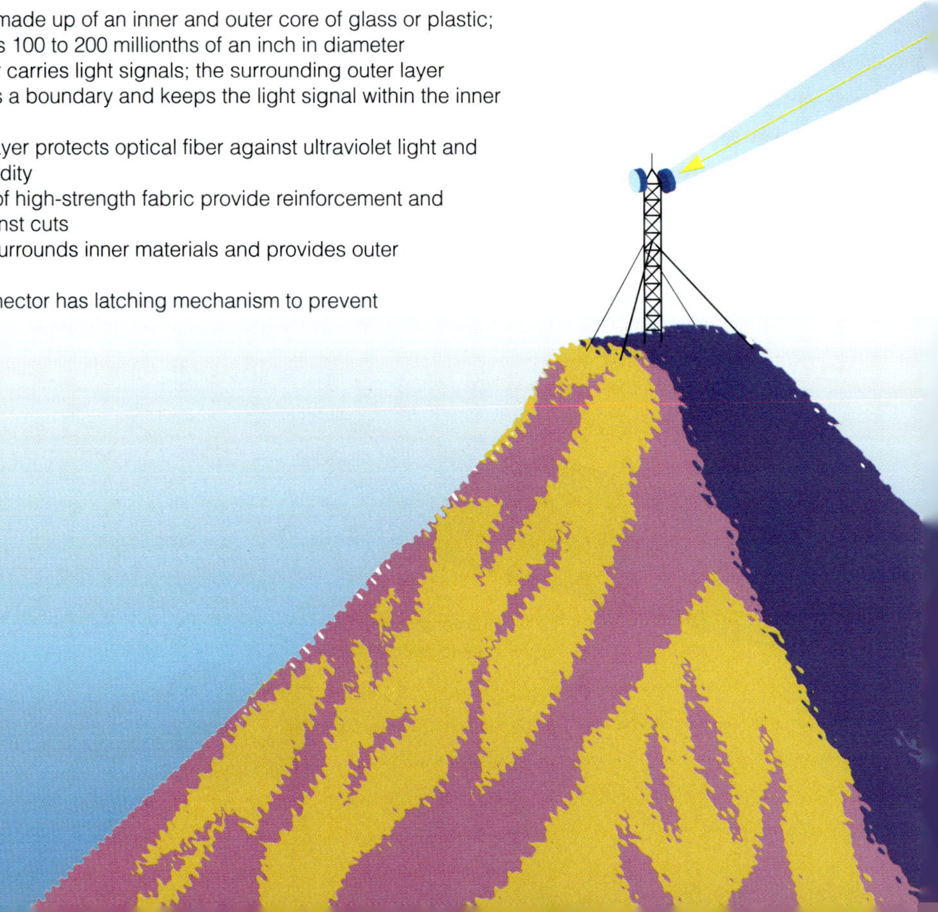

Microwave Transmission

Microwaves are radio waves that can be used to provide high-speed transmission of both voice communications and digital signals. Earth-based microwave transmission, called **terrestrial microwave**, involves sending data from one microwave station to another, similarly to the way broadcast radio signals are transmitted (Figure 6-11). Microwaves are limited to line-of-sight transmission. This means that microwaves must be transmitted in a straight line and that no obstructions can exist, such as buildings or mountains, between microwave stations. To avoid possible obstructions, microwave antennas often are positioned on the tops of buildings, towers, or mountains.

Figure 6-11
The round antennas on the tower are used for microwave transmission. Microwave transmission is limited to line-of-sight. Antennas usually are placed 25 to 75 miles apart.

25 to 75 miles

Communications satellites receive microwave signals from earth-based communications facilities, amplify the signals, and retransmit the signals back to the communications facilities. These communications facilities, called **earth stations**, use large, dish-shaped antennas to transmit and receive data from satellites (Figure 6-12). The transmission *to* the satellite is called an **uplink** and the transmission *from* the satellite to a receiving earth station is called a **downlink**.

Figure 6-12
Earth stations use large dish antennas to communicate with satellites.

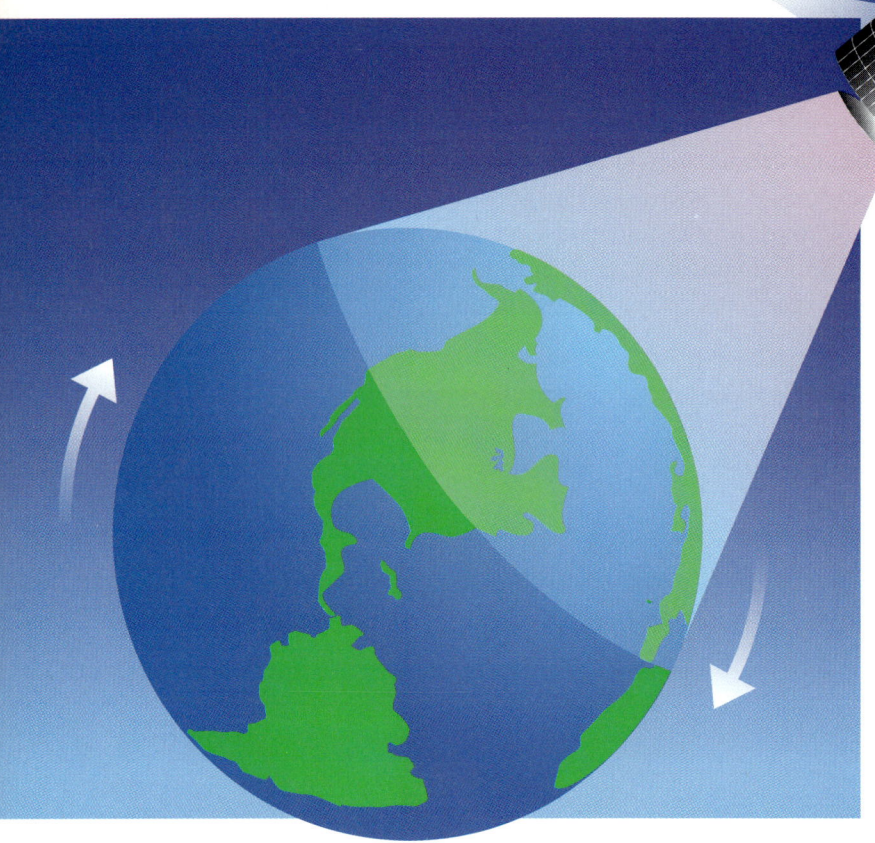

Communications satellites usually are placed about 22,300 miles above the earth in a **geosynchronous orbit** (Figure 6-13). This means that the satellite orbits at the same speed as the earth, so the dish antennas used to send and receive microwave signals remain fixed on the appropriate satellite at all times.

Businesses with operations in multiple locations often use private satellite systems to communicate information. If a business transmits only a small amount of information each day–say, daily sales results from a retail store–a small satellite dish antenna can be used. One such antenna, called a **very small aperture terminal** (VSAT) dish antenna, is only one to three meters in size, but transmits up to 19,200 bits per second. The cost of using a private satellite system with a VSAT antenna can be as low as $200 per month.

Figure 6-13
Communications satellites are placed in geosynchronous orbits approximately 22,300 miles above the earth. Geosynchronous means that the orbit of the satellite matches the rotation of the earth so the satellite is always above the same spot on the earth.

Wireless Transmission: Radio and Light Waves

Wireless transmission uses one of three techniques to transmit data: carrier-connect radio, infrared light beams, or radio waves. Carrier-connect radio and infrared light are used by companies to transmit data between devices that are in the same general area. Carrier-connect radio, for example, uses the existing electrical wiring of a building to act as an antenna, to transmit data within a building. Infrared light beams are used to transmit data between personal computer devices without connecting them with a cable (Figure 6-14). While such local wireless systems provide flexibility and portability, they are slower and more susceptible to interference than wired connections.

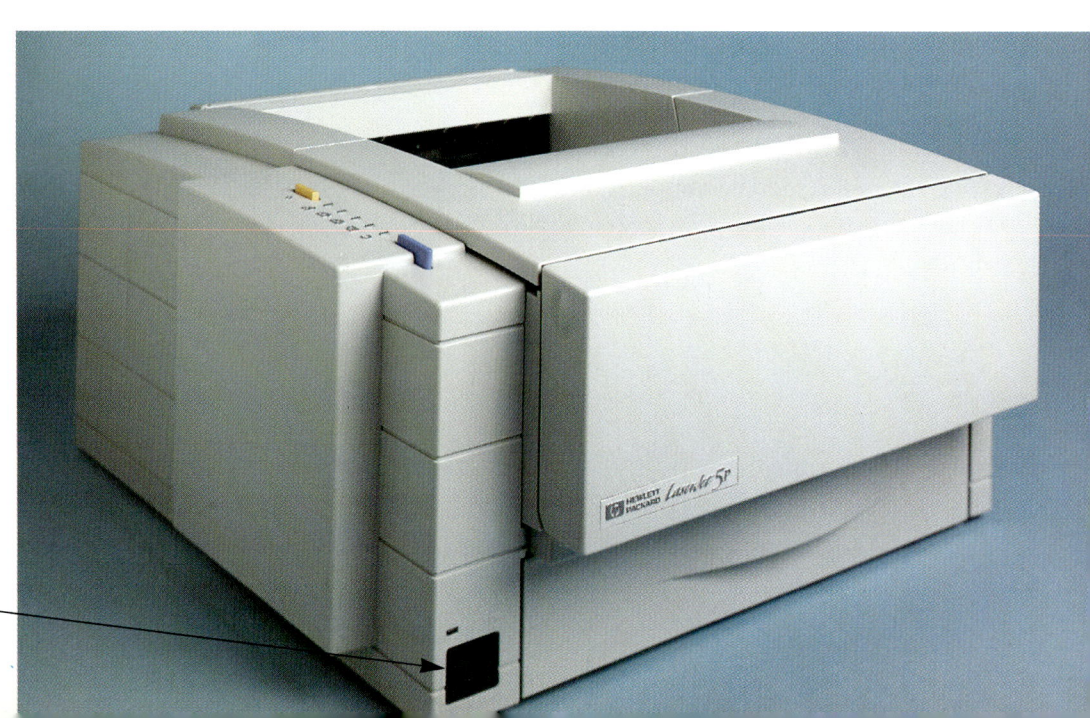

Figure 6-14
Many portable personal computers and printers come with infrared communications capabilities. This allows you to print a document without attaching the computer to the printer with a cable. The range is approximately ten feet.

infrared sensor

Radio-wave wireless systems are used to transmit data over longer distances such as cities, regions, and countries. Several companies run nationwide radio-wave networks to support mobile communications. Users include companies with large numbers of service personnel who need to access the company's databases while they are at a customer site. A repair technician, for example, might need to know the availability of a particular part. Using a portable radio data terminal (Figure 6-15), the technician can access the company's inventory database to determine the availability of the required part.

The cellular telephone system is another radio-wave wireless system widely used for mobile communications. A **cellular telephone** uses radio waves to communicate with a local antenna assigned to a specific geographic area called a cell (Figure 6-16). Individual cells range from one to ten miles in width and use between 50 and 75 radio channels. Suppose you make a call from a cellular telephone in your car. As you travel from one cell to another, a computer monitors the activity in each cell and switches the conversation from the current radio channel to an open radio channel in an adjacent cell. Cellular telephone channels can be used for both voice and digital data transmission.

Figure 6-15
This portable terminal uses radio waves to communicate with a base radio station that is connected to a host computer. Using such a terminal, service technicians can inquire instantly as to the availability of repair parts.

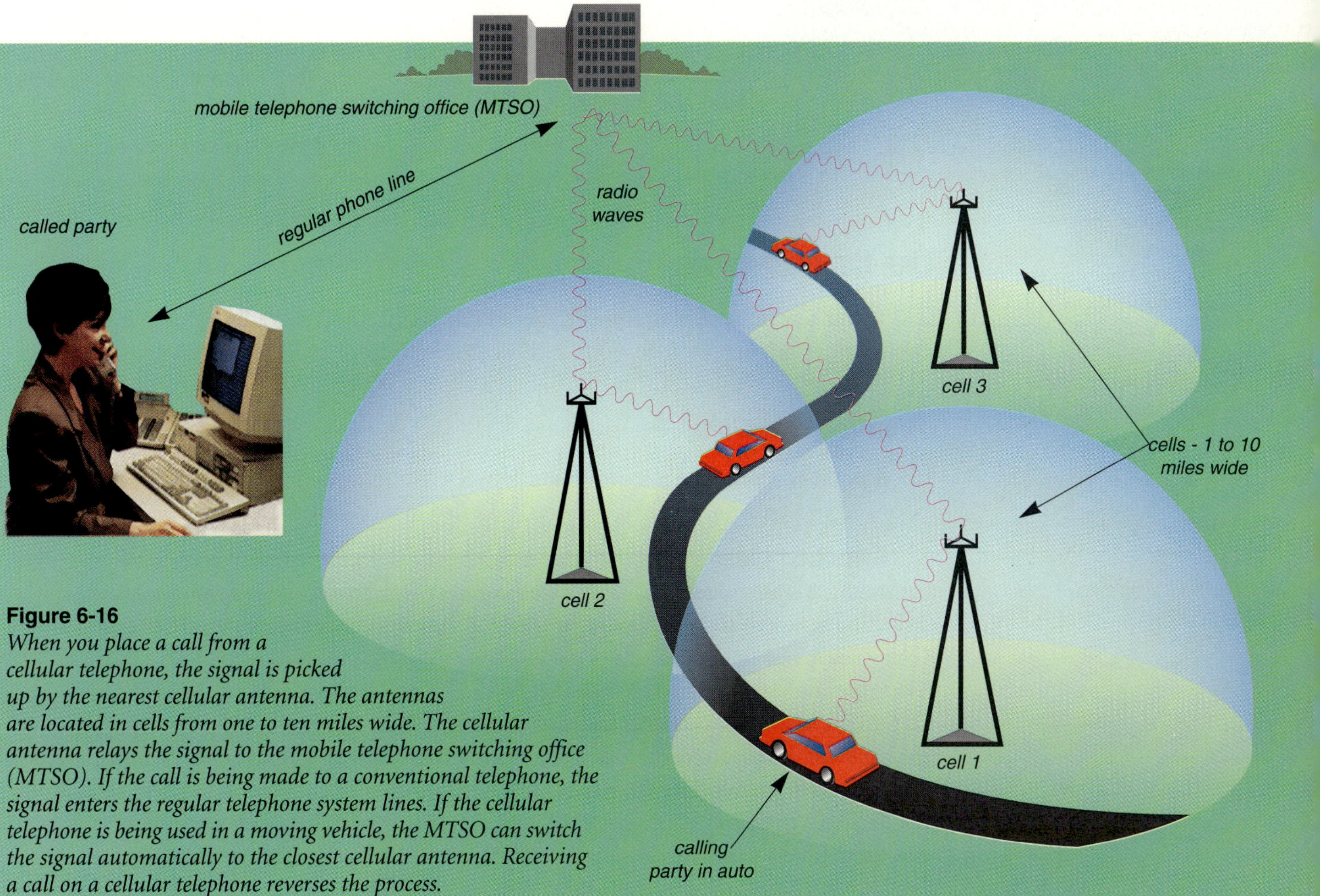

Figure 6-16
When you place a call from a cellular telephone, the signal is picked up by the nearest cellular antenna. The antennas are located in cells from one to ten miles wide. The cellular antenna relays the signal to the mobile telephone switching office (MTSO). If the call is being made to a conventional telephone, the signal enters the regular telephone system lines. If the cellular telephone is being used in a moving vehicle, the MTSO can switch the signal automatically to the closest cellular antenna. Receiving a call on a cellular telephone reverses the process.

An Example of a Communications Channel

Making a communications channel generally requires several different transmission media, especially when data is transmitted over long distances. Figure 6-17 illustrates a communications channel that uses several types of transmission media to transmit data from a personal computer to a large computer located across the country. The steps that would occur are as follows:

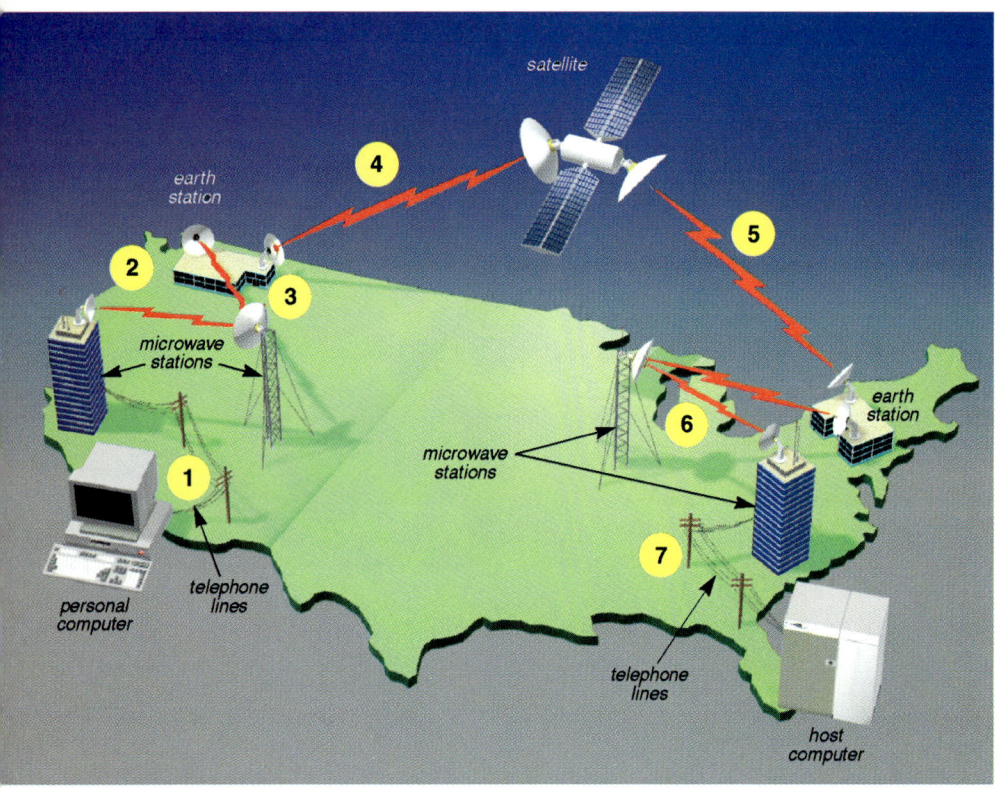

1. Data is input into the personal computer. The computer sends the data over telephone lines to a microwave station.
2. The microwave station transmits the data to another microwave station.
3. The last microwave station transmits the data to an earth station.
4. The earth station transmits the data to the communications satellite.
5. The satellite relays the data to another earth station on the other side of the country.
6. The earth station transmits the data to microwave stations.
7. The last microwave station sends the data over telephone lines to the large computer.

This entire transmission process would take less than one second.

Figure 6-17
Telephone lines, microwave transmission, and a communications satellite allow a personal computer to communicate with a large host computer.

Line Configurations

Two major **line configurations** (types of line connections) commonly used in communications are point-to-point lines and multidrop, or multipoint, lines.

Point-to-Point Lines

A **point-to-point line** is a direct line between a sending and a receiving device. It may be one of two types: a switched line or a dedicated line (Figure 6-18).

Switched Line A **switched line** uses a regular telephone line to establish a communications connection. Each time a connection is made, the telephone company switching stations select the line to be used for the call (hence the name switched line). Using a switched line to transmit data is similar to using a telephone to make a call. The communications equipment at the sending end dials the telephone number of the communications equipment at the receiving end. When the communications equipment at the receiving end answers the call, a connection is established and data can be transmitted. The process of establishing the communications connection is sometimes referred to as a **handshake**. When data transmission is complete, the communications equipment at either end terminates the call by hanging up, and the communications connection is ended.

Switched lines are relatively inexpensive. Using a switched line for data communications costs no more than making a regular telephone call. Another advantage of switched lines is that a connection can be made between any two locations with telephone service and communications equipment. For example, you could dial another computer to connect to the Internet and browse an online catalog. When you are done, you can hang up and place a second call to a different computer to check the balance in your checking account. One disadvantage of using switched lines is that line quality cannot be controlled because the line is chosen randomly by the telephone company switching equipment.

Dedicated Line A **dedicated line** is a line connection that always is established, unlike a switched line where the line connection is reestablished each time it is used. The communications device at one end always is connected to the device at the other end. Because dedicated lines maintain a constant connection, the quality and consistency of the connection is better than a switched line. You can create a dedicated line connection by running a cable between two points such as two offices or buildings; or you can lease a dedicated line from an outside organization such as a telephone company or some other communications service company. If the dedicated line is leased from an outside organization, it sometimes is called a **leased line** or a **private line**. The cost of dedicated lines varies based on the distance between the two connected points and the speed at which data will be transmitted. The charges for leased lines, however, usually are flat fees, meaning you pay a fixed monthly amount, regardless of how long you actually use the line.

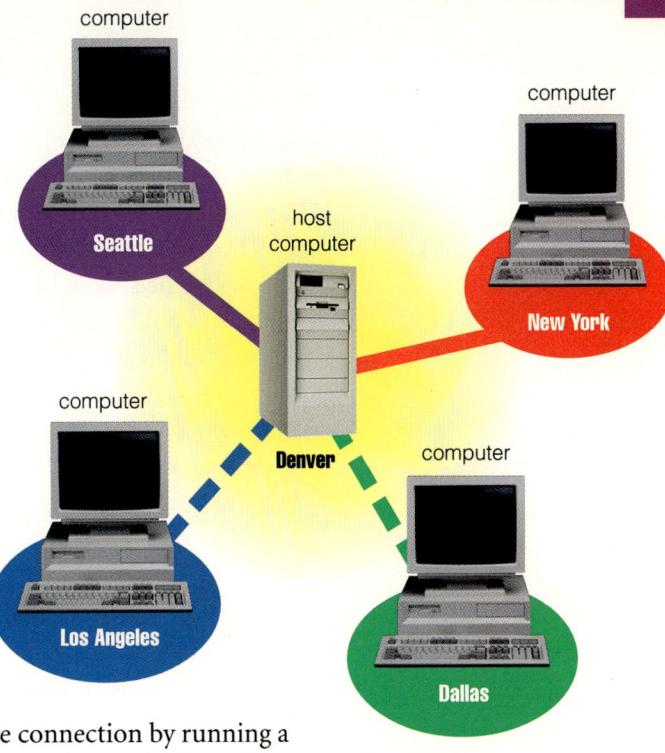

Figure 6-18
A point-to-point line configuration using both switched telephone (dial up) lines (----) and dedicated lines (——) are connected to a computer in Denver. The dedicated lines are always connected, whereas the switched lines have to be connected each time they are used.

Multidrop Lines

The second major line configuration is called a **multidrop line** or **multipoint line**. Multidrop lines commonly are used to connect multiple devices such as terminals or personal computers along a single line to a main computer, sometimes called a **host computer** (Figure 6-19).

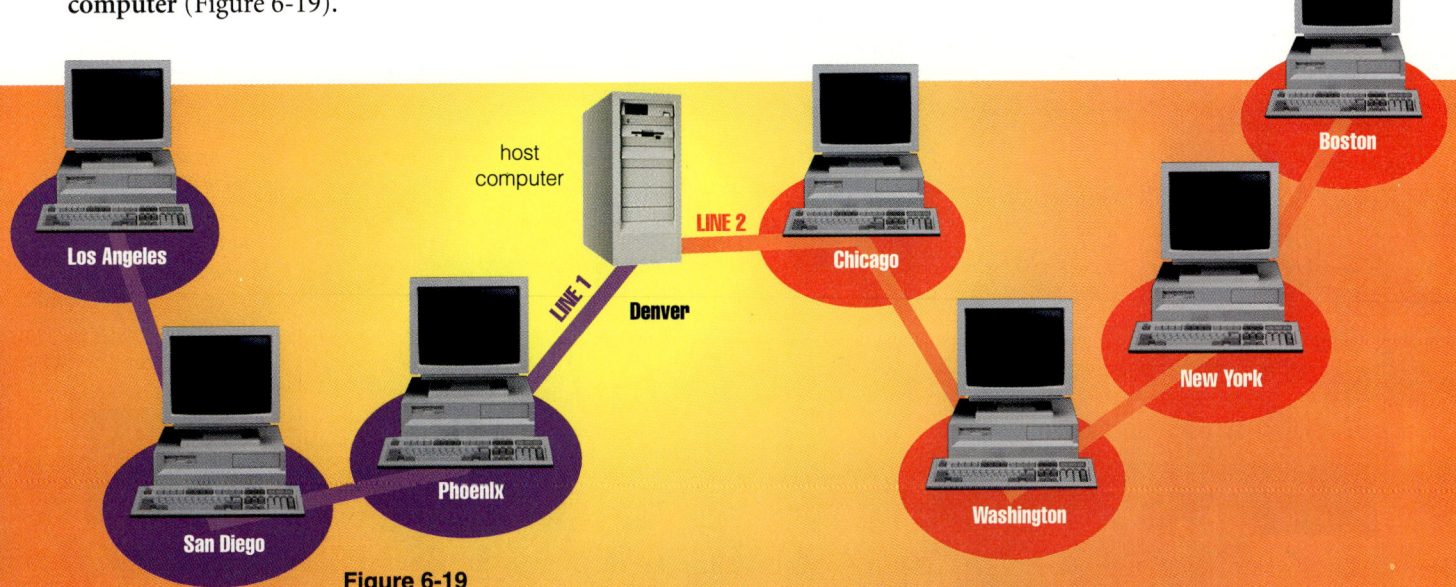

Figure 6-19
Two multidrop lines connect several cities with a computer in Denver. Each line is shared by computers at several locations. Multidrop line configurations are less expensive than individual lines to each remote location.

For example, suppose a ticket agent uses a terminal to request flight information from a database stored on a host computer. While the request is being transmitted to the main computer and the reply back to the terminal, other terminals on the line cannot transmit data. The time required to transmit the data, however, is short—most likely less than one second. Because the delays are so short, users cannot tell that other terminals are using the line.

The number of computers or terminals placed on one multidrop line is decided by the designer of the system based on the anticipated amount of traffic on the line. For example, a single line could connect 100 or more computers, provided each computer sent only short messages and used the communications line only a few hours per day. If the computers sent longer messages such as reports and used the line almost continuously, the number of computers on one line would have to be fewer.

A dedicated leased line almost always is used for multidrop line configurations. Using multidrop lines can decrease line costs considerably because many computers can share one line.

Characteristics of Communications Channels

The communications channels just described can be categorized by a number of characteristics including the type of signal, transmission mode, transmission direction, and transmission rate.

Types of Signals: Digital and Analog

Computer equipment is designed to process data as **digital signals**, which are individual electrical pulses that represent the bits that are grouped together in bytes. Telephone equipment originally was designed to carry only voice transmission, which is comprised of a continuous electrical wave called an **analog signal** (Figure 6-20). For telephone lines to carry digital signals, a special piece of equipment called a *modem* is used to convert between digital signals (0s and 1s) and analog signals. Modems are discussed in more detail later in this chapter.

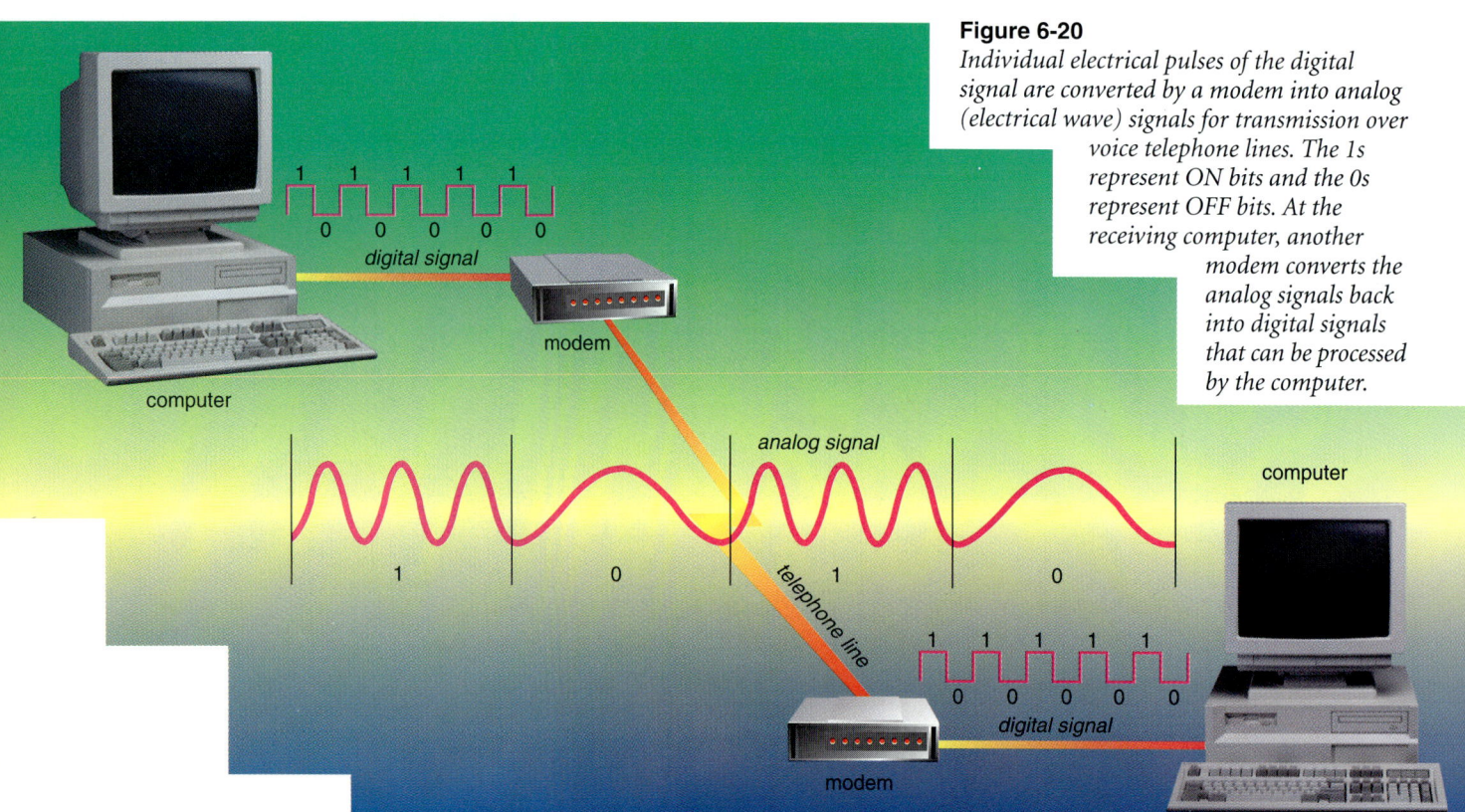

Figure 6-20
Individual electrical pulses of the digital signal are converted by a modem into analog (electrical wave) signals for transmission over voice telephone lines. The 1s represent ON bits and the 0s represent OFF bits. At the receiving computer, another modem converts the analog signals back into digital signals that can be processed by the computer.

To provide faster and clearer transmission of digital signals, many telephone companies now offer digital data service. **Digital data service** uses communications channels specifically designed to carry digital signals to provide higher speed and lower error rates than analog voice lines. Using the high-speed lines provided by digital data services is more expensive, however, than using a standard telephone line. A **T1** digital line, which transmits 1.5 megabits per second, costs several thousand dollars per month. A **T3** digital line, which transmits 45 megabits per second, costs more than $40,000 per month and requires a large investment in expensive equipment.

Digital data service, which now is available to customers in major metropolitan areas, typically is used by organizations with a consistent high-volume of communications traffic. Individuals who need fast digital data transmission can obtain an ISDN line. **ISDN (integrated services digital network)** is an international standard for the transmission of both analog voice and digital data using different communications channels and companies. Using ISDN lines, data can be transmitted over one or more separate channels at 128,000 bits per second, about four times as fast as an analog voice line. Future plans for ISDN include the use of fiber-optic cable that will provide transmission rates up to 2.2 billion bits per second—speeds high enough to allow the transmission of full-motion video images.

For a review of ISDN lines, visit the Discovering Computers Chapter 6 inCyber page (http://www.scsite.com/dc/ch6/incyber.htm) and click ISDN.

Transmission Modes: Asynchronous and Synchronous

In **asynchronous transmission mode** (Figure 6-21) data is transmitted in individual bytes (made up of bits) at irregular intervals, such as when you enter data. Start and stop bits are used to distinguish where one byte stops and another byte starts. An additional bit called a *parity bit* sometimes is included at the end of each byte to check for errors and to detect if one of the bits was changed during transmission. Because only one byte is transmitted at a time, the asynchronous transmission mode is relatively slow and is best used to send only small amounts of data. This mode is efficient enough, however, for use with most personal computer communications equipment.

In the **synchronous transmission mode** (Figure 6-21), large blocks of data are transmitted at regular intervals. Timing signals synchronize the communications equipment at the sending and receiving ends, thus eliminating the need for start and stop bits for each byte. Error-checking bits and start and end indicators called *sync bytes* also are transmitted. While synchronous transmission requires more sophisticated and expensive equipment, it provides much higher speeds and accuracy than asynchronous transmission.

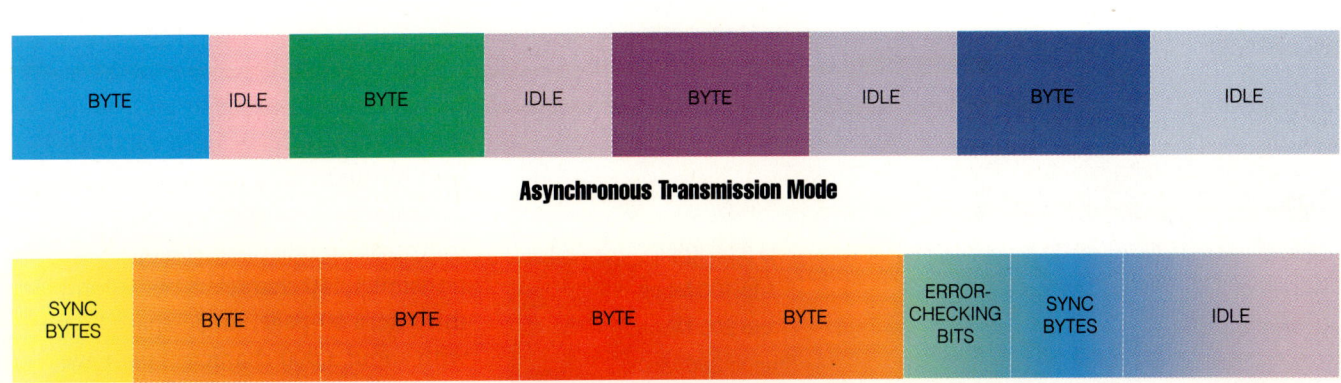

Figure 6-21
In asynchronous transmission mode, individual bytes are transmitted. Each byte has start, stop, and error-checking bits. In synchronous transmission mode, multiple bytes are sent in a block with sync bytes at the beginning of the block and error-checking bits and sync bytes at the end of the block. Synchronous transmission is faster and more accurate.

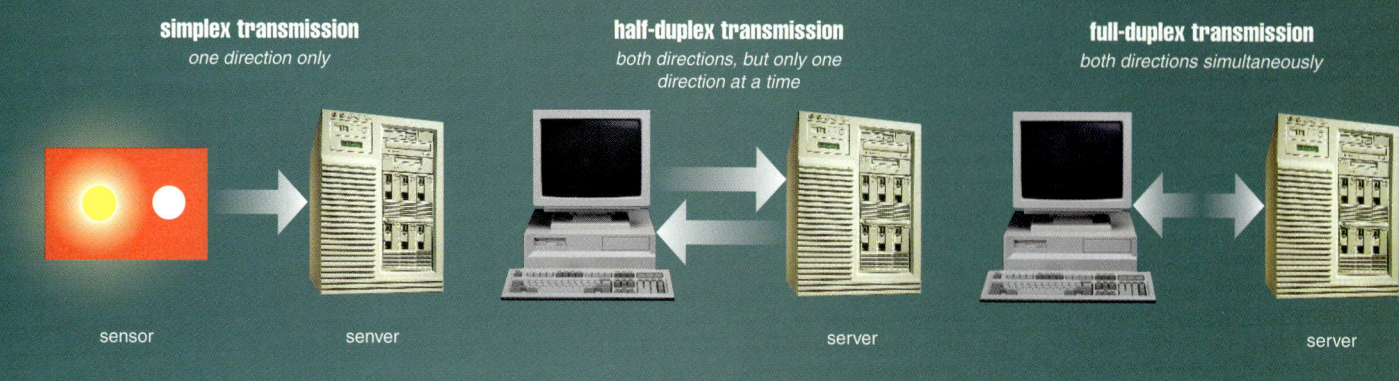

Figure 6-22
Simplex transmission allows data to flow in one direction only. Half-duplex transmission allows data to flow in both directions but not at the same time. Full-duplex transmission allows data to flow in both directions simultaneously.

Direction of Transmission: Simplex, Half-Duplex, and Full-Duplex

The direction of data transmission is classified in one of three ways: simplex, half-duplex, or full-duplex (Figure 6-22). In **simplex transmission**, data flows in one direction only. Simplex is used only when the sending device, such as a temperature sensor, never requires a response from the computer. For example, if a computer is used to control the temperature of a building, numerous sensors are placed throughout the building. Simplex transmission lines can be used to connect each sensor back to the computer because the computer needs only to receive data from the temperature sensors and does not need to send data back to the sensors.

In **half-duplex transmission**, data can flow in either direction, but can flow only in one direction at a time. Citizens band (CB) radio is an example of half-duplex transmission; you can talk or listen, but you cannot do both at the same time.

In **full-duplex transmission**, data can be sent in both directions at the same time. A normal telephone line is an example of full-duplex transmission; both parties can talk at the same time. Full-duplex transmission is used for most interactive computer applications and for computer-to-computer data transmission.

Tranmission Rate

The transmission rate of a communications channel is determined by its bandwidth and its speed. **Bandwidth** is the range of frequencies that a communications channel can carry. The larger the bandwidth of a channel, the more frequencies that channel can transmit. Because data can be assigned to different frequencies for transmission, a larger bandwidth means more data can be transmitted at one time.

The speed at which data is transmitted usually is expressed as **bits per second (bps)**, the number of bits that can be transmitted in one second. For example, using 10-bit bytes to represent each character (8 data bits, 1 start bit, and 1 stop bit), a communications channel with a transmission rate of 14,400 bps will transmit 1,440 characters per second. At this rate, a 60-page, single-spaced report with about 3,000 characters per page would be transmitted in a little more than two minutes. Figure 6-23 shows the range of transmission rates for different media. Each year, communications companies develop new methods and technologies to increase these rates.

Figure 6-23
Transmission rates of different media.

Media	Rate*
Twisted-pair wire (voice grade telephone line)	to 33.6 Kbps
Twisted-pair wire (direct connection)	1 to 100 Mbps
Coaxial cable	1 to 200 Mbps
Fiber-optic cable	up to 266 Mbps
Terrestrial microwave	5.7 Mbps
Satellite microwave	64 to 512 Kbps
Radio wave	4.8 to 19.2 Kbps
Infrared	1 to 4 Mbps

*Rate: bps — bits per second
Kbps — kilo (thousand) bits per second
Mbps — mega (million) bits per second

Communications Software

Some communications equipment is preprogrammed to accomplish its intended communications tasks. Other communications equipment must be used with a separate program to ensure proper transmission of data. These programs, referred to as **communications software**, manage the transmission of data between computers and have a number of features including dialing (if a switched telephone line is used), file transfer, terminal emulation, and Internet access.

The **dialing** feature allows you to store, review, select and dial telephone numbers of computers that can be called. The software uses wizards, dialog boxes, and other onscreen messages to help you establish a communications connection.

The **file transfer** feature allows you to move one or more files from one computer system to another. For file transfers to work, both the sending and receiving computers must have file transfer software.

Most minicomputers and mainframes are designed to work with terminals that transmit and display data differently than PCs. The **terminal emulation** feature allows a personal computer to act as a specific type of terminal so the personal computer can connect to another, usually larger, computer such as a mainframe. Terminal emulation software performs the necessary conversion of data sent from and received by the personal computer so the computers can communicate.

The **Internet access** feature allows you to use the computer to connect to the Internet to send e-mail, participate in chat rooms, visit World Wide Web sites, and more.

Communications Equipment

A variety of equipment is used to connect computers to each other. The following sections discuss some of the more common types of communications equipment.

Modems

As previously discussed, a computer's digital signals must be converted to analog signals to be transmitted along standard telephone lines. The communications equipment that performs this conversion is a modem. A **modem** not only converts the digital signals of a computer to analog signals, but also converts analog signals back into digital signals that can be used by a computer. The word modem comes from a combination of the words *mo*dulate–to change into a sound or analog signal–and *dem*odulate–to convert an analog signal into a digital signal. Modems are needed at both the sending and receiving ends of a communications channel for data transmission to occur.

An **external modem** (Figure 6-24) is a stand-alone (separate) device that attaches to a computer with a cable and to a telephone outlet with a standard telephone cord. Because external modems are stand-alone devices, they can be moved easily from one computer to another.

Figure 6-24
An external modem connects a computer to a telephone outlet.

CHAPTER 6 – COMMUNICATIONS AND NETWORKS

An **internal modem** (Figure 6-25) is contained on a circuit board that is installed inside a computer or inserted into an expansion slot. Internal modems generally are less expensive than comparable external modems, but once they are installed, internal modems are not as easy to move.

While some modems can transmit data at rates up to 56,000 bits per second (bps), most personal computers use modems of 28,800 bps. The actual amount of data transmitted by a modem can be higher than these rates through the use of data compression features built into the modem.

For details on modems, visit the Discovering Computers Chapter 6 inCyber page (http://www.scsite.com/dc/ch6/incyber.htm) and click Modem.

Figure 6-25
An internal modem performs the same functions as an external modem but is mounted inside the computer.

Multiplexers

A **multiplexer**, sometimes referred to as an MUX, combines two or more input signals from several devices into a single stream of data and transmits it over a communications channel (Figure 6-26). The multiplexer at the sending end codes each character with an identifier before combining the data streams. The multiplexer at the receiving end uses these characters to separate the combined data stream into its original parts. By combining the individual data streams into one, a multiplexer increases the efficiency of communications and reduces the cost of using individual communications channels. Multiplexers often are connected to external modems or have internal modems built in.

Figure 6-26
At the sending end, a multiplexer (MUX) combines separate data transmissions into a single data stream. At the receiving end, the multiplexer separates the single stream into its original parts.

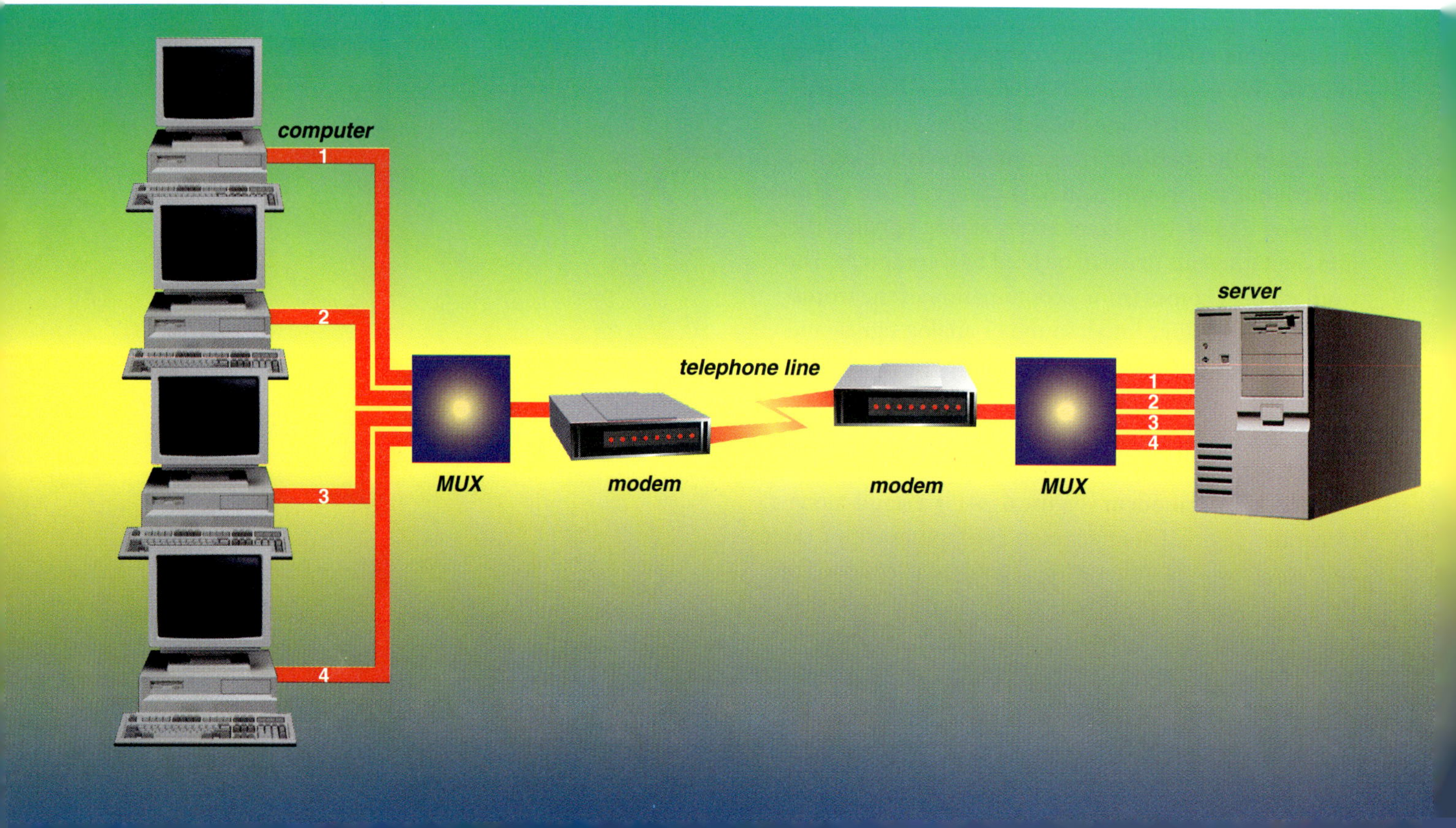

Front-End Processors

A **front-end processor** is a computer dedicated to handling the communications requirements of a larger computer. Relieved of these tasks, the large computer can be dedicated to processing data, while the front-end processor communicates the data. Tasks that a front-end processor handles include **polling** (checking the connected terminals or computers to see if they have data to send); error-checking and correction; and ensuring access security (making sure that a connected device or the user of the connected device is authorized to access the computer).

Network Interface Cards

A **network interface card**, or **NIC** (pronounced *nick*), is a circuit card that fits in an expansion slot of a computer or other device, such as a printer, so the device can be connected to the network (Figure 6-27). Most network interface cards require a cable connection and have connectors on the card for different types of cable. A NIC has circuits that coordinate the transmission and receipt of data and the error-checking of transmitted data.

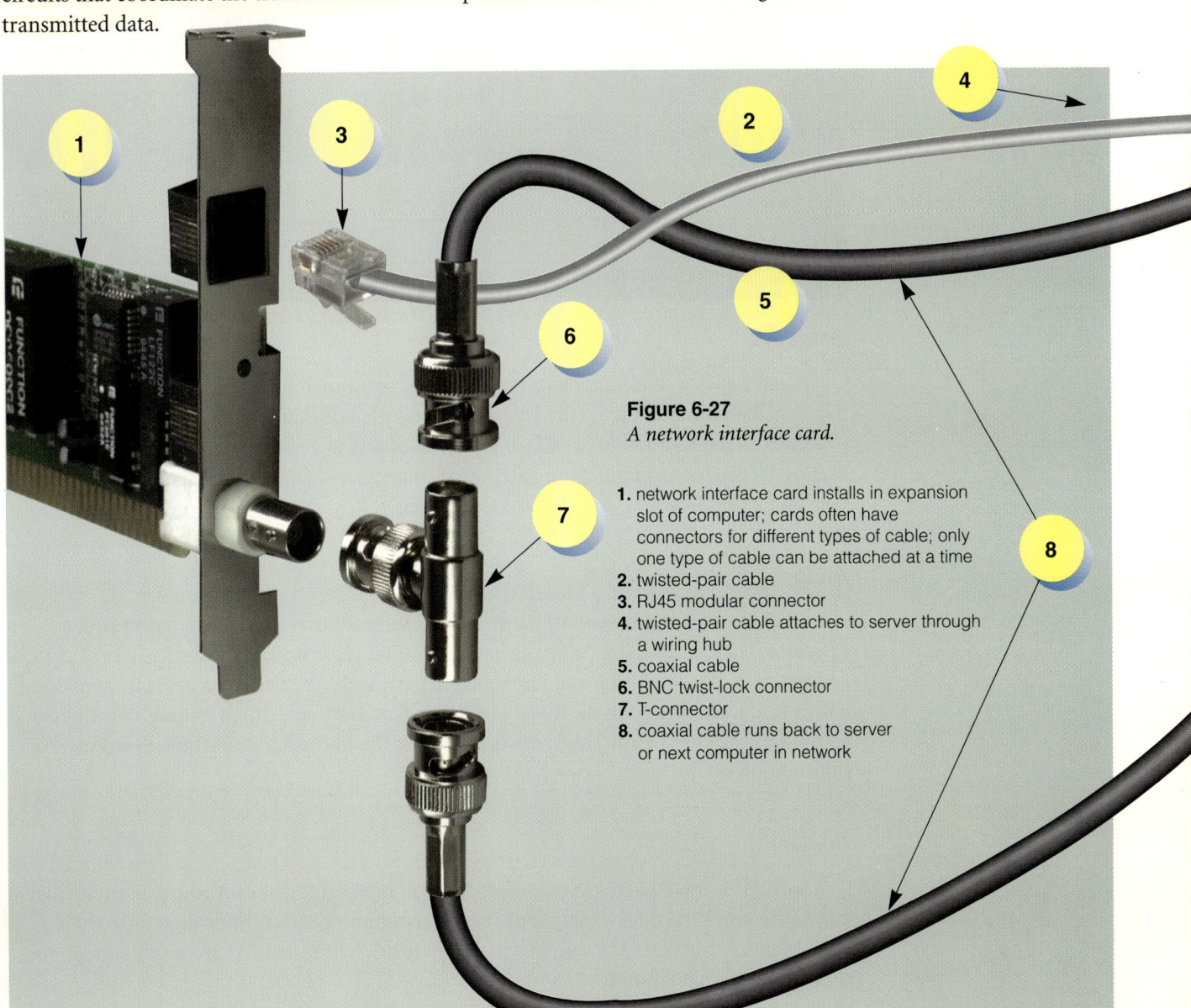

Figure 6-27
A network interface card.

1. network interface card installs in expansion slot of computer; cards often have connectors for different types of cable; only one type of cable can be attached at a time
2. twisted-pair cable
3. RJ45 modular connector
4. twisted-pair cable attaches to server through a wiring hub
5. coaxial cable
6. BNC twist-lock connector
7. T-connector
8. coaxial cable runs back to server or next computer in network

Wiring Hubs

A **wiring hub**, also called a **concentrator** or **multistation access unit** (**MAU**), allows devices such as computers, printers, and storage devices to be connected to the server (Figure 6-28). The hub acts as the central connecting point for cables that run to the server and each of the devices on a network. Hubs usually contain connectors, called ports, for eight to twelve devices plus the server. A hub that can be connected with another hub to increase the number of devices attached to the server is called a **stackable hub**.

Figure 6-28
A wiring hub acts as a central connecting point for the server and the devices in the network.

Gateways

A **gateway** is a combination of hardware and software that allows users on one network to access the resources on a *different* type of network. For example, a gateway could be used to connect a local area network of personal computers to a mainframe computer network. Many colleges, for example, use a gateway so students and faculty can access the World Wide Web and other networks outside the local region.

Bridges

A **bridge** is a combination of hardware and software that is used to connect *similar* networks. For example, if a company had similar but separate local area networks of personal computers in its accounting and marketing departments, the networks could be connected with a bridge. In this example, using a bridge makes more sense than joining all the personal computers together in one large network, because the individual departments only access information on the other network occasionally.

Routers

A router is used when several networks are connected together. A **router** is an intelligent network connecting device that sends (routes) communications traffic directly to the appropriate network. In the case of a partial network failure, routers are smart enough to determine alternate routes.

Communications Networks

A communications **network** is a collection of terminals, computers, and other equipment that uses communications channels to share data, information, hardware, and software. Networks can be classified as either local area networks or wide area networks.

Local Area Networks (LANs)

A **local area network**, or LAN, is a communications network that covers a limited geographic area such as a school computer laboratory, an office, a building, or a group of buildings. The LAN consists of a communications channel that connects a series of computer terminals connected to a central computer or, more commonly, connects a group of personal computers to one another.

For an overview of local area networks (LANs), visit the Discovering Computers Chapter 6 inCyber page (http://www.scsite.com/dc/ch6/incyber.htm) and click LAN.

LAN Applications Three common applications of local area networks are hardware, software, and information resource sharing.

Hardware resource sharing allows each personal computer on a network to access and use devices that are too costly to provide for each user or cannot be justified for each user because they are used infrequently. For example, suppose a number of personal computers on a network each needed to use a laser printer. A LAN allows you to connect a laser printer to the network, so that whenever a personal computer user on the network needs the laser printer, he or she can access it over the network. Figure 6-29 depicts a simple local area network consisting of four personal computers and a printer linked together by a cable.

Three of the personal computers (computer 1 in the sales and marketing department, computer 2 in the accounting department, and computer 3 in the personnel department) can be used at all times. Computer 4 is used as a **server**, which is a computer dedicated to handling the communications needs of the other computers in the network. The users of this LAN have connected the laser printer to the server so all computers and the server have access to the printer. In small networks, the server computer also can be used to run applications, just like other computers on the network. In large networks, the server usually is dedicated to providing network services such as hardware, software, and information resource sharing.

Local Area Network

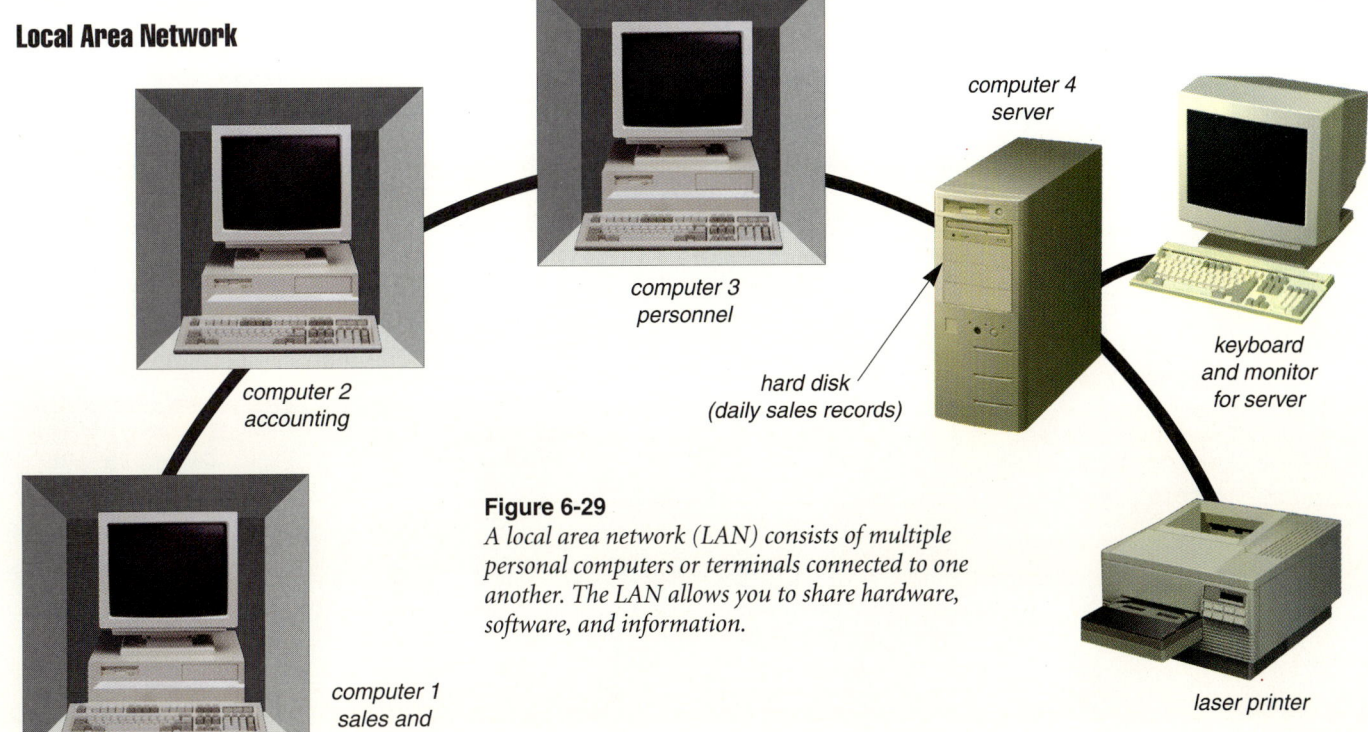

Figure 6-29
A local area network (LAN) consists of multiple personal computers or terminals connected to one another. The LAN allows you to share hardware, software, and information.

Software resource sharing involves storing frequently used software on the hard disk of the server so multiple users can access the software. Sharing the software is more cost-effective than buying and installing the software on each computer. Because sharing software is a common practice for both in-house and commercial software, most software vendors sell network versions of their software. Software vendors issue agreements called **network licenses** or **site licenses**, which allow many users to run the software package. The site license fee usually is based on the number of computers attached to the network and costs less than buying separate copies of the software package for each computer.

Information resource sharing allows anyone using a personal computer on a local area network to access data stored on any other computer in the network. In actual practice, hardware resource sharing and information resource sharing often are combined. For example, in Figure 6-29, the sales records could be stored on the hard disk associated with the server. Anyone needing access to the sales records could use this information resource. The capability of accessing and storing data on shared storage devices is an important feature of many local area networks.

File-Server and Client-Server Networks Information resource sharing usually is provided using either the file-server or client-server method. With the **file-server** method, the server sends an entire file at one time to a requesting computer, which then performs the processing. With the **client-server** method, the server completes some of the processing first and then transmits the data to the requesting computer.

Figure 6-30 illustrates how a server processes a request for information about customers with balances over $1,000, depending on the method used. With the *file-server* method, first you transmit a request for the customer file to the server (1). The server locates the customer file (2) and transmits the entire file to your computer (3). Your computer then selects customers with balances over $1,000 and prepares the report (4). With the *client-server* method, you transmit a request for customers with a balance over $1,000 from your computer (the *client*) to the server (1). The server selects the records of customers with balances over $1,000 (2) and transmits the selected records to your computer (3). Your computer then prepares the report (4). While the client-server method greatly reduces the amount of data sent over a network, it does require a more powerful server system.

For details on client-server networks, visit the Discovering Computers Chapter 6 inCyber page (http://www.scsite.com/dc/ch6/incyber.htm) and click Client-Server.

Figure 6-30
A request for information about customers with balances over $1,000 would be processed differently by file-server and client-server networks.

When a server provides selected information from files stored on the server, and the application software is run on the client system (as described in this example), the server is called a **database server**. If the server computer also runs all or part of the application software, such as a sales order entry program, it is called an **application server**.

Peer-to-Peer Networks A local area network does not have to use a single server computer. A **peer-to-peer network** allows any computer to share the hardware (such as a printer), software, or information located on any other computer in the network. Peer-to-peer networks are appropriate for a small number of users who work primarily on their own computers and need only to use the resources of other computers occasionally.

Network Operating Systems A **network operating system** (NOS) is the system software that makes it possible to implement and control a local area network and allows users to use the files, resources, and other services on that network (such as e-mail). Tasks of the network operating system include:

- **Administration** Adding, deleting, and organizing client users and performing maintenance tasks such as backup.
- **File Management** Locating and transferring files from the server to the client computers.
- **Printer Management** Prioritizing print jobs and reports sent to specific printers on the network.
- **Security** Monitoring and, when necessary, restricting access to network resources.

Different types of networks use different types of network operating systems. Simple peer-to-peer networks need a minimum amount of software to manage their activities. Often, the necessary software is provided by the operating system or by the manufacturer of the hardware used to link the networked systems. Artisoft's LANtastic, Microsoft's Windows 95 and Windows for Workgroups, and Apple's AppleTalk are examples of peer-to-peer network software. Client-server networks, however, need more sophisticated network operating systems to coordinate the number of devices on the network and keep communications running efficiently. The NOS in a client-server system runs on the server computer; the personal computer clients run their own operating systems. Novell's NetWare, Microsoft's Advanced NT Server, and IBM's LAN Server are examples of network operating systems.

CLIENT-SERVER

4. REQUESTING COMPUTER PREPARES REPORT

1. REQUEST FOR BALANCES OVER $1,000

3. RECORDS OF CUSTOMERS WITH BALANCES OVER $1,000 TRANSMITTED

2. SERVER SELECTS CUSTOMERS WITH BALANCES OVER $1,000

Figure 6-31
The control room for a regional telephone company. Telephone companies use sophisticated software and equipment to monitor and route communications traffic.

Wide Area Networks (WANs)

A **wide area network**, or WAN, covers a large geographic region (such as a city or country) and uses telephone cables, terrestrial microwave, satellites, or other combinations of communications channels (Figure 6-31).

A wide area network limited to the area surrounding a city is sometimes referred to as a **metropolitan area network**, or MAN. Wide area networks can be privately or publicly owned and operated. Electronic Data Systems (EDS), for example, has built an extensive private communications network to handle the computing needs of its computer services business.

Public wide area network companies include **common carriers** such as AT&T, Sprint, and MCI. Companies called **value-added carriers** lease communications channels from the common carriers to use in value-added networks. **Value-added networks** (VAN) enhance communications channels by adding improvements such as faster data transmission or other specialized communications services. Tymnet, Inc., for example, operates a VAN that provides packet-switching services. **Packet-switching** combines individual packets of data from various users and transmits them together over a high-speed channel. The messages are separated and distributed over lower speed channels at the receiving end. Sharing the high-speed channel is more economical than each user paying for its own high-speed channel.

Network Configurations

The way the equipment is configured in a communications network is called **topology**. A topology is determined by the *logical* connection of the devices in the network–that is, the path the data follows as it is routed from one device to another. The actual *physical* connections, including the cabling, may form a different shape than the one formed by the devices in the network. Any device directly connected to a network, such as a computer or a printer, is referred to as a **node**. Personal computers connected to a network often are referred to as **workstations**. The more common topologies are star, bus, and ring. Combinations of these topologies also are used.

Star Network

A **star network** has a central computer with one or more terminals or smaller computers connected to it, forming a star. A pure star network consists of only point-to-point lines between the central computer and the other computers on the network. Most star networks, such as the one shown in Figure 6-32, are not pure star networks and include both point-to-point lines and multidrop lines.

A star network configuration often is used when the central computer contains all the data required to process input from terminals, such as an airline reservation system.

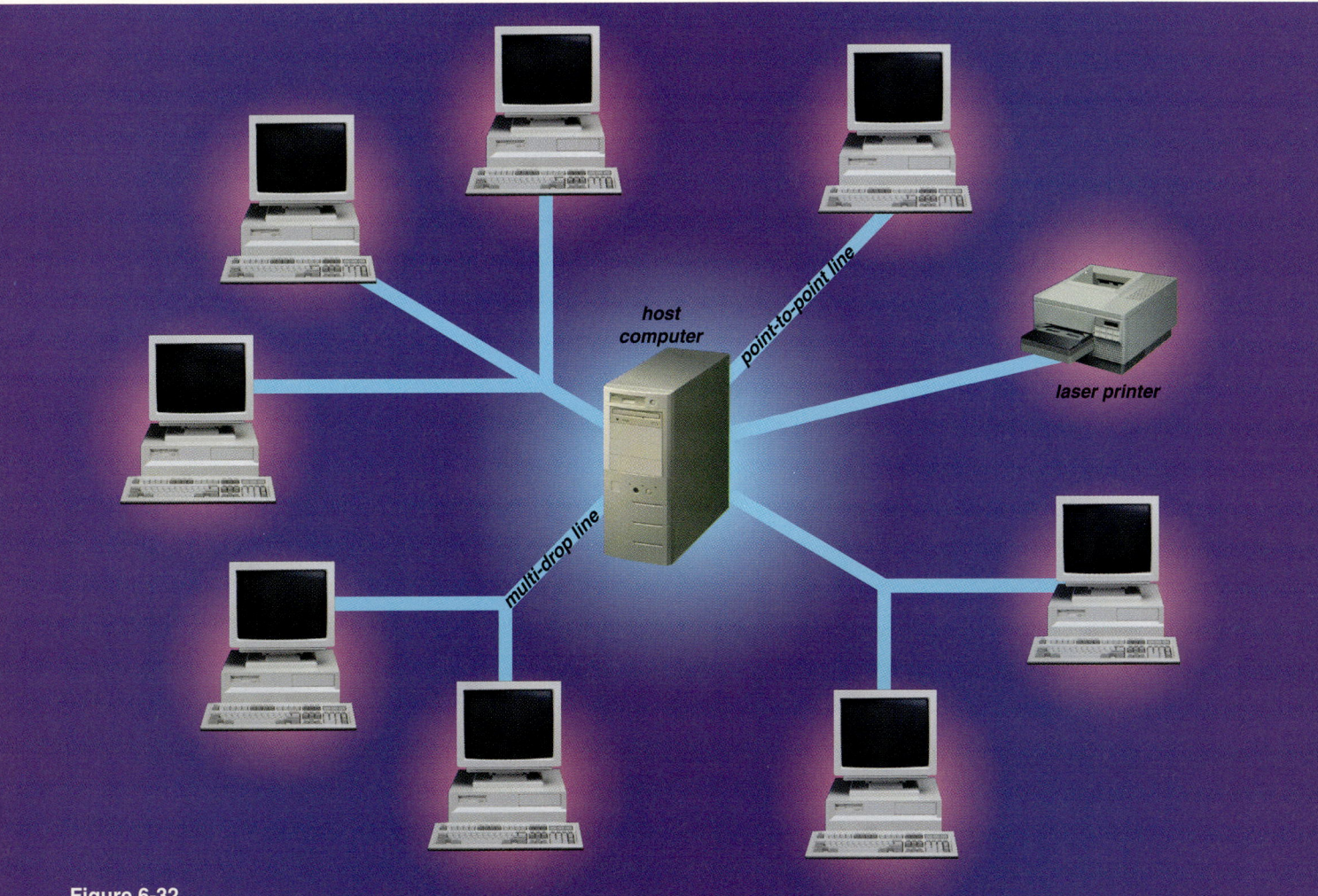

Figure 6-32
A star network contains a single, centralized host computer with which all the terminals or personal computers in the network communicate. Both point-to-point and multidrop lines can be used in a star network.

For example, if seat reservations are being processed on an airline's star network, all the data needed to confirm reservations is contained in the database stored on the central computer. Companies often use star networks to connect terminals to a mainframe or minicomputer that serves as the host computer.

Star networks are relatively efficient and provide close control of the data processed on the network. The major disadvantage of a star network is that the entire network depends on the central computer and its hardware and software. If any of these elements fail, the entire network is disabled. Therefore, in most large star networks, backup computer systems are kept available in case the primary system fails.

Bus Network

In a **bus network**, all the devices or nodes in the network are connected to and share a single data path (Figure 6-33). Bus networks allow data to be transmitted in both directions. Each time data is sent, a destination address is included with the transmission so the data is routed to the appropriate receiving device. A bus network often is physically wired using a single cable running from one device to the next. A bus network also can be wired with a wiring hub at the center so it looks like a star. It still is considered a bus network, however, because a logical bus–a single cable–exists inside the hub. An advantage of a bus network is that devices can be attached or detached from the network at any point without disturbing the rest of the network. In addition, if one computer on the network fails, this does not affect the other users of the network.

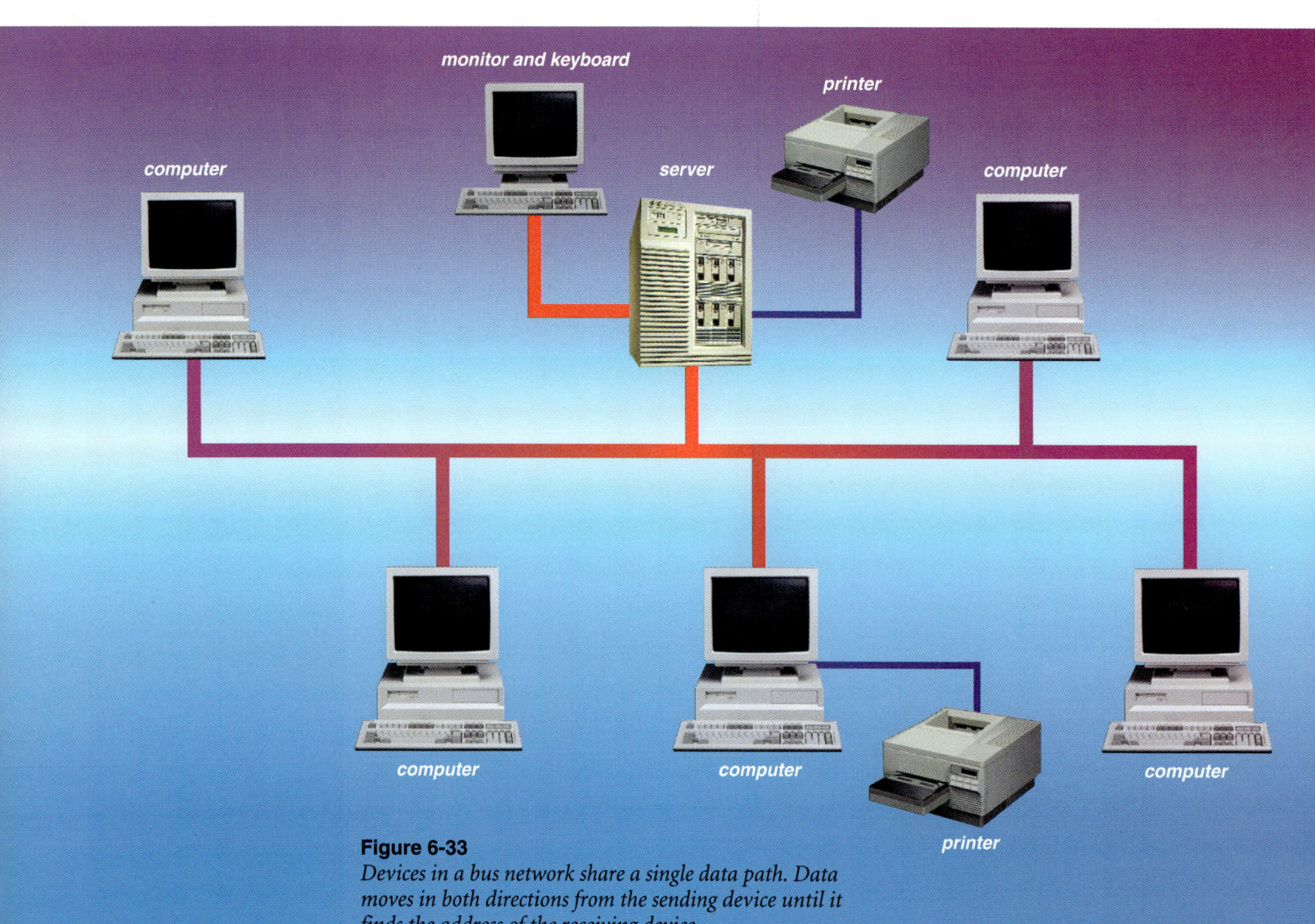

Figure 6-33
Devices in a bus network share a single data path. Data moves in both directions from the sending device until it finds the address of the receiving device.

COMMUNICATIONS PROTOCOLS 6.29

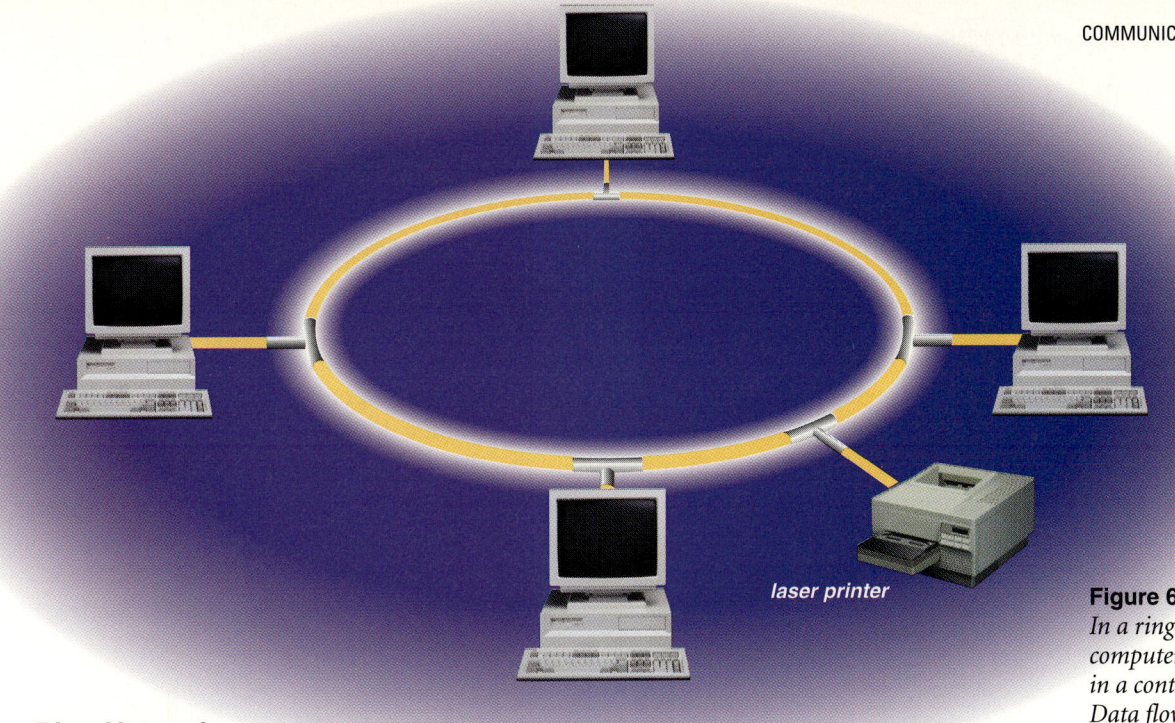

laser printer

Figure 6-34
In a ring network, all computers are connected in a continuous loop. Data flows around the ring in one direction only. The actual ring usually exists inside a wiring hub. Separate cables run from the hub ring to the individual devices connected to the network.

Ring Network

In a **ring network**, all the devices on the network are connected in a continuous loop or ring. Unlike a star network, a ring network does not use a centralized host computer. Rather, a circle of computers communicate with one another (Figure 6-34). Data travels around a ring network in one direction only and passes through each computer. Ring networks sometimes are used to connect large computers in the same area that share data frequently. One disadvantage of a ring network is that if one computer fails, the entire network fails because the data cannot be transmitted past the failed computer.

Communications Protocols

Communications software is written to work with one or more protocols. A **protocol** is a set of rules and procedures for exchanging information between computers. Protocols define how the communications link is established, how information is transmitted, and how errors are detected and corrected. Using the same protocols, different types and makes of computers can communicate with each other. Over the years, numerous protocols have been developed, some of which can be used together. The table shown in Figure 6-35 lists some of the more widely used protocols. The two most widely used protocols for networks are Ethernet and token ring.

Figure 6-35
A partial list of commonly used communication protocols. Protocols specify the procedures that are used during transmission.

PROTOCOL	DESCRIPTION
Ethernet	Most widely used protocol for LANS.
Token ring	Uses electronic token to avoid transmission conflict by allowing only one device to transmit at a time.
PowerTalk	Links Apple Macintosh computers.
FDDI	Fiber Distributed Data Interface. High-speed fiber-optic protocol.
SNA	System Network Architecture. Primarily used to link large systems.
TCP/IP	Transmission Control Protocol/Internet Protocol. Used on the Internet.
X.25	International standard for packet switching.
ATM	Asynchronous Transfer Mode. Protocol developed for transmitting voice, data, and video over any type of media.
Frame Relay	High-speed protocol used to link remote networks.
CDPD	Cellular Digital Packet Data. Protocol used for cellular phones.
IPX	Used on Novell NetWare networks.
Xmodem	PC protocol that uses 128 byte blocks.
Ymodem	PC protocol that uses 1,024 byte blocks.
Zmodem	PC protocol that uses 512 byte blocks.
Kermit	PC protocol that uses variable length blocks.

Ethernet

Ethernet is the most widely used network protocol for LAN networks. Developed in the mid-1970s by Xerox, Ethernet was approved as the first industry standard LAN protocol in 1983. Ethernet is based on a bus topology but can be wired in a star pattern by using a wiring hub. Most Ethernet networks transmit data at 10 Mbps. A higher speed version of Ethernet, called **Fast-Ethernet,** can transmit data at 100 Mbps.

Because Ethernet uses a bus topology, a packet of data can be sent in both directions along the bus whenever a node is ready to transmit. The packet of data, which contains the destination address and the sending address, travels along the network until it arrives at the designated receiving device. If the packet runs into another packet, a **collision** occurs. Ethernet uses a method called **carrier sense multiple access with collision detection (CSMA/CD)** to detect collisions and retransmit the data. This method is illustrated in Figure 6-36.

Figure 6-36
How an Ethernet network transmits data.

1. Computers on an Ethernet bus network monitor the network cable to determine if any workstations are transmitting data. Sometimes, two or more computers try to send data at the same time. In this example, computer A is trying to send data to computer D and computer C is trying to send data to computer B. Each data packet contains the sender's address, the destination address, and the data.

2. When the data packets collide, static is created and a special electronic signal is sent to all computers on the network. The signal indicates a collision has occurred and that data packets should be retransmitted.

3. Each computer waits a random amount of time to retransmit. This usually results in one computer successfully transmitting its data before the other computer starts to retransmit.

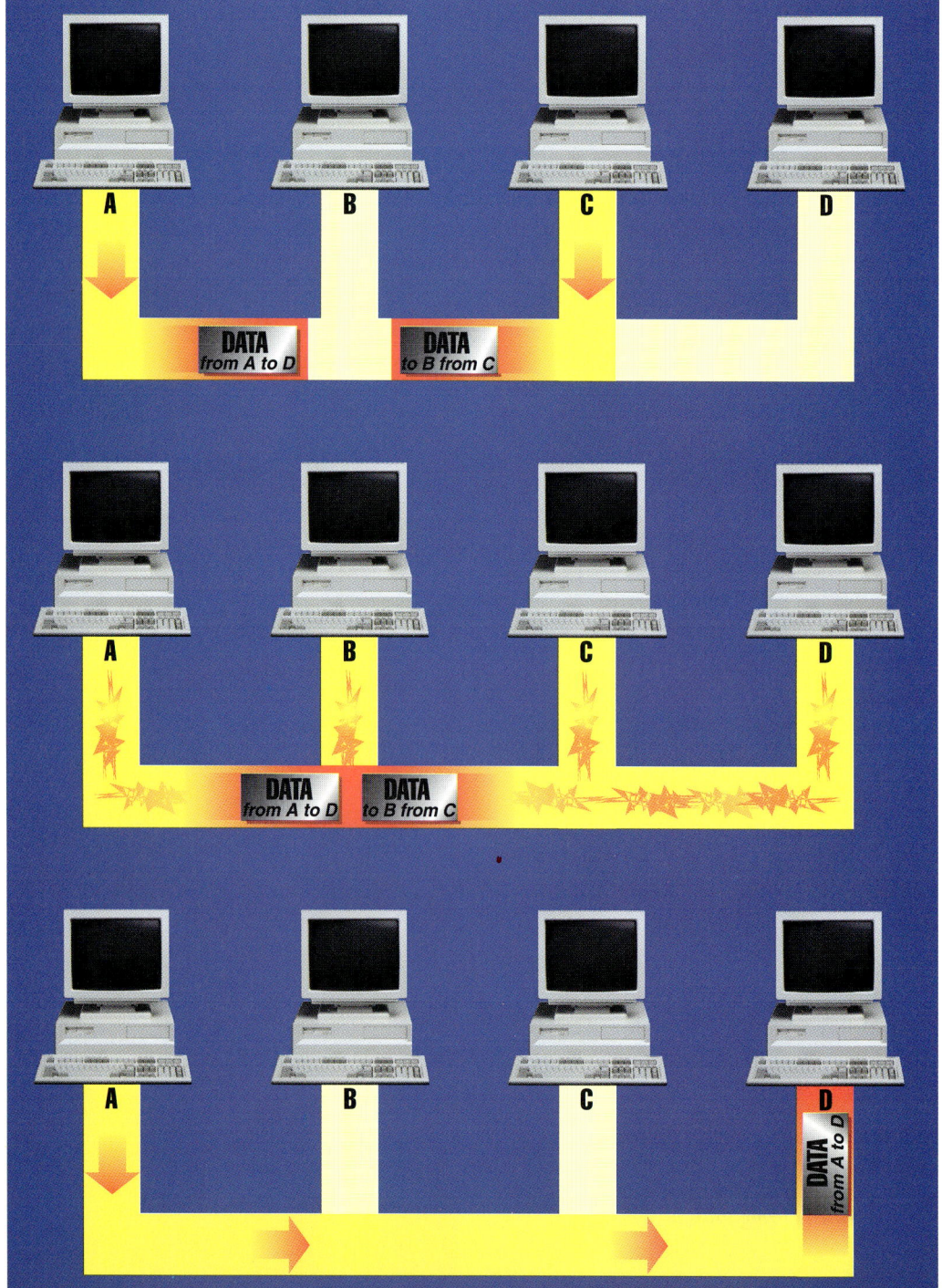

COMMUNICATIONS PROTOCOLS **6.31**

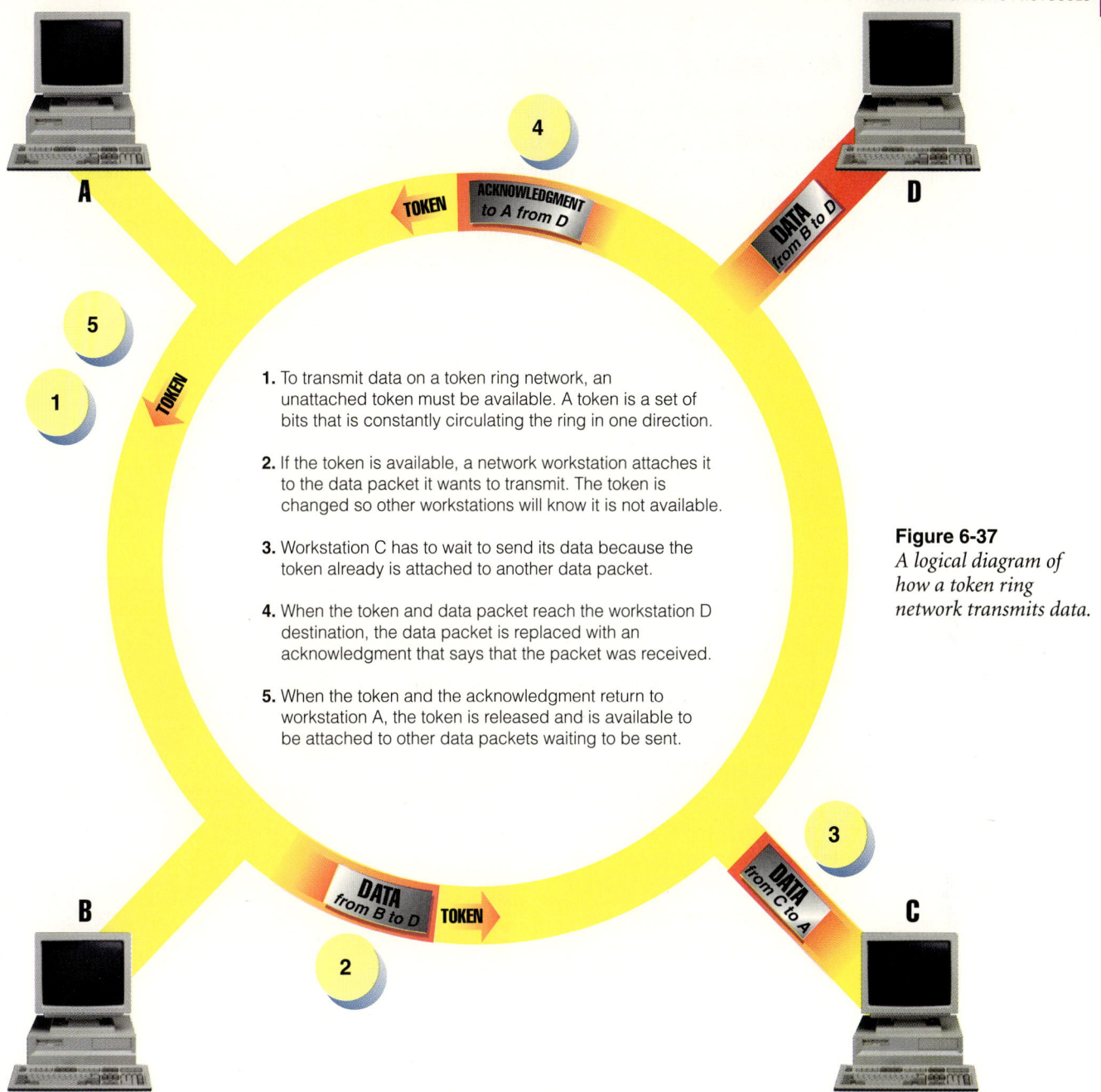

1. To transmit data on a token ring network, an unattached token must be available. A token is a set of bits that is constantly circulating the ring in one direction.

2. If the token is available, a network workstation attaches it to the data packet it wants to transmit. The token is changed so other workstations will know it is not available.

3. Workstation C has to wait to send its data because the token already is attached to another data packet.

4. When the token and data packet reach the workstation D destination, the data packet is replaced with an acknowledgment that says that the packet was received.

5. When the token and the acknowledgment return to workstation A, the token is released and is available to be attached to other data packets waiting to be sent.

Figure 6-37
A logical diagram of how a token ring network transmits data.

Token Ring

Token ring is the second most widely used protocol for LAN networks. A **token ring network** constantly circulates an electronic signal, called a **token**, around the network (Figure 6-37). Devices on the network that want to send a message take the token and attach it to their data. Once it is attached to data, the token cannot be used by other devices. When data arrives at its destination, the data is replaced with an acknowledgment that the data was received, and the token and the acknowledgment are sent back to the original sending device. When the original sending device receives the token and the acknowledgment, other devices then can use the token to send their data.

The *ring* in token ring applies to the circular sequence in which the computer checks each network node to see if it has data to send. It does not mean that a continuous loop of cable connects all of the nodes. In fact, like Ethernet, token ring networks are wired in a star pattern with separate cables connecting a central wiring hub with each node. Depending on the cabling and equipment used, token ring networks can transfer data at 4 and 16 Mbps. Token ring networks that transfer data at 16 Mbps use two tokens.

An Example of a Communications Network

The diagram in Figure 6-38 illustrates how two personal computer networks and a mainframe computer are connected to share information with each other and with outside sources.

The marketing department operates a bus network of four personal computers (1). Frequently used marketing data and programs are stored in the server (2). The personal computers in the marketing department share a laser printer (3). A modem (4) is attached to the marketing server so outside sales representatives can use a dial telephone line (5) to call the marketing system and obtain product price information.

The administration department operates a bus network of three personal computers (6) wired in a star pattern through a wiring hub. As with the marketing network, common data and programs are stored on a server (7) and the administration personal computers share a laser printer (8). Because the administration department sometimes needs information from the marketing system, the two similar networks are connected with a LAN bridge (9). The bridge allows users on either network to access data or programs on the other network.

Administration department users sometimes need information from the company's mainframe computer system (10). They can access the mainframe through the use of a gateway (11) that allows different types of network systems to be connected. All communications with the mainframe computer are controlled by a front-end processor (12). A dial telephone line (13) connected to a modem (14) allows remote users to call the mainframe and allows mainframe users to call other computers. A leased telephone line (15) and a modem (16) are used for a permanent connection to the computer at the corporate headquarters, several hundred miles away. The leased line can carry the signals of up to four different users. The signals are separated by the use of a multiplexer (17). A gateway (18) connects the front-end processor and mainframe system to a microwave antenna (19) on the roof of the building. The microwave antenna sends and receives data from a computer at the manufacturing plant located two miles away. The front-end processor also controls mainframe computer terminals located throughout the company (20).

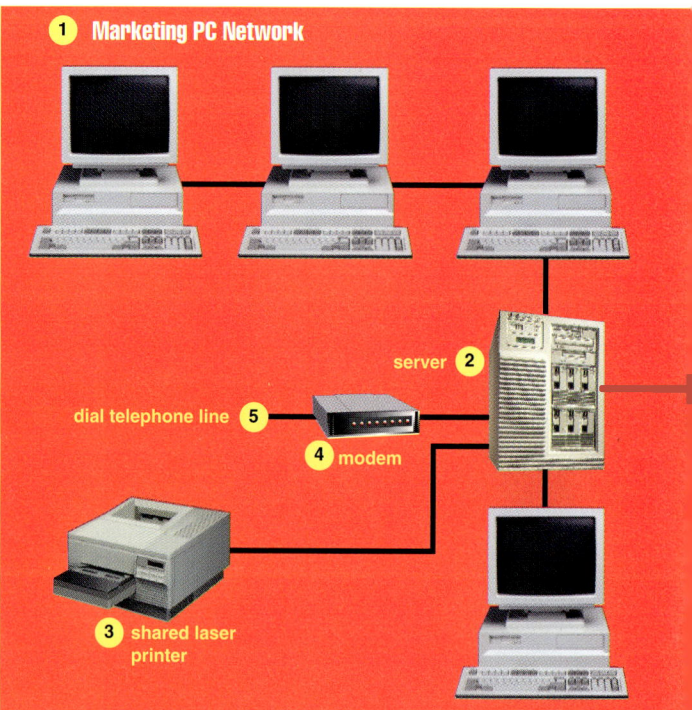

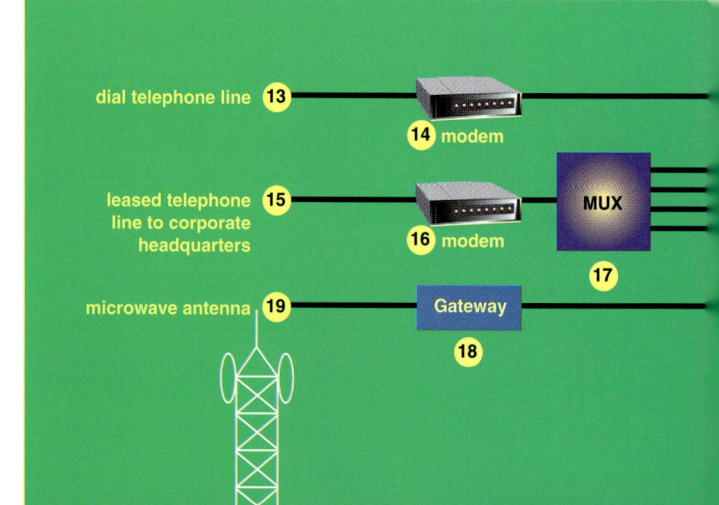

Summary of Communications and Networks

Communications will continue to affect how you work, access and use information, and use computers. Because of communications technology, individuals and organizations no longer are limited to local data resources; they can obtain information from anywhere in the world at electronic speed. Communications technology continues to change, challenging today's businesses to find ways to adapt the technology to make their operations more efficient and to provide better products and services for their customers. Networks are just one way that organizations are using communications technology to meet current business challenges. Today, many companies are focused on **enterprise computing**, which involves connecting all of the computers in an organization into one network, so everyone in the organization (the enterprise) can share hardware, software, information resources, and even processing power. By linking individual computers into networks, organizations not only expand computing resources, but also allow increased communication between workgroups and individuals. For individuals, new communications technology offers increased access to worldwide information and services and provides new opportunities in business and education.

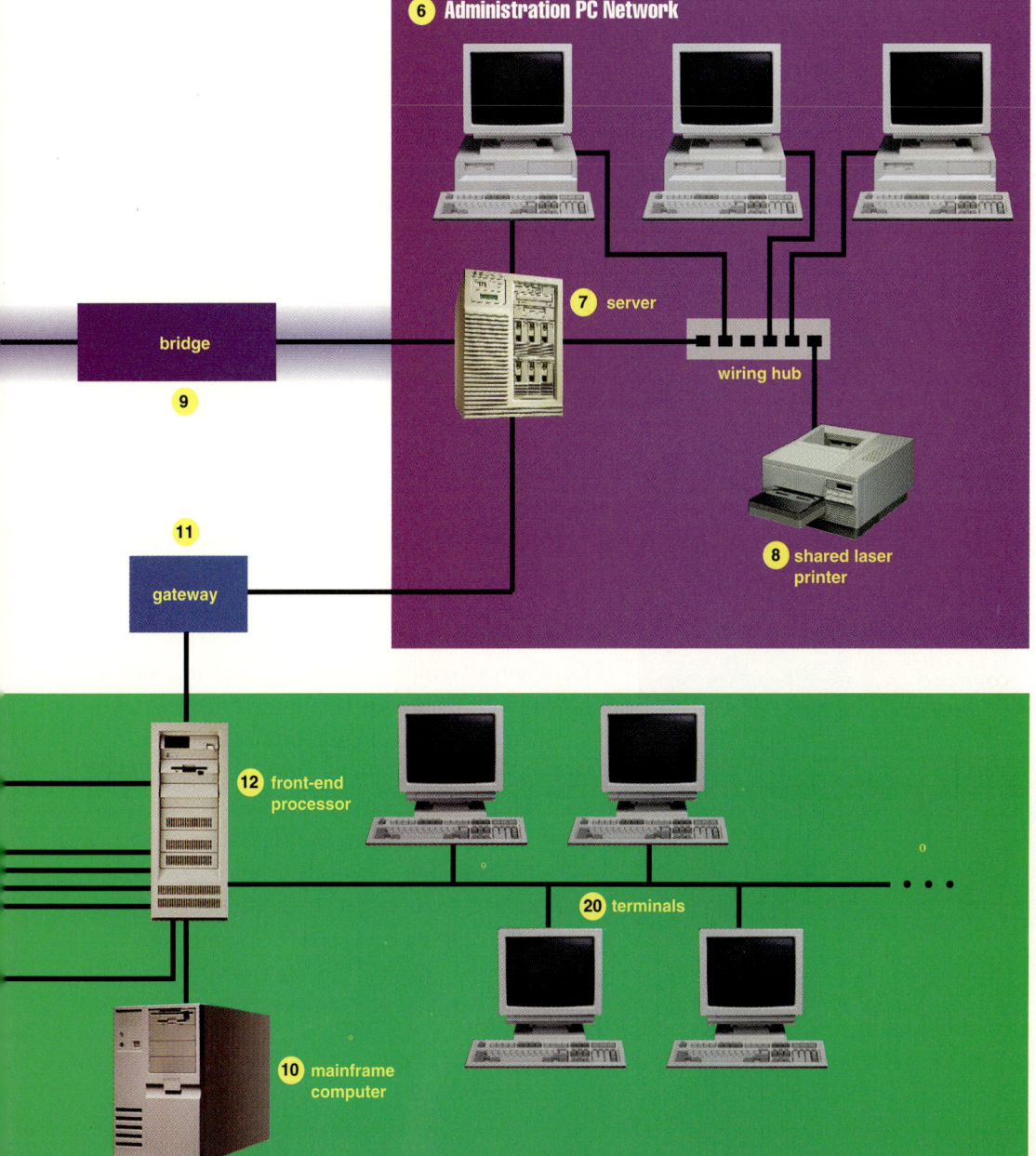

Figure 6-38
The two personal computer networks are connected together with a bridge. A gateway is used to connect the administration personal computer network with a mainframe. All communications with the mainframe are controlled by a separate computer called a front-end processor. Modems are used to connect the networks to leased and dial telephone lines.

CHAPTER 6 – COMMUNICATIONS AND NETWORKS

COMPUTERS AT WORK

GPS: Tool of the Modern Traveler

In ancient times, mariners learned to use the stars to navigate and determine their position on the globe. Today, travelers have a new constellation to help them find their way; 24 global positioning system (GPS) satellites that circle the earth. The satellites are spread across six, 12,000-mile-high orbits and circle the earth every twelve hours. At any point on the globe, at least five satellites are within range for GPS use. Every thirty seconds, each satellite broadcasts a radio signal giving its precise location over the earth and the time the signal was sent. The time is determined by an onboard atomic clock that is accurate to within one second every 70,000 years. By comparing how long it takes signals from three or more satellites to arrive, a GPS receiver on earth can use the surveying technique of **triangulation** to determine its precise location, including altitude.

The GPS system originally was developed by the U.S. government in the 1970s for military use and was not made available for commercial use until the mid 1980s. Early GPS equipment was expensive and was used primarily in aviation and marine navigation. Hand-held units were available but cost more than $3,000. Today, lower-cost components have enabled GPS technology to be incorporated into many consumer electronic products such as cellular phones and portable computers. Hand-held devices used by hikers are available for less than $200.

Trucking companies were among the first commercial users of GPS systems, usually in combination with separate two-way communications systems. The GPS system locates the truck and the communications system lets the company stay in touch with the driver. Companies can let drivers know about opportunities to pick up more freight along the way and drivers can notify the company if they are delayed or need assistance.

Several developers have combined GPS with mapping software. The latitude and longitude coordinates determined by the GPS receiver are translated into a specific map location that is displayed on a screen. Both Hertz® and Avis® have installed small screens in some of their premium rental cars that can direct a driver to his or her hotel or the nearest bank or restaurant. Deere & Company developed a GPS and mapping system for use with the its farm equipment. The system allows farmers to practice *precision farming*; working their land foot by foot instead of field by field. The potential savings in fertilizer and pesticides more than pay for the system. Eventually, GPS and mapping systems will be installed in all new vehicles. This undoubtedly will reduce the age-old problem of driving partners arguing over whether or not to stop and ask directions.

Figure 6-39

IN THE FUTURE

Anywhere, Anytime Voice and Data Communications

Existing satellite phones are expensive, more than $20,000 each, and require an electronics package the size of a small suitcase. In the near future, satellite communications systems will enable you to talk, or send and receive data, anywhere on earth with a device the size of a cellular phone. To accomplish this goal, several organizations made up of private companies and international government agencies are developing the necessary hardware and software and negotiating with countries for communication rights. Several of these organizations base their plans on using low-earth orbit (LEO) satellites that will circle the earth at an altitude of less than 500 miles. LEO satellites are less expensive to build and put into orbit compared to satellites that are placed in geosynchronous orbits up to 22,300 miles above the earth. Two of the better known organizations planning satellite systems are IRIDIUM, Inc. and Teledesic Corporation.

The IRIDIUM system is a $4 billion project led by the U.S. communications company Motorola. IRIDIUM's plan includes 66 LEO satellites that will provide global wireless telephone service in 1998. Fax, paging, and low-speed (2,400 bps) data transfer capabilities also will be available. IRIDIUM will be a worldwide version of existing cellular phone systems without the patchwork of *no service* areas that now exist.

An even more ambitious $9 billion project is being planned by Teledesic. Two of the principal backers of Teledesic are Bill Gates of Microsoft and cellular phone pioneer Craig McCaw. During a two-year period beginning in 2000, Teledesic plans to orbit 924 LEO satellites; 44 each in 21 polar orbits. The Teledesic satellites will provide high-speed communications up to 2 MB per second. This higher transfer rate will make Teledesic better suited for data communications including much of the international Internet traffic. Unlike traditional satellites that communicate only with ground stations, Teledesic satellites will transmit data from one satellite to another. If necessary, communications traffic will be rerouted to avoid nonfunctioning or overloaded satellites.

In addition to IRIDIUM and Teledesic, nine other groups currently are developing global satellite-based communications systems. Several other organizations plan regional systems to service specific areas such as India and Western Europe. Although it is unlikely that all of these groups will succeed, some will and the ability to phone and be phoned anywhere will be a reality.

Figure 6-40

6 review

chapter 1 | 2 | 3 | 4 | 5 | 6 | 7 | 8 | 9 | 10 | 11 | 12 | 13 | 14 | I

inCyber | review | terms | yourTurn | hotTopics | outThere | winLabs | webWalk | exercises | news | home

INSTRUCTIONS: *To display this page from the Web, launch your browser and enter the URL, http://www.scsite.com/dc/ch6/review.htm. Click the links for current and additional information.*

1 What Is Communications?

Communications, sometimes called **data communications** or **telecommunications**, refers to the transmission of data and information between two or more computers using a communications channel. Communications technology is necessary for **electronic mail (e-mail)**, **voice mail**, **facsimile (fax)**, **telecommuting**, **videoconferencing**, **groupware**, **electronic data interchange (EDI)**, **global positioning systems (GPSs)**, electronic **bulletin board systems (BBSs)**, **online services**, the **Internet**, and **intranets**.

2 Components of a Communications System

The basic model of a communications system consists of a computer or terminal, communications equipment that sends data, a communications channel, communications equipment that receives data, and another computer. **Communications software** also is required. A **communications channel**, which is the path that data follows as it is transmitted from the sending equipment to the receiving equipment, is made up of one or more transmission media.

3 Transmission Media

Transmission **media** are the physical materials or other means used to establish a communications channel. Two types of transmission media are physical cabling media and wireless media.

4 Physical Cabling Media

Twisted-pair cable consists of pairs of plastic-coated copper wires that are twisted together. **Coaxial cable** is a high-quality communications line that consists of a copper wire conductor surrounded by three layers: a nonconducting insulator, a woven metal outer conductor, and a plastic outer coating. **Fiber-optic cable** uses smooth, hair-thin strands of glass or plastic to transmit data as pulses of light.

5 Wireless Media

Microwaves are radio waves that can be used to provide high-speed transmission of both voice communication and digital signals. **Wireless transmission** uses carrier-connect radio, infrared light beams, or radio waves to transmit data.

6 Line Configurations

Two major **line configurations** (types of line connections) commonly used in communications are point-to-point lines and multidrop, or multipoint, lines. A **point-to-point line** is a direct line between a sending and receiving device. A point-to-point line may be a **switched line** or a **dedicated line**. A **multidrop**, or **multipoint**, **line** commonly is used to connect multiple devices along a single line to a main computer, sometimes called a **host computer**.

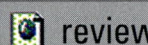

7 Characteristics of Communications Channels

Communications can be categorized by a number of characteristics including the type of signal, transmission mode, transmission direction, and transmission rate. Computer equipment is designed to process data as **digital signals**, or individual electrical pulses. Telephone lines were designed to carry voice transmission in continuous electrical waves called **analog signals**. A modem converts between digital and analog signals. In **asynchronous transmission mode,** data is transmitted in individual bytes at irregular intervals. In **synchronous transmission mode**, large blocks of data are transmitted at regular intervals.

8 Transmission Direction and Transmission Rate

The direction of data transmission is classified in one of three ways. In **simplex transmission**, data flows in one direction only. In **half-duplex transmission**, data can flow in either direction, but only in one direction at a time. In **full-duplex transmission**, data can be sent in both directions simultaneously. The transmission rate of a communications channel is determined by its bandwidth and its speed. **Bandwidth** is the range of frequencies that a communications channel can carry. The speed at which data is transmitted usually is expressed as **bits per second (bps)**.

9 Communications Software

Communications **software** is separate programs that manage the transmission of data between computers. Communications software has a number of features including **dialing**, **file transfer**, **terminal emulation**, and **Internet access**.

10 Communications Equipment

A **modem** converts digital signals to analog signals, and converts analog signals back into digital signals. A **multiplexer** combines input signals from several devices into a single stream of data and transmits it. After it passes over a communications channel, a multiplexer separates the data stream into its original parts. A **front-end processor** handles the communications requirements of a larger system. A **network interface card** fits in an expansion slot of a computer or other device so the device can be connected to the network. A **wiring hub** allows devices to be connected to the server. A **gateway** allows users on one network to access resources on a *different* type of network. A **bridge** is used to connect *similar* networks. A **router** is an intelligent network connector that sends communications traffic to the appropriate network.

11 Communications Networks

A communications **network** is a collection of terminals, computers, and other equipment that uses communications channels to share data, information, hardware, and software. Networks can be classified as either local area networks or wide area networks.

12 Local Area Networks (LANs)

A **local area network** (**LAN**) is a communications network that covers a limited geographic area. Common applications of local area networks are **hardware resource sharing**, **software resource sharing**, and **information resource sharing**. Information resource sharing usually is provided using either the **file-server method** or the **client-server method**. A **peer-to-peer network** allows any computer on a LAN to share the resources of any other computer on the LAN. A **network operating system** (**NOS**) is the system software that makes it possible to implement and control a LAN.

13 Wide Area Networks (WANs)

A **wide area network** (**WAN**) covers a large geographic region and uses telephone cables, terrestrial microwave, satellites, or other combinations of communications channels. **Common carriers** are public wide area network companies. **Value-added networks** (**VANs**) enhance communications channels leased from common carriers by adding improvements such as faster data transmission or other specialized services.

14 Network Configurations

The way equipment is configured in a communications network is called **topology**. A **star network** topology has a central computer with one or more smaller computers connected to it, forming a star. In a **bus network** topology, all the devices in the network are connected to and share a single data path. In a **ring network** topology, the devices on the network are connected in a continuous loop or ring.

15 Communications Protocols

A **protocol** is a set of rules and procedures for exchanging information between computers. Protocols define how a link is established, how information is transmitted, and how errors are detected and corrected. By using the same protocols, different types and makes of computers can communicate. The two most widely used protocols for networks are **Ethernet** and **token ring**.

6.39 terms

chapter
1 | 2 | 3 | 4 | 5 | 6 | 7 | 8 | 9 | 10 | 11 | 12 | 13 | 14 | I

inCyber | review | terms | yourTurn | hotTopics | outThere | winLabs | webWalk | exercises | news | home

INSTRUCTIONS: *To display this page from the Web, launch your browser and enter the URL, http://www.scsite.com/dc/ch6/terms.htm. Scroll through the list of terms. Click a term for its definition and a picture. Click the rocket ship for current and additional information about the term.*

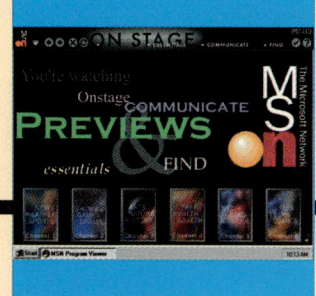

online services

DEFINITION

online services
Online services make information and services such as electronic banking, shopping, news, weather, hotel and airline reservations, investment information, and Internet access available to paying subscribers (**6.6**)

10base2 cable (6.10)
10baseT cable (6.9)

analog signal (6.16)
application server (6.25)
asynchronous transmission mode (6.17)

bandwidth (6.18)
bits per second (bps) (6.18)
bridge (6.22)
bulletin board system (BBS) (6.5)
bus network (6.28)

carrier sense multiple access with collision detection (CSMA/CD) (6.30)
cellular telephone (6.13)
client-server (6.24)
coax (6.9)
coaxial cable (6.9)
collision (6.30)
common carriers (6.26)
communications (6.2)
communications channel (6.8)
communications line (6.8)
communications link (6.8)
communications satellites (6.11)
communications software (6.8), (6.19)
concentrator (6.22)

data communications (6.2)
data link (6.8)
database server (6.25)
dedicated line (6.15)
dialing (6.19)
digital data service (6.17)
digital signal (6.16)

downlink (6.11)

earth stations (6.11)
electronic data interchange (EDI) (6.4)
electronic mail (e-mail) (6.2)
enterprise computing (6.33)
Ethernet (6.30)
external modem (6.19)

facsimile (6.2)
Fast-Ethernet (6.30)
fax (6.2)
fiber-optic cable (6.10)
file-server (6.24)
file transfer (6.19)
front-end processor (6.21)
full-duplex transmission (6.18)

gateway (6.22)
geosynchronous orbit (6.12)
global positioning system (GPS) (6.5)
groupware (6.4)

half-duplex transmission (6.18)
handshake (6.14)
hardware resource sharing (6.23)
host computer (6.15)

information resource sharing (6.24)
information services (6.6)
internal modem (6.20)
Internet (6.7)
Internet access (6.19)
ISDN (integrated services digital network) (6.17)

leased line (6.15)
line configurations (6.14)
local area network (LAN) (6.23)

metropolitan area network (MAN) (6.26)
microwaves (6.11)
modem (6.19)
multidrop line (6.15)
multiplexer (6.20)
multipoint line (6.15)
multistation access unit (MAU) (6.22)

network (6.23)
network interface card (NIC) (6.21)
network licenses (6.24)
network operating system (NOS) (6.25)
node (6.27)

online services (6.6)

packet-switching (6.26)
peer-to-peer network (6.25)
point-to-point line (6.14)
polling (6.21)
private line (6.15)
protocol (6.29)

ring network (6.29)
router (6.22)

shielded twisted-pair (STP) cable (6.9)
simplex transmission (6.18)
site licenses (6.24)
software resource sharing (6.24)

stackable hub (6.22)
star network (6.27)
switched line (6.14)
synchronous transmission mode (6.17)
sys op (6.5)
system operator (6.5)

T1 (6.17)
T3 (6.17)
telecommunications (6.2)
telecommuting (6.2)
terminal emulation (6.19)
terrestrial microwave (6.11)
thinnet (6.10)
token (6.31)
topology (6.27)
token ring network (6.31)
transmission media (6.9)
twisted-pair cable (6.9)

unshielded twisted-pair (UTP) cable (6.9)
uplink (6.11)

value-added carriers (6.26)
value-added network (VAN) (6.26)
very small aperture terminal (VSAT) (6.12)
videoconferencing (6.3)
voice mail (6.2)

wide area network (WAN) (6.26)
wireless transmission (6.12)
wiring hub (6.22)
workgroup technology (6.4)
workstations (6.27)

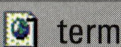 terms — 6:03 AM

6 yourTurn

inCyber | review | terms | yourTurn | hotTopics | outThere | winLabs | webWalk | exercises | news | home

INSTRUCTIONS: *To display this page from the Web, launch your browser and enter the URL, http://www.scsite.com/dc/ch6/turn.htm. Click a blank line for the answer. Click the links for current and additional information.*

Label the Figure

1. _____
2. _____
3. _____
4. _____
5. _____
6. _____
7. _____
8. _____

Instructions: Identify each part of a communication system.

Fill in the Blanks

Instructions: Complete each sentence with the correct term or terms.

1. _____ refers to the transmission of data and information between two or more computers using a channel such as a standard telephone line.
2. One application that relies on communications technology is _____, which is the direct exchange of documents from one business's computer system to another.
3. A(n) _____ is the path that data follows as it is transmitted from the sending equipment to the receiving equipment in a communications system.
4. Three kinds of physical cabling media are _____, which consists of pairs of plastic wires wound together, _____, which is composed of a copper wire conductor surrounded by three layers, and _____, which uses hair-thin strands of glass or plastic to transmit pulses of light.
5. A(n) _____ is a device that attaches to a computer and converts between digital signals and analog signals.

Short Answer

Instructions: Write a brief answer to each of the following questions.

1. How are point-to-point lines different from multidrop lines? How is a switched line different from a dedicated line? What are the advantages and disadvantages of using a switched line? _____
2. How is asynchronous transmission mode different from synchronous transmission mode? What is a parity bit? _____
3. What functions are performed by communications software? What is the purpose of each? _____
4. How are local area networks (LANs) different from wide area networks (WANs)? How is the file-server method of information resource sharing different from the client-server method of information resource sharing? _____
5. Why are communications protocols important? What are the Ethernet and token ring protocols? _____

6 hotTopics

chapter 1 | 2 | 3 | 4 | 5 | 6 | 7 | 8 | 9 | 10 | 11 | 12 | 13 | 14 | I

inCyber | review | terms | yourTurn | hotTopics | outThere | winLabs | webWalk | exercises | news | home

INSTRUCTIONS: *To display this page from the Web, launch your browser and enter the URL, http://www.scsite.com/dc/ch6/hot.htm. Click the links for current and additional information to help you respond to the hotTopics questions.*

1 *A luxury sedan is available with an electronic navigation system that uses* global positioning satellites. To use the system, a driver chooses from lists of destinations by touching a screen on the dashboard. After asking how the driver wants to travel (city streets or highway), a computer shows a map with a suggested route. As the car moves, a computer voice indicates where and when to turn. Of the applications such as the navigation system that rely on communications technology, which would you be most likely to use today? Which would you be most likely to use ten years from now? Which will have the greatest impact on society?

2 *The number of people telecommuting has increased fourfold in the past eight years.* Telecommuting offers several advantages to employees—flexible work schedules, casual dress codes, and no rush-hour traffic. Studies show employers also benefit—less office space is required and telecommuters are 10 to 20 percent more productive than their office-bound brethren. Whether telecommuting is a success, however, appears to depend on three factors: the employee's personality, the employer's willingness to make adjustments, and the nature of the job. What type of personality is necessary to telecommute successfully? What adjustments must be made by employers? Given your personality and the career you plan to pursue, could you be a successful telecommuter? Why?

3 *Many online services and bulletin board systems have taken increased* responsibility for the content of the messages they communicate. But online services and bulletin board systems cover large geographic areas, and standards vary from community to community. Some feel any attempt at control is censorship. Do online services and bulletin board systems have the obligation to decide what is communicated? What role should government take in controlling the type of information transmitted? Why? If you were head of an online service or bulletin board, what standards would you set?

4 *If you have friends or family who live out of town, you (or they) may be paying a substantial* amount to a common carrier for long-distance telephone service. Yet, with a computer, the appropriate software and hardware, and an Internet access provider, you can talk to people anywhere in the world for as long as you want, all for a monthly flat rate (usually around twenty-five dollars). Problems do exist: setting up the equipment can be difficult, conversations are somewhat choppy, and both parties must be online and using the same phone software. Will phone service via the Internet ever replace conventional telephone service? How might common carriers change to accommodate this new mode of communication? Would you be interested in using your computer to call people long distance? Why?

5 *In the course of a usual day, people communicate in different directions. Sometimes they just* listen, sometimes they listen and then respond, and sometimes everyone is able to talk at once. Make a list of interactions you have in a typical day. Classify each communication based on the direction of transmission: those comparable to simplex transmission, those comparable to half-duplex transmission, and those comparable to full-duplex transmission. Explain why you classified each communication as you did. Is there any communication that, by its nature, must have a certain direction of transmission? Would any communication improve if the direction of transmission were different? Why or why not?

6.42 outThere

chapter
1 | 2 | 3 | 4 | 5 | 6 | 7 | 8 | 9 | 10 | 11 | 12 | 13 | 14 | I

inCyber | review | terms | yourTurn | hotTopics | outThere | winLabs | webWalk | exercises | news | home

INSTRUCTIONS: *To display this page from the Web, launch your browser and enter the URL, http://www.scsite.com/dc/ch6/out.htm. Click the links for current and additional information.*

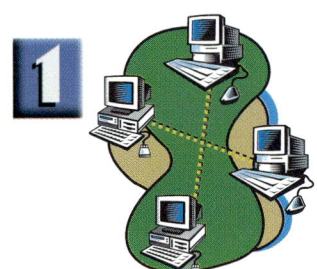

1 *Many schools and offices have a network connecting their computers. These* networks offer advantages that could not be realized if the computers were not joined. Locate a school or office that uses a network and interview someone about how the network works. For what purposes is the network used? What are the advantages of using a network? Does the organization use a single server computer or a peer-to-peer network? What network operating system is used? Why? What network configuration (star, bus, or ring) is used? Why? Is the network connected to another network? If so, how?

2 *As office networks grow increasingly commonplace, network security* has become an important issue. Networks frequently carry sensitive information — research analysis, test data, engineering designs, legal documents, and so on. No organization can afford to leave this type of information vulnerable to hackers, industrial espionage agents, or disgruntled employees. It is estimated that attacks on networks cost companies billions of dollars each year. Visit some Web sites to learn more about network security. How frequent are attacks on networks? What are the results of these attacks? What factors are important in providing network security? How can a network be secured?

3 *Facsimile equipment has become an essential component of even small businesses. Orders,* invoices, and correspondence are faxed routinely between merchants and customers. Fax machines also are becoming increasingly popular in homes. People are faxing notes to friends, letters to magazines, even song requests to radio stations! Because of this, fax machines now are available at a variety of outlets including computer stores, office supply stores, discount stores, and electronics stores. Visit three different types of stores and find similar fax machines in each. Write down the brand name of each machine, the features it offers, the store in which it was found, and the machine's cost. Where would you be most likely to purchase a fax machine? Why?

4 *Choosing a network operating system (NOS) may be one of the more important decisions made* when establishing a network. The network operating system determines the way information, software, and hardware are shared and manipulated. The efficiency and security of a network is to a large extent dependent on the network operating system. Learn about two or more network operating systems by visiting appropriate Web sites. What are the operating system's features? What are its specifications? What hardware is required? With what software is the operating system compatible? Where is the system available? How can it be learned? From what you have discovered, which network operating system do you think is best? Why?

5 *Some experts predict that online information services and the Internet eventually will be as* much a part of our lives as newspapers, magazines, and television. Are all online information services the same? Call the telephone numbers for at least three of the online information service providers listed in Figure 6-6 on page 6.7 to find out how they differ. What services are offered? Is a particular type of computer or user interface required? What is the membership fee? Are other fees charged, such as a minimum monthly charge, hourly access fee, or added cost for certain services? Is Internet access included? How? From the information you learn, in which online service are you most interested? Why?

6.43 winLabs

6 winLabs   c h a p t e r   1 | 2 | 3 | 4 | 5 | 6 | 7 | 8 | 9 | 10 | 11 | 12 | 13 | 14 | I

inCyber | review | terms | yourTurn | hotTopics | outThere | winLabs | webWalk | exercises | news | home

INSTRUCTIONS: *To display this page from the Web, launch your browser and enter the URL, http://www.scsite.com/dc/ch6/labs.htm. Click the links for current and additional information.*

1   Shelly Cashman Series Computers of the Future Lab

Follow the instructions in winLabs 1 on page 1.34 to display the Shelly Cashman Series Labs screen. Click Exploring the Computers of the Future. Click the Start Lab button. When the initial screen displays, carefully read the objectives. With your printer turned on, click the Print Questions button. Fill out the top of the Questions sheet and then answer the questions.

2   What is The Microsoft Network

Right-click The Microsoft Network (MSN) icon on the desktop. Click Properties on the shortcut menu. When The Microsoft Network Properties dialog box displays (Figure 6-41), read the information and then answer the following questions: (1) What version of The Microsoft Network are you using? Click the Connection Settings button and then answer the following questions: (1) What is the current service type? (2) What is the telephone number for this service type? (3) What modem, if any, is being used to connect to the MSN? Close the dialog boxes.

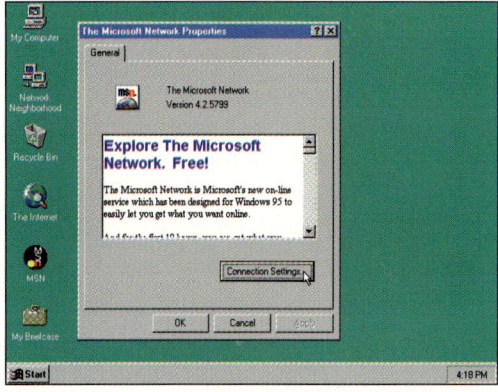

Figure 6-41

3   Understanding Your Modem

Click the Start button on the taskbar, point to Settings on the Start menu, and then click Control Panel on the submenu. Double-click the Modems icon in the Control Panel window. When the Modems Properties dialog box displays, click the General tab. Click the first modem in the list and then click the Properties button. When the modem's dialog box displays, click the General tab (Figure 6-42). Answer the following questions: (1) What is the name of the modem? (2) To which port is the modem connected? (3) What is the maximum speed of the modem? Click the Connection tab and then answer the following questions: (1) What is the number of data bits? (2) What is the parity? (3) What is the number of stop bits? (4) Which call preferences are set on your modem? Close the dialog boxes and Control Panel.

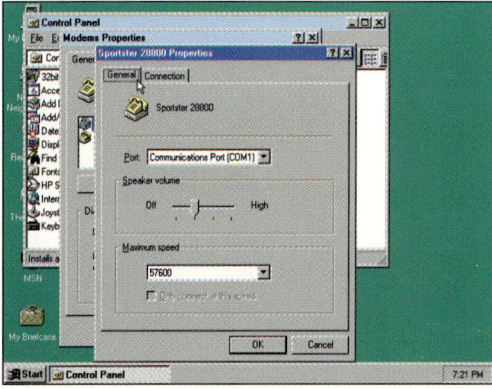

Figure 6-42

4   Using Help to Understand Networks

Click the Start button on the taskbar and then click Help on the Start menu. Click the Contents tab, double-click How To..., and then double-click Use a Network. Double-click Setting up your computer to connect to the network. In the Windows Help window, click the Options button, click Print Topic, and then click the OK button in the Print dialog box. Click the Help Topics button. One at a time, display and print each of the remaining Use a Network topics. Close any open Help window(s). Read the printouts.

6.44 webWalk

INSTRUCTIONS: *To display this page from the Web, launch your browser and enter the URL, http://www.scsite.com/dc/ch6/walk.htm. Click the exercise link to display the exercise.*

1 Desktop Videoconferencing
Desktop videoconferencing products are applications that can be used on standard desktop computer systems. You can learn more about desktop videoconferencing by completing this exercise.

3 Global Positioning System GPS
GPS is a satellite-based radio navigation system originally employed by the U.S. Department of Defense that now is used to track vehicles and goods and provide accurate position, velocity, and time. To learn more about GPS, complete this exercise.

4 Online Services
Online services, sometimes called information services, provide information and services to paying subscribers. To visit an online service (Figure 6-44), complete this exercise.

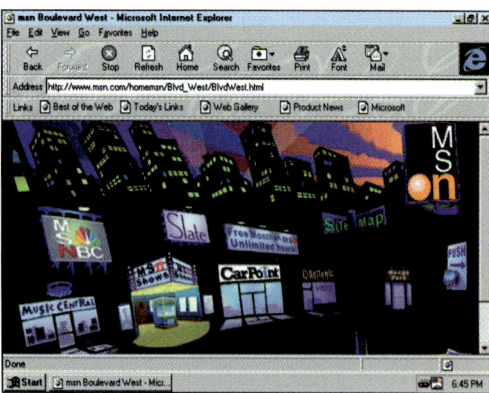

Figure 6-44

7 Real-time auction
Complete this exercise to learn about a Web site that runs a real-time auction in which you can participate.

9 Web Chat
Complete this exercise to enter a Web Chat discussion related to the issues presented in the hotTopics exercise.

2 Groupware
Groupware is software that helps multiple users collaborate on projects and share information (Figure 6-43). Complete this exercise to learn more about groupware.

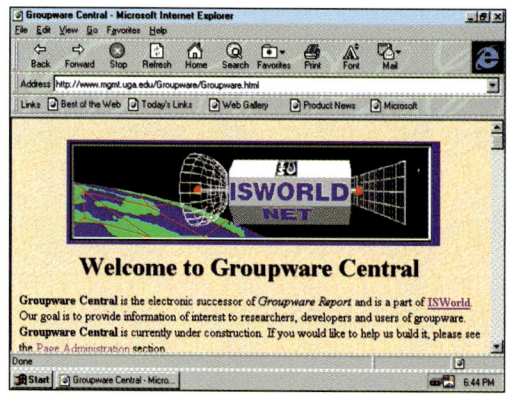

Figure 6-43

5 Information Mining
Complete this exercise to improve your Web research skills by using a Web search engine to find information related to this chapter.

6 Online Investing
Communications technology makes Web services, such as online investing possible. Complete this exercise to learn about a Web site where you can place stock and option orders and manage your portfolio around the clock.

8 Electronic Mail (E-mail)
E-mail allows you to use a computer to transmit messages to and receive messages from other computer users. Complete this exercise to visit a unique web site and send your comments via e-mail.

The Internet and the World Wide Web

OBJECTIVES

After completing this chapter, you will be able to:

- Describe the Internet and how it works
- Describe the World Wide Web portion of the Internet
- Understand how Web documents are linked to one another
- Understand how Web browser software works
- Describe several types of multimedia available on the Web
- Explain how to use a Web search tool to find information
- Describe different ways organizations use intranets and firewalls
- Explain how Internet services such as e-mail, FTP, Gopher, Telnet, Usenet, and Internet Relay Chat help you communicate and access information
- Describe how network computers are used
- Understand how to connect to the Internet and the World Wide Web

CHAPTER 7

The Internet has been described as the fastest growing area of computer technology. The popularity of the World Wide Web, which is the part of the Internet that supports multimedia, has added to this growth. Together, the Internet and the World Wide Web represent one of the more exciting uses of computers today. Already, these highly interactive applications have changed the way people gather information, do research, listen to the radio, take classes, collaborate on projects, and more. Companies and organizations now use the Internet and the World Wide Web to reach customers and vendors and to communicate with employees.

The future will bring even more exciting applications of these technologies. Millions of dollars are being invested in Internet-related hardware and software projects, and new Internet companies are being started everyday. This chapter will explain what the Internet and World Wide Web are, how they work, and how you can use them to communicate and obtain information on an unlimited number of products, services, and subjects.

What Is the Internet?

Recall that a network is a group of computers connected by communications equipment and software. When two or more networks are joined together they are called an **internetwork** or **internet** (lowercase i). The term, **the Internet** (uppercase I), is used to describe a worldwide group of connected networks that allow public access to information and services (Figure 7-1).

Some of these networks are local, some are regional, and some are national. Together, these networks create a global network that serves an estimated 40 million users (Figure 7-2). Although each of the networks that makes up the Internet is owned by a public or private organization, no single organization *owns* or controls the Internet. Some say this lack of central control is a strength of the Internet that has allowed it to grow rapidly. Others say the lack of central control is a weakness that will prevent the Internet from handling the increasing volume of users.

For an overview of the Internet, visit the Discovering Computers Chapter 7 inCyber page (http://www.scsite.com/dc/ch7/incyber.htm) and click Overview.

Figure 7-1
The Internet is a worldwide group of connected networks that allows public access to information and service.

Figure 7-2
Internet statistics. All numbers are estimates. Because the Internet is not controlled by any single organization, it is impossible to measure precisely Internet usage or growth.

Internet Statistics

40 million users

200 connected countries

100,000 connected networks

12 million host computers or sites

100,000 Web server computers

Number of users growing at 4% per month

History of the Internet

The Internet began in 1969 as a network of four computers located at the University of California at Los Angeles, the University of California at Santa Barbara, the University of Utah, and the Stanford Research Institute. The initial work was funded by an agency of the U.S. Department of Defense called the **Advanced Research Projects Agency (ARPA)**. The first network thus was called **ARPANET**. The Department of Defense had two major goals for the initial project. The first goal, which was driven by national security concerns, was to develop the hardware and software needed to create a geographically dispersed network that could function even if part of the network was disabled or destroyed. The second goal was to create a way for scientists at different locations to share information and collaborate on military and scientific projects.

Over the years, the total number of computers connected to the original network has grown steadily and, within the last five years, explosively. Within two years of its creation, more than 20 sites were connected to the Internet. Within 10 years, more than 200 sites, including several European sites, were connected; within 20 years, more than 100,000 sites were linked to the original network. Today, experts estimate more than 12 million computers distribute information over the Internet.

In addition to the computer sites linked to the original network, whole networks also were added. One of these networks was operated by the National Science Foundation (NSF) and was called **NSFnet**. The NSFnet included the five United States-based supercomputer centers. NSFnet served as the major U.S. Internet network from 1987 until 1995 when other companies took over responsibility. Figure 7-3 shows a map produced by the NSF that shows the major U.S. Internet connections.

For the history of the Internet, visit the Discovering Computers Chapter 7 inCyber page (http://www.scsite.com/dc/ch7/incyber.htm) and click History.

Figure 7-3
This map was prepared by the National Science Foundation and shows the major U.S. Internet connections.

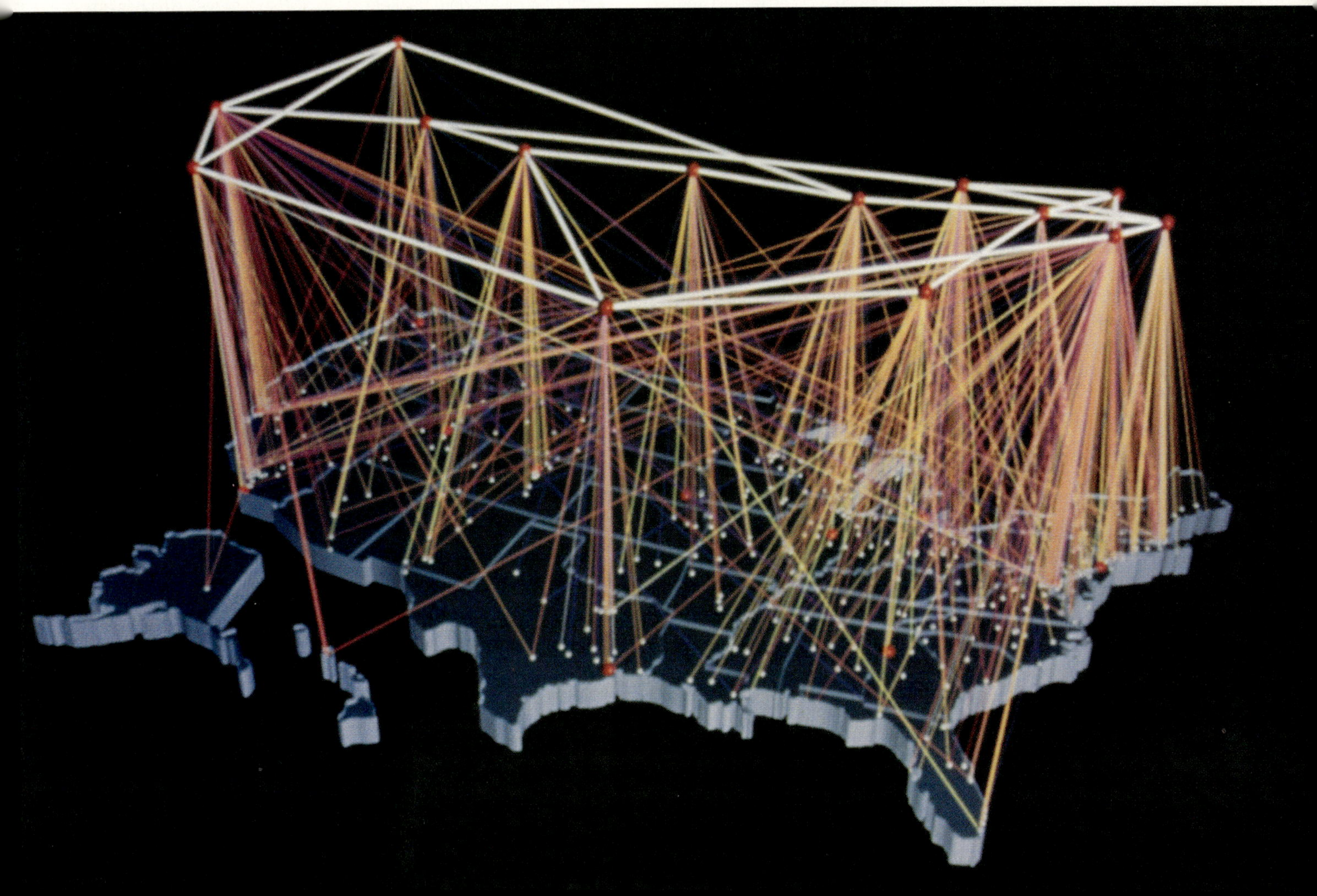

How the Internet Works

As illustrated in Figure 7-4, the Internet operates by taking data, dividing it into separate parts called packets, and sending the packets along the best route available to a destination computer. The data might be an e-mail message, a file, a document, or a request for a file. Each packet contains the data and the destination, origin, and sequence information used to reassemble the data at the destination. Although each packet may arrive out of sequence, the receiving computer reassembles the original message. Usually, some data, such as a file or document, is sent back to the computer that sent the original data.

The technique of breaking a message into individual packets, sending the packets along the best route available, and reassembling the data is called *packet switching*. The software used for packet switching on the Internet is a communications protocol named **TCP/IP** (**transmission control protocol/Internet protocol**). As you learned in Chapter 6, a communications protocol specifies the rules, or standards, that are used to transmit data.

The physical part of the Internet includes networks and communications lines owned and operated by many companies. You can connect to these networks in one of several ways.

Figure 7-4
How data is sent over the Internet.

PHASE 1 – Request is sent

1. Individuals connecting from home typically dial in to an Internet service provider (ISP) using a modem over regular telephone lines. Once connected, you can send information or requests over the Internet. You can request a Web page, for example, by typing its Internet address (called a URL).

2. Data sent over the Internet is divided into packets. Each packet has destination and origin information.

3. An Internet service provider (ISP) has a permanent connection to the Internet and provides temporary connections to others for a fee. ISPs use T1 lines leased from local telephone companies to connect to regional host computers.

4. Regional host computers are operated by national Internet service providers. National ISPs consolidate local ISP traffic and provide connections to the Internet backbones, which are the fastest Internet communication lines. If necessary, the regional host computer routes data packets along different paths to their final destinations.

5. National ISPs are connected to one another by metropolitan area exchanges (MAEs), which are facilities where Internet traffic carried by one backbone provider is transferred to another backbone provider.

6. Your request is transferred by another regional host and local ISP to a server, which is any computer directly connected to the Internet that stores and serves data. All of the information on the Internet originates within servers, which are operated by schools, companies, and other organizations. Upon receipt, the server reassembles and interprets the data packets and takes the appropriate action, such as sending a Web page back to your computer.

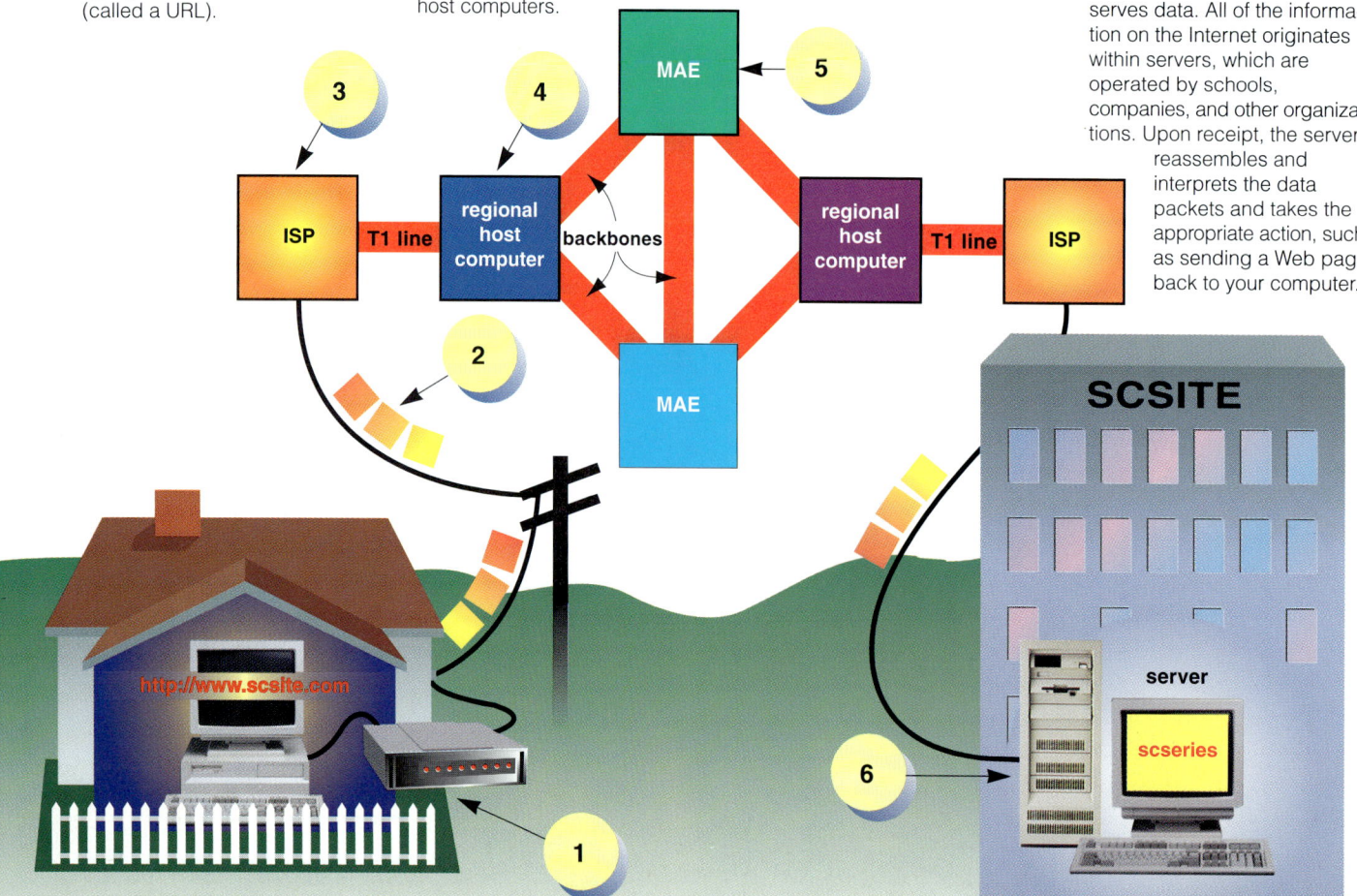

HOW THE INTERNET WORKS **7.5**

Organizations such as schools and companies often provide Internet access for students and employees. You also can connect through an online service such as America Online. Finally, you might connect to the Internet through an Internet service provider. An **Internet service provider (ISP)** is an organization that has a permanent connection to the Internet and provides temporary connections to others for a fee. Local ISPs connect to regional host computers operated by national Internet service providers.

Regional host computers are connected to the major networks that carry most of the Internet communications traffic by high-speed communications lines called **backbones**. Backbones are like highways that connect major cities across the country. **Metropolitan area exchanges** (**MAEs**), located in major cities, are used to transfer data packets from one backbone provider to another. MAEs function like highway interchanges. Smaller, slower speed networks extend out from the backbone into regions and local communities like roads and streets. Internet traffic control is provided by routers, located throughout the Internet, which contain network maps. If the most direct path to the destination is overloaded or not operating, routers send the packets along an alternate path. If necessary, each packet can be sent over a different path to the destination.

inCyber

For a list of Internet service providers (ISPs), visit the Discovering Computers Chapter 7 inCyber page (http://www.scsite.com/dc/ch7/incyber.htm) and click ISP.

PHASE 2 – Data is received

1. The server retrieves the requested file, divides it into packets, and sends it back to the local ISP.

2. The local ISP then routes the packets to the national ISP and so on over the Internet, back to your computer. The packets can be routed over the same or a different path than the original request.

3. The requested file displays on your computer screen.

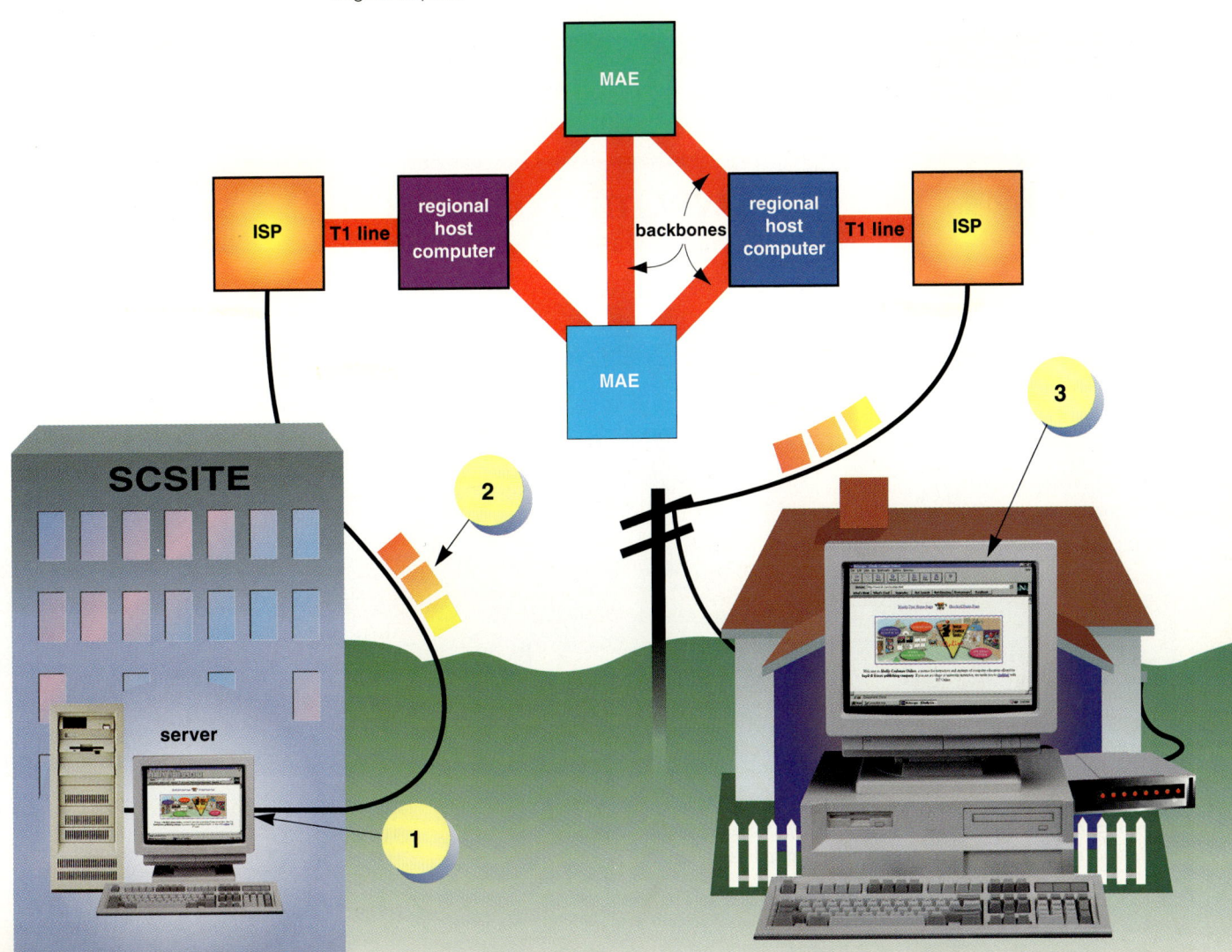

Internet Addresses

Like the postal service, the Internet relies on an addressing system to send data to its destination. Each location on the Internet has a four-part numeric address called an **IP** (**Internet protocol**) **address**. The first part of the IP address identifies the geographic region, the second part the company or organization, the third part the computer group, and the fourth and last part, the specific computer.

Because these all-numeric IP addresses are hard to remember and use, the Internet supports the use of a text name that can be substituted for the IP address. The text version of the IP address is called a **domain name**. Figure 7-5 is an example of an IP address and its associated domain name. Like IP addresses, domain names also are separated by periods. For domestic Web sites, the rightmost portion of the domain name contains a domain type abbreviation that identifies the type of organization. For international Web sites, the domain name also includes a country code, such as uk for the United Kingdom or ca for Canada. Figure 7-6 is a list of domain type abbreviations. Domain names are registered in the **domain name system** (**DNS**) and are stored in Internet computers called domain name servers. **Domain name servers** use the domain name to look up the associated IP address.

Because the rapid growth of the Internet is expected to continue, an expanded IP addressing scheme is being implemented. The new address scheme will increase the number of addresses by a factor of four and will provide added security for data transfers.

For information about registering domain names, visit the Discovering Computers Chapter 7 inCyber page (http://www.scsite.com/dc/ch7/incyber.htm) and click DNS.

Figure 7-5
The IP address and associated domain name for Microsoft Corporation.

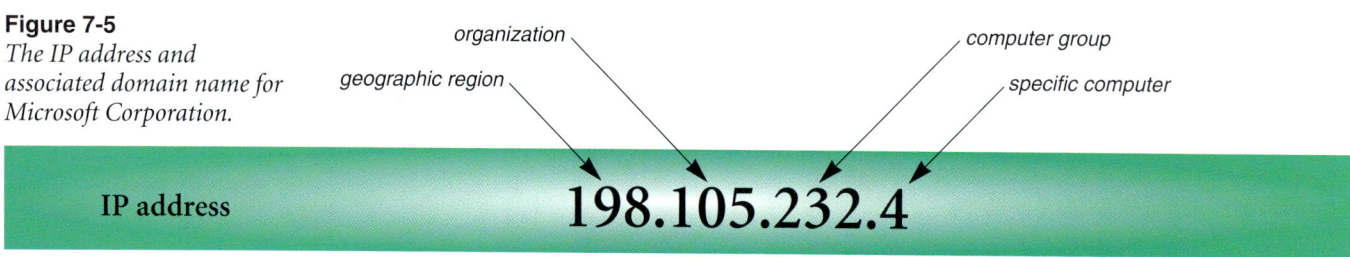

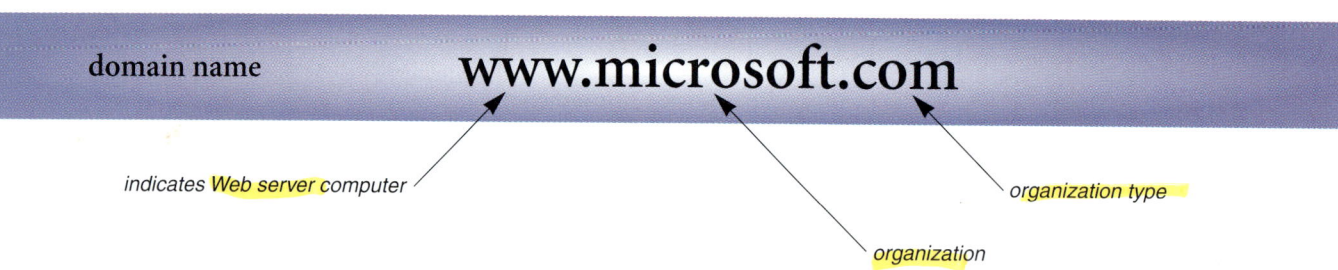

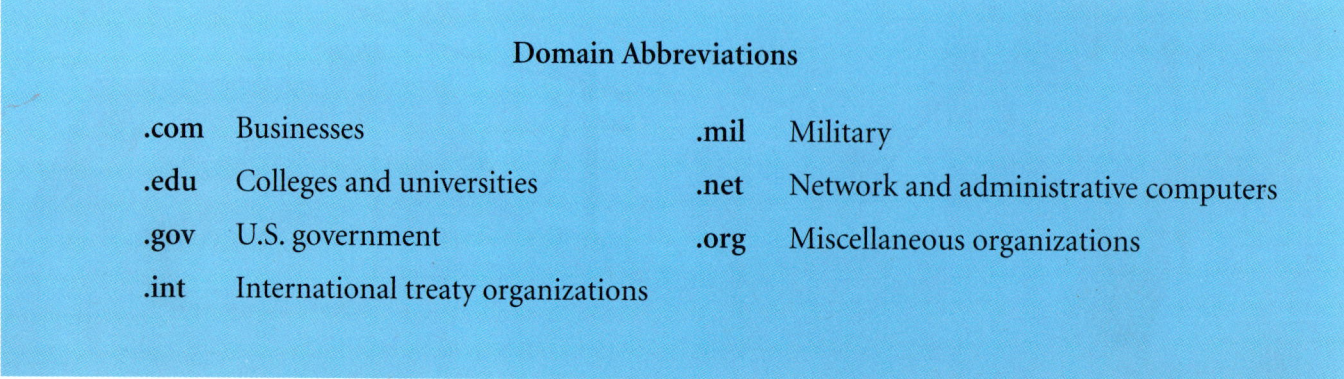

Figure 7-6
Abbreviations used in domain names indicate the organization type. The majority of domain names are registered to businesses.

The World Wide Web (WWW)

In 1991, software was developed in Europe that made the Internet easier to use. Tim Berners-Lee, a programmer working at the European Particle Physics Laboratory (CERN) in Geneva, Switzerland, released a program that allowed you to create a document called a Web page that had built-in links to other related documents. These links, called **hyperlinks**, allowed you to move quickly from one document to another, regardless of whether the documents were located on the same computer or on different computers in different countries. The collection of hyperlinked documents accessible on the Internet has become known as the **World Wide Web, WWW, W3**, or simply the **Web**. Internet locations that contain hyperlinked documents are called **Web sites**. Multiple Web sites may be on the same computer. For example, many small companies or individuals can have their Web sites located on a single server operated by an Internet service provider.

> inCyber
>
> For information about international standards for the World Wide Web (WWW), visit the Discovering Computers Chapter 7 inCyber page (http://www.scsite.com/dc/ch7/incyber.htm) and click WWW.

How a Web Page Works

A **Web page** (Figure 7-7) is a hypertext or hypermedia document residing on an Internet computer that contains text, graphics, video, or sound. A **hypertext** document contains text hyperlinks to other documents. A **hypermedia** document contains text, graphics, video, or sound hyperlinks that connect to other documents.

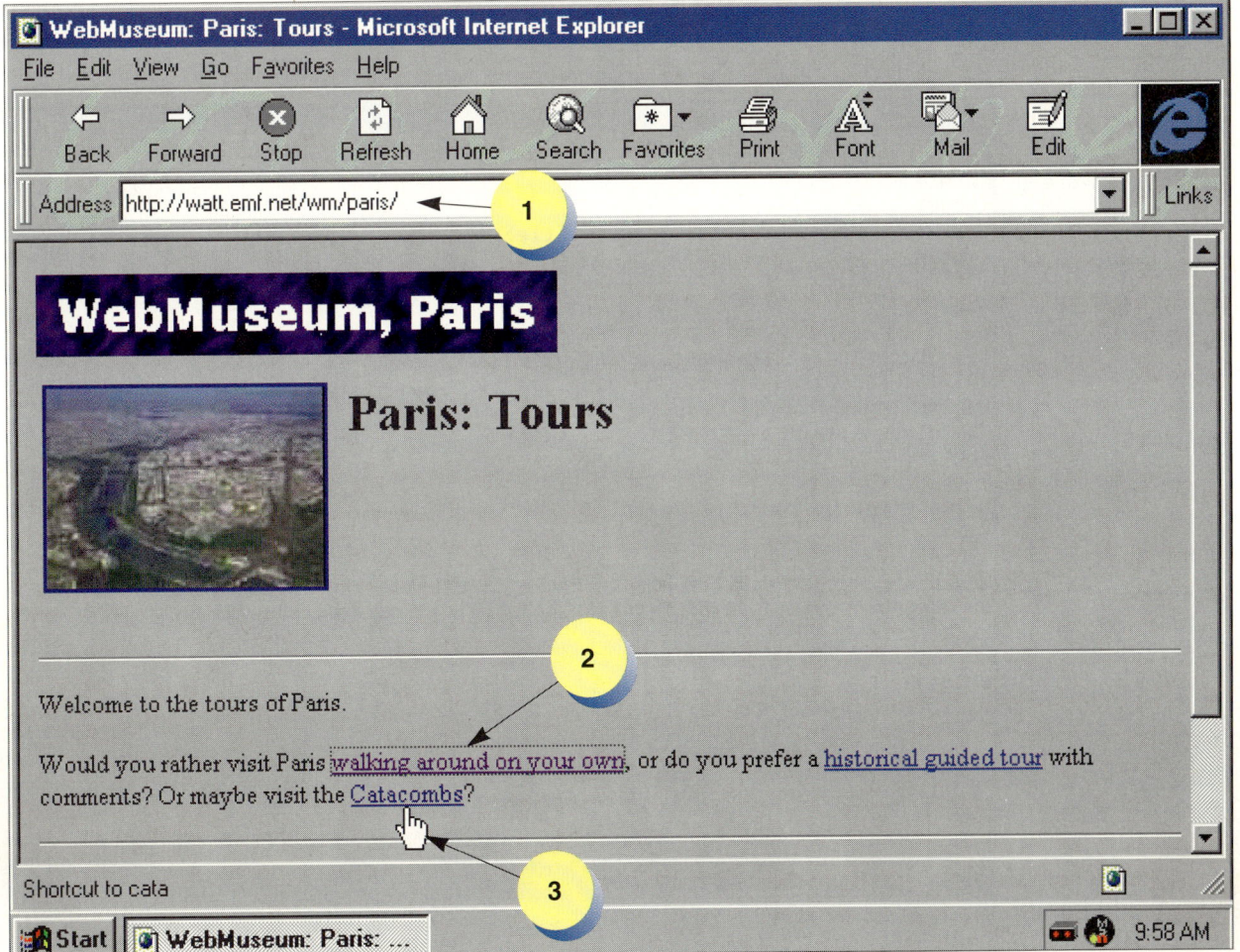

Figure 7-7
An example of a Web page.

1. address of Web page; also called location or URL
2. different color indicates document associated with this hypertext link has been viewed
3. pointer positioned over a hypertext link changes shape to a hand with a pointing finger

Three types of hyperlinks exist. **Target hyperlinks** move from one location in a document to another location in the same document. **Relative hyperlinks** move from one document to another document on the same Internet computer. **Absolute hyperlinks** move to another document on a different Internet computer.

Hypertext and hypermedia allow you to learn in a nonlinear way. Reading a book from cover to cover is a linear way of learning. Branching off and investigating related topics as you encounter them is a nonlinear way of learning. For example, while reading an article on geology, you might want to learn more about mining. Reading about mining might interest you in old mining towns. Reading about old mining towns might inspire you to read about a particular person who made his or her fortune in mining. The ability to branch from one related topic to another in a nonlinear fashion is what makes hyperlinks so powerful and the Internet such an interesting place to explore. Displaying pages from one Web site after another is called **Web surfing** and is like using a remote control to jump from one TV channel to another.

Web pages are created using **hypertext markup language** (HTML), which is a set of special instructions, called **tags**, or **markups**, that specify links to other documents and how the page is displayed. Figure 7-8 shows how the Web page shown in Figure 7-7 looks as text coded with HTML tags. You can generate HTML tags by using Web page authoring software specifically designed for this task or by using Web authoring features included in many applications such as word processing and desktop publishing. Your computer interprets the text coded with HTML tags by using Web browser software.

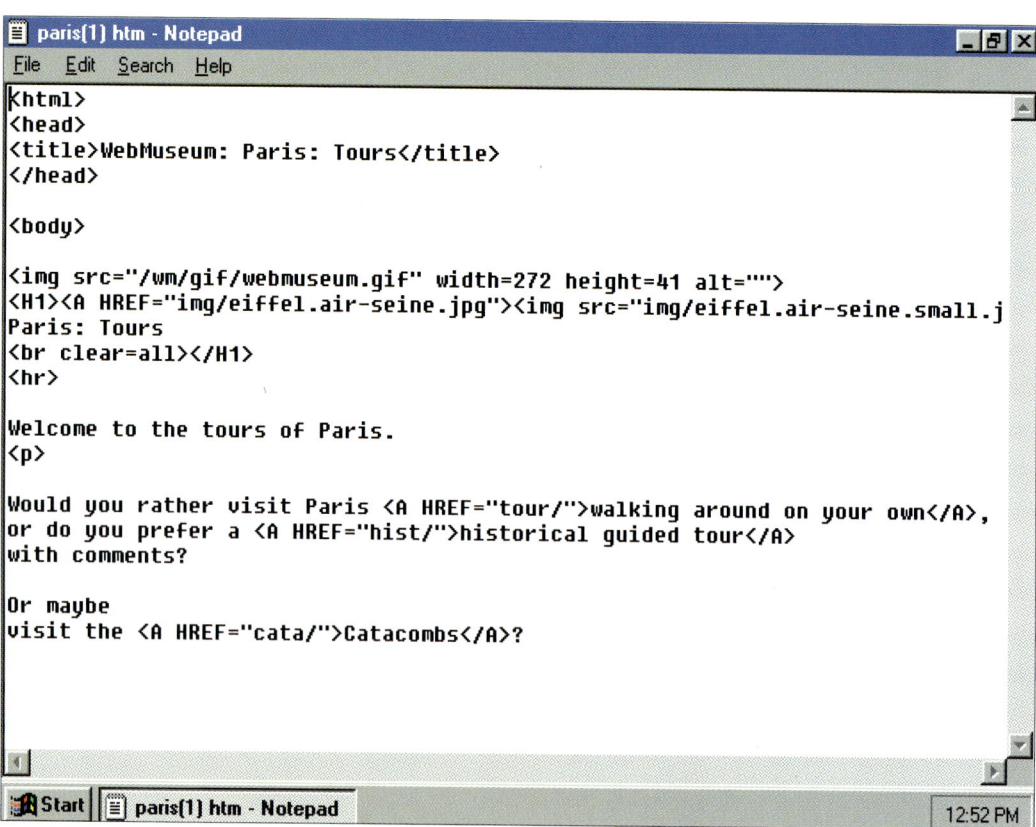

Figure 7-8
This screen shows the HTML text for the Web page in Figure 7-7. Web browser software interprets the HTML instructions inside the angle brackets < > and displays the text, graphics, and hyperlinks accordingly.

THE WORLD WIDE WEB (WWW) 7.9

Web Browser Software

Web browser software, also called a **Web browser** or simply a **browser**, is a program that interprets and displays Web pages and enables you to link to other Web pages. The first Web browsers used text commands and displayed only text documents. In 1993, however, Marc Andreessen, a student at the University of Illinois, created a graphical Web browser called **Mosaic**. Mosaic displayed documents that included graphics _and_ used a graphical interface. The graphical interface, just as it did with other application software programs, made it easier and more enjoyable to view Web documents and contributed to the rapid growth of the Internet. Andreessen later went on to be one of the founders of Netscape, a leading Internet software company that developed the Netscape Navigator Web browser. Figure 7-9 is an example of another Web browser, Microsoft Internet Explorer.

Before you can use a Web browser to view pages on the World Wide Web, your computer has to connect to an Internet computer through an Internet access provider. The Internet connection is established by an Internet communications program. Once the connection to the Internet is established, the browser program is started.

> inCyber
>
> For a list of Web browsers, visit the Discovering Computers Chapter 7 inCyber page (http://www.scsite.com/dc/ch7/incyber.htm) and click Browser.

Figure 7-9
Microsoft Internet Explorer Web browser software.

1. Back and Forward buttons – display previously viewed pages
2. Stop button – interrupts transmission
3. Refresh button – reloads current page
4. Home button – returns to designated Home page
5. Search button – displays Web search tool
6. Favorites button – stores locations of favorite Web pages; also called bookmarks
7. Print button – prints all or portion of current page
8. Web address (URL) of current page
9. Links – connections to other sites
10. Address text box – entering a URL in Address text box retrieves that page

When the browser program starts, it retrieves and displays a Web page called a home page. A **home page** is the Web page designated as the page to display each time you launch your browser. Most browsers use the manufacturer's Web page as the default, but you can change your browser's home page at any time. While the term home page often is used to describe the first page at a Web site, technically, the first page at a Web site is called a **welcome page**. A Web site's welcome page often serves as a table of contents for the other pages at the Web site.

The browser retrieves Web pages by using a **Uniform Resource Locator**, or **URL**, which is an address that points to a specific resource on the Internet. URL is pronounced either "you are ell" or "earl," like the man's name. As shown in Figure 7-10, the URL can indicate an Internet site, a specific document at a site, and a location within a document at a site. All Web page URLs begin with **http://**, which stands for **hypertext transfer protocol**, the communications standard used to transfer pages on the Web.

Figure 7-10
Web pages are found and referenced using their address, called a Uniform Resource Locator (URL).

1. protocol – used to transfer data; for Web pages is always http:// (hypertext transfer protocol)
2. domain name – identifies computer that stores Web pages; often, but not always, begins with www
3. directory path – identifies where Web page is stored on computer
4. document name – name of Web page
5. anchor name – reference to a specific part of a long document; always preceded with #

Displaying the Web page on your screen can take anywhere from a few seconds to several minutes, depending on the speed of your connection and the amount of graphics on the Web page. To speed up the display of pages, most Web browsers let you turn off the graphics and display only text.

Browsers display hyperlinks to other documents either as underlined text of a different color or as a graphic. When you position the pointer over a hyperlink, the mouse pointer changes to a small hand with a pointing finger. Some browsers also display the URL of the hyperlinked document at the bottom of the screen. You can display the document by clicking the hyperlink with your pointing device or by typing its URL in the Location text box of the Web browser. To remind you that you have seen a document, some browsers change the color of a text hyperlink after you click it.

Two ways to keep track of Web pages you have viewed are available: a history list and a bookmark list. A **history list** records the pages you have viewed during the time you are connected to the Web (a session). The history list is cleared when you exit your browser program. If you think you might want to return to a page in a future session, you can record its location with a bookmark. A **bookmark** consists of the title of a Web page and the URL of that page. Unlike history lists, bookmark lists, also called *hotlists* or *favorites*, are stored on your computer and can be used in future Web sessions. A bookmark list and a history list both allow you to display a Web page quickly by clicking its name in the list.

Some Web browser programs display only Web pages. Other browsers allow you to use Internet services such as e-mail, file transfers, and others discussed later in this chapter. Two widely used browsers that support these services are Microsoft Internet Explorer and Netscape Navigator.

Multimedia on the Web

Some of the most exciting Web developments involve multimedia, which is the integration of text, graphics, video, animation, and sound. These developments increase the types of information available on the Web, expand the Web's potential uses, and make the Internet a more entertaining place to explore.

To run a multimedia application on the Web, your browser might need an additional program called a plug-in or helper application. **Plug-ins** run multimedia within the browser window; **helper applications** run multimedia in a window separate from the browser. Plug-ins and helper applications can be downloaded from many sites on the Web. Links to these sites often are found with Web multimedia applications. Figure 7-11 is a list of popular plug-ins and helper applications.

A programming language called **Java** is being used to develop much of the multimedia on the Web. Developers use Java to create small programs called **applets** that can be downloaded and run in your browser window. Unlike other programs you download from the Web, applets can be used by any type of computer and are relatively safe from viruses and other tampering. Java is discussed in more detail in the programming chapter.

For links to popular plug-ins, visit the Discovering Computers Chapter 7 inCyber page (http://www.scsite.com/dc/ch7/incyber.htm) and click Plug-In.

Multimedia Plug-in and Helper Application Programs

Category	Program Name	Web Site	Comment
Graphics	N/A	N/A	Separate plug-ins usually not required. All browsers display most graphics.
Audio	RealAudio Internet Phone	www.realaudio.com www.vocaltec.com	Streaming audio Internet phone service
Animation	Shockwave	www.macromedia.com	Interactive animation with sound
Video	VivoActive CU-SeeMe	www.vivo.com www.wpine.com	Video viewer Videoconferencing
Virtual Reality	Live3D WebSpace	www.netscape.com www.sd.tgs.com	VRML viewer VRML viewer

Figure 7-11
Plug-in and helper application programs often are required to experience multimedia material on the Web. This table lists popular plug-ins and helper applications and Web sites where they can be obtained.

7.12 CHAPTER 7 – THE INTERNET AND THE WORLD WIDE WEB

The following sections discuss multimedia Web developments in the areas of graphics, audio, animation, video, and virtual reality.

Graphics Graphics were the first media used to enhance the text-based Internet. The introduction of graphical browsers enabled illustrations, logos, and other images to be incorporated into Web pages. Today, many Web pages, especially those created by consumer product companies, use colorful graphic designs and images to reinforce their text messages (Figure 7-12). Even prior to the introduction of the Web, the Internet was an excellent source of graphic material. Today, the Web contains thousands of image files on countless subjects that can be downloaded free and used for noncommercial purposes.

Animation Using animation on a Web page adds media without greatly increasing download time. Animated graphics can make Web pages more visually interesting or draw attention to important information or links. Text even can be animated to scroll across the page like a ticker used for stocks, news, or sports scores (Figure 7-13). Scrolling text even can contain hyperlinks to a different page. Animation also is used for many Web-based games. Figure 7-14 shows an animated game that was developed with the Java programming language.

Figure 7-12
Many companies use colorful graphics and images on their Web pages.

Figure 7-13
Animation is used to scroll sports news across the screen of this ticker. To learn more about a sports story, you can click the Get Story hyperlink or the scrolling headline itself.

1. sports headlines scroll across the screen

THE WORLD WIDE WEB (WWW) 7.13

Audio Simple **audio** Web applications consist of individual sound files that must be downloaded before they can be played. More advanced audio Web applications use **streaming audio**, which allows you to hear the sound as it downloads to your computer. Music companies often include audio files on their Web sites to provide samples of the latest hits. Other companies use streaming audio to provide Internet radio channels that broadcast music, interviews, and talk shows (Figure 7-15). Web-based audio also is used for Internet audioconferencing. **Internet audioconferencing**, also called **Internet telephone service** or **Internet telephony**, enables you to talk to other people over the Web. As you speak into a microphone, audioconferencing software and your computer sound card digitize and compress your conversation. Software and equipment at the receiving end reverse the process. Some software allows only one person to speak at a time, but newer packages support two-way simultaneous conversations. Audioconferencing allows you to talk to friends or colleagues for just the cost of your Internet connection. **Internet voice mail** enables you to send and retrieve voice messages.

For links to streaming audio, visit the Discovering Computers Chapter 7 inCyber page (http://www.scsite.com/dc/ch7/incyber.htm) and click Streaming Audio.

Figure 7-14
An example of a game developed with the Java programming language.

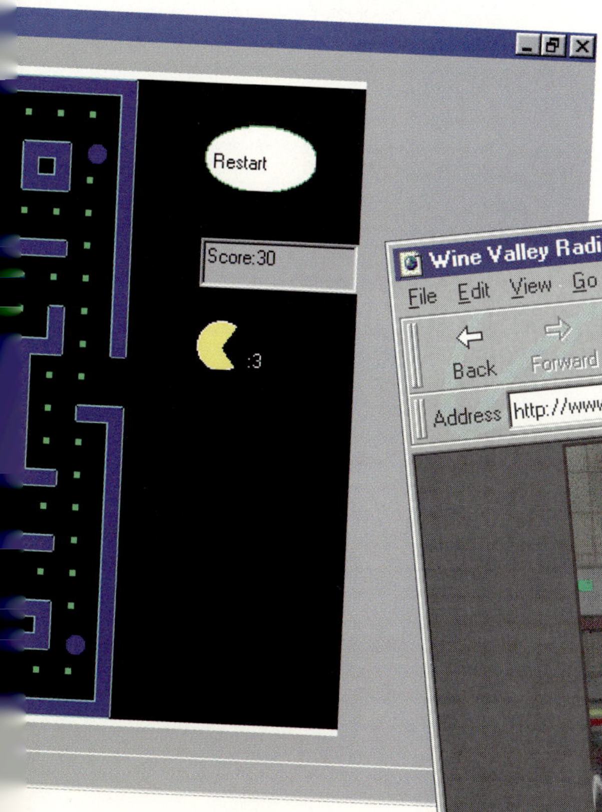

Figure 7-15
Wine Valley Radio is one of several Internet radio stations. When you click an audio file, such as a conversation or music, an audio control box displays. The control box has start, stop, and volume controls and displays information about the file.

Video Like audio, simple **video** Web applications use individual video files such as movie clips that can be downloaded and played on your computer. Because video files often are large and can take a long time to download, these movie clips usually are quite short. **Streaming video** allows you to view longer or live video images as they are downloaded to your computer. Streaming video also allows you to conduct Internet videoconferences similarly to Internet audioconferences. As you are filmed by a video camera, videoconferencing software and your computer's video board capture, digitize, and compress the images and sounds. This data is divided into packets and sent over the Internet. Equipment and software at the receiving end assemble the packets, decompress the data, and present the image and sound as video. Like traditional videoconferencing, live Internet videoconferences can be choppy and blurry depending on the speed of the slowest communications link.

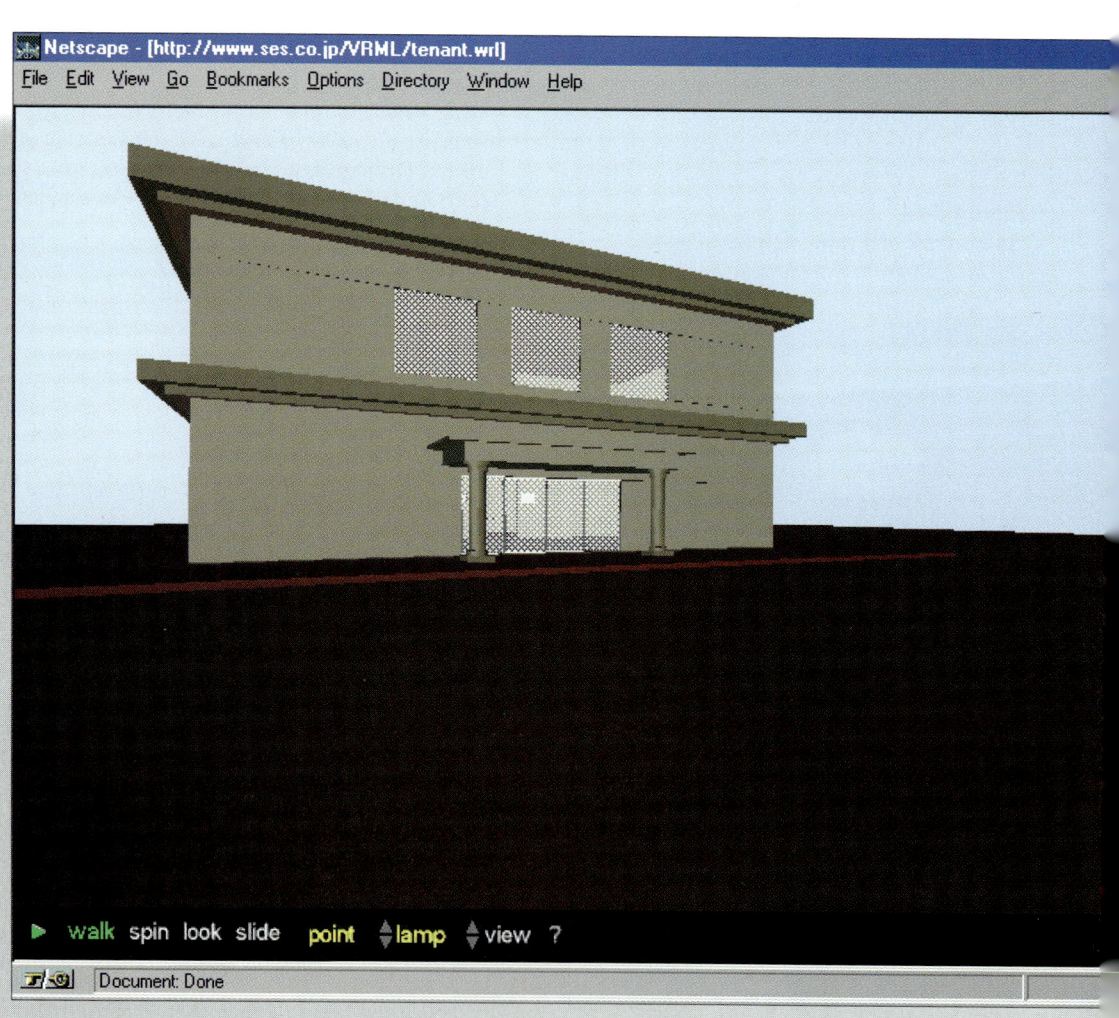

Virtual Reality Virtual reality (VR) is the creation of an artificial environment that you can experience. On the Web, VR involves the display of three-dimensional (3-D) images that you can explore and manipulate interactively. Most Web-based VR applications are developed using **VRML (virtual reality modeling language)**. VRML allows a developer to create a collection of 3-D objects, such as a room with furniture. You can walk through such a VR room by moving your pointing device forward, backward, or to the side.

VR often is used for games, but it has many practical applications as well. Architects create VR models of buildings and rooms so they can show their clients how a completed construction project will look before it is built. Figure 7-16 is an example of a building model created with VRML.

For links to virtual reality resources, visit the Discovering Computers Chapter 7 inCyber page (http://www.scsite.com/dc/ch7/incyber.htm) and click Virtual Reality.

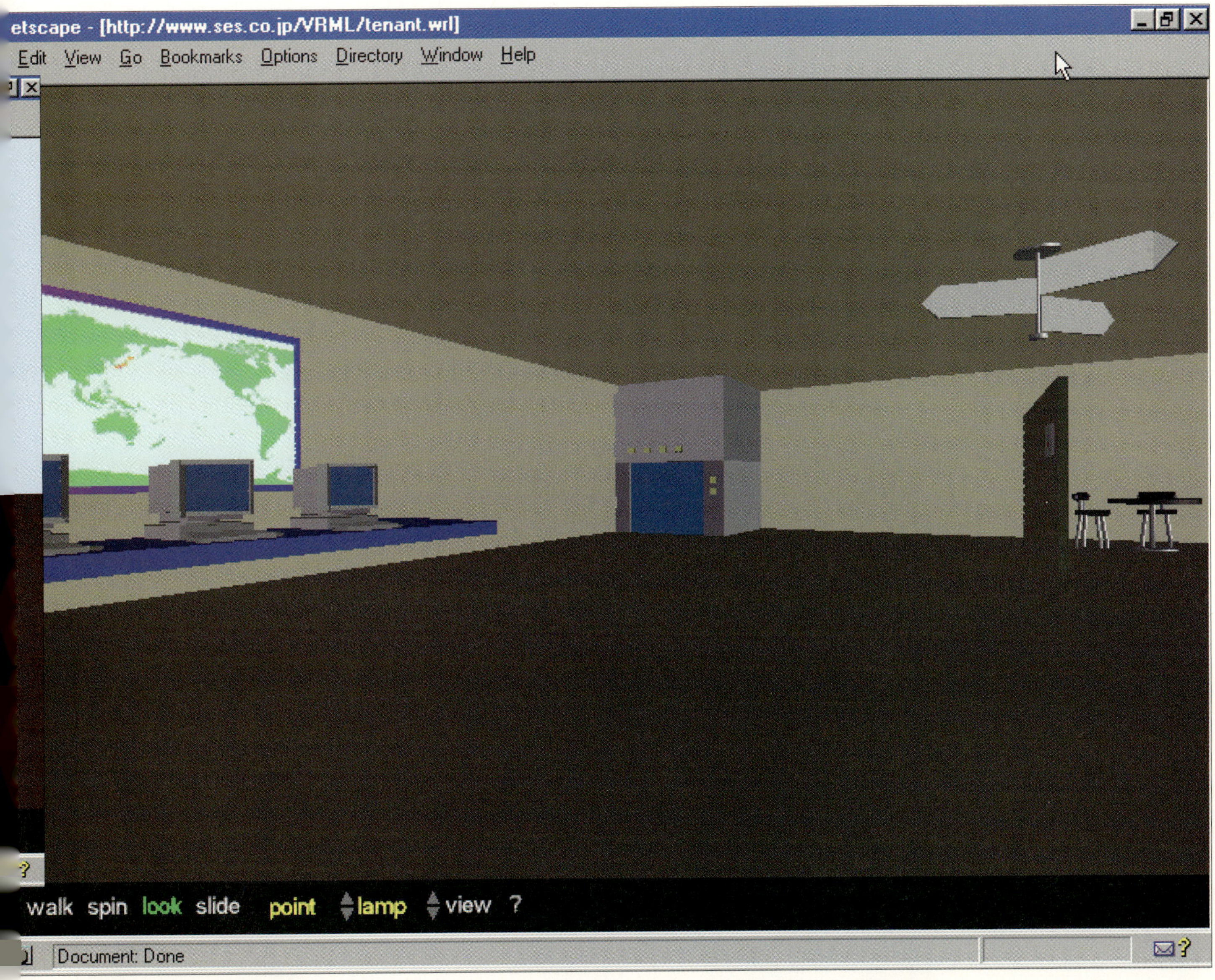

Figure 7-16
These virtual reality images of a building were developed using VRML software. You use your mouse and the controls in the lower-left portion of the screen to walk around or enter the building. As you enter the building, a different image is displayed.

Searching for Information on the Web

Because no single organization controls additions, deletions, and changes to Web sites, no central menu or catalog of Web site content and addresses exists. Several companies, however, maintain organized directories of Web sites and provide search tools to help you find information on specific topics. A **search tool**, also called a **search engine**, is a software program that finds Web sites, Web pages, and Internet files that match one or more keywords that you enter. Some search tools look for simple word matches and others allow for more specific searches on a series of words or an entire phrase. Figure 7-17 is an example of the Yahoo! search tool. Search tools do not actually search the entire Internet — such a search would take an

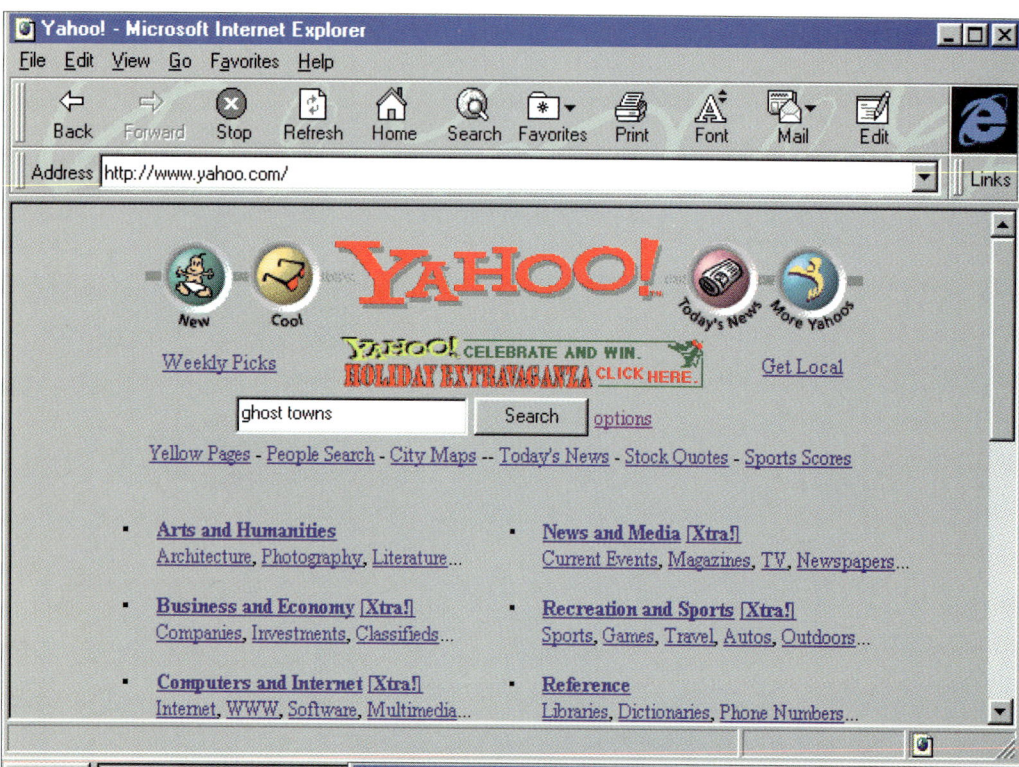

Figure 7-17
Yahoo! combines a search tool and a directory of Web sites. To use the search tool, you enter one or more keywords. The second screen shows that 13 matches were made to the keywords, ghost towns.

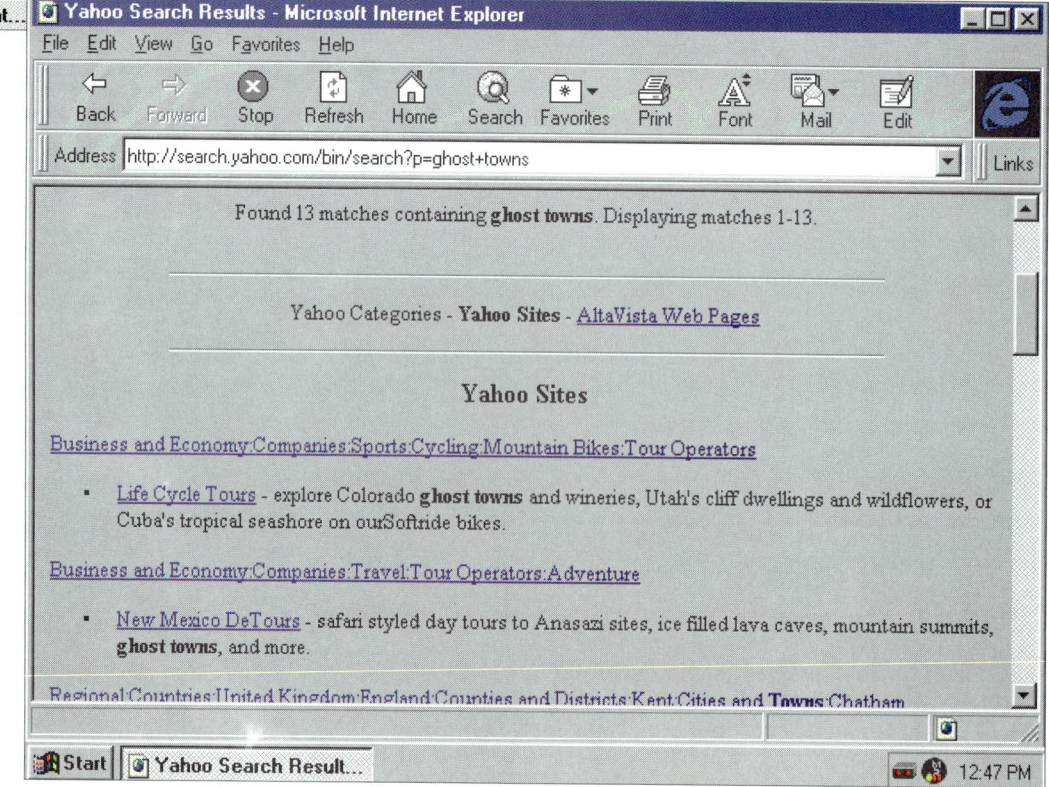

For links to search tools, visit the Discovering Computers Chapter 7 inCyber page (http://www.scsite.com/dc/ch7/incyber.htm) and click Search Tool.

extremely long time. Instead, they search an index of Internet sites and documents that constantly is updated by the company that provides the search tool. Figure 7-18 lists the Web site addresses of several Internet search tools. Most of these sites also provide directories of Web sites organized in categories such as sports, entertainment, or business.

Web Search Sites

Name	Web Site Location	Comment
Yahoo!	www.yahoo.com	One of the first. Updated daily.
Infoseek	guide-p.infoseek.com	Searches Web or Usenet for words and phrases.
Lycos	www.lycos.com	Comprehensive catalog plus multimedia content searches.
AltaVista	www.altavista.digital.com	Creates indexes from more than 30 million Web pages.
Excite	www.excite.com	Concept-based search tool.
WebCrawler	www.webcrawler.com	Natural language search tool.
Four11	www.Four11.com	Finds user-IDs.
BigBook	www.bigbook.com	Yellow pages for more than 16 million businesses.

Figure 7-18
These search tools and directories can help you find products, services, information, and other Internet users.

Intranets and Firewalls

Recognizing the efficiency and power of the Web, many organizations have applied Web technology to their own internal networks. Internal networks that use Internet and Web technology are called **intranets** (*intra* means inside). Simple intranet applications include electronic publishing of basic organizational information such as telephone directories, event calendars, and employee benefit information. More sophisticated uses of intranets include groupware applications such as project management, group scheduling, and employee conferencing.

Sometimes an organization will allow other organizations to access its internal, private network. For example, a manufacturing company might want to share information with its suppliers, or members of a particular profession such as real estate brokers might decide to share a private network. These are examples of **extranets**, which are private networks that include more than one organization.

While some intranets operate on a LAN at a single location, some intranets and most extranets use many public and private networks to connect remote locations. Anytime a private network connects to a public network, an organization must be concerned about security and unauthorized access to organizational data. To prevent unauthorized access,

For intranet resources, visit the Discovering Computers Chapter 7 inCyber page (http://www.scsite.com/dc/ch7/incyber.htm) and click Intranet.

7.18 CHAPTER 7 — THE INTERNET AND THE WORLD WIDE WEB

organizations implement one or more layers of security called a firewall. A **firewall** is a general term that refers to both hardware and software used to restrict access to data on a network (Figure 7-19). Firewalls are used to deny network access to outsiders and to restrict employees' access to sensitive data such as payroll or personnel records.

A common way to implement a firewall is to place a computer called a **proxy server** between two separate networks. For example, a proxy server might separate an organization's internal network from an Internet network used to share data with remote locations. The proxy server can be programmed to allow access to and from only specific network locations, such as a company office in another state.

A proxy server also makes using the Web more efficient through a process called caching (pronounced cash-ing). **Caching** involves storing a copy of each Web page that is accessed in local storage. When another person requests the same page, the proxy server checks to see if the page has been updated on the Web. If the page has changed, a new file is retrieved from the Web. If the page has not changed, the proxy server retrieves a copy of the page from cache. Retrieving a page from cache is faster than retrieving the page from its original Web location. Caching is similar in concept to cache memory and disk cache explained in earlier chapters.

For details on the Microsoft Proxy Server, visit the Discovering Computers Chapter 7 inCyber page (http://www.scsite.com/dc/ch7/incyber.htm) and click Proxy Server.

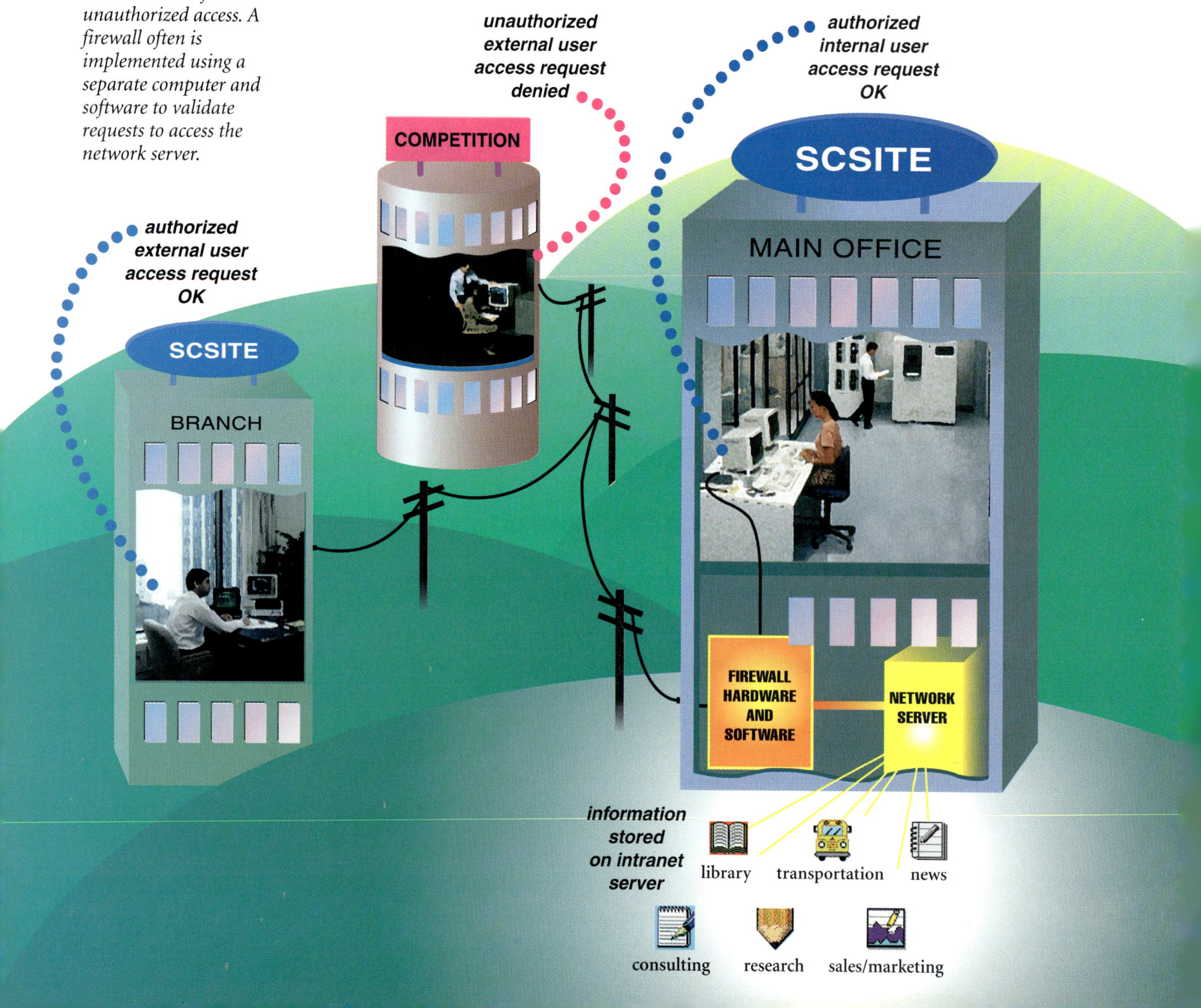

Figure 7-19
Firewall hardware and software protect the network server from unauthorized access. A firewall often is implemented using a separate computer and software to validate requests to access the network server.

Other Internet Services

Although the World Wide Web is the most talked about part of the Internet, many of the Internet services developed prior to the creation of the Web still are used widely. These Internet services include e-mail, FTP, Gopher, Telnet, Usenet, and Internet Relay Chat (IRC).

E-mail

E-mail, the electronic exchange of messages from one person to another, was one of the original features of the Internet. E-mail enabled scientists and researchers working on government-sponsored projects to communicate with their colleagues at other locations. Today, e-mail still is a widely used Internet feature.

Internet e-mail works essentially the same as e-mail on other systems — messages can be created, sent, forwarded, stored, printed, and deleted. To receive e-mail over the Internet, you must have a **mailbox**, which is a file used to collect your messages on an Internet computer. Although your mailbox can be located anywhere on the Internet, it usually is located on the computer that connects you to the Internet, such as the server operated by your Internet service provider (ISP). Most ISPs and online services provide an Internet e-mail program and a mailbox as a standard part of their Internet access services.

An **Internet mailbox address** is a combination of a user name and the domain name that identifies the location of the mailbox computer (Figure 7-20). Your **user name**, or **user-ID**, is a unique combination of characters that identifies you. It must be different from the other user names located on the same mailbox computer. A user name sometimes is limited to eight characters and often is a combination of your first and last names, such as the initial of your first name plus your last name. You also can use a nickname or any combination of characters for your user name, but others may find it harder to remember.

Although no complete listing of Internet e-mail addresses exists, several Internet sites list addresses collected from public sources. These sites also allow you to list your e-mail address voluntarily so others can find it. The site also might ask for other information, such as your high school or college, so others can determine if you are the person they want to reach.

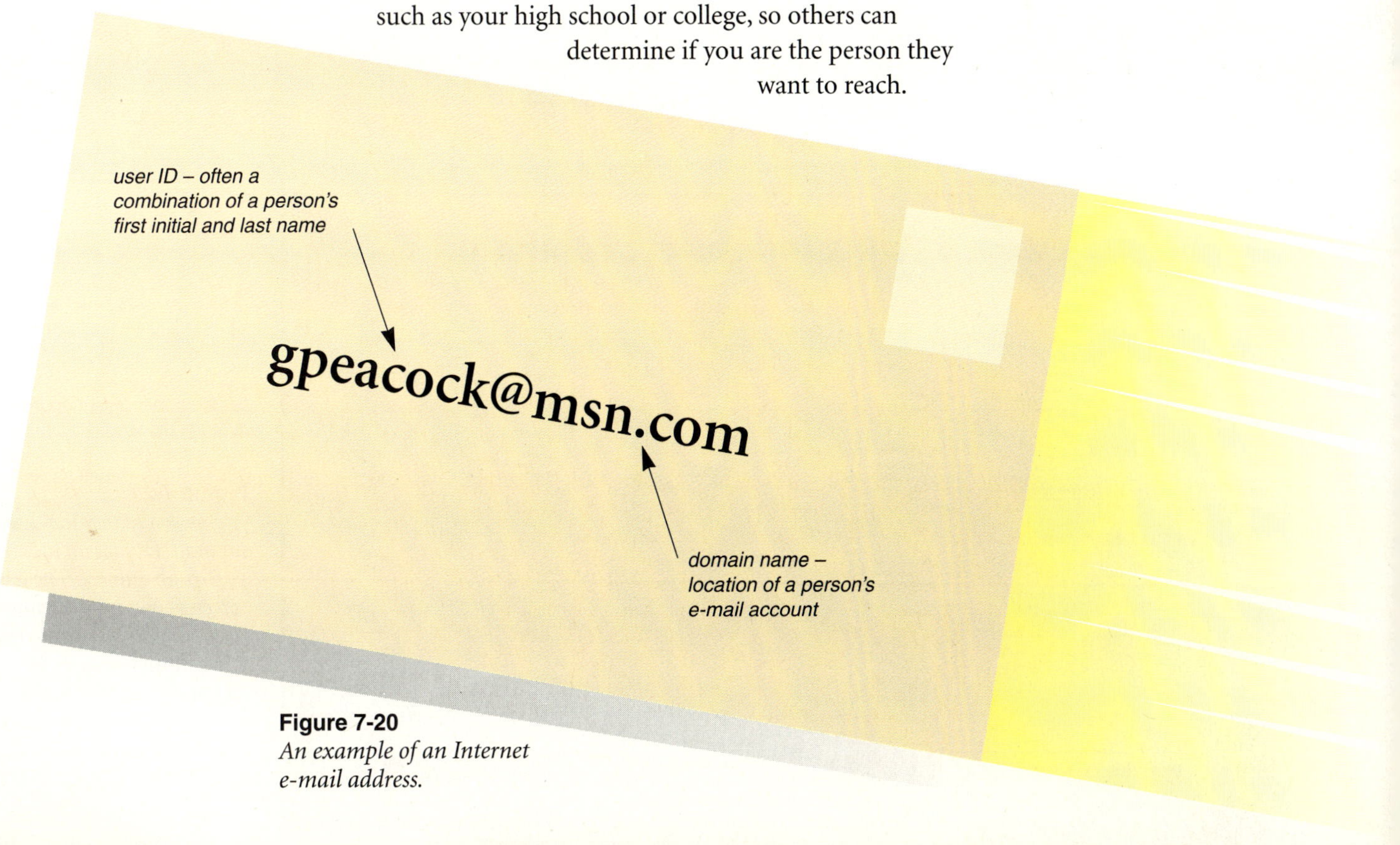

user ID – often a combination of a person's first initial and last name

gpeacock@msn.com

domain name – location of a person's e-mail account

Figure 7-20
An example of an Internet e-mail address.

FTP

FTP (file transfer protocol) is an Internet standard that allows you to exchange files with other computers on the Internet. Computers that contain files available for FTP are called **FTP sites** or **FTP servers**.

FTP sites contain a wide variety of file types including text, graphics, audio, video, and program files. Many of these program files can be downloaded at no cost. Others, called **shareware**, are programs you can download and try free but must pay a license fee if you decide to keep them. Some FTP sites limit file transfers to persons who have authorized accounts on the computer. Many FTP computers, however, allow **anonymous FTP**, whereby anyone can log in and transfer some, if not all, available files.

To view or use a FTP file you must first download it to your computer. Many large FTP files are compressed to reduce storage space and download transfer time. Before you use a compressed file you must expand it with a decompression program. Decompression programs usually are available at the FTP site.

Some computers, called **Archie sites** (Figure 7-21), maintain directories of files on the Internet that can be downloaded with FTP. A FTP file search tool called **Archie** can be used to find files on a particular subject. Archie, named after the comic book character, finds files whose names at least partially match a keyword that you enter. An **Archie gateway** is a Web page that provides an easy-to-use interface to the Archie search function.

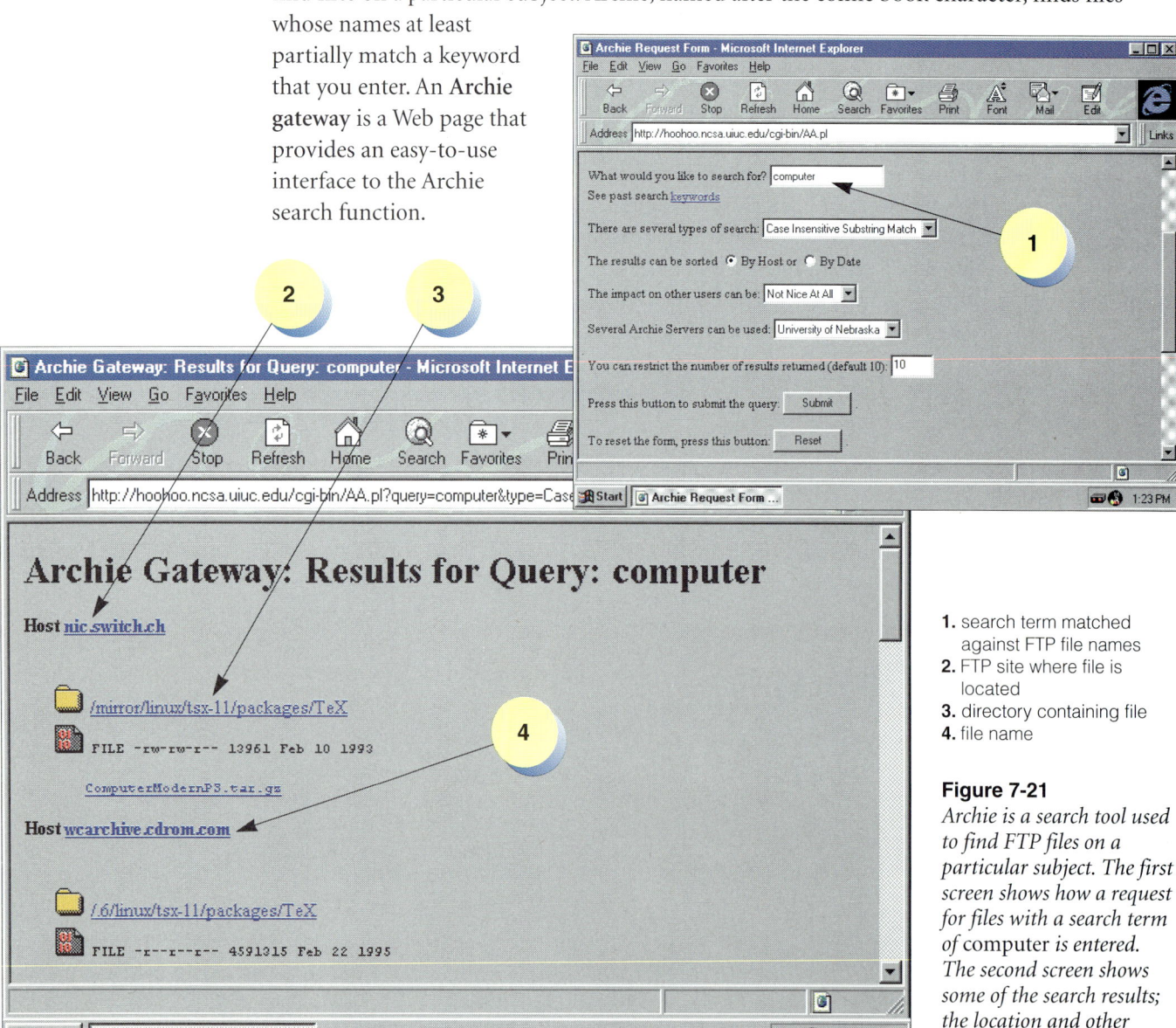

1. search term matched against FTP file names
2. FTP site where file is located
3. directory containing file
4. file name

Figure 7-21
Archie is a search tool used to find FTP files on a particular subject. The first screen shows how a request for files with a search term of computer *is entered. The second screen shows some of the search results; the location and other information for two files.*

OTHER INTERNET SERVICES **7.21**

Gopher

Before Web-based search tools were developed, Gopher was the primary method used to locate information on the Internet. **Gopher** is a menu-driven program that helps you locate and retrieve files on the Internet. Gopher originally was developed at the University of Minnesota and is named after the school mascot, the Golden Gopher. Internet computers called **Gopher servers** maintain Gopher directories.

Unlike FTP and Archie, Gopher does not require you to know the details of FTP sites and files names. Instead, you browse through Gopher menus, which usually start with a list of topics (Figure 7-22). Choosing an item on the list leads to one or more menus that break down the topic into more specific areas. Eventually, you reach a menu listing individual files you can download. Unlike FTP files, you can view Gopher files before you decide to download. In addition to the menu system, most Gopher servers offer **Veronica** or **Jughead** search programs that search Gopher directories for files on a specific subject. Like Archie, the FTP search tools, Veronica and Jughead, are named after Archie comic book characters.

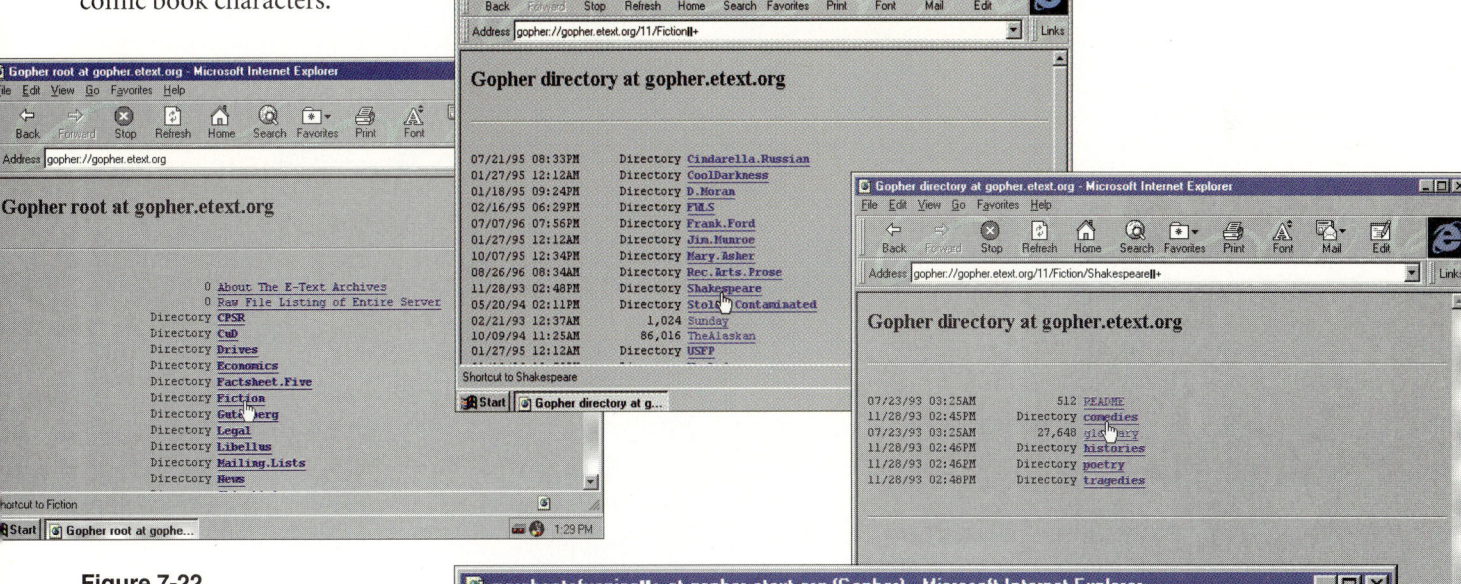

Figure 7-22
With the Gopher file retrieval program, you click a series of menus to narrow in on a subject until you find the document you want. These screens show the search progression from Fiction to Shakespeare to comedies to The Merchant of Venice.

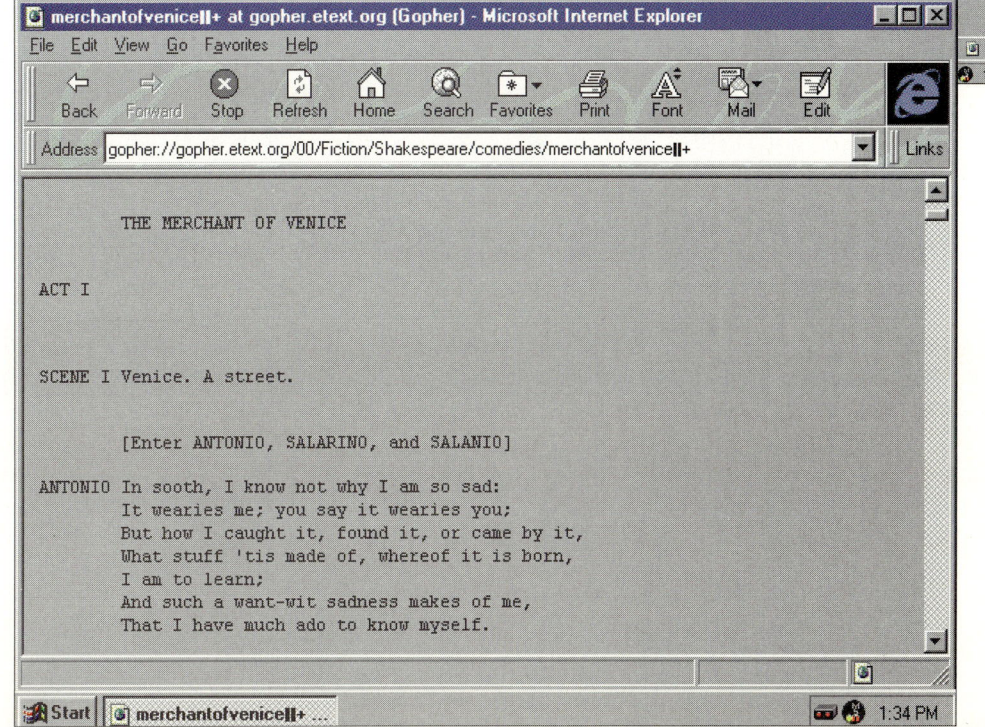

Telnet

Telnet is an Internet protocol that enables you to log into a remote computer on the Internet. Once you make a Telnet connection, you can use the remote computer as if you had a direct, local connection. Telnet often is used to play games on the Internet. One of the more popular types of Internet games is called a MUD. A **MUD** (**multiuser dimension**) is a role-playing game in which you and other participants assume the identity of specific characters. With some MUDs, the computer provides a text description of the characters and situations you encounter as you play the game. Another type of MUD, called a **MOO** (**multiuser object oriented**), allows you to create new characters and game locations, such as a wizard in a castle. Some MOOs have graphics and sound like arcade games. Figure 7-23 is an example of a MOO.

Figure 7-23
An example of a MOO (multiuser object oriented) game that can be played on the Internet using Telnet.

Usenet

Usenet is a collection of news and discussion groups, called **newsgroups**, that are accessed via the Internet. Each of the more than 6,000 newsgroups operates as if it were a bulletin board devoted to a particular subject. Newsgroup subjects are organized in a hierarchical order with a major subject divided into one or more levels of subgroups. Each subgroup is separated by a period. Figure 7-24 shows an example of a Usenet newsgroup discussion.

To participate in a newsgroup, you must use a program called a **newsreader**. The newsreader enables you to access a newsgroup to read a previously entered message, called an **article**, and add an article of your own, called **posting**. A newsreader also keeps track of which articles you have and have not read. Newsgroup members often post articles as a reply to another article — either to answer a question or to comment on material in the original article. These replies often cause the author of the original article, or others, to post additional articles related to the original article. This process can be short-lived or go on indefinitely depending on the nature of the topic and the interest of the participants. The original article and all subsequent related replies are called a **thread**.

1. newsgroup subject
2. original posting asking for information on cycling computers; text of original message is shown in lower portion of screen
3. replies to original posting
4. text of original posting

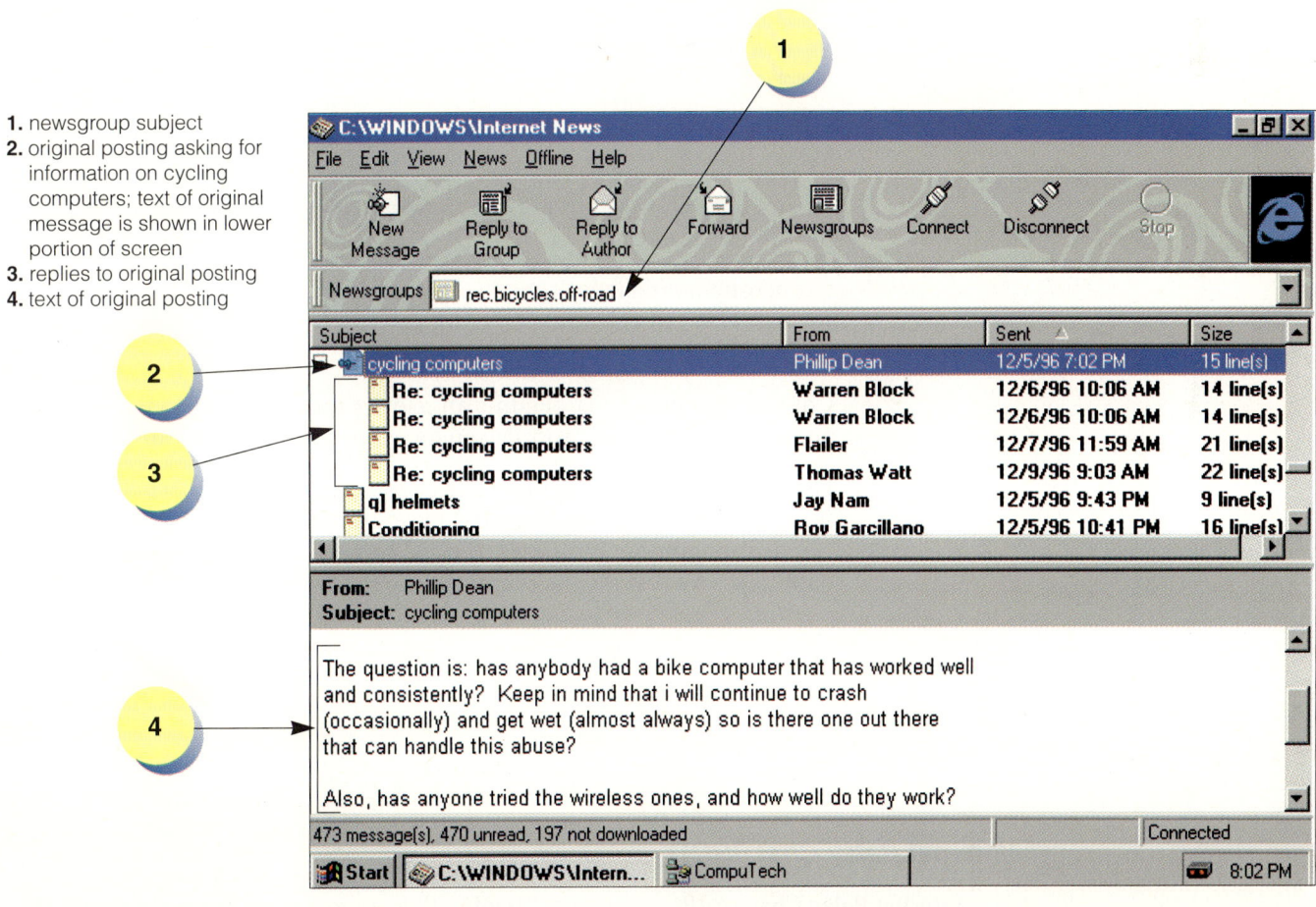

Figure 7-24
An example of a Usenet discussion. The top part of the screen shows articles that have been posted in the rec.bicycles.off-road newsgroup. The article posted on 12/5/96 by Phillip Dean, shown in the lower portion of the screen, received several replies.

Some newsgroups are supervised by a **moderator**, who reads each article before it is posted to the newsgroup. If the moderator thinks an article is appropriate for the newsgroup, the moderator posts the article for all members to read. Over time, newsgroup members have developed certain guidelines for posting articles called **netiquette** (short for network etiquette). These guidelines, shown in Figure 7-25, also are appropriate for other communications such as e-mail.

Figure 7-25
Netiquette – guidelines for communicating on a network.

Netiquette (Network Etiquette)

1. Choose your words carefully. Hundreds, maybe thousands, of people may read your article. Say what you mean, keep it brief, and use correct grammar and spelling. Be careful about using sarcasm, humor, or any other language that might be misinterpreted.

2. Read the FAQs. An **FAQ** is a list of frequently asked questions and their answers. FAQs are available for many newsgroups and for other areas on the Internet. For example, most hardware and software companies have FAQ files as part of their support programs. FAQs prevent new users, called **newbies**, and others from asking the same question over and over.

3. Choose a meaningful subject heading. Give the potential reader a good idea of the contents of your article.

4. Do not **SHOUT!** Do not use all capital letters — it is considered the same as shouting.

5. Use acronyms and emoticons to convey meaning quickly. Acronyms such as BTW (by the way) and emoticons such as smileys :) save time and add personality to your message.

6. Control your emotions. Sending an abusive message is called **flaming** and is considered inappropriate and a waste of network resources.

7. Post your article to the appropriate newsgroup. Posting an article (especially one soliciting business) to several inappropriate newsgroups is called **spamming**. It is frowned upon heavily and often results in flames (see 6 above) being sent to the offending person.

Internet Relay Chat (IRC)

Internet Relay Chat, or **IRC**, allows you to join others in real-time conversations on the Internet. To start an IRC session, you must connect to an Internet server using an IRC client program. (Many free IRC clients can be downloaded from the Web.) You then can create or join a conversation group called a **channel** on the Internet server to which you are attached. The channel name should indicate the topic of discussion. The person who creates a channel acts as the **channel operator** and has responsibility for monitoring the conversation and disconnecting anyone who becomes disruptive. Operator status can be shared or transferred to someone else.

You can find IRC channels using the /list command. You can participate by using the /join command and entering a nickname for yourself. Unless you specify the nickname of another IRC participant, any messages you send go to everyone in the channel. Figure 7-26 is an example of a discussion during an IRC session. Most online services include chat channels as one of their services.

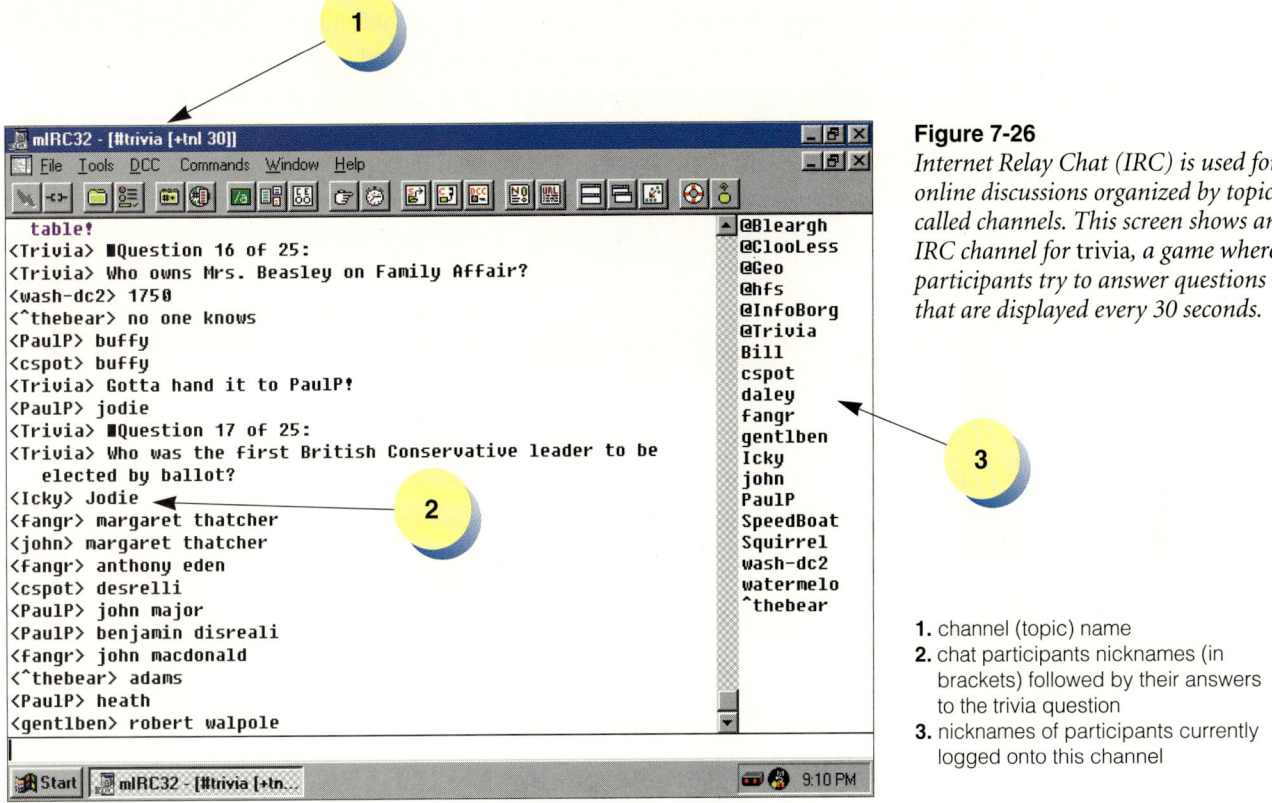

Figure 7-26
Internet Relay Chat (IRC) is used for online discussions organized by topics called channels. This screen shows an IRC channel for trivia, *a game where participants try to answer questions that are displayed every 30 seconds.*

1. channel (topic) name
2. chat participants nicknames (in brackets) followed by their answers to the trivia question
3. nicknames of participants currently logged onto this channel

Network Computers

As a way of reducing the total cost of ownership and the complexity associated with fully configured personal computer systems, many businesses and home users are turning to network computers. A **network computer**, or **NC**, is a computer designed to work while connected to a network, but not as a stand-alone computer. Network computers have limited, if any, built-in storage, because storage is provided by the server to which the network computer is attached. Because they have fewer components and less software than typical PCs, network computers sometimes are referred to as **thin-client** computers. The following sections discuss the types of network computers used in business and the home.

Network Computers for Business

For many business applications, a personal computer has more capability than the application requires. Jobs that primarily involve entering transactions or looking up information in a database, do not need floppy disks, CD-ROMs, or large hard disks. These extra components contribute to both the cost and complexity of the PC and, the more complex a system is, the more expensive it is to maintain. Studies have shown that the average cost to maintain a desktop computer over a three-year life is approximately $8,000 a year. This amount includes the cost of the equipment, software, repairs, training, and support, which usually is provided by someone from the Information Systems department.

Network computers for business reduce these costs in several ways. To begin with, NCs are less expensive to purchase, typically costing $500 to $1,000 compared with $2,000 to $3,000 spent on the average desktop PC. NCs cost less because they have fewer components. NCs have less memory than typical PCs and have no hard, floppy, or CD-ROM disk drives. All storage is done on the server. For software, NCs rely on Java-based applications downloaded from a server. Because all software is stored on the server, software is easier to maintain. A new version of the software has to be upgraded only once, on the server, instead of on all of the individual computers. Figure 7-27 shows a network computer manufactured by Sun Microsystems, Inc.

An alternative to the network computer is the network personal computer. A **network personal computer**, or **netPC**, primarily relies on the server for software and storage but does have a hard disk for storing some data and programs. A netPC can run Java and other programs such as Microsoft Windows applications.

Figure 7-27
JavaStation™, business network computer manufactured by Sun Microsystems, Inc.

Network Computers for the Home

Many potential home computer users do not want the features and components of a personal computer. All they want is the ability to access the information on the Internet they hear about and read about every day. Previously, the only way to access the Internet from home was with a personal computer that new cost at least $1,000 and an average of $2,000. A network computer for the home, sometimes called an **information appliance**, is a device that incorporates Internet access into a device with which you are familiar already, such as a television, a telephone, or a video game console. Instead of costing thousands of dollars, home network computers cost hundreds of dollars, comparable to other mid-range consumer electronics devices. To keep the cost down, manufacturers have eliminated standard computer features, such as any type of disk drive. Instead of a separate monitor, you use your television set. If you want to use the device to enter e-mail, you can use an optional wireless keyboard. One of the more popular home network computers uses a device that looks and acts like a cable TV box (Figure 7-28). This **set-top box** uses your telephone line to connect to an Internet service provider. To navigate Web pages, you use a device that looks like a large TV remote control (Figure 7-29).

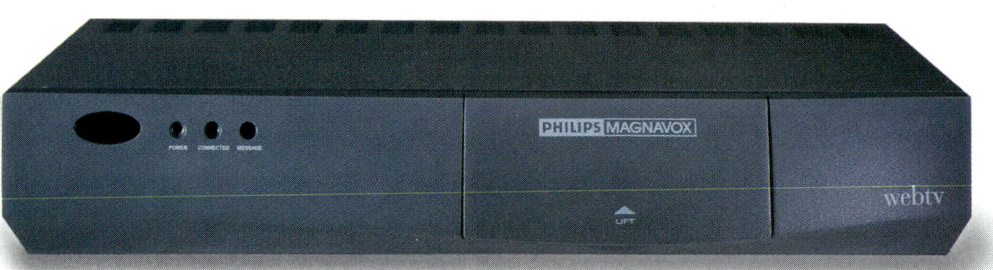

Figure 7-28
One type of home network computer uses a set-top box, similar to a cable TV box.

NETWORK COMPUTERS 7.27

Figure 7-29
This remote control device is used to navigate Web pages on a home network computer.

Summary of Network Computers

Figure 7-30 shows a comparison of the network and personal computer features. In reviewing this table, you should keep in mind that network computers are a quickly evolving category of personal computers. Features and descriptions will likely change over time.

COMPARISON OF NETWORK COMPUTERS AND A PERSONAL COMPUTER

	Home Network Computer	**Business Network Computer (NC)**	**Network Personal Computer (netPC)**	**Personal Computer**
Cost	$200 - $500	$500 - $1,000	$1,000 - $2,000	$2,000 - $3,000
Hardware differences	• set-top box • hand-held remote control • uses TV for monitor	• 8 MB	• 16 MB • small hard disk	• 32 MB • hard, floppy, and CD-ROM disks
What's missing	• hard disk • floppy disk • CD-ROM • keyboard (optional)	• hard disk • floppy disk • CD-ROM	• floppy disk • CD-ROM	• nothing
Software	• Web browser software	• Java-based software downloaded from server	• primarily on server • some software on hard disk • can run Windows	• software applications on hard drive • can download from server • can run Windows
Advantages	• low cost • easy to use • entertainment oriented	• low cost • easy to administer	• lower cost than PC • local storage	• full capabilities
Disadvantages	• unable to run easily productivity software such as wp, ss, db	• no local storage • totally dependent on server • limited software available	• may be more or less computer than needed	• high cost • high maintenance

Figure 7-30
Comparison of different types of network computers and a personal computer.

How to Connect to the Internet and the World Wide Web

The following steps describe how you can connect to the Internet and the World Wide Web.

1. **Determine how you will obtain access to the Internet.** The three more common ways that people connect to the Internet are through their school or work, through an online service, or through an Internet service provider (ISP).

    Through school or work: Most schools and many organizations have direct, high-speed connections to the Internet. Check with the department that operates the computer labs at school or the department that supports the network at work to obtain details about obtaining an Internet account.

    Through an online service: Most online services, such as America Online and CompuServe, offer Internet access as one of their services. If you already use an online service, this is an excellent way to begin using the Internet. Keep a record of the amount of time you spend on the Internet and the effect it has on your online service bill. You may find that it would be less expensive to use an Internet service provider.

    Through an Internet service provider (ISP): As described earlier in the chapter, an Internet service provider (ISP) has a permanent connection to the Internet and provides temporary connections to others for a fee. The most common fee arrangement is a fixed amount, usually about $15 to $30 per month. You may receive a discounted fee if you sign up for an extended period of time, such as a year. The fee usually includes up to a certain number of Internet access hours, say 100 per month. If you use more than this number of hours, you will be charged an additional amount.

    ISPs include many types of organizations, including private companies such as EarthLink and common carriers such as AT&T. Different Internet service providers offer access services to geographic regions of different sizes: some are local or regional, and others serve users nationwide. Figure 7-31 is a list of national Internet service providers. Before choosing an ISP, check the telephone number you will use to connect to the ISP to see if it will be a local or long-distance call. If you live in a medium to large city, most ISPs will provide a local telephone number.

National Internet Service Providers

Name	Telephone	Web Site
AT&T WorldNet[SM]	800-967-5363	www.att.com/worldnet/wis
EarthLink Network	800-395-8425	www.earthlink.net
network MCI	800-550-0927	www.mci.com
NETCOM	800-538-2551	www.netcom.com
SPRYNET	800-777-9638	www.sprynet.com

Figure 7-31

These companies are national Internet service providers (ISPs). You can find local ISPs in your telephone book yellow pages under Computers-Networks.

If you know existing ISP users, ask them how often they are unable to log on to the network and the level and quality of technical support. Ask to see the ISP's account setup and software installation instructions. The quality, clarity, and content of these instructions will give you an idea of how well the ISP is organized.

Your ISP probably will set up your account using **PPP (point-to-point protocol)**, a widely used version of the Internet communications protocol TCP/IP. Avoid using a **SLIP (serial line Internet protocol)** connection, because SLIP is an older protocol that does not offer the same degree of error checking as PPP.

2. **Obtain the necessary equipment.** You probably already have the equipment necessary to connect to the Internet. At a minimum, you need a computer, a modem, and a telephone line. (If you want to print information, you also will need a printer.) The speed of you computer, modem, and telephone line will affect how rapidly you can access and display information.

   For the computer, any system less than two-years old should suffice. If your system is more than two years old, consult your ISP.

   For the modem, the higher your modem speed the better. Although 14.4 Kbps or 9,600 bps will work, you need a 28.8 Kbps or faster modem to enjoy the features of the Internet. If you do not have a modem, buy the highest speed you can afford. If you have a slower modem, consider replacing it. A slow modem will act as a bottleneck and lead to frustrating delays as Web pages and information download.

   For most users, a normal analog telephone line will be sufficient. You may want to consider adding a second telephone line so your regular telephone line is not tied up while you are online. If you plan to do serious work using the Internet, such as telecommuting, consider installing a digital ISDN line. An ISDN line can transmit data at up to 128 Kbps, which is more than four times faster than a 28.8 Kbps modem. ISDN lines are more costly to install and maintain but can be worth it if you can offset the expense with greater earnings.

3. **Obtain the necessary software.** You need at least two pieces of software to access the Internet and the World Wide Web through an ISP; a communications program and a Web browser program. You also may want software for e-mail, FTP, and other Internet services, although most Web browsers include some or all of these programs. If your browser does not have these functions, your ISP may provide the programs free. Many also can be downloaded from the Internet or purchased from the developers or software retailers. Why would you want to purchase software you can get free? You may need technical support, which is rarely available for free software.

4. **Install the software.** You should be familiar with the ISP's installation instructions if you reviewed them prior to choosing the ISP. Before starting the installation, however, re-read the instructions in full: exceptions or important information sometimes are placed out of sequence in the instructions. Then, follow the instructions for your operating system. Depending on the Internet software, the installation procedure can be simple, using wizards and dialog boxes or complex, requiring changes to confusing system files. If you run into problems, return to installation step one and start over. If the software still does not work, call your ISP for support.

5. **Explore the Internet and the World Wide Web.** The best way to learn how to use the Internet and Web is to log on and explore. Pick a subject and use a search tool to see what is on the Web. Look up your school's home page and see if it describes the place you know. To help you explore, the section following this chapter lists some useful, interesting, and unusual Web sites. Good exploring!

7.30 CHAPTER 7 – THE INTERNET AND THE WORLD WIDE WEB

COMPUTERS AT WORK

Doing Business on the World Wide Web

The rapid growth of the World Wide Web is being accelerated by businesses rushing to establish Web sites to promote their products and services. More than 50 percent of the existing Web sites are commercial (as indicated by their .com domain type), and an even higher percentage of new sites are being set up by businesses. These companies recognize that the Web offers a number of unique advantages over traditional ways of doing business. These advantages include:

- Twenty-four-hour access — Your Internet site can be open around the clock. Customers can reach you according to their schedules and time zones, not yours.
- Global presence — Your product message can be read by customers around the world.
- Lower marketing costs — An electronic product brochure or catalog is less expensive to produce than one on paper. In addition, it can be updated quickly.
- Two-way communications — Compliments, complaints, suggestions, and other customer feedback can be recorded and distributed for follow-up.

For retailers, additional advantages include:

- Lower product display and storage costs — Costs associated with displaying a product, such as a showroom or storefront, are eliminated. Storage costs also can be reduced by eliminating the need to store inventory at multiple locations.
- Lower salesperson costs — For many products, customers obtain sufficient information to make a purchase without the assistance of a salesperson. Even if a salesperson is required to close the sale, presales information provided over the Internet increases the salesperson's efficiency.

The volume of product sales over the Web is growing even faster than the number of companies establishing Web sites. For 1996, Forrester Research, Inc. estimated that products in excess of $500 million were sold via online shopping (a combination of Internet and online service providers). By 2000, they estimate that online product sales will be more than $6 billion, which is a twelve-fold increase. It appears that the business and customer rush to the World Wide Web will continue for some time.

Figure 7-32

IN THE FUTURE: THE FUTURE OF THE INTERNET AND THE WORLD WIDE WEB 7.31

The Future of the Internet and the World Wide Web

What is the future of the World Wide Web? Will increasing traffic cause a catastrophic collapse as predicted by some experts, or will the Web continue to evolve as a primary communications channel? Or both? The following are some of the current predictions about the future of the Internet and the World Wide Web:

- Business use of the Web for electronic commerce will be the driving force of the Web's expansion. Businesses will learn how to make money on the Web, and the Web will become self-supporting.
- Within 10 years, the Web will operate at speeds 100 to 1,000 times faster than today.
- Browser capabilities will be incorporated into most software applications. Stand-alone browsers rarely will be used.
- Using the Web will become an integral part of all education.
- By the year 2000, 80 percent of the world's computers will be connected.
- The ability to connect to the Internet will be built into everyday home and office appliances and other devices that use embedded computers, such as automobiles.
- Web search capabilities will be more intelligent and focused.
- Separate proprietary networks for telephone, television, and radio will merge with the Internet. Eventually, a single, integrated network will exist, made up of many different media, that will carry all communications traffic.

To paraphrase the Sun Microsystems, Inc. corporate slogan; the **Internet will be the computer.**

Figure 7-33

7 review

chapter
| 1 | 2 | 3 | 4 | 5 | 6 | 7 | 8 | 9 | 10 | 11 | 12 | 13 | 14 | I |

inCyber | review | terms | yourTurn | hotTopics | outThere | winLabs | webWalk | exercises | news | home

INSTRUCTIONS: *To display this page from the Web, launch your browser and enter the URL, http://www.scsite.com/dc/ch7/review.htm. Click the links for current and additional information.*

1 The Internet

The term, **the Internet**, is used to describe a worldwide group of connected networks (some local, some regional, and some national) that allows public access to information and services. Together, these networks create a global network that serves approximately 40 million users.

2 How the Internet Works

The Internet operates by dividing data into separate parts, called **packets**, and sending the packets along the best route available to a destination computer. The software used to perform this technique, called *packet switching*, is a communications protocol named **TCP/IP (transmission control protocol/Internet protocol)**. People can connect to the Internet through an organization such as a school or company, an online service, or an **Internet service provider (ISP)**.

3 Internet Addresses

Each location on the Internet has a four-part numeric address called an **IP (Internet protocol) address**. Because IP addresses are difficult to remember and use, the Internet supports a text version, called a **domain name**, that can be substituted for the IP address. Domain names are registered in the **domain name system (DNS)** and are used by **domain name servers** to look up the associated IP address.

4 The World Wide Web

The **World Wide Web (WWW, W3,** or the **Web)** is a collection of hyperlinked documents accessible on the Internet. **Hyperlinks** can be used to move quickly from one document to another, regardless of whether the documents are located on the same computer or on different computers in different countries. Internet locations that contain hyperlinked documents are called **Web sites**.

5 How a Web Page Works

A **Web page** is a **hypertext** document (document with text hyperlinks) or **hypermedia** document (document with text, graphics, video, or sound hyperlinks) residing on an Internet computer. The three types of hyperlinks are **target hyperlinks** that move from one location in a document to another location in the same document; **relative hyperlinks** that move from one document to another document on the same computer; and **absolute hyperlinks** that move from one document to another document on a different Internet computer. Displaying pages from one Web site after another is called **Web surfing**. Web pages are created using **hypertext markup language (HTML)**, which is a set of special instructions that specify links to other documents and how the page is displayed.

7.33 review

inCyber | review | terms | yourTurn | hotTopics | outThere | winLabs | webWalk | exercises | news | home

6 Web Browser Software

Web browser software is a program that interprets and displays Web pages and enables you to link to other Web pages. Each time a browser is launched, a **home page** is displayed. The browser retrieves Web pages using a **Uniform Resource Locator** (**URL**), which is an address that points to a specific resource on the Internet. Browsers display hyperlinks either as underlined text of a different color or as a graphic. Linked documents can be displayed by clicking the hyperlink or by typing its URL in the Location text box. Two ways to keep track of Web pages that have been viewed are a **history list** and a **bookmark** list.

7 Multimedia on the Web

Some of the more exciting Web developments involve multimedia. To run a multimedia application, a browser may need an additional program called a **plug-in** or **helper application**. A programming language called **Java** is being used to develop much of the multimedia on the Web. Developers use Java to create small programs called applets that can be downloaded and run in a browser window. Multimedia Web developments have been made in the areas of **graphics**, **animation**, **audio**, **video**, and **virtual reality** (**VR**).

8 Web Search Tools

A **search tool**, also called a **search engine**, is a software program that finds Web sites, Web pages, and Internet files that match one or more keywords entered. Search tools search an index of Internet sites and documents that is constantly updated.

9 Intranets

Internal networks that use Internet and Web technology are called **intranets**. Intranet applications include electronic publishing and groupware applications. **Extranets** are private networks that include more than one organization. To prevent unauthorized access, organizations implement one or more layers of security called a **firewall**, which refers to both hardware and software used to restrict access to data on a network.

10 Internet Services

Internet services include e-mail, FTP, Gopher, Telnet, Usenet, and Internet Relay Chat (IRC). **E-mail** is the electronic exchange of messages from one person to another. To receive e-mail, you must have a **mailbox**, which is a file used to collect messages on an Internet computer. An **Internet mailbox address** is a combination of a **user name** (a unique combination of characters that identifies you) and the domain name that identifies the location of the mailbox computer.

11 FTP and Gopher

FTP (file transfer protocol) is an Internet standard that allows you to exchange files with other computers on the Internet. Computers that contain files available for FTP are called **FTP sites** or **FTP servers**. An FTP search tool called **Archie** can be used to find files on a particular subject. **Gopher** is a menu-driven program that helps you locate and retrieve files on the Internet. Internet computers called **Gopher servers** maintain Gopher directories. Most Gopher servers offer **Veronica** or **Jughead** search programs.

12 Telnet, Usenet, and Internet Relay Chat (IRC)

Telnet is an Internet protocol used to log into a remote computer on the Internet. **Usenet** is a collection of news and discussion groups, called **newsgroups**. Each newsgroup operates as if it were a bulletin board devoted to a particular subject. **Internet Relay Chat (IRC)** allows you to join in real-time conversations on the Internet.

13 Network Computers

A **network computer** is designed to work while connected to a network, but not as a stand-alone computer. Network computers are also called **thin-client** computers. A **network personal computer**, or **netPC**, relies on the server but does have a hard disk. A **set-top box**, using a phone line, can connect your TV to the Web.

14 Connecting to the Internet

You must perform five steps to connect to the Internet and the World Wide Web. First, determine how you will obtain access to the Internet (through school or work, an online service, or an Internet service provider). Second, obtain the necessary equipment (a computer, a modem, and a telephone line). Third, obtain the necessary software (a communications program and a browser). Fourth, install the software. Fifth, explore the Internet and the World Wide Web.

chapter 1 | 2 | 3 | 4 | 5 | 6 | 7 | 8 | 9 | 10 | 11 | 12 | 13 | 14 | I

inCyber | review | terms | yourTurn | hotTopics | outThere | winLabs | webWalk | exercises | news | home

INSTRUCTIONS: *To display this page from the Web, launch your browser and enter the URL, http://www.scsite.com/dc/ch7/terms.htm. Scroll through the list of terms. Click a term for its definition and a picture. Click the rocket ship for current and additional information about the term.*

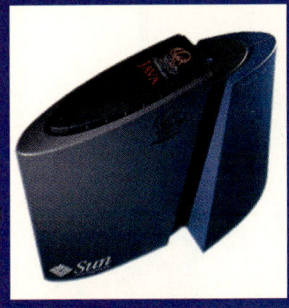

network computer ▼

D E F I N I T I O N

network computer
Relies on the server for software and storage. Does not have a hard disk. **(7.25)**

absolute hyperlinks (7.8)
Advanced Research Projects
    Agency (ARPA) (7.3)
animation (7.12)
anonymous FTP (7.20)
applets (7.11)
Archie (7.20)
Archie gateway (7.20)
Archie sites (7.20)
ARPANET (7.3)
article (7.23)
audio (7.13)

backbones (7.5)
bookmark (7.11)
browser (7.9)

caching (7.18)
channel (7.25)
channel operator (7.25)

domain name (7.6)
domain name servers (7.6)
domain name system (DNS) (7.6)

e-mail (7.19)
extranets (7.17)

FAQ (7.24)
firewall (7.18)
flaming (7.24)
FTP (file transfer protocol) (7.20)
FTP servers (7.20)
FTP sites (7.20)

Gopher (7.21)
Gopher servers (7.21)
graphics (7.12)

helper application (7.11)
history list (7.11)
home page (7.10)
http:// (7.10)
hyperlinks (7.7)
hypermedia (7.7)
hypertext (7.7)
hypertext markup language
    (HTML) (7.8)
hypertext transfer protocol (7.10)

information appliance (7.26)
internet (7.2)
the Internet (7.2)
Internet audioconferencing (7.13)
Internet mailbox address (7.19)
Internet Relay Chat (IRC) (7.25)
Internet service provider (ISP)
    (7.28)
Internet telephone service (7.13)
Internet telephony (7.13)
Internet voice mail (7.13)
internetwork (7.2)
intranet (7.17)
IP (Internet protocol) address
    (7.6)
IRC (7.25)

Java (7.11)
/join (7.25)
Jughead (7.21)

/list (7.25)

mailbox (7.19)
markups (7.8)
metropolitan area exchanges
    (MAEs) (7.5)

moderator (7.24)
MOO (multiuser object oriented)
    (7.22)
Mosaic (7.9)
MUD (multiuser dimension)
    (7.22)

NC (7.25)
netiquette (7.24)
network computer (7.25)
network personal computer (7.26)
net PC (7.26)
newbies (7.24)
newsgroups (7.23)
newsreader (7.23)
NSFnet (7.3)

online service (7.28)

packets (7.4)
plug-in (7.11)
posting (7.23)
PPP (point-to-point protocol)
    (7.29)
proxy server (7.18)

relative hyperlinks (7.8)

search engine (7.16)
search tool (7.16)
set-top box (7.26)
shareware (7.20)
SHOUT! (7.24)
SLIP (serial line Internet protocol)
    (7.29)
spamming (7.24)
streaming audio (7.13)
streaming video (7.14)

tags (7.8)
target hyperlinks (7.8)
TCP/IP (transmission control
    protocol/Internet protocol)
    (7.4)
Telnet (7.22)
thin-client (7.25)
thread (7.23)

Uniform Resource Locator (URL)
    (7.10)
URL (7.10)
Usenet (7.23)
user name (7.19)
user-ID (7.19)

Veronica (7.21)
video (7.14)
virtual reality (VR) (7.15)
VRML (virtual reality modeling
    language) (7.15)

W3 (7.7)
Web (7.7)
Web browser (7.9)
Web browser software (7.9)
Web page (7.7)
Web sites (7.7)
Web surfing (7.8)
welcome page (7.10)
World Wide Web (7.7)
WWW (7.7)

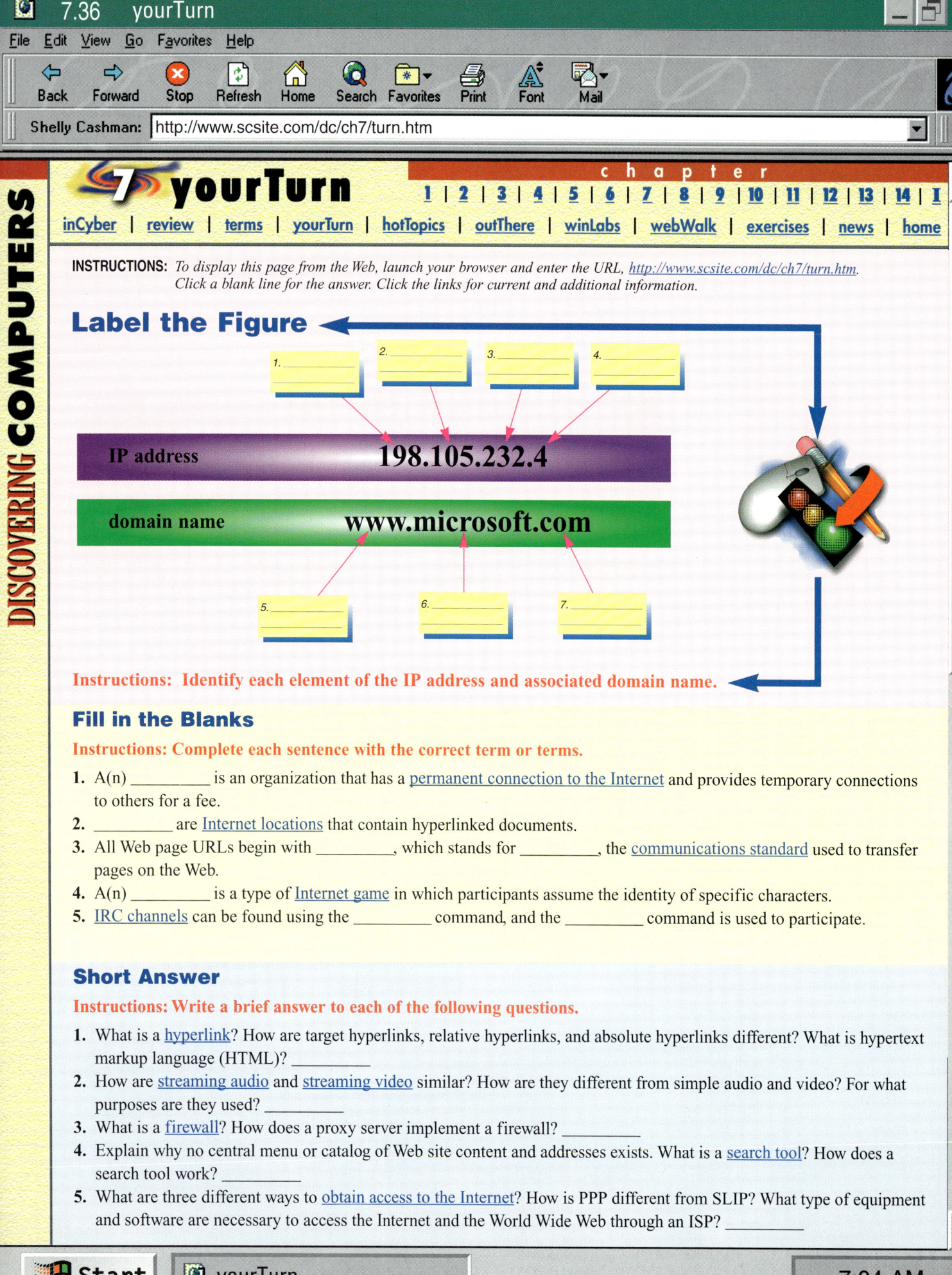

7.37 hotTopics

Shelly Cashman: http://www.scsite.com/dc/ch7/hot.htm Links

7 hotTopics   chapter 1 | 2 | 3 | 4 | 5 | 6 | 7 | 8 | 9 | 10 | 11 | 12 | 13 | 14 | I

inCyber | review | terms | yourTurn | hotTopics | outThere | winLabs | webWalk | exercises | news | home

INSTRUCTIONS: *To display this page from the Web, launch your browser and enter the URL,* http://www.scsite.com/dc/ch7/hot.htm. *Click the links for current and additional information to help you respond to the hotTopics questions.*

1 *When Chess Grand Master Gary Kasparov played Big Blue the computer,* IBM created a Web site to follow the chess tournament. It is estimated that at times more than *one million* people saw some of the match online. Experts feel the site was successful because visitors got what they wanted (exciting games with respected analysis), and the event lent itself to the site's design (a view of the chessboard with the capability to interact). Considering these two factors, desirability and appropriateness, what other events could be covered successfully at a Web site? Why? How would you design the Web site? What advantages would coverage at a Web site have over coverage in other media?

2 *An increasing number of doctors is going online as volunteer medical consultants. People* suffering from almost any disease can find relevant support groups, mailing lists, and Web sites. These forums may help reduce feelings of isolation and provide invaluable information. Many doctors, however, still are reluctant to go online. They fear online forums can raise false hopes, repeat unsubstantiated claims, or promote quack remedies. If someone you knew had a serious condition, would you suggest trying the Internet? Why? What cautions would you recommend when exploring a health issue online? How would you advise someone to act on medical information received from the Web?

3 *After hearing a girl had been mistreated by her mother, a student posted a message to Internet* newsgroups urging readers to call the girl's family. The family received several threatening telephone calls. The girl's angry father insisted the allegations were exaggerated and feared the telephone calls could destroy an already vulnerable family. The message's author admitted no wrong doing and claimed people should be free to write what they want on the Internet. While conventional laws regarding libel, slander, and harassment may apply, Internet communications ultimately depend on the writer's sense of responsibility. Are these remedies enough? What, if anything, should be done to guarantee a message's veracity? What obligations do the writers and readers of messages have?

4 *While seeking an explanation for a recently doubled dropout rate, educators at a major* university found that 43 percent of the dropouts disclosed late-night Internet connections, neglecting their studies and failing to attend class. Some colleges have expressed concern about excessive use of the Internet, occasionally called cyberaddiction. Unsure whether this condition is a true addiction or merely a sympton of other problems, colleges have offered a range of solutions, including support groups, turning off computers, and slowing down the machines. Is *cyberaddiction* really a problem? Why? If it is, what can be done? How would you determine if a friend is spending too much time online? What would you do to help?

5 *The freedom and anonymity of the Internet may be both its most appealing and disturbing* characteristics. These features may encourage a woman suffering from ochlophobia (fear of crowds) to discover help in a newsgroup, but these same features allow lawbreakers to send obscene materials, arrange illicit meetings, and swindle unsuspecting readers. What controls should be placed on the Internet? Why? Should people be subject to local ordinances (a California couple recently was prosecuted for violating Tennessee law with pictures downloaded from their bulletin board), or should regulations be global? Why?

Start | hotTopics | 7:05 AM

outThere

INSTRUCTIONS: To display this page from the Web, launch your browser and enter the URL, *http://www.scsite.com/dc/ch7/out.htm*. Click the links for current and additional information.

1  *News and information about a wide range of events are available at various* Web sites. News mavens complain, however, that they are forced to spend too much time surfing the Web trying to track down the material they want. A solution to the complaint is called invited push media, a continuous stream of information that you request be sent to your personal computer. Visit one or more Web sites to find out about a push media application. What is the name of the application? How much does it cost? How does the application work? What type of information is broadcast? How current is it? Does every user get the same information? Would you be interested in downloading a push media application? Why?

2 *Most communities have a number of Internet Service Providers (ISPs) that offer access to the* Internet. Because the monthly rates, the features offered, and the quality of the connection may vary, however, it is wise to do some comparison shopping before signing on with an ISP. Contact at least two ISPs to learn more about each service. What are the rates? Are invoices sent or is a charge automatically billed to a credit card? How many people can use the account? Is disk storage space available for a personal Web page? If so, does the page contain any restrictions? Is the service not accessible at any time? When is technical support available? Try to find users of each ISP and ask them about the quality of the connection. Which ISP do you feel is the better buy? Why?

3 *Eighty percent of the work in preparing a research report is locating the* necessary information. Search tools can help to find relevant information at Web sites, but they fail to cover other possible resources such as magazines, newspapers, and books. To make their inquiries more inclusive, many students are turning to online research services available on the World Wide Web. Visit a Web site to learn more about an online research service. What resources are used by the service? How is using the service similar to using a library? How is it different? Who uses the service? How safe is the service for kids? How much does it cost? Would you use an online research service? Why?

4 *Web browsers are an essential tool when exploring the World Wide Web. If you plan to* spend time on the Internet, it is important to use a browser with which you are comfortable. Visit a software vendor and compare two or more Web browsers. What is the name of each browser? How much does each cost? What types of hardware and software are required? What features are offered by each browser? If possible, try each browser. How are they similar? How are they different? Is one browser easier to use than the other? Why? Which browser does the salesperson recommend? Why? Which would you be more likely to buy? Why?

5 *Not only do teachers suggest that their students use the Internet, more and more teachers are* using the Internet themselves to improve their presentations. Visit one or more Web sites that suggest lesson plans, projects, and activities and look at the available material from a student's point of view. What lesson plans, projects, or activities do you think a student would find most interesting? Why? What suggestions look least promising? Why? What types of teachers would be most likely to benefit from visiting each site? Why? Using the available lesson plans, projects, or activities, how would you teach a lesson in your favorite subject?

7 winLabs

chapter 1 | 2 | 3 | 4 | 5 | 6 | 7 | 8 | 9 | 10 | 11 | 12 | 13 | 14 | I

inCyber | review | terms | yourTurn | hotTopics | outThere | winLabs | webWalk | exercises | news | home

INSTRUCTIONS: *To display this page from the Web, launch your browser and enter the URL, http://www.scsite.com/dc/ch7/labs.htm. Click the links for current and additional information.*

1 Shelly Cashman Series Internet Lab
Follow the instructions in winLabs 1 on page 1.34 to display the Shelly Cashman Series Labs screen. Click Connecting to the Internet. Click the Start Lab button. When the initial screen displays, carefully read the objectives. With your printer turned on, click the Print Questions button. Fill out the top of the Questions sheet and then answer the questions.

2 Shelly Cashman Series World Wide Web Lab
Follow the instructions in winLabs 1 on page 1.34 to display the Shelly Cashman Series Labs screen. Click The World Wide Web. Click the Start Lab button. When the screen displays, read the objectives. With your printer turned on, click the Print Questions button. Fill out the top of the Questions sheet and answer the questions.

3 Understanding Your Internet Properties
Right-click The Internet icon on the desktop. Click Properties on the shortcut menu. When The Internet Properties dialog box displays, click the General tab. Click the question mark button on the title bar and then click Show pictures. Read the information in the pop-up window and then click the pop-up window to close it. Repeat this process for other areas of the dialog box and then answer the following questions: (1) What are three ways to make pages display more quickly? (2) In what color do visited links display? Unvisited links? (3) What is the address bar? Click the Navigation tab and then answer the following questions: (1) What is the Internet address of the start page? (2) How many days of pages display in history? Click the Cancel button.

4 Determining Dial-Up Network Connections
Click the Start button on the taskbar, point to Programs on the Start menu, point to Accessories on the Programs submenu, and then click Dial-Up Networking on the Accessories submenu. When the Dial-Up Networking window displays, right-click a connection in the list (e.g., The Microsoft Network) and then click Connect on the shortcut menu. Write down the User name and the Phone number. Close the dialog box and open window.

5 Using Help to Understand the Internet
Click the Start button on the taskbar and then on the Start menu, click Help. Click the Contents tab, double-click Introducing Windows, and then double-click Welcome to the Information Highway. Double-click An introduction to the Internet (Figure 7-34). In the Windows Help window, click the Options button, click Print Topic, and then click the OK button to print the topic. Click the Help Topics button. Double-click Taking a test drive on the information highway. Print the topic. Close any open window(s).

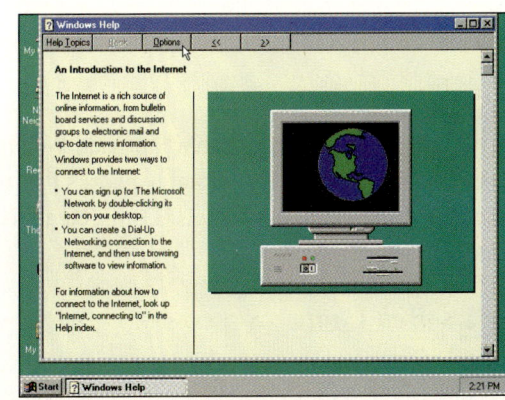

Figure 7-34

webWalk

chapter 7

1 | 2 | 3 | 4 | 5 | 6 | 7 | 8 | 9 | 10 | 11 | 12 | 13 | 14 | I

inCyber | review | terms | yourTurn | hotTopics | outThere | winLabs | webWalk | exercises | news | home

INSTRUCTIONS: *To display this page from the Web, launch your browser and enter the URL, http://www.scsite.com/dc/ch7/walk.htm. Click the exercise link to display the exercise.*

① Web Chat
A chatting application allows Web users to have real-time conversations with each other via the Web (Figure 7-35). To learn more about Web Chatting, complete this exercise.

② Internet Congestion
The expanding population of the Internet is raising concern that the Net will suffer a catastrophic collapse. You can learn more about these concerns by completing this exercise.

③ Real-Time Information
Through the network of computers known as the World Wide Web, complex data can be queried and reported through user-friendly interfaces (Figure 7-36). To visit a Web site where you can access complex, real-time information, complete this exercise.

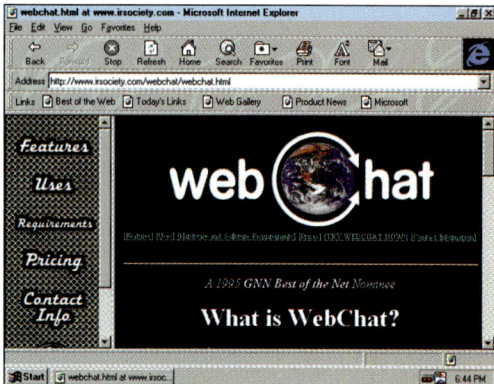

Figure 7-35

④ Web TV
In the near future when you are watching television and an interesting new product is shown, you will be able to click and be connected instantly to the product's Web site. To learn more about Web TV, complete this exercise.

⑤ Information Mining
Complete this exercise to improve your Web research skills by using a Web search engine to find information related to this chapter.

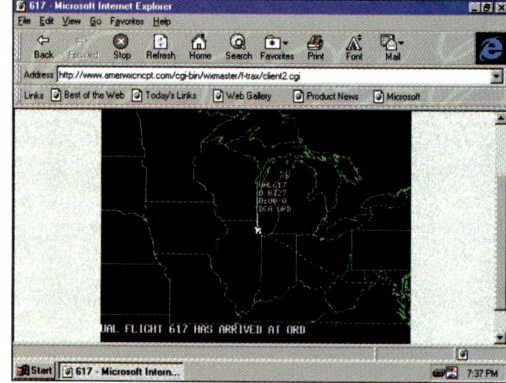

Figure 7-36

⑥ Web Domain Names
A Domain Name such as www.scsite.com that identifies a computer on the web must be registered. Complete this exercise to learn more about how domain names are registered.

⑦ Intranets
Many organizations have applied Web technology to their own internal networks. Internal networks that use Internet and Web technology are called Intranets. Complete this exercise to learn more about Intranets.

⑧ Cable Modem
A cable modem is a device that allows high-speed access to the Internet via a cable TV network. Complete this exercise to learn more about cable modems.

⑨ Web Chat
Complete this exercise to enter a Web Chat discussion related to the issues presented in the hotTopics exercise.

Guide to World Wide Web Sites

The World Wide Web is an exciting and highly dynamic medium. Every day, new Web sites are added, existing ones are changed, and still others cease to exist. Because of this, you may find that a URL listed here has changed or no longer is valid. A continually updated Guide to World Wide Web Sites, which links to the most current versions of these sites, can be found at http://www.scsite.com/dc/ch7/websites.htm.

CATEGORIES

Art	Government and Politics	Reference
Business and Finance	Health and Medicine	Science
Careers and Employment	History	Shopping
Computers and Computing	Humor	Sports
Education	Internet	Travel
Entertainment	Museums	Unclassified!
Environment	News Sources	Weather

7.42 GUIDE TO WORLD WIDE WEB SITES

CATEGORY/SITE NAME	LOCATION (all site locations begin with http://)	COMMENT
Art		
The WebMuseum	sunsite.unc.edu/louvre/net/	Web version of Louvre Museum, Paris
Art Links on the Web	amanda.physics.wisc.edu/outside.html	Links to many art sites
Leonardo da Vinci	www.leonardo.net/museum	Works of the famous Italian artist and thinker
World Art Treasures	sgwww.epfl.ch/BERGER	100,000 slides organized by civilization
The Andy Warhol Museum	www.clpgh.org/warhol	Famous American pop artist
ArtServe	rubens.anu.edu.au	More than 18,000 images
Business and Finance		
Imperative!™	www.tig.com/IBC	How to do business on the web
All Business Network	www.all-biz.com	Links to Web business information
FinanCenter, Inc.	www.financenter.com	Personal finance information
The Wall Street Journal	update.wsj.com	Financial news page
Stock Research Group	www.stockgroup.com	Investment information
PC Quote	www.pcquote.com	Free delayed stock quotes
Careers and Employment		
CareerMosaic®	www.careermosaic.com	Jobs from around the world
E-Span Employment Database	www.espan.com	Searchable job database
CareerMagazine	www.careermag.com	Career articles and information

For an updated list: http://www.scsite.com/dc/ch7/websites.htm

The Andy Warhol Museum

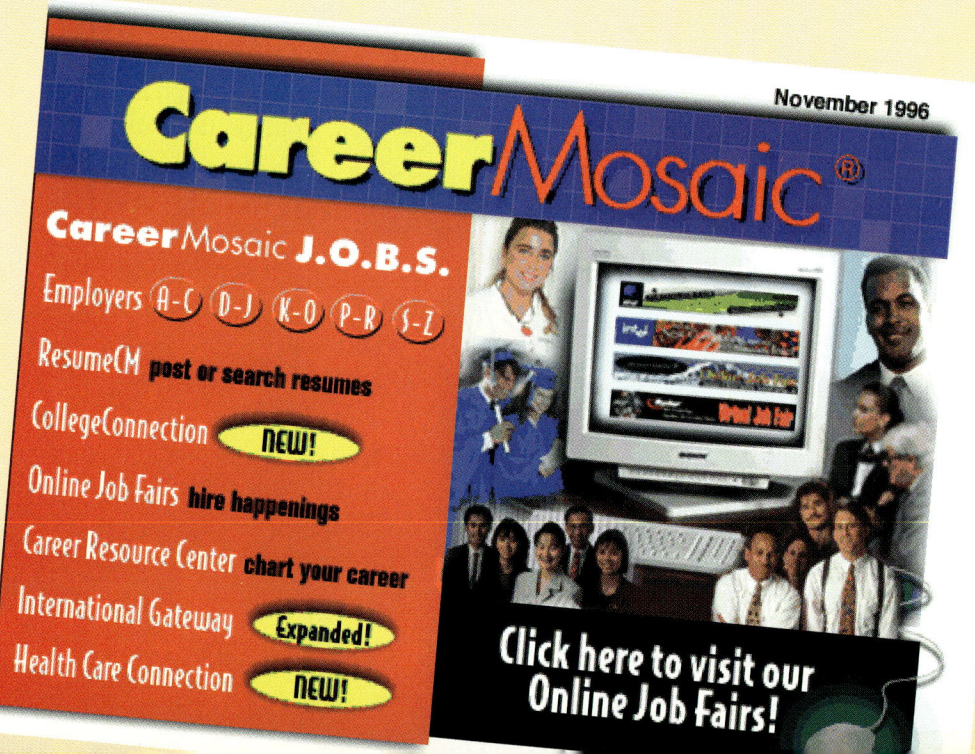

GUIDE TO WORLD WIDE WEB SITES 7.43

CATEGORY/SITE NAME	LOCATION (all site locations begin with http://)	COMMENT
Computers and Computing		
Computer companies	Insert name or initials of most computer companies between www. and .com to find their Web site. Examples: www.ibm.com, www.microsoft.com, www.dell.com.	
The Computer Museum	www.net.org	Exhibits and history of computing
MIT Media Lab	www.media.mit.edu	Information on computer trends
Virtual Computer Library	www.utexas.edu/computer/vcl	Information on computers and computing
Education		
CollegeNET	www.collegenet.com	Searchable database of more than 2,000 colleges and universities
EdLinks	www.marshall.edu/~jmullens/edlinks.html	Links to many educational sites
The Open University	www.open.ac.uk	Independent study courses from U.K.
Entertainment		
Mr. Showbiz	web3.starwave.com/showbiz	Information on latest films
Rock & Roll Hall of Fame	www.rockhall.com	Cleveland museum site
Classics World	www.classicalmus.com	Classical music information
Metaverse	metaverse.com	Music and entertainment news
Playbill On-Line	www.playbill.com	Theater news
Music Boulevard	www.musicblvd.com	Search for and buy all types of music

For an updated list: http://www.scsite.com/dc/ch7/websites.htm

7.44 GUIDE TO WORLD WIDE WEB SITES

CATEGORY/SITE NAME	LOCATION (all site locations begin with http://)	COMMENT
Environment		
U.S. Environmental Protection Agency (EPA)	www.epa.gov	U.S. government environmental news
EnviroLink Network	www.envirolink.org	Environmental information
Greenpeace	www.greenpeace.org	Environmental activism
Government and Politics		
U.S. Census Bureau	www.census.gov	Population and other statistics
CIA	www.odci.gov/cia	Political and economic information on countries
The White House	www.whitehouse.gov	Take tour and learn about occupants
FedWorld	www.fedworld.gov	Links to U.S. government sites
The Library of Congress	www.loc.gov	Variety of U.S. government information
Canada Info	www.clo.com/~canadainfo	List of Canadian Web sites
United Kingdom	www.coi.gov.uk/coi	U.K. Central Office of Information
United Nations	www.un.org	Latest UN projects and information
Health and Medicine		
The Interactive Patient	medicus.marshall.edu/medicus.htm	Simulates visit to doctor
Centers for Disease Control and Prevention (CDC)	www.cdc.gov	How to prevent and control disease
Solutions	disability.com	Resource for disability products and services
Women's Medical Health Page	www.best.com/~sirlou/wmhp.html	Articles and links to other sites

For an updated list: http://www.scsite.com/dc/ch7/websites.htm

GUIDE TO WORLD WIDE WEB SITES 7.45

CATEGORY/SITE NAME	LOCATION (all site locations begin with http://)	COMMENT
History		
American Memory	rs6.loc.gov/amhome.html	American history
Virtual Library History Index	history.cc.ukans.edu/history/www-history_main.html	Organized links to history sites / Links to history sites
Historical Text Archive	www.msstate.edu/Archives/History/USA/usa.html	U.S. documents, photos, and database
Humor		
Comedy Central Online	www.comcentral.com	From comedy TV network
The Dilbert Zone	www.unitedmedia.com/comics/dilbert	Humorous insights about working
Calvin & Hobbes Gallery	eus.kub.nl:2080/calvin-hobbes	Comic strip gallery
Late Show Top 10 Archive	www.cbs.com/lateshow/ttlist.html	David Letterman Top 10 lists
Internet		
EFF's Guide to the Internet	www.eff.org/papers/bdgtti/eegtti.html	Comprehensive guide to the Internet
WWW Frequently Asked Questions	www.boutell.com/faq	Common Web questions and answers
Internet Glossary	www.matisse.net/files/glossary.html	Definitions of Internet terms

For an updated list: http://www.scsite.com/dc/ch7/websites.htm

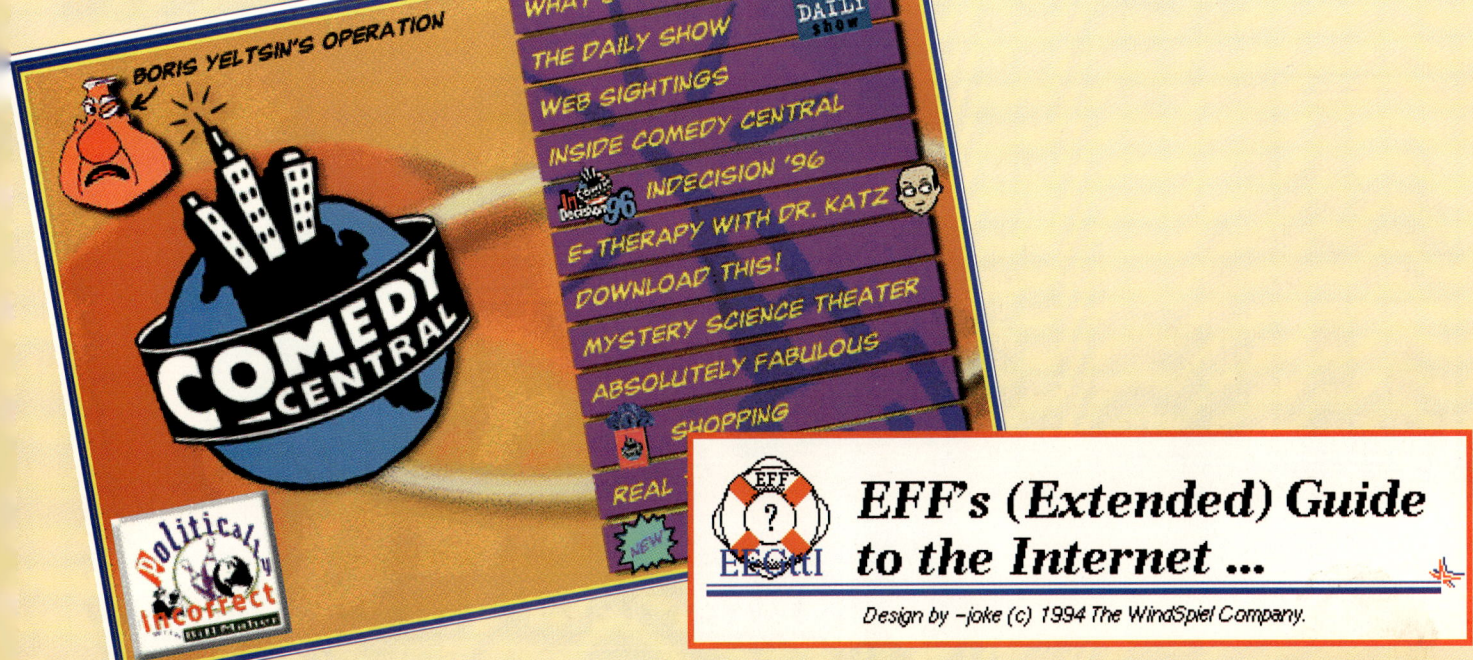

GUIDE TO WORLD WIDE WEB SITES

CATEGORY/SITE NAME	LOCATION (all site locations begin with http://)	COMMENT
Museums		
The Smithsonian	www.si.edu	Information and links to Smithsonian museums
U.S. Holocaust Memorial Museum	www.ushmm.org	Dedicated to World War II victims
University of California Museum of Paleontology	ucmp1.berkeley.edu/welcome.html	Great information on dinosaurs and other exhibits
News Sources		
The Electronic Newsstand	www.enews.com	Articles from worldwide publications
Pathfinder	www.pathfinder.com	Excerpts from Time-Warner magazines
Wired News	www.wired.com	*Wired* magazine online and HotWired Network
CNN Interactive	www.cnn.com	CNN all-news network
USA TODAY	www.usatoday.com	Latest U.S. and international news
C/NET	www.cnet.com	Technology news
Reference		
Internet Public Library	ipl.sils.umich.edu	Literature and reference works
The New York Public Library	gopher.nypl.org	Extensive reference and research material
Dictionary Library	math-www.uni-paderborn.de/HTML/Dictionaries.html	Links to many types of dictionaries
Bartlett's Quotations	www.cc.columbia.edu/acis/bartelby/bartlett	Organized, searchable database of famous quotes

For an updated list: http://www.scsite.com/dc/ch7/websites.htm

GUIDE TO WORLD WIDE WEB SITES   7.47

CATEGORY/SITE NAME	LOCATION (all site locations begin with http://)	COMMENT
Science		
The Nine Planets	seds.lpl.arizona.edu/nineplanets/nineplanets/nineplanets.html	Tour the solar system
American Institute of Physics	www.aip.org	Physics research information
Internet Chemistry Index	www.chemie.fu-berlin.de/chemistry/index	List of chemistry information sites
Exploratorium	www.exploratorium.edu	Interactive science exhibits
The NASA Homepage	www.nasa.gov	Information on U.S. space program
Shopping		
BizWeb	www.bizweb.com	Search for products from more than 1,000 companies
CommerceNet	www.commerce.net	Index of products and services
Ventana Online	www.vmedia.com	computer books and software
Internet Book Shop	www.bookshop.co.uk	780,000 titles on more than 2,000 subjects
Internet Shopping Network	www.internet.net	Specialty stores, hot deals, computer products
The Internet Mall™	www.internet-mall.com	Comprehensive list of Web businesses
Consumer World	www.consumerworld.org	Consumer information
Sports		
ESPNET SportsZone	www.espn.com	Latest sports news
NBA Basketball	www.nba.com	Information and links to team sites
NFL Football	www.nfl.com	Information and links to team sites
Sports Illustrated	www.pathfinder.com/si	Leading sports magazine

For an updated list: http://www.scsite.com/dc/ch7/websites.htm

7.48 GUIDE TO WORLD WIDE WEB SITES

CATEGORY/SITE NAME	LOCATION (all site locations begin with http://)	COMMENT
Travel		
InfoHub WWW Travel Guide	www.infohub.com	Worldwide travel information
Excite City.Net	www.city.net	Guide to world cities
Virtual Tourist II	wings.buffalo.edu/world/vt2	World map links to information database
TravelWeb℠	www.travelweb.com	Places to stay
Travelocity℠	www.travelocity.com	Online travel agency
Lonely Planet Travel Guides	www.lonelyplanet.com	Budget travel guides and stories
Unclassified!		
Cool Site of the Day	cool.infi.net	Different site each day
Cupid's Network™	www.cupidnet.com/cupid	Links to dating resources
Pizza Hut	www.pizzahut.com	Order pizza online (limited areas)
Weather		
The Weather Channel	www.weather.com	National and local forecasts
INTELLiCAST Guides	www.intellicast.com	International weather and skiing information

For an updated list: http://www.scsite.com/dc/ch7/websites.htm

Operating Systems and System Software

OBJECTIVES

After completing this chapter, you will be able to:

- Describe the three major categories of system software
- Define the term operating system
- Describe the functions of an operating system
- Understand what happens when an operating system is loaded
- Explain the difference between proprietary and portable operating systems
- Name and briefly describe the major operating systems that are being used today
- Discuss utilities and language translators

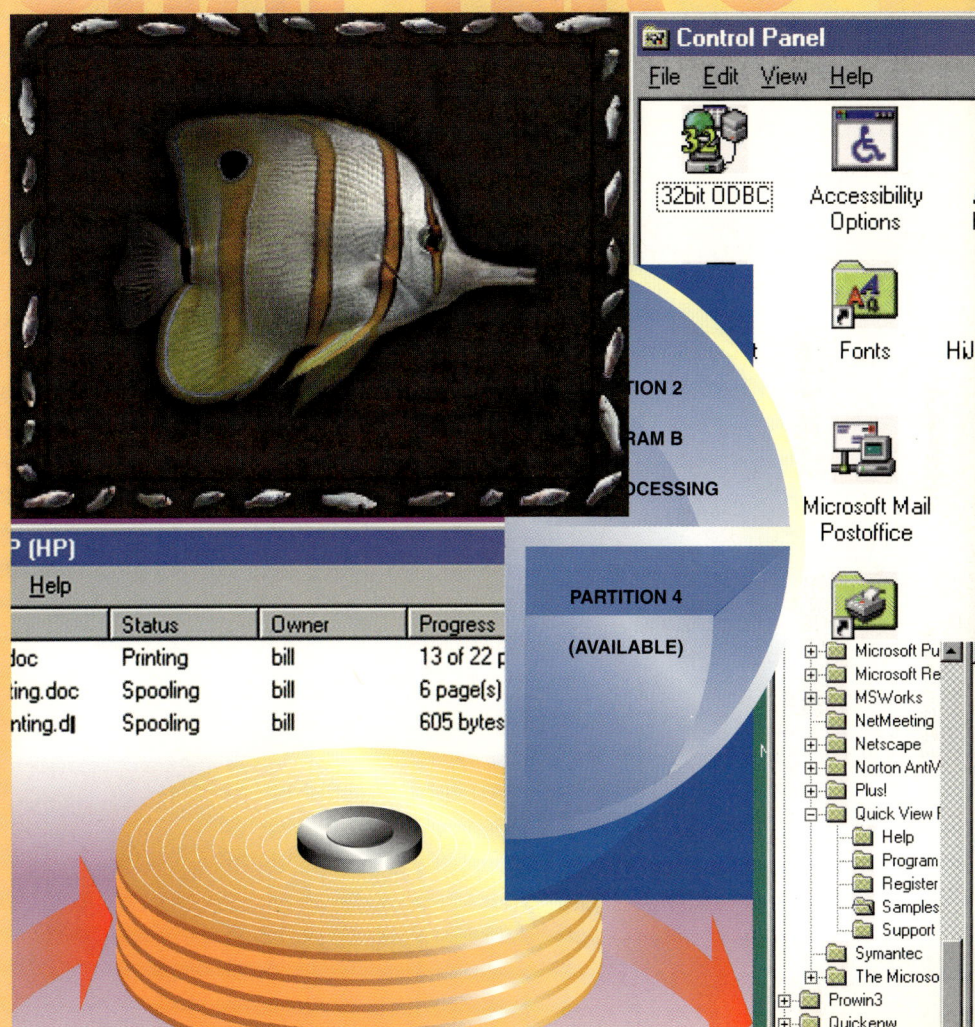

When most people think of software, they think of applications such as word processing, spreadsheet, and database. To run an application on a computer, however, another type of software is needed to serve as an interface between the user, the application, and the hardware. This software consists of programs that are referred to as the operating system. The operating system is just one example of a type of software called system software, which controls the operations of the computer hardware.

This chapter discusses functions performed by system software with a focus on the operating system, its functions, and what happens when the computer loads an operating system. Popular operating systems, utility programs, and language translators also are reviewed.

What Is System Software?

System software consists of all the programs, including the operating system, that are related to controlling the operations of the computer hardware. Some of the functions that system software performs include starting up the computer; loading, executing, and storing application programs; and storing and retrieving files. System software also performs a variety of other functions such as formatting disks, sorting data files, and translating program instructions into binary code that the computer can understand. System software can be classified into three major categories: operating systems, utilities, and language translators.

What Is an Operating System?

An **operating system (OS)** is a set of programs that manages the operations of a computer and functions as an interface between the user, the application programs, and the computer hardware (Figure 8-1). A computer cannot operate without an operating system.

The operating system usually is stored on the computer's hard disk drive. Each time you start the computer, the essential and more frequently used instructions in the operating system are copied from the disk and stored in the computer's memory. This set of essential instructions always resides in memory while you operate the computer and is called the *resident* portion of the operating system. The resident portion of the operating system is called by many different names: the **kernel**, **supervisor**, **monitor**, **executive**, **master program**, or **control program**. The individual instructions, or commands, contained in the resident portion of the operating system are called **internal commands**. The *nonresident* portion of the operating system consists of the less frequently used instructions, called **external commands**. The nonresident portion of the operating system remains on the disk while you operate the computer, ready to be loaded into memory whenever an external command is needed.

Figure 8-1
The operating system and other system software act as an interface between the user, the application software, and the computer hardware. As shown in this illustration, you can work with application software that interfaces with the operating system or you can interact directly with the operating system and other system software.

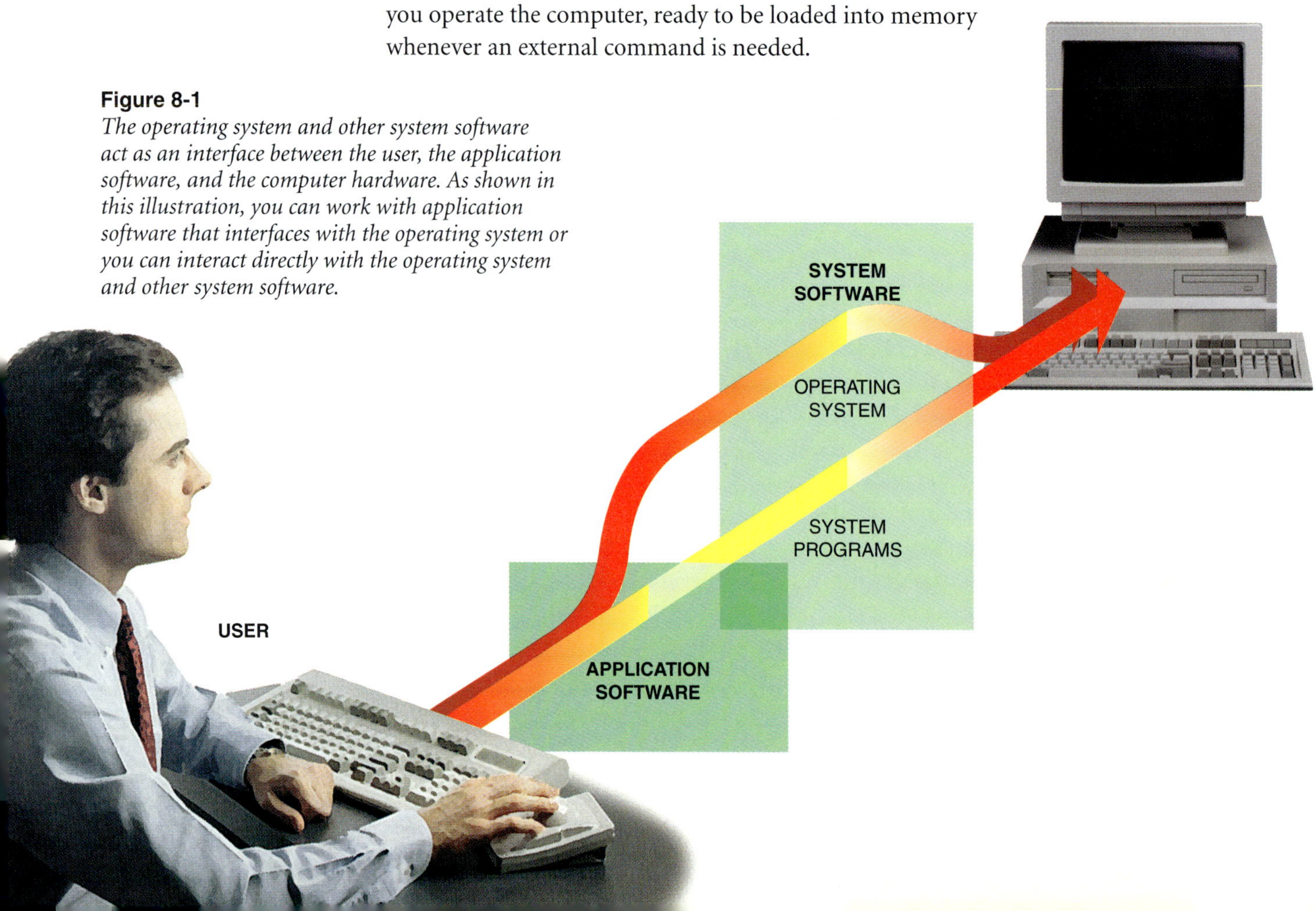

The **user interface** is the feature of the operating system that determines how you interact with the computer. The user interface controls how you enter data and commands (input) and how information is presented on the screen (output). The three types of user interfaces are command-line, menu-driven, and graphical (Figure 8-2). Many operating systems use a combination of these types.

If you are using a **command-line user interface,** you enter keywords (commands) that cause the computer to take a specific action, such as copying a file or sending a file to the printer. The set of commands you use to interact with the computer is called the **command language**.

A **menu-driven user interface** uses menus that present a set of commands or options that causes the computer to take a specific action. You can use the keyboard or a pointing device to select a menu item.

A **graphical user interface** (**GUI**) uses visual clues, such as icons, to help you perform tasks. Icons are small pictures that represent actions, programs, tasks, and other objects, such as documents. An icon of a printer, for example, might represent the Print command. Icons are helpful because they are memorable, use little space on-screen, and can be understood by most people.

Today, many graphical user interfaces incorporate browser-like features, which make them even easier to use. In these browser-like interfaces, icons function like Web hyperlinks, toolbar buttons resemble those used in graphical Web browsers, and multimedia applets can run directly on your screen.

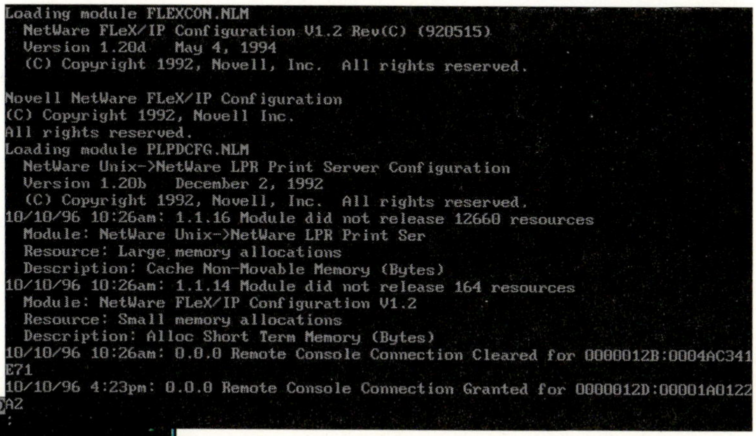

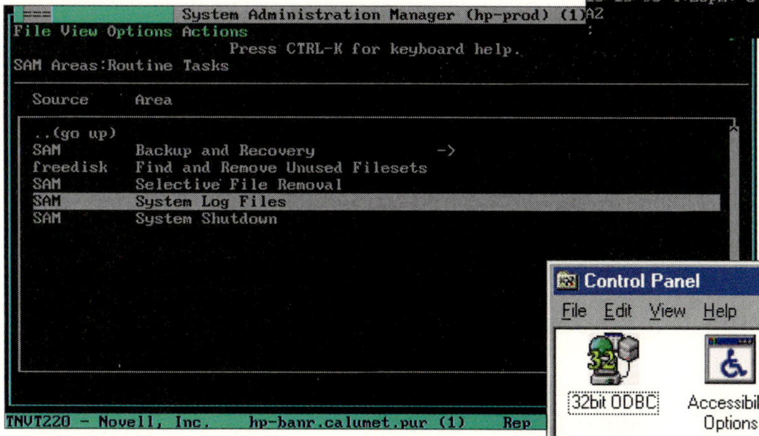

Figure 8-2
Examples of command-line, menu-driven, and graphical user interfaces. The user interface determines how information is presented on the screen and how you enter data and commands.

Functions of an Operating System

The operating system performs four functions that allow you and the application software to interact with the computer: process management, memory management, input and output management, and system administration.

Process Management

In operating system terms, a **process**, also called a **task**, is a program or part of a program that can be executed (run) separately. Different methods of managing processes include single tasking, multitasking, and multiprocessing (Figure 8-3).

Single Tasking Single tasking operating systems allow only one user to run one program at one time. Single tasking operating systems were the first type of operating systems developed; they still are used on some personal computers today. If you are working on a personal computer with a single tasking operating system, you can load only one application, such as a spreadsheet, into memory. If you want to work on another application, such as word processing, you must exit the spreadsheet application and load the word processing application into memory.

Multitasking Multitasking operating systems allow the computer to work on more than one process or task at a time. Multitasking operating systems used on personal computers usually support a single user running multiple programs at one time. The multitasking operating systems used on larger computers such as servers, minicomputers, and mainframes, usually are **multiuser timesharing** operating systems that allow multiple users to run the same program at one time. A World Wide Web search engine server, for example, would use a multiuser timesharing operating system to allow hundreds of users to enter search requests at one time.

For a description of multitasking, visit the Discovering Computers Chapter 8 inCyber page (http://www.scsite.com/dc/ch8/incyber.htm) and click Multitasking.

Operating System Process Management

Single Tasking:	Single user can run one program at a time
Multitasking:	Multiple programs can run
Context switching	User switches back and forth between programs
Cooperative multitasking	Programs switch when they reach a logical break point
Preemptive multitasking	Operating system switches programs based on allocated amount of time and priority
Multiprocessing:	Multiple CPUs
Asymmetric multiprocessing	Tasks assigned to specific CPUs; each CPU has its own memory
Symmetric multiprocessing	Tasks assigned to available CPUs; CPUs share memory

Figure 8-3
Operating systems divide work to be done into processes or tasks. This table summarizes the different methods operating systems use to manage processes.

Multitasking is accomplished in three ways: context switching, cooperative multitasking, and preemptive multitasking.

With **context switching**, multiple processes can be open but only one process is active. A context switch happens when one process relinquishes control of the CPU (stops executing) and another starts. For example, suppose you have two windows open, one with a word processing document and the other with a spreadsheet. As you switch back and forth between these applications, the operating system suspends activity on one task to allow you to work on the other. The operating system saves information about the currently running process so it can restart the process later from exactly where it left off.

With **cooperative multitasking**, multiple processes switch back and forth automatically when they reach logical break points, such as waiting for input. This method of multitasking relies on the processes to relinquish control to other processes. If the processes of one application require substantially more CPU time than those of other applications, problems can arise. Programs must be designed to cooperate in order to work together effectively in this environment.

With **preemptive multitasking**, the operating system prioritizes the processes to be performed and assigns a set amount of CPU time for the execution of each process. Certain processes, such as keyboard input or mouse movement, are given higher priority than other processes, such as sending data to the printer. Every few milliseconds, the CPU evaluates the processes waiting to be executed and chooses the one with the highest priority. This process then is assigned one or more increments of CPU time called a **time slice** (Figure 8-4). When the process finishes its work or the assigned time slice expires, the CPU executes the next highest priority process. If two or more processes have the same priority, such as two users inputting data at the same time, the CPU executes the process that was least recently worked on. Eventually, each process receives a time slice and is executed. Unless the system has a heavy workload, you may not even be aware that your program process was set aside temporarily. Before you notice a delay, the operating system has allocated your program process another time slice and processing continues.

Figure 8-4
A time slice is a brief amount of CPU time given to a process by the operating system. Higher priority (more important) processes receive more consecutive slices than lower priority applications. In this example, process B is the lowest priority, thus it receives only one time slice. Process A is the highest priority and receives three time slices.

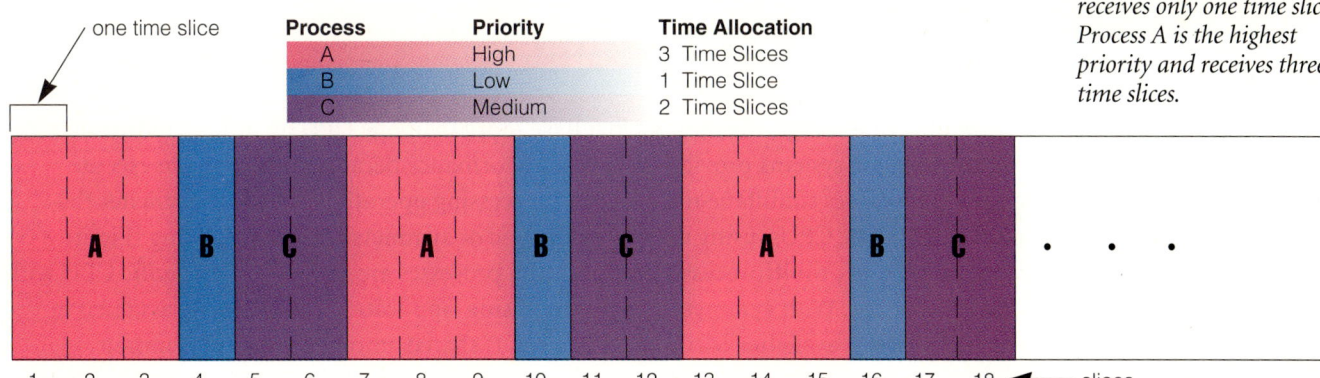

Some multitasking operating systems permit **multithreading**, which essentially is multitasking within a single program. A **thread** is the smallest amount of program code that can be executed; each thread contains a different action or command. Multithreading allows multiple threads to execute simultaneously within the same program, which frees the program to continue accepting commands (threads). You can continue entering commands without waiting until the previous command is finished processing. Your computer thus seems to run faster.

The terms foreground and background often are used to explain a process's priority in a multitasking operating system. A process is in the **foreground** if it is the currently active process or the process with the highest priority. A process is in the **background** if it has been suspended or has a lower priority.

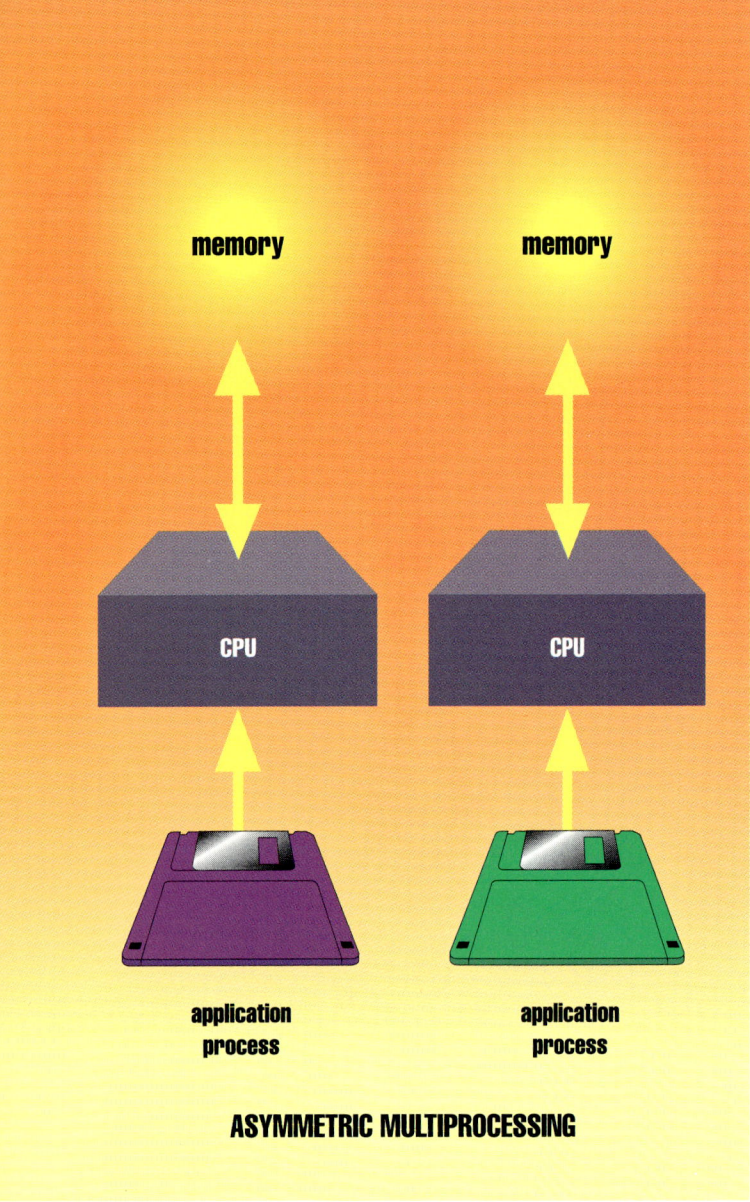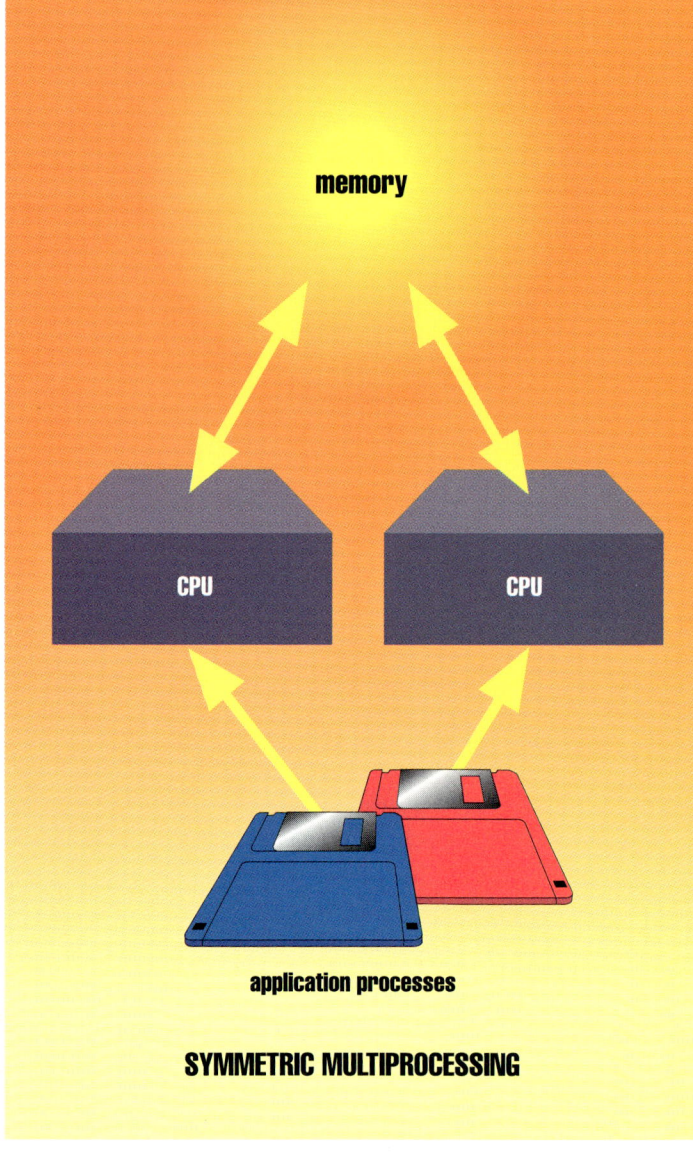

Figure 8-5
In asymmetric multiprocessing, application processes are assigned to a specific CPU that has its own memory. In symmetric multiprocessing, application processes are assigned to the first available CPU. Memory is shared by all of the CPUs.

Multiprocessing Computers that have more than one CPU are called **multiprocessors**. Multiprocessing systems provide increased performance because the CPUs can execute different processes simultaneously. A **multiprocessing operating system** coordinates the operations of the CPUs, using either asymmetric or symmetric multiprocessing (Figure 8-5). With **asymmetric multiprocessing**, application processes are assigned to a specific CPU with its own memory. With **symmetric multiprocessing**, application processes are assigned to whatever CPU is available. Memory, as needed, is shared among the CPUs. Symmetric multiprocessing is more complex, but achieves a higher processing rate because the operating system has more flexibility in assigning processes to available CPUs.

A unique advantage of multiprocessing systems is that, if one CPU fails, the operating system can shift work to the remaining CPUs. As discussed in Chapter 3, some multiprocessor systems have multiple CPUs designed into a single chip, while others have physically separate CPUs. A system with separate CPUs can serve as a **fault-tolerant computer**; that is, one that can continue to operate even if one of its components fails. Fault-tolerant computers are built with duplicate, or redundant, components such as CPUs, memory, input and output controllers, and disk drives. If any one of these components fail, the system continues to operate using the duplicate component. Fault-tolerant computers are used for airline reservation systems, communications networks, bank teller machines, and other systems that are of critical importance and must be operational at all times.

Memory Management

During processing, some areas of memory are used to store the operating system kernel, application program instructions, and data waiting to be processed. Other areas of memory are used temporarily for calculations, sorting, and other intermediate results. It is the operating system's job to allocate, or assign, each of these items to an area of memory. Data that has just been read into memory from an input device and data that is waiting to be sent to an output device is stored in areas of memory called **buffers**. The operating system assigns the buffers a location in memory and manages the data that is stored in them.

Operating systems also allocate at least some portion of memory for fixed areas called **partitions** (Figure 8-6). Some operating systems allocate all memory for partitions; others allocate only some memory for partitions and use the partitions to store only the kernel and the data held in buffers.

Another way of allocating memory is called virtual memory management, or virtual storage. **Virtual memory management** increases the amount of memory the operating system can use by allocating a set amount of disk space to be used to store items during processing, in addition to the existing memory. The amount of disk space allocated for use as memory is sometimes called the **swap file**.

Virtual memory management is used with multitasking operating systems to maximize the number of programs that can use memory at one time. Without virtual memory management, the operating system loads an entire program into memory during execution. With virtual memory management, the operating system loads only the portion of the program that currently is being used into memory. The most common way operating systems perform virtual memory management is by using a process called paging.

With **paging**, a fixed number of bytes, called a **page**, is transferred from the disk to memory each time data or program instructions are needed. The size of a page, or *frame*, generally ranges from 512 to 4,000 bytes; the exact page size is determined by the operating system. Each time data or instructions are needed, the operating system transfers a page into memory. The operating system continues to bring pages into memory until the

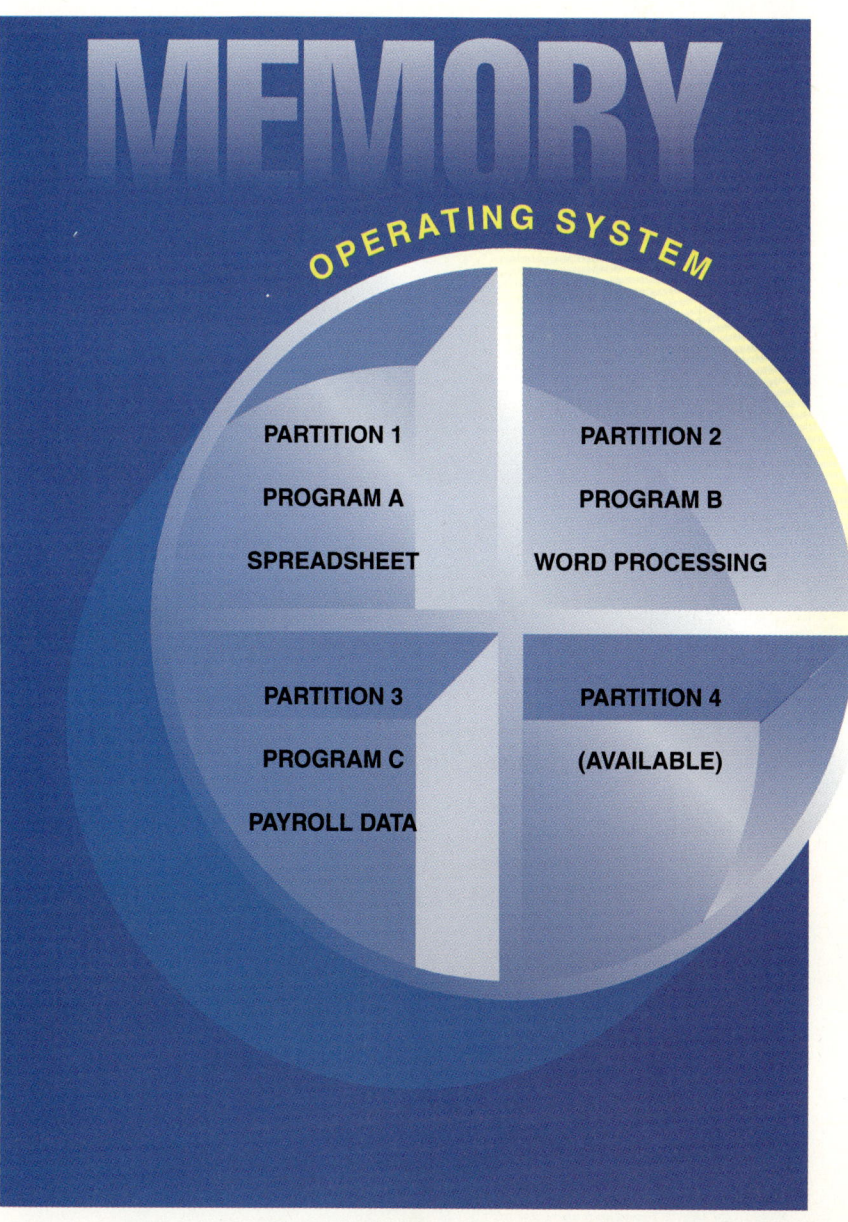

Figure 8-6
Operating systems keep track of programs and their related data by assigning them to a portion of memory called a partition.

area reserved for pages is full. If additional pages are required, the operating system makes room for them by writing one or more of the pages currently in memory back to the disk. This process is referred to as **swapping** (Figure 8-7). The operating system usually swaps the least recently used page back to the disk.

Input and Output Management

At any given time, a computer has to handle many different input and output processes. Two input devices, for example, might be sending data to the computer at the same time that the CPU is sending data to an output or storage device. The operating system is responsible for managing these input and output processes.

The operating system manages these processes differently, depending on the device. If an output device, such as a tape drive, is allocated to a specific user or application, the operating system has to manage input and output requests from only one user or application. If a device such as a disk drive is allocated to multiple users and applications, the operating system has to monitor and prioritize requests from multiple users and applications. The operating system keeps track of disk read and write requests, stores these requests in buffers along with the associated data for write requests, and usually processes them sequentially.

Figure 8-7
With virtual memory management, the operating system expands the amount of memory to include disk space. Data and program instructions are transferred in fixed amounts called pages. Pages are transferred to and from memory and disk as needed. To make room in memory for a new page, the least recently used page is swapped back to the disk or swap file.

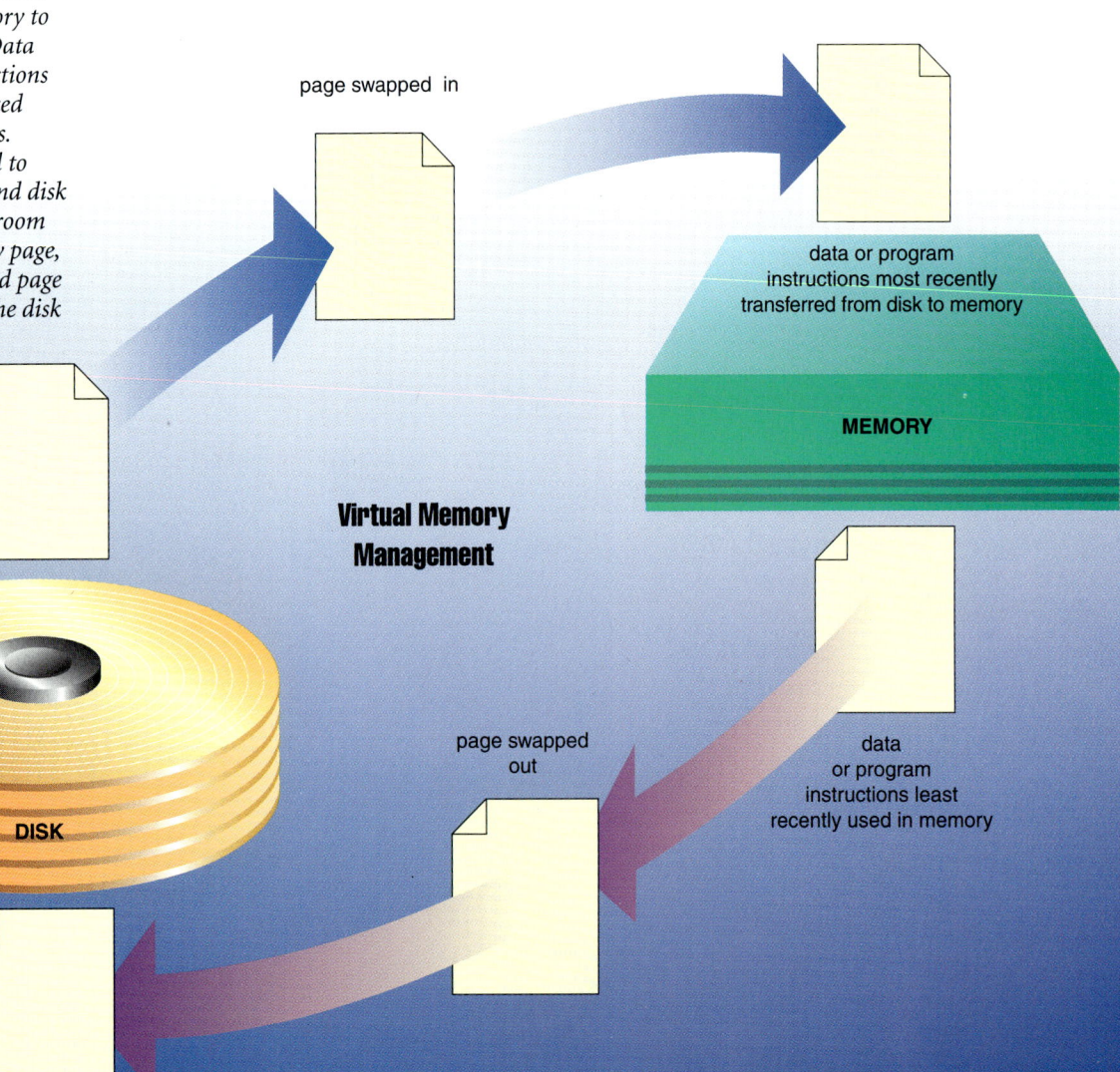

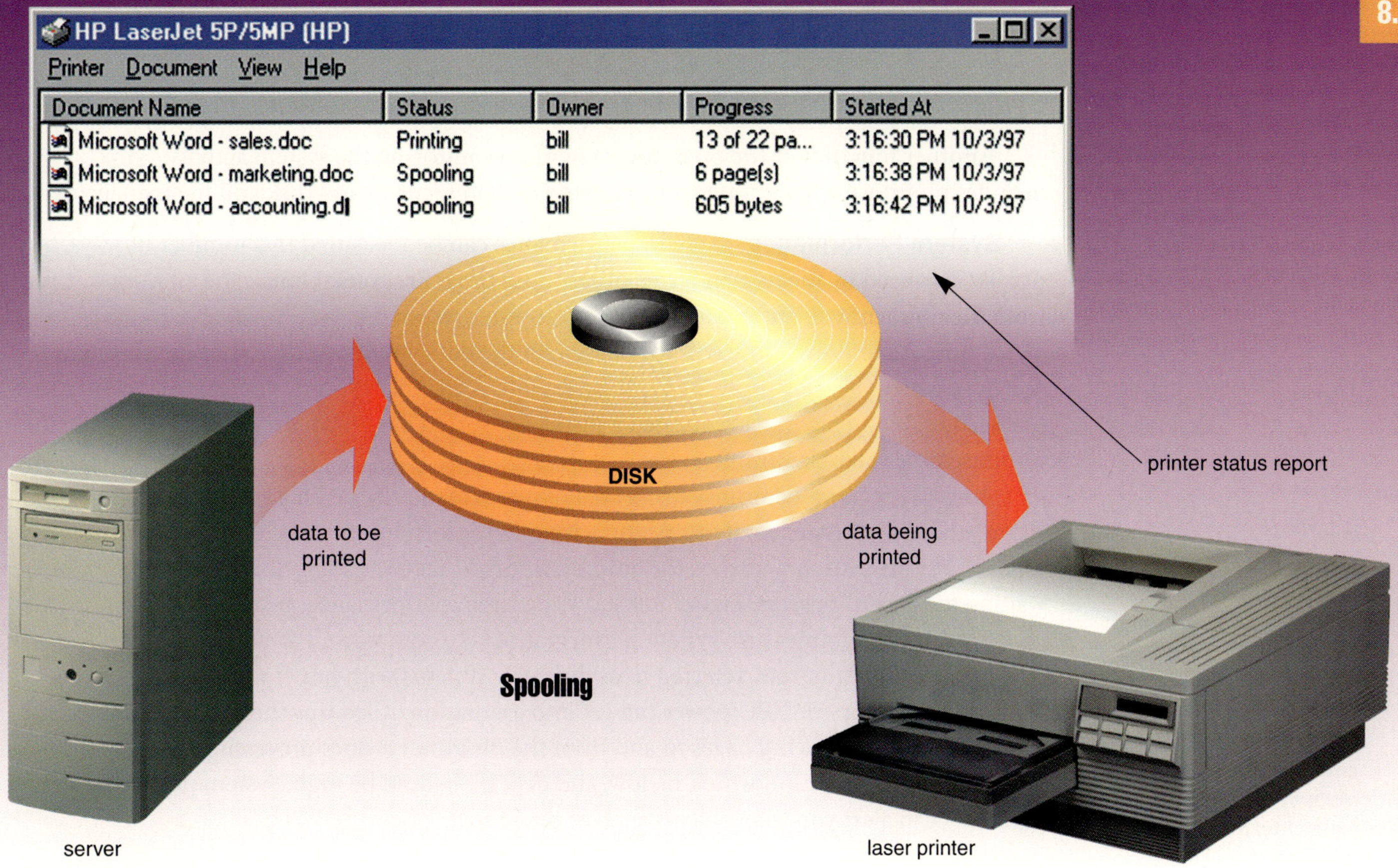

Figure 8-8
Spooling increases both CPU and printer efficiency by writing reports to the disk before they are printed. Writing to the disk is much faster than writing directly to the printer. After the reports are written to the disk, the CPU can begin processing other programs while the report is printing. A printer status report shows the reports in the print spool (the reports waiting to be printed).

Because printers are relatively slow devices compared to other computer system devices, the operating system uses a technique called spooling to increase printer efficiency. With **spooling** (Figure 8-8), a report is first written (saved) to the disk before it is printed. Writing to the disk is much faster than writing to the printer. For example, a report that averages one-half hour of printing time may take only one minute to write to the disk. After the report is written to the disk, the CPU is available to process other programs. The report saved on the disk can be printed at a later time or, on a multitasking operating system, a print program is started. The print program processes the **print spool**, which are the reports on the disk waiting to be printed, while other programs are running. The terms *spool* and *spooling* come from the idea that storing reports temporarily on the disk is like winding thread onto a spool so it can be unwound at a later time.

Because hardware devices use different commands to input and output data, the operating system uses programs called **device drivers** to communicate with each device. The mouse, keyboard, monitor, printer, and other peripheral devices all require separate device drivers. If one of these devices is changed or a new hardware device is added to the system, a new device driver is needed. Installation of new devices is easier if the device and the operating system support Plug and Play technology. With **Plug and Play technology**, the operating system recognizes any new devices and assists in the installation of the device by automatically loading the necessary driver programs and checking for conflicts with other devices. Because they are specific to a hardware device, most device drivers are supplied by the hardware device manufacturer. Some device drivers, especially for common devices such as the mouse, come with the operating system.

inCyber

For reviews of Plug and Play technology, visit the Discovering Computers Chapter 8 inCyber page (http://www.scsite.com/dc/ch8/incyber.htm) and click Plug and Play.

System Administration

Another function of the operating system is monitoring the system activity. This includes monitoring system performance and system security and disk and file management.

System Performance System performance can be measured in a number of ways, but usually is gauged by the user in terms of response time. **Response time** is the amount of time from the moment you enter data until the computer responds.

A system's response time will vary based on the data you have entered or the command you have issued. If you simply are typing data into a file, the response time usually is less than one second. If you have just requested a display of sorted data from several files, however, the response time might be minutes.

A more precise way of measuring system performance is to run a program designed to record and report system activity. Along with other information, these programs usually report **CPU utilization**, which is the amount of time that the CPU is working and not idle, waiting for data to process. Figure 8-9 shows a system performance measurement report.

Another way to measure system performance is to compare CPU utilization with the disk input and output rate, referred to as disk I/O. Systems with heavy workloads and insufficient memory or CPU power can get into a situation called **thrashing**, where the system spends more time moving pages to and from the disk than it does processing data. In this situation, CPU utilization would be low, and disk I/O would be high. System performance reporting can alert you to problems such as thrashing.

Figure 8-9
Most operating systems come with programs that help you monitor system performance. This screen, from the Windows 95 operating system, graphically displays the amount of CPU utilization and disk activity.

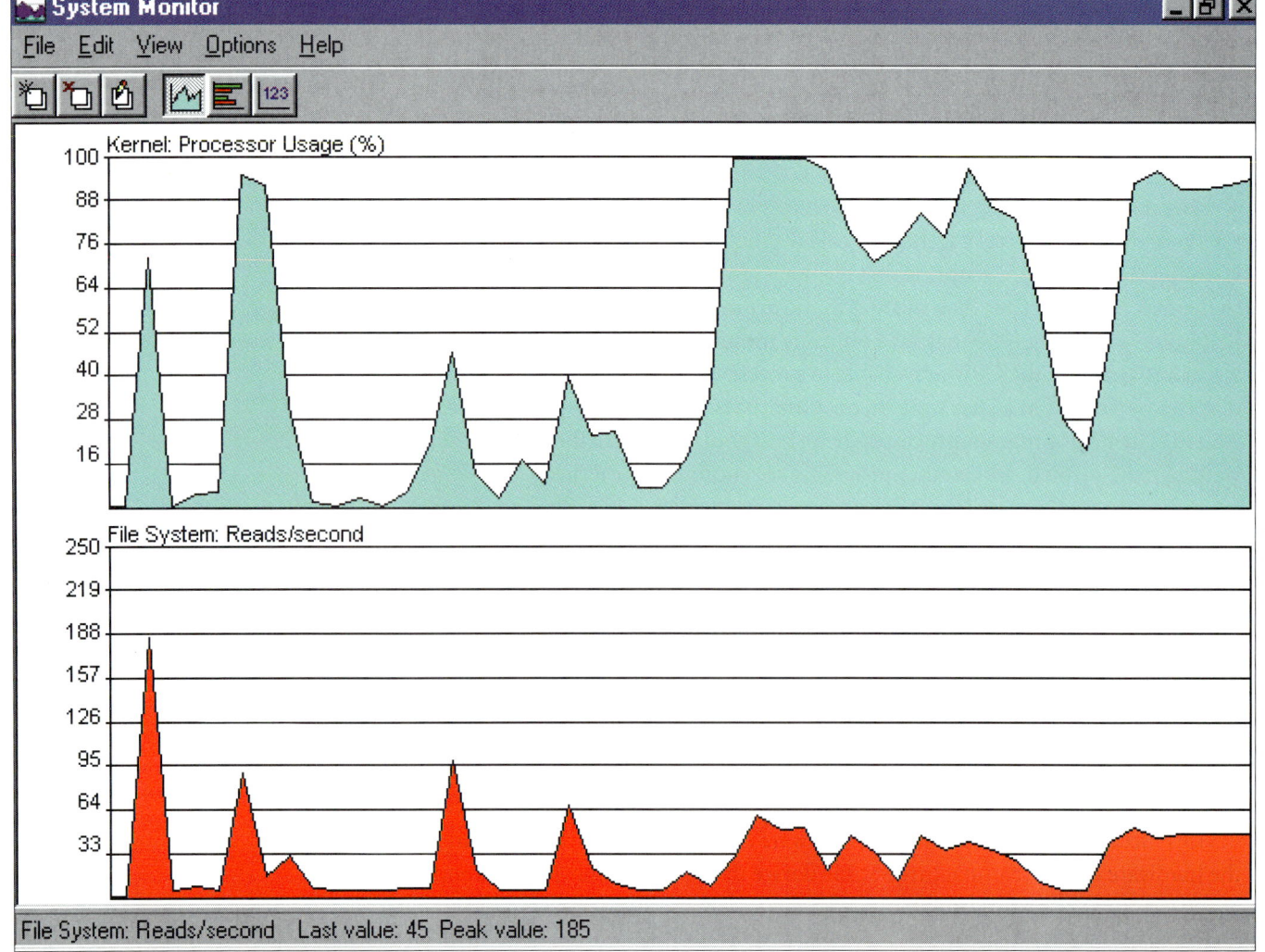

FUNCTIONS OF AN OPERATING SYSTEM **8.11**

Logon code; usually specifies application to be used

User ID; usually name of user

Password; unique word or combination of characters known only to user

Figure 8-10
The logon code, user ID, and password all must be entered correctly before the user is allowed to use the computer. To hide the password, an asterisk usually is displayed as each password character is typed.

System Security Most multiuser operating systems allow each user to have a logon code, a user ID, and a password. Each is a word or series of characters (Figure 8-10). A **logon code** usually identifies the application that will be used, such as accounting, sales, or manufacturing. A **user ID** identifies the user, such as Jeffrey Ryan or Mary Gonzales. The **password** usually is confidential; often it is known only to you and the computer system administrator. As you enter your password, most systems will hide the actual password characters by displaying a series of asterisks.

Before you are allowed to use a system or an application, you must enter your logon code, user ID, and password correctly. Your entries are compared with entries stored in an authorization file. If they do not match, you are denied access. Both successful and unsuccessful logon attempts often are recorded in a file so management can review who is using or attempting to use the system. These logs also can be used to allocate computer system expenses based on the percentage of system use by an organization's various departments.

For a list of security tools available on the Internet, visit the Discovering Computers Chapter 8 inCyber page (http://www.scsite.com/dc/ch8/incyber.htm) and click Security System.

Disk and File Management All operating systems contain programs that perform functions related to disk and file management. Some of these functions include formatting hard and floppy disks, listing files stored on the system, deleting files from a disk, copying files from one storage device to another, renaming stored files, and creating folders and directories to organize files.

Loading an Operating System

The process of loading an operating system into memory is called **booting** the system. Figure 8-11 shows information that is displayed during this process. The actual information displayed will vary depending on the make of the computer and the equipment installed. The boot process is similar for large and small computer systems. The following steps explain what occurs during the boot process on a personal computer using the Windows 95 operating system.

1. When you turn on your computer, the power supply distributes current to the motherboard and the other devices located in the system unit case.

2. The surge of electricity causes the CPU chip to reset itself and look to the BIOS chip for instructions on how to proceed. **BIOS**, which stands for **Basic Input/Output System**, is a set of instructions that provides the interface between the operating system and the hardware devices. The BIOS is stored in a read-only memory (ROM) chip.

3. The BIOS chip begins a set of tests to make sure the equipment is working correctly. The tests, called the **POST**, for **Power On Self Test**, check the memory, keyboard, buses, and expansion cards. After some of the early tests are completed, the BIOS instructions are copied into memory where they can be executed faster than in ROM.

4. The results of POST tests are compared with data in a CMOS chip on the motherboard. The CMOS chip contains key information about system components, such as the amount of memory and number and type of disk drives available. The CMOS chip is updated whenever new components are installed.

5. After the POST tests are completed successfully, the BIOS begins looking for the boot program that will load the operating system. Usually, it first looks in floppy disk drive A.

For information about BIOS and CMOS, visit the Discovering Computers Chapter 8 inCyber page (http://www.scsite.com/dc/ch8/incyber.htm) and click BIOS.

BIOS version number and copyright notice

total amount of memory displays after memory test

device detected and tested

message indicating Windows 95 operating system beginning to load

sound card and CD-ROM device drivers loaded

If an operating system disk is not loaded in drive A, the BIOS looks in drive C, which is the drive letter usually given to the first hard disk drive.

6. The boot program is loaded into memory and executed. The boot program then begins loading the resident portion, or kernel, of the operating system into memory.

7. The operating system then loads system configuration information. System configuration information is contained in several files called the registry. The **registry** files contain information on which hardware and software is installed and individual user preferences for mouse speed, passwords, and other user-specific information. In earlier versions of the Windows operating system, hardware and software configuration information was contained in the **CONFIG.SYS** and **AUTOEXEC.BAT** files and other files ending in the letters *ini*.

8. For each hardware device identified in the registry, such as the sound card, a CD-ROM drive, or a scanner, the operating system loads a device driver program. A device driver tells the computer how to communicate with a device.

9. The remainder of the operating system is loaded and the desktop and icons display on the screen. The operating system executes programs in the Start Up folder, which contains a list of programs to start automatically when you start Windows 95.

Figure 8-11
An example of information displayed during the boot process.

Popular Operating Systems

The first operating systems were developed by manufacturers specifically for the computers in their product line. These operating systems, called **proprietary operating systems**, were limited to a specific vendor or computer model. When manufacturers introduced another computer or model, they often produced an improved and different operating system. Because programs are designed to be used with a particular operating system, users who wanted to switch computer models or vendors had to convert their existing programs to run under the new operating system.

Today, however, the trend is toward **portable operating systems** that will run on many manufacturers' computers. The advantage of portable operating systems is that you can change computer models or vendors, yet retain existing software and data files, which usually represent a sizable investment in time and money.

New versions of an operating system usually will run software written for the previous version of the operating system. If an application written for the old version of the operating system can run under the new version, it is said to be **upward compatible**. If an application written for the new version of an operating system also can run under the previous version, it is said to be **downward compatible**.

The following section discusses some of the more popular operating systems.

DOS

For information about DOS, visit the Discovering Computers Chapter 8 inCyber page (http://www.scsite.com/dc/ch8/incyber.htm) and click DOS.

DOS (Disk Operating System) refers to several single tasking operating systems that were developed in the early 1980s for IBM-compatible personal computers. The two more widely used versions of DOS were MS-DOS and PC-DOS. Both were developed by Microsoft Corporation and were essentially the same. Microsoft developed **PC-DOS (Personal Computer DOS)** for IBM; IBM installed and sold it on its computer systems. At the same time, Microsoft marketed and sold **MS-DOS (Microsoft DOS)** to makers of IBM-compatible personal computer systems.

New versions of DOS have been and continue to be developed. Improvements to the later versions of DOS include the capability of running with a command-line or menu-driven user interface and better memory and disk management. Because it does not offer a full graphical user interface and it cannot take full advantage of modern 32-bit microprocessors, DOS no longer is a top-selling operating system. DOS does, however, still have a large installed base of users. An estimated 70 million computers used some version of DOS during its peak.

POPULAR OPERATING SYSTEMS **8.15**

Windows 3.x

Windows 3.x refers to three versions of Microsoft's Windows operating system: Windows 3.0, Windows 3.1, and Windows 3.11. Sometimes, these versions also are referred to as Microsoft Windows or simply Windows (with a capital W). **Windows 3.0** was the first widely used graphical user interface for IBM-compatible personal computers. **Windows 3.1** (Figure 8-12) provided a number of improvements to version 3.0. Windows 3.11, also called **Windows for Workgroups**, is a networking version of Windows 3.1. Although the 3.x versions commonly are referred to as operating systems, actually they are operating environments. An **operating environment** is a graphical user interface that works in combination with an operating system to simplify its use. The operating environment of Windows 3.x, for example, was designed to work with DOS, which is the actual operating system. Common features of an operating environment (such as Windows) include support for mouse usage, icons, and pull-down menus. Windows 3.x also supports cooperative multitasking, so you can have several applications open at the same time.

Closely related to operating environments are operating system shell programs. Like an operating environment, a **shell** acts as an interface between you and the operating system. Operating system shells, however, usually do not support applications windowing or graphics and have only a limited number of utility functions such as file maintenance.

inCyber

For links to resources for Windows 3.x, visit the Discovering Computers Chapter 8 inCyber page (http://www.scsite.com/dc/ch8/incyber.htm) and click Windows 3.x.

Figure 8-12
Microsoft Windows 3.1 is a widely used graphical user interface for IBM-compatible personal computers.

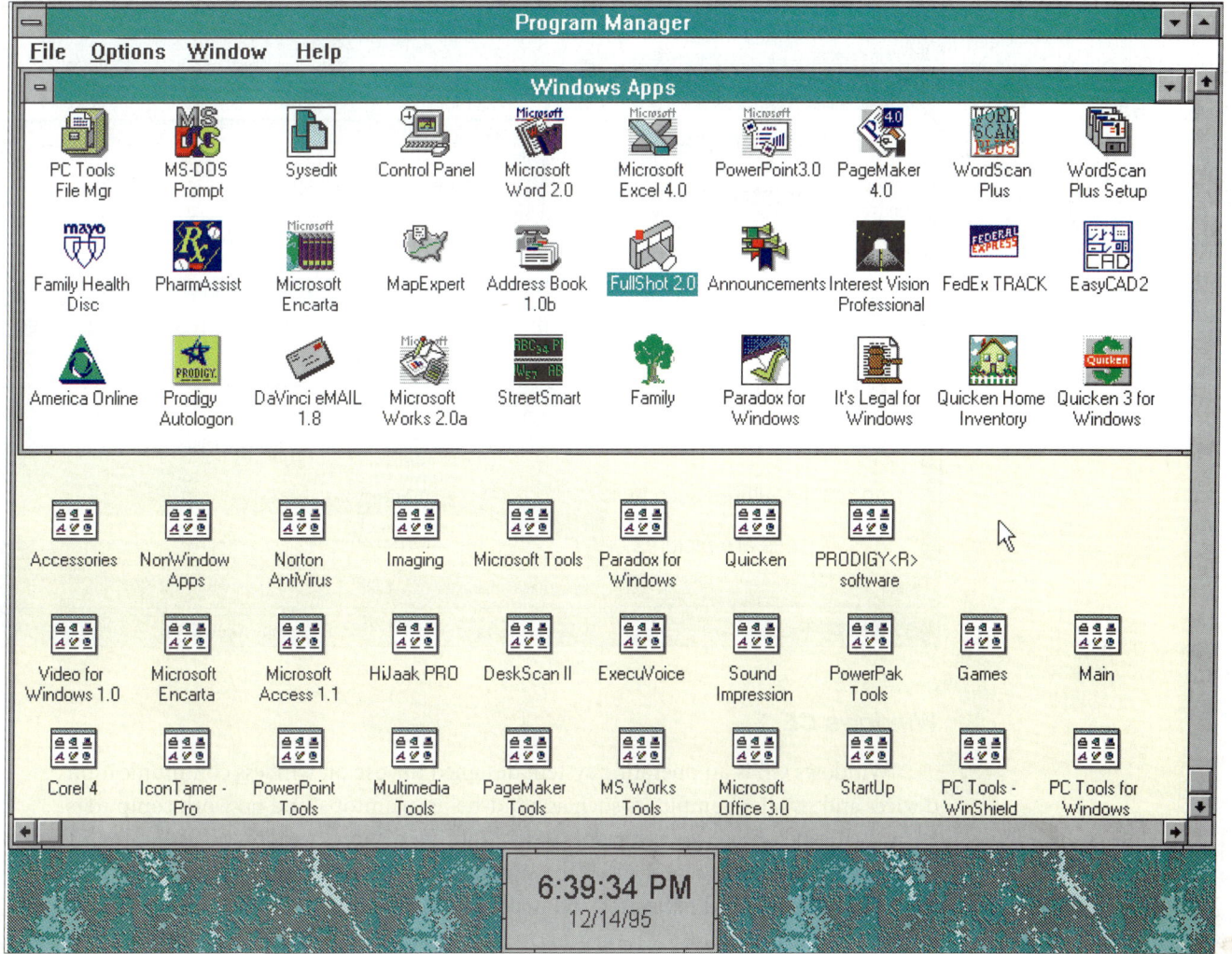

Windows 95 and Beyond

Instead of naming the next major version of its operating system Windows 4.0, Microsoft named it Windows 95, indicating the year it was released. **Windows 95**, also referred to as **Win 95**, is a true operating system and not an operating environment as were the 3.x versions of Windows. Windows 95 thus does not require a separate version of DOS, although some DOS features are included for compatibility. One advantage of Windows 95 is its improved graphical user interface, which makes working with files and programs easier than earlier versions (Figure 8-13). Another advantage is that most programs run faster under Windows 95, because it is written to take advantage of newer 32-bit processors and supports preemptive multitasking. For older, 16-bit programs, Win 95 also supports cooperative multitasking. Windows 95 includes support for peer-to-peer networking and e-mail.

Newer versions of Windows support several different user interfaces, including the traditional Windows interface and new, browser-like interfaces. These new interfaces combine the functionality of Windows with a Web browser and a multimedia Web page. Icons work like hyperlinks; a small window displays television-style news; and an animated ticker provides stock updates, news, or other information. You can display three different files at once in small windows, called **frames**, and move through files by clicking browser-like toolbar buttons. You also can use the interface as a regular Web browser to view Web pages, create Web shortcuts that are updated automatically, and more.

> **inCyber**
>
> For a comprehensive source of Windows 95 tools and information, visit the Discovering Computers Chapter 8 inCyber page (http://www.scsite.com/dc/ch8/incyber.htm) and click Windows 95.

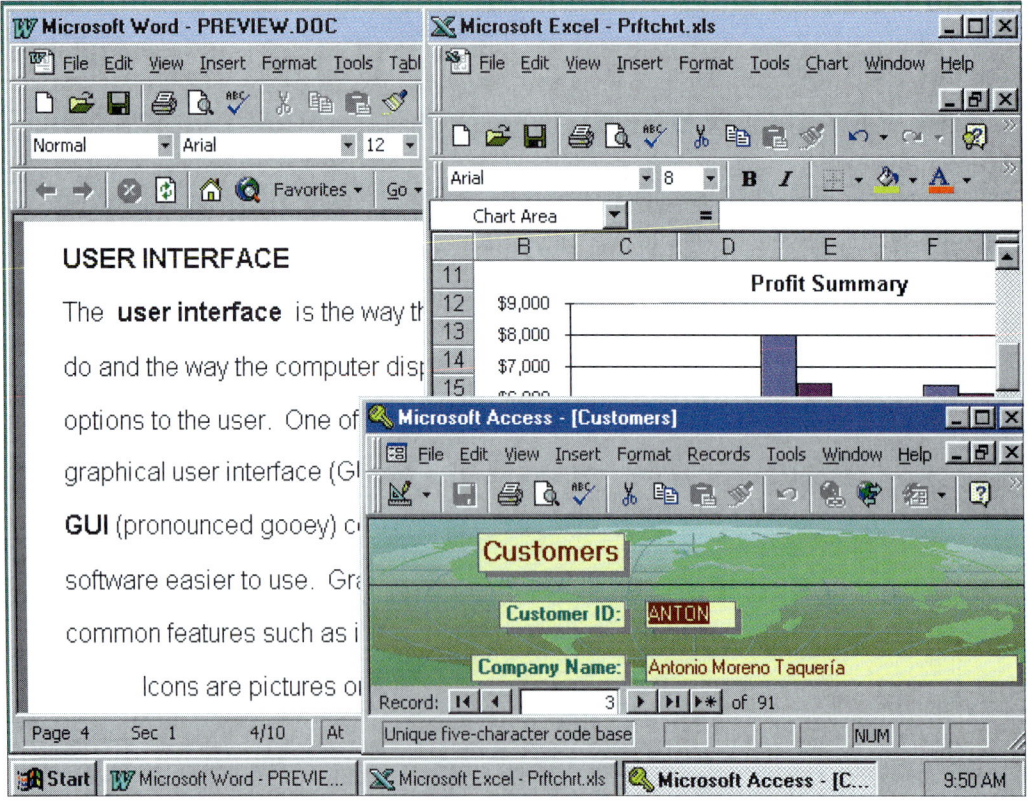

Figure 8-13
Microsoft Windows 95 is a sophisticated graphical user interface operating system that offers built-in peer-to-peer networking and e-mail.

Windows CE

Windows CE is an operating system designed for use on wireless communication devices and smaller computers such as hand-helds, palmtops, and network computers. Because it is designed for use on smaller computing devices, Windows CE requires little memory. On most of these devices, the Windows CE interface incorporates many elements of the Windows graphical user interface. It also has multitasking, multithreading, and e-mail and Internet capabilities.

POPULAR OPERATING SYSTEMS   8.17

Windows NT

Microsoft's **Windows NT** (for New Technology), also referred to as **NT**, is a sophisticated graphical user interface operating system designed for client-server networks. Like Windows 95, NT is a complete operating system, not an operating environment. Two versions of NT exist: the Server version for network servers and the Workstation version for computers connected to the network. NT uses a modular design. The central module, called the Executive, contains the kernel and implements virtual memory management, process management, and other basic operating system functions. All other operating system functions are performed by separate modules, which are started by the Executive when they are needed. Other NT features include the following:

- Capability of working with multiple CPUs using symmetric multiprocessing
- Preemptive multitasking and multithreading
- Support of most major networking communications protocols
- System performance measurement
- User and account system security

Windows NT Server also includes tools for developing Internet Web pages and operating a Web page server. Because they are more complex than other versions of Windows, both versions of Windows NT require more disk space, memory, and faster processors.

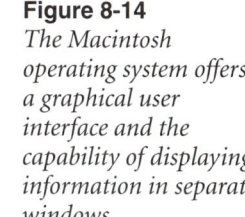

inCyber

For descriptions of Internet resources for Windows NT, visit the Discovering Computers Chapter 8 inCyber page (http://www.scsite.com/dc/ch8/incyber.htm) and click Windows NT.

Macintosh

The Apple **Macintosh** multitasking operating system was the first commercially successful graphical user interface (Figure 8-14). It was released with Macintosh computers in 1984; since then, it has set the standard for operating system ease of use and has been the model for most of the new graphical user interfaces developed for non-Macintosh systems. For most of its history, the Macintosh operating system was available only on computers manufactured by Apple. In recent years, however, Apple has licensed the operating system to other computer manufacturers. Distinctive features of the latest version of the operating system, called **MacOS**, include built-in networking support, electronic mail, and an extensive step-by-step Help system called Apple Guide.

Figure 8-14
The Macintosh operating system offers a graphical user interface and the capability of displaying information in separate windows.

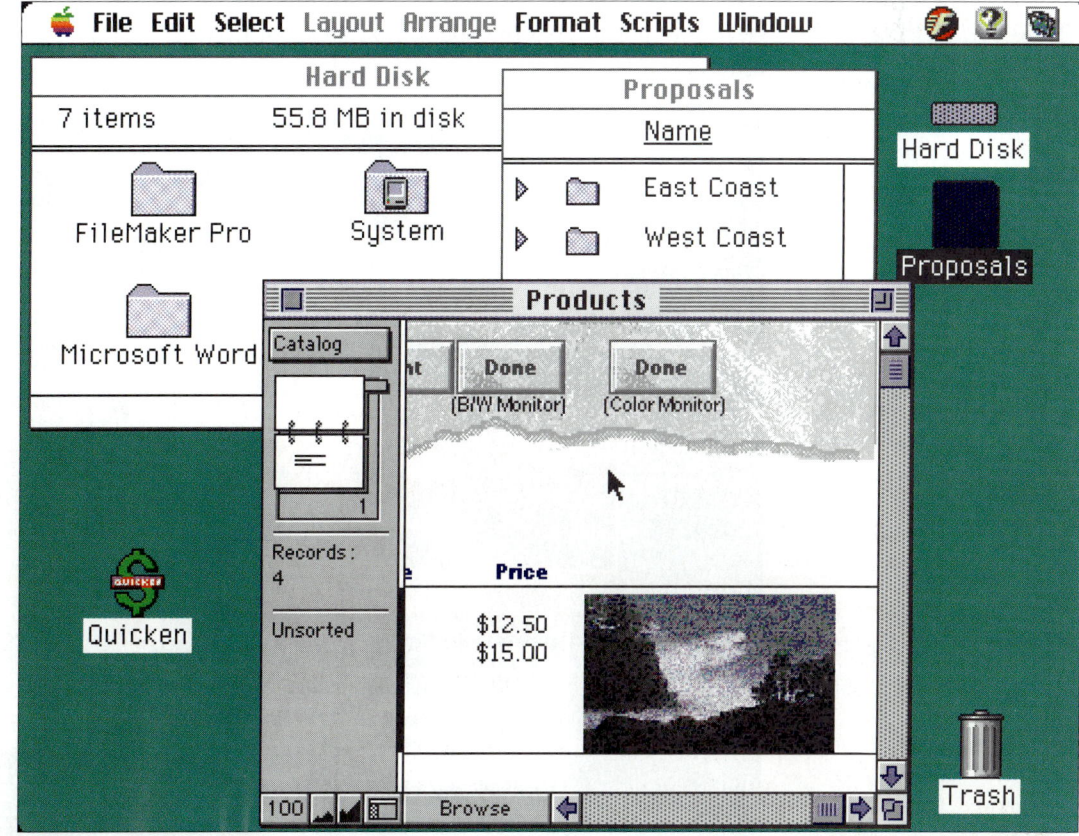

OS/2

For links to OS/2 resources on the Internet, visit the Discovering Computers Chapter 8 inCyber page (http://www.scsite.com/dc/ch8/incyber.htm) and click OS/2.

OS/2 is IBM's graphical user interface operating system designed to work with 32-bit microprocessors (Figure 8-15). In addition to its capability of running programs written specifically for OS/2, the operating system also can run programs written for DOS and most Windows 3.x programs. The latest version of OS/2, called OS/2 Warp 4, includes the following features:

- Graphical user interface that displays 3-D shadowed icons
- Capability of running Java applets without a Web browser
- Capability of working with multiple CPUs using symmetric multiprocessing
- Preemptive multitasking and multithreading
- Speaker-independent voice recognition that you can use to input data and commands
- Desktop objects that allow you to connect directly to Internet documents and services

Because of IBM's long association with business computing and OS/2's strong networking support, OS/2 has been most widely used by businesses. Like Windows NT, a separate version of OS/2 exists for use on a server.

UNIX

UNIX is a multiuser, multitasking operating system developed in the early 1970s by scientists at Bell Laboratories. Because of federal regulations, Bell Labs (a subsidiary of AT&T) was prohibited from actively promoting UNIX in the commercial marketplace. Bell Labs instead licensed UNIX for a low fee to numerous colleges and universities where it obtained a wide following and was implemented on many different types of computers. After deregulation of the telephone companies in the 1980s, UNIX was licensed to many hardware and software companies. Today, a version of UNIX is available for most computers of all sizes. This widespread availability of UNIX is just one of its advantages. Another advantage is UNIX's capability of handling a high volume of transactions in a multiuser environment. UNIX often is used as the operating system for network servers, especially servers that use multiple CPUs.

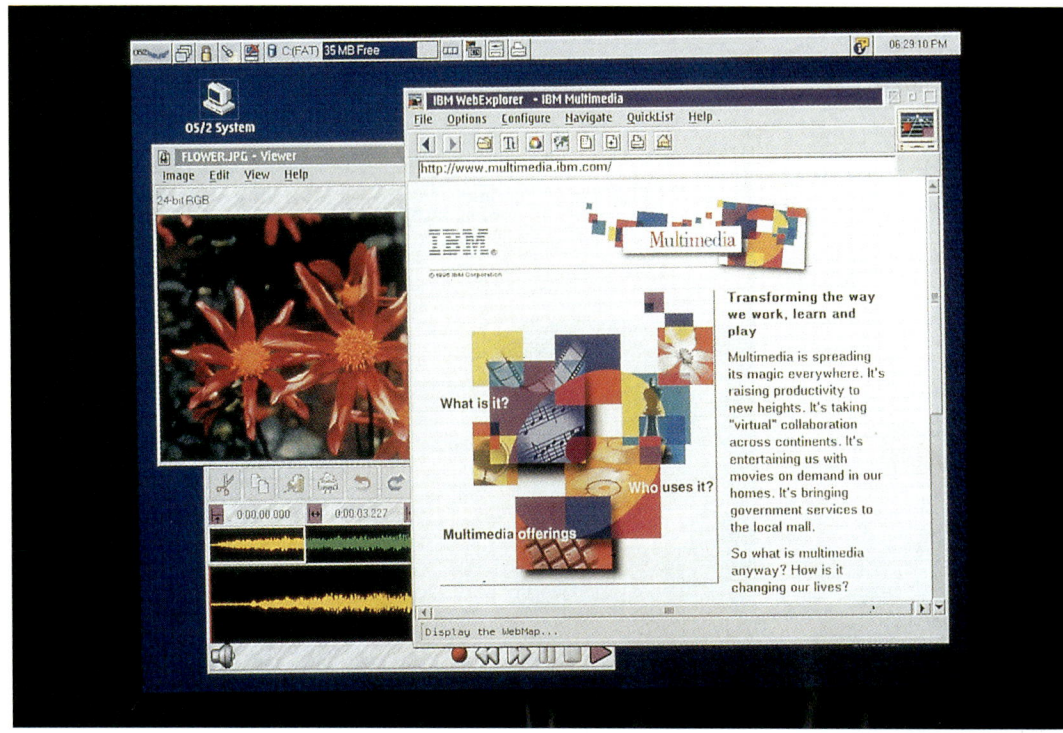

Figure 8-15
IBM's OS/2 operating system is used primarily by businesses and organizations. The latest version includes speech recognition technology.

UNIX does have some weaknesses, however. UNIX is a command-line operating system and many of its commands are difficult to remember and use. Some versions of UNIX do offer a graphical user environment to help reduce this problem. UNIX also lacks some of the system administration features offered by other operating systems. Finally, several widely used versions of UNIX exist, each of which is slightly different. To move application software from one of these UNIX versions to another, you must convert some programs.

NetWare

NetWare from Novell is a widely used network operating system designed for client-server networks. NetWare has two parts; a server portion that resides on the network server, and a client portion that resides on each client computer connected to the network. The server portion of NetWare allows you to share hardware devices attached to the server (such as a printer), as well as any files or application software stored on the server. The main job of the client portion of NetWare is to communicate with the server. Client computers also have a local operating system, such as Windows.

For information on Novell NetWare, visit the Discovering Computers Chapter 8 inCyber page (http://www.scsite.com/dc/ch8/incyber.htm) and click NetWare.

Utilities

Utility programs perform specific tasks related to managing computer resources or files. Most operating systems include many utility programs. These utility programs usually handle frequently performed tasks such as copying and moving files and formatting disks. You also can purchase single, stand-alone utility programs or a package of utility programs designed to work together. These utility programs usually are improvements over the utilities that come with the operating system. A brief description of some of the tasks performed by utility programs follows:

- **File Viewer** The file management programs of some operating systems merely list the names and size of files. To view the contents of a file, you have to start an application program and open the file. Figure 8-16 shows a file viewer utility screen.

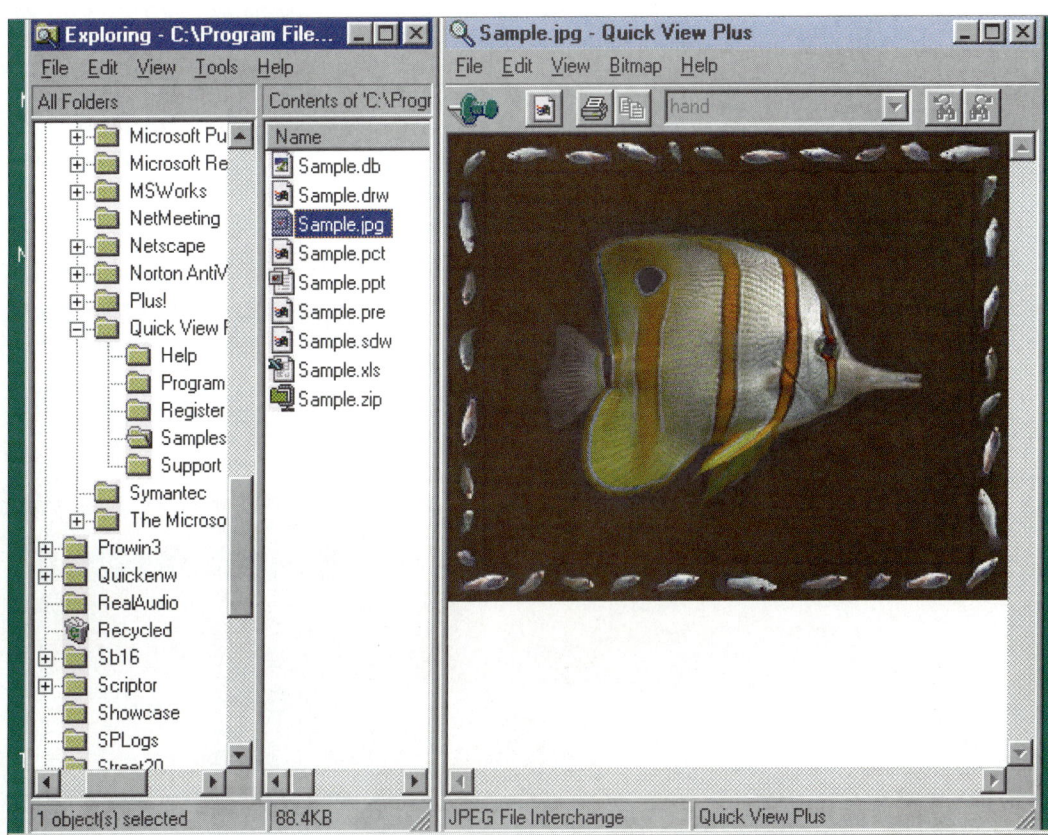

Figure 8-16
Quick View Plus is a file viewer utility that lets you quickly see the contents of a file, such as a document or graphic image, without starting an application software package.

A **file viewer** identifies a file by its name and a three-character extension (the three characters after the period in the file name) and displays the text and graphic contents of a file. You can view the contents of a file without starting the related application.

- **File Conversion** Application software programs create files in many different formats, as identified by the three-character extension after the period in the file name. For example, all Microsoft Word documents have the letters *doc* after the period. **File conversion software** allows you to convert a file from one format to another so the file can be used by another application.

- **File Compression** If you download files frequently or exchange large files with others, you will benefit from **file compression software**, which reduces (compresses) the size of files. Compressed files take less room on a disk (hard drive or floppy) and require less time to download or upload. File compression software also performs decompression routines that can return a compressed file to its original size. More information on data compression can be found in Chapter 5.

- **Backup** **Backup software** allows you to copy files or your entire hard disk on tape or disk cartridges (Figure 8-17). The backup software monitors the copying process and alerts you if you need an additional disk cartridge or tape. Restore programs, which are included with backup software, reverse the process and allow you to reload the copied files to another storage medium.

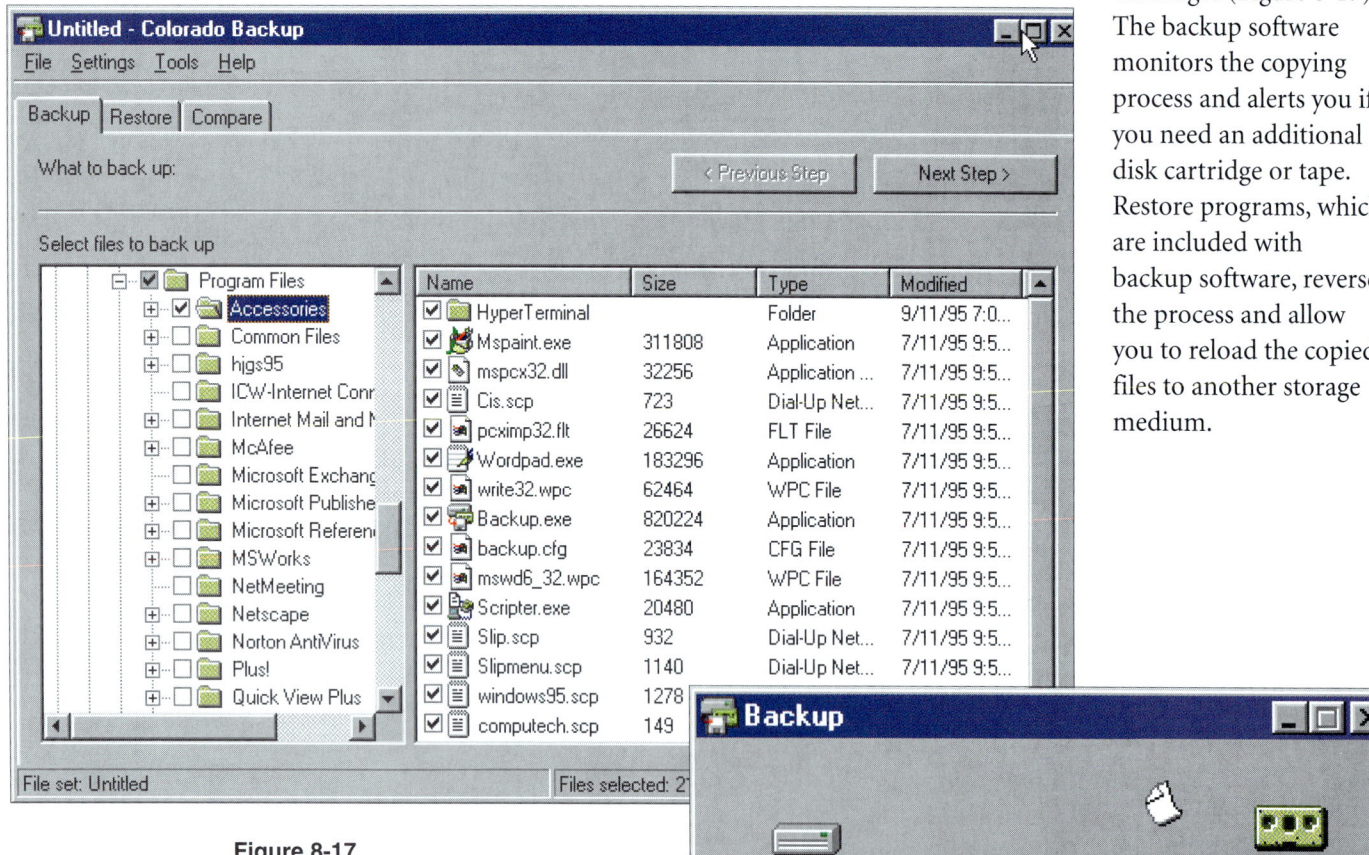

Figure 8-17
Backup software allows you to copy important files on tape or disk cartridges. If system files are damaged, backup copies can be used to restore the data.

- **Diagnostics** Because a computer is a combination of many sophisticated hardware and software components, it is difficult to monitor the operations of every part. A **diagnostic program** helps you determine if the hardware and certain system software programs are installed correctly and functioning properly (Figure 8-18).
- **Uninstaller** When software applications are installed, entries often are made in the system files that are used to help the operating system run the software. If you delete or remove the software application from your computer, these system file entries remain. An **uninstaller** (Figure 8-19) deletes unwanted software and any associated entries in system files.
- **Antivirus** A computer **virus** is a program that copies itself into other programs and spreads through multiple computer systems. Most viruses cause damage to files on the system where the virus is present. **Antivirus programs** prevent, detect, and remove viruses. Viruses and antivirus software also are discussed in Chapter 13, Security, Ethics, and Privacy.

For various diagnostic software packages, visit the Discovering Computers Chapter 8 inCyber page (http://www.scsite.com/dc/ch8/incyber.htm) and click Diagnostic Program.

Figure 8-18
This diagnostic program displays information graphically that helps you determine if hardware devices and software programs are installed properly.

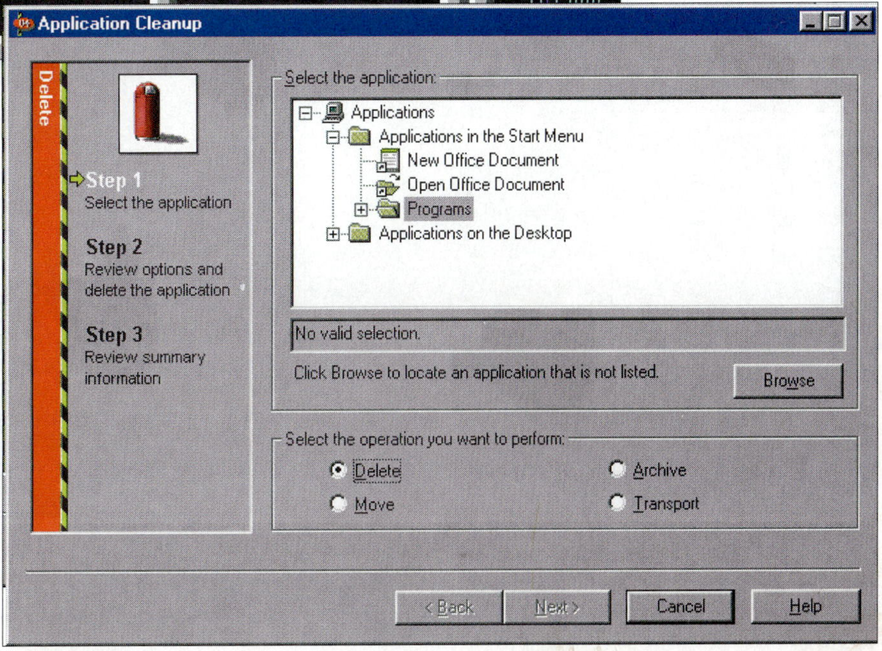

Figure 8-19
An uninstaller utility removes all unnecessary files and system file entries when you remove an application from your system.

For files of shareware screen savers, visit the Discovering Computers Chapter 8 inCyber page (http://www.scsite.com/dc/ch8/incyber.htm) and click Screen Saver.

- **Screen Saver** If your computer remains idle for a certain period of time, a **screen saver** automatically displays a moving image on your screen (Figure 8-20). Screen savers originally were developed to prevent a problem called *ghosting*, where a dim image of the current display was etched permanently on the monitor if the display remained on-screen too long. Ghosting is not a problem with today's monitors, but screen savers still are used, primarily for entertainment and security. A screen saver, for instance, prevents someone else from seeing work on your screen if you leave your computer. If you touch any key or your mouse, the screen saver disappears. Screen savers can, however, be set up so that a password is needed to clear it and display the work that was previously on the screen.

- **Desktop Enhancer** A **desktop enhancer** (Figure 8-21) allows you to change the look and organization of your *desktop*, which is the on-screen work area that uses icons and menus to simulate the top of a desk. You can add individual application icons to a taskbar so you can start them quickly or place frequently used applications in separate panels on your desktop. Desktop enhancers also include programs that help you find and manage files more efficiently.

- **Internet Organizer** An **Internet organizer** helps you manage and use your list of favorite Web sites (Figure 8-22). Internet organizers are improved versions of the bookmark or favorites feature included with all Web browser software. Some organizers even will search the Web and report if any of your favorite sites have changed since you last visited them.

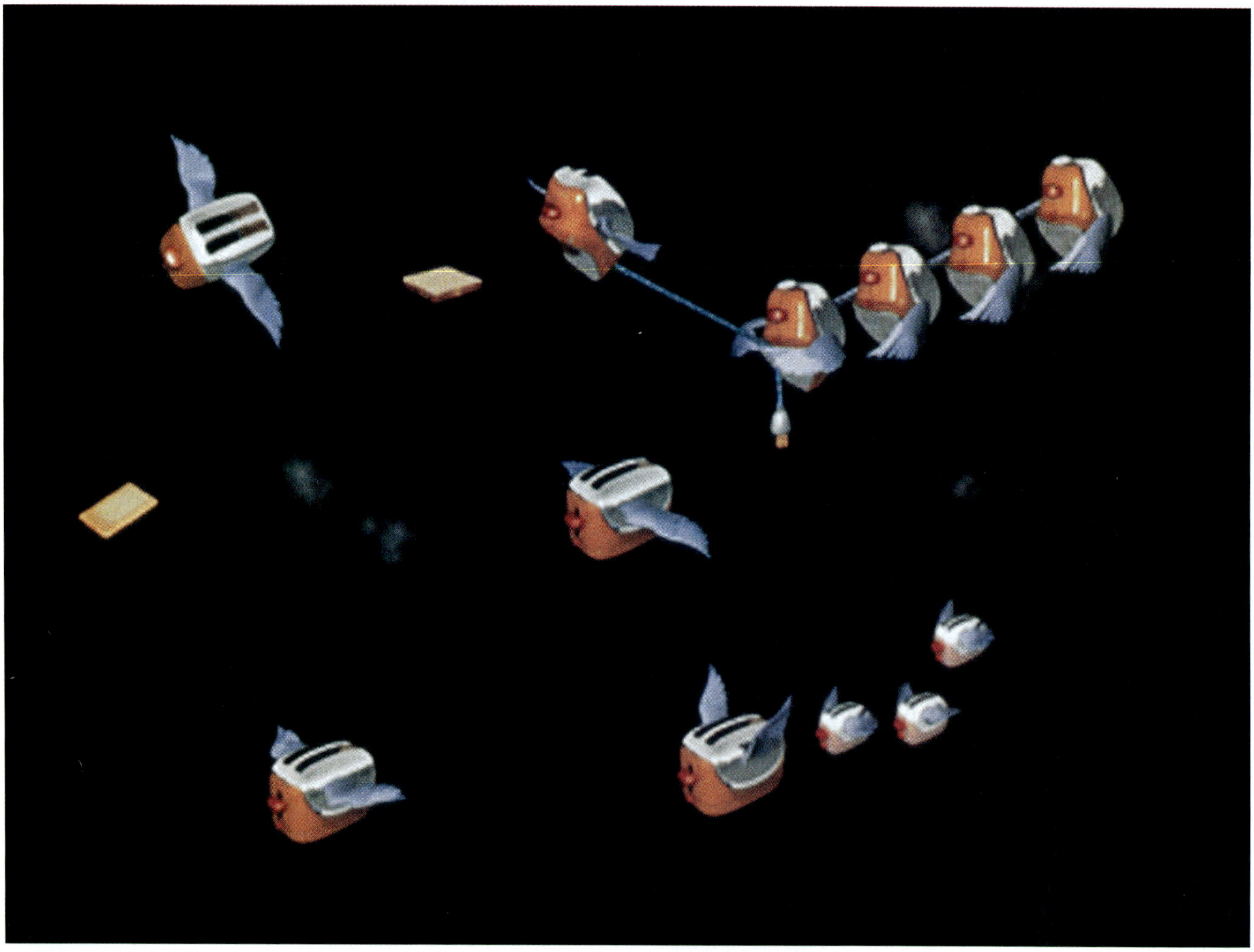

Figure 8-20
If your computer is idle for a while, a screen saver displays a moving image on your monitor. Most screen savers are used for entertainment, but they can be set up to require a password.

SUMMARY OF OPERATING SYSTEMS AND SYSTEM SOFTWARE   8.23

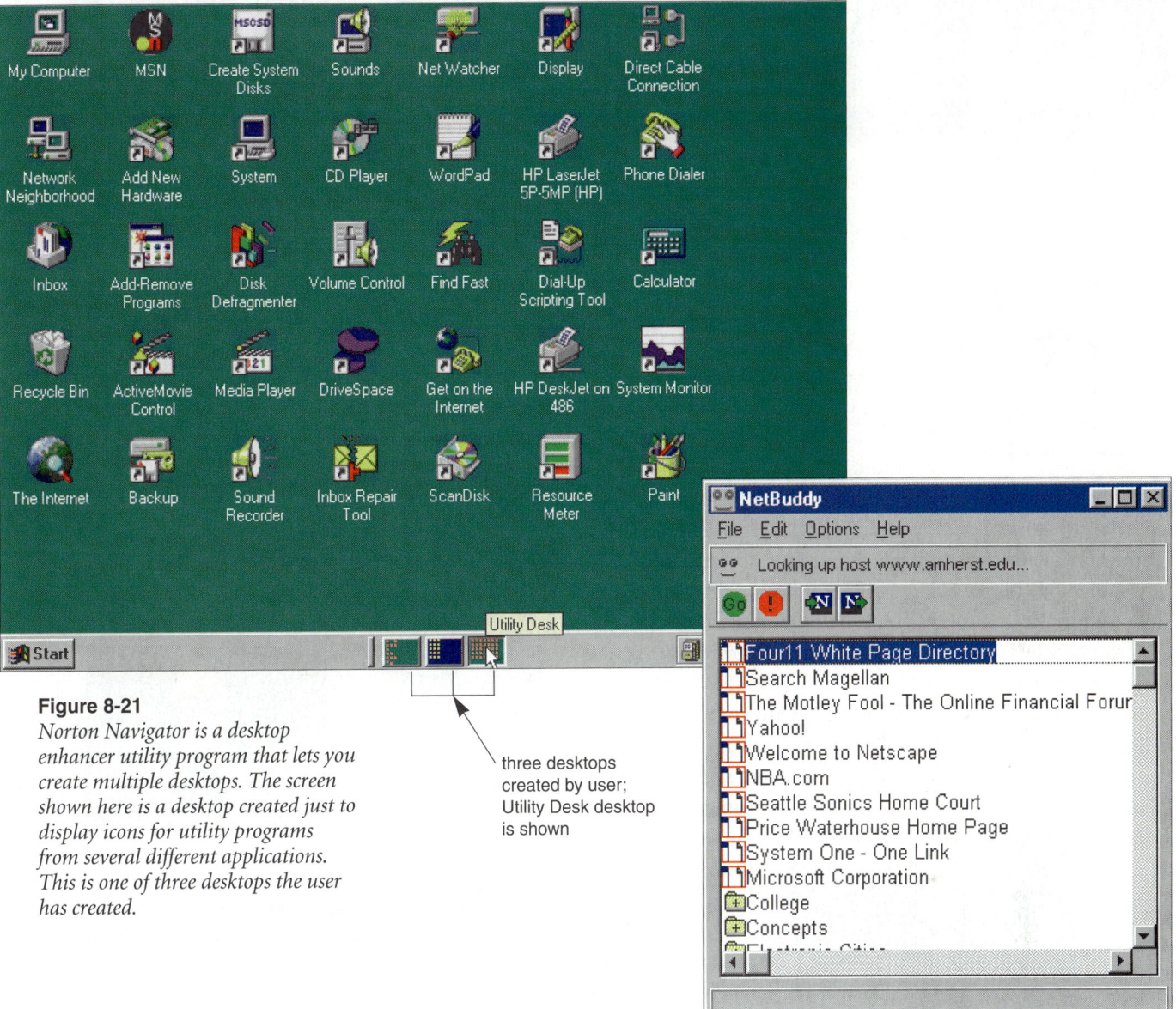

Figure 8-21
Norton Navigator is a desktop enhancer utility program that lets you create multiple desktops. The screen shown here is a desktop created just to display icons for utility programs from several different applications. This is one of three desktops the user has created.

three desktops created by user; Utility Desk desktop is shown

Figure 8-22
An Internet organizer utility program helps you manage your list of favorite Web sites. The Internet organizer shown on this screen will check your favorite Web pages automatically to see if they have changed.

Language Translators

Special-purpose system software programs called **language translators** are used to convert the programming instructions written by programmers into the binary code that a computer can understand. Language translators are written for specific programming languages and computer systems. Chapter 12, Program Development, explains language translators in more detail.

Summary of Operating Systems and System Software

System software, including the operating system, utilities, and language translators, is an essential part of a computer system. To obtain maximum benefits from your computer system, you should understand all of these well. This is especially true for the latest personal computer operating systems, which include features such as virtual memory management and multitasking. Understanding and being able to use these and other features will allow you to exercise more control over your computer resources.

CHAPTER 8 – OPERATING SYSTEMS AND SYSTEM SOFTWARE

COMPUTERS AT WORK

The Social Interface

Are you tired of reading those plain software and operating system messages in dialog boxes of the same size, shape, and color? With Microsoft's Office 97 Office Assistant, you now have a choice of nine cartoon-like characters, called Assistants, that answer questions, offer tips, and provide Help. The on-screen character makes the message less intimidating, more personal, and hopefully, more fun. These electronic Assistants are a type of **social interface** that use objects with human characteristics to communicate information. Each Assistant, some of which are shown on this page, has a different personality that is reflected in the way the Assistant delivers messages. Some Assistants deliver long, detailed explanations, while others are brief and to the point.

An early version of electronic assistants was used in Microsoft's BoB program. BoB was an operating system interface that displayed a picture of what looked like a home office. If you wanted to schedule something, you clicked the calendar on the wall. If you wanted to write a letter, you clicked the paper and pencil on the desktop. Although BoB was discontinued, the idea of the electronic assistants was incorporated into Office 97.

Eventually, software will make it possible for you to pick your own on-screen assistant, or perhaps have an entire team of electronic assistants with different skills. For example, you might have Albert Einstein help with math, William Shakespeare help with that short story you have to write, and Martha Stewart help with party planning, cooking, gardening, decorating, or practically anything else. Imagine the possibilities if one day soon you are able to choose the likeness of your favorite celebrity as an electronic assistant.

Figure 8-23

The Next User Interface

Using the graphical user interfaces of today, you are able to communicate with a computer using a keyboard and a pointing device. Next-generation operating systems will be more natural and *human-centric*, meaning that they will allow you to interface with the computer using most of the methods you now use to communicate with other humans. These methods include hand gestures, facial expressions, and, of course, spoken words.

The computer will use a video camera to recognize hand gestures and facial expressions. Small cameras already are used by many people for personal videoconferencing and in the future, will be built into most systems just like microphones are built into many systems today. You will train the system to match your gestures and expressions with a limited set of commands. For example, moving your hand one way could indicate forward, a command you could use when reviewing pages of a document. Placing your hand with the palm towards the screen could indicate stop or halt. Nodding your head up and down could indicate yes in response to a dialog box message. Training these systems will be similar to training the simple voice recognition systems that now exist.

Future operating system voice recognition, however, will go beyond today's limited systems. Next-generation operating systems will support continuous speech voice recognition and will use artificial intelligence to determine the meaning of what you are saying. If the computer does not understand something, it will ask you to explain it, just as another person would. When the computer speaks to you, it will be through an on-screen presence that may resemble a person, animal, or other object. IBM and Apple have prototype interfaces that resemble a human head. The head *speaks* to you, asking questions about what you want to do or sharing information about something, such as an error condition. To maintain the consistency of this interface, you respond verbally. To turn off the IBM system, you simply tell the character to go to sleep. The character closes it eyes and droops its head before shutting down the system.

Pen gestures now used with personal digital assistants (PDAs) and pen computers also will be recognized by the operating system. Mousepads also will function as graphics tablets and enable you to input drawings or use a pen stylus instead of a mouse.

All of these operating system and user interface changes are designed to make the computer easier to use, especially for people who still feel uncomfortable using a keyboard. Voice, gesture, and pen input will give everyone more command options and not only make computers easier to use, but also more interesting.

Figure 8-24

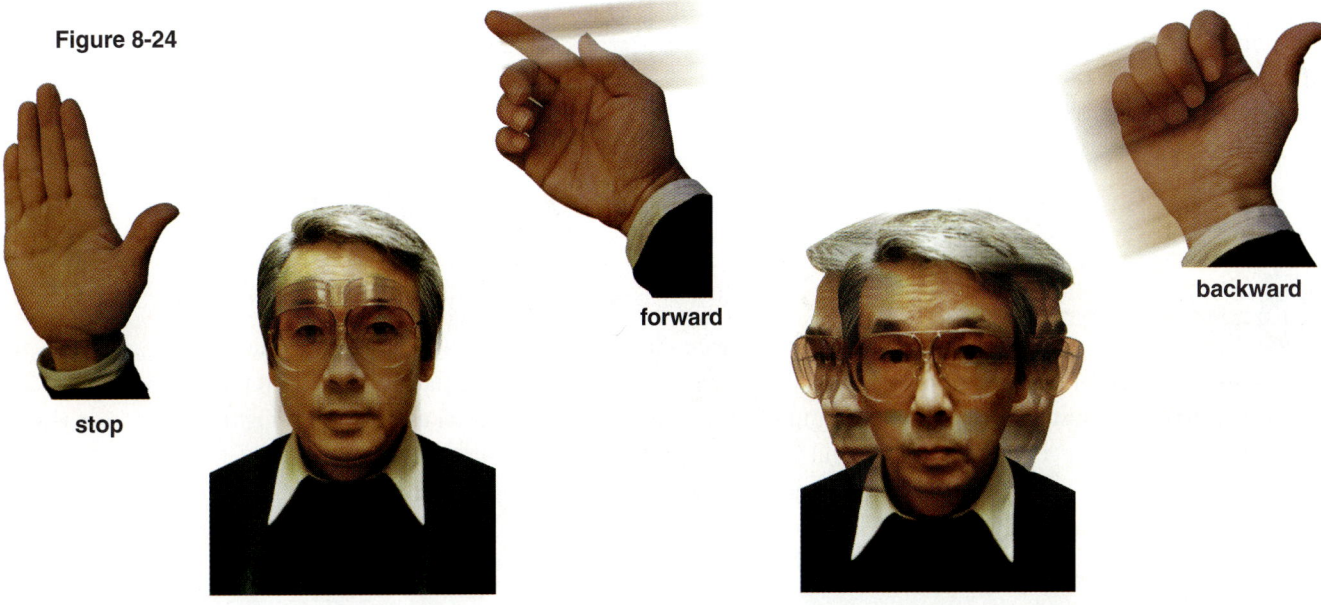

review

chapter 1 | 2 | 3 | 4 | 5 | 6 | 7 | 8 | 9 | 10 | 11 | 12 | 13 | 14 | I

inCyber | review | terms | yourTurn | hotTopics | outThere | winLabs | webWalk | exercises | news | home

INSTRUCTIONS: *To display this page from the Web, launch your browser and enter the URL, http://www.scsite.com/dc/ch8/review.htm. Click the links for current and additional information.*

1 System Software

System software consists of the programs, including the operating system, that control the operations of the computer. The three major categories are: operating systems, utilities, and language translators.

2 Operating Systems

An **operating system (OS)** is a set of programs that manages the operations of a computer and functions as an interface among the user, the application programs, and the computer hardware. The **user interface** determines how users interact with the computer. A **graphical user interface (GUI)** uses visual clues to help perform tasks. An operating system performs four functions: process management, memory management, input and output management, and system administration.

3 Process Management

In operating system terms, a **process** is a program or part of a program that can be executed (run) separately. **Single tasking** operating systems allow only one user to run one program at a time. **Multitasking** operating systems allow the computer to work on more than one process at a time.

4 Memory Management

The operating system assigns the operating system **kernel**, application program instructions, data, and intermediate results to areas of memory. Data that has just been read into memory or is waiting to be sent to an output device is stored in areas called **buffers**. At least some portion of memory is allocated for fixed areas called **partitions**, which are used to store the operating system and programs and their related data. **Virtual memory management** increases the amount of memory by using a set amount of disk space to store items during processing, in addition to the existing memory.

5 Input and Output Management

The operating system manages input and output processes differently depending on the device. **Spooling** increases both CPU and printer efficiency. The operating system uses programs called **device drivers** to communicate with each input and output device. With **Plug and Play technology**, the operating system recognizes any new devices and assists in their installation.

6 System Administration

The operating system monitors system performance and system security. System performance usually is gauged by the user in terms of **response time**, which is the amount of time from when data is entered until the system responds. To ensure system security, most multiuser operating systems allow each user to have a **logon code**, a **user ID**, and a **password**. All operating systems contain programs that perform functions related to disk and file management. These functions include formatting disks, listing files, deleting files, copying files, renaming files, and organizing files.

7 Loading an Operating System

Loading an operating system is called **booting**. With the Windows 95 operating system, when the computer is turned on the CPU looks to the BIOS **(Basic Input/Output System)** chip for instructions. The BIOS chip tests the system and then looks for the boot program. The boot program is loaded into memory and begins loading the resident portion of the operating system. The operating system then loads system configuration information. A device driver is loaded for each hardware device. The remainder of the operating system is loaded and the desktop and icons display on the screen.

8 Portable Operating Systems

The trend is toward **portable operating systems** that will run on many manufacturers' computers. Users can change computer models or vendors, yet retain existing software and data files.

9 DOS and Windows 3.X

DOS (Disk Operating System) refers to several single tasking operating systems that were developed for IBM-compatible personal computers. **Windows 3.x** refers to versions of Microsoft's Windows operating system.

10 Windows 95, Windows CE, and Windows NT

Windows 95 is a 32-bit operating system. It has an improved graphical user interface, is written to take advantage of newer 32-bit processors, and supports **preemptive multitasking**. **Windows CE** is an operating system designed for use on wireless communications devices and smaller computers. **Windows NT** is a sophisticated operating system designed for client-server networks.

11 Macintosh, OS/2, UNIX, and Netware

The Apple **Macintosh** multitasking operating system was the first commercially successful graphical user interface. **OS/2** is IBM's graphical user interface operating system designed to work with 32-bit microprocessors. **UNIX** is a multiuser, multitasking operating system available for most computers of all sizes. **NetWare** from Novell is a widely used network operating system designed for client-server networks.

12 Utilities

Utility programs perform specific tasks related to managing computer resources or files. Utility programs include **file viewers**, **file conversion** software, **file compression software**, **backup software**, **diagnostic programs**, **uninstallers**, **antivirus programs**, **screen savers**, **desktop enhancers**, and **Internet organizers**.

13 Language Translators

Special-purpose system software programs called **language translators** convert the programming instructions written by programmers into binary code that a computer can understand.

8.28 terms

chapter 1 | 2 | 3 | 4 | 5 | 6 | 7 | 8 | 9 | 10 | 11 | 12 | 13 | 14 | I

inCyber | review | terms | yourTurn | hotTopics | outThere | winLabs | webWalk | exercises | news | home

INSTRUCTIONS: *To display this page from the Web, launch your browser and enter the URL, http://www.scsite.com/dc/ch8/terms.htm. Scroll through the list of terms. Click a term for its definition and a picture. Click the rocket ship for current and additional information about the term.*

screen saver ▼

DEFINITION

screen saver
Automatically displays an image on your screen if your computer remains idle for a certain period of time. **(8.22)**

antivirus program (8.21)
asymmetric multiprocessing (8.6)
AUTOEXEC.BAT (8.13)

background (8.5)
backup software (8.20)
Basic Input/Output System (8.12)
BIOS (8.12)
booting (8.12)
buffers (8.7)

command language (8.3)
command-line user interface (8.3)
CONFIG.SYS (8.13)
context switching (8.5)
control program (8.2)
cooperative multitasking (8.5)
CPU utilization (8.10)

desktop enhancer (8.22)
device drivers (8.9)
diagnostic program (8.21)
DOS (Disk Operating System) (8.14)
downward compatible (8.14)

executive (8.2)
external commands (8.2)

fault-tolerant computer (8.6)
file compression software (8.20)
file conversion (8.20)
file viewer (8.19)
foreground (8.5)
frames (8.16)

graphical user interface (GUI) (8.3)

internal commands (8.2)
Internet organizer (8.22)

kernel (8.2)

language translators (8.23)
logon code (8.11)

Macintosh (8.17)
MacOS (8.17)
master program (8.2)
menu-driven user interface (8.13)
monitor (8.2)
MS-DOS (Microsoft DOS) (8.14)
multiprocessing operating system (8.6)
multiprocessors (8.6)
multitasking (8.4)
multithreading (8.5)
multiuser timesharing (8.4)

NetWare (8.19)
NT (8.17)

operating environment (8.15)
operating system (OS) (8.2)
OS/2 (8.8)

page (8.7)
paging (8.7)
partitions (8.7)
password (8.11)
PC-DOS (Personal Computer DOS) (8.14)
Plug and Play technology (8.9)
portable operating systems (8.14)
POST (8.12)
Power On Self Test (8.12)
preemptive multitasking (8.5)

print spool (8.9)
process (8.4)
proprietary operating systems (8.14)

registry (8.13)
response time (8.10)

screen saver (8.22)
shell (8.5)
single tasking (8.4)
spooling (8.9)
supervisor (8.2)
swap file (8.7)
swapping (8.8)
symmetric multiprocessing (8.6)
system software (8.2)

task (8.4)
thrashing (8.?)
time slice (8.?)

uninstaller (8.21)
UNIX (8.18)
upward compatible (8.14)
user ID (8.11)
user interface (8.2)
utility programs (8.19)

virtual memory management (8.7)
virus (8.21)

Win 95 (8.16)
Windows 3.0 (8.15)
Windows 3.1 (8.15)
Windows 3.x (8.15)
Windows 95 (8.16)
Windows CE (8.16)
Windows for Workgroups (8.15)
Windows NT (8.17)

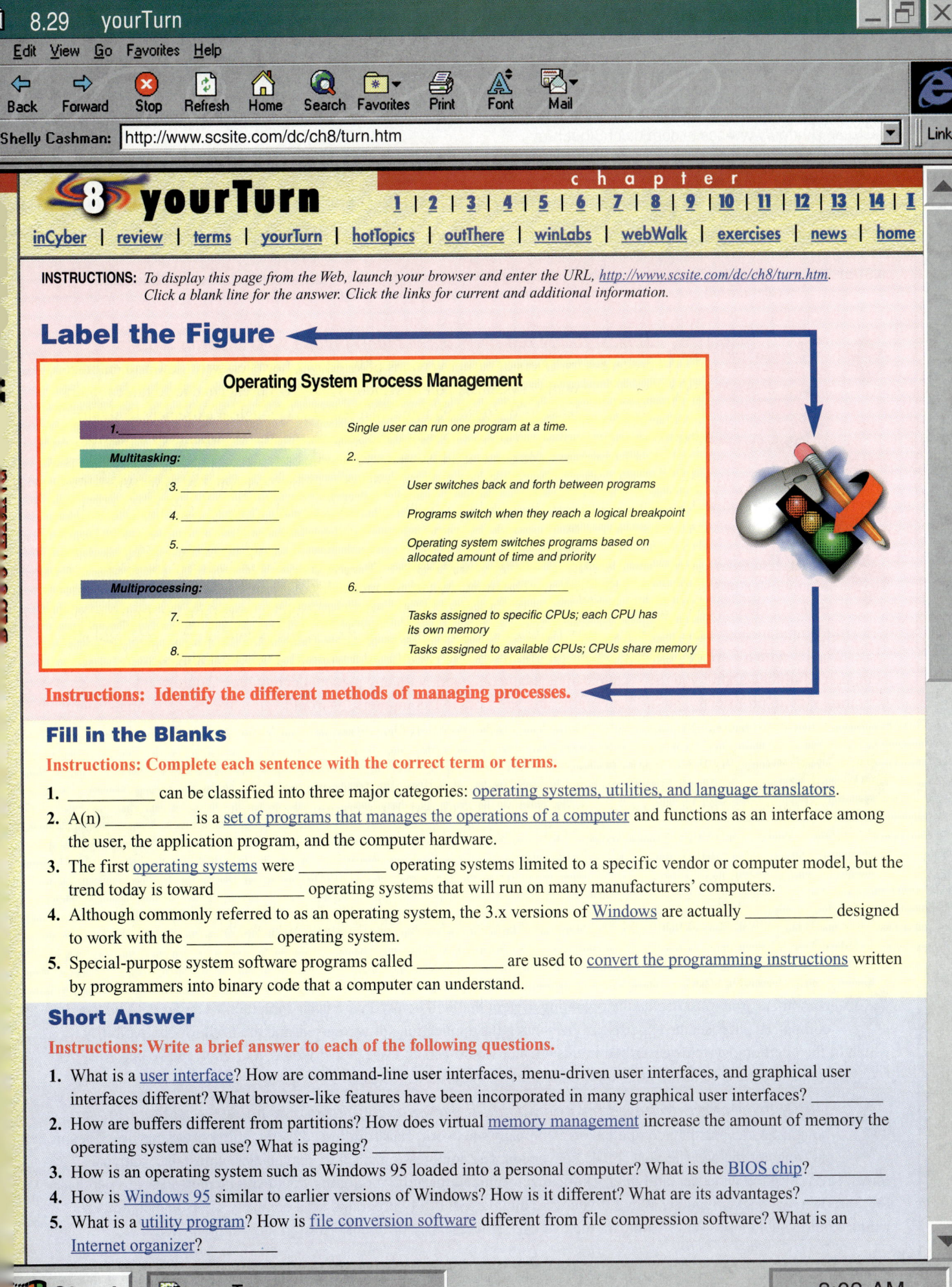

8.30 hotTopics

DISCOVERING COMPUTERS

8 hotTopics — chapter
1 | 2 | 3 | 4 | 5 | 6 | 7 | 8 | 9 | 10 | 11 | 12 | 13 | 14 | I

inCyber | review | terms | yourTurn | hotTopics | outThere | winLabs | webWalk | exercises | news | home

INSTRUCTIONS: *To display this page from the Web, launch your browser and enter the URL,* http://www.scsite.com/dc/ch8/hot.htm. *Click the links for current and additional information to help you respond to the hotTopics questions.*

1 *Most software reviewers agree that Windows 95 is superior to its* predecessors. Users of earlier versions of Windows, however, were slower to embrace the new operating system. A poll of Windows and DOS users conducted three months after the release of **Windows 95** found that only 10% thought it extremely likely they would upgrade to Windows 95 within the next six months, 35% believed it possible, and 53% felt it was not likely at all. Why might people be reluctant to adopt new versions of an operating system? What features would be most apt to hasten the acceptance of a new operating system? Why? If you generally were satisfied with a current version of an operating system, how likely would you be to upgrade your system with a new and perhaps superior version? Why?

2 **Steve Wozniak**, *cofounder of Apple Computer, feels the company erred in initially making* Macintosh a proprietary operating system. The intent was to enhance sales of Apple hardware, but Wozniak now believes the company should have licensed the operating system to other manufacturers for a fee. Imagine you are CEO of Computers and Advanced Technology (CAT), a company that specializes in laptop computers (company slogan: "Life is better with a CAT on your lap"). Your programmers have developed a wonderful new operating system for CAT computers, but they assure you the system can be adapted to work with any personal computers. Would you keep the operating system proprietary, possibly strengthening sales of CAT computers, or would you make the operating system portable and license it to other manufacturers? Why? What factors, if any, might make you change your decision?

3 *New utility programs are being developed constantly to meet user needs. One new program* guards against **computer theft** by once a week making a silent call to a control center. If the call emanates from an appropriate number, the call is logged. If the computer has been reported stolen, however, the center traces the call to locate the missing computer. What other needs could be addressed by a utility program? What are three specific tasks (not addressed in this chapter) related to managing computer resources or files that all computer users or a specific group of users would like to have performed? What would a utility program do to perform each task? How would the program make a user's computing life easier? If you were to market the program, what would you call it?

4 *Suppose you start a small company. The company uses several different types of personal* computers. You must decide the **operating system** that will be used with each computer. Keeping in mind the company's purpose, the expertise of personnel, the application software used, and the need for compatibility, which of the operating systems described in this chapter would you choose? Why? Would your choice have been different five years ago? Might it be different five years from now? Why?

5 *Utility programs purchased for an individual personal computer may be different from those* bought for the personal computers on a company's network. Tasks addressed by the **utility programs** described in this chapter include file viewer, file conversion, file compression, backup, diagnostics, uninstaller, antivirus, screen saver, desktop enhancer, and **Internet** organizer. Which four utility programs would you be most likely to purchase for your own personal computer? Why? If you were buying four utility programs for a company's personal computers, which would you choose? Why? Compare the two lists. How are they different? How are they similar? Why?

Start | hotTopics   8:04 AM

outThere

chapter 8

1 | 2 | 3 | 4 | 5 | 6 | 7 | 8 | 9 | 10 | 11 | 12 | 13 | 14 | I

inCyber | review | terms | yourTurn | hotTopics | outThere | winLabs | webWalk | exercises | news | home

INSTRUCTIONS: *To display this page from the Web, launch your browser and enter the URL, http://www.scsite.com/dc/ch8/out.htm. Click the links for current and additional information.*

1. *Transferring the notes taken in class or the term paper scratched out on the bus* to a desktop computer usually involves puzzling over illegible handwriting and typing for hours. Windows CE, which is an operating system available on numerous personal digital assistants, may make life easier. A representative PDA unit comes with a small keyboard, a touch-sensitive screen, and mini Word, Excel, and Schedule+ applications. Weighing less than a pound and running on two AA batteries, it transfers work done to a desktop PC through a simple cable connection. Visit a computer vendor and try a PDA that uses Windows CE. What PDA did you use? How does it work? What are its strengths? What are its weaknesses? Would you consider purchasing the PDA? Why or why not?

2. *Virus protection programs can detect known computer viruses and clean them from a system.* Yet, because new viruses are developed every day, virus protection programs must be updated frequently to handle recently created threats. Fortunately, help is available on the World Wide Web. For a monthly fee, subscribers can download antivirus software that is renewed periodically to deal with the latest viruses. Visit a Web site to learn more about virus protection software. Who provides the software? Who created the software? How is the online virus protection software better than the utility programs available in stores? With what operating systems is the software compatible? How often can it be used? How much does it cost? What other types of utility programs are available?

3. *Just as it is important to get out and kick the tires before deciding on a new car,* it is a good idea to test several operating systems before choosing one for a personal computer. Find two personal computers that use different operating systems. Compare the two operating systems. What is the name of each operating system? What type of interface does each use? What type of operating system (single tasking, context switching, cooperative multitasking, or preemptive multitasking) is each? How does each manage memory, manage input and output, and monitor system activity? What utilities are available? What application software is used with each operating system? Based on what you have learned, which operating system would you choose for your own personal computer? Why?

4. *Operating systems often develop loyal followings. The introduction of Windows 95 led to* renewed controversy concerning the merits of various operating systems, and the debate has been fueled on the World Wide Web by the originators of each operating system. Visit one or more Web pages that compare various operating systems. Who authored the Web page? What operating systems are being compared? How are they compared? According to the Web page, what are the advantages and disadvantages of each operating system? After reviewing the page, are you convinced of the superiority of one operating system? Why or why not?

5. *Bill Gates, a founder of Microsoft Corporation, is the wealthiest man in America.* The $20 billion CEO leads a company that is said to have a greater reach than any organization since the Roman Empire; more than 90 percent of all personal computers have a Microsoft operating system. The story of Bill Gates and Microsoft has been chronicled in several books, including *Hard Drive: Bill Gates and the Making of the Microsoft Empire* (James Wallace), *Accidental Empire: How the Boys of Silicon Valley Make Their Millions and Still Can't Get a Date* (Robert X. Cringely), *Gates* (Stephen Manes), and *The Road Ahead* (Bill Gates). Read one of these books and prepare a brief report. What qualities or factors led to the success of Bill Gates and Microsoft? Why? Will Microsoft's success continue? Why or Why not?

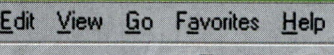 

winLabs

chapter
1 | 2 | 3 | 4 | 5 | 6 | 7 | 8 | 9 | 10 | 11 | 12 | 13 | 14 | I

inCyber | review | terms | yourTurn | hotTopics | outThere | winLabs | webWalk | exercises | news | home

INSTRUCTIONS: *To display this page from the Web, launch your browser and enter the URL, http://www.scsite.com/dc/ch8/labs.htm. Click the links for current and additional information.*

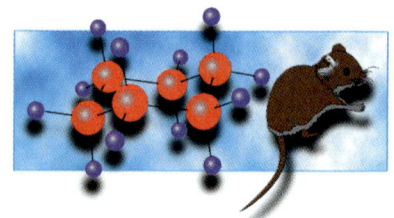

1 Shelly Cashman Series System Software Lab
Follow the instructions in winLabs 1 on page 1.34 to display the Shelly Cashman Series Labs screen. Click Evaluating **Operating Systems**. Click the Start Lab button. When the initial screen displays, carefully read the objectives. With your printer on, click the Print Questions button. Fill out the top of the Questions sheet and then answer the questions.

2 Shelly Cashman Series Ergonomics Lab
Follow the instructions in winLabs 1 on page 1.34 to display the Shelly Cashman Series Labs screen. Click **Working** at Your Computer. Click the Start Lab button. When the initial screen displays, carefully read the objectives. With your printer on, click the Print Questions button. Fill out the top of the Questions sheet and then answer the questions.

3 Using a Screen Saver
Right-click an empty area on your desktop and then click Properties on the shortcut menu. When the Display Properties dialog box displays, click the **Screen Saver** tab. To activate or modify a screen saver, click the Screen Saver box arrow and then click Mystify Your Mind or any other selection. Click the Preview button to display the actual screen saver (Figure 8-25). Move the mouse to make the screen saver disappear. Answer the following questions: (1) How many screen savers are available in your Screen Saver list? (2) How many minutes does your system wait before activating a screen saver? Click the Cancel button in the Display Properties dialog box.

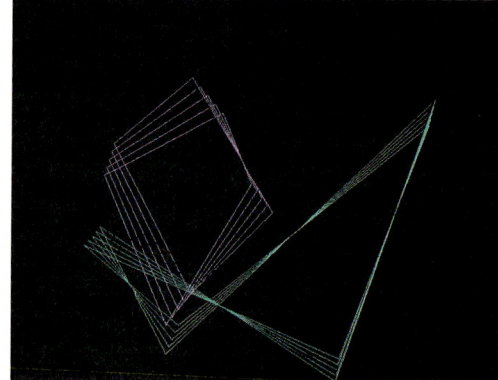

Figure 8-25

4 Changing Desktop Colors
Right-click an empty area on your desktop and then click Properties on the shortcut menu. When the Display Properties dialog box displays, click the Appearance tab. Perform the following tasks: (1) Click the question mark button on the title bar and then click the Scheme box. When the pop-up window displays, right-click it. Click Print Topic on the shortcut menu and then click the OK button in the Print dialog box. Click anywhere to remove the pop-up window. (2) Click the Scheme box arrow and then click Rose to display the color scheme in Figure 8-26. Find a color scheme you like. Click the Cancel button.

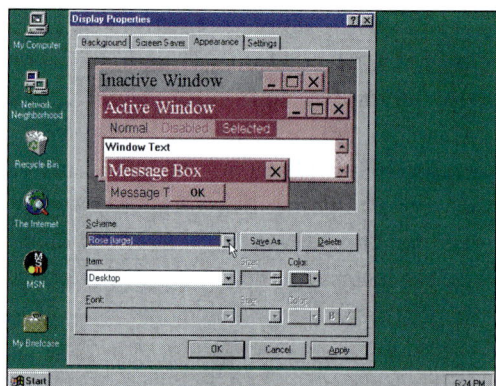

Figure 8-26

5 About Windows 95
Double-click the My Computer icon on the desktop. When the My Computer window displays, click Help on the menu bar and then click About Windows 95. Answer the following questions: (1) To whom is Windows 95 licensed? (2) How much physical memory is available to Windows? Click the OK button. Close My Computer.

8.33 webWalk

chapter 8 webWalk
1 | 2 | 3 | 4 | 5 | 6 | 7 | 8 | 9 | 10 | 11 | 12 | 13 | 14 | I

inCyber | review | terms | yourTurn | hotTopics | outThere | winLabs | webWalk | exercises | news | home

INSTRUCTIONS: *To display this page from the Web, launch your browser and enter the URL, http://www.scsite.com/dc/ch8/walk.htm. Click the exercise link to display the exercise.*

1. Screen Save Utilities
Ghosting is not a problem with today's monitors, but screen savers still are used for entertainment and security. To learn more about screen savers, complete this exercise.

2. File Compression Utilities
If you frequently download files or trade large files with others, you will benefit from file compression software (Figure 8-27). You can learn more about file compression software by completing this exercise.

3. Graphical User Interfaces
A graphical user interface (GUI) uses visual clues such as icons to help you perform tasks. You can learn more about GUIs by completing this exercise.

4. All About BIOS
The Basic Input/Output System (BIOS) is a set of instructions that provides the interface between the operating system and the hardware devices (Figure 8-28). Complete this exercise to learn more about BIOS.

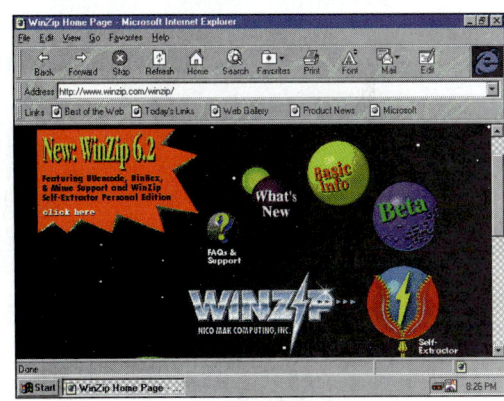

Figure 8-27

5. Information Mining
Complete this exercise to improve your Web research skills by using a Web search engine to find information related to this chapter.

6. Windows CE
Windows CE is an operating system designed for use on wireless communication devices and smaller computers such as hand-helds, palmtops, and network computers. To learn more about Windows CE, complete this exercise.

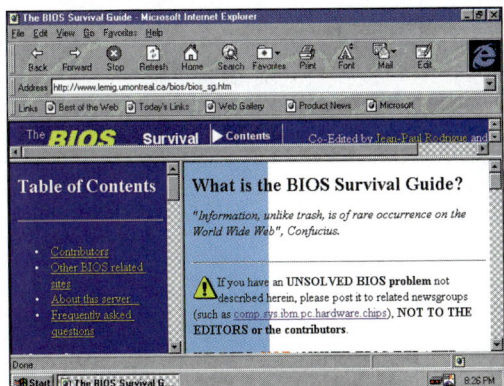

Figure 8-28

7. Antivirus Utilities
A computer virus is a program that causes damage by copying itself into other programs and spreading through multiple computer systems. Utility programs include virus protection programs that prevent, detect, and remove viruses. Complete this exercise to learn more about computer virus protection.

8. Offline Web Browsing
Offline Web Browsing can save time, money and slow, frustrating Internet connections by organizing scheduled downloads and keeping them updated. Complete this exercise to learn more about offline web browsing.

9. Web Chat
Complete this exercise to enter a Web Chat discussion related to the issues presented in the hotTopics exercise.

How to Purchase, Install, and Maintain a Personal Computer

    At some point in time, perhaps during this course, you probably will decide to buy a computer system. It may be your first system or a replacement system. The decision is an important one and will require an investment of both time and money. The following guidelines are presented to help you purchase, install, and maintain your system. The guidelines assume you are purchasing a desktop personal computer, often referred to as a PC. It is further assumed that the computer will be used for home or light business use. Because it is the most widely purchased type of system, some of the guidelines assume an IBM-compatible computer is being purchased. Most of the guidelines, however, may be applied to the purchase of any personal computer including a Macintosh or other non-Windows system. The type of system you purchase should be determined by your software requirements and the need to be compatible with other systems with which you work.

    Many of the guidelines also can be applied to purchasing notebook computers. A separate section on notebook computer requirements also is included. A notebook computer may be an appropriate choice if you need computing capability when you travel.

How to Purchase a Computer System

1 Determine what applications you will use on your computer. This decision will guide you as to the type and size of computer. Artists and others who work with graphics will need a larger, better quality monitor and additional disk space.

2 Choose your software first. Some packages run only on Macintosh computers, others only on a PC. Some packages run only under the Windows operating system. In addition, some software requires more memory and disk space than other packages. Most users will want at least word processing and access to the Internet and World Wide Web. For the most software for the money, consider purchasing an integrated package or a software suite that offers reduced pricing on several applications purchased at the same time. Be sure the software contains the features that are necessary for the work you will be performing.

3 Be aware of *hidden* costs. Realize that some additional costs are associated with buying a computer. Such costs might include an additional telephone line or outlet to use a modem, computer furniture, consumable supplies such as floppy disks and paper, floppy disk holders, reference manuals on specific software packages, and special training classes you may want to take. Depending on where you buy your computer, the seller may be willing to include some or all of these in the system purchase price.

4 Buy equipment that meets the *Energy Star* power consumption guidelines. These guidelines require that computer systems, monitors, and printers reduce electrical consumption if they have not been used for some period of time, usually several minutes. Equipment meeting the guidelines can display the *Energy Star* logo.

5 Consider buying from local computer dealers or direct mail companies. Each has certain advantages. The local dealer can more easily provide hands-on support, if necessary. With a mail-order company, you usually are limited to speaking to someone over the telephone. Mail-order companies usually, but not always, offer the lowest prices. The important thing to do when you are shopping for a system is to make sure you are comparing identical or similar configurations. Local companies can be found in the telephone book. Call first to see if they sell regularly to individual customers; some sell only or primarily to businesses. Telephone numbers for mail-order companies can be found in their advertisements that run in PC periodicals. Most libraries subscribe to several of the major PC magazines. If you call a mail-order firm, ask if it has a catalog that can be sent to you. If you do not buy a system right away, call for another catalog; prices and configurations change frequently.

SYSTEM COST COMPARISON WORKSHEET

Category	Item	Desired	#1	#2	#3	#4
Base System	Mfr	–				
	Model					
	Processor	Pentium with MMX				
	Speed	200 MHz				
	Power supply	200 watts				
	Expansion slots	5				
	Local bus video	yes				
	Operating system	Windows				
	Price					
Memory	RAM	32 MB				
	L2 Cache	512 K				
	Price					
Hard Disk	Mfr					
	Size	2.0 GB				
	Price					
Floppy Disk	3 1/2 inch					
Video Graphics	Mfr/Model	64-bit				
	Memory	4 MB				
	Price					
Color Monitor	Mfr/Model					
	Size	17 inch				
	Dot Pitch	0.26 mm				
	Price					
Sound Card	Mfr/Model	16-bit				
	Price					
Speakers	Mfr/Model					
	Number	3 pc				
	Price					
CD-ROM Drive	Mfr/Model					
	Speed	12X				
	Price					
Mouse	Mfr/Model					
	Price					
Fax Modem	Mfr/Model					
	Speed	33.6 Kbps				
	Price					
Printer	Mfr/Model					
	Type	ink jet				
	Speed	6 ppm				
	Price					
Surge Protector	Mfr/Model					
	Price					
Tape Backup	Mfr/Model					
	Price					
UPS	Mfr/Model					
	Price					
Other	Sales Tax					
	Shipping					
	1 YR Warranty	standard				
	1 YR On-Site Svc					
	3 YR On-Site Svc					
	TOTAL					
Software	List free software					

Figure 1
A spreadsheet is an effective way to summarize and compare the prices and equipment offered by different system vendors. List your desired system in the column labeled Desired. Place descriptions on the lines and enter prices in the boxes.

6 **Use a spreadsheet, such as the one shown in Figure 1, to compare purchase alternatives.** Use a separate sheet of paper to take notes on each vendor's system and then summarize the information on the spreadsheet.

7 **Consider more than just price.** Do not necessarily buy the lowest cost system. Consider intangibles such as how long the vendor has been in business, its reputation for quality, and reputation for support.

8 **Do some research.** Talk to friends, coworkers, and instructors. Ask what type of system and software they bought and why. Would they recommend their system and the company they bought it from? Are they satisfied with their software? Spend some time at the library or on the Internet reviewing computer periodicals. Most periodicals have frequent articles that rate systems and software on cost, performance, and support issues. Check out the Web sites of different system manufacturers for the latest information on equipment and prices.

9 **Look for free software.** Many system vendors include free software with their systems. Some even let you choose which software you want. Free software only has value, however, if you would have purchased it if it had not come with the computer.

10 **Buy a system compatible with the one you use elsewhere.** If you use a personal computer at work or at some other organization, make sure the computer you buy is compatible. That way, if you need or want to, you can work on projects at home.

11 **Consider purchasing an on-site service agreement.** If you use your system for business or otherwise are unable to be without your computer, consider purchasing an on-site service agreement. Many of the mail-order vendors offer such support through third-party companies. Agreements usually state that a technician will be on-site within 24 hours. Some systems include on-site service for only the first year. It usually is less expensive to extend the service for two or three years when you buy the computer instead of waiting to buy the service agreement later.

12 **Use a credit card to purchase your system.** Many credit cards now have purchase protection benefits that cover you in case of loss or damage to purchased goods. Some also extend the warranty of any products purchased with the card. Paying by credit card also gives you time to install and use the system before you have to pay for it. Finally, if you are dissatisfied with the system and are unable to reach an agreement with the seller, paying by credit card gives you certain rights regarding withholding payment until the dispute is resolved. Check your credit card agreement for specific details.

13 **Avoid buying the smallest system available.** Studies show that many users become dissatisfied because they did not buy a powerful enough system. Plan to buy a system that will last you for at least three years. If you have to buy a smaller system, be sure it can be upgraded with additional memory and devices as your system requirements grow. Consider the following as a minimum recommended system. Each of the components will be discussed separately.

Base System Components

Pentium processor with MMX technology, 200 MHz
200 watt power supply
5 open expansion slots
1 open expansion bay
1 parallel and 2 serial ports
keyboard
512 K level 2 (L2) cache memory
32 MB of RAM
2.0 GB hard disk drive
$3^{1}/_{2}$-inch floppy disk drive
64-bit video graphics card with 4 MB memory
17-inch SVGA color monitor
16-bit sound card and speakers
12X CD-ROM drive
mouse or other pointing device
33.6 kbps fax modem
ink-jet or personal laser printer
surge protector
latest version of operating system
FCC Class B approved

Optional Components

color ink-jet printer
multifunction device (printer, scanner, copier, fax machine)
tape backup
cartridge disk drive
ergonomic keyboard
uninterruptable power supply (UPS)

Processor: A Pentium processor with MMX technology with a speed rating of at least 200 megahertz is needed for today's more sophisticated software, even word processing software. Buy a system that can be upgraded to the next generation processor.

Power Supply: 200 watts. If the power supply is too small, it will not be able to support additional expansion cards that you might want to add in the future. The power supply should be UL (Underwriters Laboratory) approved.

Expansion Slots: At least five open slots. Expansion slots are needed for scanners, tape drives, video capture boards, and other equipment you may want to add in the future as your needs change and the price of this equipment becomes lower.

Expansion Bay: At least one open bay. An expansion (drive) bay will let you add another disk drive or a tape drive.

Ports: At least one parallel and two serial ports. The parallel port will be used for your printer. The serial ports can be used for additional printers, external modems, joysticks, a mouse, and certain network connections.

Keyboard: Almost always included with the system. If you can, check out the feel of the keys before you buy. If you like the way another keyboard feels, ask the vendor if you can have it instead. Consider upgrading to an ergonomic keyboard that has built-in wrist rests. Ergonomic keyboards take up more space but are more comfortable and help prevent injuries.

Cache Memory: 512 K of level 2 cache will boost the performance of many applications.

Memory (RAM): 32 megabytes (MB) Each new operating system release recommends (requires) more memory. It is easier and less expensive to obtain the memory when you buy the system than if you wait until later.

Hard Disk: 2.0 gigabytes (GB). Each new software release requires more hard disk space. Even with disk compression programs, disk space is used up quickly. Start with more disk than you ever think you will need.

Floppy Disk Drive: A $3^1/_2$-inch floppy disk drive is standard on most systems.

Video Graphics Card: A 64-bit local bus video card with 4 MB of memory will provide crisp colors and support full-motion video.

Color Monitor: 17 inch. This is one device where it pays to spend a little more money. A 17-inch super VGA (SVGA) monitor with a dot pitch of 0.26 mm or less will display graphics better than a 15-inch model. For health reasons, make sure you pick a low-radiation model. Also, look for a monitor with an antiglare coating on the screen or consider buying an antiglare filter that mounts on the front of the screen. If you work frequently with graphics, consider a larger 20-inch or 21-inch unit.

Sound Card and Speakers: 16-bit sound card with FM or wavetable synthesis, or both. Powered speakers use batteries to produce a fuller sound. If music is important to you, consider three-piece speakers with a separate subwoofer unit for better bass sounds.

CD-ROM Drive: Much software and almost all multimedia are distributed on CD-ROM. Get at least a 12X speed model.

Pointing Device: Most systems include a mouse as part of the base package. Some people prefer to use a trackball.

Fax Modem: 33.6 kbps. Volumes of information are available on the Internet and from online databases. In addition, many software vendors provide assistance and free software upgrades via their Web sites. For the speed they provide, 33.6 kbps modems are worth the extra money. Facsimile (fax) capability is included in almost all modems. Buy a modem that can be software upgraded. Internal modems cost less but external modems are easier to move to another computer.

Printer: Ink-jet and personal laser printers produce excellent black and white graphic output. Inexpensive color ink-jet printers also are available. If your office space is limited, or you want the additional features, consider a multifunction device that combines a printer, scanner, copier, and fax machine.

Surge Protector: A voltage spike literally can destroy your system. It is low-cost insurance to protect yourself with a surge protector. Do not merely buy a fused multiple plug outlet from the local hardware store. Buy a surge protector designed for computers with a separate protected jack for your telephone (modem) line.

Operating System: Almost all new systems come with an operating system, but it is not always the most current. Make sure the operating system is the one you want and is the latest version.

FCC Class B Approved: The Federal Communications Commission (FCC) provides radio frequency emission standards that computer manufacturers must meet. If a computer does not meet the FCC standards, it could cause interference with radio and television reception. Class B standards apply to computers used in a home. Class A standards apply to a business installation.

Tape Backup: Large hard disks make backing up data on floppy disks impractical. Internal or external tape backup systems are the most common solution. Some portable units, great if you have more than one system, are designed to connect to your printer port. The small tapes can store the equivalent of hundreds of floppy disks.

Cartridge Disk Drive: Removable cartridge disk drives are a fast and portable way to store large amounts of data.

Uninterruptable Power Supply (UPS): A UPS uses batteries to start or keep your system running if the main electrical power is turned off. The length of time they provide depends on the size of the batteries and the electrical requirements of your system but is usually at least 10 minutes. The idea of a UPS is to give you enough time to save your work. Get a UPS that is rated for your size system.

Remember that the types of applications you want to use on your system will guide you as to the type and size of computer that is right for you. The ideal computer system you choose may differ from the general recommendation presented here. Determine your needs and buy the best system your budget will allow.

How to Purchase a Notebook Computer System

Many of the guidelines previously mentioned also apply to the purchase of a notebook computer. The following are some of the considerations unique to notebooks.

1. **Carefully determine how you want to use your notebook system.** Notebook computers can be divided into three categories: desktop replacement systems, value notebooks, and subnotebooks. *Desktop replacement systems* have all the features and functionality of a full-sized desktop system and are designed for the person who wants only one system or who needs a full-featured system for on-the-road presentations. They include a large hard drive, floppy disk drive, high-speed CD-ROM drive, built-in speakers, PC card slots, and a large (12 inches or larger) active-matrix display. Desktop replacement systems often weigh seven pounds or more and cost between $5,000 and $8,000. *Value notebooks* have lower speed and capacity components than desktop replacement systems but keep most of the functionality. Value notebooks generally weigh between five and seven pounds and cost between $2,500 and $4,000. *Subnotebooks* save weight and size by making the floppy disk drive an optional external device and by having a smaller display screen and keyboard. Subnotebooks generally weigh less than five pounds and cost less than $2,500.

2. **If your system frequently will be used to display animation or video or will be used to display information to others, obtain a notebook with an active-matrix screen.** Active-matrix screens present a better quality picture that can be seen from the side. Less expensive passive matrix screens sometimes are hard to see in low-light conditions and can be viewed only straight on.

3. **If your unit does not have one built-in, consider purchasing a separate CD-ROM drive.** Loading software, especially large software suites, is much faster if done from CD-ROM. A separate CD-ROM drive has the advantage of being left behind to save weight.

4. **If you will use your system both on the road and at home or in the office, consider a docking station.** A docking station usually includes a floppy disk drive, a CD-ROM drive, and a connector for a full-sized monitor and is an alternative to buying a full-sized system when you work at home or in the office.

5. **Experiment with different pointing devices and keyboards before you buy.** Notebook computer keyboards are not nearly as standardized as keyboards on desktop systems. Some notebooks have wide wrist rests and others have none. The same is true for pointing devices. Options include pointing sticks, touchpads, and trackballs.

One manufacturer offers a small mouse that pulls out from the notebook case. Try them all before you buy.

6. **Upgrade memory and disk storage at the time of purchase.** As is true with desktop systems, memory and disk upgrades usually are less expensive if done at the time of initial system purchase. Disk storage systems often are custom designed for notebook manufacturers and may not be available two or three years after the notebook was sold.

The following points apply if you plan to travel with your notebook computer.

7. **If you are going to use your notebook on an airplane, purchase a second battery.** Two batteries should be enough power to work through most flights. If you think you will be working off batteries frequently, choose a system that uses lithium-ion batteries, which last longer than nickel cadmium or nickel hydride batteries.

8. **Purchase a well-padded and well-designed carrying case.** A well-padded case can protect your notebook from the bumps it will receive while traveling. A well-designed carrying case will have room for accessories, spare disks, pens, and some amount of paperwork.

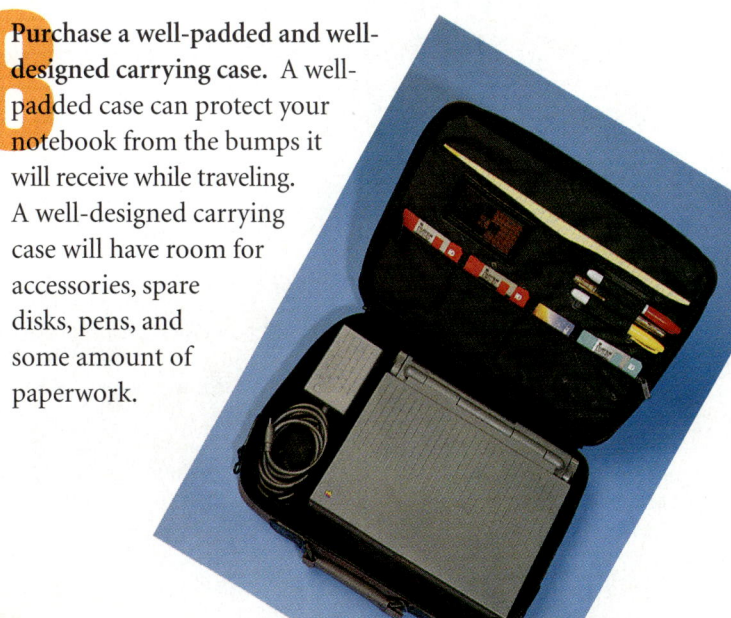

8.40 HOW TO PURCHASE, INSTALL, AND MAINTAIN A PERSONAL COMPUTER

9 If you travel overseas, obtain a set of electrical and telephone outlet adapters. Overseas electrical and telephone connections use different outlets. Several manufacturers sell sets of adapters that will work in most countries.

How to Install a Computer System

1. **Read the installation manuals *before* you start to install your equipment.** Many manufacturers include separate installation instructions with their equipment that contain important information. Take the time to read them.

2. **Allow for adequate workspace around the computer.** A workspace of at least two feet by four feet is recommended.

3. **Install bookshelves.** Bookshelves above and/or to the side of the computer area are useful for keeping manuals and other reference materials handy.

4. **Install your computer in a well-designed work area.** An applied science called ergonomics is devoted to making the equipment people use and surrounding work area safer and more efficient. Ergonomic studies have shown that the height of your chair, keyboard, monitor, and work surface is important and can affect your health. See Figure 2 for specific work area guidelines.

5. **Use a document holder.** To minimize neck and eye strain, obtain a document holder that holds documents at the same height and distance as your computer screen.

6. **Provide adequate lighting.** Use nonglare light bulbs that illuminate your entire work area.

7. **While working at your computer, be aware of health issues.** See Figure 3 for a list of computer user health guidelines.

8. **Have a telephone nearby that can be used while you are sitting at the computer.** Having a telephone near the computer is helpful if you need to call a vendor about a hardware or software problem. Oftentimes, the vendor support person can talk you through the correction while you are on the telephone. To avoid data loss, however, do not place floppy disks on the telephone or near any other electrical or electronic equipment.

9. **Obtain a computer tool set.** Computer tool sets are available from computer dealers, office supply stores, and mail-order companies. These sets will have the right size screwdrivers and other tools to work on your computer. Get one that comes in a zippered carrying case to keep all the tools together.

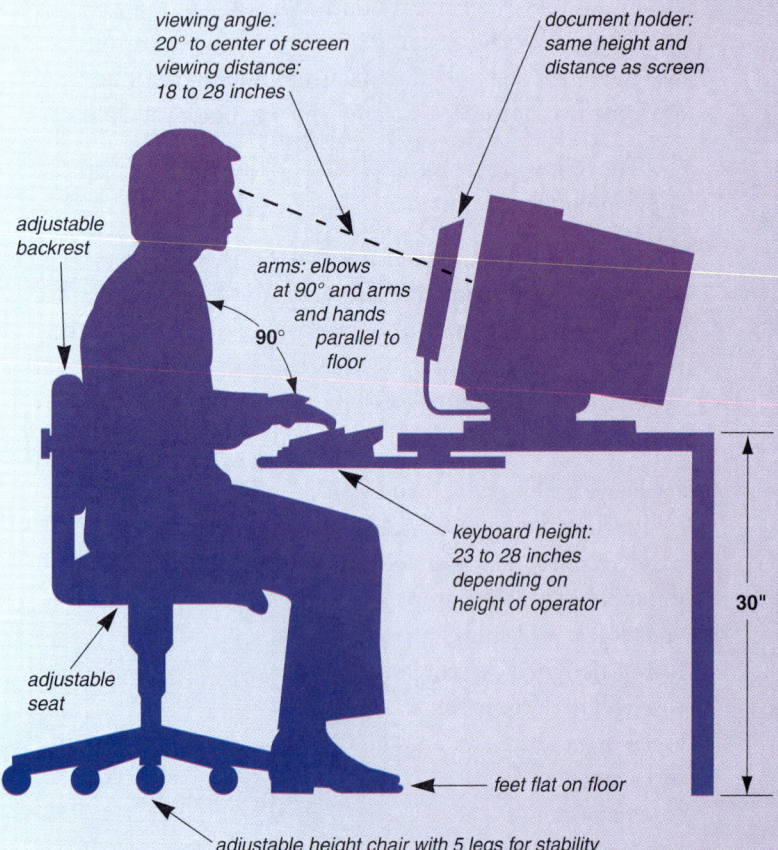

Figure 2
More than anything else, a well-designed work area should be flexible to allow adjustment to the height and build of different individuals. Good lighting and air quality also should be considered.

HOW TO INSTALL A COMPUTER SYSTEM 8.41

10. **Save all the paperwork that comes with your system.** Keep it in an accessible place with the paperwork from your other computer-related purchases. To keep different size documents together, consider putting them in a sealable plastic bag.

11. **Record the serial numbers of all your equipment and software.** Write the serial numbers on the outside of the manuals that came with the equipment as well as in a single list that contains the serial numbers of all your equipment and software.

12. **Keep the shipping containers and packing materials for all your equipment.** This material will come in handy if you have to return your equipment for servicing or have to move it to another location.

13. **Look at the inside of your computer.** Before you connect power to your system, remove the computer case cover and visually inspect the internal components. The user manual usually identifies what each component does. Look for any disconnected wires, loose screws or washers, or any other obvious signs of trouble. Be careful not to touch anything inside the case unless you are grounded. Static electricity permanently can damage the chips on the circuit boards. Before you replace the cover, take several photographs of the computer showing the location of the circuit boards. These photos may save you from taking the cover off in the future if you or a vendor has a question about what equipment controller card is installed in what expansion slot. If you feel uncomfortable performing this step by yourself, ask a more experienced computer user to help. If you buy your system from a local dealer, have the dealer perform this step with you before you take possession of your system.

14. **Identify device connectors.** At the back of your system, you will find a number of connectors for the printer, the monitor, the mouse, a telephone line, and so forth. If the manufacturer does not already identify them, use a marking pen to write the purpose of each connector on the back of the computer case.

15. **Complete and send in your equipment and software registration cards right away.** If you already are entered in the vendor's user database, it can save you time when you call with a support question. Being a registered user also makes you eligible for special pricing on software upgrades.

16. **Install your system in an area where the temperature and humidity can be maintained.** Try to maintain a constant temperature between 60 and 80 degrees Fahrenheit when the computer is operating. High temperatures and humidity can damage electronic components. Be careful when using space heaters; their hot, dry air has been known to cause disk problems.

17. **Keep your computer area clean.** Avoid eating and drinking around the computer. Smoking should be avoided also. Cigarette smoke quickly can cause damage to the floppy disk drives and floppy disk surfaces.

18. **Check your home or renters insurance policy.** Some policies have limits on the amount of computer equipment they cover. Other policies do not cover computer equipment at all if it is used for a business (a separate policy is required).

COMPUTER USER HEALTH GUIDELINES

1. Work in a well-designed work area. See Figure 2 on page 8.40 for guidelines.
2. Alternate work activities to prevent physical and mental fatigue. If possible, change the order of your work to provide some variety.
3. Take frequent breaks. Every 15 minutes, look away from the screen to give your eyes a break. At least once per hour, get out of your chair and move around. Every two hours, take at least a 15-minute break.
4. Incorporate hand, arm, and body stretching exercises into your breaks. At lunch, try to get outside and walk.
5. Make sure your computer monitor is designed to minimize electromagnetic radiation (EMR). If it is an older model, consider adding EMR reducing accessories.
6. Try to eliminate or minimize surrounding noise. Noisy environments contribute to stress and tension.
7. If you frequently use the telephone and the computer at the same time, consider using a telephone headset. Cradling the telephone between your head and shoulder can cause muscle strain.
8. Be aware of symptoms of repetitive strain injuries: soreness, pain, numbness, or weakness in neck, shoulders, arms, wrists, and hands. Do not ignore early signs; seek medical advice.

Figure 3
All computer users should follow these guidelines to maintain their health.

How to Maintain Your Computer System

1. **Start a notebook that includes information on your system.** This notebook should be a single source of information about your entire system, both hardware and software. Each time you make a change to your system, adding or removing hardware or software, or when you change system parameters, you should record the change in your notebook. Keep a separate section for user IDs, passwords, and nicknames you use for Web sites and online services. Items you should include in the notebook are the following:
   - Serial numbers of all equipment and software.
   - Vendor support telephone numbers. These numbers often are buried in user manuals. Look up these numbers once and record all of them on a single sheet of paper at the front of your notebook.
   - User IDs, passwords, and nicknames for Web sites and online services.
   - Date and vendor for each equipment and software purchase.
   - Trouble log; a chronological history of any equipment or software problems. This history can be helpful if the problem persists and you have to call for support several times.
   - Notes on discussions with vendor support personnel (can be combined with trouble log).

   See Figure 4 for a suggested outline of notebook contents.

2. **Periodically review disk directories and delete unneeded files.** Files have a way of building up and quickly can use up your disk space. If you think you may need a file in the future, back it up to a floppy disk. Consider using an uninstaller utility program.

3. **Any time you work inside your computer, turn off the power and disconnect the equipment from the power source.** In addition, before you touch anything inside the computer, touch an unpainted metal surface such as the power supply. This will help to discharge any static electricity that could damage internal components.

4. **Reduce the need to clean the inside of your system by keeping the surrounding area dirt and dust free.** Floppy disk cleaners are available but should be used sparingly (some owners never use them unless they experience floppy disk problems). If dust builds up inside the computer, remove it carefully with compressed air and a small vacuum. Do not touch the components with the vacuum.

5. **Backup key files and data.** Use the operating system or a utility program to create an emergency or rescue disk to help you restart your computer if it crashes. Important data files should be copied regularly to disks, tape, or another computer.

6. **Periodically, defragment your hard disk.** Defragmenting your hard disk reorganizes files so they are incontiguous (adjacent) clusters and makes disk operations faster. Always back up your system before you run a defragmentation program.

7. **Protect your system from computer viruses.** Computer viruses are programs designed to *infect* computer systems by copying themselves into other computer files. The virus program spreads when the infected files are used by or copied to another system. Virus programs are dangerous because often they are designed to damage the files of the infected computer. You can protect yourself from viruses by installing an antivirus program on your computer.

8. **Learn to use system diagnostic programs.** If your system did not include diagnostic programs, obtain a set. These programs help you identify and possibly solve problems before you call for technical assistance. Some system manufacturers now include diagnostic programs with their systems and ask that you run the programs before you call for help.

PC OWNER'S NOTEBOOK OUTLINE

1. **Vendors**
   Vendor
   City/State
   Product
   Telephone #
   URL

2. **Internet and online services information**
   Service provider name
   Logon telephone number
   Alternate logon telephone number
   Technical support telephone number
   User ID
   Password

3. **Web site information**
   Web site name
   URL
   User ID
   Password
   Nickname

4. **Serial numbers**
   Product
   Manufacturer
   Serial #

5. **Purchase history**
   Date
   Product
   Manufacturer
   Vendor
   Cost

6. **Software log**
   Date installed/uninstalled

7. **Trouble log**
   Date
   Time
   Problem
   Resolution

8. **Support calls**
   Date
   Time
   Company
   Contact
   Problem
   Comments

9. **Vendor paperwork**

Figure 4
This suggested notebook outline will keep important information about your computer on hand and organized.

Index

Absolute hyperlinks: Hyperlinks that move to another document on a different Internet computer. **7.8**
Absolute referencing: In spreadsheet programs, when a formula is copied to another cell, the formula continues to refer to the same cell location. **2.19**
Absolute referencing, used by graphics tablets, 4.11
Access arms: Contain the read/write heads and move the heads across the surface of the disk. **5.10**
Access speed: The time it takes to find data and retrieve it. **3.13-14**
Access time: The time required to locate data on floppy disk and transfer it to memory. **5.7**
 CD-ROM, 5.15
 floppy disk, 5.7
 hard disk, 5.10
Accounting department, 1.23
Accounting software: Software that is used by companies to record and report financial transactions. **2.30**
Accuracy, 1.8
Active matrix: LCD screens that use individual transistors to control each crystal cell. **4.29**
Adapter cards, *see* **Expansion board**
Ad hoc report: Report created whenever needed to provide information that is not required on a scheduled basis; also called on-demand report. **4.24**
Advanced Research Projects Agency (ARPA), *see* **ARPA**
Aldus Freehand, 2.13
Aldus Persuasion, 2.25
Alignment: Formatting of document, dealing with how text is positioned in relation to a fixed reference point, usually a right or left margin; also called justification. **2.9**
Alphanumeric: Type of field in database; data includes letters, numbers and special characters. **2.22**
AltaVista search tool, 7.17
America Online, 1.9, 2.26, 2.28, 6.7, 7.5, 7.28
American Standard Code for Information Interchange (ACSII): The most widely used coding system to represent data, primarily on personal computers and many minicomputers. **3.4**
Analog computers: Computers designed to process continuously variable data, such as electrical voltage. **3.3**
Analog signal: A signal used in communications lines that consists of a continuous electrical wave. **6.16**
Analytical graphics: The charts provided by spreadsheet software. **2.20**
Animation: Graphics that can make Web pages more visually interesting or draw attention to important information or links. **7.12**
Animation, presentation graphics and, 2.24
Annotations: Editing feature of word processing programs; marks are made directly in document to make editing comments without changing document. **2.8**
Anonymous FTP: FTP site that allows anyone to log in and transfer some, if not all, available files. **7.20**
Antivirus program: Utility program that prevents, detects, and removes viruses. **8.20**

Applets: To assist in running multimedia applications on the Web, small programs that can be downloaded and run in browser window. **7.11**
Application server: Server computer that provides database information and runs all or part of the application software, such as a sales order entry program. **6.25**
Application software: Programs that tell a computer how to produce information, and reside permanently in storage, such as a disk. **1.18**
 accounting, 2.30
 communications, 2.26
 computer-aided design, 2.31
 database, 2.21-23
 desktop publishing, 2.12-14
 downward compatible, 8.14
 electronic mail, 2.27-28
 groupware, 2.30-31
 illustration, 2.13
 integrated, 2.32-33
 learning aids, 2.36-37
 multimedia authoring, 2.32
 personal finance, 2.29
 personal information management, 2.28
 presentation graphics, 2.24-25
 project management, 2.29
 spreadsheet, 2.14-21
 support tools, 2.37
 upward compatible, 8.14
 user tools, 2.1-42
 Web browsers, 2.26
 word processing, 2.4-12
Application software packages: Programs purchased from computer stores or software vendors. **1.18, 2.4**-37
Archie: FTP search tool that is used to find files on a particular subject. **7.20**
Archie gateway: Web page that provides an easy-to-use interface to the Archie search function. **7.20**
Arithmetic/logic unit (ALU): Part of the CPU that performs math and logic operations. **1.6, 3.8**
Arithmetic operations: Numeric calculations performed by the arithmetic/logic unit in the CPU that includes addition, subtraction, multiplication, and division. **3.8**
ARPA (Advanced Research Projects Agency): Agency of the U.S. Department of Defense; funded initial work on the Internet. **7.3**
ARPANET: The first Internet network. **7.3**
Arrow control keys, *see* **Arrow keys**
Arrow keys: Keys on a keyboard that move the cursor up, down, left, or right on the screen. **4.3**
Art, Web sites on, 7.42
Article: In a newsgroup, a previously entered message. **7.23**
Assistants, Office 97 and, 8.24
Asymmetric multiprocessing: Type of processing whereby application processes are assigned to a specific CPU in computers that have more than one CPU. **8.8**
Asynchronous transmission mode: Communications transmission mode that transmits data in individual bytes at irregular intervals; relatively slow method that is best used to send only small amounts of data. **6.16**
AT&T WorldNet, 7.28
Audio: Web applications consisting of individual sound files that must be downloaded before they can be played. **7.13**

Audio output: Consists of sounds, including words and music, produced by the computer; audio output device on the computer is a speaker. **4.25**
AutoCAD, 2.31
AutoCorrect: Editing feature in word processing programs that corrects common spelling errors automatically in words as they are entered. **2.7**
AUTOEXEC.BAT: File containing hardware and software configuration information in earlier versions of Windows operating system. **8.13**
AutoFormat: Formatting feature in word processing programs; formats document automatically as it is being typed. **2.10**
Automatic teller machines (ATMs), 4.18
AutoSave: Feature that automatically saves open documents at specified intervals. **2.4**
AutoSum button: Used in spreadsheet program to automatically calculate totals. **2.16**
Auxiliary storage, *see* **Storage**
Auxiliary storage devices, *see* **Storage devices**

Backbones: High-speed communications lines connecting regional host computers to the major networks carrying most of the Internet communications traffic. **7.5**
Background: Jobs assigned a lower processing priority in a multitasking operating system. **8.5**
Backup: Procedures that provide for storing copies of program and data files so that in the event the files are lost or destroyed, they can be recovered. **5.12**
Backup software: Utility program that allows copying files or entire hard disk on tape or disk cartridges. **8.20**
Band printer: Impact printer that uses a horizontal, rotating band and can print in the range of 600 to 2,000 lines per minute. **4.34**
Bandwidth: The range of frequencies that a communications channel can carry. **6.18**
Banking, online, 2.26, 6.6
Bar charts: Charts that display relationships among data with bars of various lengths. **2.20**
Bar code: A type of optical code consisting of vertical lines and spaces, found on most grocery and retail items; usually scanned to produce price and inventory information about the product. **4.14**
Basic Input/Output System (BIOS): Set of instructions that provides the interface between the operating system and the hardware devices, stored on ROM chip. **8.12**
 loading operating system and, 8.12
Bay: An open area inside the system unit used to install additional equipment. **3.6, 3.18**
Bernoulli disk cartridge: Removable hard disk storage device that works by using a cushion of air to keep the flexible disk surface from touching the read/write head. **5.11**
BigBook search tool, 7.17
Binary code, 5.7
Biological feedback input: Devices that work in combination with special software to translate movements, temperature, or even skin-based electrical signals into input; include devices such as gloves, body suits, and eyeglasses. **4.21**
BIOS, *see* **Basic Input/Output System**
Bit(s): An element of a byte that can represent one of two values, on or off. There are 8 bits in a byte. **3.3**
 parity, 3.5, 6.17

Bits per inch (bpi): Number of bits that can be recorded on one inch of track on a floppy disk. **5.6**

Bits per second (bps): A measure of the speed of data transmission; the number of bits transmitted in one second. **6.18**

Bookmark: The title and URL of a Web page, recorded in the browser so the user can return to the Web page in a future session. **7.11**

Booting: The process of loading an operating system into memory. **8.12-13**

Border: Decorative line or box used with text, graphics, or tables. **2.10**

Bridge: A combination of hardware and software that is used to connect similar networks. **6.22**

Browser, *see* **Web browser software**

Buffers: Areas of memory used to store data that has been read or is waiting to be sent to an output device. **8.7**

Built-in style: Feature of word processing program that allows font and format information to be saved so it can be applied to new documents. **2.10**

Bulletin board system (BBS): A computer system that maintains a centralized collection of information in the form of electronic messages, accessed using a personal computer and communications equipment. **6.5**

Bunny suits: Special protective clothing worn during chip manufacturing process in clean rooms. **3.26**

Bus: Any line that transmits bits between the memory and the input/output devices, and between memory and the CPU. **3.14-15**

Business graphics, *see* **Analytical graphics**
Businesses
 network computers for, 7.25-26
 on World Wide Web, 7.30, 7.31
Business Web sites, 7.42

Bus network: A communications network that has all devices connected to and sharing a single data path. **6.28**

Button: Icon (usually a rectangular or circular shape) that when clicked, causes a specific action to take place. **2.3**

Byte: Each storage location within main memory, identified with a memory address. **3.3**
sync, 6.17

Cache: High-speed memory between the CPU and the main RAM memory; stores the most frequently used instructions and data, and increases processing efficiency. **3.12**
disk, 5.10
RAM, 3.13
speed and, 3.13
Cache memory chip, 3.7

Caching: Process of storing a copy of each Web page that is accessed in local storage by a proxy server. **7.18**

Cage: Two or more bays together. **3.18**
Career Web sites, 7.42
Carrier-connect radio, 6.12

Carrier sense multiple access with collision detection (CSMA/CD): Method used by Ethernet network protocol to detect data collisions and retransmit data. **6.30**

Cartridge tape: Frequently used storage medium for backup on personal computers, contains magnetic recording tape in a small plastic housing. **5.16**

Cathode ray tube (CRT): The large tube inside a monitor or terminal. **4.27, 4.31**

CD-E (compact disk-erasable): Erasable CD-ROM drive. **5.15**

CD-R (compact disk-recordable): Recordable CD-ROM drive. **5.15**

CD-ROM (compact disk read-only memory): A small optical disk that uses the same laser technology as audio compact disks; used for storage. 1.5, 1.7, 3.6,**5.14**
access time, 5.15

CD-ROM drive: Storage device that uses a low-powered laser light to read data from removable CD-ROMs. 1.5, **1.7**, 3.6

Cell: Intersection of a row and column on a spreadsheet. **2.15**

Cellular telephone: A wireless telephone that uses radio waves to communicate with a local antenna assigned to a specific geographic area called a cell. **6.13**

Centered alignment: Alignment that divides text equally on either side of a reference point, usually the center of the page. 2.9

Central processing unit (CPU): Processing unit located on motherboard; contains a control unit that executes instructions that guide the computer through a task, and an arithmetic/logic unit that performs math and logic functions. These two components work together using the program and data stored in memory to perform the processing operations. **1.6**, 3.6, **3.8-10**
components of, 3.8
loading operating system and, 8.12
microprocessor and, 3.7
multiple, 8.6
multitasking and, 8.5
superscalar, 3.21
use of multiple, 3.21
word size and, 3.9
Central processing unit (CPU) chip, 3.7
Central processing unit (CPU) upgrade sockets, 3.10

Channel: Conversation group involved in Internet Relay Chat. **7.24**

Channel operator: The person who creates a channel for Internet Relay Chat, and has responsibility for monitoring the conversation. **7.24**

Characters per second (cps): Speed measurement of impact printers that have movable print heads. **4.33**

Chart: In spreadsheet software, a graphic representation of the relationship of numerical data. **2.20**
presentation graphics, 2.24
Check disk, 5.20
Chip, *see* **Integrated circuit**

CISC (complex instruction set computing/computers): Computers that have hundreds of commands in their instruction sets; describes most computers. **3.19**

Clean rooms: Special laboratories where chips are manufactured to avoid contamination of the chip surface. **3.25-26**

Clicking: Describes process of pressing and releasing mouse button. **4.5**

Client-server: In information resource sharing on a network, process of the server completing some of the processing first, and then transmitting data to the requesting computer. **6.24**

Clip art: Previously created illustrations and pictures that are sold in collections, and inserted as graphics into word processing documents. **2.10,** 4.25

Clipboard: Temporary storage location for text during cut and copy operations. **2.6**

Cluster: Two to eight track sectors on a floppy disk; the smallest unit of floppy disk space used to store data. **5.5**

CMOS (complementary metal-oxide semiconductor): Type of memory used to store information about the computer system, such as the amount of memory, the type of keyboard and monitor, and the type and capacity of disk drives. **3.13**

Coax, *see* **Coaxial cable**

Coaxial cable: A high-quality communications line consisting of a copper wire conductor surrounded by a nonconducting insulator that is in turn surrounded by a woven metal outer conductor, and finally a plastic outer coating. **6.9-10**
Code
 ASCII, 3.4
 binary, 5.7
 EBCDIC, 3.4
 operation, 3.20
 thread, 8.5
 Unicode, 3.4-5

Collision: In data communications, describes occurrence of a transmitted packet of data running into another packet. **6.30**

Color libraries: Included in desktop publishing programs; standard sets of colors used by designers and printers to ensure that colors will print exactly as specified. **2.13**

Color monitor: Monitor that can display text or graphics in color. **4.28,** 4.31

Columns: Data that is organized vertically on a spreadsheet. **2.15**

Command(s): Keywords and phrases input to direct the computer to perform certain activities. Commands are either chosen with a pointing device, entered from the keyboard, or selected using another type of input device. **2.3, 4.2**

Common carriers: Public wide area network companies such as the telephone companies. **6.26**

Command language: The set of commands used to interact with the computer in a command-line user interface. **8.3**

Command-line user interface: Type of user interface that has user enter keywords (commands) that cause the computer to take a specific action, such as copying a file or sending a file to the printer. **8.3,** 8.19

Communications: The transmission of data and information between two or more computers using a communications channel such as a standard telephone line; also called data communications, or telecommunications. 1.8, **6.2-36**
 communications channels, 6.8-18
 equipment, 6.19-22
 line configurations, 6.14-16
 networks, 6.23-32
 software, 6.18
 transmission media, 6.8-14
 uses of, 6.2-7

Communications channel: The path that data follows as it is transmitted from the sending equipment to the receiving equipment in a communications system. **6.8**
 characteristics of, 6.16-18
 example of, 6.14
 Internet, 7.4, 7.5
 line configurations, 6.14-16
 transmission direction, 6.18
 transmission media, 6.8-14
 transmission modes, 6.17
 transmission rate, 6.18
 types of signals, 6.16-17

Communications devices: Devices that enable a computer to connect to other computers; includes modems, and network interface cards. **1.7**

Communications line, *see* **Communications channel**
Communications link, *see* **Communications channel**
Communications satellites: Satellites that receive microwave signals from earth-based communications facilities, amplify the signals, and retransmit the signals back to the communications facilities. **6.11**
Communications software: Programs that perform data communications tasks such as dialing, file transfer, terminal emulation, and Internet access, allowing data to be transmitted from one computer to another. **2.26, 6.8, 6.19**
 Internet and, 7.29
 Web browsers, *see* Web browser software
Compact disk read-only memory, *see* **CD-ROM**
Compel, 2.25
Compound document: In object linking and embedding applications, a document that contains objects from more than one application. **2.34**
CompuServe, 2.28, 6.6, 6.7, 7.28
Computer(s): An electronic device, operating under the control of instructions stored in its own memory unit that can accept data (input), process data arithmetically and logically, produce results (output) from the processing, and store the results for future use. **1.4**
 analog, 3.3
 categories of, 1.10-15
 components of, 1.4-7
 connectivity, 1.9
 digital, 3.3
 example of use, 1.20-25
 fault-tolerant, 8.6
 host, 6.15
 network, 7.25-27
 neural network, 3.22
 operations of, 1.7
 overview of using, 1.1-30
 power, 1.8
 proxy server, 7.18
 speed of, 3.9, 3.13-14
Computer-aided design (CAD): Design method that uses software to aid in product and structure design. 1.23, **2.31**
 graphics tablets used in, 4.11
Computer-assisted retrieval (CAR): Process in which microfilm readers perform automatic data lookup. **4.41**
Computer drawing programs: Graphics programs that allow an artistic user to create works of art. **4.25**
Computer graphics: Any nontext pictorial information. **4.25**
Computer literacy: Knowing how to use a computer. **1.2**
Computer output microfilm (COM): An output technique that records output from a computer as microscopic images on roll or sheet film. **4.41**
Computer paint programs, *see* **Computer drawing programs**
Computer program, *see* **Software**
Computer programmers: People who design, write, test, and implement programs necessary to direct the computer to process data into information. **1.16**
Computer system: Collection of devices that function together to process data. **1.4**
Computer users, *see* **User(s)**
Computing Web sites, 7.43
Concentrator, *see* **Wiring hub**
CONFIG.SYS: File containing hardware and software configuration information in earlier versions of Windows operating system. **8.13**

Connectivity: The capability of connecting a computer to other computers. **1.9**
Connectors: Couplers contained in ports, used to attach cables to peripheral devices. 3.6, **3.16-18**
Context-sensitive: Help information that is about the current command or operation being attempted. **2.36**
Context switching: Multitasking method in which multiple processes can be open but only one process is active; it happens when one process relinquishes control of the CPU and another starts. **8.5**
Contiguous clusters, 5.12
Continuous-form paper: A type of paper that is connected together for a continuous flow through the printer. **4.32**
Continuous-speech recognition: Voice input system that allows the user to speak in a flowing, conversational tone. **4.20**
Controller cards, *see* **Expansion board**
Control program: The resident portion of the operating system, also called kernel, supervisor, monitor, executive, or master program. **8.2**
Control unit: Part of the CPU that repeatedly executes the fetching, decoding, executing, and storing operations, called the machine cycle. **1.6, 3.8**
Cooperative multitasking: Multitasking method in which multiple processes switch back and forth automatically when they reach logical break points, such as waiting for input; this method relies on the processes to relinquish control to other processes. **8.5, 8.16**
Coprocessor: A special microprocessor chip or circuit board designed to perform a specific task, such as numeric calculations. **3.14**
Copy: Makes a copy of marked text and stores it on the Clipboard, leaving original marked text where it was. **2.6**
CorelDRAW!, 2.13
Corel Quattro Pro, 2.20
CPU, *see* **Central processing unit**
CPU utilization: The amount of time that the CPU is working and not idle, waiting for data to process. **8.10**
CRT, *see* **Cathode ray tube**
Currency: Type of field in database; contains dollars and cents amounts. **2.22**
Cursor *see* **Insertion point**
Cut: Removing portion of document and storing it in the Clipboard. **2.6**
Cylinder: All the tracks on a disk that occupy the same position on the top and bottom of the disk that have the same number. **5.4**

Data: The raw facts, including numbers, words, images, and sounds, given to a computer during the input operation, that is processed to produce information. **1.7, 4.2**
 reading, 5.2
 represented in computer, 3.3-5
 storage, *see* **Storage**
 writing or recording, 5.2
Data automation, source, 4.12-17
Database: Collection of data that is stored in related files. **2.21**
Database server: Network server that provides selected information from files stored on the server, but does not run the application software; contrast with application server. **6.25**
Database software: Software that allows the user to create, maintain, and update the data that is stored in it. **2.21-23**
Data collection devices: Input devices used for obtaining data at the site where the transaction or event being reported takes place. **4.17**
Data communications, *see* **Communications**

Data compression: Method of storing data on a disk that reduces storage requirements by substituting codes for repeating patterns of data. **5.13, 7.20**
Data link, *see* **Communications channel**
Data transfer rate: The time required to transfer data from disk to main memory. **5.7**
Date: Type of field in database containing month, day, and year information. **2.22**
dBASE, 2.23
Decimal number system, 3.22-23
Decoding: Control unit operation that translates the program instruction into the commands that the computer can process. **3.8**
Decompressing files, 7.20
Dedicated line: A communications line connection between devices that is always established. **6.15**
Dedicated word processing systems: Computers that are used only for word processing. **2.4**
Defragmentation: Storage method that reorganizes stored data so files are located in contiguous clusters, improving the speed of the computer. **5.12**
Delete: Removing text from a document. **2.6**
Desktop computer: The most common type of personal computer, designed to fit conveniently on the surface of a desk or workspace, and has separate keyboard and display screen. **1.13**
 floppy disk drives in, 5.4
Desktop enhancer: Utility program that allows user to change the look and organization of a desktop (on-screen work area). **8.22**
Desktop publishing (DTP): Software that allows user to design and produce high-quality documents that contain text, graphics, and unique colors. **2.12-14**
 Web authoring features, 7.8
Destination document: In object linking and embedding applications, the document into which to object is placed. **2.34**
Detail report: A report in which each line usually corresponds to one record that has been processed. **4.23**
Device drivers: Programs used by the operating system to control input and output devices. **8.9**
Diagnostic program: Utility program that helps in determining if hardware and certain systems software programs are installed correctly and functioning properly. **8.21**
Dialing: Communications software that stores, reviews, selects, and dials telephone numbers. **6.19**
Dicing: Step in chip manufacturing process where wafers are cut into individual chips. **3.27**
Die: In chip manufacturing, name given to wafers that are cut into individual chips. **3.27**
Diffusion oven: In chip manufacturing, oven that bakes first layer of material onto the wafer surface. **3.26**
Digital audio tape (DAT): Method of storing large amounts of data on tape using helical scan technology to write data at high densities across the tape at an angle. **5.18**
Digital cameras: Cameras that record photographs in the form of digital data that can be stored on a computer. **4.21**
Digital computers: Computers that process data, including text, sound, graphics, or video, into a digital (numeric) value; describes most computers. **3.3**
Digital data service: Offered by telephone companies, communications channels specifically designed to carry digital signals. **6.17**

Digital signal: A type of signal for computer processing in which individual electrical pulses that represent bits are grouped together in bytes. **6.16**

Digital signal processing (DSP): In voice input systems, a board that is added to the computer to convert the voice into digital form. **4.20**

Digitizer: Converts points, lines, and curves from a sketch, drawing, or photograph to digital impulses and transmits them to a computer. **4.10**

Digitizing: The process a computer uses to convert data into a digital form. **3.3**

DIMM (dual in-line memory module): Small circuit board that holds multiple RAM chips. **3.12**

Direct-access storage devices, *see* **Fixed disks**

Directory, formatting floppy disk, 5.5

Discrete-speech recognition: Voice input system that requires the user to pause slightly between each word spoken to the computer. **4.20**

Discussion database, 2.30, 2.31

Disk cache: An area of memory set aside for data most often read from the disk. **5.10**

Disk cartridges: Hard disk storage devices that can be inserted and removed from the computer, offering the storage and fast access features of hard disks and the portability of floppy disks. **5.11**

Disk compression programs, 5.13

Diskette, *see* **Floppy disk**

Disk management, operating system and, 8.11

Disk mirroring, *see* **Redundant array of inexpensive disks**

Display device: The visual output device of a computer, such as a monitor. **4.27**-31

Display terminals: A keyboard and a screen. **4.18**

Document
 hyperlinked, *see* Hyperlinks
 hypermedia, 7.7
 hypertext, 7.7

Document, object linking and embedding applications
 compound, 2.34
 destination, 2.34
 source, 2.34

Document, word processing, *see* Word processing document

Domain name: The text version of the Internet protocol address. **7.6**

Domain name servers: Internet computers that use the domain name to look up the associated Internet protocol address. **7.6**

Domain name system (DNS): System that domain names are registered in. **7.6**

Dopants: Materials that are added to surface of wafer during chip manufacturing, and will conduct electricity. **3.26**

DOS (Disk Operating System): Several single tasking operating systems developed in the early 1980s for IBM-compatible personal computers; most widely used versions were MS-DOS and PC-DOS. **8.14**

Dot matrix printer: An impact printer that has a print head consisting of a series of small tubes containing pins that, when pressed against a ribbon and paper, print small dots closely together to form characters. **4.32**

Dot pitch: The distance between each pixel on the computer screen. **4.30**

Dots per inch (dpi): Measurement of laser printer resolution. **4.37**

Double-clicking: Pressing and releasing mouse button twice without moving the mouse. **4.5**

Downlink: The transmission from a satellite to a receiving earth station. **6.11**

Downward compatible: Describes application that is written for the new version of an operating system and can also run under the previous version. **8.14**

Dragging: Using mouse to move data from one location in document to another. **4.5**

Drive bay, *see* **Bay**

Drivers, device, 8.9

Drum plotter: Plotter that uses a rotating drum, or cylinder, over which drawing pens are mounted. **4.38**

Dual scan: A type of passive matrix LCD screen frequently used on lower cost portable computers. **4.29**

Dumb terminal: A keyboard and a display screen that can be used to enter and transmit data to, or receive and display data from, a computer to which it is connected, and has no independent processing capability or secondary storage. **4.18**

DVD (digital video disk): Revised format for CD-ROM disks that eventually will increase the capacity of CD-ROM size disks to 4.7 gigabytes. **5.14**

Dye diffusion: Process used by a special type of thermal printer; chemically treated paper is used to obtain color print quality equal to glossy magazines. **4.37**

Dynamic RAM (DRAM): A type of RAM memory that has access to speeds of 50 to 100 nanoseconds; comprises most memory. **3.13**

EarthLink Network, 7.28

Earth stations: Communications facilities that contain large, dish-shaped antennas used to transmit and receive data from satellites. **6.11**

Ecco Pro, 2.28

Editing: Making changes and corrections to content of a document. **2.6-8**

Editing, sound, 4.19

Education, Web used for, 7.8, 7.31, 7.38

Education Web sites, 7.43

Electronic data interchange (EDI): The direct electronic exchange of documents from one business's computer system to another. **6.4**

Electronic mail, *see* **E-mail**

Electronic meetings, 6.3

Electronic whiteboard: Input device that is a modified conference room whiteboard that uses a built-in scanner to record text and drawings in a file on an attached computer. **4.22**

Electrostatic plotter: Plotter in which the paper moves under a row of wires (styli) that can be turned on to create an electrostatic charge on the paper. **4.39**

E-mail (electronic mail): Electronic exchange of messages to and from other computer users. **6.2, 7.19**
 acronyms, 2.28
 emoticons, 2.28

E-mail etiquette, 2.28

E-mail software: Software that allows users to send messages to and receive messages from other computer users. **2.27-28, 6.2**

Embedded object: Object that user can make changes to in the destination document using tools from the application that originally created the object; only the destination document is changed, while the source document is not affected. **2.34**

Employment Web sites, 7.42

Embedded processors: Un*seen* computers that are built into equipment such as radios, cellular telephones, ATMs, and automobiles. **3.28**

End users, *see* **User(s)**

Enterprise computing: Connecting all of the computers in an organization into one network, so everyone in the organization can share computing resources. **6.33**

Entertainment Web sites, 7.43

Environment, Web sites on, 7.44

ESCAPE (ESC) key, 4.4

Etching: During chip manufacturing, process of removing channels in layers of materials on wafer. **3.26**

Ethernet: The most widely used network protocol for LAN networks; can transmit data at 10 Mbps. **6.30**

Eudora, 2.28

Even parity: The total number of on bits in the byte (including the parity bit) must be an even number. **3.5**

Exception report: A report containing information that is outside of normal user-specified values or conditions, called the exception criteria. **4.24**

Excite search tool, 7.17

Executing: Control unit operation that processes the computer commands. **3.8**

Execution cycle: Together, executing and storing operations of the machine cycle. **3.8**

Executive, *see* **Control program**

Executive information system (EIS), 1.25

Expansion board: Circuit board for add-on devices. 3.6, **3.15**

Expansion bus: Bus that carries data to and from the expansion slots. **3.14**

Expansion card, *see* **Expansion board**

Expansion slot: A socket designed to hold the circuit board for a device, such as a sound card, that adds capability to the computer system. 3.6, **3.15-16**

Extended Binary Coded Decimal Interchange Code (EBCDIC): A coding system used to represent data, primarily on mainframes. **3.4**

External commands: Less frequently used instructions in the nonresident portion of the operating system. **8.2**

External modem: A separate, or stand-alone device attached to the computer with a cable and to the telephone outlet with a standard telephone cord. **6.19**

External report: A report used outside the organization. **4.23**

Extranets: Private networks that include more than one organization. **7.17**

Facsimile, *see* **Fax**

FAQ: Stands for frequently asked questions, about the Internet. **7.24,** 7.45

Fast-Ethernet: A higher-speed version of Ethernet network protocol; can transmit data at 100 Mbps. **6.30**

Fault-tolerant computer: Computer built with redundant components to allow processing to continue if any single component fails. **8.6**

Favorites, 7.11

Fax (facsimile): Communications method that uses equipment to transmit and receive a document image over telephone lines. **4.42, 6.2**

Fetching: Control unit operation that obtains the next program instruction from memory. **3.8**

Fiber-optic cable: High-speed transmission media for communications channel that uses smooth, hair-thin strands of glass or plastic to transmit data as pulses of light. **6.10**

ISDN lines, 6.17

Fields: A special item of information, such as a name or Social Security number, in a record of a database file. **2.21**

File(s): A collection of related records. **2.21**
 compressed, 5.13, 7.20, 8.20
 uncompressing, 5.13, 7.20, 8.20

File allocation table (FAT): On personal computers, a directory that stores information such as the file name, file size, the time and date the file was last changed, and the cluster number where the file begins. **5.5**

File compression software: Utility program that reduces (compresses) the size of files. **8.20**

File conversion: Utility program that converts file from one format to another so the file can be used by another application. **8.20**

File management
 operating system and, 8.11
 utility programs, 8.19-21

File-server: In information resource sharing on a network, method that uses a server to send an entire file at one time to a requesting computer, and then the requesting computer performs the processing. **6.24**

File transfer: Communications software that allows the user to move one or more files from one computer system to another. The software generally has to be loaded on both the sending and receiving computers. **6.19**

File transfer protocol, *see* **FTP**

File viewer: Utility program that lists the names and size of files. **8.19**

Finance Web sites, 7.42

Financial transactions, accounting software and, 2.30

Firewall: Refers to both the hardware and software used to restrict access to data on a network. **7.18**

Firmware: Instructions that are stored in ROM memory; also called microcode. **3.13**

Fixed disks: Hard disks on minicomputers and mainframes; also called direct-access storage devices. **5.9**

Flaming: Sending an abusive message on the Internet. **7.24**

Flash memory: Type of RAM that can retain data even when power is turned off. **3.11**

Flash RAM, *see* **Flash memory**

Flatbed plotter: Plotter that uses software to instruct the pens to move to the down position so the pens contact the flat surface of the paper. **4.38**

Flat panel display: A thin display screen that uses liquid crystal display or gas plasma technology; often used in portable computers. **4.29**

Floppy disk: Type of small, removable magnetic disk storage consisting of a circular piece of thin mylar plastic, which is coated with an oxide material that is recorded on, storing data as magnetic areas. The plastic disk is enclosed in a rigid plastic shell for protection from debris; most widely used portable storage medium. **1.7, 5.3-8**
 access time, 5.7
 care of, 5.8
 formatting, 5.4
 storage capacity, 5.6

Floppy disk drive: Drive used to contain inserted floppy disk. 1.5, **1.7**, 3.6, 5.3, 5.6

Floptical: Floppy disk that combines optical and magnetic technologies to achieve high storage rates (currently up to 120 megabytes) on a disk similar to a 3½-inch magnetic floppy disk. **5.15**

Font: A specific combination of typeface and point size. **2.9**

Footers: Information printed at the bottom of every page. **2.10**

Foreground: In a multitasking operating system, describes process that is currently active or process that has the highest priority. **8.5**

Formatting disk: Process that prepares a floppy disk for storage by defining the tracks, cylinders, and sectors on the surface of the floppy disk. **5.4**

Format/formatting documents: Changing the appearance of a document. **2.8**
 word processing document, 2.8-11

Formulas: Perform calculations on the data in a spreadsheet. **2.15**

Four11 search tool, 7.17

FoxPro, 2.23

Fragmented: File stored in clusters that are not next to each other; also describes the condition of a disk drive that has many files stored in noncontiguous clusters, slowing down the computer's speed. **5.12**

Frames: Division of screen into small windows that allows multiple files to be displayed on the screen at the same time. **8.16**

Front-end processor: A computer dedicated to handling the communications requirements of a larger computer. **6.21**

FTP (file transfer protocol): Internet standard that allows the exchange of files with other computers on the Internet. **7.20**
 anonymous, 7.20

FTP servers, *see* **FTP sites**

FTP sites: Computers that contain files available for transfer on FTP; many files can be downloaded at no cost. **7.20**

Full-duplex transmission: Data transmission method in which data can be sent in both directions at the same time. **6.18**

Function(s): Stored formulas that perform common calculations in a spreadsheet. **2.16**

Function keys: A set of numerical keys preceded by an "F", included on keyboards as a type of user interface. Pressing a function key causes a command to take place in an application program. **4.4**

Games
 MOO (multiuser object oriented), 7.22
 MUD (multiuser dimension), 7.22
 virtual reality, 7.15
 Web-based, 7.12

Gas plasma: Screens that use neon gas deposited between two sheets of polarizing material. **4.29**

Gateway: A combination of hardware and software that allows users on one network to access the resources on a different type of network. **6.22**

Geosynchronous orbit: Orbit about 22,300 miles above the earth that communications satellites are placed in, causing the satellite to orbit at the same speed as the earth, so the dish antennas used to send and receive microwave signals remain fixed on the appropriate satellite at all times. **6.12**

Gestures: Special symbols made with a pen input device that issue commands to the computer. **4.8**

Ghosting, 8.22

Gigabyte (GB): A measurement of memory space, equal to a billion bytes, or one million kilobytes. **3.11**, 5.9

Gigaflops (GFLOPS): Billions of floating-point operations per second. **3.20**

Global positioning system (GPS): Communications system that uses satellites to determine the geographic location of earth-based GPS equipment; often used for tracking and navigation by all types of vehicles. **6.5**

Gopher: Menu-driven program that assists users in locating and retrieving files on the Internet. **7.21**

Gopher servers: Internet computers that maintain Gopher directories. **7.21**

Government Web sites, 7.44

Grammar checker: Editing feature of word processors that is used to check for grammar, writing style, and sentence structure errors. **2.8**

Graphical user interface (GUI): A user interface that provides visual clues, such as symbols called icons, to help the user when entering data or running programs. **1.17, 2.2-3, 8.3**
 browser-like features, 8.3
 Macintosh, 8.17
 OS/2, 8.18
 Windows 3.x, 8.15
 Windows 95, 8.15
 Windows NT, 8.17

Graphical Web browser, 7.9-11, 7.12

Graphics: The incorporation of pictures in documents; some graphics are included in word processing packages, but are usually created in separate applications, and imported (brought into) the word processing document, and can often be modified by the user; also describes designs and images used in Web pages to reinforce text messages. **2.10**, 4.25, **7.12**
 light pen used with, 4.10
 Web page, 7.10, 7.12

Graphics objects, used in desktop publishing, 2.13

Graphics tablet: Converts points, lines, and curves from a sketch, drawing, or photograph to digital impulses and transmits them to a computer; also contains unique characters and commands. **4.11**

Gray scaling: Used by monochrome monitors to convert an image into pixels that are different shades of gray. **4.28**

Groupware: Software that helps multiple users work together by sharing information. **2.30-31, 6.4**
 intranets, 7.17

Half-duplex transmission: Data transmission method that allows data to flow in both directions, but in only one direction at a time. **6.18**

Hand-held computers: Small computers used by workers who are on their feet instead of sitting at a desk, such as meter readers or inventory counters. **1.10**
 Windows CE and, 8.16

Hand-held scanner, 4.13

Handshake: The process of establishing the communications connection on a switched line. **6.14**

Handwriting recognition software: Software that can be taught to recognize an individual's unique style of writing. **4.8**

Hard copy: Output that is printed. **4.23**

Hard disk(s): Storage devices containing high-capacity disk or disks, providing faster access time and greater storage capacity than floppy disks. **5.8-11**
 access time, 5.10
 hierarchical storage management using, 5.24
 maintaining data stored on, 5.12-13
 storage capacity, 5.9

Hard disk controller: Collection of electronic circuits that manage the flow of data to and from the hard disk. **5.10-11**

Hard disk drive: Secondary storage device containing nonremovable disks. 1.5, **1.7**, 3.6
 disk cartridges, 5.11

Hardware: Equipment that inputs, processes, outputs, and stores data, consisting of input devices, a system unit, output devices, storage devices, and communications devices. **1.4**
 communications, 6.19-22
 configuration information, 8.13
 device drivers, 8.9
 Internet connection, 7.27, 7.29
 network computers, 7.25-27
 network connections, 6.14-15, 6.22, 6.27-29
 operating system and, 8.8-9, 8.12

Hardware resource sharing: Used in local area networks, allowing each personal computer on a network to access and use devices that are too costly, or used too infrequently to provide to each user. **6.23**

Head crash: Describes process of a read/write head colliding with the hard disk surface, usually resulting in a loss of data. **5.10**

Headers: Information that is printed at the top of every page. **2.10**

Health Web sites, 7.44

Helical scan technology: Used by digital audio tape to record data at high densities across the tape at an angle. **5.18**

Helper application: Used for Web applications; allows multimedia to be run in a window separate from the browser. **7.11**

Hexadecimal (base 16): Number system that represents binary in a more compact form; used by the computer to communicate with a programmer when a problem with to program exists. **3.22**

Hierarchical storage management (HSM): Process of automating the transfer of data by moving files from online devices to different categories and speeds of storage devices. **5.24**

High-definition television (HDTV): Television sets designed for digital signals; may eventually replace computer screens. **4.26**

High-density (HD) floppy disk: Floppy disk that can store 1.44 megabytes on a 3fi-inch floppy disk; most widely used floppy disk. **5.6**

Highlighting tool: Revision feature that allows user to mark text in color to call out key parts of a document for others. **2.8**

History, Web sites on, 7.45

History list: Records list of Web pages that are viewed during the time user is connected to the Web. **7.11**

Holographic storage, 5.25

Home, network computers for, 7.26

Home page: First page of information located at a Web site, located through the Internet. **1.8, 2.26**

Home page: The Web page designated as the page to display each time a browser is launched. **7.10**

Host computer: In a data communications system, a main computer that is connected to several devices, such as terminals or personal computers. **6.15**

number of, on Internet, 7.2

Hotlists, 7.11

HTML, *see* **Hypertext markup language**

http:// (hypertext transfer protocol): The communications standard used to transfer pages on the Web. **7.10**

Human-centric operating systems, 8.25

Human resources department, 1.24

Humor Web sites, 7.45

Hyperlinks: In Web documents, built-in links to other related documents, allowing user to move quickly from one document to another. 1.8, **7.7**
 absolute, 7.8
 icons as, 8.16
 relative, 7.8
 target, 7.8

Hypermedia: Web document that contains text, graphics, video, or sound hyperlinks to other documents. **7.7**

Hypertext: Web document that contains text hyperlinks to other documents. **7.7**

Hypertext markup language (HTML): Set of special instructions used to create Web pages; the special instructions are called tags, or markups, that specify links to other documents and how the page is displayed. **7.8**

Hypertext transfer protocol, *see* **http://**

Icon: In a graphical user interface, on screen pictures that represent an application software program where data is stored. **1.17, 2.2**
 as hyperlinks, 8.16

Ideograms: Symbols used by Asian and other foreign languages to represent multiple words and ideas. **3.4**

Illustration software: Software that is designed for use by artists. **2.13**

Image libraries, 2.24

Image processing systems: In source data automation, systems that use scanners to capture and electronically file exact copies of documents. **4.13**

Image scanner: An input device that electronically captures an entire page of text or images such as photographs or art work, converting the information on the original document into digital data that can be stored on a disk and processed by the computer; also called page scanner. **4.13**

OCR software used with, 4.16

Impact printers: Printers that transfer images onto paper by some type of printing mechanism striking the paper, ribbon, and character together. **4.32-34**

Information: Data that has been processed by computer into a form that has meaning and is useful. **1.7**

accurate, timely, and useful, 1.19

Information appliance: Network computer for the home, that incorporates Internet access into a device normally found in the home, such as a television, telephone, or video game console; costs less than a personal computer. **7.26**

Information literacy: Knowing how to find, analyze, and use information. **1.2**

Information processing: The production of information by processing data on a computer. **1.7**

Information processing cycle: Input, process, output, and storage operations. Collectively, these operations describe the procedures that a computer performs to process data into information and store it for future use. **1.7**

Information resource sharing: Allows LAN users to access the data stored on any other computer in the network. **6.24**

Information services, *see* **Online services**

Information system: Elements required for information processing, including software, hardware, data, users, procedures, and information systems personnel. **1.19**
 elements of, 1.19

Information systems department, 1.24

Info*seek* search tool, 7.17

Infrared light wave transmission, 6.12

Ink: Describes the darkened location on screen where a pen input device touches it. **4.8**

Ink-jet printer: Nonimpact printer that forms characters by using a nozzle that shoots droplets of ink onto the page, producing high-quality print and graphics. **4.34-36**

Input: First step in information processing cycle; the process of entering data (including numbers, words, images, and sounds), programs, commands, and user responses into memory of computer for processing. Input can also refer to the media (such as disks, tapes, and documents) that contain input data. **1.7, 4.2-22**
 biological feedback, 4.21
 digital camera, 4.21
 keyboard, 4.2-4
 mouse, 4.5
 operating system management of, 8.8-9
 pen, 4.8
 pointing devices, 4.5-11
 sound, 4.19
 source data automation, 4.12-17

terminals, 4.18
video, 4.22
voice, 4.19-21

Input devices: Hardware used to enter data into a computer, such as a keyboard and a mouse. **1.4**

storage devices used as, 5.2

Insert: Adding characters to existing text. **2.6**

Insertion point: A symbol such as an underline character, rectangle, or vertical bar that indicates where on the screen the next character entered will appear; also called cursor. **2.6, 4.3**

Insert mode, 2.6

Instruction cycle: Together, name given to fetching and decoding operations of the machine cycle. **3.8**

Instruction set: The collection of commands, such as ADD or MOVE, that the computer's circuits can directly perform. **3.19**

Integrated circuit (IC): A complete electronic circuit that has been etched on a thin slice of nonconducting material such as silicon; also called chip. **3.8, 3.25**
 cache memory, 3.7
 CPU, 3.7
 manufacturing, 3.25-27

Integrated drive electronics (IDE): Controllers that can operate one or two hard disk drives. **5.11**

Integrated services digital network, *see* **ISDN**

Integrated software: Software that combines applications such as word processing, spreadsheet, database, and communications into a single, easy-to-use package. **2.32-33**

Intelligent features, word processors with, 2.4

Intelligent terminal: Terminal that contains not only a keyboard and screen, but also has built-in processing capabilities and storage devices. **4.18**

Intel Pentium Pro microprocessor, 1.6, 3.7, 3.12

Interface cards, *see* **Expansion board**

Interlaced monitors: Monitors that display images by illuminating every other line and then return to the top to illuminate lines that were skipped. **4.31**

Internal cache, *see* **Level 1 (L1) cache**

Internal commands: Instructions to the computer included in the resident portion of the operating system. **8.2**

Internal modem: A circuit board containing a modem that is installed inside the computer or inserted into an expansion slot. **6.20**

Internal report: Report used by individuals in the performance of their jobs and only by personnel within an organization. **4.23**

Internet, *see* **Internetwork**

Internet, The: Worldwide group of connected networks that allows the public access to information on thousands of subjects, gives users the ability to send messages, and obtain products and services. **1.3, 1.9, 6.7, 7.1, 7.2**
 addresses, 7.6
 connecting to, 7.28-29
 future of, 7.31
 history of, 7.3
 operation of, 7.4-5
 statistics, 7.2
 traffic control, 7.5
 Web sites about, 7.45

Internet access: Communications software feature that allows the computer to connect to the Internet. **6.19, 7.5**

Internet access provider, 7.9

Internet audioconferencing: Used by Web-based audio for conversations with other people over the Web; generally less expensive than regular telephone long-distance rates; also called Internet telephone service, or Internet telephony. **7.13**

Internet mailbox address: In e-mail, describes the combination of a user name and the domain that identifies the location of the mailbox computer. **7.19**

Internet organizer: Utility program that helps user manage and use list of favorite Web sites. **8.22**

Internet radio channel, 7.13

Internet Relay Chat (IRC): Service allowing user to join others in real-time conversations on the Internet; used by connecting to an Internet server with an IRC client program. **7.24-25**

Internet service provider (ISP): Company that has a permanent connection to the Internet, and offers access to the Internet as one of its services. 2.26, 2.28, **7.28-29**

  e-mail and, 7.19
  software, 7.29

Internet telephone service, see **Internet audioconferencing**

Internet telephony, see **Internet audioconferencing**

Internet videoconferences, 7.14

Internet voice mail: Internet audioconferencing feature that enables the sending and retrieving of voice messages. **7.13**

Internetwork: Two or more networks joined together; also called internet. **7.2**

Intranet: Internal networks that use Internet and Web technology. **7.17**

Intuit QuickBooks, 2.30

Investment information, online, 6.6

Ion implantation: Process of adding materials to the surface of a wafer that will conduct electricity. **3.26**

IP (Internet protocol) address: Addressing system for the Internet consisting of a four-part numeric address, identifying the geographic region, company, computer group, and the specific computer location. **7.6**

IRC, see **Internet Relay Chat**

ISDN (integrated services digital network): An international standard for the transmission of both analog voice and digital data using different communications channels and companies. **6.17,** 7.29

Isometric pointing device, see **Pointing stick**

Java: Programming language used to develop multimedia on the Web. **7.11**

/join: Command used to participate in IRC channels. **7.25**

Joystick: Pointing device that uses the movement of a vertical stem to direct the pointer. **4.7**

Jughead: Program that searches Gopher directories for files on a specific subject. **7.21**

Justification, see **Alignment**

Justified alignment: Placement of text that aligns text with both the left and right margins. **2.9**

Kernel, see **Control program**

Keyboard: Input device that contains alphabetic, numeric, cursor control, and function keys. Used to enter data. **1.4,** 1.5, **4.2-4**

Kilobyte (K or KB): A measure of memory equal to 1,024 bytes, usually rounded to 1,000 bytes. **3.11**

Labels: Text that is entered in the cell of a spreadsheet. **2.15**

LAN, see **Local area network**

Landscape: Page orientation that is wider than it is tall. **2.11**

Language translators: Special-purpose systems software used to convert the programming instructions written by programmers into the binary code that a computer can understand. **8.23**

Laptop computers: Larger versions of notebook computers that weigh between 8 and 15 pounds. **1.13**

Laser
  holograms using, 5.25
  optical disk using, 5.14

Laser printer: Nonimpact page printer that converts data from the computer into a laser beam aimed at a positively charged revolving drum. Each position on the drum touched by the beam becomes negatively charged and attracts toner, which is transferred and fused to paper by heat and pressure to create the text or image. **4.36**

Latency, see **Rotational delay**

LCD projection panels: Data projection devices that use liquid crystal display (LCD) technology, and are designed to be placed on top of an overhead projector. **4.40**

LCD projectors: Self-contained data projection devices that have their own light source, and do not require a separate overhead projector. **4.40**

LCS (liquid crystal shutters) printers, 4.36

Learning, hypermedia and, 7.8

Learning aids, software, 2.36-37

Leased line: A dedicated communications line provided by an outside organization; also called private line. **6.15**

LED (light emitting diode) printers, 4.36

Left alignment: Placement of text aligning it with left margin only. **2.9**

Level 1 (L1) cache: Cache memory built into the microprocessor chip; also called internal cache. **3.12**

Level 2 (L2) cache: Cache that is not part of the CPU chip; usually found on the motherboard. **3.12**

Light pen: Pen used as an input device by touching it on the display screen to create or modify graphics. **4.10**

Light wave transmission, 6.12-13

Line charts: Graphic charts that indicate a trend over a period of time by use of a rising or falling line. **2.20**

Line configurations: The types of line connections used in communications systems. The major line configurations are point-to-point and multidrop, or multipoint lines. **6.14**

  multidrop lines, 6.15-16
  point-to-point lines, 6.14-15

Line spacing: The vertical distance from the bottom of one line to the next line. **2.9**

Lines per minute (lpm): Measurement of the rate of printing of line printers. **4.33**

Linked object: Object that user can make changes to in the source document, using the original software application, and the changes are reflected in both the source document and the linked destination document. **2.35**

Liquid crystal display (LCD): Type of flat panel display screen that has liquid crystal deposited between two sheets of polarizing material. When an electrical current passes between crossing wires, the liquid crystals are aligned so light cannot shine through, producing an image on the screen. **4.29**

/list: Command used to find IRC channels. **7.25**

Local area network (LAN): A communications network that covers a limited geographic area; consists of a communications channel connecting a series of computer terminals connected to a central computer, or connects a group of personal computers to one another. **6.23**

  intranets on, 7.17
  protocols for, 6.30-31

Local bus: An expansion bus that connects directly to the CPU. **3.14**

Logical operations: Comparisons of data by the arithmetic/logic unit of the central processing unit, to determine if one value is greater than, equal to, or less than another. **3.8**

Logon code: In multiuser operating systems, a code consisting of a word or series of characters must be entered correctly before a user is allowed to use an application program. **8.11**

Longitudinal recording: Magnetic tape storage method used by quarter-inch-cartridge devices by recording data up and down the length of the tape. **5.18**

Lossless compression, 5.13
Lossy compression, 5.13
Lotus 1-2-3, 2.20
Lotus cc:Mail, 2.28
Lotus Freelance Graphics, 2.25
Lotus Notes, 2.30, 2.31
Lotus Organizer, 2.28
Lotus SmartSuite, 2.33
Lycos search tool, 7.17

Machine cycle: The four steps that the CPU carries out for each machine language instruction: fetch, decode, execute, and store. **3.8**

Machine language instructions: Program instructions are translated into a form that the electronic circuits in the CPU can interpret and convert into one or more of the commands in the computer's instruction set. **3.19-20**

Macintosh: Multitasking operating system first released with Macintosh computers in 1984; the first commercially successful graphical user interface. **8.17**

MacOS: Latest version of Macintosh operating system. **8.17**

Macro: A sequence of commands and keystrokes that are recorded and saved, to be performed when the macro is run. **2.16**

Magnetic disk: A round piece of plastic or metal, the surface of which is covered with a magnetic material; data is written to (recorded on) or read from the magnetic surface. The most widely used storage medium for all types of computers, offering high storage capacity, reliability, and fast access to data, include floppy disks, hard disks, and removable disk cartridges. **5.3-13**

Magnetic ink character recognition (MICR): Characters using a special ink that is magnetized during processing; used primarily by banking industry for processing checks. **4.17**

Magnetic tape: Sequential storage media consisting of a thin ribbon of plastic, coated on one side with a material that is magnetized to record bit patterns representing data; primary means of backup for most systems. **5.16-18**

  hierarchical storage management using, 5.24

Magneto-optical (MO): Drives that record data by using a magnetic field to change the polarity of a spot on a disk that has been heated by a laser. **5.15**

Mailbox: A file used to collect messages on an Internet computer, needed to receive e-mail over the Internet. **7.19**

Main board, see **Motherboard**

Mainframes: Large computers that can handle hundreds of users connected at the same time, process transactions at a very high rate, and store large amounts of data; range in price from several hundred thousand to several million dollars. 1.10, **1.14**

  hard disks in, 5.9

Main memory, see **RAM (Random Access Memory)**

Maintaining data, stored on disk, 5.12-13
Manufacturing department, 1.22
Map software, 6.5

Margins: The space in the border of a page. **2.9**
Marketing department, 1.20
Markups, *see* **Tags**
Massively parallel processors (MPPs): Processors that use hundreds or thousands of microprocessor CPUs to perform calculations. **3.21**
Mass storage: Systems that provide automated retrieval of data from a library of storage media such as tape or cartridges. **5.21**
Master pages, 2.13
Master program, *see* **Control program**
Medicine Web sites, 7.44
Megabyte (MB): A measure of memory equal to one million bytes, or 1,000 kilobytes. **3.11**, 5.9
Megaflops (MFLOPS): Millions of floating-point operations per second. **3.20**
Megahertz (MHz): A measurement used to describe the speed of the system clock; it is equal to one million cycles (or pulses) per second. **3.9**
Memo: Type of field in database; contains freeform text of any type or length. **2.22**
Memory: Contained in the processor unit of the computer; temporarily stores data that can be retrieved and program instructions when they are being processed. **1.6, 3.11.**
  cache, 3.7, 3.12, 3.13
  CMOS, 3.13
  location of, 3.6
  nonvolatile, 3.13, 5.2
  operating system management of, 8.7-8, 8.10
  speed, 3.13-14
  volatile, 3.11, 5.2
  See also **RAM; ROM**
Memory address: The location of a byte in memory. **3.11**
Memory buttons: Small storage devices the size of a dime that can be read or updated using a pen-like probe attached to a hand-held terminal. **5.21**
Menu: A screen display that provides a list of processing options for the user and allows the user to make a selection. **2.3**
Menu-driven user interface: User interface that uses menus to present a set of commands or options, selected with a keyboard or pointing device, that cause the computer to take a specific action. **8.3**
Metropolitan area exchanges (MAEs): Exchanges located in major cities, that carry Internet communications traffic; used to transfer data packets from one backbone provider to another. **7.5**
Metropolitan area network (MAN): A wide area network limited to the area surrounding a city. **6.26**
Micro, *see* **Personal computer(s)**
Microcode, *see* **Firmware**
Microcomputer, *see* **Personal computer(s)**
Microfiche: Sheet film used by computer output microfilm. **4.41**
Microprocessor: The smallest processor, which is a single integrated circuit that contains the CPU, located on the motherboard. **3.7**
  comparison of types, 3.10
Microsoft Access, 2.23
Microsoft Corporation, 1.8
Microsoft Excel, 2.20
Microsoft Internet Explorer, 1.8, 7.9, 7.11
Microsoft Mail, 2.28
Microsoft Money, 2.29
Microsoft Network, The, 2.26, 6.6, 6.7
Microsoft Office, 2.33
Microsoft Office 97 Office Assistant, 8.24
Microsoft PowerPoint, 2.25
Microsoft Project, 2.29
Microsoft Schedule+, 2.28

Microsoft Windows: The most popular graphical user interface for personal computers. **2.2**
Microsoft Windows 95, 1.17
Microsoft Word, 2.12
Microwaves: Radio waves that can be used to provide high-speed transmission of both voice communications and digital signals. **6.11-12**
MIDI, *see* **Musical instrument digital interface**
Millisecond: A thousandth of a second. **3.14**
Minicomputers: More powerful than personal computers and can support a number of users performing different tasks; cost from approximately fifteen thousand to several hundred thousand dollars. 1.10, **1.14**
  hard disks in, 5.9
MIPS (million instructions per second): Measure of the processing speed of computers. **3.20**
Mobile workers, pen input devices used by, 4.8
Modem: Communications device that converts digital signals of a computer to analog signals, and converts analog signals back into digital signals that can be used by a computer; used to connect computers over telephone lines. 1.5, **1.7, 6.19**
  external, 6.19
  fax, 6.2
  internal, 6.20
  Internet connection, 7.29
  speed of, 7.29
Moderator: Person who supervises a newsgroup by reading each article before it is posted to the newsgroup. **7.24**
Monitor: Output display device that looks like a television and consists of a display surface, called a screen, and a plastic or metal case to house the electrical components. 1.5, **1.6, 4.27-31**
  resolution of, 4.30
Monochrome monitor: Monitor that displays a single color such as white, green, or amber characters on a black background, or black characters on a white background. **4.28**
Monospacing: Each character on a page or screen takes up the same amount of horizontal space. **2.9**
MOO (multiuser object oriented): A type of MUD (role-playing game) that allows the user to create new characters and game locations. **7.22**
Motherboard: A circuit board that contains most of the electronic components of the system unit; also called the system board. **1.6**, 3.6, **3.7**
Mouse: Small, palm-sized input device that is moved across a flat surface, such as a desktop, to control the movement of the pointer on a screen. **1.4, 1.5, 4.5**
Mouse pad: Rectangular piece of cushioned material that the mouse rests on, providing better traction for the mouse than a desktop. **4.5**
Mouse pointer: On screen symbol moved to select processing options or information; can be many shapes but is usually in the shape of an arrow. **1.4**
MS-DOS (Microsoft DOS): A single tasking operating system originally developed by Microsoft Corporation for IBM personal computers. **8.14**
Multidrop line: Communications line configuration using a single line to connect multiple devices, such as terminals or personal computers to a main computer; also called multipoint line. **6.15-16**
Multifunction device (MFD): Output device that is a single piece of equipment that can print, scan, copy, and fax. **4.42**

Multimedia authoring software: Software that allows user to create a presentation that can include text, graphics, video, sound, and animation. **2.32**
Multimedia format: Format for presentation of information; combines text and graphics, and can include video and sound. **1.9**
  Web and, 7.11-15
Multimedia presentation: An interactive computer presentation created using multimedia authoring software, in which the user can choose what amount of material to cover and in what sequence it will be reviewed. **2.32**
Multimedia ToolBook, 2.32
Multiplexer (MUX): An electronic device that converts multiple input signals from several devices into a single stream of data that can be transmitted over a communications channel. **6.20**
Multiple zone recording (MZR): Storage method that records data a the same density on all tracks. **5.6**
Multipoint line, *see* **Multidrop line**
Multiprocessing operating system: Operating system that coordinates the operations of computers with more than one CPU. **8.6**
Multiprocessors: Computers with more than one CPU. **8.6**
Multiscanning monitors: Monitors that are designed to work within a range of frequencies and thus can work with different standards and video adapters. **4.30**
Multistation access unit (MAU), *see* **Wiring hub**
Multisync monitors, *see* **Multiscanning monitors**
Multitasking: Operating systems that allow the computer to work on more than one process or task at a time. **8.4**
  cooperative, 8.5, 8.16
  preemptive, 8.5
  virtual memory management, 8.7
Multithreading: Multitasking within a single program, allowing multiple threads to execute simultaneously within the same program, freeing the program to continue accepting commands. **8.5**
Multiuser timesharing: Operating systems that allow multiple users to run the same program at one time. **8.4**
Museum Web sites, 7.46
Musical instrument digital interface (MIDI): Serial port interface designed to be connected to a musical device such as an electronic music keyboard. **3.18**

Nanosecond: Measure of time equal to one billionth of a second. **3.13**
Narrative report: Report that is primarily text-based, but may contain some graphic or numeric information. **4.23**
National Science Foundation, 7.3
Natural language voice interface: Interface that allows the user to ask a question and have the computer not only convert the question to understandable words but interpret the question and give an appropriate response. **4.21**
NCs, *see* **Network computers**
Near-line storage: Hierarchical storage management method consisting of high-capacity optical disks. **5.24**
NETCOM, 7.28
Netiquette: Guidelines developed for posting articles to newsgroups, and are also appropriate for other communications, such as e-mail. **7.24**
NetPC, *see* **Network personal computer**
Netscape Navigator, 7.9, 7.11

INDEX

NetWare: Widely used network operating system designed for client-server networks, from Novell. **8.19**
Network: Collection of terminals, computers, and other equipment that uses communications channels to share data, information, hardware, and software. **1.7**, 1.9, **6.23-32**
 configurations, 6.27-29
 connected, 7.2
 example of, 6.32
 extranets, 7.17
 intranets, 7.17
 operating system, 6.25
 protocols, 6.29-31
 security and, 7.17-18
 servers, 1.10, 1.13
 types of, 6.23-26
 word processing documents shared on, 2.4
Network computers (NCs): Low-cost computers designed to work while connected to a network, but not as stand-alone computers. They have limited processing capability and little, if any, storage. **1.13, 7.25**-27
 Windows CE and, 8.16
Network interface card (NIC): Circuit card that fits in an expansion slot of a computer or other device, such as a printer, so the device can be connected to the network. **1.7, 6.21**
Network licenses: Special agreements, obtained from software vendors, that allow a software package to be shared by many users within the same organization. **6.24**
Network MCI, 7.28
Network operating system (NOS): System software that makes it possible to implement and control a LAN and allows users to use the files, resources, and other services on that network. **6.25**
Network personal computer: Personal computer designed to work while connected to a network, primarily relying on a server for software and storage but has a hard disk used for storing some data and programs and able to run some programs; also called netPC. **7.26**
Neural network computers: Computers that use specially designed circuits to simulate the way to human brain processes information, learns, and remembers. **3.22**
Newbies: New users on the Internet. **7.24**
News, online, 6.6, 7.46
Newsgroups: A collection of news and discussion groups accessed via the Internet. **7.23**-24
Newsreader: Program used to access a newsgroup. **7.23**
Node: Device connected to a network, such as a computer or printer. **6.27**
Nonimpact printing: Printing that occurs without having a mechanism strike against a sheet of paper. **4.34-39**
Noninterlaced monitors: Monitors that illuminate each line on screen sequentially so the entire screen is lighted in a single pass. **4.31**
Nonvolatile: Type of memory (ROM) that retains its contents even when the computer is turned off. **3.13, 5.2**
Notebook computers: Personal computers that are small enough to be carried in a briefcase but are often transported in their own carrying case; they weigh between four and eight pounds. **1.11**
Novell, 8.19
NSFnet: Network operated by the National Science Foundation that served as the major U.S. Internet network from 1987 until 1995. **7.3**
NT, see **Windows NT**
Number systems, 3.22-24
Numeric: Type of field in database containing number data only. **2.22**

Numeric keypad: Keypad, usually contained within the keyboard, where numeric keys are arranged in an adding machine or calculator format to aid the user with numeric data entry. **4.3**

Object: Any piece of information created with a Windows program, which is linked or embedded in another application. **2.34**
 desktop publishing, 2.13
 embedded, 2.34
 linked, 2.35
 3-D, 7.15
Object linking and embedding (OLE): Describes ways to transfer and share information among software applications, by placing objects created in one application into another application. **2.34**-35
OCR (optical character recognition): Scanning devices that read typewritten, computer-printed, and in some cases hand-printed characters from ordinary documents, compare the characters with a predefined shape stored in memory, and convert the character into the corresponding computer code. **4.15**-16
OCR-A, 4.15
OCR-B, 4.15
OCR software: Software that is used with image scanners to convert text images into data that can be processed by word processing software. **4.16**
Odd parity: The total number of on bits in the byte (including the parity bit) must be an odd number. **3.5**
Offline storage: Hierarchical storage management method consisting of automated tape libraries. **5.24**
OLE, see **Object linking and embedding**
On-demand report, see **Ad hoc report**
Online Help: Feature of most applications software that evaluates questions from user and displays a list of related topics. **2.36**
Online information service, 1.9
Online research, 7.38
Online services: Information and services provided to users who subscribe to the services for a fee; accessed with communications equipment and software. 2.26, 2.28, **6.6,** 7.5, **7.28**
Online storage: Hierarchical storage management method usually consisting of hard disks, or sometimes RAM disks, providing fast, direct access to data. **5.24**
Online vendor support, 6.5
Operand: Specifies the data or location of the data that will be used by machine language instructions. **3.20**
Operating environment: A graphical user interface between the user and the operating system. **8.15**
Operating system: Set of programs containing instructions that manage the operations of a computer such as loading, storing, and executing a program, and transferring data among the system devices and memory. **1.17, 2.2, 8.2-19**
 functions of, 8.4-11
 input and output management, 8.8-9
 loading, 8.12-13
 memory management, 8.7-8
 multiprocessing, 8.6
 multitasking, 8.4-5
 network, 6.25
 next-generation, 8.25
 popular, 8.14-19
 portable, 8.14
 proprietary, 8.14
 single tasking, 8.4
 system administration, 8.10-11

Operation code: First part of machine language instruction; tells the computer what to do and matches one of the commands in the instruction set. **3.20**
Optical character recognition, see **OCR**
Optical codes: In source data automation, codes that use a pattern or symbol to represent data, such as a bar code. **4.14**
Optical disks: Storage medium in which data is written using lasers to burn microscopic holes on the surface of a hard plastic disk; able to store enormous quantities of information. **5.14**-15
 hierarchical storage management using, 5.24
Optical mark recognition (OMR): Input devices that often are used to process questionnaires or test answer sheets. Carefully placed marks on the form indicate responses to questions that are read and interpreted by a computer program. **4.15**
Optical memory cards: Special purpose storage consisting of plastic cards the size of a credit card that can store up to 4.1 MB of digitized text or images using a laser beam. **5.22**
Optical recognition: Devices that use a light source to read codes, marks, and characters and convert them into digital data that can be processed by a computer. **4.14**-16
OS/2: IBM's graphical user interface operating system designed to work with 32-bit microprocessors. **8.18**
Output: The data that has been processed into a useful form called information that can be used by a person or machine. **1.6, 1.7, 4.23**-43
 audio, 4.25
 computer output microfilm, 4.41
 data projectors, 4.40
 display devices, 4.27-31
 fax, 4.42
 multifunction devices, 4.42
 operating system management of, 8.8-9
 printers, 4.32-39
 types of, 4.23-26
 video, 4.26
 voice, 4.25-26
Output devices: Devices that convert the results of processing into a form that can be understood by users; most common devices are printers, monitors, and speakers. **1.6**
 storage devices used as, 5.2
Overtype mode, 2.6

Package: In chip manufacturing, ceramic or plastic case containing die that have passed all tests. **3.27**
Packets: Internet operation that divides data into separate parts including the data and the destination, origin, and sequence information, that is sent along the best route available to a destination computer, where the information is reassembled into the original message. **7.4**
Packet-switching: In communications networks, process of combining individual packets of data from various users and transmitting them over a high-speed channel. **6.26,** 7.4
Page: In virtual memory management, the fixed number of bytes that are transferred from disk to memory each time data or program instructions are needed. **8.7**
Page composition and layout: In desktop publishing, the process of arranging text and graphics on a document page. **2.12**
Page definition language: In desktop publishing, language describing the document to be printed that the printer can understand. **2.14**
Page makeup, see **Page composition and layout**
Page scanner, see **Image scanner**

Pages per minute (ppm): Measure of the speed of printers that can produce an entire page at one time. **4.37**
Paging: In virtual memory management, a fixed number of bytes (a page) is transferred from disk to memory each time data or program instructions are needed. **8.7**
Palmtop computers: Small computers that often have several built-in or interchangeable personal information management functions, such as a calendar and an address book; do not have disk storage devices and usually have a nonstandard keyboard. **1.10**
  Windows CE and, 8.16
Paradox, 2.23
Parallel ports: Ports most often used to connect devices that send or receive large amounts of data such as printers or disk and tape drives. **3.16**
Parallel processing: The use of multiple CPUs, each with its own memory, that work on their assigned portion of a problem simultaneously. **3.21**
Parametric, 2.31
Parity (even and odd), 3.5
RAID technology, 5.20
Parity bit: One extra bit for each byte that is used for error checking. **3.5**
  asynchronous transmission, 6.17
Partition(s): Portions of memory allocated by operating system into fixed areas. **8.7**
Partitioned disk: Separate areas that hard disk is divided into before it is formatted. **5.9**
Passive matrix: LCD screens that use fewer transistors, one for each row and column. **4.29**
Password: In multiuser operating systems, a value, such as a word or number, that must be entered correctly before a user is allowed to use an application program. **8.11**
Paste: An option used after performing either the cut or copy command, where the selected data is placed elsewhere in the document. **2.6**
PC, *see* **Personal computer(s)**
PC Card: Small, credit-card sized device that fits into PCMIA expansions slots; often used with portable computers for storage, communications, and additional memory. **3.16, 5.19**
PC-DOS (Personal Computer DOS): Single tasking operating system developed by Microsoft for IBM. **8.14**
PCMIA (Personal Computer Memory Card International Association): Association that developed specifications for PC Cards. **3.16**
Peachtree Accounting, 2.30
Peer-to-peer network: Local area network that allows any computer to share the software, data, or hardware (such as a printer) located on any other computer in the network. **6.25**
Pen computers: Specialized personal computers that use a pen-like device to enter data, and have special software that allows the system to recognize handwritten input. **1.10**
Pen input: Input by device that can be used in three ways: to input data using hand-written characters and shapes that the computer can recognize, as a pointing device like a mouse to select items on the screen, and to gesture, which is a way of issuing commands. **4.8**
Pen plotter: Plotter used to create images on a sheet of paper by moving one or more pens over the surface, or by moving the paper under the top of the pens. **4.38**
Periodic reports: Reports that are produced on a regular basis such as daily, weekly, or monthly; also called scheduled reports. **4.24**
Peripheral device: Any device connected to the system unit. **1.7**

Personal communicator, *see* **Personal digital assistant (PDA)**
Personal computer(s) (PCs): Small systems that have become widely used in recent years. Depending on their size and features, personal computer prices can range from several hundred to several thousand dollars. **1.10-13**
  hard disks in, 5.8, 5.9
  network, 7.26
  terminal emulation software, 6.19
  videoconferences using, 6.4
Personal digital assistant (PDA): Small pen input device designed for workers on the go; often has built-in communications capabilities that allows the PDA to use voice, fax, or data communications. **1.11**
  pen input devices used with, 4.8
Personal finance software: Software used to track income and expenses, pay bills, complete online transactions, and evaluate financial plans. **2.29**
Personal information management (PIM) software: Software that helps users keep track of miscellaneous bits of personal information, such as notes to self, phone messages, and appointment scheduling. **2.28**
Photographs
  digital camera, 4.21
  used as graphics, 4.25
Photolithography: Process in chip manufacturing, where an image of the chip design, called a mask, is used as a negative. The photoresist is exposed to the mask using ultraviolet light. **3.26**
Photoresist: A soft gelatin-like emulsion that is added to the wafer during chip manufacturing. **3.26**
Picture element, *see* **Pixel**
Pie chart: A graphic representation of proportions used for showing the relationship of parts to a whole, depicted as slices of a pie. **2.20**
Pipelining: Describes the CPU starting a new instruction as soon as the preceding instruction moves to the next stage, providing rapid throughput. **3.21**
Pixel (picture element): On screen, the dots that can be illuminated. **4.30, 4.31**
PKZIP, 5.13
Placeholder, hierarchical storage management using, 5.24
Platters: Part of hard disk that is coated with a material that allows data to be recorded magnetically on the surface; enclosed in an airtight, sealed case. **5.8**
Plotter: Output device used to produce high-quality line drawings and diagrams. **4.38**
Plug and Play technology: Technology that allows the operating system to recognize any new devices and assists in the installation of the device by automatically loading the necessary driver programs and checking for conflicts with other devices. **8.9**
Plug-ins: Applications that run multimedia within the browser window; can be downloaded from many sites on the Web. **7.11**
Point: Measure of character size, approximately equal to 1/72 of one inch. **2.8**
Pointer, *see* **Mouse pointer**
Pointing devices, 4.5-11
Pointing stick: Small input device shaped like a pencil eraser that moves the insertion point as pressure is applied to the device; also called isometric pointing device, or trackpoint. **4.7**
Point-of-sale (POS) terminal: Allows data to be entered at the time and place where the transaction with the consumer occurs, such as in fast-food restaurants or hotels. **4.18**

Point-to-point line: A line configuration used in communications that is a direct line between a sending and receiving device; may be a switched line or a dedicated line. **6.14-15**
Politics, Web sites on, 7.44
Polling: Used by front-end processor to check the connected terminals or computers to *see* if they have data to send. **6.21**
Port: A socket used to connect the system unit to a peripheral device such as a printer or a modem. 3.6, **3.16-18**
Portable computers
  floppy disk drives, 5.4
  input devices for, 4.6
Portable operating systems: Operating systems that will run on many manufacturers' computers. **8.14**
Portrait: Page orientation that is taller than it is wide. **2.11**
POST (Power On Self Test): Tests run by the BIOS chip when the computer is turned on to make sure the equipment is working properly. **8.12**
Posting: Process of adding an article to a newsgroup. **7.23**
PostScript: A page definition language. **2.14**
Power On Self Test, *see* **POST**
Power supply: Converts the wall outlet electricity to the lower voltages used by the computer. 3.6, **3.18**
PPP (point-to-point protocol): A version of the Internet communications protocol TCP/IP, widely used by Internet service providers. **7.29**
Preemptive multitasking: Multitasking method in which the operating system prioritizes the processes to be performed and assigns a set amount of CPU time for the execution of each process. **8.5**
Presentation graphics: Software that allows the user to create documents called slides that are used in making presentations before a group. **2.24-25**
Printer/printing: Output device used to produce permanent hard copy. 1.5, **1.6, 4.32-39**
  impact, 4.32-34
  nonimpact, 4.34-39
  word processing document, 2.11
Print preview: Allows the user to *see* on the screen how a document will look when it is printed. **2.11**
Print spool: The reports stored on disk that are waiting to be printed. **8.9**
Private line, *see* **Leased line**
Process/processing: Part of the information processing cycle; the procedures a computer performs to process data into information. **1.7**
  options, 2.2
Process, *see* **Task**
Process management, operating system and, 8.4-6
Processor, *see* **Central processing unit (CPU)**
Prodigy, 6.6, 6.7
Product design department, 1.23
Program(s): The detailed set of instructions that tells the computer exactly what to do, so it can perform the operations in the information processing cycle; also called program instructions, or software. **4.2**
  applets, 7.11
Programmable terminal, *see* **Intelligent terminal**
Project management software: Software that allows users to plan, schedule, track, and analyze the events, resources, and costs of a project. **2.29**
Proportional spacing: On a page or screen, wide characters, such as a W or M are given more horizontal space than narrow characters. **2.9**
Proprietary operating systems: Operating systems that are limited to a specific vendor or computer model. **8.14**

INDEX I.11

Protocol: In communications, a set of rules and procedures for exchanging information between computers. **6.29**
  FTP, 7.20
  hypertext transfer (http), 7.10
  Internet, 7.4, 7.20, 7.22, 7.29
  point-to-point, 7.29
  serial line Internet, 7.29
  TCP/IP, 7.4
  Telnet, 7.22
Proxy server: A computer that is placed between two separate networks; used to implement a firewall that restricts access to data.
Push media, 7.38

Quarter-inch-cartridge (QIC): Tape device, often used with PCs, that records data in narrow tracks along the length of the tape. **5.18**
Query: The ability to retrieve database information in a report, based on criteria specified by the user. **2.23**
Quicken, 2.29

Radio, Internet, 7.13
Radio wave transmission, 6.12-13
RAID, *see* **Redundant array of inexpensive disks**
RAID levels, 5.19-20
Rails: Mounting brackets needed to install a device in a bay inside the system unit. **3.18**
RAM (Random Access Memory): Contained in the processor unit of the computer; temporarily stores data and program instructions when they are being processed. Also called main memory. **1.6, 3.11**-12
RAM cache memory, speed and, 3.13
Reading data: The process of retrieving data. **5.2**
  from floppy disk, 5.7
Read only memory, *see* **ROM**
Read/write head: Recording mechanism in the drive that rests on the top and bottom surface of the rotating disk, generating electronic impulses that change the polarity, or alignment of magnetic areas along a track on the disk. **5.7**
  floppy disk, 5.7
  hard disk, 5.10
  tape drives, 5.18
Reception, 1.20
Record(s): Collection of related facts or fields in a database. **2.21**
Recording data: The process of storing data. **5.2**
  on floppy disk, 5.7
Recording density: Number of bits that can be recorded on one inch of track on a disk, referred to as bits per inch. **5.6**
Redundant array of inexpensive disks (RAID): Storage technique that uses small disks which are connected into an integrated unit that acts like a single large disk drive. **5.19**
Reel-to-reel tape: Magnetic storage tape device that uses two reels: a supply reel to hold the tape to be read from or written to, and the take-up reel to temporarily hold portions of the supply reel tape as it is being processed. **5.17**
Reference Web sites, 7.46
Refresh rate: Speed at which the entire screen is redrawn. **4.31**
Registers: Storage locations in the CPU that temporarily store specific data such as the address of the next instruction. **3.8**
Registry: Operating system files that contain information about which hardware and software is installed, and information about individual user preferences. **8.13**
Relative hyperlinks: Hyperlinks that move from one document to another document on the same Internet computer. **7.8**

Relative referencing: In spreadsheet programs, when a formula is copied to another cell, the formula is automatically updated to the new location. **2.19**
Reliability, 1.8
Remote workers, 2.28
Replace: Used with search feature, that allows substitution of new letters or words for the old. **2.6**
Report(s): Information presented in an organized form. **4.23**
Research, online, 7.38, 7.46
Resolution: Measure of a screen's image clarity, and depends on the number of individual dots (pixels) displayed on the screen, and the distance between each pixel. **4.30**
Response time: The amount of time measured from the moment data is entered into the computer until the computer responds. **8.10**
Restore programs, 8.20
Revision marks: Editing feature of word processing program that allows changes to be made directly in a document, by marking additions and deletions with underlines, strikethroughs, or different colors and fonts. **2.8**
Right alignment: Placement of text aligning it with right margin only. **2.9**
Ring network: Communications network that has a series of computers connected to one another in a continuous loop or ring. **6.29**
RISC (reduced instruction set computing): Technology that involves reducing the computer's instruction set to only those instructions that are most frequently used, allowing the computer to operate faster. **3.19**
ROM (read only memory): Describes chips that store data or instructions that do not change. This data is permanently recorded in the memory when it is manufactured. ROM memory retains its contents even when the power is turned off. **3.13**
Rotational delay: The time it takes for the sector containing the data to rotate under the read/write head; also called latency. **5.7**
Router: An intelligent network connecting device that sends (routes) communications traffic directly to the appropriate network; used when several networks are connected together. **6.22**
  Internet, 7.5
Rows: Data which is organized horizontally on a spreadsheet. **2.15**

Sales department, 1.20
Satellites
  communications, 6.11-12
  global positioning system, 6.5
Scanners
  hand-held, 4.13
  image, 4.13, 4.16
  optical character recognition, 4.15
Scheduled reports, *see* **Periodic reports**
Scheduling, group, 2.31
School, connecting to Internet through, 7.28
Science Web sites, 7.47
Screen(s): Term used to refer to both the surface of any display device and to any type of display device. **4.27**
  touch, 4.9
Screen saver: Utility program that automatically displays a moving image on the screen if the computer remains idle for a certain period of time; primarily used for entertainment and security. **8.22**
Scrolling: The movement of screen data up or down one line or screen at a time. **2.6**
Scroll tips: Small page labels beside the scroll box, that show the current page during scrolling operations. **2.6**

SCSI (small computer system interface): Port that can be used to attach seven to fifteen different devices to a single port. **3.16**
SCSI (small computer system interface) controllers: Controllers that can support multiple disk drives or a mix of other SCSI-compatible devices. **5.11**
Search: Feature that allows user to find all occurrences of a particular character, word, or combination of words. **2.6**
Search engine, *see* **Search tool**
Search tool: Software program that finds Web sites, Web pages, and Internet files that match one or more keywords that are entered by searching an index of Internet sits and documents. **7.16**-17
  FTP, 7.20-21
Secondary storage, *see* **Storage**
Sector: A pie-shaped section of the floppy disk. **5.4**
Security
  network, 7.18
  operating system and, 8.11
Seek **time:** The time it takes to position the read/write head over the proper track. **5.7**
Sequential storage: Name given to magnetic tape as storage media because the computer must write and read tape records one after another (sequentially). **5.16**
Serial port: Port that transmits data one bit at a time and is considerably slower than a parallel port. **3.18**
Serpentine recording, *see* **Longitudinal recording**
Server, *see* **Server computers**
Server computers: Computers designed to support a computer network that allow users to share files, application software, and hardware. **1.10, 1.13**
  FTP, 7.20
  operating system for, 8.18
  proxy, 7.18
  Web, 7.2
Set-top box: Home network computer that uses a device that looks and acts like a cable TV box, and uses a telephone line to connect to an Internet service provider. **7.26**
Shading: Formatting feature that allows darkening of the background area of a section of a document or table. **2.10**
Shadow mask, 4.31
Shareware: Program that can be downloaded from FTP sites and tried out for free, but a license fee must be paid if the programs are kept. **7.20**
Shelf storage: Hierarchical storage management method where data has been stored on a tape or other removable media and stored in a cabinet or rack. **5.24**
Shell: Program that acts as an interface between the user and the operating system, and offers a limited number of utility functions such as file maintenance. **8.15**
Shielded twisted-pair (STP) cable: Communications cable consisting of pairs of plastic-coated copper wires that are twisted together, covered by a foil wrapper around each wire to reduce electrical interference. **6.9**
Shipping and receiving department, 1.22
Shopping, online, 2.26, 6.6, 7.30, 7.47
SHOUT!: Use of all capital letters in Internet communications. **7.24**
Shutter, floppy disk, 5.4
SIMM (single in-line memory module): Small circuit board that holds multiple RAM chips. **3.12**

Simplex transmission: Data transmission method in which data flows only in one direction, used when the sending device never requires a response from the receiving computer. **6.18**

Single large expensive disks, *see* **SLEDs**

Single tasking: Operating systems that allow only one user to run one program at one time. **8.4**

Site licenses, *see* **Network licenses**

SLEDs (single large expensive disks): Single large disk storage systems. **5.20**

Slides: Documents created by presentation graphics software that are used in making presentations before a group. **2.24**

SLIP (serial line Internet protocol): Older protocol that does not offer a high degree of error checking. **7.29**

Small computer system interface, *see* **SCSI**

Smart cards: Special purpose storage devices about the size and thickness of a credit card that contain a thin microprocessor capable of storing data. **5.22**

Smart terminal, *see* **Intelligent terminal**

Social interface: Operating system interface that uses objects with human characteristics to deliver messages to users. **8.24**

Soft copy: Output displayed on a screen. **4.23**

Software: The detailed set of instructions that tells a computer what to do. **1.16-18**
application, *see* Application software
communications, 6.8, 6.19
configuration information, 8.13
Internet service provider, 7.29
map, 6.5
network computers, 7.25-27
OCR, 4.16
sound editing, 4.19
system, 1.17
Web page authoring, 7.8

Software packages, *see* **Application software packages**

Software resource sharing: Describes sharing of software by multiple users; frequently used software is stored on the hard disk server in a LAN for access by users. **6.24**

Software suite: Individual applications are packaged in the same box and sold for a price that is significantly less than buying the applications individually. **2.33**

Sound, used in presentation graphics, 2.24

Sound board: Expansion board that enhances the sound-generating capacity of computer. **3.18**
lossy compression, 5.13

Sound card: Multimedia device containing electronics that capture sound data input; installed in the computer. **4.19**

Sound editing software, 4.19
Sound files, audio Web applications and, 7.13
Sound input, 4.19

Source data automation: Procedures and equipment designed to make the input process more efficient by eliminating the manual entry of data; the equipment captures data directly from its original form such as an invoice or inventory tag. **4.12-17**

Source data collection, *see* **Source data automation**

Source document: In source data automation, the original form that data is captured from. **4.12**

Source document: In object linking and embedding applications, the document from which the object originates. **2.34**

Spacing: Describes how far apart individual letters and lines of text are placed. **2.9**

Spamming: Process of posting an article (especially one soliciting business) to several inappropriate newsgroups. **7.24**

Speaker(s): Device used for audio output. **1.5, 1.6**

Speaker dependent: Voice input system that has to be trained to recognize the speaker's individual speech pattern. **4.20**

Speaker independent: Voice input system that has voice templates for each word, so the system does not have to be trained to recognize the speaker's individual speech pattern. **4.20**

Special effects, presentation graphics, 2.24

Special-purpose terminal: Terminal that performs specific jobs and contains features uniquely designed for use in a particular industry, such as a point-of-sale terminal. **4.18**

Speed, 1.8

Spelling checker: Feature that allows user to review individual words, sections of a document, or the entire document for correct spelling. **2.6**

Spooling: Process in which a report is first written (saved) to the disk before it is printed; used to increase printer efficiency. **8.9**

Sports Web sites, 7.47

Spreadsheet: Organization of numeric data in a worksheet or table format, by spreadsheet software. Data is organized horizontally in rows, and vertically in columns. **2.14**

Spreadsheet software, 2.14-21
SPRYNET, 7.28

Stackable hub: Communications wiring hub that can be connected to another hub to increase the number of devices attached to the server. **6.22**

Star network: Communications network that contains a central computer and one or more terminals or computers connected to it, forming a star configuration. **6.27**

Static RAM: A type of RAM memory that is larger than dynamic RAM and has access times of 10 to 50 nanoseconds. **3.13**

Storage: Part of the information processing cycle in which data and programs are stored when not being processed; also called secondary storage, or auxiliary storage. **1.7, 1.8, 5.2-26**
CD-ROM, 5.14-15
holographic, 5.25
magnetic disk, 5.3-13
magnetic tape, 5.16-18
mass systems, 5.21
memory buttons, 5.21
optical disks, 5.14-15
optical memory cards, 5.22
PC Cards, 5.19
RAID systems, 5.19-20
smart cards, 5.22

Storage devices: Hardware that stores instructions and data when they are not being used by the system unit; often function as input source when previously stored data is read into memory. **1.7**

Storing: Control unit operation that takes place when the result of the instruction is written to memory. **3.8**

Streaming audio: Feature used by advanced audio Web applications that allows sounds to be heard as they are downloaded to the computer. **7.13**

Streaming video: Feature used by Web applications that allows viewing of longer or live video images as they are downloaded to the computer. **7.14**

Striping: Storage technique that divides a logical piece of data, such as a record or word into smaller parts and writes those parts on multiple drives. **5.20**

Style: Specific combination of features affecting the appearance of a document, such as bold, italic, or underline formatting, applied to a font to make it stand out. **2.9**

Style sheet, *see* **Built-in style**

Subnotebook computers: Smaller versions of notebook computers that weigh less than 4 pounds. **1.13**

Summary report: Report that summarizes data, containing totals from detailed input data. **4.24**

Supercomputers: The most powerful category of computers, and the most expensive; can process hundreds of millions of instructions per second, and cost several million dollars. 1.10, **1.15**
NSFnet and, 7.3

Superscalar CPUs: CPUs that have two or more pipelines that can process instructions simultaneously. **3.21**

Supervisor, *see* **Control program**

Support tools, software, 2.37

SVGA (super video graphics array): Standard for monitors and video adapter cards that display high resolutions, typically 800 x 600 or 1,024 x 768 pixels, producing images that are almost equivalent to the quality of a photograph. **4.30**

Swap file: In virtual memory management, the name given to the amount of disk space allocated for use as memory. **8.7**

Swapping: When using paging, the process of the operating system making room for additional pages by writing pages currently in memory back to the disk. **8.8**

Switched line: Point-to-point line using a regular telephone line to establish a communications connection. **6.14-15**

Symmetric multiprocessing: In computers that have more than one CPU, the process of assigning application tasks to whatever CPU is available. **8.6**

Sync bytes, 6.17

Synchronous transmission mode: Data communications method that transmits large blocks of data at regular intervals using timing signals to synchronize the sending and receiving equipment. **6.17**

Sys op, *see* **System operator**

System administrator, 1.19
System administration, operating system and, 8.10-11

System board, *see* **Motherboard**

System clock: A chip used by the control unit to synchronize, or control the timing of all computer operations. **3.8**

System operator: Person who maintains and updates the bulletin board system. **6.5**

System performance, measuring, 8.10

Systems analyst: Person who works with both the user and the programmer to determine and design the desired output of a program. **1.16**

System software: All the programs including the operating system that are related to controlling the operations of the computer hardware. **1.17, 8.2-28**
language translators, 8.23
operating systems, 8.2-19
utility programs, 8.19-23

System unit: Part of the computer containing the electronic circuits that cause the execution of program instructions and manipulation of data to occur; includes the central processing unit, memory, and other electronic components. 1.5, **1.6, 3.2-28**
bays, 3.18
buses, 3.14-15
components of, 3.6-19
connectors, 3.16-18
coprocessors, 3.14
CPU, 3.7-10
expansion slots, 3.15-16
machine language instructions, 3.19-20
memory, 3.11-14
microprocessor, 3.7-10

motherboard, 3.7
ports, 3.16-18
power supply, 3.18
sound components, 3.18
types of processing, 3.21
upgrade sockets, 3.10

T1: Digital communications line that transmits 1.5 megabits per second, costing several thousand dollars per month. **6.17**
T3: Digital communications line that transmits 45 megabits per second, costing more than $40,000 per month. **6.17**
Tables: Arrangement of information in rows or columns, allowing user to easily add and change table information and move the entire table as a single item, instead of as individual lines of text. **2.10**
Tags: Set of special instructions in HTML that specify links to other documents and how the Web page is displayed; also called markups. **7.8**
Tape density: The number of bits that can be stored on one inch of tape. **5.18**
Tape libraries, hierarchical storage management using, 5.24
Target hyperlinks: Hyperlinks that move from one location in a document to another location in the same document. **7.8**
Task: In operating system, a program or part of a program that can be executed separately; also called process. **8.4**
TCP/IP (transmission control protocol/Internet protocol): Communications protocol used for packet switching on the Internet. **7.4**
Telecommunications, see **Communications**
Telecommuting: The capability of individuals to work at home and communicate with their offices by using personal computers and communications equipment and software. **6.2, 7.29**
Telephone
  cellular, 6.13
  dialing feature of communications software, 6.19
  fiber-optic cable, 6.10
  full-duplex transmission, 6.18
  modem and, 6.19
  switched line, 6.14
  voice mail, 6.2
Telephone companies, wide area networks and, 6.26
Telephone line, Internet connection and, 7.29
Telnet: An Internet protocol that enables user to log onto a remote computer on the Internet, and use the remote computer as if it were a direct, local connection. **7.22**
Template: Formatting feature of word processing software that uses a predefined style sheet, containing font, style, spacing, and formatting information, and usually includes text that is always used, such as title and headings. **2.10**
desktop publishing, 2.13
10base2 cable, see **Thinnet**
10baseT cable, see **Unshielded twisted-pair (UTP) cable**
Terabytes, 5.9, 5.25
Terminal(s), see **Display terminals**
Terminal emulation: Communications software feature that allows a personal computer to act as a specific type of terminal so the personal computer can connect to another, usually larger, computer such as a mainframe. **6.19**
Terrestrial microwave: Earth-based microwave transmission; involves sending data from one microwave station to another in line-of-sight transmissions. **6.11**
The Microsoft Network, see Microsoft Network, The

Thrashing: Process that takes place in a computer system with a heavy workload and insufficient memory, where the system spends more time moving pages to and from the disk that it does processing data. **8.10**
Thermal printer: Printer that uses heat to transfer colored inks from ink sheets onto the printing surface; also called thermal transfer printer. **4.37**
Thermal transfer printer, see **Thermal printer**
Thesaurus: Allows the user to look up synonyms for words in a document. **2.8**
Thin-client, see **Network computer**
Thinnet: Coaxial cable with a small diameter often used with computer networks; also called 10base2 cable. **6.10**
Thread: In newsgroups, name given to the original article and all subsequent related replies. **7.23**
3-D objects, 7.15
Timeline, 2.29
Time slice: Increments of CPU time. **8.5**
Toggle key: Key that switches, or toggles, the keyboard between two different modes, such as the CAPS LOCK key. **4.3**
Token: Electronic signal used for transmitting messages in a token ring network by constantly circulating around the network, allowing devices on the network to attach messages to the token. **6.31**
Token ring network: A type of ring network that constantly circulates an electronic signal, called a token, around the network, that allows devices on the network to send messages by taking the token and attaching it to data. **6.31**
Toolbar, 2.3
Topology: The configuration, or physical layout, of the equipment in a communications network. **6.27**
Touchpad: Input device with a flat rectangular surface that senses the movement of a finger on its surface to control the movement of the insertion point. **4.6**
Touch screen: Input device that allows user to touch areas on the screen to enter data. **4.9**
Tower computers: Personal computers in an upright case, that provides room for expanding the system and adding optional equipment. **1.13**
Track: A narrow recording band forming a full circle around the floppy disk. **5.4**
Trackball: Pointing device like a mouse, only with the sensing ball on top of the device, so the cursor can be moved by rotating the ball with a finger. **4.6**
Trackpad, see **Touchpad**
Trackpoint, see **Pointing stick**
Track sector: Section of track within a sector. **5.4**
Tracks per inch (tpi): The number of tracks on the recording surface of a floppy disk. **5.6**
Trade books: Books that are available to help users in learning to use the features of personal computer application packages, and can be found where software is sold and are usually carried in regular bookstores. **2.37**
Transmission media: Physical materials or other means used to establish a communications channel. **6.9-14**
Transmission modes, of communications channels, 6.16
Travel planning, online, 6.6
Travel Web sites, 7.48
Triangulation: Technique used by global positioning systems to determine the precise geographical location of a GPS receiver on earth by comparing the time it takes for signals from three or more satellites to arrive. **6.34**

Turn-around documents: Documents designed to be returned to the organization that created them, and when returned (turned around), the data is read by an OCR device. **4.16**
Tutorials: Step-by-step instructions using real examples showing users how to use an application. **2.36**
Twisted-pair cable: Communications cable consisting of pairs of plastic-coated copper wires that are twisted together. **6.9**
Typeface: A specific set of characters that are designed the same, such as Helvetica or Times New Roman. **2.8**
Typeover mode, 2.6

Unclassified! Web sites, 7.48
Uncompressing data, 5.13
Unicode: A 16-bit code that has the capacity to represent more than 65,000 characters and symbols; represents all the world's current languages. **3.4-5**
Uniform Resource Locator (URL): Address that points to a specific resource on the Internet; can indicate an Internet site, a specific document at a site, and a location within a document at a site. **7.10**
  guide to Web sites, 7.41-48
Uninstaller: Utility program that deletes unwanted software and any associated entries in system files. **8.21**
Universal product code (UPC): Type of bar code, used for input information about grocery and retail items. **4.14**
Universal Serial Bus (USB): Bus that allows up to 128 devices to be connected to a serial port. **3.18**
UNIX: Multiuser, multitasking operating system developed in the early 1970s. **8.18**
Unshielded twisted-pair (UTP) cable: Communications cable consisting of pairs of plastic-coated copper wires that are twisted together; also called 10baseT cable. **6.9**
Upgrade socket: Empty socket in motherboard that can be used to install more power CPUs. **3.10**
Uplink: The transmission to a satellite. **6.11**
Upward compatible: Describes application that is written for the old version of an operating system and can also run under the new version. **8.14**
URL, see Uniform Resource Locator
Usenet: Collection of news and discussion groups accessed via the Internet. **7.23-24**
User(s): The people who either use the computer directly, or use the information it provides; also called computer users, or end users. **1.7**
  number of, 1.10
User-ID, see User name
User interface: Combination of hardware and software that allows user to communicate with a computer system. **1.17, 2.2, 8.3**
  types of, 8.3
User name: A unique combination of characters identifying user for e-mail; also called user-ID. **7.19, 8.11**
User responses: The data that a user inputs to respond to a question or message from the software. **4.2**
User tools, 2.1-42
Utility programs: Programs that perform specific tasks related to managing computer resources or files; often contained in operating systems. **8.19-23**

Validation: In database programs, the comparison of data entered against a predefined format or value. **2.23**

Value(s): Numerical data contained in the cells of a spreadsheet. **2.15**
Value-added carriers: Companies that lease channels from common carriers to provide specialized communications services. **6.26**
Value-added network (VAN): Network provided by companies that lease channels from common carriers to provide specialized communications services. **6.26**
Vendors, online support, 6.5
Veronica: Search programs that search Gopher directories for files on a specific subject. **7.21**
Very small aperture terminal (VSAT): Satellite antenna measuring only one to three meters in size that can transmit up to 19,200 bits of data per second. **6.12**
VGA (video graphics array): Standard for monitors and video adapter cards that display resolutions of 640 x 480 pixels. **4.30**
Video: Web applications that use individual video files such as movie clips that can be downloaded and played on a computer. **7.14**
Video card: Multimedia device containing electronics that capture and process video data; installed in the computer. **4.19**
Videoconferencing: The use of computers, television cameras, and communications software and equipment to conduct electronic meetings with participants at different locations. **6.3**-4
Internet, **7.14**
Video display terminals (VDTs), see **Display terminals**
Video expansion board, lossy compression and, 5.13
Video input: Input to the computer using a video camera or a video recorder using previously recorded material, requiring tremendous amounts of storage space. **4.22**
Video output: Output consisting of visual images captured with a video input device, and directed to an output device, such as a monitor. **4.26**
Virtual file allocation table (VFAT): File allocation table on Windows 95 systems. **5.5**
Virtual memory management: Process used by multitasking operating system that increases the amount of memory the operating system can use by allocating a set amount of disk space to be used to store items during processing, in addition to the existing memory. **8.7**
Virtual reality (VR): Creation of an artificial environment that can be experienced by the user as 3-D images that can be explored and manipulated interactively, using a pointing device. **7.15**
Virtual reality modeling language, see **VRML**
Virus: A program that copies itself into other programs and spreads through multiple computer systems; can cause damage to files on the system where the virus is present. **8.21**
Voice input: Input that allows the user to enter data and issue commands to the computer with spoken words. **4.19**-21
Voice mail: Verbal electronic mail that allows the caller to leave a message via telephone that is digitized so it can be stored on disk like other computer data, and accessed by the recipient. **6.2**
Internet, 7.13
Voice output: Spoken words that are conveyed to the user from the computer. **4.26**
Voice synthesis: A type of voice generation that can transform words stored in memory into speech, which is played through speakers attached to the computer. **4.26**
Voice templates: Used by voice input systems to recognize patterns of sounds. **4.20**

Volatile: Describes RAM memory because the programs and data stored in RAM are erased when the power to the computer is turned off. **3.11, 5.2**
VRML (virtual reality modeling language: Language used by Web-based virtual reality applications that allows a developer to create a collection of 3-D objects. **7.15**

W3, see **World Wide Web**
Wafers: In chip manufacturing process, silicon ingot is sliced into wafers that eventually will become computer chips. **3.25**
Weather, online, 6.6, 7.48
Web, see **World Wide Web**
Web browser, see **Web browser software**
Web browser software: Software running on Internet-connected computers that interpret and display Web pages, enabling users to access Web sites that have text, graphics, video, and sound and have hypertext links to other information and Web sites. 1.8, **1.9, 2.26, 7.9**-11, 7.29
graphical, 7.9-11, 7.12
Windows and, 8.16
WebCrawler search tool, 7.17
Web page: Hypertext or hypermedia document residing on an Internet computer that contains text, graphics, video, or sound. **2.26, 7.7**-8
bookmark, 7.11
caching, 7.18
creating using word processor, 2.12
history list, 7.11
home page, 7.10
Web page authoring software, 7.8
Web server computers, number of, 7.2
Web sites: Internet locations that contain hyperlinked documents. **1.9, 7.7**
domain names, 7.6
guide to, 7.41-48
list of favorite, 7.11, 8.22
organized directories of, 7.16
Web surfing: Process of displaying pages one Web site after another; similar to using a television remote control to jump between channels. **7.8**
Welcome page: The first page on a Web site; often serves as a table of contents for the other pages on the Web site. 1.8, **7.10**
What-if analysis: The capability of a spreadsheet to recalculate when data is changed. **2.19**
Wide area network (WAN): Communications network that covers a large geographical area, and uses telephone cables, microwaves, satellites, or a combination of communications channels. **6.26**
Win 95, see **Windows 95**
Window: A rectangular area of the screen that is used to display information. **2.2**
Windows 95: Operating system developed by Microsoft for IBM-compatible personal computers that takes advantage of 32-bit processors. Windows 95 has an improved graphical user interface and supports preemptive multitasking; also called Win 95. **8.16**
Windows 3.0: Operating system developed by Microsoft; the first widely used graphical user interface for IBM-compatible computers. **8.15**
Windows 3.1: Operating system that includes a number of improvements to Windows 3.0. **8.15**
Windows 3.x: Refers to these versions of Microsoft's Windows operating system: Windows 3.0, Windows 3.1, and Windows 3.11. **8.15**
Windows CE: Operating system used on wireless communication devices and smaller computers such as hand-helds, palmtops, and network computers; requires little memory. **8.16**

Windows for Workgroups: Networking version of Windows 3.1. **8.15**
Windows NT: Sophisticated graphical user interface operating system designed for client-server networks; uses a modular design. **8.17**
Wireless communications, Windows CE and, 8.16
Wireless transmission: In communications systems, used to connect devices in the same general area such as an office or business park, using one of three transmission techniques: infrared light beams, radio waves, or carrier-connect radio. **6.12**
Wiring hub: A central connecting point for devices such as computers, printers, and storage devices that are connected to the server; also called concentrator, or multistation access unit. **6.22**
Wizard: Automated assistant that helps user complete a task by asking questions and then automatically performing actions based on the given answers. **2.36**
Word processing: The most widely used computer application; involves the use of a computer to produce or modify documents that consist primarily of text. **2.4**-12
creating Web pages using, 2.12
dedicated systems, 2.4
Web authoring features, 7.8
Word processing document
creating, 2.4-6
editing, 2.6-8
formatting, 2.8-11
printing, 2.11
WordPerfect, 2.12
Word size: The number of bits that the CPU can process at one time. **3.9**
Word wrap: An automatic line return that occurs when text reaches a certain position on a line in a document, such as the right-hand margin. **2.5**
Work, connecting to Internet through, 7.28
Workflow support, 2.31
Workgroup technology: Equipment and software that help group members communicate, manage activities, and make group decisions. **2.30, 6.4**
Worksheet, see **Spreadsheet**
Workstations: Personal computers connected to a network; often have powerful calculating and graphics capabilities and are frequently used by engineers. **1.13, 6.27**
World Wide Web (WWW): Portion of the Internet containing Web sites, where information can be accessed electronically; the collection of hyperlinked documents accessible on the Internet. **1.9, 7.1, 7.7**-17
connecting to, 7.28-29
doing business on, 7.30
future of, 7.31
guide to sites, 7.41-48
multimedia on, 7.11-15
searching for information on, 7.16-17
Write-protect window: On a floppy disk, a small hole in the corner of the floppy disk that protects data from being erased accidentally. **5.5**
Writing data: The process of storing data; also called recording data. **5.2**
WWW, see **World Wide Web**
WYSIWIG: An acronym for What You See Is What You Get. A feature that displays the document on the screen exactly as it will look when it is printed. **2.5**

Yahoo! search tool, 7.16, 7.17

Zero insertion force (ZIF) socket, 3.10

Photo Credits

Cover Credits: Background, ticket, graduation cap, and diploma provided by PhotoDisc Inc © 1996; **Chapter 1:** *Chapter opener: upper left*, Sotographs/Liaison International; *right*, David Young Wolff/Tony Stone Images; *bottom right*, Greg Pease/Tony Stone Images; *Figure 1-1 upper right*, David Mason/Woodfin Camp & Associates; *Figure 1-1a bottom right*, Sotographs/Liaison International; *Figure 1-1b middle*, Charlie Westerman/Liaison International; *Figure 1-1d bottom left*, Courtesy of AST Research, Inc.; *Figure 1-1e upper left*, Mitch Kezar/Tony Stone Images; *Figure 1-2* Courtesy of Henry Blackham; *Figure 1-3* Courtesy of Intel Corporation; *Figure 1-6a* Courtesy of Omnidata International, Inc.; *Figure 1-6b* Courtesy of Hewlett-Packard Company; *Figure 1-6c* Yoav Levy/Phototake, Inc.; *Figure 1-6d* Courtesy of U.S. Robotics; *Figure 1-6e* Courtesy of Texas Instruments, Inc.; *Figure 1-6f* Courtesy of International Business Machines Corporation; *Figure 1-6g* Courtesy of Toshiba America Information Systems, Inc.; *Figure 1-6h* Courtesy of Gateway 2000, Inc.; *Figure 1-6i* Courtesy of International Business Machines Corporation; *Figure 1-6j* Courtesy of Sun Microsystems, Inc.; *Figure 1-6k* Courtesy of International Business Machines Corporation; *Figure 1-7* Courtesy of Hewlett-Packard Company; *Figure 1-8* Courtesy of International Business Machines Corporation; *Figure 1-9* Courtesy of International Business Machines Corporation; *Figure 1-10* Courtesy of Cray Research, Inc.; *Figure 1-11* Courtesy of Minnesota Supercomputer Center; *Figure 1-14* Scott Goodwin Photography, Inc.; *Figure 1-15* International Business Machines Corporation; *Figure 1-16* Walter Hodges/Tony Stone Images; *Figure 1-17* Tom McCarthy/PhotoEdit; *Figure 1-18* David Young Wolff/Tony Stone Images; *Figure 1-19* Richard Pasley/Stock Boston; *Figure 1-21* Comstock, Inc.; *Figure 1-22* Courtesy of John Deere & Company; *Figure 1-23* Courtesy of Cannondale, Inc.; *Figure 1-24* Jeff Dunn/Stock Boston; *Figure 1-25* Courtesy of Hewlett-Packard Company; *Figure 1-26* Courtesy of International Business Machines Corporation; *Figure 1-27* Jose L. Pelaez/The Stock Market; *Page 1.33*, Anxious computer and carriage, Courtesy of Corel Professional Photos CD-ROM Image usage; **Timeline:** *1937* ABC, Courtesy of Iowa State University; *1937* Dr. John Atanasoff, Courtesy of Iowa State University; *1937* Clifford Berry, Courtesy of Iowa State University; *1943* ENIAC, Courtesy of the University of Pennsylvania Archives; *1945* Dr. John von Neumann, Courtesy of the Institute for Advanced Studies; *1951* UNIVAC, Courtesy of Unisys Corporation; *1951* Newspaper, Courtesy of Unisys Corporation; *1952* Dr. Grace Hopper, Courtesy of Harvard University Archives; *1952* COBOL, Courtesy of the Department of the Navy; *1952* IBM Model 650, Courtesy of International Business Machines Corporation; *1952* Core memory, Courtesy of M.I.T. Archives; *1957* FORTRAN, Courtesy of the Department of the Navy; *1957* Vacuum tubes, Courtesy of International Business Machines Corporation; *1957* Transistor, Courtesy of M.I.T. Archives; *1964* IBM System/360, Courtesy of International Business Machines Corporation; *1964* Dr. John Kemeny, Courtesy of Dartmouth College News Service; *1964* DEC, Courtesy of Digital Equipment Corporation; *1964* Pascal, Shelly R. Harrison; *1970* LSI, Courtesy of International Business Machines Corporation; *1971* Dr. Ted Hoff, Courtesy of Intel Corporation; *1971* Pentium chip, Courtesy of Intel Corporation; *1971* Altair, Boston Computer Museum; *1975* Robert Metcalfe, Courtesy of *InfoWorld*; *1976* Apple logo, Courtesy of Apple Computer, Inc.; *1976* Steve Wozniak and Steve Jobs, Courtesy of Apple Computer, Inc.; *1976* Apple, Courtesy of Apple Computer, Inc.; *1979* VisCalc, Courtesy of Software Arts, Inc.; *1980* Bill Gates, Courtesy of Microsoft Corporation; *1981* IBM PC, Courtesy of International Business Machines Corporation; *1983 TIME* magazine cover © 1982, Time, Inc.; *1983* Lotus 1-2-3, Courtesy of Lotus Development Corporation; *1983* Mitch Kapor, Courtesy of Lotus Development Corporation; *1984* IBM, Courtesy of International Business Machines Corporation; *1984* Apple Macintosh, Courtesy of Apple Computer, Inc.; *1987* Intel 80386, Courtesy of Intel Corporation; *1987* Intel 486, Courtesy of Intel Corporation; *1990* Windows, Courtesy of Microsoft Corporation; *1992* PDA, Courtesy of Apple Computer, Inc.; *1993* Pentium chip, Courtesy of Intel Corporation; *1993* Energy Star logo, Courtesy of the Environmental Protection Agency; *1995* Pentium Pro, Courtesy of Intel Corporation; *1996* Dr. Andrew Grove, Courtesy of Intel Corporation; *1997* Microsoft Office 97, Courtesy of Microsoft Corporation; **Chapter 2:** *Figure 2-8* Courtesy of T/Maker Company; *Figure 2-12* Courtesy of Corel Corporation; *Figure 2-25* Scott Goodwin Photography, Inc.; *Figure 2-41* Courtesy of International Business Machines Corporation; *Figure 2-48* Scott Goodwin Photography, Inc.; *Pages 2.44-45*, Chessmen, disk, pen, package, and giraffe, Courtesy of Corel Professional Photos CD-ROM Image usage; **Chapter 3:** *Chapter opener: upper right*, R. Ian Lloyd/West Light; *middle right*, Scott Goodwin Photography, Inc.; *lower right*, Scott Goodwin Photography, Inc.; *lower left*, David Parker/Seagate Microelectronics LTD/Science Photo Library/Photo Researchers, Inc.; *upper left*, Michael Rosenfeld/Tony Stone Images; *Figure 3-8* Courtesy of Intel Corporation; *Figure 3-9* Courtesy of Intel Corporation; *Figure 3-10* Courtesy of International Business Machines Corporation; *Figure 3-13* Scott Goodwin Photography, Inc.; *Figure 3-15* Scott Goodwin Photography, Inc.; *Figure 3-20* Scott Goodwin Photography, Inc.; *Figure 3-21* Scott Goodwin Photography, Inc.; *Figure 3-22* Scott Goodwin Photography, Inc.; *Figure 3-26* Scott Goodwin Photography, Inc.; *Figure 3-35* R. Ian Lloyd/West Light; *Figure 3-36* Alfred Pasieka/Peter Arnold, Inc.; *Figure 3-37* Charles D. Winters/Photo Researchers, Inc.; *Figure 3-38* Courtesy of Texas Instruments; *Figure 3-39* Dick Lurie/Tony Stone Images; *Figure 3-40* David Parker/Seagate

Microelectronics LTD/Science Photo Library/Photo Researchers, Inc.; *Figure 3-41* Dr. Jeremy Burgess/Science Photo Library/Photo Researchers, Inc.; *Figure 3-42* John Maher/The Stock Market; *Figure 3-44* Dr. Jeremy Burgess/Science Photo Library/Photo Researchers, Inc.; *Pages 3.34-35*, Chip, calculator, brain, Courtesy of Corel Professional Photos CD-ROM Image usage; **Chapter 4:** *Chapter opener top,* Courtesy of International Business Machines Corporation; *lower left,* Courtesy of HEI, Inc.; *middle left,* Courtesy of NEC Technologies, Inc.; *Figure 4-1* Scott Goodwin Photography, Inc.; *Figure 4-4* Kevin Horan/Tony Stone Images; *Figure 4-5* Courtesy of NEC Technologies, Inc.; *Figure 4-6* Scott Goodwin Photography, Inc.; *Figure 4-7* Courtesy of International Business Machines Corporation; *Figure 4-8* Courtesy of Logitech, Inc.; *Figure 4-9* Scott Goodwin Photography, Inc.; *Figure 4-11* Courtesy of International Business Machines Corporation; *Figure 4-12* Courtesy of HEI, Inc.; *Figure 4-13* Courtesy of International Business Machines Corporation; *Figure 4-14* Peter Vadnai/The Stock Market; *Figure 4-16* Courtesy of Logitech, Inc.; *Figure 4-17* Courtesy of International Business Machines Corporation; *Figure 4-19a* John Coletti/Stock Boston; *Figure 4-19b* Jim Pickerell/Tony Stone Images; *Figure 4-19c* David Frazier/Tony Stone Images; *Figure 4-20* Courtesy of Scantron Corporation; *Figure 4-23* Scott Goodwin Photography, Inc.; *Figure 4-24* Courtesy of Hewlett-Packard Company; *Figure 4-25* Peter Vadnai/The Stock Market; *Figure 4-26* Tony Freeman/PhotoEdit; *Figure 4-28* Martin Schneider Associates; *Figure 4-30* Courtesy of VideoLabs, Inc.; *Figure 4-31* Courtesy of Softboard Microfield Graphics, Inc.; *Figure 4-37* AT&T Corporation; *Figure 4-38* Courtesy of Portrait Display Labs, Inc.; *Figure 4-39* Courtesy of NEC Technologies, Inc.; *Figure 4-40* Courtesy of International Business Machines Corporation; *Figure 4-41* Courtesy of International Business Machines Corporation; *Figure 4-43* Courtesy of Evans & Sutherland Computer Corporation; *Figure 4-45* Scott Goodwin Photography, Inc.; *Figure 4-50* Courtesy of Lexmark International Inc.; *Figure 4-52* Courtesy of Epson America, Inc.; *Figure 4-53* Courtesy of Siemens Nixdorf Printing Systems, L.P.; *Figure 4-54* Courtesy of CalComp Inc.; *Figure 4-55* Courtesy of Hewlett-Packard Company; *Figure 4-56* Courtesy of CalComp Inc.; *Figure 4-57a* Courtesy of Seiko Instruments USA, Inc.; *Figure 4-57b* Courtesy of Zebra Technologies Corporation; *Figure 4-57c* Courtesy of Citizen America Corporation; *Figure 4-58* Courtesy of 3M Visual Systems Division; *Figure 4-59* Courtesy of In Focus Systems; *Figure 4-60* Courtesy of Eastman Kodak Co.; *Figure 4-61* Courtesy of Hewlett-Packard Company; *Figure 4-62* Courtesy of Hewlett-Packard Company; *Figure 4-64* James D. Wilson/Woodfin Camp & Associates; *Figure 4-65* © Jim Pickerell/West Light; *Pages 4.51-52*, Car, typewriter, and pen, Courtesy of Corel Professional Photos CD-ROM Image usage; **Chapter 5:** *Chapter opener: upper left,* Scott Goodwin Photography, Inc.; *middle left,* Courtesy of Drexler Technology Corporation; *middle,* Courtesy of GemPlus; *bottom left,* Courtesy of Imation Enterprises Corporation; *bottom right,* Courtesy of International Business Machines Corporation; *Figure 5-2* Scott Goodwin Photography, Inc.; *Figure 5-4* Scott Goodwin Photography, Inc.; *Figure 5-6* Scott Goodwin Photography, Inc.; *Figure 5-10* Courtesy of Western Digital Corporation; *Figure 5-11* Courtesy of International Business Machines Corporation; *Figure 5-14* Courtesy of Iomega Corporation; *Figure 5-18* Tony Cordoza/Liaison International; *Figure 5-19* Courtesy of Imation Enterprises Corporation; *Figure 5-20* Scott Goodwin Photography, Inc.; *Figure 5-21* Courtesy of International Business Machines Corporation; *Figure 5-22* Courtesy of Imation Enterprises Corporation; *Figure 5-24* Courtesy of Kingston Technology Corporation; *Figure 5-27* Rob Crandall/Folio, Inc.; *Figure 5-28* Courtesy of Dallas Semiconductor; *Figure 5-29* Courtesy of GemPlus; *Figure 5-30* Courtesy of Drexler Technology Corporation; *Pages 5.30-31*, Hand, disks, apple, optical disk, and movie board, Courtesy of Corel Professional Photos CD-ROM Image usage; **Chapter 6:** *Chapter opener: upper right,* Bob Krist/Tony Stone Images; *middle right,* Matthew Borkoski/Folio, Inc.; *middle,* Uniphoto, Inc.; *lower left,* Jeff Zaruba/The Stock Market; *Figure 6-1* Uniphoto, Inc.; *Figure 6-2* Robert Reichert/Liaison International; *Figure 6-3* Matthew Borkoski/Folio, Inc.; *Figure 6-4* Larry Mulvehill/Rainbow; *Figure 6-11* Jeff Zaruba/The Stock Market; *Figure 6-12* Harry M. Walker/Liaison International; *Figure 6-14* Scott Goodwin Photography, Inc.; *Figure 6-15* Courtesy of Motorola, Inc.; *Figure 6-16* Courtesy of Hewlett-Packard Company; *Figure 6-24* Scott Goodwin Photography, Inc.; *Figure 6-25* Courtesy of U.S. Robotics; *Figure 6-31* Bob Krist/Tony Stone Images; *Figure 6-39* David Parker/Science Photo Library/Photo Researchers, Inc.; *Pages 6.41-42*, Car, satellite, sign, pencil, hand, computers, lock, and file, Courtesy of Corel Professional Photos CD-ROM Image usage; **Chapter 7:** *Figure 7-3* Courtesy of Donna Cox and Robert Patterson/NCSA/UIUC; *Figure 7-19a* Catherine Noren/Stock Boston; *Figure 7-19b* Courtesy of Cray Research, Inc.; *Figure 7-19c* Courtesy of International Business Machines Corporation; *Figure 7-27* Courtesy of Sun Microsystems, Inc.; *Figure 7-28* Courtesy of Philips Consumer Electronics Company; *Figure 7-29a* Courtesy of Philips Consumer Electronics Company; *Figure 7-29b* Courtesy of Philips Consumer Electronics Company; *Figure 7-33* Courtesy of Donna Cox and Robert Patterson/NCSA/UIUC; *Pages 7.37-38*, Humor computer, striker, and world map; Courtesy of Corel Professional Photos CD-ROM Image usage; **Chapter 8:** *Figure 8-1* Courtesy of International Business Machines Corporation; *Figure 8-12* Courtesy of Microsoft Corporation; *Figure 8-13* Courtesy of Microsoft Corporation; *Figure 8-14* Fredrick D. Bodin; *Figure 8-15* Courtesy of International Business Machines Corporation; *Figure 8-20* Courtesy of Berkeley Systems, Inc.; *Page 8.30*, Television, Courtesy of Corel Professional Photos CD-ROM Image usage; **Buyers Guide:** *Figure a* Courtesy of International Business Machines Corporation; *Figure b* Courtesy of CompUSA; *Figure c* Scott Goodwin Photography, Inc.; *Figure f* Scott Goodwin Photography, Inc.; *Figure g* Courtesy of Toshiba America, Inc.; *Figure h* Scott Goodwin Photography, Inc.; *Figure i* Courtesy of Xircom, Inc.; *Figure k* Scott Goodwin Photography, Inc.